Capt. Peter D. G.
Hg & Hg C 682 Eng. Bn.
47 Inf. Div.

Col. Peter Grossman
Retired Jan. 1987

# THE MINUTE MAN
# IN PEACE AND WAR

# THE MINUTE MAN
# IN PEACE AND WAR

## *A History of*
## *The National Guard*

By **Jim Dan Hill,** Ph.D., D.Litt.

Foreword by George Fielding Eliot

THE STACKPOLE COMPANY
HARRISBURG, PENNSYLVANIA

Illustrated by Louis James Nolan

Library of Congress Catalog Card Number: 63-22141

*Printed and bound in the United States of America*
by THE TELEGRAPH PRESS, *Established 1831*
*Harrisburg, Pennsylvania*

# DEDICATED

## to

## THE OFFICERS AND MEN

of Wisconsin's 120th and Pennsylvania's 190th Field Artillery Regiments, October, 1940—August, 1945. The latter was re-designated 190th Field Artillery Group, in England, Winter of 1944, with an additional Guard Battalion, the 997th (Kansas) assigned in augmentation of the Regiment's two original Pennsylvania Battalions. These officers and men not only maintained the highest military traditions of their States and their Nation but they also often made their Colonel appear better than he really was, which he deeply appreciated.

*Books by the Author*

SEA DOGS OF THE SIXTIES: Farragut and Seven Contemporaries

THE TEXAS NAVY: Forgotten Battles and Shirtsleeve Diplomacy

THE MINUTE MAN IN PEACE AND WAR: A History of the
National Guard

# Preface

This book is the first published effort to bring an historical survey of the Volunteer Organized Militia, the National Guard, as an American defense institution, into a single volume. Furthermore, no multi-volume work is dedicated to the same objective. The author rather light-heartedly embarked upon the project six or seven years ago as a leisure time, avocational project that might easily be completed within two years at most. He was aware that American historians had been prone to neglect the less dramatic aspects of warfare. He was hardly prepared for the massive, time consuming, undigested sources in some areas of the project and the paucity of information of any kind on other important aspects of the subject. The search relative to the latter was equally time consuming and often more frustrating. Frequently a State has far more to offer in its Colonial archives than it does for the eve of, or even during, the American Civil War.

Actually, the highly complex subject from 1607 to the present is too big and too paragraph consuming with modifications of general patterns and practices within the Thirteen Colonies and the successor United States to be fully covered in a single volume. In any event, after wallowing in English precedents, analyzing the different laws and often conflicting military policies of the American Colonies, the author found he had written ten or twelve chapters before getting into the American Revolution. If any space emphasis toward modernity was to be achieved within a single volume, a new approach was obviously necessary. The introductory technique of definitions by historical examples and summaries found in the first chapter is the result. Through this device, the emphasis of the survey properly falls upon the past hundred years, which include the eras of America's greatest military manpower efforts. Such emphasis is required if one is to bring into historical focus, the role of the State-organized Regiments and Divisions of volunteer, avocational, citizen-soldiers in the American military efforts of our own day.

The Civil War policies and results are necessarily reviewed in some detail. In terms of military manpower, that war is the essential link between the military past and the present. Present practices stem from the military experience both of the Confederacy and the Union. Likewise, the concept of a Federal Organized Milita, euphoniously dubbed the U.S. Volunteers and known today as the U.S. Army Reserve, but patterned closely upon the procedures within the Volunteer Organized Militia of the States, began manifesting itself before the end of the four years of the Civil War.

Oddly enough, the National Guard, or Volunteer Organized Militia of the States (the terms are synonymous), is likewise the parent of the Naval Reserve and through it a progenitor of the U.S. Marine Corps and Coast Guard Reserve. Some of the States still have an Organized Naval Militia, but on terms vastly different from those under which their original units were formed. But the same can be said of the Air National Guard and Army National Guard units now organized by and within the several States of the United States. Moreover, next to the active duty Divisions, Wings, Battalions, Squadrons, Companies and Flights of the Regular Air Force and the Regular Army, the Air National Guard and Army National Guard units of the States continue to be America's top priority forces for emergency combat and immediate field service.

All of which adds up to the National Guard being a unique, complex and at times an unfathomable defense institution when viewed from the outside. Unless memory is in error, it was Colonel Frederick G. Todd, Curator of the Military Museum at West Point, who once said, or wrote, that no one could ever really understand the National Guard and its membership without having been a Guardsman; and even a three-year hitch was no guarantee that a young Guardsman would understand it. Accordingly, one of the purposes of this book is an historical presentation of the American National Guard with the hope that all Guardsmen will completely understand their own institution and that all non-Guardsmen may have the means of a thorough acquaintance and some understanding without the arduous responsibilities of an enlistment. If the book, with its emphasis upon the past hundred years, fully accomplishes this purpose, no additional tears or anguish will be expended for those unused chapters.

No historian can write a book of this length without being indebted to many sources, many other historians, numerous libraries, scores of librarians and some extremely competent clerical assistance. Some of the authors are mentioned in the bibliographical notes found at the end of each chapter. Even so, there are so many oversights that trying to mention all others here would result in additional paragraphs of little interest to the general reader. Moreover, everyone, it is hoped, has been the recipient of personal thanks with the additional assurance that he will be blamed with none of the errors of minor fact or major interpretation that some reviewer inevitably finds or attributes to an opus of this scope.

Nevertheless, a few names must be mentioned in connection with the basic research. A manuscript entitled *The National Guard of the United States,* by the well known, scholarly, military author and soldier, Colonel

Elbridge Colby, Infantry, U. S. Army (Ret.), covers the period since 1902 to and including World War II with extreme accuracy and lucidity. Its approach was of indispensable assistance, most particularly in constitutional and legislative problems and the philosophies that made possible their ultimate solution. His manuscript is now available to readers, graduate students and authors in the Martin Library of Military History, maintained by the National Guard Association of the United States, 1 Massachusetts Avenue N. W., Washington, D. C. It has been constantly in the possession of this author during the writing of the pertinent sections of this book. To that end it has been drawn upon.

Miss Martha Derthick, brilliant, young political scientist, graciously made available a copy of her Harvard, doctoral thesis on the National Guard Association of the United States. While she appears to view most associations that have legislative programs with a dubious eye, her research is indeed thorough and her manuscript is rich in factual and bibliographical lore. Mr. Edward Greve, Reference Librarian, Wisconsin State College, Superior, has been an unerring assistant toward obscure sources and in arranging inter-library loans of materials not locally available. Colonel Allan G. Crist, Editor of *the National Guardsman,* has rendered indispensable assistance in processing the manuscript for publication, but neither he nor any of the above are responsible for errors in either content or interpretation.

Additional remarks should be made concerning the informal bibliographical notes at the end of each chapter. Without exception, they are far from all-inclusive. For some there is even a guilty fear that there may be several grave omissions. The areas most frequently slighted are in the nature of newspaper files, contemporary magazine articles, and studies in learned quarterlies. Some are mentioned but many more should have been, space permitting. But the purpose of the informal bibliographical notes is not so much to express gratitude and appreciation as it has been to provide additional reading for those with a continuing interest in the subject of that chapter; and, further, to serve as springboards for research and more detailed writing and analysis by others. At least one title in each bibliographical note is endowed with sufficient footnotes and source material guides to launch a graduate student toward a Master's or Doctoral thesis should he feel inclined toward a subject within the compass of that chapter. And here it is well to suggest that the scope of Chapter I alone offers enough elbow room for a score of Ph.D. theses without any one encroaching upon the zone of the other. Other chapters likewise offer opportunities.

In any event, it is hoped others will be intrigued to explore some historical areas before and since the Civil War, upon which this single volume has of necessity touched but lightly. Any idea that anyone might ever have entertained that any single volume can rightly be considered definitive, or even more than a broad overview, of such a great narrative as the National Guard and the citizen-soldier in the history of America will most certainly be dissipated by this survey.

The military history of America is too big for any one man to write the definitive narrative. In that great story, the citizen in uniform, serving his Country through dire days of grave emergencies, is the biggest single factor. The Organized Militia, the National Guard, as the parent institution not only of the American Army in its broadest sense but also of the Naval Reserve, is likewise too big. Not for a moment has the author flattered himself that in writing this book he is pre-empting an historical field, as he appears once to have done accidentally by writing *The Texas Navy*, another story that was too long neglected in the public domain. But that was not a very big story. Indeed, there were days when he willingly would have relinquished pre-emption thereto (except for royalties purposes) because too many non-historical, short-tempered customers made their purchase thinking it was another Texas joke book.

JIM DAN HILL  
Superior, Wisconsin  
26 May 1963

# Foreword

By George Fielding Eliot

The Organized Militia system of the United States—of which the National Guard is the modern outgrowth—is a military institution which has survived for more than three centuries because it has proven equal to the successive challenges of history in each generation of our National existence. It is distinctively an American institution—there is nothing quite like it in any other country. From its origins as the Militia Companies or "Trained Bands" upon which the earliest Colonial settlements in North America depended for survival against hostile Indians, to the Companies, Batteries and Air Squadrons which are the "building blocks" of today's National Guard Divisions and Air Wings, ready for combat anywhere in the World, the roots of its strength and of its inextinguishable vitality have ever been in the home communities of the American people. Its key organizational principle is now as always that of the development of military units manned and officered at the community level, deriving spiritual cohesion from home town associations and neighborly sentiments.

In all our wars, the American people have found it necessary to rely extensively—in some cases almost exclusively—on citizen-soldiers. Never have we maintained, or been able to think of maintaining in time of peace, a sufficient Military Establishment to meet the needs of war. Even today, when we are compelled to keep up a permanent level of nuclear armament adequate to deter any other nuclear power from launching a nuclear surprise attack against us, we must also be ready for a wide variety of global military emergencies which would require prompt reinforcement of our active forces. And today as in times past, the first-line reinforcements which are ready to hand are the organized units of the National Guard.

It is difficult to understand why no military historian has hitherto set himself the task of writing an objective history of this great American military organization, which has borne so honorable a share in the National defense. Happily, this omission has at last been repaired, and the Country owes a debt of gratitude to the author of this present work—which I am proud indeed to have the opportunity of introducing with these few preliminary comments. As a soldier of talent and perception, and an historian of wide accomplishment, General Hill brings to this task unusual abilities supported by a flaming loyalty to the National Guard in which he served with such distinction for many years. The story he has to tell has long needed telling; the myths he deals with so trenchantly have long needed refutation. And at every high point of his narrative the same questions will recur to the reflective reader: If we had not had these units of organized citizen-soldiers *then*—whether in 1775 or 1917 or 1941—what might have happened? What would we have done to meet our sudden need? And what if such another need beset us tomorrow morning?

One of the great merits of General Hill's history is that he never loses sight of the essential difference between Organized and Unorganized Militia. This has been a stumbling block to many an historian. Few indeed have understood the real meaning of the term "Minute Man" as distinguished from "Militiaman." Yet this distinction is vital and has been with us from the earliest dawn of our history. In the early settlements it was indeed a condition of survival in a wilderness peopled by hostile savages that every able-bodied man should be available to bear arms in the common defense—young men and old, and even at times the women. But it soon became apparent that something more than a last-ditch defense of the town stockade was required if the community was to survive and flourish. The outlying farmsteads, the mill on the river, the wagon on the road bringing produce to market, these too required defense—a defense that could only be assured by convincing the enemy that attacking them entailed drastic consequences; or, if need be, destroying by offensive operations his capability of attack. For such operations, young and active men alone could be used; one of the earliest examples was the special contingent of 1,000 men organized in 1675 by the Colonies of Massachusetts Bay, Plymouth and Rhode Island to penetrate the Great Swamp and destroy the stronghold of the Wampanoag Indians in "King Philip's War" of 1675. Later, special units of "Provincial" troops were organized to participate, sometimes in company with the British Regulars, sometimes by themselves, in the Frontier wars with the French and the Indians: one notable instance being the capture in 1745 of the great French fortress of Louisbourg by Colonial troops commanded by William Pepperell of Maine. From more than a century of experiences such as these, our forebears derived the concept of what we call today a "ready reserve"—units of citizen-soldiers organized, armed and officered to be ready for action promptly in case of need. It was this concept which produced the "Minute Man" Companies of the New England Militia during the "cold war" days of the 1770s when armed resistance to the British Crown was foreseen as a rising possibility, and when it was also foreseen that the necessity for such resistance might arise so suddenly that there would not be time to train and arm and organize for it after the event. It is this concept of the first-line or ready reserve as a special and selected element of our citizen forces that governs the mission of the National Guard today.

Readiness as a military quality is of course measured by the time gap between anticipated warning and need for commitment to action under the conditions prevailing at the time. This is further affected by such factors as the quality of the enemy forces and the conditions under which action may be expected. In applying these requirements to the organization and training of part-time soldiers—citizen-soldiers who volunteer to devote a portion of their own leisure to preparing to defend their Country—political and economic considerations must also be taken into account. In America at least, no plan for raising citizen forces, whatever its military merits, is worth the paper on which it is written unless it is politically acceptable in terms of the mood and spirit of the times. This fact is often forgotten by critics who harp on how much better it would have been had the United States just provided itself with a strong Regular Army right after the adoption of the Constitution and kept such an Army in being thereafter.

In fact the prevailing sentiment about the dangers of a "standing army" to republican liberties was such that only with the utmost difficulty did George Washington and other clear-sighted statesmen induce a majority of the Constitutional Convention to include provision for Federal armed forces in that document, as well as the provisions for Militia forces to be raised and officered by the States. In such a political climate it was clear that the Militia would have to be the chief military reliance of the new Nation, and Washington wisely bent his efforts toward making the Militia a well-organized and effective force. His masterly "Sentiments on a Peace Establishment," written at Newburgh in 1783 after considering the views of his senior General Officers, follows the lines already suggested by experience: to have a ready reserve chosen from the general body of the Militia, composed of selected young men who might "form a Corps in every State, capable of resisting any sudden impression which might be attempted by a foreign Enemy, while the remainder of the National forces would have time to assemble and make preparations for the Field." Given such a ready reserve, Washington thought that a Regular Army of some 2,600 men might be enough for controlling the Indian Frontier and that any additional funds available for permanent armed forces could be spent to the best advantage in creating a navy. For the Militia units, Washington wanted a uniform system of organization and training, under Federal supervision, with a specified number of training days each year. But when this scheme was presented to Congress in 1792, everything was knocked out except a general obligation to serve in time of need. It would be more than a hundred years until, in 1903, the first Federal law was passed to implement the Constitutional provision allowing Congress to "provide for organizing, arming and disciplining the militia."

What remained was a State-controlled Militia, and the States did continue to provide Militia units of varying degrees of capability. It was upon the State Governments that the Federal Government relied, under the Constitution, to obtain citizen reinforcements for the Regular Army whenever the occasion arose. Indeed it is hard to see how any citizen force could have legally been kept in being except through the workings of the Constitutional machinery of government, or recruits obtained for such a force except through the traditional grass-roots sentiments by which the needs of the common defense are harmonized with local sentiments and community or State loyalties.

After the turn of the last century, as the full impact of modern technology on the conduct of war and the armament of military forces began to be understood in parallel with the enormous expansion of American World responsibilities, the political climate was sufficiently changed by the pressures of the times so that Federal supervision (accompanied and supported by Federal financial aid) began to be accepted by the States—not the least of the pressures to this end being supplied by the officers and men of the National Guard themselves, eager for the weapons, the equipment and the training which would enable them to meet the military requirements and the more exigent time limits of the new era.

But the stubborn fact remained that though Federal assistance was needed to make the National Guard a truly ready reserve, it was only by continuing to depend upon long-established local and State loyalties and unit traditions that a sufficient flow of volunteer manpower could be made available to keep up a respectable level of forces.

To many of the able military logicians of the new General Staff of the Army, the Constitutional system of dual control—Federal and State—by which the National Guard was governed appeared complicated and untidy. What they wanted was a ready reserve for the Army entirely controlled and administered by the Federal Government—meaning by the War Department and the War Department General Staff. They could not understand that this was politically infeasible and practically impossible as well—because such a reserve could not then (or now, for that matter) obtain a sufficient flow of volunteers to support it in adequate strength. Moreover it would have little assurance against the future ebb and flow of political and economic tides, whereas the National Guard, strongly entrenched in the confidence and the affection of its home town bases, possessed above all other virtues the crowning quality of durability.

How the National Guard lived through these storms and subsequently proved its battle-worthiness in two World Wars and in Korea is a story which General Hill has told in glowing detail, and I do not intend to try to anticipate his story by any capsulized account. But I would like to underline this one quality which the Guard still possesses and will continue to possess—the quality of political durability. To anyone who has truly at heart the military security of the United States, this is a quality which should be uniquely attractive. We live in an era when changes both technological and psychological come upon us with unprecedented velocity and variety. In consequence, we live in an era when the validity of experience as a guide to the future has never been more persistently, indeed savagely challenged. Just the experience of the past two years in the development of the military policy of the United States has provided sufficient evidence of that fact, and it is not a fact which is wholly reassuring. The current "Whiz kid" era in the Pentagon finds military officers of all the Services required to defend the concepts of a lifetime of professional accomplishment against the pert and sometimes disdainful challenges of young "systems analysts" who have never heard so much as a cap pistol fired in anger; and there is reason to fear that in some cases the voice of the slide-rule slickers rather than the voice of experience prevails in decisions upon which the Nation's future safety depends. Behind all this lies the basic philosophy of the nuclear age—that everything is changed, everything is new, and experience need no longer be deferred to by anyone.

This, then, is a time of peculiar and unprecedented danger to our Country. At such a time, an established military institution which possesses strong roots deeply imbedded in the affections and the confidence of our people, which has a strength and a solidity which are its own birthright born of three centuries and more of proven service, has a value as a stabilizing influence which is beyond estimation. The National Guard has already gone through one major encounter with the "Whizkid" system, and it did not come out second-best by a long shot. Loyally supported by the Governors of fifty sovereign States and by the Congressional veterans who know its worth, the National Guard has emerged from this contest with its head not wholly unbloodied but certainly unbowed. It may be doubted that the contest will be renewed as eagerly as it was entered upon by the advocates of changes for the sake of change. Here, then, is an element of stability in our Military Establishment which cannot be deranged soon again by the click of a computer. To the professional military officer fighting to preserve the values and the concepts which he knows to be essential to the National safety, here is a beacon light of encouragement—and a helping hand from his brothers-in-arms of the citizen forces.

The National Guard stands today at a peak of readiness such as has never been demanded of a citizen force before in all our history. It is capable of attaining even a higher level of readiness if that should be required of it, as may very well prove to be the case. If trial by battle comes its way again, its officers and men will meet that trial as worthily as the Guardsmen of earlier generations. But perhaps the greatest service which the National Guard can now perform for the Nation is to help to preserve the confidence of our people in the great military traditions to which it is heir, and to steady the course of the ship of state amidst the rocks and shoals of a perilous future.

New York, New York
September 9, 1963

# Table of Contents

# CHAPTER I

# The National Guard:
# Oldest of Army Components

AMERICAN MILITARY HISTORY offers a confusion of terms applicable to the official and legal status of sundry categories of soldiers. An example that readily comes to mind is *militia* in its overall historic and generic meaning, and the same word, *the Militia,* more specifically as the unorganized, militarily-obligated manpower of a given Colony, State or Nation. But *Militia,* with various adjectives, is a term that necessarily recurs again, again and again. No noun in the military lexicon has been more frequently abused and more thoroughly misunderstood.

1

Other historical terms that invite critical scrutiny because they contribute to misunderstanding are *Trainbands, Colonial Levies, Minute Men, Continental Line,* and the *Line* of various States, or Colonies in revolt, such as the *Maryland Line* and the *Pennsylvania Line.* Contemporaneous with the foregoing in early American history are such terms as *Crown troops, Crown commissions,* and *British Regulars.*

More modern but equally confusing to the non-military, and often confused within the Defense Department today, are such terms as *Organized Militia, Volunteer Militia,* and the *National Guard* of a given State, such as *Colorado National Guard* and the *National Guard of the United States.* There are also *volunteers, State Volunteer Regiments, U.S. Volunteers, U.S. Veteran Volunteers, U.S. Veteran Reserve Corps,* as well as the *National Army* of World War I and the *Army of the United States, U.S. Army* and the *Regular Army* as of today. Added to these in recent years are the *Officers Reserve Corps, U.S. Army Reserve, Home Guard, Draftees,* and *Selectees.* Moreover, today in the Pentagon there is much talk of the *Obligors,* which, oddly enough, is a substitute word for *Militia* in its basic meaning.

To the casual reader of military history, some of these are readily recognized as more-or-less synonymous. Others are quite specific, but some are almost as generic in scope as the often-misunderstood term *Militia.* For example, *Regular Army* and *U.S. Army* are specific, and generally accepted as being identical in meaning, though capable of confusion to less discerning laymen. On the other hand, the *Army of the United States* is a rather sweeping phrase that in its World War II meaning signifies all Army personnel currently on active duty irrespective of origin, component, or whether serving voluntarily or involuntarily. During and since the Korean Affair, *Active Army* has been supplanting the longer, more awkward term.

Perhaps the easiest approach to a delineation and complete understanding of the above-italicized, and other wide-ranging similar terms, would be to review briefly America's military personnel policies and at the same time cite some outstanding names in American military history, fitting each into his proper category. Thereafter some rather specific definitions can be achieved with a high degree of clarity.

## COLONIAL ORIGINS

All components of the American Army, Navy and Marine Corps would happily claim Captain John Smith, Colony of Virginia, 1607, as an honored and revered prototype and historical forerunner of their own category. He certainly had the versatility, qualities of leadership, military knowledge and skills, afloat and ashore, for coping with military, naval and civilian government problems. He was a man of whom even the Air Force would be proud, but its claiming him as its very

2

own would offer some difficulties. Actually, the doughty Captain cannot be catalogued under any of the terms, or categories, mentioned above. He held neither a National nor a King's commission to qualify him for either the Regular Army or Regular Navy or Marine Corps of his day. Moreover, Captain John Smith held no Colonial commission, or status in an English Trainband, that could categorize him as a prototype of our modern National Guardsmen.

Captain Smith was a soldier of fortune following his profession under the military powers granted to a chartered corporation of merchant ventures. His commission and authority came from the corporation through its charter from the Crown. Legally his military status was on a parity with that of Captain Robert Clive, Army of the East India Company, whose sword at Arcot and aptitude for diplomacy among the nabobs laid the foundations for Great Britain's Viceroyalty of India. That Clive ultimately was integrated into the English Regular Army as a Lieutenant Colonel in order that his authority would extend to the small detachments of Crown Troops, or British Regulars, supporting East India Army formations, is irrelevant. Clive was a "John Company" officer throughout his military and administrative career. In our military parlance and history there is no equivalent to the large military forces of some of the English chartered companies. With this exception, all English military institutions and the legal concepts upon which they rested were transplanted to and took root in America. In matters military, England is indeed the mother country.

Captain Miles Standish, 1620, Massachusetts, and his little band of armed volunteers, who ventured ashore to explore, select, defend and hold their future homesteads, were to the civil body politic, created by the Mayflower Compact, what the Trainbands of England were to their respective Counties, Towns, and Cities. Since there is a direct and unbroken lineage from the Trainbands of Britain to the modern National Guard, it can be said with historical accuracy that the allegedly-rejected suitor of Priscilla Alden most likely was America's first National Guard Captain. Admittedly, in 1620, Lafayette had not yet coined the term "National Guard." But all sociologists, political scientists and historians agree that many institutions have existed under sundry names decades and centuries prior to their modern designation. This is conspicuously true of the National Guard, though some States were resisting the present name as late as 1905. In Boston, for example, the Commonwealth's Adjutant General stood pat on "Massachusetts Volunteer Militia" as a more honored and historic term extending back to Colonial days.

Nathaniel Bacon, Virginia, 1673-76, a top-flight Indian-fighter and leader of Bacon's Rebellion, was hardly a prototype of any modern military category. He was a rebel who achieved his Indian-fighting

3

commission by putting the Governor under duress, which, if anything, might identify Bacon as an unduly aggressive National Guardsman. Bacon, however, was a rebel, first, last and always. But his vest pocket revolt brought to America the first full Regiment of Regulars, 1,000 strong, to enter the stage of American history. This was the King's First Guards (Grenadier Guards since 1815), commanded by Colonel Herbert Jeffreys. The Regiment's sojourn was short. Bacon had died of natural causes. The Revolt was over. Three hundred of the Regiment deserted to become Colonists. Swamp fever and miasma accounted for casualties of 2% per month. The remaining 600 were, at the end of five months, hustled back to Britain to get them off the Colonial budget. America has been resisting Regular Army costs ever since.

King William's War, 1689-97; Queen Anne's War, 1701-13; King George's War, 1744-48, and the French-and-Indian War, 1754-63, added new names to military history. They came from both the King's Regulars and the rosters of the Colonial Organized Militia, which was displacing the old English term, "Trainbands." Indeed, some Regiments of King's Regulars were recruited and partially officered in America. Young George Washington's older brother, Lawrence Washington, received a Crown, or Regular, commission as Captain in 1740. He rated half-pay, and was subject to the King's call the remainder of his life, though his Regiment, "Spotswood's Americans," was "disembodied," or inactivated, with approach of peace from King George's War, 1748.

Captain Lawrence Washington died on the eve of the French-and-Indian War. An inspired, youthful George felt it a duty to carry on. He sought a commission in the Organized Militia, Colony of Virginia. With Braddock, and after, he yearned for and often sought a Regular, or Crown commission, especially when he found a Regular Captain always outranked a provincial Lieutenant Colonel. In hopes of admission to the Regulars, he wrote to an influential friend: ". . . mention me in favorable terms to General Forbes [the King's General in Pennsylvania] . . . as a person who would gladly be distinguished in some measure from the common run of provincial officers." Young Washington never achieved that distinction in the form of a commission in the King's Regulars.

But soon thereafter his own Virginia made Washington a full Colonel commanding her 1st Regiment. Forbes recognized merit, and before George Washington had reached the age of 27 he was commanding a Brigade in successful offensive operations. Thus he apparently lost interest in the Regulars. Besides, the war was over!

## THE REVOLUTIONARY WAR

It has been suggested that it was an evil day for the British Empire when it lost the services of George Washington through failure to give

4

him status with a Regular commission. The idea is of little validity. Charles Lee, a soldier of fortune at heart, renounced a Regular Lieutenant Colonelcy to join the Maryland Line and fight against his King. Horatio Gates did likewise with his half-pay, Regular Major's commission. Moreover, his love for and loyalty to his adopted country never has been questioned, as in Lee's case. Richard Montgomery, a King's Regular Captain in New York, most likely paraphrased what Washington's thoughts and words would have been. A friend wrote Montgomery apologetically because the Continental Congress had not given Montgomery a Major Generalcy. The King's Captain replied: "I submit in great cheerfulness to any regulation they [Continental Congress] in their prudence shall judge expedient. Laying aside the punctilio of the soldier, I shall endeavor to discharge my duty to society, considering myself as the *citizen,* reduced to the necessity of taking up arms for the public safety." Thus Montgomery, who died fighting under the walls of Quebec, was a British Regular when he voiced well the philosophy of the Organized Militia of his adopted New York. We can safely assume Colonel George Washington, of the Old Dominion's Organized Militia, would have said as much had he held a commission in the King's Regulars.

When Washington and his Generals accepted commissions from the Continental Congress, their status was that of modern National Guard General Officers being inducted into extended active duty for a major emergency. Some already held a higher, or lower, prior rank in the Volunteer Militia of their respective States. All initial Continental appointments necessarily were nominated, or sponsored, formally or informally, by their State Governors and/or Congressional Delegations. Later there were a few exceptions in favor of some foreigners whom Benjamin Franklin, or Silas Deane, in Paris, had promised high commissions.

The armed revolt against England naturally was opened by Colonial, organized units, the equivalent of modern National Guardsmen, who acted under the authority of their Revolutionary governments rather than those of the King's officials. The local application of the term "Minute Men" to the Lexington Company of Massachusetts Voluteer Militia that helped the British Regulars in triggering the Revolutionary War should confuse no one as to their basic status.* In any event, the volunteer units of Minute Men from Massachusetts quickly became integrated with Washington's Eight-Months Army, which besieged and captured Boston. His forces at Boston in turn became the nucleus of the subsequent Continental Line, composed of units from all the revolting States, or Colonies.

---

* A more detailed examination of the *Minute Men* is included in the glossary of terms at the end of this chapter.

The Regiments of the resulting Continental Line were recruited within the States by Commanders named by the Revolutionary State Governments. Personnel procurement was through volunteering expedited by bounties and pressures of State laws for compulsory military service. The resulting Regiments carried their State designations throughout the War. They were perfect prototypes of the Organized Militia, or National Guard, Regiments that as units, up to Divisional size, have been called or ordered into extended Federal service for a definite period, or for the duration, in every American war.

But if some writers have been confused, they have an honorable precedent. General Washington himself had trouble explaining the character of his Army to puzzled members of the Continental Congress. In 1780 he responded to some queries: "If in all cases ours was *one* army, or *thirteen armies* allied for the common defense, there would be no difficulty in solving your question; but we are occasionally both, and I should not be much out if I were to say that we are sometimes neither but a compound of *both.*" At all times Washington and other leading Americans thought of his Army only as a provisional force of citizen-soldiers with Militia obligations to their own States, who were absolving those duties voluntarily by active service in the Regiments of their respective States.

In any event, these formations of volunteering officers and men, recruited and officered by the 13 States to form the Maryland Line, Pennsylvania Line, etc., to an aggregate for the Continental Line, or Army, definitely proved good enough to keep America in the war and to defeat the British in detail when the Redcoats waxed bold enough, or careless enough, to divide their forces.

But what of the Militia units of the States, of whose quality the officers of the Continental Line occasionally complained, but whose presence they always welcomed, except when supplies were low and no fighting was in sight? They were the Home Guard units, the Civil Defense establishment, of their day. Since the Revolution was a home front war, these local limited-duty units were often in evidence when homes actually were threatened. In such cases they often reinforced the Continental Line. When the Redcoats and/or hostile Indians were defeated or went elsewhere, the personnel of such formations automatically demobilized themselves back to the towns and farms. They occasionally fought and won battles of major significance, with little or no help from Continental Line troops. The names of General Stark, victor at Bennington, and General Herkimer, of Oriskaney, for example, appear nowhere in the Continental Line. They and their men fought, and won, purely in their local Home Guard status, under State commissions and without any Congressional recognition or confirmation whatsoever.

There was, however, an element of strong compulsion upon their service from their respective State Governments. Under Colonial statutes, stemming from the Common Law from England, every able-bodied citizen within specified ages had an arms-bearing responsibility—his Militia obligation to his State! This obligation was utilized in pressuring volunteers for the States' contributions to the Continental Line, or Army, just as Selective Service stimulates a certain amount of volunteering today. It is upon this Common Law principle that the Draft and Selective Service Laws of World Wars I and II became the law of the land, which, in effect, recognizes and specifies a corresponding Militia responsibility to the modern Federal Government, though this last concept was of slow evolution.

It was the local objectives of the Home Guard units that destroyed their value in extensive maneuver operations and for a pursuit phase following a victory. It was for this, and occasional failure to protect the flanks of the thinly-deployed Continental Line, that Washington and his commanders occasionally vented their spleen upon "the Militia." Actually, as is conspicuously obvious, Washington and all the officers and men of the Continental Line were merely Militiamen themselves. The only difference was that they were voluntarily and transitorially in Continental service for a more extended and far-flung active service against the common enemy. Some friction between active duty components and home front elements is inevitable, however, in any war. It is surprising that there was not more mutual recrimination. That there was so little was most likely because there was such constant flow of personnel, back and forth, between the continuously-organized and serving Continental Line Militiamen and the home front Militiamen that both had some understanding of the problems of the other.

Indeed, the Revolution could not have been won without the home front Militiamen. More than once, it was through them, with their loyalty and the speed with which they could embody themselves into quasi-tactical, auxiliary formations for dealing with civil dangers as well as military operations, that the Revolutionary Governors were able to stay in office against the Tory forces of reaction. In but one State, Georgia, were the forces and friends of the King ever able to create so much as the semblance of a loyal State Government! These home front facts are less dramatic, but nevertheless just as important in the winning of the Revolution as were some of the major battles.

## ORIGINS OF THE REGULAR ARMY

With independence won, the Continental Line was disbanded. No provision was made for an American Regular Army. But units had to become caretakers for the surplus equipment and supplies concentrated at Fort Duquesne (Pittsburgh) and at West Point, New York. In 1784 Congress provided for such small housekeeping and guard details.

In 1776 Alexander Hamilton had begun his military career by organizing, under a New York commission, an Artillery Battery for service in the New York Line, Continental Army. He commanded it two years, but soon became a Lieutenant Colonel and Washington's military Secretary. At war's end, Hamilton's old Battery was the parent unit whence came the caretaking detail of 55 men for West Point in 1784. Thus an Artillery Battery in America's modern Regular Army proudly traces its ancestry over a zig-zag course back to Hamilton's New York Battery. This tenuous thread is the only direct relationship between the Continental Army and the United States Regular Army. But, of course, as Americans and men of all Services aloft, afloat and ashore, we share and glory in the heritage that has come down to us from Washington and his Continental Line.

Jefferson argued there could be no permanent, or Regular, Army in America because there were not enough paupers to fill the ranks. But the Indians in the West and the refusal of Canadian frontier post commanders to withdraw behind their boundary ultimately took care of that fanciful idea. If there were not enough paupers, some non-paupers to fill ranks would have to be hired at a proper wage.

The need for a strong central government, with military and naval power to cope with these problems, was one of the potent forces back of the creation and adoption of the Federal Constitution. Thus in the first session of the First Congress, the Act of September 29, 1789, recognized the need for "the establishment for the troops in the service of the United States" in which all officers were appointed by Federal authority and swore allegiance to the United States only. This law is the birth certificate of America's Regular Army.

We hardly can leave George Washington, however, without noting that before he died he did achieve a United States military commission, but it hardly qualified him as a Regular. During the naval war with France, in the Adams Administration, there was legislation authorizing a provisional Army of volunteer Militia units to be drawn from the States, to a total of 50,000 officers and men, for offensive operations against Louisiana and Florida. Washington was tendered and he accepted, July 3, 1798, a commission as Lieutenant General. He was to be Commander-in-Chief. The modern status most nearly equivalent to this unexpected rank would be the temporary National Army commissions of World War I, or the World War II commissions in the Army of the United States, such as the Lieutenant Generalcy President Roosevelt procured for William S. Knudsen, President of General Motors, while America was mobilizing prior to Pearl Harbor.

In any event, when Washington died 18 months later, he still was holding that partial-mobilization commission of Lieutenant General. It is here suggested that the next time Congress finds itself in another series of posthumous promotions and decorations, as it did at the end of World War II, some thoughtful Senator may introduce a Bill restoring George Washington's final rank to the highest held while on active duty. And such a Bill might as well make General Washington a Regular. He did so badly want that status back in his days under Braddock when the King's Regular Captains gave orders to him, a 23-year-old Virginia Lieutenant Colonel; and, worse yet, made the orders stick.

When the little war with France ended, with no more than a few naval engagements, the partial military mobilization which had brought ex-President Washington out of retirement, was demobilized. Few units had left their home Counties. But the War of 1812 was to bring a new mobilization.

Generally speaking the military manpower policies for the War of 1812 followed the pattern and lines that prevailed through the American Revolution, except for one conspicuous exception. An American Regular Army component, small though it was, participated for the first time in other than an Indian frontier war. Moreover, some of its units earned more than passing distinction. Others were paper Regulars. Also present, and equivalent to the old Continental Line, were the Regiments of the States on extended active duty. Efforts to supplant these with a rapidly-expanded Regular Army, as we shall see, were considerably less than successful.

## MILITARY OBLIGATIONS IN THE NEW NATION

Meanwhile, the earlier efforts of the States to implement a Federal Militia Act of 1792 had given America's obligated manpower a semblance of organization that was no more than a system for a continuing military census. Like much other legislation of the era, it was predicated upon the sovereignty-of-the-States philosophy of the era and its details had the blessing of George Washington and other prominent military leaders of the day. As of that era it looked good. Indeed, it was good enough that its principles prevailed without major revision until 1903. Under the continuing pressures of a cold war, it might have developed even more meritorious features comparable to the work of modern Draft and Selective Service Boards. But in a soothing climate of peace at home, an Indian frontier increasingly far to Westward, and the striking forces of potential European enemies a wide ocean away and then busily engaged in fighting one another, the Militia Act of 1792, with amendments, became a static symbol of the status quo, to the ultimate confusion of Brevet Major General Emory

9

Upton, U. S. Army, whose writings in turn have confused many others.

The Militia Act of 1792 created a degree of uniformity among the States as to the ages of military obligation (18 to 44, inclusive) and gave its primary attention to registration, or *enrollment*, of able-bodied men within those ages. The law presumed that each State would create Company-size *districts* with specific metes and bounds throughout each County, Town and City. A designated civilian "Captain" would be responsible for *enrolling* and convening an annual muster of all obligated male citizens who came "to reside within his bounds." Of course, the perimeter of the bounds of 10 Companies constituted the bounds of a Regiment, Regimental areas were consolidated into those of Brigades, and those of Brigades into Divisions, each with civilian "commanders" for the proliferating Military Areas with tactical designations.

For each Division there was to be one Troop of Horse and one Company of Artillery. And who was to pay for all the uniforms, side and shoulder arms, and artillery with accessories? In times of peace, these were responsibilities and areas of legislation by the States. Only in time of war and only for the Regiments inducted into Federal service would the central government become responsible for them. An amending law in 1808 made annual appropriations of $200,000 for arms or ordnance, to be made available to the Military Departments of the several States. It was one of the first of many Federal subsidies that are today commonplace.

The practical military men of that era who endorsed this manpower plan did not conceive these geographical districts of enrolled, obligated personnel as *de facto* armies. To these framers of the law it was a plan for an orderly arrangement of the manpower pool of the Nation whence could be skimmed the elite for the creation of field forces. But to many of the inexperienced civilians of the post-Revolution generations and to many historians of that era and after, there was created the illusion of an enormous and grossly-incompetent civilian Army in being. In reality it was no more than a military manpower bookkeeping arrangement with functions more comparable to those of the modern Selective Service than to functional combat Companies, Regiments, Brigades and Divisions in being.

For example, the comparatively small State of Maryland, in its efforts to implement the Militia Act of 1792, soon found the White male citizenry, within the obligated ages, enrolled on the rosters of no less than 50 Infantry Regimental Areas, which in turn were consolidated into 10 or 12 Brigade Areas and three Divisional Areas, or regions. Confusing such a set-up with an army is almost comparable to confusing the numbered, administrative Corps Areas of 1940, such as the V Corps Area headquartered at Indianapolis, with the highly-tactical

V Corps of Third Army which was formed that year and which soon was destined for North Ireland. Nevertheless, that confusion has been carried into many histories and occasionally by military writers who should have known better.

In any event, the implementation of this law in all the States, by 1811, was revealing a military manpower total of 719,499 "officers and men" on the rosters of the *Enrolled Militia* (unorganized Militia) of that year. They were shown to be in more than 1,000 "Regiments" under more than 300 "Generals." The population of the United States in 1810 was 7,239,000, or a half-million less than that of modern Michigan. Most of the "Generals" and "Colonels" in these manpower statistics were undoubtedly just as reluctant about assuming the field duty implications of such ranks and titles as most of the men on their mass rosters were reluctant to buy their own arms, uniforms and ammunition. And the pecuniary resistance to this last idea was nothing short of massive.

The implementation of the Militia Act of 1792, within the States by their own legislation, did have the effect of stimulating some voluntary military associations which organized themselves into active units of the *Organized Militia*, the equivalent of the Colonial Minute Men Companies and of today's National Guard. And they often did buy their own uniforms, accessories and horses. Some States provided firearms to these volunteer Companies, extended tax exemptions and gave them the monies resulting from *Enrolled* Militiamen who did not appear on annual "Muster Days."

The conventional pattern was for the Governor's State Adjutant General to strive for the voluntary organization of at least enough Artillery units to man coastal defense Batteries within his State. In Western States, like Tennessee, with no coast to guard, the initial emphasis was on volunteer Ranger Companies, in being at all times, for immediate defense against Indians. Normally, the Adjutant General's next objective was one voluntary military association, organized into a self-equipped, weekly or biweekly or even monthly drilling Company of Infantry, in each of the State's Regimental roster areas of enrollees. In the armies of that era, the two flank Companies of each Regiment were of picked men. One normally was called the Grenade Company, or Grenadiers, which drew the post of honor and danger in attacks and assaults on fixed positions. The other flank unit was the Light Infantry Company, whence came detachments for skirmishers, advance guard and other local security arrangements when the Regiment was in march order. It was a reasonably satisfied State Adjutant General who could show one voluntarily-organized, active and functional Infantry Company of the Organized Militia that could be designated in advance as one of the flank Companies for each of the Regimental roster areas proposed for his State by the Federal Militia Act of 1792. Available evidence suggests that few States achieved this comparatively ambitious goal in the rural districts.

In the cities with busy harbors and in an age when all men of means rode horses, it was comparatively easy to organize a sociable-minded Company of coastal Cannoneers, three or four Company-size units of Cavalry and even an occasional Battery of light Field Artillery. In any event, these objectives, and the partial achievements thereof, explain the plethora of apparently separate County and City Companies of "Light Infantry," "Grenadiers," "Sea Fencibles," "Rifle Rangers," and "City Troops" that were the peacetime Organized Militia, or National Guard units, from 1795 to the eve of the Civil War.

Came the War of 1812 and subsequent Indian troubles with their sudden calls upon the States for troops. Quite naturally the several Adjutants General of their respective States showed their Governors how an immediate quota could be met by organizing the scattered but volunteer Light Infantry and Grenadier units into volunteer Regimental formations of 10 Companies each. Thus could be and were provided promptly a State's contribution to a National field force.

In the districts thus stripped of active, drilling and self-equipped units of Organized Militia, the Governor's Adjutant General strove to create Home Guard Companies for riots, storms, local security and as a nucleus whence could be created new units of *Volunteers,* should there be an additional call before the return of those then on extended active duty pursuant to the earlier National call. Sometimes the threats of invoking the terms of the State's military Draft Law expedited the volunteering to create the subsequent units. Such practices left in final reserve the geographically distributed, enrolled but unorganized Militia, or military manpower pool. And in one significant instance, they had to fight as such.

## THE ENROLLED MILITIA AT BLADENSBURG

In the case of Maryland, the District of Columbia and Virginia, when a powerful amphibious expedition under Britain's Admiral Sir George Cockburn appeared at the mouth of the Potomac River, the Federal Government did call upon those States for immediate, spot defense levies. In effect, this sudden alarm activated into militarily-labeled mobs the enrolled, Unorganized Militia that participated in the confused and so often-misunderstood Battle of Bladensburg. This debacle, as all know, was a fast-running prelude to the disastrous burning of the National Capitol and White House, Summer of 1814.

Bladensburg was the only major battle in the War of 1812 that was fought by an alarm-bell, overnight, civilian levy on the towns and countryside. Actually, the so-called Army was a mass *posse comitatus*, with the nomenclature of the parade ground substituted for that of the Sheriff's Office. To be sure, there was an under-strength Regiment of short-term Regulars and a Company or more of Marines on the battlefield that day, but there is no evidence that they influenced the outcome any more than did Captain J. I. Stull's "Georgetown Rifles." His was a Home Guard outfit that had been drilling with unserviceable squirrel guns. There was reason to expect new rifles from War Department supplies en route to action. But there was a miscue somewhere along the line. They appeared on the field of battle with only their "sidearms"—tomahawks, to be specific!

Oddly enough, a famous, crack Regiment of the British Army, the King's Own, rates Bladensburg the bloodiest day of action in its history. It had the bad luck to run afoul of the uncoordinated roadblock set up by the Navy's Commodore Joshua Barney. He had nothing else for his crews and guns to do after he prematurely blew up his flotilla of gunboats. One could award him a D.S.C. for the courage of his leadership that day. It would be impossible, however, to write for him a Distinguished Service Medal citation for his strategic concepts. The destruction of his flotilla was the first and primary objective of the British landing force. Had Barney fought from his ships instead of from his belated roadblock, the English commander would not have been allowed the rapid, concentrated singleness of mission toward Washington.

But what else could one expect in a battle in which the President of the United States galloped about with a brace of horse pistols as his only military identification as Constitutional Commander-in-Chief; and while the Secretary of State modified deployments for battle without the knowledge of intervening field commanders? Presumably the Secretary of State might have worked through the Secretary of War. But the latter was attempting the task of the Commanding General, Fifth Military District, who, in turn, was assiduously confusing any immediate coordination of the sundry columns of sailors, Marines and rabble of all categories converging on Bladensburg. They were still converging when the British launched the attack that routed them in detail.

As an unequalled, gigantic, farcical comedy of errors, one could argue that Bladensburg was almost worth the price of production; but as a battle it was a tragic travesty, in which the quality and category of the troops had the lesser roles. In any event, when the English fleet and army bombarded Baltimore's Fort McHenry, and the over-land advance on Baltimore was launched, the Maryland skirmishers, who killed England's General Ross in an advance guard action that stopped the British Army in its tracks, were the same kind of troops who, under too much leadership at Bladensburg, had performed so badly. The major difficulty at Bladensburg was that there were too many highly-talented, articulate chiefs and also too many under-equipped and utterly confused warriors. But because of the notoriety of Bladensburg, "the Militia" became the historians' whipping boy for all the land warfare failures of 1812-14. The historical fact that, for this war, the Federal Government authorized and mustered the largest Regular Army America was to see prior to 1898, has too long been ignored in favor of acceptance of General Upton's ideal and arguments for an "expansible Regular Army."

Regular Army peak strengths, officers and men, in subsequent Nineteenth Century American wars were: Mexican War, November, 1847, 21,686; Civil War, June, 1862, 25,480; Spanish-American War, June, 1898, 47,867. All military personnel statistics for 1812-15 are deplorable. The maximum authorized Regular Army strength was 62,674. The peak muster strength most likely was reached in late 1814, or early 1815. Upton cites an AGO return for February, 1815, of 33,424. Some historians have estimated a peak mustering figure of 38,000.

### THE "EXPANSIBLE REGULAR ARMY" IN THEORY AND PRACTICE

Before the actual opening of hostilities, the War Department embarked upon a military manpower policy that later was labeled as the "concept of an expansible Regular Army." Professional soldiers, most particularly Emory Upton, toward the end of the Century, began endorsing the concept. They seldom, if ever, have cited the War of 1812 as being the manner in which the theory would or should work when put into practice.

In early 1805, the Regular Army stood at 187 officers and cadets and 2,385 men in two Regiments of Infantry and 20 Batteries of Artillery. The latter were grouped into one Artillery Regimental command. War clouds with Britain were seen far enough in advance that military expansion began as early as 1808. In that year eight Regiments of all Arms were added, by appropriate legislation. Enlistments were for five years. In January, 1812, there was legislation for an additional 13 Regular Army Regiments. The terms of enlistment were similar. Since the size of the Regiments was increased simultaneously, this authorized a Regular Army of 35,603; and the shooting had not yet started.

But enlistments were slow in 1812 to the point of uncertainty. Accordingly, the President was authorized to accept from the States six Companies of volunteer Frontier Rangers for a period of a year. This was to relieve Regular Army units on the Indian frontier. Within a month, February 6, 1812, the President was authorized to accept

14

volunteer units of Organized Militiamen from the States up to an aggregate of 30,000 officers and men. In April the terms of Regular Army enlistments were reduced to 18 months. The Governors further were instructed to be prepared to respond to a Call for Companies and Regiments for their Organized Militia units to an aggregate of 80,000 officers and men. But at the end of 1812 (following six months of hostilities) there appear to have been less than 20,000 Regular Army officers and men in uniform. At the same time there were perhaps 30,000 Volunteers on extended active duty in the units of Organized Militia, or National Guard. They had been inducted into Federal service for varying terms of duty, often determined by State statutes to be longer than the Federal Call.

Came January, 1813, and troops in Organized Militia, or National Guard, units were particularly invited to join the Regular Army formations for one-year enlistments. Enlistment bounties were increased with an appeal to all and sundry. The Regular Army's organizational structure was increased to 44 Regiments of Infantry, four of Artillery, two of Dragoons, one Regiment of Rifles, and an expansion of the Corps of Engineers. These formations called for a strength of 57,351 officers and men in the Regular Army. Subsequent legislation, February 10, 1814, added three Regiments of Rifles and other minor modifications for an authorized strength of 62,274. This figure never was reached. It was one thing to vote an "expansible Regular Army," but expanding it adequately and effectively was something else. Obviously the big mistake in manpower planning in this war was failure to give heed to the military needs of the Organized Militia and make plans for tapping the great reservoir of volunteer potential, as early as 1808, when the Regular Army expansion began.

There are no accurate figures for either the Regular Army Regiments or the Organized Volunteer Militia Regiments on extended active duty as of each day, week and month of the war period. It does not appear, however, that the ambitious structure of Regular Regiments ever achieved a peak strength of more than 34,000. Nor did the Volunteers in States' Regiments on field duty (ignoring short-term, static, defense missions on bays, rivers and harbors and locally-garrisoned Indian frontier forts) reach more than near the same figure, approximately 33,000. The hundreds of thousands of Militiamen often said to have served during the War of 1812 appear to have been local short-termers of one to 12 weeks. Their response was to such alarms as the sudden appearance of English warships off the Coast or false rumors of Indian raids inland. Thus, the day-to-day field campaigning and fighting through the War of 1812 appears to have been done by a force that at peak strength, and toward the war's end, approximated 67,000 officers and men. They were divided almost equally between Regular Army and what we would today call volunteer, National Guardsmen from the States.

But in examination of Troop Lists of engaged units, it often appears the Regulars were in the minority. At New Orleans, for example, which was America's most significant victory of the war, the American Order of Battle included 66 Marines, 22 Regular Army Artillerymen, and two Regular Army Infantry Regiments, the 7th and 44th. The former mustered 465 officers and men; the latter 331.*

These figures were approximately par for the Regular Regiments of that war, though the authorized, paper strength of the Regiments was slightly more than 1,000 officers and men each. Organized Militia Regiments on extended active duty were also of identical authorized war strength. However, they were usually about the size of the two Regular formations mentioned above. The backbone of Jackson's force at New Orleans consisted of the 2,982 officers and men in the Tennessee and Kentucky Regiments, and the 515 Louisiana Artillerymen and Infantrymen in the "Battery St. Domingo Men of Colour" and Major Planche's Battalion. The remainder (1,309 officers and men) of Jackson's aggregate of 5,690 were hastily-recruited levies from the local military manpower pool, or Unorganized Militia. The last, of course, included the much-publicized Lafitte contingent of Barataria pirates, smugglers and blackbirders.

On the Detroit-Niagara-Lake Champlain frontier there was a military stalemate throughout most of the war. Once again Organized Militia, or volunteer Regiments from the States, mustered more men in the field than did their Regular Army counterparts. And the Northwest Indian frontier was almost entirely controlled by the Civilian Components. But at Queenstown Heights, a Regiment of Regulars, and later a Brigade of Regulars, under Winfield Scott, at Lundy's Lane, fought with such distinction that the Regular Army's potential for disciplined valor under fire was sparked first in this war. Nevertheless, their shortened terms of enlistment, the majority for only one year, and the necessity for so many spot commissions direct from civil life, caused a later-day Regular Army officer to lament that by-and-large there was

---

* The 7th U.S. Infantry was commanded by a Maj. H. D. Peire, U.S. Army. He was breveted to the next higher rank for outstanding service in this battle. He had been a Regular since Aug. 1, 1813, on which date he was commissioned Major from the same rank and assignment he had held in a Volunteer Regiment of Louisiana Organized Militia, or Volunteers. Capt. Isaac L. Baker commanded the 44th U.S. Infantry. His original commission as a Regular was dated July 6, 1812, 12 days before war was declared. Examination of these and other Regular Army Regimental rosters clearly indicates little difference in quality and experience of comparable Regiments of the civilian component and the professional component of the 1812-15 forces. The former did often complain that the latter enjoyed preferences in matters of supplies, equipment and regularity of pay. Actually, all the field forces were sadly neglected in these matters throughout the war.

little difference between the Regular Army professionals and the Civilian Components of America's Army that fought the War of 1812-15. In any event, when peace brought immediate reduction to a small permanent establishment, all ranks and commissions of the retained, or integrated, officers were not by seniority, or prewar service. The test for Regular Army integration was one of combat record, from Generals down to Ensigns and Lieutenants.

## REORGANIZATION ON MERIT

It is interesting to note that of the two Major Generals retained to command the reduced, peacetime Regular Army, both were from the Organized Militia, or National Guard. Neither had any peacetime service except within the Volunteer Militia units of their respective States.

The senior officer chosen, and Commanding General of the postwar Army, was Jacob Brown. He began the war as Colonel of a New York Volunteer Regiment, Organized Militia. The second and junior Major General in the new postwar Regular Army was Andrew Jackson. As a General Officer in Tennessee's Organized Militia, thence to active duty commanding that State's contingent of Volunteer Regiments, all of Jackson's war service was in the grade of a General Officer. To clarify command status over Regular Army units assigned to their field forces, both Brown and Jackson had been given wartime Federal commissions, comparable to modern A.U.S. ranks, as Brigadier Generals in 1813 and 1814 respectively.

The postwar organization also called for four permanent Brigadier Generals. Of those chosen, Edmund P. Gaines and Alexander Macomb had sufficient prior service to rate them as professional soldiers. Their original commissions were dated in early 1799; thus, both could show 16 years of continuous service. Winfield Scott and Eleazer W. Ripley, the two other Brigadiers retained for their brilliant war records, were strictly short-timers.

Scott, trained as a lawyer, had wangled an appointment from civil life as an Artillery Captain in Regular Army expansion legislation of 1808. He lost one of the four years prior to hostilities in 1812 because of suspension from "all rank, pay and emoluments for the space of 12 months." In 1810 he had faced a court-martial. To a specification of mutiny and threatening the life of his Commanding Officer, Scott had conceded his having said he would have to carry two pistols should he go into battle under his current commander, General James Wilkinson. One pistol would be "for his enemy and one for his General." Scott's defense had been that he was justified in saying it. The light sentence suggests the Court thought his logic had some merit. But as a Regimental and Brigade Commander on the Niagara frontier, Scott had proved himself to be a terrific trainer and leader of men. In the 50 years ahead of him as a General Officer, Scott was to become virtually the father of American military professionalism. But in 1815, he was about the most irregular Regular who ever pinned a single star on his shoulder.

Except for experience in the Organized Militia units of New Hampshire and Massachusetts, Eleazer W. Ripley had no service record prior to outbreak of hostilities in 1812. Like Scott, he was a lawyer. His original commission, at age 30, was Lieutenant Colonel, 21st U.S. Infantry, which was backdated to rank him from March 12, 1812. In 1820, Ripley became bored with peacetime soldiering and resigned to reenter the legal profession.

The foregoing brief review of leaders emerging from the War of 1812 is primarily to illustrate further the legal origins of their commissions and thereby differentiate with further clarity the two components that constituted the active field forces of the United States during that war. These, of course, were composed of the Volunteers in the Regiments inducted from the Organized Militia of the several States and the approximately 50 understrength Regiments of the "expansible" Regular Army. It was only at Bladensburg that overnight levies of the unorganized but enrolled Militia of Maryland and the District of Columbia appeared in such numbers that they dominated the military scene. In the operational field forces, one could hardly say there was enough difference between the performance of the Regulars as a whole and the Volunteers as a whole to warrant material historical notice, except for some specific Regiments of each component on a specifically good or an exceptionally poor day, dependent on the viewpoint. Certainly the forefathers of that era saw no basis for differentiation when they reorganized the Army in 1815. Moreover, the theory of the "expansible" Regular Army, as a war measure, was not to be proposed again seriously until after 1900, when the disciples of the deceased Emory Upton embraced the idea from his posthumous book.

That the 1812-15 forefathers were not satisfied with their own solutions to the wartime military manpower problems is quite evident. At the war's end, newer Regular Army Regiments were being broken-up necessarily to create replacements for understrength older units. Volunteer Regiments often were weakened in the field by Regular Army recruiting within their ranks. In late 1814, the Administration was so concerned over manpower for field operations that it was considering three or four conscription plans. It is well the war ended without their having to pursue such ideas any further. None of the proposals they had under advisement would have been successful. A workable Draft plan that decentralized to the States and their lesser governmental agencies the responsibility of selection was slightly more than 100 years in the future.

With the peacetime Regular Regiments totalling less than 10,000, and committed to distant Indian frontiers, the military-minded civilians returned to their voluntary, patriotic, military associations. They indulged in such drilling, shooting, riding, and social amenities as might be found in local units of the "Georgia Hussars," "Governor's Grenadiers," "Coastal Cannoneers," "Lawrence Minutemen," "City National Guard" or, farther West, the "Raccoon Roughs." In this manner they maintained the Organized Militia traditions from Colonial days.*

The remainder of American mankind in ages of 18 to 45, unconsciously and unwittingly, reverted to "enrollees" (if they went to the annual Muster Day at all) in the Unorganized Militia, or militarily-obligated manpower, of their respective States. Annual mustering days continued in the statutes to remind them of an obligation and to maintain the yearly census of a State's manpower pool of men in military age. By 1840 these mustering days of the unorganized but enrolled Militia had become occasions for political speeches, picnics and the consumption of much raw whiskey. Thus the annual musters fell into such disrepute that they gradually were discontinued in most States, often without so much as formal repeal of the law requiring the musters. Nevertheless, those military, manpower census days of the Unorganized Militia too long and too often have been considered the annual training period of the volunteer Companies. They were by no means the same.

Meanwhile, the Indian wars after 1815 were fought by the Regulars, aided by civilian contingents ranging from a Sheriff's Posse to Companies, Regiments and even Brigades sent on active duty by Governors, pursuant to limited-service Calls from Washington. The largest of these was the Seminole War, but it involved Organized Militia units and levies from no more than a few States. The next Federal Call that went to all the States was caused by the War with Mexico, April, 1846—March, 1848.

## FIELD FORCES FOR THE MEXICAN WAR

This was essentially a foreign war. Not even in Texas, the Border State, were home towns threatened by hostile columns. Hence, this was the first war in which all the engaged United States troops were away from home. There was no fighting for Home Guard units. There were no sudden levies on the militarily-obligated manpower of an area, such as took place in Virginia and Maryland when Washington was captured and the Capitol was burned in the Summer of 1814.

---

* A few historic unit titles survive, as non-military social organizations, Boston's Ancient and Honorable Artillery Company is of this character.

In short, for the United States, the Mexican War was fought exclusively by the Volunteers in the States' voluntarily-organized Militia units (National Guardsmen) and the Regular Army.

In May, 1846, the latter numbered 734 officers and 7,885 enlisted men. Of these, 803 were not present for duty. But of those available, 3,554 officers and men were right where they should have been. They constituted Brevet Brigadier General Zachary Taylor's Army of Occupation, concentrated just North of the Rio Grande near Brownsville. Initially, General Taylor thought all he needed was this force plus such volunteer Organized Militia Regiments as Texas might provide. With such reserve potential, he felt he hardly could lose a war with Mexico. Since the citizen-soldiers of the Republic of Texas had won their independence in a war with Mexico, this was a fairly safe assumption. But Taylor did want to be sure of adequate supplies. Logistical support for his existing command and for future reinforcements was his primary concern.

Taylor's superior, Brevet Major General Edmund P. Gaines, commanding the Department of the West from his Headquarters in New Orleans, had plans of his own for calling upon the Governors of other nearby States. Came the Mexican offensive, which gave Americans a mild scare at Resaca de la Palma, and both Generals activated their respective plans. Taylor called on Texas for three-months units; Gaines upon Texas and other regional States for Volunteer units for six months of service. Such plans and actions were in line with what had happened in the Seminole War. Obviously, to Generals Gaines and Taylor, Mexico appeared to be no more than an oversized, frontier, Indian problem.

Taylor's call to Texas quickly brought 1,390 officers and men in one Regiment and a separate Battalion. Until his logistical problems were better in hand, this was about all Taylor wanted. The Gaines call for six-months units mobilized 11,211 officers and men in sundry volunteer State Regiments. Of these about 6,000 reported to Taylor at Brownsville before he had adequate logistical support.

Fortunately, the remainder of the "Gaines Army" never arrived. Meanwhile, the President, Secretary of War, and Congress were making plans of their own. The Gaines calls were halted. He was reprimanded repeatedly for exceeding authority. To these official frowns the 69-year-old veteran Regular responded: "I carelessly submit to them, as they seem to be a source of pleasure to the War Department, and certainly inflict no injury on me." Gaines was relieved and court-martialed in his permanent grade of Brigadier General. He brilliantly and vehemently beat the rap, was given a new assignment appropriate to his brevet rank, and died, in active duty status, at age 72.

Meanwhile the Washington plans, with which Gaines had been interfering, were taking form rapidly. The Federal Militia Act did not authorize the President to draft from the States any Militia units for extended compulsory service beyond three months. But there was nothing to keep Congress from changing the law. It had happened in the past and soon was to occur again. Meanwhile, volunteering units of the Organized Militia could be supplied in properly-formed tactical units for as long a term as the men joining those units might willingly obligate themselves as a unit. This was one of the constructive lessons learned from the War of 1812. Some of the States occasionally had put on the line Regiments of their citizens who volunteered in advance for much longer terms. Tennessee, in particular, learned, with Andrew Jackson's campaigns so far from home towns, that short-term rotation of personnel did not make sense. And President James K. Polk was from Tennessee.*

The President, Secretary of War William L. Marcey, and the C. G. of the Army, Winfield Scott, collaborated with the Congress to call on the States for tactical formations of Battery, Battalion, and Regimental size comparable to Tables and ranks prevailing in the Regular Army. These units were to be officered and manned by not more than 50,000 Volunteers for "twelve months," or "for the war," at the option of the President. The President was authorized to apportion Field, Staff and General Officers among the States furnishing Volunteers. Companies, Battalions and Regiments of the Volunteers were to be organized and officered pursuant to the Militia laws of the States. States and individuals were to be reimbursed for costs of fitting-out these volunteering Regiments. At the discretion of the President, Militia levies, similar to those called-out for the defense of Washington, might be retained compulsorily on active duty for six months, instead of the three months in the existing law.

The strength ceiling for the Regular Army was raised to allow recruiting of all Company-size units to war strength of 100 men each. A new Regiment of Regular Army Mounted Riflemen was to be created. The inflation of the unit structure beyond the recruiting capabilities of the Regular Army was not repeated. These purely war measures were supported by an appropriation of $10,000,000.

For reasons unknown, the President defaulted on his "one-year or duration of war" option for the Volunteer units. He published the law as passed. This was interpreted as leaving the option up to the Volunteer units and/or the States organizing the Regiments. This proved to be a

---

* In the usage and popularization of the word "Volunteers" in American military history, Tennessee has an undeniable claim, hence validating its nickname "The Volunteer State." That the War Department, as we shall see, later adopted the word as its very own and gradually diverted its meaning so that by 1901 it was descriptive of another procedure for recruiting troops, does not deny the original meaning of the term or Tennessee's early claim thereto.

mistake and a basis for much criticism by some historians, who projected the same criticisms just as bitterly against the three-year enlistment of Volunteers in 1861. All volunteering should be "for the duration," they properly insisted. But these errors were not the fault of the Volunteers in either instance. The fault was and is in National policy. And professional military planners appear to be just as capable of the same errors as were the politicians of 1845 and 1861. The same sort of thing happened through the Korean "Police Action" with former General of the Army George C. Marshall as Secretary of Defense and Generals Omar N. Bradley and J. Lawton Collins as Chairman of the Joint Chiefs of Staff and Army Chief of Staff, respectively. Their basic policy was not more than two years of active duty for individual citizen-soldiers in a war that lasted more than three years. They called it "Rotation of Service," with emphasis on rotation. It normally precluded a soldier's being in Korea more than six months, and many were in active operations only a matter of weeks. Historians often are astounded by the extent to which a new and happy phrase can make a discredited and worthless old practice look like something new and good.

## ROTATION IN MEXICO

Even so, the Mexican War results were somewhat more happy than those of our own day in Korea. The flow of volunteering Organized Militia units to the front was immediate. Initially they were in advance of adequate logistical arrangements. The battles that followed were fought by units of Regulars and Volunteers with an aggregate of 104,284 officers and men of all components, including a Battalion of Marines numbering 548 officers and men. But the net daily operational numbers were much smaller. The names of many officers and men first occur in three-months or six-months unit lists of the Taylor or Gaines calls. They then recur in one-year, and later in duration-of-war Regiments, or on the rosters of a Regular Army unit. For example, 30,476 of the above aggregate served in Regular Army formations. Of these, however, 15,736 officers and men joined the Regulars in Mexico.

Almost without exception these 15,736 officers and men were from one-year and six-months Regiments from the "Gaines Army" that were going back to the States to be mustered-out for expiration of enlistments. One way to stay until the show was over, and without missing anything, was to join-up with one of the Regular Regiments. All of them were in chronic need of fillers.

Moreover, not all who thus joined the Regular Army in Mexico were enlisted men. Samuel H. Walker, the famous Texas Ranger who gave his name to the Walker model of the first, truly successful Colt revolver, left Texas as a Lieutenant Colonel of John C. Hays' 1st Regiment of Texas Mounted Rifle Volunteers. He died in action, between Vera Cruz

22

and Mexico City, as Captain Samuel H. Walker, U. S. Mounted Rifles, Regular Army. The same was true of a number of lesser-known names. Such men and their 15,734 associates were not of the stripe who would permit expiration of a contract, or a false sense of pride in matter of rank, keep them out of a fight until it was finished.

It is thus quite apparent that slightly more than half of the officers and men who constituted the Regular Army of the Mexican War actually were displaced citizen-soldiers from the Regiments and Battalions sent on active duty from the Organized Militia of the States. Moreover, the statistical aggregate of Americans in uniform who went to Mexico should be diminished by that number, as they obviously were counted twice, and a few of them at least three times.

Within the various categories of three-months (Taylor's call) and six months ("Gaines' Army"), one-year and duration-of-war Regiments from the States, there is a similarly high duplication of names within the aggregate of 73,532 Volunteers from the States. Within this aggregate, 1,390 were in Taylor's three-months call; 11,211 in "Gaines' Army" call for six months, but all were mustered-out sooner. But many such short-time Volunteers thus became a part of the 27,063 Volunteers on rosters of the one-year Regiments. Then came the duration-of-war Regiments of Volunteers with a subtotal of 33,596. Considering the duplication of names on successive rosters, it does not appear likely that the officers and men in the Volunteer formations from the States ever exceeded, as of any one date, the 50,000 in the President's Call. With this number as a base, and subtracting the 15,736 officers and men fed into the Regular Army's war aggregate of 31,024, and adding the same to the Volunteer Regiments whence they originally came, it is quite apparent that the ratio of citizen-soldier effort to that of the Regular Army, in personnel terms, was about 65 to 15. This certainly gives little support to the constantly-recurring inference by most military historians that the short, brilliant war with Mexico was essentially a professional performance.

One such historian flatly attributes American victories to the "simple fact" that we "used no militia in Mexico." In the sense of Home Guard units and geographical, Regimental, and district levies such as the conscripts of the Enrolled Militia who turned out to defend Washington, D.C., only to be routed at Bladensburg, the statement is perhaps correct. But the allegation ignores the fact that the Volunteer Regiments from the States were part and parcel of the Militia of the States whose names they bore, i.e., the Organized Militia, National Guard Regiments of their day, placed on active duty pursuant to requisitions (or Calls) upon the Governors of the several States by the Federal Government. Every Regiment was officered, recruited, often armed, equipped and frequently clothed on State authority, but subject to reimbursement from the Federal Treasury for the service to the Nation as a whole.

The Regiments, separate Battalions, Batteries and Companies of the States' Volunteers that fought and sustained casualties in the Mexican War are tabulated below.

## ORGANIZED MILITIA (NATIONAL GUARD) UNITS

| | Regiments | Separate Battalions | Separate Companies and Batteries |
|---|---|---|---|
| Alabama | 1 | 2 | 4 |
| Arkansas | 1 | | 2 |
| California | | 1 | |
| Florida | | | 2 |
| Georgia | 1 | 2 | 1 |
| Illinois | 5 | | 4 |
| Indiana | 5 | | |
| Iowa | | 1* | |
| Kentucky | 4 | | |
| Louisiana | 7 | 4 | 1 |
| Maryland and D.C. | 1 | 1 | 1 |
| Massachusetts | 1 | | |
| Michigan | 1 | | |
| Mississippi | 2 | 1 | 1 |
| Missouri | 4 | 6 | 9 |
| New Jersey | | 1 | |
| New York | 2 | | |
| North Carolina | 1 | | |
| Ohio | 5 | | 3 |
| Pennsylvania | 2 | | 1 |
| South Carolina | 1 | | |
| Tennessee | 6 | | 1 |
| Texas | 7 | 2 | 11 |
| Virginia | 1 | | |
| Total | 58 | 21 | 41 |

* Iowa, with perhaps less than 100,000 population, became a State the first year of the war. Its lone Battalion was known as the "Iowa Mormon Volunteers." It was the only unit in the Mexican War to proclaim a religious preference. Not included in these totals was the so-called "Santa Fe Battalion," of Rocky Mountain trappers and traders. It was organized by Col. Sterling Price, 2nd Missouri Infantry Volunteers, who provided the officer leadership from his Regiment. The famous Kit Carson served in the "Santa Fe Battalion" as a 2nd Lt. The Mexican War was unpopular in anti-slavery New England, hence there was but one Volunteer Regiment from that region.

The full-strength Regimental Tables of that era approximated 1,000 officers and men. The above-tabulated 21 separate Battalions and the 41 Companies constituted a full, fair equivalent of an additional 12 Regiments, for a total of 70 Regiments and Regimental equivalents of Volunteers, or Organized Militiamen, for the war. Actually, some Regiments were well under 1,000, as were the Regular Regiments through most of the War. But while some Organized Militia, or Volunteer, Regiments left for the Theater of War under-strength, there were others that anticipated their own need for replacements by leaving home with more than 1,400 officers and men. In any event, the equivalent of the 70 State Regiments of all categories listed above balances-out rather closely to the aggregate of 73,260 Volunteers in State units who saw Federal duty during the Mexican War. Since not all the tabulated units were active simultaneously and throughout the war, this offers no conflict with the estimate that no more than 50,000 Volunteers were in Federal service as of a given date.

In the same way that not all these men were on duty simultaneously, not all the tabulated Regiments and smaller units of Volunteers were simultaneously in Federal service. But neither were all the Regular Army Regiments in being throughout the period of hostilities. Some were created, or reactivated, under earlier numbers, after the shooting had started. All the Regiments of Regulars, however, were chronically and sadly under-strength throughout the war. The nearest to a solution of the replacement problem Generals Scott and Taylor ever found was to recruit vigorously among the men of State units whose terms were expiring. As indicated above, this yielded 15,736 officers and men as fillers for the Regular Army formations.

The Regular Army units that fought in the Mexican War were as follows: Mounted troops (Dragoons and Mounted Rifles), four Regiments; Infantry, 17 Regiments; Artillery, four Regiments, for a total of 25 Regiments. In the field, the Troop Lists of both Taylor and Scott reveal an occasional special Company of Engineers and even a rocket unit, but these were created in the Theater of Operations from personnel pinched from older formations. Incidentally, the Organized Militia, or National Guard, component of the Mexican War's Army of the United States was weak in Artillery, the equivalent of hardly more than 11 Batteries. On the other hand, 16,887 of the Volunteers in State Regiments were in mounted units comparable to the Dragoons and Mounted Riflemen in the Regular formations.

## PERSONNEL AFTERMATH OF THE WAR

Along with their Regiments, the States fielded two Major Generals and 11 Brigadier Generals, of whom among the latter, four were breveted to Major General for gallantry and distinguished service in the presence of the enemy. Likewise, the Regular Army fielded two Major Generals and six Brigadiers, among whom one Major General (Scott) and five Brigadiers were breveted to the next higher rank.

Actually, none but Scott and Taylor came out of the war with significant military reputations. The latter became President. The former was often a best man but never the bridegroom at White House inaugurals. From among the Volunteers in the Regiments of the States, only Brigadier General Franklin Pierce and Colonel Jefferson Davis, Commander of the 1st Mississippi Rifles, played major roles in subsequent political history. Pierce, of course, was President, 1853-57. Davis became Pierce's Secretary of War and later served in the Senate, thence to the Presidency of the short-lived Confederate States of America.

Much has been written in the memoirs and biographies of professional soldiers and further commented upon by historians in general concerning the Mexican War as a training experience and "dress rehearsal" for the professional soldier leadership of the impending Civil War. At the same time, everyone has overlooked the equally obvious fact that the same war provided the Governors of the States, North and South, with large numbers of experienced citizen-soldiers from among whom were drawn Field Grade and General Officers who led Regiments, Brigades, Divisions and Army Corps through all the bitter campaigns of 1861-65.

The oft-fostered impression that the Governors in the Mexican War, and particularly in the Civil War, ignored military experience to pay-off political debts with Colonelcies and Regimental commands, is not supported by closer scrutiny of the facts. It is quite clear that military experience normally was utilized in such instances as it was competent and willing to serve. It is easy to find exceptions to this general rule within the States. But it likewise is easy to find worse exceptions in which the Federal War Department and the President, in both the Mexican and Civil Wars, used commissions much higher than Colonel to satisfy a political patronage claimant.*

## DEFINITIONS—PAST AND PRESENT

In the light of the foregoing brief historical review of the origins of the civilian and professional components of the armies of the United States prior to 1861 (those components known today as the National Guard and the Regular Army) it is now possible to offer intelligently and with greater clarity a brief glossary of the more confusing terms with which this review was opened. The arrangement is chronological, rather than alphabetical. When practicable, definitions also progress from the generic to the specific.

ARMY, in its original and generic sense, is any armed land force, friendly, hostile or neutral, American or foreign, that is just sufficiently armed and organized to distinguish it from the horde of its own mankind.

MILITIA stems from the Latin *miles*, meaning soldier, hence *militia*, indicating military service. It came to England in the French form, *milice*, during the Elizabethan mass mobilization to defend England

---

* In the Civil War the Federal Major Generalcies to N. P. Banks, Benjamin F. Butler and E. D. Morgan, the first two dated May 16, 1861 and that of Morgan Sept. 28, 1861, are the most flagrant examples.

against the Armada, 1588. It signified the obligation of every able-bodied Englishman to defend his country. Of course, that concept in England long antedated the appearance of the word *militia* in the English language. The primitive hue-and-cry that rallied the tribal, and later the feudal, *Fyrd* to restore order and to resist danger, is older than English written history. In short, *militia* was and is the concept of duty and obligation which makes all citizens vulnerable to army service should the need become sufficiently great and urgent. This concept was fundamental. In further application, the word took on an added, more tangible connotation. Hence it early came to mean all the able-bodied adult males within proclaimed, or statutory, ages who were obligated to perform military duty on call.

THE MILITIA (of a specific American Colony, or State) is merely the transition of the English Common Law concept to the Colony and its successor State. The Militia of Virginia, for example, was and is the able-bodied manpower of that State within the arms-bearing ages set forth in laws. Colonial and State Draft laws were quite common, but they were effective only to the extent of expediting volunteering. That the Federal Constitution should not be an abridgement of a State's right to Militia service of its citizens was written into the Bill of Rights of the Constitution, thereby somewhat abridging the basic Army and Navy Clauses of the Federal Constitution.

ENROLLED MILITIA were mere local lists of names and addresses of men within the statutory ages for military service. The concept extended back to the early English Assize of Arms. In America, after 1792, the term is associated with efforts of the several States to implement, in law and practice, the Federal Militia Act of May 8, 1792.

FEDERAL MILITIA in the sense of an able-bodied male citizen's military obligation to render service directly to the United States is quite modern. The concept of such obligation was specifically challenged by the Justices of the Massachusetts Supreme Court in supporting their Governor in resisting the Call on that State for troops in 1812. Connecticut concurred. Hence the mass acceptance of the idea of a Federal Militia came out of the titanic war effort of the North to preserve the Union. The Massachusetts objections were more completely negated by the concept of an American duality of citizenship, State and Federal, with a corresponding duality of obligation. Successful implementation of the concept has been slow, the evolution of which is reserved for subsequent chapters.

NAVAL MILITIA as a literary simile has been associated with and confused with privateering and ships sailing under letter of marque and reprisal. Such use of the term is mere poetic license at best and grossly inaccurate at worst. There was no Naval Militia until 1889, when Massachusetts State legislation authorized Organized Naval Militia units, as potential ships' crews and a seagoing counterpart to the Massachusetts Volunteer Militia. Other coastal and Great Lakes States soon followed suit. See Chapter V.

TRAINBANDS as a military term appears to have originated in the reign of James I. Institutionally, and in practice, they go back to Alfred the Great, and perhaps to even earlier periods in English history. The concept arises from the Militia obligation, or duty, to serve. For greater security, certain men in or near each settlement or City, who volunteered or were selected otherwise, were given, or agreed to procure, arms in advance of any emergency. They were to become skilled in their use. They were obligated to hasten to a designated strongpoint or rendezvous for defensive or offensive action upon the sounding of danger alarms. The Trainbands of the cities, particularly of London, became the nuclei of the armed, Cromwellian revolt that achieved the beheading of Charles I. Charles II, thoughtful of his own neck, abolished the Trainbands to create England's Regular Army. But the British Territorials continue today as the direct institutional descendants of the Trainbands. Some British Regular Regiments, however, trace their heritage to certain Trainbands, just as a modern Battery of Artillery in the Regular Army proudly claims Alexander Hamilton's New York Battery as its lineal ancestor. In Colonial America the term was quite common for comparable units of a Colony's voluntary military associations that organized themselves into chartered or otherwise recognized units of the Organized Militia. Current editions of Webster's Dictionary err in the statement: "These bands developed into the militia." To be correct it should read ". . . *from* the militia."

ORGANIZED MILITIA, in the specific sense, is synonymous with the earlier Colonial Trainbands and chartered Companies. See above. The term began supplanting Trainbands when the Colonies began turning-out Regimental-size units for participation in the American phases of the Eighteenth Century wars. Service in the Organized Militia normally was considered evidence of patriotism above and beyond the normal requirement of Militia responsibility.

MINUTE MEN Companies were part and parcel of the Organized Militia. They were not a new or essentially different American military component. They were Colonial Militiamen voluntarily associated into Trainbands, or Organized Militia, who, because of known dangers, further had agreed to turn-out, with arms, for immediate service, upon a minute's notice. Neither this concept nor its practice originated among the Revolutionary Fathers of Massachusetts with whom the term is so vividly associated. Indeed, these Fathers did not even coin the word. They borrowed it and its fullest implications from the comparatively distant Canadian and Indian frontiers where the word and the practice of urgency were in vogue through the French-and-Indian War. The Companies of Longfellow's "embattled farmers" who at Lexington and Concord "fired the shot heard 'round the world," were merely the volunteer Organized Militia Companies of Massachusetts who acted under the authority of their Provincial Congress in resisting a raid against their civil liberties by the King's Regulars. These Massachusetts Minute Men Companies were a part of a momentous incident in American history that became enshrined in the rich traditions and heritage of the Massachusetts Volunteer Militia; because of which heritage that Commonwealth was the last of the States to accept the comparatively new-fangled term, "Massachusetts National Guard."

NATIONAL GUARD is synonymous with Organized Militia, Volunteer Militia, Active Militia and Uniformed Companies. See above. Lafayette coined the phrase *Garde Nationale* for his French Revolution Army, and structured it as nearly as possible upon the Continental Line in which he had commanded a Virginia Brigade. On his 1824 visit he popularized the term in America by applying it to all Organized Militia units in America. The term immediately began appearing in ephemeral writings and popular parlance. New York, by statute, adopted the term during the Civil War. The further evolution of the National Guard *as a dual force,* State and National, is reviewed in subsequent chapters.

VOLUNTEERS, specifically and with a capital V, denoted men in *units* of the Organized Militia "called" into active Federal Service. Such Companies, Battalions and Regiments were made available to the Federal Government by State authorities, and through the State machinery of government, for all National emergencies beginning with the Whiskey Rebellion. The State's name, until 1917, normally appears in the unit's official designation such as "1st Michigan Corps" or "3rd Ohio Volunteer Infantry." The extent to which some States may have "stimulated" volunteering by coordinated offers of bounties and threats of draft is immaterial to the definition.

U.S. VOLUNTEERS properly applies only to men and emergency Regiments directly recruited by the Federal Government outside of State channels. This began, within the narrowest meaning of the term, with four Regiments recruited from Confederate prisoners-of-

29

war for service restricted to the Indian frontier only. Actually the same direct recruiting procedures also were applied to most of the U.S. Colored Troops recruited in the last two years of the Civil War, and to the 10 Regiments of U.S. Veteran Volunteers in the twilight of the war. The evolution from these beginnings to some specialized Regiments for the Spanish War, which became the precursors of the U.S. Organized Reserve, the Officers Reserve Corps and the present-day U.S. Army Reserve (in other words, a Federally-organized Militia) is discussed in the following chapters.

COMMISSIONS IN U.S. VOLUNTEERS constituted a temporary, war-time rank device whereby Field, Staff and General Officers, irrespective of their basic component, could be clothed with proper military authority from the Federal Government for the performance of their duties without regard to the origin of the troops over whom they might be called upon to exercise that authority. In addition to the system of brevet ranks, it became a device for much higher war ranks for Regulars than they were to enjoy in the postwar peacetime establishment. The practice became notable in the Mexican War, but was most conspicuous in the Civil War. By the end of the Pacification of the Philippines, the confusion of Regular Army brevet ranks and brevet U.S.V. ranks was so complete that before World War I it wisely was decided to erase everything and begin over. Details are reviewed in chapters that follow.

U.S. ARMY, currently abbreviated U.S.A. or USA, is synonymous with the Regular Army, in the sense that it is a fulltime, permanent professional force.* That the Revolutionary Founding Fathers so soon imitated the British Regulars, with whom so many of them had first soldiered and later fought against, was prompt, though perhaps unconscious, flattery to the King's Regiments.

ARMY OF THE UNITED STATES (AUS) currently includes all the components of America's land forces; i.e., Regular Army, National

---

* A highly-persuasive political scientist in a recent volume insists there were no armed forces professionals prior to industrialization and modern technology. In brief, fighting for one's King and Country was hardly a profession. He could have gotten the idea from some of the provocative and interesting writings of Capt. Hoffman Nickerson, best known for his *The Armed Horde* (1940). Capt. Nickerson often appears to have considered all men-at-arms prior to our own age as mere amateurs. Whether soldiering was historically a profession, a career, or a trade is pretty much a matter of semantics. It is not urged here that Webster's reference to the "profession of arms" suggests it is the oldest profession. That claim has been long preempted by others. But, land soldiering is certainly one of the oldest *honored* professions. How else can one explain the soldier caste in India and the older civilizations? The Crusaders were religious as well as military in their profession. The laboratory techniques of the physician, William Harvey, arguing for the circulation of blood in 1616, are undoubtedly amateurish to modern eyes, but no one has indicted the medical profession for that reason, or suggested Harvey was not a professional.

Guard, and U.S. Army Reserve. The term is associated largely with the era of World War II and is becoming obsolete in the light of subsequent legislation. When it is desired to indicate all components of the American Army on active duty, and excluding those available for call but not yet with the Colors, the conventional phrase is America's Active Army, or merely "The Active Army." Otherwise components are referred to by names as above, though there is a careless tendency in the Pentagon to merge the National Guard with the U.S. Army Reserve and vice versa, particularly for statistical purposes.

NATIONAL ARMY is the same as Army of the United States, except that it is of World War I vintage. National Army commissions and ranks were temporary and for the war only. Further details are in a subsequent chapter.

OFFICERS RESERVE CORPS AND ENLISTED RESERVE CORPS were World War I terms for the original elements of the present-day U.S. Army Reserve which, as indicated above, is basically a Federal Organized Militia; i.e., officers and men who hold themselves in readiness to serve their Country above and beyond the minimum required of the obligated, unorganized Militiaman within the military age manpower pool—the same concept that created the Trainbands, the Organized Militia and National Guard units of the Colonies and the States. Creating an American army in which all three components, the Army National Guard (the oldest and from which the others are descendants), the Regular Army, and the U.S. Army Reserve work together as one, is considerably more than the achievements of today's generation. It is a part of the unification of this Nation and an evolution of defense practices and institutions that are a part of the great American chronicle.

# Bibliographical Note For Chapter I

For a chapter spanning three centuries, only a few of the more significant sources and titles to which an author is indebted may be cited. Dr. Herbert L. Osgood's, *The American Colonies in the Seventeenth Century*, 3 vols., 1904-07, and his *American Colonies in the Eighteenth Century*, 4 vols., 1924-25, is a source of the minutiae of American Colonial origins. Dr. Osgood was not a military man. One occasionally suspects he did not always best select and interpret the martial facts he examined and recorded, but his copious citations and bibliographies offer effective guides to those who launch independent investigations. Accordingly, students are led quickly to such State collections as *Colonial Records of North Carolina*, 10 vols., 1886-1907, and *Documents Relative to the Colonial History of the State of New York*, 15 vols., 1856-87. They are illustrative of similar series edited, indexed and published by most of the older States, New Jersey, Virginia, Massachusetts and Pennsylvania in particular. They are rich in military information. Much of the writing is of a lively character that belies the dry and ponderous titles of such series. W. W. Hening, *The Statutes-at-Large Being a Collection of all the Laws of Virginia (1619-1792)*, 13 vols. 1823; *Acts and Laws of His Majesty's Province of Massachusetts Bay in New England*, 1754; *Secret Journals of Acts and Proceedings of* [Continental] *Congress*, 4 vols., and the United States *Statutes at Large* since 1789, are likewise indispensable sources but must be used with extreme caution. Acts of legislative bodies and the results therefrom, if any, are often quite different. In the stresses and strains for a satisfactory peace, there are more compromises between legislative theory and practical implementation than perhaps in any other field of Government activity. Edward A. Freeman, *History of the Norman Conquest*, 6 vols., 1867-79, in the chapters pertinent to the Battle of Hastings, or Senlac, reveals the essential difference in the military obligation of the *Fyrd* levies, a primitive Militia, and King Harold's *Huscarles*, the primitive professionals. Sir John W. Fortescue's *History of the British Army*, 13 vols., 1899-1930, further reveals the extent to which America has been influenced by English Common Law, military customs, traditions and organization. The titles of other standard works reflect their pertinence to certain sections of the foregoing chapter: Stanley M. Pargellis, *Military Affairs in North America, 1748-1765; Selected Documents from the Cumberland Papers in Windsor Castle*, 1936; Stanley M. Pargellis, *Lord Loudoun in North America*, 1933; Douglas S. Freeman, *George Washington*, 7 vols. (last volume completed by John A. Carroll and Mary Wells Ashworth) 1949-1957; Louis C. Hatch, *Administration of American Revolutionary Army*, 1904; Brig. Gen. John McA. Palmer, *General von Steuben*, 1937; Francis V. Greene, *The Revolutionary War and Military Policy of the United States*, 1911; Christopher Ward, *The War of the Revolution*, 1952; Cols. R. Ernest Dupuy and Trevor N. Dupuy, *Military Heritage of America*, 1956. The last named is an able and significant, encyclopedic compendium of U.S. military history from early times, but emphasizes operations, with increasing attention to modern events. Henry Adams, *History of the United States*, 9 vols., 1909-11, is an indispensable work for the Administrations of Jefferson and Madison, to which all nine volumes are devoted. Glenn Tucker, *Poltroons and Patriots,* 2 vols., 1954, is a popular but superior history of the War of 1812 as a whole, but, like Adams and some others, the author does not achieve a sharp delineation between the compulsorily *Enrolled Militia* and the *Organized Militia* of volunteers that sustained the traditions of the Revolution's Continental Line, the equivalent of today's National Guard. James Parton, *Life of Andrew Jackson,* 3 vols., 1861, is certainly not the most recent, hardly the most readable and perhaps not the best of the several extended biographies of this great citizen-soldier, but for its attention to details and closeness to the spirit of the times it never has been fully displaced, particularly in the military narrative. George R. Gleig, *Narrative of the Campaigns of the British Army at Washington and New Orleans,* 1821, is the personal memoirs of a highly-articulate English officer who was there. Francis B. Heitman, *Historical Register and Dictionary of the United States Army,* 2 vols., 1903, is an indispensable reference. Brevet Maj. Gen. Emory Upton, *Military Policy of the United States,* 1904, is not a history, but is a brief in support of prior concepts. Brig. Gen. John McA. Palmer's indictments of Upton's scholarship and often erroneous concepts are conclusive, hence the book should be used with extreme caution by modern historians, though the volume's impact upon professional thinking prior to World War I cannot be denied. Justin H. Smith, *The War with Mexico,* 2 vols., 1919, is unequaled for meticulous scholarship from Mexican as well as American sources. Maj. Gen. Cadmus M. Wilcox, C.S.A., *History of the Mexican War,* 1892; Robert S. Henry, *The Story of the Mexican War,* 1950, and Alfred H. Bill, *Rehearsal for Conflict; the War with Mexico, 1846-1848,* 1947, constitute additional meritorious titles on this period. Of these three, Wilcox is massive with important troop details accumulated both from research and his own participation in the War. Henry and Bill are accurate authors who bring literary skill to a most difficult narrative. Maj. Charles W. Elliott, *Winfield Scott: The Soldier and the Man,* 1937, is a superb biography by a superb scholar. C. Joseph Bernardo and Eugene H. Bacon, in their *American Military Policy: Its Develophent since 1775,* 1955, present an excellent and well-documented study of overall defense policies, particularly as reflected by Federal departmental reports and the United States *Statutes at Large.* Thus the viewpoint is essentially from Washington rather than from the States where the volunteer, Organized Militia, in the era of this chapter, flourished as a decentralized defense institution. William E. Connelley, *Doniphan's Expedition: The Hughes Reprint,* 1907, is essentially a unit history of the 1st Missouri Mounted Volunteers. It is the best and most revealing narrative of any unit out of the Mexican War. It shows the Organized Militia, or National Guard of that era, at its gallant best and at its ill-fed worst.

## CHAPTER II

# Presidents Davis and Lincoln
# Call for State Regiments

THAT IN 1861 AMERICA was utterly unprepared for war has been repeated so often it has become a *cliché*. But like some other axiomatic observations, the apparent truth of which largely rests upon unchallenged repetition, it will do no harm to examine the idea rather closely. Bear in mind that being prepared for war is always a comparative condition. When both contestants are unprepared, both are adequately prepared.

Actually, on February 28, 1861, America was better prepared to resist a European aggressor and otherwise to put teeth in the Monroe Doctrine than she ever had been. Thanks to technical progress, the erstwhile, enormous, powerful fleets of Europe were obsolete. Longer-range naval ordnance, steam and advances in naval architecture had disposed of them. American designers knew the armored man-of-war to be practical and already were sure they could improve upon the rapidly-groping French and slower English efforts. Thus with five 40-gun steam frigates of the *Minnesota* class, six "first class screw sloops" of the famous *Hartford* class, eight "second class screw sloops" of the *Wyoming* class, five *Mohawk*-class "screw gunboats" and four "large paddle-wheel sloops" of the *Mississippi* class, the American Navy had ships, guns and speed that could give pause to any nation of Europe, including proud Britannia. For supplies, patrols and police work on distant coasts and seas, on some of which the United States had completely supplanted the English, America normally kept in commission a number of old-fashioned sailing men-of-war in addition to the modern steamers.*

The Regular Army had been expanded from the 10,035 officers and men as of the post-Mexican War reorganization of 1848. In December, 1860, it numbered 16,435 officers and men. There was no foreign force in Canada or Mexico that could challenge it. Thus the expansion had been largely a result of Indians and the opening of the West to the Pacific. About a seventh of the Army was under Brevet Major General David E. Twiggs in Texas. His command was the nearest approach to a Federal "striking force" in being. Except for a few details of Topographic Engineers and a number of Batteries of Coast Artillerymen along the Gulf and Atlantic seaboards, the remainder were scattered in small garrisons throughout the great West of cattlemen, gold-seekers, trappers, Mormons, and Indians. To one of those coastal Batteries and to Twiggs' comparatively large command, it will be necessary to return later.

In addition to these land forces, every Governor of each of the 33 sovereign States, as some of them most certainly conceived themselves to be, had a not-always small, volunteer, part-time army of his own. Each had traditions and legal machinery for rapid expansion of what he had. Presumably units of peacetime Organized Militia would be at the immediate disposal of the President of the United States should the Nation be threatened by a foreign aggressor. And so they would have been in most instances. But had not Massachusetts and Connecticut, 1812-15, declined to turn-out such Regiments of volunteer Organized Militia in support of Mr. Madison's "unworthy war" with England? Had not some unsympathetic New England States dragged their feet on the subject of Regiments of their Volunteer Militia to support Mr. Polk's "unholy war" with Mexico? What would be the status of these

---

* As of a week prior to Lincoln's inauguration, the American naval strength listed 76 warships of all ages, classes and armaments. Of these, 42, with an aggregate of 555 guns and 7,600 officers and men, were in commission, afloat and manned to a state of readiness. The Home Squadron, largely deployed in the Gulf of Mexico and the Caribbean, numbered 12 ships. All but a few of the men-of-war previously on distant stations were arriving home or were en route home in recognition of the impending domestic chaos. The warships not then in commission had caretaking details aboard. In most instances they were capable of being commissioned within two to six weeks if promptly given the manpower. Many Regular Navy Officers were ashore on the "Awaiting Orders" list.

armies of voluntarily-organized Militia Companies, Batteries, and Regiments should the President call upon them to punish one or more of their own recalcitrant member States? Who would be the aggressor in such a case?

And some of these State armies, actually in being, were not exactly small. New York's Governor Edwin D. Morgan, alone and overnight, could turn out more armed, uniformed, voluntarily-organized, well-officered, drilling and marching units of Infantry, Cavalry and Artillery than could the Federal Government. Moreover, they could be concentrated more readily. The Draft Laws and the calls upon the militarily-obligated citizens were in the hands of the State Governments, just as in Colonial times.

There was no machinery for a Federal Organized Militia. This is the most valid basis for the cliché that America was utterly unprepared. The Founding Fathers had not considered such to be necessary. Had not the Continental Line, composed of Regiments requisitioned from the States, achieved independence? Had not the Regiments from the States turned out in 1794 to crush the Whiskey Insurrection? Within recent memories, as of 1860, the efficacy of Regiments of States' Organized Militia, the Volunteers, had been fully proved in Mexico. Thus America, on land and sea, was never more powerful than in 1860 if the enemy should be the conventional one from across the Canadian or Mexican boundaries, or from Europe.

Accordingly, when historians record that America was unprepared, they are correct only when they mean the Federal Government of the United States was not organically equipped to cope with a revolt within its member States. Moreover, no benign government of, for and by the people ever is fully prepared to cope with a mass revolt activated by such a sharp and uncompromising clash of basic concepts and ideologies as prevailed in the America of 1860. Furthermore, the individual States, North and South, were *de facto* just sovereign enough, militarily and otherwise, to ally themselves into powerful, opposing groups of States under their respective central banners and governments; the North to preserve the Union in the form that they thought it should be and the South to preserve the Constitution as Southerners considered it to have been conceived and written. At the same time, the irresolute Border States experienced the hapless fate that often befalls those who would be neutral. They became the true centers of bloody civil strife and provided the battlefields for the more determined Titans. In short, the Federal Government was unprepared, but the several States, North and South, were well prepared for staging the four years of well-organized definitive warfare that makes the American Civil War unique in the histories of rebellions and civil strife.

# THE DRIFT TO SECESSION

The quick crisis of Secession, disunion, denial of Secession, and war came as a surprise to many but not to all. The men of the South, thoroughly indoctrinated by the orderly, persuasive, relentless logic of John C. Calhoun and his disciples, had been seriously considering an orderly procedure of Secession for 32 years—since the Tariff of 1828— but they actually had done nothing about it except for occasional threats that created political leverage. Many men of the North came to the logical conclusion that it was all political action, in which the posturing and performances were so loud one could not hear the words, hence there was no point in trying to follow the logic. Many other Northern men agreed with Southern theory and logic, but thought the benefits of the Union so obvious that no responsible Southern leadership ever actually would implement Secession. Almost everyone in the North long since had ceased taking Secession seriously.

Came the election of 1856. A burgeoning third party under an old and honored name, Republicanism, appeared on the National scene. These new Republicans further bolstered their party and their cause by such of Thomas Jefferson's Republican philosophy as served the purpose of restraints upon and the early abolition of Slavery, which was the Party's principal objective—its *raison d'etre*. Most thoughtful Whigs and Democrats, North and South, considered the new Republican party a transitory, one-plank organization that soon would go the way of the Anti-Masons, the Freesoilers and the Know-Nothings. Those who viewed the new party and its one burning issue with concern breathed a sigh of relief when a quiet, gentlemanly, safe-and-sane bachelor from Pennsylvania, Mr. James Buchanan, on March 4, 1857, entered the White House. All would be well before the next election.

But came 1860 and all was *not* well. Mr. Buchanan had proved to be too gentlemanly, too logical, too sane, and too unimaginative to be safe. The growing Republican party fattened itself on the disintegration of the old Whig organization. President Buchanan's dominant Democratic party allowed itself the luxury of a disastrous split upon Slavery, the very platform plank upon which the blossoming Republicans were measuring their greatest growth and strongest purpose. Abraham Lincoln, a political unknown, except for one term in the House of Representatives 12 years earlier, and a record for brilliant political debating against Senator Stephen A. Douglas of Illinois in 1858, was elected President, Autumn, 1860. There is ample evidence that neither Mr. Lincoln nor his best-informed supporters, advisers and friends then knew or faintly realized the drift of the Union toward the brink. That they were so uninformed is often a part of the thesis supporting the Nation's unpreparedness cliché. Actually, it is no more than an indictment of their qualifications for National leadership as of 1860 and early 1861. That Lincoln matured rapidly as a leader has obscured this patent fact.

Conversely, the South often has been credited with better leadership, particularly in military affairs, than was actually the case. In the sad Winter of 1860-61, the distressed Nation was bankrupt for adequate leadership, North and South.

December 20, 1860, South Carolina legally and openly convened a plenary State Convention that in truth was as thoroughly logical and legal as the State Convention of May 23, 1788, that, by ratifying the Constitution, had put South Carolina in the Union. By this due process the Convention of late 1860 solemnly and unanimously repealed the action of the earlier convention and thereby declared that "the Union now subsisting between South Carolina and the other States, under the name of the United States of America, is hereby dissolved." Most Southerners actually thought Secession was that simple, that easy! Most thoughtful Northerners considered it just another political power play for another one-sided compromise on Slavery to which the free States need not and should not submit. By February 1, 1861, however, Mississippi, Florida, Alabama, Georgia, Louisiana and Texas had taken like actions to "dissolve the bonds."

And having dissolved them, they took immediate steps to create new bonds within a new union to be called the Confederate States of America. Having inaugurated Jefferson Davis as its Provisional President, February 18, 1861, in Montgomery, Alabama, the Provisional Congress of the new, if smaller, republic continued in session.

It was a far-from-warlike, revolutionary body. Four more weeks were leisurely spent finishing a final draft of a Constitution that for the most part was a paraphrasing of the Constitution of the Union whence they had departed. Where it differed was from suspicion of a central government of too much strength and a President with too much power. It was certainly no document under which to plan a quick war and a sweeping victory. Commissioners were sent to Washington to negotiate. A blanket enactment made all laws of the United States as of November, 1860, that were not in conflict with the new Confederate Constitution, the laws of the Confederacy. This, of course, enacted for the Confederacy the well-known Militia Acts of 1792 and 1795, the same, identical, legal framework and terms of reference under which President Lincoln necessarily would work in rejecting Secession.

## CONFEDERATE MILITARY LEGISLATION

But Forts Sumter and Pickens and the situation created by the Twiggs Force of U.S. Regulars in San Antonio, Texas, forced the Confederate Congress to give further attention to the subject of armaments.

39

The Executive Branch, C.S.A., was designated receiving agent of all erstwhile Federal assets and properties, such as arsenals and forts. Executive authority to receive into Confederate service State troops tendered, or who might volunteer as units, for a period of 12 months, was enacted on February 28. The next day, Secretary of War L. R. Walker, C.S.A., instructed Brigadier General P. G. T. Beauregard to induct *not more than 5,000 South Carolina troops* into the Provisional Army, Confederate States, and to take command at Charleston, South Carolina. But a week later, two days after Lincoln was inaugurated and six weeks before surrender of Fort Sumter, the Confederate Congress took a second apprehensive look at these open-ended powers for a President. A ceiling was set at 100,000 men on the overall strength of those units that might be tendered, or which might volunteer, for as long as 12 months. The Act also stipulated six months as the period of compulsory time the men of a unit inducted *on requisition* from a State could be held in the Provisional Army, Confederate States.

On the same date the South's Congress got around to creating a Regular Army of a maximum size consisting of Engineers, (one Company of Sappers and Miners); "forty companies of artillerists and artificers;" six Regiments of Infantry, one of Cavalry, and Staff Departments of officers and men to a grand total of all Arms and Staffs of less than 11,000. Vacancies for only four, later five, Brigadier Generals were authorized, with no rank higher. This was only 64% of the actual strength of the Union's Regular Army as of the preceding January. On the whole, this legislation was more restrictive on a Confederate President who might become too powerful than it was in preparation for the all-out war that came. Certainly Mr. Lincoln, under United States laws and precedents for war powers, had a larger Army *in being* than that for which Davis merely had authority. Lincoln also had and soon exercised more freedom of action than could, or did, President Davis.

Meanwhile, difficulties were arising in Texas, Florida and South Carolina over the vacating of forts and installations occupied by troops of the old Union. South Carolina had been beefing-up and increasing her units of State Organized Militia. Further flexing her muscles of sovereignty, she had begun organizing a little standing army of her own—the South Carolina Regular Army. The United States garrison of Fort Sumter was indeed offering some difficulties. Nevertheless, it was March 11, a week after Mr. Lincoln's inauguration in Washington, before the Provisional Confederate Congress got around to appropriating money to support a Presidential requisition of a mere 3,000 Confederate Provisional Army troops (Organized Militia, or National Guard units, requisitioned by the Confederacy) for reinforcing the South Carolina troops in the Charleston area.

Brigadier General P. G. T. Beauregard, C.S.A., was their commander.

As of six weeks earlier, he had been a United States Regular Army officer on duty as Superintendent of West Point. When his native State of Louisiana had "dissolved the bonds," he had been permitted to resign with dignity and openly to proceed Southward to accept his commission in the small, authorized, but purely paper Regular Army of the Confederacy. Many people, North and South, wondered why Major Robert Anderson, U.S.A., commanding the tiny Fort Sumter garrison, did not, with equal dignity and graciousness, withdraw and proceed Northward to a new and more appropriate assignment under the new scheme of things.

## CRISIS AT FORT SUMTER

But Major Anderson, a pro-slavery man at heart, was a sickly, aging, West Pointer with nearly 40 years in the uniform. He had little imagination and less graciousness in matters that ran counter to his sense of duty. He elected to hold the fort, as ordered, pending the arrival and landing of the supplies and reinforcements he was sure were on the way. It was to preclude that landing that the South's Beauregard was there with a growing strength. The situation stood in stalemate until 4:30 A.M., Friday, April 12.

At that hour and on that date Beauregard committed the last of a vast series of errors, North and South, that could have been comic except that the stage was not set for comedy. America's greatest historical tragedy was the result. Beauregard, with a lack of necessity he did not appreciate, pounded the fort to rubble in a bloodless bombardment. Anderson surrendered on terms still considered quite generous. But the lack of casualties and the presence of chivalry were lost in the tidal wave of emotions that swept the North and soldified opposition to the South.

The Stars and Stripes had been fired upon. The States Rights philosophy could not be more than a cloak for treason. If naught but bayonets could save the Union, then bayonets it must be. There could be no compromise with neutralism such as that being mouthed by Border States Governors from Maryland and Virginia to Missouri. It was thus that Fort Sumter inflamed the North. Henceforth, the fat was in the fire—for four long years!

In the same way that Pearl Harbor solved sundry problems for President Franklin D. Roosevelt, Fort Sumter paved the way for decisive action by President Lincoln. Prior to April 12, his Administration had been stymied by a National political stalemate. As a President-elect, November to March, he had wisely, or unwisely, refused to go along with any of the compromises intended to pacify the South, then being debated in the U.S. Congress. From Christmas to March 4, the outgoing President Buchanan had done little more than bicker with seceding States over bits of real estate. The Border States, such as Virginia, Kentucky, Tennessee, Arkansas, had declined to secede, but clearly said they would join the Confederacy should their "neutrality" be violated by invasion from the North. Lest it tip them into the arms of the eager Southern Confederacy, Lincoln did not dare publicly to plan and certainly not to mobilize, or concentrate forces, in the North for readiness to preserve the Union through coercive measures. But Sumter ended all that. The South had taken the sword. The storm of opinion in the North was that since the Confederacy had taken the sword it might well perish by it. For Mr. Lincoln it was a time for decisive action.

Congress was not in session. The lame duck session of the outgoing 36th Congress had ended March 4. The 1st Special Session of the 37th Congress was called for July 4. Why Mr. Lincoln did not set an earlier date is not clear. Presumably he wanted a margin of time for some functioning and action of his Executive Department before convening a new Congress for emotional debates. In any event, he assumed the war powers normally inherent in the Presidency, and under those powers he launched a program for coping with the situation. Thus when Congress did convene, he was prepared to submit a policy and some accomplished facts that they could confirm or reject.

## THE NORTH RETAINS THE REGULAR ESTABLISHMENTS

The foregoing more-or-less well-known events are briefly reviewed here, with emphasis upon the military aspects, to clarify the views and actions of leaders who were so far removed from our modern concepts that, at times, it is difficult to sympathize with either side as each unwittingly drifted to complete division and conflict. In the split, the North retained practically all the Regular Army's 15,259 enlisted men as of that date. But they were widely dispersed. General David E. Twiggs, at San Antonio, had surrendered his command, stores and munitions to secessionist Texan forces, February 18, but on condition that they be permitted, if they chose, to return North. As a result, 102 officers and practically all the men, 2,328, stood with the Union. About 1,200 of them were moved out as units, under their officers, in time to fight at Bull Run and in Missouri. The remainder were held, because of Sumter, to become prisoners but were soon exchanged.

Only 29% of the Regular Army's 1,098 officers "went South." These resignations were not sufficient in number to sustain the myth that their defection to their native States caused the utter demoralization of the old Regular Army, as is claimed by many apologists for the North's humiliating defeat in the first major battle, Bull Run. What many mistook for demoralization was perhaps no more than the healthy flux that occurs when a long-static military machine is hurriedly being expanded and simultaneously regrouped in distant areas. In any event, the South's proposed Regular Army was not demoralized because no

42

such Army was in existence except for the 313 former U.S. Regulars who had resigned, and practically all of whom had applied for commissions in the Confederate States Regular Army. It existed only in the Confederate Statutes.

In naval strength, the Confederacy had nothing except a law on the books and a list of 321 warrant officers, Marine Corps officers, Engineers, Paymasters, Surgeons, and Line officers who had resigned from the U.S. Navy to "go South." This number was only 20% of the comparable commissioned and warrant ranks in the Regular Navy as of January, 1861. More Naval officers of Southern heritage had remained in the Union Navy than had resigned. The Union retained all ships in operational condition; lost only a few decommissioned, unmanned ships in Norfolk and other Southern naval yards and stations. All navies of that era, as noted earlier, were in transition from sail to steam. The Navy retained by the Union was one of the most modern then afloat and by no means the smallest, but it was far from adequate for an immediate blockade of the long and varied Southern coasts. It could and did execute and support early operations in force against strategic points at Roanoke Island, Hilton Head and New Orleans.

## MOBILIZATION OF THE CITIZEN-SOLDIERS BEGINS SLOWLY

It was thus early apparent that if any major fighting was to be done to preserve the Union, on the one hand, and to sustain the right of Secession, on the other, it must, as usual in American history, fall upon the citizen-soldiers. Most naturally the first mobilization Calls were to the units of the Organized Militia, or National Guardsmen, of the several States, North and South. As noted above, both the Confederacy and the Union had laws providing for the central government to requisition Organized Militia units from the individual States. Hence Messrs. Lincoln and Davis had at their disposal the same philosophies and the same procedures for creating armies with which to fight a war; i.e., requisition Regiments, Companies and Batteries from the States of their respective republics. And, odd as it may seem, both Presidents necessarily looked to the same organic statutes—the Militia Acts of May 2, 1792, and of February 28, 1795, for basic authority.

The only difference was that the South's modifications of February 28, 1861 allowed Mr. Davis to accept *volunteering units for 12 months* that might be tendered by the States, but under the ceiling of 100,000 when "called" or requisitioned by the Confederate Government. However, any non-volunteering units requisitioned from the Southern States could not be held in service beyond six months. These were, in effect, Confederate amendments to the Militia Act of 1792, which they had blanketed into their statutes from the old Federal Code.

The Confederacy's military legislation of the preceding February and March has been taken by many to mean President Davis had a full mobilization well advanced before President Lincoln's Call for units totalling 75,000 volunteers for three months. This is not supported by the official records. The first appropriation to pay and maintain units in the Confederate Provisional Army was on March 11, and was to care for 3,000 men in the South Carolina units being inducted for 12 months' service under Beauregard at Charleston. The same Act anticipated induction of 2,000 additional troops in the immediate future. These were the Beauregard forces, augmented by an additional two or three Regiments still in South Carolina State service, to whom Fort Sumter surrendered. Had President Davis truly had large and fast-growing Confederate forces in being on April 15, 1861, Mr. Lincoln undoubtedly would have called upon his States for Regiments in excess of the 75,000 Organized Militiamen he actually requisitioned to the Colors on that date. Certainly he was restricted by no ceiling, as was Davis.

How many Southerners were on the active rolls of the seceded States' fast-growing Organized Militia units? Southern State records are too fragmentary to answer that question. There is ample evidence that as the tensions grew at Fort Sumter, there was a tendency among the seceding States to flex their muscles of sovereignty by enacting State military laws and organizing new units and expanding old formations. Most of the arms and equipment for these additional units of Organized Militiamen, or Southern National Guardsmen, came from the arsenals of the seized Federal forts, such as those given up by Twiggs in San Antonio. A wealthy cotton broker from South Carolina, living in London, did ship a secession gift, consisting of one engraved English Blakely 12-pounder rifle, complete with ammunition and accessories, in time for it to participate in the reduction of Fort Sumter.

In Texas, where the refusal of all Batteries, Battalions and Regiments of the United States Regular Army to team-up with the Confederacy created more tension than in most seceding States, it does not appear that State volunteer units in excess of three or four thousand officers and men were activated immediately. How many of these, if any, immediately were tendered to the Confederate Administration, does not appear to be of record today. In any event, as of April 15, 1861, the South was little-advanced in her mobilization. However, the Confederate Congressional authorization to President Davis four weeks before firing on Sumter to *accept* units for a year to an aggregate strength of 100,000, had excited many Northern leaders as much as did the subsequent hostile act.

The Confederate States did have one outstanding asset not initially enjoyed by the North in 1861. The Southerners had a social solidarity and an instinctive commonality of purpose that stemmed from complete indoctrination that Secession was legal, logical and necessary to their

44

freedoms, ill-advised though it was that among those freedoms was the right to practice Slavery. This solidarity as to rights of the States constituted an invisible tower of strength of imponderable durability and dimensions. Its power and intensity was the great unknown as Mr. Lincoln read the telegraphic reports on Sumter and pondered a mobilization to save the Union.

## THE MARTIAL SPIRIT IN THE STATES

There is a myth, eagerly accepted by apologists for early Union defeats, and further magnified, disseminated and perpetuated by Emory Upton and his subsequent disciples, that the loyal States of the Union in no way were prepared to honor troop requisitions. In the same breath they infer that the South was efficient in creating its armies, but are vague as to details. The obsolete rolls of the decadent Enrolled Militia in the North are accentuated. Furthermore, they suggest the Regiments the Northern States did field were utterly worthless compared with those the Southerners so suddenly had brought to combat excellence. That such could be achieved by the mere 29% of former Regular officers who went South, and that without the aid of any trained, enlisted formations, is certainly no compliment to the professional competence of the 71% of the Regulars and all their units who had remained true to the Old Flag. But Colonel Frederick P. Todd was undoubtedly correct when he wrote that Upton never learned the difference between the Volunteer Organized Militia units and the mass of Enrolled Militia manpower—not even when the historical document being handled revealed the difference.

The enrollment and annual musters of all males with Militia obligations, contemplated in the Militia Act of 1792, had indeed fallen into forensic and alcoholic desuetude prior to the Mexican War. Nevertheless, another section of the old law recognized and encouraged volunteer units of Organized Militia in being, drilling units of serious-minded, socially-conscious and public-spirited Companies, in peace as well as war. Their grouping into Regiments and Battalions was recognized. State laws and practices further implemented and often emphasized and subsidized this concept at the expense of the decadent and abandoned lists of mass Militia enrollees.

Actually, within the decade that preceded the Civil War, forces were present that gave a great stimulus to voluntary military associations that blossomed throughout America into uniformed, armed, regularly-drilling units of all Arms. Throughout the South the growing tensions arising from the great Slavery controversy had created fears of slave revolts. In the absence of modern State Troopers or any other fulltime law-and-order Constabulary that a Slave State Governor could call upon should civil disorders exceed the powers of a County Sheriff to quell, there was no other immediate agency to which he could turn except

Companies of the uniformed, armed and regularly-drilling Organized Militia. For this reason, Southern Governors and legislators through the 1850's gave more attention to fostering and supporting such units than did their predecessors through the two preceding decades. Indeed, frequent night patrols along the highways and back roads, to make sure that bondmen were observing the curfew laws for slaves, could count as the equivalent of a drill period for some Squads and Platoons of local Companies. Arkansas and Texas also had the constant threats of Indian frontiers. Texas kept one or two Battalions of State Rangers on active duty through all seasons, backed by Organized Militia Regiments of Mounted Rifles, available from the home towns of certain Organized Militia units.

But in the industrial and urban growth of some of the Northern States there were still stronger stimuli to the organization and perfecting of Companies, Battalions and Regiments of voluntarily-organized citizen-Soldiers. Those States were likewise without State Constabularies for coping with riots and civil disorders beyond the powers of a Sheriff to handle. At the same time, uninhibited immigration was filling Northern cities with unemployed and unemployables. Native resentment was manifesting itself with such secret, disorderly, bigoted movements as the Know-Nothings. Riots and property destruction were common, even in the smaller, mill towns.

It was in New York City, however, that the Nation was treated to the spectacle of the Astor Place Riot of May 10, 1849. Believe it or not, the spark plug for this incredible incident was the rivalry of the two actors; one an American with a robust, mass appeal, and the other an Englishman with a more restrained, traditional technique. Each fancied himself the better Macbeth, not to mention Hamlet and sundry other Shakespearean characters. The cleavage between New York's burgeoning, highbrow culture as exemplified by the Astor Opera House, starring the Englishman, and the gallery lowbrows of the Bowery Theater, starring the American, was easily whipped into class hatreds. These were readily augmented by Irish animosities against England. Moreover, the City was filled with refugee revolutionists from the 1848 street barricades that had filled the avenues of Central Europe's major capitals. They instinctively associated street riots with freedom.

With Macready, the English Macbeth, playing to a packed audience in the Astor Opera House, it was quite easy for the Know-Nothings and other dissident groups to create a maddened mob into storming that Bastille of culture and class. The rioters were taking the Opera House apart, beginning with door jambs and window frames, with occasional corner bricks pried loose for missiles, when New York's famous 7th Infantry Regiment arrived not only to restore law but primarily to save the lives of the English actor and his audience of white ties and tails. Even so, before order was restored, the casualty score was 22 killed and 36 wounded, with the mob taking the greater punishment.

Equally dramatic and even more alarming were events in California. Between lawlessness on the one hand and self-appointed, secret Vigilante Committees on the other, civil authority collapsed. In desperation, the Governor prevailed upon a middle-aged San Francisco banker to accept the post of State Adjutant General, with the mission of creating and commanding enough additional Organized Militia Companies and Regiments to restore civil control. This the banker did, though the emboldened Vigilantes had cast off the veil of secrecy and were so well-organized that they gave him some anxious moments. His name was William Tecumseh Sherman.* He had resigned his Regular Army Captaincy in 1853.

Had San Francisco and New York been the only demonstrations to Mayors and Governors of the need they might have for an effective force of National Guardsmen, or Organized Militiamen, the interest in such units might not have been felt so keenly. But from Boston to Baltimore and Albany to Chicago there were similar minor incidents that convinced all that civil unrest was a part of the price of the much-desired railroad expansion and industrial development.

There was also the anti-English disposition of the Irish to dabble in Britain's Canadian troubles. Thus, when a Governor of Connecticut

* Most American military historians have emphasized by reiteration the concept that leadership in the Union and Confederate armies was by Regular Army officers. It is an interpretation of American military history that perhaps should be reexamined. U. S. Grant, William T. Sherman, George B. McClellan, Ambrose E. Burnside, Daniel Tyler, Henry W. Halleck, John C. Fremont, William S. Rosecrans, Joseph J. Reynolds, Henry W. Slocum, and Joe Hooker are but a few of the so-called Regulars who provided that oft-repeated battlefield leadership. Actually, all the above, like Grant, were civilians through most of the decade of the 1850's. Furthermore, most of them, like Slocum, McClellan, Burnside, and Grant, returned to civil life at the first favorable opportunity following the end of hostilities. Sherman, Halleck and Hooker are representative of a few who elected to stay in the postwar Regular Army, as did many highly-successful citizen-soldiers from the Organized Militia, or National Guard, among whom Nelson A. Miles, S. B. M. Young, Arthur MacArthur, Lloyd Wheaton, and Ewell Otis are significant names. That such non-professional officers were integrated into the Regular Army with ranks equal to or above their own was gall and wormwood to ambitious and tested young professionals like George A. Custer, Emory Upton, Adelbert Ames, and particularly to an aging professional like Abner Doubleday, who had been with Robert Anderson in Fort Sumter and who had an uninterrupted active commissioned service record from 1838.

In the Confederate armies, Robert E. Lee, P. G. T. Beauregard, Joseph E. Johnston and J. E. B. Stuart are among those who never turned their backs upon their chosen profession of arms. But often linked with their names as "Regulars" are ex-professors Thomas J. (Stonewall) Jackson, Daniel Harvey Hill, former attorney Jubal A. Early and sundry others. All of these were truly great leaders. But ranking with them, and better than some, are the Confederates, John B. Gordon, Patrick R. Cleburne, John T. Green, Richard Taylor, and Nathan Bedford Forrest, none of whom ever held a Regular commission. Their genius for leadership, however, is acknowledged by all. But to return to Sherman and Grant. They were civilians, with temporary, active duty U.S.V. commissions until July 4, 1863. Their rewards for Vicksburg were a Brigadier Generalcy for Sherman and the next higher rank for Grant, in the Regular Army they had left 10 years earlier. They welcomed their new status. It clarified their future official relations with old Regulars who long had outranked them.

found some of his newly-chartered and authorized units of Organized Militia were composed exclusively of recently-arrived Irish, he cancelled their charters. The State adopted a policy that no units should be composed entirely of recently-arrived foreigners. But this did no more than to stimulate enlistments in older units and toward the creation of new units composed of duly-naturalized citizens. The civil disorders in Northwestern Missouri and "Bleeding Kansas," combined with scores of lesser incidents in the Border States incident to enforcement, or non-enforcement, of the emotional and controversial Fugitive Slave Act, kept their Governors on tenterhooks. They gave a corresponding interest to the improvement of their units of voluntarily-organized military associations that might be used in major emergencies.

Likewise overlooked by too many historians, the decade prior to the Civil War also had an external stimulus to a new interest in matters military. This was the Crimean War, 1854-56. Its gallantries, such as the Charge of the Light Brigade, combined with its numerous, varied, and gaudy uniforms and precision drills, captured the imagination of many Americans. In Chicago a young law clerk from upstate New York found himself a member of a duly-authorized Illinois Infantry Company known as "the National Guard Cadets." Through lack of interest, the unit was suffering. He became Captain and proved conclusively what all National Guardsmen today accept as axiomatic; i.e., there is nothing that cures a unit's ills like a brilliant and imaginative training program. Young Elmer E. Ellsworth, for such was the law clerk's name, introduced not only the complicated and precise formations, drills and arms manuals of the French Zouaves, but he worked-out an American adaptation of their baggy uniforms.

In but a matter of months, the new Captain of Chicago's "National Guard Cadets" had reached full war strength for his unit, with a long waiting list of recruits. With it as a lever, he was able to enforce a discipline reminiscent of Cromwell and his Roundheads. Members were pledged to "abstain from liquor, tobacco, profanity and all excesses." Ere long the Company's drill periods were attracting such immense crowds of spectators that Captain Ellsworth decided to put the show on the road. Back from a triumphal tour of the East, he was promoted to Major and later Colonel on the Staff of the State Adjutant General. His old Company, for its excellence, was selected as the Governor's Guard.

Meanwhile, young Ellsworth had moved to Springfield and was reading law in the office of Abraham Lincoln. Of course, he was active in the election campaign, 1860. The next year, he went to Washington with the President-Elect, where he was working on the details of a proposed Federal Militia Bureau, with himself as Chief. The outbreak of hostilities brought him a Regimental command from his native State.

It appropriately was named "Ellsworth's Zouaves," but officially designated 11th New York Infantry. On May 24, 1861, a month prior to Bull Run, Ellsworth was killed by a civilian as he removed a Confederate flag from above a large hotel in Alexandria, Virginia.

Were Ellsworth's only claim to fame that of the first Regimental Commander to be killed by gunfire, his name hardly would be worthy of mention here. It is cited because of the overall effect of his prewar demonstrations and exhibition tours. Between 1857 and 1860 he had created almost a craze for crack Drill Companies and revitalized National Guard Regiments and Battalions. In Indiana, Lew Wallace, for whom "Ben Hur" was two decades in the future, dusted-off his Mexican War commission as a citizen-soldier and pulled together a Regiment of such crack units. Zouave Companies and Regiments blossomed throughout the Mid-West and along the Atlantic seaboard well in advance of the outbreak of the Civil War.

Of even greater significance was an earlier development within New York. The officers of that State's National Guard had organized a professional society for the improvement of themselves in the performance of their duties and to study ways and means for improving the efficiency of their units. The Military Association of the State of New York held regular meetings, and read, discussed, and later published in their Proceedings scholarly papers on arms, techniques and European solutions to military manpower problems. For quality and range of military interest, it does not appear that the Regular Army of that day was doing anything of a professional character comparable to the studies of these dedicated citizen-soldiers.

None knew better than they the obsolete character of the allegedly-enrolled Militia that was presumed to assemble on Muster Days to bring the manpower rolls up to date. About the only merit the New Yorkers could see in the Enrolled Militia idea was its yield in fines and forfeitures. These funds automatically became available to the zealous citizen-soldiers in the volunteer, uniformed units. This was also true in some other States. If sluggards would be sluggards, let them pay a special tax toward the self-sacrificing military efforts of more responsible citizens. Actually, in most States the farce of the annual musters of the unorganized, or enrollment of men with Militia responsibility, had been discontinued by common consent. If anyone wanted to know the strength of military manpower pools of the individual States, he necessarily went to the last Census return of the male population by ages.

NATIONAL GUARD STRENGTHS PRIOR TO MARCH, 1861

It is far more difficult to approximate the combined strengths of the voluntary Organized Militia units of all the States, North and South, at the time it belatedly dawned upon Presidents Lincoln and Davis that they really had a war on their hands. Records are incomplete in the Northern States and when available are not of the same date. In Southern and Border States they are not only incomplete but in some instances they are non-extant. The little Border State, Delaware, apparently had none. At least her reluctant, neutral-minded Governor did not admit any when later confronted by Lincoln's proposed quota of one Regiment of 780 men in the first three-months Call, April 15, 1861. What had happened to several Delaware Companies known to have been active prior to Lincoln's Call is not of record. On the other hand, smaller but more populous and militant-minded Rhode Island had about 2,000 officers and men in her volunteer uniformed units of drilling Organized Militia as of January 24, 1861. The strength of the Massachusetts Volunteer Militia as of December 31, 1860, was 5,593 officers and men.

Wisconsin had no Indian frontier. Moreover, it was geographically removed from the rising tide toward strife, so that 1860 was a more-or-less normal year. On June 30, 1860, that State had Volunteer Companies as follows: 42 of Infantry and "Rifles," two of Cavalry and six Batteries of Field Artillery, for an aggregate strength of 1,993 officers and men. With an 1860 population of 776,000, this allows a ratio of better than 3.8 National Guardsmen per thousand of population. The Empire State of New York had a population in 1860 of 3,881,000. With a long and cherished military tradition and under the alert stewardship of her professional-minded military leaders, New York voluntarily was evidencing great military interest. Its uniformed National Guard units, as of January, 1859, had aggregate strengths as follows: Cavalry, 1,614; Artillery, 2,076; Light Infantry, 1,808; Infantry, 10,184; Engineers, 194, and a General Staff of 194, for an aggregate of 17,756 officers and men. In ratio to the State's population there were, in 1859, about 4.6 uniformed National Guardsmen for each thousand population. By December 31, 1860, the official returns showed an aggregate of 18,955.

But on a population basis Pennsylvania was doing even better. Her returns for December 31, 1860, reveal nearly 19,000 officers and men in 339 Infantry, 84 Artillery and 53 Cavalry units. All were of Company size but organized to the Division level.

Ohio, with an 1860 population of 2,340,000, had, in 1860, more than 150 Company-size units, according to one historian, for an aggregate strength of more than 4,000 officers and men, or a ratio of 2.3 Guardsmen per thousand of population. On the other hand, the Adjutant General's report for that year recognizes but 40 Company-size units with an aggregate of only 1,523 officers and men. Ohio is known to have had a number of quasi-military associations of uniformed, marching, drilling and shooting, Company-size associations, who armed themselves without deference to the Government and ignored the State's

Military Department. That there could have been 100 or more such free-wheeling para-military societies in the Buckeye State is rejected in the estimated totals that follow. The situation, however, reveals the difficulties in arriving at precise figures. Many States have exact unit lists of volunteer, active and uniformed units, but the annual strength returns have been lost. Existing strength returns from States with complete records suggest that 40 to 60 men per Company, dependent on the degree of urbanization, would appear to be good estimates for the hard core of each Company. Through this means and by population ratio for comparable States, it appears that the loyal States, excluding distant California and Oregon, had well over 75,000 officers and men in Active, or Organized Militia units, as of 1860.

The Border States, Maryland, Delaware, Kentucky and Missouri, could have turned out collectively between six and seven thousand Organized Militiamen. But within the Southern States the problem becomes even more obscure. Virginia and South Carolina, with their superb State Military Academies, led the South in active Company-size units. Virginia had 342. At 40 officers and men each, they would have shown returns of 13,680. Out of Virginia's 1860 population of 1,596,000, the Adjutant General officially reported, September 30, 1860, a capability of fielding 20,000 officers and men without undue delay. His concern was for arms, though he recently had acquired 13 rifled six-pounder field guns and 5,000 "excellent percussion muskets." There is no comparable report for South Carolina. On a population ratio approach, the Palmetto State should have had half as many units and men in her Active Militia; i.e., about 7,000 officers and men in 1860. Unofficial sources sustain this estimate. But Georgia, with an 1860 population of 1,057,000, did not conform to the South's military pace. In 1860 she appears to have had only 33 Company-size units for an estimated aggregate of less than 1,500 officers and men. On a population basis, Louisiana was doing better with 40 units with an estimated strength of 1,600 out of a population of 700,000. This is close to Wisconsin's ratio, ignoring the percentage of Colored men who were ineligible —whether free or slaves. All in all, it appears the 11 States which soon were to form the Confederacy could in 1860 have produced Active Militiamen, in units, aggregating 35,000 to 40,000 officers and men.

From fragmentary evidence, exact for some States and outright extrapolation for others, it thus appears that in 1860—months before the passions of Fort Sumter—the volunteer, active units of all the States could not have been less than 110,000 officers and men. And most likely, including California and the Territories, the figure was closer to 130,000, from a National population of 31,443,000.*

---

* In offering this estimate, it is fully realized that compilation of "Correspondence,

In any event, the martial spirit, measured in terms of statistics, was far higher in 1860 than in 1897, the eve of the Spanish War. In that year the aggregate of the National Guard unit strengths from the 45 States and three Territories, with a total population of 72,000,000, was only 115,000.

From the foregoing it is clear that the States, North and South, were well-organized for fighting exactly the stubborn sort of well-defined war that came upon them—better-organized than was the Federal Government for suppressing it. The citizen-soldiers were, of course, poorly-armed, often with muskets or non-issue rifles procured privately. They seldom had more military clothing than their drill night uniforms and gold braided regalia for dress parades and social occasions. All horses, like the uniforms and some of the weapons, were privately-owned. Companies and Batteries were sometimes as small as 30 men, but they became cadres for war strength units which in turn provided future officers and cadres for Battalions and Regiments. As one State official explained to the War Department, he was recruiting as many lumberjacks as possible for a high-priority unit because they more readily could sustain the hardships. At the same time, he was saving his Organized Militia units for officers because they were composed of "our best but less hardy city and towns people." But, generally speaking, the day after Fort Sumter was fired upon, the war spirit in the North reached such heights that Armories and drill fields were filled to overflowing with would-be recruits for the existing units.

## LINCOLN'S CALL FOR STATE REGIMENTS TO AN AGGREGATE OF 75,000

The White House had made no military moves except to recall the far-cruising warships and to concentrate scattered Regular Army formations, while the small Provisional Army of the Confederate States was

Orders, etc., from Nov. 1, 1860, to March 31, 1862," in Vol. I, Sec. III, *Official Records, War of the Rebellion,* by omission if not in other ways, often conveys the impression that there was nothing within the States except the States' Draft Law, obligated, military manpower pools, represented by the out-of-date Enrolled Militia lists, whence the Governors were to recruit their volunteers. About the only mentions of existing units occur when Governors and States' Adjutants General are clamoring for modern rifles with which to replace obsolete weapons then in the hands of their Regiments. They naturally reflect considerable activity in regroupment and expansion of existing and new units that add to the concept that the States were building from nothing. The omission of such basic data as is sought here could be interpreted as a deliberate intent to aggrandize and emphasize the Federal role in the war effort at the expense of the States. The author likewise is aware of the many official and quasi-official State publications and compilations which deprecate the States' military situation, Spring of 1861, to such a degree that one is led to think there was no Military Establishment at all. But these writings and selected documents and tables, like the compilation mentioned above, for the most part were performed 1866 to 1895 when alibis were being stabilized, egos were being flattered, and praise of the mighty war efforts of all Towns, Cities, States and individuals was in order. The war efforts of the States, North and South, were astoundingly Gargantuan, but the fertile military seed whence came the fifty-fold increases should not be overlooked or discounted.

assembling, piecemeal, under Beauregard at Charleston, because of the Fort Sumter problem. Beauregard's force had come into existence not so much by a Confederate Presidential Call as by the Confederate Congressional authorization that Jefferson Davis accept into Confederate service for 12 months such units as the Southern States might tender, but not to exceed 100,000. On the day following the Fort's surrender, the entire Provisional Army, Confederate States, was represented by Beauregard's forces at Charleston. They consisted of the gun crews for the 70 pieces of heavy artillery that had demolished the Fort and a few Regiments, mostly from South Carolina, that had been tendered and accepted. Recruiting for the Provisional Army, Confederate States (P.A.C.S.) did not begin in Texas until a month after Fort Sumter. That State's first Regiment was not formed until June 13, 1861.

The White House thus experienced no major degree of alarms as of April 15, the date of Lincoln's First Call. A brief proclamation asking for short-service Regiments, such as George Washington's for the 1794 Whiskey Rebellion, seemed appropriate. But in the same way that President Davis misjudged the frenzy of war fever that would sweep the North once the Union flag had been fired upon, President Lincoln in no way was prepared for the corresponding frenzy of preparations for a long, determined, mass resistance in the South, once his Call went forth for augmentation of the Union Regular Army by 75,000 Volunteers in Regiments from the loyal States.

Accordingly, the two Presidents found themselves committed to an all-out Civil War that neither anticipated nor wanted. Dr. William B. Hesseltine's scholarly volume, *Lincoln and the War Governors,* shows clearly that the executives of the Northern States had a far keener perception of the temper of the people and the crisis toward which the Republic was hastening unwittingly than did Mr. Lincoln and his Administration in Washington. Some had given detailed thought to troop plans in advance of the Call. Moreover, Mr. Davis would have been better-advised had he harkened unto the opinions of such shrewd, grassroots, Southern politicians as his Secretary of State, Robert Toombs, before Beauregard was given a blank check with reference to Fort Sumter. However, this is no place for things that might have been. Throughout the North, the demolition of Fort Sumter by gunfire, April 12-14, though bloodless, was war! To Southerners, Lincoln's Call for 75,000 men from the loyal States was a gigantic mobilization for aggressive operations against their liberties. They were not to be allowed to "depart in peace." The Provisional Army, Confederate States, must be made powerful without delay. The State Regiments of Organized Militia in the South began tendering their services to the Confederacy, for 12 months "unless sooner discharged."

Lincoln's First Call, as did some others subsequent thereto, took the form of a proclamation. It was dated April 15 and telegraphed to the Governors. "Whereas the laws of the United States have been for some time past and now are opposed and the execution thereof obstructed in the States of South Carolina, Georgia, Alabama, Florida, Mississippi, Louisiana and Texas by combinations . . . Now, therefore, I, Abraham Lincoln, President . . . hereby do call forth the militia of the several States of the Union to the aggregate number of 75,000 . . . The details of this object will be immediately communicated to the State authorities through the War Department."

These details were sent the same day. By way of giving each Governor and his Adjutant General an objective easily within his capabilities and for equitable distribution of the burden, Regimental quotas were initially assigned as follows: Maine, 1; New Hampshire, 1; Vermont, 1; Massachusetts, 2; Rhode Island, 1; Connecticut, 1; New York, 17; Pennsylvania, 16; New Jersey, 4; Delaware, 1; Maryland, 4; Virginia, 3; North Carolina, 2; Tennessee, 2; Arkansas, 1; Kentucky, 4; Missouri, 4; Illinois, 6; Indiana, 6; Ohio, 13; Michigan, 1; Wisconsin, 1; Iowa, 1; Minnesota, 1. California and Oregon were so far removed from the prospective Theater of Operations that they were not included in this First Call.

Most units were to be of Infantry, clearly indicating a police or Constabulary operation, though most of the Governors were of a contrary opinion. Regiments were to be of 10 Companies, each conforming to then-current Tables of the Regular Army. These called for 74 enlisted men, a Captain, with First and Second lieutenants, in each Company. The Colonel, a Lieutenant Colonel, a Major and seven other Regimental Staff officers and noncommissioned officers raised the total strength of the Regiment to 780. At least one to 10 supernumeraries normally were allowed.

The small Slave State of Delaware was not the only Border State to look hard at the Call and drag its feet. As noted above, it offered the excuse it had no complete Regiment. Virginia, North Carolina, Tennessee and Arkansas fell from their neutrality fence into the arms of the waiting Confederacy. Out of appreciation for the Old Dominion's belated decision, the Capital of the Confederacy was moved from Montgomery, Alabama, to Richmond. Lincoln's Call, an admitted preparation for invasion, was the excuse given by the Secession Conventions of these four States when they, too, "absolved the bonds." The failure of Virginia, Tennessee, Kentucky and Missouri to stand firmly with the Union was far more serious than today meets the eye. They were among the Nation's most populous States.

Rump Secession Conventions in Missouri and Kentucky were valid enough that historians still disagree as to whether they did or did not properly represent the will of the majority within their Commonwealths.

Richmond was sure they did. Congressional Delegations from these States were received and seated in the Confederate Congress.* The two States were plunged into the bitterest little civil wars of their own in the armed struggles, between Union and Secession adherents, for control of the State Governments.

With such conditions within the Slave-holding Border States, there were sundry and obvious reasons why Mr. Lincoln did not expect their Governors to come forth with Regimental quotas.

Meanwhile, the Governors of the non-Slave States, under the stimulus of the "firing on the flag" at Fort Sumter, were pressing for expansion of their quotas to accommodate the superfluity of volunteering units. Reallocations to them were simple. A few of the more cautious Northern Governors made little clamor, but quietly "stockpiled" the enthusiasm of the moment. This was done through enlistments to the State for terms far in excess of three months, which obligated the volunteers and their units for future Calls. In the opinions of these Governors, a long, hard Winter lay ahead.

New York's Governor Edwin D. Morgan exemplifies the outcry for an expanded quota. Thereby also hangs a unique tale which is of some significance here. It offered the first instance in which there was a serious, direct, operating proposal that the Second Amendment to the Constitution** was not exclusive to the several States of the Union. Further, that citizens likewise had a direct Militia responsibility to the Federal Government. Moreover, there was no reason why men with such obligation should not be recruited into Regiments for temporary emergency active duty by the War Department and without deference to historic Colonial and State Militia channels.

The manner in which that concept grew through the course of the Civil War, became fully accepted in 1899, was written into the Dick Act of 1903, and reached full floriation in the Defense Act of 1916 creating a Federal Organized Militia, officially known as the Organized Reserve Corps of the Army, are topics for review in subsequent chapters. Because it was the first large, practical effort to apply the principle, the contretemps between New York's Governor and Daniel E. Sickles is highly pertinent.

## NEW YORK EXCEEDS HER QUOTA

Mr. Sickles, age 42, had been an ambitious New York boy who abandoned the printer's trade to read law in the office of the subsequent Major General Benjamin F. Butler. It was the meeting of an apt student and a most unscrupulous, able teacher if the subsequent

---

* Territorial Delegates from the Choctaw Nation, Seminole Nation, Cherokee Nation, and Arizona Territory also were seated.

** ARTICLE II. A well regulated militia being necessary to the security of a free state, the right of the people to keep and bear arms shall not be infringed.

bizarre military and political records of both men be accepted as evidence.

By 1857 young Sickles was in the Federal House of Representatives from New York. He previously had been Corporation Counsel for the City. He achieved his greatest ill-repute as a Congressman when he shot and killed Philip Barton Key. The latter's principal claim to fame was inherited from a father who wrote "The Star-Spangled Banner," plus his own apparent success as a part-time extracurricular suitor to a beautiful, dark-eyed Italian brunette of 24 Summers. She also happened to be Mrs. Sickles.

Unto our own day, the gossip-loving scandal mongers of Washington, D.C., never have been more agog. The jury cleared the Congressman, but his New York City Democratic constituents did not draft him to the new term beginning March 4, 1861. Lincoln's need for troops reminded Sickles that prior to election to Congress he had been a Colonel in the New York National Guard.

The State already had more than enough men and units in being to meet the comparatively modest quota the War Department had assigned, but Governor Morgan could not resist the persuasive enthusiasm of Dan Sickles. He authorized the Colonel to recruit a new war-strength Regiment. This was achieved so readily that the authority was increased to a Brigade. To Sickles it brought the glittering hope of a quick, if single, star. Thus was born New York's "Excelsior Brigade." It is with reluctance that one admits Sickles had done a good job. He had inveigled no less than 12 better-qualified, seasoned officers of the Mexican War to serve under him in Field and Staff grades. But the new Brigadier General and the Governor parted company when the "Excelsior Brigade" was not among those tendered the Federal Government for the immediate march against the new and rival Confederacy of seceding States. Worse yet, Sickles was ordered to disband part of the Brigade. Upstate New York was complaining the City was getting more than its share of the units. Sickles headed for Washington and the White House.

He proposed to Mr. Lincoln that since New York would not clear his units for activation, why should they not be inducted directly into Federal service? As for his own part, he would be satisfied with a temporary Federal commission as Brigadier General of Volunteers, without any State label attached. He glibly quoted the vague Army and Navy Federal powers under Paragraphs 12, 13 and 15, Section 8, Article I, of the Constitution.*

Mr. Lincoln was impressed, appears to have been intrigued by both

* The Article empowered the Congress "12. To raise and support armies . . . 13. To provide and maintain a navy . . . 15. To provide for calling forth the militia to execute the laws of the Union, suppress insurrections and repel invasions."

the man and the procedure. Insofar as he was concerned, eagerness to serve covered a multitude of other shortcomings. But the ebullient Dan Sickles' proposal was outside the existing formula prescribed by the U.S. Statutes. The President already had greatly exceeded his legal powers as Commander-in-Chief of the Army and Navy, pending Congressional approval. Although reluctant to add straws to the camel's back, the President readily promised the Brigadier Generalcy, was sure he would find a way to keep the Brigade in being. Thereupon he gave Sickles a warm goodbye and passed the buck downward to the desk of the prime bungler in his Administration, Secretary of War Simon Cameron.

Following needless delays, through which Sickles received from New York State authorities all the obstructions reserved for those who are caught ignoring military channels, the "Excelsiors" were still in nebulous status when the Bull Run debacle suggested the immediate need for more men. They were inducted initially as the 3rd, 4th and 5th Infantry Regiments of the "Excelsior Brigade." To mollify New York they were credited to that State's next Call quota and renumbered the 72nd, 73rd and 74th Regiments, New York Infantry.* But seeds had been planted for invoking a citizen's direct Militia obligation to the Federal Government. In the Draft Act of March 3, 1863 it was to prove disastrous. But it offered a formula, as noted in the following chapter, for enlisting Freedmen who as slaves had not been bothered with a Militia obligation to any Government. As Freedmen, theirs was a right and duty to serve the Government that had liberated them. Such logic was followed easily when manpower became scarce.

## SMALLER STATES WITH SMALLER PROBLEMS

Though Massachusetts' Benjamin F. Butler, under whom Sickles had read law, staged a contretemps with his Governor Andrew that had some points in common with the foregoing New York difficulties, most Governors and their Adjutants General functioned with as much smoothness as the temper of the times and the sudden sense of urgency permitted. And most of them were less prodigal with their offerings than were New York and Massachusetts. Thinly-populated Maine, for example, quietly made available her quota of one Regiment by expanding to war strength 10 Companies. Colonel Nathaniel J. Jackson, a Guardsman without a Federal active duty record, was designated to

---

* All else notwithstanding, Sickles as a combat soldier had qualities of leadership that nature denied to many well-educated and trained professionals. Out of the Peninsula Campaign he became a Major General, U.S.V. As C.G., III Corps at Chancellorsville, he definitely did better than most. At Gettysburg, in the famous Peach Orchard, he either won or nearly threw away the victory, dependent upon whether one is reading the reports of Sickles or Meade. Neither witness is convincing. Integrated into the Regular Army as Colonel, 42nd Inf., 1866, he retired as Major General, 1869, to embark upon an unbelievably amorous diplomatic career in Spain. In and out of trouble all his life, he died in 1914.

command. Within 18 days the Regiment was ready to leave. With little faith in the three-months Call idea, Governor Israel Washburn had enlisted the Regiment into State service for a minimum of two years, but the War Department at the end of three months returned it to the State. The men were held to their State enlistments for a brief period and then released for volunteering into units of the Second Call. The names of Jackson and many of his officers and men appear on the rosters of the 5th Maine, mustered-in June 24. Colonel Jackson, at the war's end, was a Major General, U.S.V., and a Division Commander. His record was not unusual.

Indiana did likewise in making available her quota of six Regiments. But unlike Maine, which had sent no units into the Mexican War, the prosperous and populous State of Indiana had turned-out five Regiments. Though not all of them had reached Mexico, the State was comparatively rich in citizen-soldiers who, as officers and men, had been combat-seasoned 13 years earlier. Out of deference to the State's earlier war record, the six Regiments for the First Call were numbered from five and commanded as follows: 6th Indiana Volunteers, Colonel Thomas T. Crittenden; 7th, Ebenezer Dumont; 8th, William P. Benton; 9th, Robert H. Milroy; 10th, Joseph J. Reynolds; 11th, Lew Wallace. The six Colonels were combat seasoned; five as officers in Mexico. Colonel Dumont, of the 7th, was a successful lawyer and judge who had left college to enlist for Mexico. At the age of 19 he had distinguished himself at Contreras, Churubusco and Chapultepec. Colonel Reynolds was a West Pointer, Class of 1839, who like William T. Sherman and many others, between the wars, had left the stagnant promotion lists of the Regulars. He, too, had become a member of a college faculty. As might well be expected, all six of these Indiana Colonels become General Officers to command Divisions and Army Corps during the four years of combat that followed. All returned to civil pursuits at the end of the war except Reynolds, who was integrated into the Regulars as a Colonel, 26th Infantry, U.S. Army.

As in Maine, all six Regiments were returned to Indiana as soon as practicable following the three-months term of Federal service. They were not, however, inactivated to reappear as personnel under higher-number Regiments as in Maine, Massachusetts and some other States. Indiana's three-months Regiments merely were beefed-up to comply with the Tables of Organization for Regiments of the Second Call,* and returned to Federal active duty as three-year Regiments with the

---

* The Regimental organization of 10 letter Companies, designated A to K, inclusive, with J omitted, was continued, but each Company was required to have 98 enlisted men in lieu of the 74 men in the Companies of the First Call. This change with additional enlisted Musicians, Medical and Staff officers, raised the war strength of newly-inducted Regiments to slightly more than 1,050 officers and men. This figure prevailed for all Calls subsequent to the First.

same numbers and the same Commanding Officers, except for the replacement of Colonel Reynolds, of the 10th. He had accepted a U.S.V. commission as Brigadier General and a field assignment from Washington. His successor as commander of the 10th Indiana was Mahlon D. Manson of the same Regiment. Colonel Manson was also an officer with Mexican War service as a Captain in the Indiana Volunteers. As a Major General of Volunteers, he ultimately commanded the XXIII Corps and was disabled out of service incident to wounds in the Atlanta campaign. In Indiana, as in other States, the newer Regiments resulting from subsequent Calls to the States for Volunteers normally found their Field and Staff officers from among the Company-grade officers of the earlier Regiments.

Wisconsin, fifteenth in population among the 31 States of the disjoined Nation, had a First Call quota of but one Regiment. It immediately and smoothly was organized by regimenting 10 existing separate Companies into the 1st Wisconsin Infantry. The State was like Maine in that it had sent no units to the Mexican War. The best available Guardsman for the command was a young Milwaukee attorney, John C. Starkweather. He had been active in the State's Organized Militia since his arrival in Wisconsin in 1850. He was the son of a New York Congressman who long had served as Colonel of that State's 12th Regiment.

Starkweather's promotion and assignment proved to be a good choice. The Regiment did well in the West Virginia campaign and was back home just in time to find all the men and units who were disappointed at not being accepted in the First Call were being grouped into the 2nd, 3rd, 4th, 5th, 6th, 7th and 8th three-year Regiments in response to the Second Call. A number of Starkweather's officers and men achieved quick promotions by accepting assignments in one of the seven new Regiments. The remainder stayed with Starkweather in their original Companies and Regiment to become the 1st Wisconsin (Reorganized) and as such a part of the State's quota for the Second Call. By Summer, 1863, Starkweather was a Brigadier General, U.S.V., in which rank he served to the war's end.

In the military literature of the Civil War there is a semi-myth that flatters Wisconsin. It seems to have stemmed from a postwar statement of General Sherman that in the last year of the war a Wisconsin Regiment was the equivalent of most Brigades because old Regiments were kept at war strength by replacements instead of sending out new Regiments. Actually, the problem of replacements never was solved by the War Department for its own Regular Regiments. For the States, the replacement policy was set by the Federal Government's system of intermittent Calls upon the States, which contemplated new or reorganized units. A few States had a system of rotating Regiments in response to Presidential Calls. Each time such a Regiment was sent out, it counted statistically as a new Regiment though it kept its old number. An examination of many Regimental rosters, however, reveals officers and men rotated home often maintained a record of continuous war service by immediately going back to active duty with one of the Regiments being rotated back to active duty in Federal service. This practice prevailed in Massachusetts.

As noted above, Indiana followed the same pattern of reorganizing under an old number that Wisconsin did. For replacements, while in Federal service, however, Regimental Commanders each sought to solve the problem in his own way. The most effective was to send recruiting parties back to the home towns of the units. Every officer and man who drew a furlough for illness, or otherwise, was urged to bring along a recruit or two when he returned to duty. Colonels, their Adjutants and Company Commanders, being no more than human, early got into the habit of thinking the best recruiters were the Lieutenants, Sergeants and men most needful of furloughs. Officers and men desiring furloughs quickly became impressed with the same stimulating idea. Recruiting from within a nearby short-term Regiment that soon was to be mustered-out was also a fruitful source of replacements. Some Indiana and Wisconsin three-year Regiments, with a Table of Organization strength of 1,050 officers and men, had an aggregate of 1,900 to 2,300 men on their rosters during their periods of service. The difference between the basic strength and the aggregate, of course, represents the number of men recruited as replacements.

Wisconsin's Adjutant General did keep recruiters and organizers busy on the home front. He thus rendered yeoman service to the Regimental Commanders in keeping units at functional strengths, but the Military Departments of most other States did likewise. In the record, Wisconsin did neither better nor worse than Indiana, which was checked in close comparison.

Wisconsin's Governor A. W. Randall and his Adjutant General, William L. Utley, were not so fortunate in finding Mexican War veterans for Regimental Commanders as was Governor O. P. Morton of Indiana. There is ample evidence that they made efforts to find and interest such officers, particularly after the first Colonel of the 2nd Wisconsin did not do too well. He promptly was replaced. Governor Randall did prevail upon Rufus King, a West Pointer who had left the Regular Army 10 years before the Mexican War. Since resignation he had become a civic leader and Editor in Milwaukee. King reluctantly accepted the State's Brigadier Generalcy to command the Regiments later known as the Civil War's "Iron Brigade." It became legendary under his command, but ill health drove him to resignation, October, 1863, without a second star. Charles S. Hamilton,

60

West Point, 1843, left a flourishing business in Fond du Lac to accept command of the 3rd Wisconsin. He became a Major General and Army Corps Commander, but resigned to return to civil life in 1863. Colonel Starkweather and a score or more of his fellow Regimental Commanders, who likewise had no prior Federal active duty, became General Officers and as such achieved more than passing distinction. States that had sent Regiments to the Mexican War do appear to have had higher ratios of promotions beyond the rank of Colonel.

## OHIO LAUNCHES AN OFFENSIVE

One of the best mobilization jobs executed in the North was by Governor William Dennison of Ohio. The original quota for his thickly-populated State, in the First Call, was one Major General, three Brigadier Generals, 13 Staff officers and 13 Regiments of Infantry. But Virginia, Tennessee, North Carolina and Arkansas had left the Union in response to the Call for them to provide eight Regiments. Some of the disrupted Border States also defaulted. It was up to the more populous of the Union States to exceed their original allocations if Mr. Lincoln was to get his Regiments totalling 73,391 officers and men in the unit quotas assigned. Governor Dennison readily agreed to field 22 Regiments instead of the initially-planned 13. War fever was running so high in Abolition-minded Ohio that he filled them with ease.

For Major General, Governor Dennison wanted a native son of Ohio, out of the Regular Army; specifically, Major Irvin McDowell. Luckily for Dennison, the War Department held the Major was too valuable to be released; hence, McDowell was promoted and retained to lose the Battle of Bull Run. In lieu of McDowell, the commission was tendered to a citizen of Cincinnati, recently arrived in the State from the Illinois Central Railroad to accept the Presidency of the Ohio and Mississippi. The transportation executive accepted. He was George B. McClellan, civil engineer and former Captain, U.S. Army.

Though Ohio's Governor has been criticized more than most for political appointments in the State's fast-burgeoning Organized Militia, today there appears to be little basis for the charge except that in accepting the enormous task of an overnight creation of 22 fully-organized Regiments, he also accepted more opportunity for errors in personnel. Moreover, that three of his officers from this era became Presidents has furthered the idea that Ohio Regiments were filled with more competent politicians than from elsewhere. But such logic is hardly impressive. Most political scientists would agree there were other potent, non-military factors that made Ohio the mother of post-Civil War Presidents.

Moreover, as of that date, Ohio's Governor had more forceful ideas and vision than did the Administration in Washington. Dennison insisted his new Major General invade, without undue delay, western Virginia. The mission was to liberate the Union-minded, non-slave-holding mountaineers who had been "dragooned out of the United States by the Tidewater Democrats." McClellan gave the same excuses (ill-prepared and not enough troops) to Dennison he later gave to Lincoln, but Dennison was a great executive though a poor politician. He knew how to answer excuses. He teamed-up with Governor Morton of Indiana for that State's available Regiments. He also put at Mc-Clellan's disposal some of his surplus Regiments not in Federal service but which he was holding and training in prospect of a future Call. He was sure it would be soon. McClellan then gave the excuse that the project had not been cleared in Washington. Dennison cleared it sufficiently to get McClellan moving.

Dennison's clear vision and the campaign that followed not only created a new Free State for the Union, but it gave a lasting and crippling blow to Virginia, the Confederacy's most industrialized, most populous and, withal, the most powerful of the Southern States. It further created a mountainous breach in the South's Northern military frontier that greatly reduced the Confederacy's advantage from interior lines of communications. This too-often-ignored and fruitful campaign also had much to do with Kentucky remaining officially within the Union, though at heart it still had Confederate impulses.

All-in-all, the results of this Indiana-supported Ohio offensive with three-months Regiments, plus State units not yet in Federal service, were of far more significance that fateful Summer than who won or lost the overpublicized Battle of Bull Run. But in groping for face-saving explanations as to why McDowell lost Bull Run, the West Virginia successes normally are forgotten or ignored. At the same time, "the Militia" is too often the scapegoat for McDowell's incompetent leadership.

## BRIEF CRITIQUE ON BULL RUN

That the same "Militia" in mountain terrain, led by the less-than-brilliant McClellan and confronted by Robert E. Lee, the South's best commander, liberated 375,000 mountaineers to form a new State in the Union, should suggest searching elsewhere for a Bull Run scapegoat. McDowell's Headquarters, with his own actions and orders, proves revealing. With reasonable discernment, one need search no further. But through the past century, such a climate of opinion has been created as to the poor quality of the North's First Call Regiments (with Bull Run as Exhibit A) that it is not likely a few paragraphs here and elsewhere will stem the tide of acceptance by repetition.

That these first Regiments from the States were improperly-clothed and poorly-fed, and often were issued obsolete muskets and inadequate training manuals, is conceded. But these were the responsibilities of the professionals and the Federal Government. Could it be argued that the still-aborning Confederacy, with no Regular Establishment except a list of 312 recently-resigned professionals from the Old Army, was able to do more for its recently-inducted State Regiments? Hardly. For equipment and clothing they were in greater need than General McDowell's Federals. It is true that the Confederates were better-commanded. Generals Beauregard, Joseph E. Johnston and T. M. Holmes were the top officers in gray at Bull Run. Any one of the three was superior to McDowell. None of them, however, gained many tactical laurels in the four years of command and fighting that followed, but they were certainly good enough to trounce McDowell.

Governor Dennison of Ohio was indeed fortunate that he necessarily appointed George B. McClellan as State Commanding General of Ohio troops, rather than McDowell. We now know McDowell's retention and high promotion in Washington were under the political influence and patronage of the Secretary of the Treasury, S. P. Chase of Ohio. Thus one is reminded again and again that Washington. D.C., had more coveted plums for the ambitious politicians and palace soldiers than did the Governors who seldom could offer more than a Colonelcy with a harsh field future. That the typical Union Governor appreciated this, and was conscientious and non-political in his efforts to find competent Regimental Commanders, there is a vast body of evidence. When seasoned military talent was not available, Governors often accepted the recommendation (election) of the officers of the Regiment being organized. The remaining procedure was to choose a friend in whom the Governor had great confidence. In public life, that means a politician. But Governor Dennison's confidence was not always misplaced. His Colonels James A. Garfield and Rutherford B. Hayes proved to be better soldiers than Presidents, the latter being the highly-specialized job that it is.

## SUBSEQUENT CALLS TO THE STATES FOR REGIMENTS

Mr. Lincoln's Second Call for troops came hard on the heels of the First. It was but one of a series of calls that punctuated the following years of fratricidal warfare. True, the First Call for 75,000 had produced Volunteer Regiments from the States to an aggregate of no less than 91,816 officers and men. This was 16,816 more than had been allocated. Massachusetts, like Ohio, had oversubscribed, with five Regiments instead of the two allocated. Connecticut had delivered three Regiments instead of one. Little Rhode Island, with thoughts of Nathaniel Greene in the Revolution, had really flexed her muscles; instead of one Regiment of 780 officers and men allocated, she had put four on the line.

Missouri and Kentucky were rich, flourishing Border States of nearly 1,200,000 each. Both had been asked for four Regiments. Kentucky delivered none, and Lincoln considered it extremely good fortune that she technically stayed in the Union.

Missouri more than compensated for Kentucky. Instead of the 3,123 officers and men for a Brigade of four Regiments, Missouri delivered to Mr. Lincoln the equivalent of 13 Regiments. Missouri had to. In a little, internal civil war all her own, the Unionists of that State had to turn-out 10,591 officers and men, without delay, to keep their State out of the Confederacy. But oversubscribed though the First Call was, it was only a matter of weeks until it was apparent a Volunteer Army from the loyal States of only 91,816 was not enough.

The next military manpower proclamation was dated May 3, 1861. With Southern military manhood flocking to the Stars and Bars, the Border States in chaos, and four more States "absolving the bonds" to join the seven in revolt, Lincoln at last knew he needed not tens of thousands but hundreds of thousands, if the Union was to be preserved. On the above date he issued a Call for sutained strength. Lincoln wanted 18,000 men for the Navy. The Regular Army, numbering 16,422 officers and men, was to be expanded by Executive Order, with additional Regiments and Battalions of all Arms. This was intended to add 22,714 officers and men to the Regular Army. Forty additional Volunteer Regiments from the States, for a period of three years or the war, whichever might occur earlier, also were requested immediately. Instead of an aggregate of 780 to the Regiment, the new Tables called for approximately 1,050. This figure prevailed for all subsequent Regimental Calls and allocations.

Congress not only confirmed the foregoing but in additional legislation of July 22 and 25, the ante was raised to 500,000. Further provision was made for 30,950 men for two-year enlistments, 9,147 for one year and 3,715 for six months. The short terms, of a year or less, were to cope with special situations, particularly in Border States and their immediate neighbors and Indian threats on the frontier. Actually the Second Call under the July legislation sometimes is referred to as a summons for 500,000 men. In reality it was a sort of fragmented proposition with a far greater yield of manpower. First and last, 700,680 men were put in uniform, most of them for three years, as a result of the Summer of 1861 Call and the associated legislation.

In May and June, 1862, New York, Indiana, and Illinois were authorized to put on active duty at Federal expense units for three months to the number of 15,007. By Summer of 1862, Stonewall Jackson's Shenandoah campaign had badly frightened Washington. McClellan's Peninsula campaign against Richmond not only had bogged down, but was in serious trouble. The Call of July 2, 1862, was for 300,000 men in three-year Regiments. The States once again came through with the total oversubscribed.

## STANTON'S EXPERIMENTAL ORDER

But before the Regiments could be delivered, everyone in Washington was reaching for a bell rope to sound an alarm. The Nation was being invaded. Antietam was at hand. Under date of August 4, 1862, Secretary of War Edwin M. Stanton published a War Department *Order* for 300,000 *Militia* in *Regiments* for nine months. In its usage within this *Order,* the term *Militia* was more-or-less synonymous with the later words *Draftees* or *Selectees*. Obviously Stanton had been reading Paragraph 15, Section 8, Article I of the Constitution with a subtle hope that he could substitute it for Article II of the Bill of Rights as the basis for dealing with the States in matters of military manpower. Stanton boldly assigned quotas for 334,885, all in properly-organized State Regiments, in addition to the Call for 300,000 three-year men only a month previously.

Note again that this was an *Order* over the signature of Edwin M. Stanton—not a traditional Call of a President. Congress had enacted a law two weeks earlier that in effect amended the old Militia Act of February 28, 1795. It increased the power of the Executive to call on the States for *compulsory* Regiments to nine months of service instead of the historical three months. It also reiterated the Constitutional phrase about the President making "all necessary rules and regulations" incident to such mandatory requisition against the States. The bureaucratic and power-hungry Mr. Stanton saw in it the authority to set up a Federal direct Draft within a State by no more than an Executive Order. Namely: ". . . if any state shall not, by the fifteenth of August, furnish its quota of the additional three hundred thousand . . . the deficiency of volunteers in that State will also be made up by a special draft from the militia. The Secretary of War will establish regulations for that purpose." It was a dishonest War Departmental effort at an Executive, direct Draft. The yield in manpower was only 87,588. But thereafter Regiments from the States for less than a year became referred to indiscriminately as both Volunteers and Militia, even though, for the most part, the individuals were as much Volunteers as those in three-year Regiments; there was merely a difference in the time factor. Moreover, their Regiments were referred to as Volunteers in most States as well as in most Federal official correspondence.

Meanwhile, the three-year Regiments for the Call of July 2, 1862 were coming in. It has been suggested that this contingent represented the best of the Volunteers. On a man-for-man basis, this is highly subjective and much to be doubted. But these Regiments were the beneficiaries of a seasoning of officers and men from older Regiments.

Leadership at all levels was more experienced. Training was on a more informed and realistic basis. Supplies and equipment were more abundant. Channels were better-established and better understood. The Regiments did shape-up well and rapidly through the Autumn and Winter of 1862-63. Theoretically, the President's Call of July 2, 1862 was for 300,000 in three-year Regiments. The allocations to the States were for Regiments of an aggregate of 335,835 officers and men. According to Captain Frederick Phisterer, U.S.A., the best personnel statistician of the Civil War, the yield was 421,465.

This eased the manpower situation for a year. Came the Spring campaigns of 1863, climaxed by Chancellorsville and followed by Lee's regroupments for the offensive that ended at Gettysburg. These events brought forth a new Presidential Proclamation calling upon the States of Maryland, Ohio, Pennsylvania, and West Virginia to turn-out Home Guard units to an aggregate of 100,000 officers and men to resist the invasion. The early manpower yield was only 16,361. Most of them came from New York and passed to the control of Major General Darius N. Couch, commanding the Department of the Susquehanna, to shore-up his Zone of Interior defenses against the Confederate invasion. Lee's defeat and withdrawal from Gettysburg removed the pressure. These quickie units, so briefly called and for no specified term, were more in the nature of the Revolutionary War and 1812 Home Guard Militia than any other Union augmentation during the Civil War.

## THE SOUTH AND NORTH ENACT DRAFT LAWS

Meanwhile, and along the same general pattern, the Southern States had been utilizing their Organized Militia and Draft powers to provide the Confederacy with field armies. At times, from the Northern viewpoint, the results were disgustingly successful. When last mentioned in this chapter, an apprehensive Confederate Congress had put a 100,000-man ceiling on the strength of the one-year units Mr. Davis might receive into the Provisional Army of the Confederate States, should those "tendered" by the States exceed that number. He could not *demand* units from the States for longer service than six months. While the showdown at Fort Sumter was in progress, Mr. Davis sought the equivalent of eight Regiments, P.A.C.S., for taking over the many forts, arsenals, frontier posts, and Army installations that had fallen, promptly and easily, into the hands of the seceding States. They, in turn, were handing-over the real estate and supplies to the Confederacy. When Fort Sumter did not follow this easy pattern, Beauregard had taken into the P.A.C.S., the properly-tendered South Carolina Brigades, about 5,000 men, concentrated at Charleston to prevent landings by the off-shore fleet, the size of which often had been exaggerated.

Thus, by April 8, 1861, a week before Sumter, Mr. Davis thought his Provisional Army of Volunteers from the States should be expanded to at least 27,200 officers and men of all Arms. Came hostilities at Fort Sumter, and the day after Lincoln's First Call for the 75,000, Davis called for 32,000 from his seven States. Virginia, North Carolina, Tennessee, and Arkansas had not yet joined Secessia.

But while these four States were leaving the Union, they simultaneously were recruiting armies of their own. The Lincoln Call that had tipped them from the Union was considered a thrown gauntlet of battle. It behooved them to get an army of their own without delay. Moreover, allies were needed. As one officer explained, his State had become his *nation;* "We were *allied* with the other Southern States, not *indissolubly* joined." But the arming of the North had an immediately-unifying effect. Virginia and her three sisters joined more than an alliance; they tendered Regiments to the Confederacy. The victory at Bull Run, in which a Brigade of former Regiments of the South Carolina "Regular Army" fought alongside Virginia Volunteers and others from Mississippi and Louisiana, created a military sense of unity within the politically loosely-conceived Confederacy. It also brought great prestige to the Provisional Army of the Confederacy. A flood of correspondence from Brigades, Regiments, separate Battalions and even independent Companies flowed into the Confederate War Department. All were tendering their services, *with the approval of their respective States.*

Accordingly, on August 8, 1861, the Confederate Provisional Congress removed the ceiling. The President was authorized to call upon the States for units totalling 400,000 for three years. It was the Confederate answer to the Federal legislation of the preceding July 22 and 23 authorizing 500,000 for three years. But this was a game in which the South could lose quickly. The North had a manpower pool, Census of 1860, of 4,559,872. With each White man in the 11 States of the recently-expanded Confederacy called to active duty, the Provisional Army of the Confederacy could have mustered only 1,064,193 officers and men. Slaves had no Militia obligation; citizens "of color" were not accepted into units.

Moreover, by early Spring of 1862, the terms of service of the first 100,000 men, accepted for 12 months, began expiring. Summer and early Autumn were always seasons of heavy combat. But the officers and men of the South's one-year Volunteer units were pretty much of a mind to take a breather at home before embarking upon new adventures and dangers. Grant's successes at Forts Henry and Donelson and deep thrust into Tennessee from Shiloh, April, 1862, were discouraging. McClellan was landing for his Peninsula Campaign but had not yet met with disaster. In Richmond, the Confederate Congress decided it was faced by a condition rather than a theory. The concept of the Confederate States of America, an alliance, all with sovereign rights, was thrown out the window.

On April 16, 1862, was passed the first Conscription Act by a central government in American history. In effect, the historic concept that the Militia responsibility was a relation between a man and his State Government was abridged and superseded, and that in a loosely-organized American republic, created for and dedicated to States Rights. In the Confederacy, according to the new concept, men and units owed their obligation directly to Richmond. The Draft ages were for men between 18 and 35. *Terms of all men then in uniform were extended to three years.* This automatically elongated the terms of service of all the one-year units. The administration of the Confederate Draft followed State lines, but with the Confederate War Department in close supervision. Substitutes might be employed from among those not vulnerable to Draft. Any man drafted as an individual could demand service in a unit from his own State. Moreover, the traditional Southern right for the men to elect their own Company, Battalion and Regimental officers was preserved in the law. Here we find both Democracy and States Rights rampant. Subsequent amendments to the law wrote-in all manner of exemptions, but the age of obligation was extended to 45. Boys of 17 and men between 45 and 50 were vulnerable for draft into local Home Guard units. These latter went by all sorts of names such as "the Choctaw (County) Minutemen" and "Shelby Avengers." By February 17, 1864, the South began drafting free Negroes and slaves into home front labor units. A few days before Appomattox, the use of slaves as soldiers became a Confederate law.

Since Mr. Davis was driven to conscription within exactly a year following his first Call to the States for Battalions and Regiments, the North had considerable time for a mental conditioning to a Draft idea before the Union Administration decided to take the same bold, and almost equally revolutionary, step. The string of phenomenal Confederate victories in the Eastern Theater except for the Antietam Campaign, the Federal "recoil from Vicksburg," accentuated by Bragg's October penetration almost to Cincinnati, and the cold, depressing months of early 1863, all combined to leave responsible leaders and citizens in the North asking what the Confederacy had that the Union did not have.

The North's ever-expanding War Department, headed by the power-mad Stanton and filled with bureaucracy-minded empire-builders, among whom Brigadier Generals Lorenzo Thomas and James B. Fry were not the least, hardly could be expected to admit there might be some factors other than manpower. True, there were critics who mentioned General Lee's consistently smaller armies, and that Major

General Don Carlos Buell had 137,000 men with whom to destroy Bragg's abbreviated and converging columns of only 49,000. But such ideas could come only from the mouth of a Copperhead. That was a label no patriotic, self-respecting citizen was willing to flirt with. From this vantage point, the War Department inspired a climate of legislative opinion that the South's Draft Law was the one thing that the Confederacy had that the Union did not have.

Proponents of a Union Draft would not admit the patent fact that the returns from all the long-service Calls Mr. Lincoln had made had far exceeded the strengths he had stipulated. Nor was it readily noted that it was only Mr. Stanton's sneaky, short-service Draft *Order* that, in terms of results, had fallen on its face. But opponents of the Bill could not deny that quotas had not been compulsory on the States, and that some of the States had not been carrying their full share compared with others. That Minnesota, Iowa, and Kansas were economically poor and had Indian problems more menacing than the Confederates, was mentioned but not accepted as valid excuses. Given plenty of men under a Draft Law, the Federal War Department would protect them, retorted the Draft Bill's supporters. Just how to get adequate Federal quotas from Maryland, Kentucky, and Missouri, in which and behind the Federal lines the Confederates constantly were recruiting Companies and even Battalions, was something no one attempted to explain. In any event, the situation called for more men. That meant a Draft Law. Mr. Stanton had said so. Moreover, it should be better and therefore more militarily-bureaucratic than the one drawn by the Confederates.

The result was the most startling governmental abortion in the annals of American history. The Draft Act of March 3, 1863 created a Militia obligation to the Federal Government by all citizens and declarant aliens between 20 and 45, except for certain highly-restricted categories. The States of the Union were completely bypassed. Draft Districts were conventionally identical with Congressional Districts; which, in turn, were divided into Sub-Districts by the District Enrollment Board. The entire machinery was under the Provost Marshal General of the Army. One of his officers, normally a Captain, was to be President and principal administrative officer for each District. The Enrollment Board should consist of no more than the Army officer, a practicing physician, and one citizen. Each of the Board's Sub-Districts was to have an officer who would do the actual enrolling and transmit his list to the District Board. Future Draft quotas would be set by the President (in other words, the War Department) in the light of population and numbers of men each District already had on active duty. All enrollees were vulnerable to this door-knocking bureaucracy for two years after their enrollment. Once sent to active duty by the District

69

Board, enrollees were in the Army for three years, or the war, whichever might be sooner. The American people today are not ready to vest the Army with doorbell-ringing authority for coercion of citizenry. Can there be any wonder that 100 years ago the law was a failure from the date of its publication?

There were other features equally objectionable. The District Boards would summon 50% in excess of the district quota. Normally, these would be entirely from Class I, which was every male 20 to 35 years of age and all unmarried men to age 45. The only other group was Class II and it included everyone not in Class I. Anyone thus summoned who was lucky enough to deceive the one physician on the Board was off the military hook, and the decision was final. From the remaining list of able-bodied men, the quota was filled by the Board, and any remaining overage returned to their homes, pending future quotas. Any busy citizen who considered himself needed at home, and who had an un-encumbered $300, could put the money on the line instead of himself, and thereby forget about the entire unpleasant business. If he could hire someone else to take his place for less than the $300, he could congratulate himself on even better luck than the law had intended. Enlistment bounties facilitated such negotiations.

The hired-substitute provision could have been copied from the Confederate Draft Law. In the South it had not proved to be so disastrous, largely for two reasons. Some communities were so stripped of manpower by volunteering into their State-organized Regiments that no one remained who was physically fit for functioning as a Draftee substitute and Bounty-jumper. With so few available, the business abuse could not become so flagrant as it was to be in the North. The other reason was that the violent community reactions against a man who had to be drafted into doing his duty, were further compounded should he publicly admit he was such a coward that he would pay money to avoid the dangers of combat. Further comparison of the two laws is fruitless. Both were immediate failures except insofar as they may have stimulated some volunteering in certain manpower age brackets that otherwise might not have put on the uniform. But whether this was enough to justify the laws, North and South, and the trouble they created and the men diverted to their attempted enforcement, is open to question. Most of the volunteering after 1863 was by adventurous young men who, through the early war years, grew into the idea that anyone with hair on his chest could best proclaim it by carrying a gun with bayonet.

The well-known Draft Riots and bounty-jumping in the North, the frictions between the Southern Governors and President Davis over "Sovereign, State exempted categories of State citizens," are oft-told narratives that merit no repetition or evaluation here. It is enough to record that of the two laws, perhaps that of the Confederacy was the better. It was set up along State lines, as that in America today. The only redeeming feature of the Federal statute was its splendid demonstration of what a military service Draft Law should *not* be. On the positive side, Lieutenant Colonel James Oakes, 4th Cavalry, U.S. Army, who spent most of the war as a Mustering Officer for the State of Illinois, combined scholarship, imagination and experience to write a treatise on what he thought a military Draft Law ought to be should America again be confronted by the problem. President Woodrow Wilson's Secretary of War, Newton D. Baker, and his legally-trained Staff officer, Enoch H. Crowder, as will be reviewed in a later chapter, were to draw heavily upon the Oakes document on the eve of World War I. The principles that Oakes prescribed are operative today. Annie Oakley, the circus sure-shot, is in the Dictionary of Biography, but for some reason James Oakes was overlooked. It could be because he was perhaps the only West Pointer and Regular Army veteran of the Mexican War, either North or South, who flatly refused a Brigadier Generalcy. This alone should be distinction sufficient for his immortalization in that continuing Who's Who of America's grave somebodies and gay nobodies. Combined with his constructive critique on the Union's Draft Law, Oakes certainly should be in the Dictionary of Biography alongside "Oakley, Annie (Aug. 13, 1860-Nov. 3, 1926), markswoman, . . ."

## CALLS FOR VOLUNTEERS CONTINUE

Notwithstanding the bloody Draft Riots in New York City, Troy and Boston, July 13-16, 1863, while the Armies of Meade and Lee were licking their wounds from Gettysburg, the Union Draft *did* yield 35,883 men. It also brought in $15,686,400 from those who bought-off. But it was General Henry W. Halleck who wrote the Law's epitaph in a letter to General Sherman. "Your ranks cannot be filled by the present draft . . . It takes more soldiers to enforce than we get by it." Mr. Lincoln had no choice but to issue another Call to the States for Volunteer Regiments.

The Proclamation was dated October 17, 1863. It followed the accepted pattern of a "Proclamation and Call" to the Governors of the different States rather than the "Order" of August 4, 1862, signed by Secretary of War Stanton and which had been so non-productive. This newest Call's only reference to compulsion was that failures to reach assigned quotas would result in drafts upon those districts and States that might show deficiencies. The number sought was 500,000. The yield was 369,280. But the Draft machinery was not trusted to make up the deficit, or to equalize quotas.

Another Call was made under date of March 14, 1864, by which time the periods of service were expiring for the three-year Regiments from the Call of May 3, 1861. Heroic efforts and sundry inducements, State and Federal, were offered. Strong appeals were made to pride in Regiments, home regions and the States. The response was good. Regiments that had been decimated by battle casualties, deaths and disabling sickness, exposure and disease, were dropped from the unit lists. Physically-fit surviving veterans normally were urged to enlist in an adjacent or nearby Regiment from their own home County or City.* The response of these veterans of three years of the most bitter service was good. The Call was for 200,000. The yield was 259,515 by volunteering. At the same time, 32,678 citizens were still sufficiently worried about the Draft that they paid commutation.

Between April 23 and July 18, 1864, there were mustered into Federal service, for 100 days, Home Guard units, which, with the customary abuse and misuse of the word, were referred to unofficially and officially as "the Militia" of those States. These units were from only 12 States and numbered an aggregate of 83,612, though the assigned quotas were for 113,000. Most of these short-term Home Guard outfits drew duty at prisoner-of-war installations, rear area forts, and as railtrain and wagon-train escorts and other Line-of-Communications assignments. The older and better-trained units that they relieved were thrown into action with Grant's heavily-engaged forces in Northern Virginia, or were fed into the campaign to take the Shenandoah Valley away from the South's General Jubal A. Early.

As the drain of warfare in the last year of bitter fighting continued, on July 18, 1864, Mr. Lincoln made another major Call for long-service Regiments. Unlike most other Calls, it was not to the States and their Governors. It cited a law passed two weeks earlier that authorized the Union to take into its service Volunteers for one, two or three years, "as they may elect, and will be entitled to the bounty provided by law for the period of service for which they enlist." The number sought was 500,000, with quotas assigned. Credits were allowed to the States for men in the Navy and for previously-exceeded quotas.

In short, the Secretary of War at last had sold the President and the Congress the idea that the fertile-brained and mercurial-minded Daniel Sickles had brought to Lincoln when he was having trouble getting his "Excelsior Brigade" into active duty the early Summer of 1861. A Federal Organized Militia was in the making. The War Depart-

---

* The old three-year Regiments that were continued, thanks to having consolidated with them reenlisting survivors from one or more other discontinued Regiments, became known as "regiments for three years and longer." They also were flattered by official designation as a Veteran unit, such as 13th Wisconsin Veteran Volunteer Infantry" A few Regiments from most States, because of light casualties and highly-effective recruiting during the course of the War, were able to reenlist all their men and continue as a "Veteran Regiment" without the more conventional consolidations or replacements from other Regiments. Men of less than three years' service but in a three-year Regiment being deactivated, were rated as "non-veterans" and were transferred to a unit of the same State that had not yet completed its full period of service.

ment had met with phenomenal success in the organization of Colored Regiments and in officering them with White Sergeants from neighboring White commands for the grades of Lieutenant and Captain. Captains and Majors in seasoned State Regiments had readily accepted promotions to Field grades for duty with the Regiments of Colored Freedmen. With more logic than understanding, Stanton and his Staff officers apparently reasoned the White citizenry and veterans being released from the expiring State Regiments could be brought into purely Federal formations and dealt with in the same manner. The impact of the new policy and its failure are reserved for the following chapter. The veterans did not go for it. The term-of-service option was popular, but they preferred reenlisting in older outfits from their own States. Younger men coming of age preferred to go into new Regiments from their States, under seasoned officers from older Regiments.

The States quickly accommodated themselves to the new ground rules by organizing Regiments for one year. For the most part they were filled by voluntary enlistments of young men who had come of military age since April, 1861. Most of them were in the field long enough to experience some hard campaigning, but few of them saw any really hard fighting. With the disdain that seasoned combat soldiers always have for the Johnny-Come-Latelies, many memoir-writers in the postwar years spoke lightly of them. The records of those few Regiments in this Call that did have full chance to show their mettle fought quite well. But the yield credited to this Call was only 386,461, practically all in State Volunteer Regiments, rather than as direct Enlistees.

The last major Presidential Call, that of December 19, 1864, for 300,000 men, was no more than a supplement to that of the preceding July. It gave the same options as to length of service and cited the same statute. For the most part its yield was in additional one-year Regiments from the States. As will be noted later, Major General Winfield Scott Hancock, in an all-out effort to recruit veterans directly into Regiments of "U.S. Veteran Volunteers," was able to create only nine Regiments. But all of them were for one year and none of them fired a shot in anger.

The need for more men ceased before this Call was finished. The response was exceptionally favorable. With the end of the fighting in sight, recruits were being turned away. Nevertheless, this Call accounted for 212,212, of whom only 54,967 were for three years.

On May 1, 1865, three weeks after Appomattox and three days before Lieutenant General Richard Taylor, P.A.C.S., surrendered all remaining Southern forces East of the Mississippi to Major General E.R.S. Canby, U.S.V., the Union Army numbered 1,100,516 officers and men, of all components, ranks and ratings. Deducting small credits to the Navy in some of the foregoing Calls, no less than 2,850,000 Army enlistment blanks had been completed for short or long periods of Union service. And that is where the indefatigable personnel statistician, Captain Frederick Phisterer, decided to call a halt. "In this number, men who re-enlist are counted twice, or even more often. To give the number of individual persons who served in the army during the war is not practicable, nor is it of any practical benefit."

## SUMMARY OF CIVIL WAR MILITARY EFFORT AND POLICIES

In the course of the four years of strife, the Union and the Confederacy were guided by the same basic traditions, concepts, military institutions, and customs. It was natural that they should attempt to solve the same military personnel and organizational problems in much the same manner and within the same terms of reference. Often they followed the same formulae, with varying degrees of success, dependent upon variables inherent North and South as compared with each other.

If more attention has been given here to the Union, in comparison with the South, it is because the North prevailed in the great appeal to arms and the Union's laws, policies and practices constitute the connecting links between military affairs in ante-bellum America and the legislation and practices in the America of our own times.

The armies of both the South and the North were created under Colonial, early Statehood, and National laws and philosophies that the Militia responsibility (military obligation) of the citizen was to his State. Each of the central governments, in Richmond and in Washington, accepted this historic principle in theory and practice by calling upon their component States for Companies, Battalions, and Regiments of Organized Militia, the equivalent of the modern National Guard. Indeed, the term "National Guard" received statutory recognition as being identical with "State Volunteers" and "Organized Militia" during this war.

In both the North and the South, the munitions, clothing and pay of all units so inducted became the immediate responsibility of the central government. Command and leadership above the Regimental level was likewise the duty and responsibility of the higher, or central, government. In the disruption of the ante-bellum Old Regular Army, the South's patrimony included an appreciable portion of arsenals, arms and munitions. The Confederacy inherited no Regiments, Batteries or Companies in being and practically no individual enlisted men from the prewar Regulars; less than a third of the officer personnel went South. The Union retained all else.

President Davis made comparatively few Proclamation Calls to his States for troops. Those he made were effective, but due to manpower limitations the South necessarily took earlier recourse to a centralized Draft of military manpower. It was not a success. In Presidential Calls to the loyal States for Organized Militia Regiments of Volunteers, the North met with phenomenal success, with over-subscribed responses, but from a much larger manpower pool than the South had. As fast as the conventional State, North or South, met its quota of units, Home Guard and other reserve military units of the States were created for internal Constabulary use, if needed, and for resisting local invasion should a hostile offensive penetrate its borders. Moreover, such Home Guard units in part-time State service served as training cadres and a possible reserve against a sudden future Federal Presidential or Confederate demand for short-service Regiments.

The first Calls of Davis and Lincoln took into active duty most of the peacetime Organized Militia, or National Guard units, North and South. Existing units thus mustered to active Federal or Confederate duty were replaced promptly by new State units in inactive status pending domestic or local emergencies and the possibility of a future Presidential Call. Earlier Calls provided military leaders at home and in the field for later Regiments. In some States this was done with foresight and reasonable efficiency, but not always so in all States, North or South. Faced by invasion threats, Mr. Lincoln called on certain States for immediate short-term service by ill-prepared units of the Organized Militia. Erroneously these sometimes were called "the Militia" in differentiation from the longer-service Regiments of Organized Militia, or National Guard, already on duty and commonly referred to as "Volunteer Regiments." Actually, the one was no more a volunteer unit than was the other. Both types were of the same legal status and origin. Only the term of service and most likely the degree of experience were different. All Regiments with State designations were the Organized Militia of the States, or National Guard, in active service, pursuant to Presidential Calls, of the Federal Government. And that is what the National Guard is today.

The War Departments of both the Union and the Confederacy occasionally were irked by having to deal with military personnel through the States. The North's efforts to free itself of this relationship through a quasi-administrative Draft, and later by a disastrous Draft Law, were unsuccessful. For reasons that did not prevail in the North, the failure of the Confederacy's Draft Law was not so spectacular, but was anything but successful. Legislation for direct recruitment of a Federal Organized Militia, or U.S. Volunteers, was enacted for the first time in this war. The results were negligible, but the failure was not so notable as was the Union's Draft Law. In the direct recruitment and organization of Federal, volunteer Negro Regiments, however, the Union War Department met with marked success.

Throughout all these personnel problems, efforts to expand the U.S. Regular Army to its authorized war strength of 40,000 met with only partial success, never attaining strength as of a given date of more than 26,000 officers and men. The Confederacy at no time was able to implement its modest legislation for a small Regular Army, though Lee, Beauregard, Joseph E. Johnston and more than 300 other officers of the Old Army who resigned to "go South" were carried on a Confederate Regular Army list. Most of them fought their share of the war in higher "temporary" Provisional Army ranks.

The self-sufficient martial spirit within the several States, North and South, inherent in the very existence of their uniformed and active Organized Militia units, immediately implemented the conflicting ideologies: local autonomy versus centralization; States Rights versus Federalism; Slavery versus violent Abolitionism; the right of Secession versus an Indissoluble Union. This implementation was done, North and South, in such size and rapidity of expansion of military formations from within the States that the normal role of the professional establishment in the North was greatly minimized and the South never had a chance to create one of a truly professional character. This explains the comparatively insignificant role of professional formations in this greatest struggle within the Western Hemisphere. Indeed, the indispensability of the career soldiers as battlefield leaders has been greatly exaggerated by many historians. Most of the top commanders in the North had left the profession of arms for civil pursuits, and the same was true of a number in the South: Stonewall Jackson, Jubal A. Early and D. H. Hill, for example. Moreover, most of them returned to civil life when the war ended.

At the same time, the wide influence of West Point and similar institutes such as Norwich, Virginia Military Institute and the Citadel, can hardly be exaggerated. Likewise, the military experience and training that the Mexican War brought to adventurous, military-minded civilians cannot be ignored. The military influence of peacetime training in Volunteer Militia and Organized Militia units of the States in the creation of battlefield leaders was also of great significance. To take an outstanding example, the 7th New York was famous early in the war for its prompt arrival in Washington as a crack, three-months outfit, with an emergency mission. Back in New York, at the end of its brief, bloodless tour, the Regiment was reverted to home station for future rotations to active duty, none for more than three months. As a result, the 7th New York's only fighting *as a unit* was at home on State call to suppress the New York City Draft Riots. Meanwhile, its original personnel had sought continued active duty in other New York Regiments for three years and longer. Through service in other Regiments, nearly 600 of the 7th's original personnel became officers. Its strength, January 1, 1861, was 991. The distribution by highest ranks held by those who became officers was: Staff ranks, such as Surgeons,

Paymasters, etc., 38; Lieutenants, 158; Captains, 205; Majors, 58; Lieutenant Colonels, 68; Colonels, 29; Brigadier Generals and Major Generals, 35. It is a record of which any alumni association would be proud.

# Bibliographical Note For Chapter II

The basic and most voluminous single source for all military aspects of the Civil War is *The War of the Rebellion: A Compilation of the Official Records of the Union and Confederate Armies*, Series I, 111 vols.; Series II, 8 vols.; Series III, 5 vols., and Series IV, 3 vols. There are also a General Index and a two-volume Atlas. It was published by the U.S. Government, under the direction of the War Department, 1880-1902. These *Rebellion Records*, or *Official Records . . . Armies*, as the several series often are abbreviated, are far more complete for the Union than for the Confederacy. Series I is for military operations. Series II consists of P.O.W. and State prison correspondence. The Call proclamations, basic organizational laws, correspondence on personnel policies, difficulties with the Draft, etc., for the Union are found in Series III and for the Confederacy in Series IV. Voluminous though this compilation is, it allows no more than frequent glimpses, but never a comprehensive view, of details within the Military Departments of the several States, North and South. For this information one must turn to long-neglected and overlooked quasi-official and official State publications such as *Maine in the War, 1865*, and the *Annual Report of the Adjutant General of the State of Wisconsin for the Year Ending December 31st, 1865*, September, 1866. More deliberate and thoroughly-exhaustive are *Reports of the Adjutant General, State of Illinois, Containing Reports for 1861-1866*, (with rosters of units), 8 vols., 1882; The Adjutant General's Office, State of Iowa, *Roster and Record of Iowa Soldiers in the War of the Rebellion with Historical Sketches of Volunteer Organizations, 1861-66*, 6 vols., 1908-1911; William Schouler, the Adjutant General, State of Massachusetts, *Annual Reports, 1861, 1862, 1863, 1864, 1865*, and later from the office of A.G., State of Massachusetts, *Record of Massachusetts Volunteers, 1861-65*, 2 vols., 1868-70; State of New York, Office of the A.G., *Acts, General Orders and Proclamations, 1861-62; Annual Reports of the A.G.O., 1862, 1863, 1864, 1865, 1866*, 75 vols., 1876, 1894, 1893-1906 (most volumes are rosters and tabulated data); State of Missouri, *Report of the Adjutant General* (Confederate), 1861, and of *Adjutant General* (Union), *1863, 1864, 1865;* Maryland Military Records Commission, *History and Roster of Maryland Volunteers*, 2 vols., 1898-99; State of Ohio, *Annual Reports of the Adjutant General, 1861, 1862, 1863, 1864, 1865*, and The Roster Commission, *Official Rosters of Soldiers of the State of Ohio, 1861-1866*, 12 vols., 1886-95; and *Report of the Adjutant General of Indiana*, 8 vols., 1869. The above States often listed their war effort down to Company rosters, names and addresses of deceased and prisoners-of-war, as well as names and last known addresses of deserters. There are comparable official publications for all the Union States, including Oregon and California. Space does not allow full listings here. Write your State

Historical Society Librarian for guidance if you are primarily interested in your own State. These official publications, and State histories based upon them, have one common weakness: a tendency to ignore completely, or to play-down all resources and potential resources prior to Lincoln's First Call, April, 1861. They thus provide excuses in the North for early reverses and further emphasize the mammoth war efforts thereafter. The war left Southern States with military records destroyed or incomplete, and no funds for cataloguing and publication until after 1877. Compilations and writings of the era, official and private, have suffered accordingly. Alabama, South Carolina, Texas, Mississippi and Florida have no comparable official reports of compilations of public, military documents. Those of Georgia, Virginia, Arkansas and Tennessee are fragmentary, greatly abbreviated. North Carolina and Louisiana are more fortunate. Belatedly, these two States have been able to assemble and publish records that approach those of the Union States in comprehensive completeness. Among the best and most indispensable of many histories pertinent to the Union and Confederate armies are: Samuel P. Bates, *History of the Pennsylvania Volunteers, 1861-65*, 5 vols., 1869-71, and *Martial Deeds of Pennsylvania*, 1865; Capt. Frederick Phisterer, U.S.A., *New York in the War of the Rebellion*, 3 vols., 1912; Brig. Gen. R. H. Orton, *Records of (Cal. N.G.) California Men in the War of the Rebellion*, 1890; Clement A. Evans, ed., *Confederate Military History*, 12 vols., 1899; Whitelaw Reid, *Ohio in the War*, 2 vols., 1893; Maj. J. T. Sprague, U.S.A., *Treachery in Texas*, 1862, (a rare account of the arrest and expulsion of Regular Army formations from Texas, 1861); Fred A. Shannon, *The Organization and Administration of the Union Army, 1861-65*, 2 vols., 1928, and Col. James B. Fry, U.S.A., *A Sketch of the Adjutant General's Department, United States Army, 1775-1875*, 1877. Robert V. Johnson and Clarence C. Buel, eds., *Battles and Leaders of the Civil War*, 4 vols., 1887, are essentially operational military history, but Order of Battle lists and secondary incidents often have bearing on personnel problems. For problems peculiar to the Border States see J. T. Scharf, *History of Maryland from the Earliest Period to the Present Day*, 3 vols., 1879; E. Merton Coulter, *The Civil War and Readjustment in Kentucky*, 1926; and Floyd C. Shoemaker, *Missouri and Missourians; Land of Contrasts and People of Achievements*, 5 vols., 1943.

## CHAPTER III

# The Civil War Armies

AMERICA'S CIVIL WAR produced a profusion and confusion of Regimental origins and designations, both North and South. But this is in keeping with everything else incident to that great conflict. Even today informed men disagree as to the proper name for this war. In New England, "The War of the Rebellion" is a favored term. In the deep South, "The War Between the States" is the official phrase. Cagey politicians in Maryland, Kentucky, and Missouri, conscious of the divided sentiments of their voters, play it safe with "The Irrepressible Conflict." Some political scientists likewise have sought refuge in "The Second American Revolution." Others have offered a persuasive phrase, "The War for Southern Independence."

While the designation, "The Civil War," is widely accepted and today seems to be the preferable term, the very words "civil war" are synonymous with confusion. Thus if well-informed military men, not to mention casual laymen, still are confused as to the nature and origin of the Batteries, Regiments and other component units of the Civil War armies, perhaps it is because no one has bothered to pinpoint some salient differences, and to reduce the status of each type of unit to current terminology.

The crazy-quilt pattern of contrasting units of different States, varied origins and often colorful names, such as the "National Guard Zouaves" (officially the 10th New York Volunteer Infantry) and the "Stonewall Brigade" (actually the 1st Brigade, 1st Division, Left Wing, Army of Northern Virginia), has led to many uninformed statements in print. There have followed erroneous, mass impressions that have a tenacity for long and false lives. There is the customary derision of Militia and praise of Volunteers, often in a context that reveals the writer does not realize that the full scope and meaning of the former includes the latter. For example, one Mid-Western political science professor, who was presumed to know enough about the military that a non-profit organization recently published his thin little volume on military personnel, failed to see any similarity between the State-organized National Guard Regiments of Volunteers that mobilized for the Spanish War and the 1,800 identically-created State Regiments of Organized Militia Volunteers that for the Union and the Confederacy fought the bitterest and most courageous campaigns of the Civil War.

In addition to these hundreds of Regiments, both the North and the South were beneficiaries of the aggressive operations of sundry regional bands of guerrillas, bushwhackers, border ruffians, and jayhawkers. Though plunder and pillage were normally their means of support and their principal motive, they usually were covered by some legal symbol from either their own central government or a State Government of their sympathy.

Thus it seems appropriate that an analytical approach be made toward the types of units that appear in the Troop Lists of the armies that fought the Civil War. Because the scattered bands of guerrillas, bushwhackers, border ruffians and jayhawkers recognized no chain of command, and seldom coordinated their forays with any major military effort, we can dismiss them as mere flotsam on the tides of war.

The organized land forces of the Union included in their Troop Lists 1,981 full Regiments of Infantry, Cavalry and Artillery, with enough separate Companies, Troops and Batteries to constitute an additional 66 similar Regiments. This establishes a total of 2,047 combat Regiments, or equivalents. These do not include 24 Regiments and 187 separate Companies of service troops organized from the wounded and others with service-connected disabilities. Thus the grand total approximated 2,080 Regiments, or equivalents in separate lesser units.

More than 90% of these Union Regiments volunteered into the Organized Militia (National Guard) of the individual States and thence were inducted into Federal service pursuant to the series of Presidential Calls. The remaining 10% of the Regiments of the Union Armies were

80

U.S. Regulars or in one of the components of the U.S. Volunteers. These last were the origin of a Federal Organized Militia of volunteers, which thus appear on a large scale for the first time in American military history.

## THE PROVISIONAL ARMY, CONFEDERATE STATES

The combat elements of the Provisional Army, Confederate States of America, reached the aggregate equivalent of only 764 Regiments comparable with those cited above for the North; i.e., counting 10 separate Companies or Batteries a Regimental equivalency. The South's White military manpower pool was only 1,064,193, compared with the North's 4,559,872. Hence the South's ratio of combat units to the manpower pool was higher than that of the North. This should do something toward dispelling the myth that Northern military effort was nullified by creation of too many Regiments, while the South better organized its more limited manpower. In this respect, if the North was in error, the South was guilty of compounding the same error.

The organization and activation of the Confederate States Regiments followed the same general pattern as did those of the North, except for one additional link in the chain of events. Most Southern States had several months of more or less complete sovereignty between their secession from the Union and the full functioning of the Richmond Government. During this period of individual State sovereignty, most of the Governors went about the business of creating miniature armies and navies of their own States. Major General Benjamin J. Cheatham, Provisional Army of Tennessee, for example, initially was commissioned no higher than Brigadier General, Provisional Army, C.S.A., July 9, 1861. This appears to have been because he brought with himself no more than one Brigade from his State into the growing Provisional Army, Confederate States. Moreover, West Pointer Jefferson Davis was saving most of the top wartime ranks for the officers of the small Regular Army he was planning for the South. Even so, Generals Lee and Joseph E. Johnston, of Virginia Forces, took demotions to Brigadier Generalcies upon entry into the Regular Army officer list of the Confederacy. But by the end of Summer, 1861, this had been rectified by promotion of all five of the South's Regular Army Brigadiers to full General. This across-the-board promotion was to make sure these top Regulars from the Old Regular Army were not outranked by such Major Generals as Leonidas Polk of Louisiana and Stirling Price of Missouri, who were bringing Divisions to duty pursuant to President Davis's invitation for Regiments, Brigades and Divisions, to an aggregate strength of 100,000 officers and men, for provisional service up to one year.

Few, if any, Southern States immediately tendered all their fully-organized Brigades or Divisions. Actually, at the time of the first Battle of Bull Run, the aggregate strengths of all mobilized armies of the several Confederate States probably outnumbered the officers and men on the payrolls of the Richmond Government. This rapidly changed as the war progressed and the Provisional Army, Confederate States, grew accordingly.

Governors of the seceded States, under constant peril of invasion by either land or sea, naturally were reluctant to release all their weapons and manpower to the Richmond Government. Thus, as they lost Divisions, Brigades, Regiments and Battalions of their State forces to the theaters of action, the Southern Governors gave increasing attention to organizing "Home Guards," "Militiamen," "Reserve Militia," and other local defense units under sundry State or local names. These were in reality the old Enrolled Militia, with guns and an obligation to serve near their homes.

When invasion actually came, many of these local units reinforced the embattled formations of the P.A.C.S., operating in their area; as in the battles for Atlanta. In such cases of joint operations of the P.A.C.S. and local forces within a State's borders, discrimination between home front formations and those of the P.A.C.S. is not always apparent. Nevertheless, 669 Regiments, 139 Battalions (of all Arms) and 261 separate Batteries of Light Artillery, for an equivalency of a grand aggregate of 764 Regiments, appear to be as precise an estimate of the P.A.C.S. as Confederate records permit. Only 11 of these Regiments, four of Cavalry and seven of Infantry, carried Confederate States Army designations. They hardly could be considered Southern Regulars. Some were created from casuals remaining from disbanded units. Others were recruited belatedly in Border States under commissions issued from Richmond. The above aggregate of Southern Regiments also includes eight Regiments and one Battalion of "Partisan Rangers," credited to various States but which were raised largely under authority and commissions issued direct from Richmond. All other Confederate Army formations, which constituted 99.71% of the South's fighting units, were from war-expanded Volunteer Militia units of the States, or essentially National Guardsmen within the modern meaning of the term.

## THE REGULAR ARMY COMPONENTS

For the North, let us look first at the Regular Army elements. They are the easiest to identify, classify and enumerate. The day Mr. Lincoln took office, March 4, 1861, the Regular Army consisted of 10 Regiments of Infantry, four of Artillery, two of Cavalry, two of Dragoons, and one of Mounted Riflemen, for a total of 19 Regiments. The aggregate strength of the entire Regular Army was 1,108 officers and 15,259 enlisted men. Only 313 of its officers "went South" to accept commissions in the legislatively-authorized paper Confederate Regular Army of 10,600 officers and men.

The United States Regulars also temporarily lost the services of the loyal officers and 2,328 loyal enlisted men when Texas went out of the Union. General Twiggs surrendered them to Texan forces, provided that these officers and men might return North with personal effects and organizational arms should they so desire. This they eventually did, almost to an officer and man. But only 1,500 of them cleared Texas, via Mississippi River steamers North, in time to fight at Bull Run or help keep Missouri in the Union. The remainder became prisoners-of-war until exchanged, because the Fort Sumter affair found them still in Texas. The South accordingly got Twiggs and about 30 of his officers, who are included in the 313 mentioned above. The South also fell heir to all Federal supplies in Texas but received no share of this big slice of the prewar Regular Army's largest frontier force of enlisted men. Actually, many serving in the Old Regular Regiments were of foreign birth or of a recent overseas heritage and had little or no State allegiance. Hence the number of enlisted Regulars who "went South" was inconsequential. The idea that the Old Regular Army was wrecked by personnel defections to the South is not sustained by the facts. It was, as noted earlier, merely too small and too dispersed for the crisis of Secession.

President Lincoln by Executive Order, with Congress subsequently concurring, immediately increased the authorized strength of the Regular Regiments and increased the number of Regiments. The Regulars were enlisted or reenlisted for only three years, as were the troops in most of the State Regiments, but as noted in the preceding chapter, they never reached their authorized strength during the four years of the war. Their peak strength was reached on or about January 1, 1863, for a total of 25,463 officers and men. Their average daily strength through the four years was only 22,929.

Even so, a grand aggregate of 70,000 officers and men saw short or long terms of service in Regular Army units through the war years. They were distributed among 30 Regiments, of which six were Cavalry, five were Artillery and 19 were Infantry. Their killed-in-action for the four years was 2,047, a ratio quite comparable to State-organized Regiments mustered-in for similar terms of service. Eight of the 30 Regular Regiments, however, do not appear on Frederick H. Dyer's list of more than 900 Union Regiments that had 50 or more men killed or mortally wounded in action. It is thus quite apparent that no major Civil War battle was either won or lost by the firepower, or lack of firepower, from the North's small, far-flung and scattered Regular Army units, many of which fought their small share of actual combat as separate Batteries, Squadrons or detached Battalions.

The South, as suggested above, never got its proposed Regular Army of 10,600 officers and men completely off the planning table. It continued to be pretty much a paper proposition throughout most of the four years. The 313 former United States Regulars who resigned to go with their States were commissioned into it, if they so desired, with dates of rank that preserved their relative seniority as of their departure from the earlier Federal service. With a few exceptions, this rule was followed. Slightly less than 100 additional West Pointers and former Regulars, who, like T. J. (Stonewall) Jackson, Jubal A. Early and D. H. Hill, had left the Army for civil pursuits in the South, also tendered their swords to their respective States, and later to the Stars and Bars. Some, but not all, of them received commissions in the Confederate Regulars. From among these former United States officers, eight (Beauregard, Bragg, Cooper, Hood, the two Johnstons, Lee and E. Kirby Smith) became full Generals. Fifteen became Lieutenant generals, 48 Major Generals and 111 Brigadier Generals. Hence more than 200 former U. S. Regulars and West Pointers never achieved a Confederate rank of Brigadier General or higher. Moreover, these high commissions were in the Confederate Provisional Army, as were the appointments of the remainder of the 463 General Officers whose names appear in Confederate records.

Some of these latter, like Benjamin H. Cheatham, were strictly citizen-soldiers but had seen active duty in the Mexican War. Others, of great eminence, such as Lieutenant Generals Richard Taylor, John B. Gordon, and Nathan B. Forrest, entered the Confederate service as volunteer members of their respective States' Organized Militia (National Guardsmen) without prior military service. They, of course, had no status in the legislation providing for seniority on the Confederate Regular Army list. The 11 C.S.A. Regiments mentioned earlier occasionally have been considered Confederate Regulars. They were, for the most part, organized rather late in the war. None appear on Colonel William F. Fox's list of the South's high-casualty Regiments. Thus Brigadier General John McA. Palmer, U.S.A., in countering some of Upton's erroneous opinions in his *Military Policy of the United States,* was fundamentally accurate in writing: "Lee and Stonewall Jackson . . . managed to get along pretty well without any Regulars at all." Certainly there were no Confederate Regular units to exemplify good discipline and training, for tactical demonstrations and whence officers and key enlisted men could be drawn, such as Generals Irvin McDowell and George McClellan had when they were shaping, organizing, equipping and training the early combat elements of the Union Army.

## THE U.S. VOLUNTEERS BEGIN TO APPEAR

From the foregoing it is quite apparent that the armies, North and South, that fought, won and lost, in the great conflict, were composed almost entirely of State Regiments, created from their Organized Militia and inducted into the Federal service in the same manner as, but at times with greater haste than, were the National Guard Regiments of the Spanish-American War, Mexican Border mobilization of 1916 and World Wars I and II.

Such official Regimental designations as the "1st Regiment of Infantry, U.S. Volunteers," or "1st Regiment of Engineers, U.S. Veteran Volunteers," and "2nd Sharpshooters, U.S.V.," with no State origin indicated, do increasingly appear in Union Troop Lists after the Winter of 1863-64. These designations of U.S. Volunteers do clearly reveal the beginnings of a directly-organized Militia of the Federal Government, some Regiments of which came into Civil War active service through other than State-organized Militia, or National Guard, channels.

About 200 Regiments, plus approximately 220 separate Batteries and Companies, at one time or another were known officially as U.S. Volunteers, U.S. Veteran Volunteers, U.S. Veteran Reserve Corps, *Corps d'Afrique* and U.S. Colored Volunteers. This last term soon transitioned into "U.S. Colored Troops" or U.S.C.T. Approximately 155 of these U.S. Volunteer Regiments—less than 8% of all the Regiments that were activated and served in the Union armies—were recruited, officered and organized by the Federal Government with little or no deference to or consideration of any State Government. They were indeed U.S. Volunteers in the sense that the term was used to designate the additional, temporary U.S.V. Regiments specially recruited in 1899 for pacification of the Philippines. In these Militia units organized by the Federal Government, which became known technically as U.S. Volunteers, to differentiate from the State Volunteer Regiments (National Guard), we find the origins, the germ seed of the U.S. Army Reserve in the National Defense Act of 1916, the Officers Reserve Corps of World War I and after, down to the modern U.S. Army Reserve of current legislation. But it was a gradual evolution, and not all of those with a U.S.V. designation were truly Federal in origin.

The 1st and 2nd Regiments of Sharpshooters, U.S. Volunteers, the first to be so designated officially, actually were not U.S. Regiments. They were from State Organized Militia sources. They were separate Companies of the late Summer, 1861, response of Maine, Michigan, Minnesota, New Hampshire, New York, Pennsylvania, Vermont and Wisconsin to the Federal Call for three-year units. Most responding units, of course, were of Regimental size, but State quotas were not always easily divisible by Regimental Tables of 10 Companies each; some Companies were left over. It was of these unregimented Companies that the 1st and 2nd Sharpshooters, U.S. Volunteers, were created. Except for being of components from several States and their Field officers being by direct Federal appointment, these two original Regiments of "U.S. Volunteers" were identical with all other State Regiments of that War. Losses by combat, sickness and failure to reenlist at the end of the three years resulted in the consolidation of remnants of the 1st U.S.V. Regiment with the 2nd on December 31, 1864. But these two Regiments, not to mention General Sickles' tiff with the Governor of New York, had given the Union War Department an idea for directly-recruited Regiments that had borne considerable fruit long before the 1st Sharpshooters, U.S. Volunteers, vanished from the Union Troop Lists.

In April, 1863, the I.C., or Invalid Corps, U.S. Volunteers, came into existence. It was a highly successful effort to utilize the severely wounded, and other men with service-connected disabilities. Each I.C. Regiment had a 1st Battalion of six Companies capable of bearing arms, executing light marches, doing guard duty and constituting an emergency reserve. The other four Companies in the 2nd Battalion of each I.C. Regiment provided cooks, rear area wagoners, and hospital nurses. Since I.C. was confused, often purposely, no doubt, with the stamp for "inspected and condemned," the name was changed to Veteran Reserve Corps, U.S. Volunteers. This organization gave the Union 24 Regiments and 186 separate Companies. Captain Phisterer quite correctly credits the above-mentioned U.S.V. Sharpshooters and these Veteran Reserve Regiments to the war efforts of their various States, because they originally entered the service as members of State-recruited, officered and organized Regiments. In any event they were not a true Federal Organized Militia, or U.S. Volunteers, as were most of the subsequent temporary U.S. Regiments.

## THE U.S.C.T. ORIGINATES WITHIN THE STATES

Came the manpower shortages after 1862, and there followed a rising agitation among the Abolitionists to give the former bondmen a chance to fight for their own freedom. Various Northern States had met part of their earlier quotas with a Regiment or more of free, or allegedly free, Negro inductees. Thus by late 1863 there were already 31 Negro Regiments from the States with their duly-numbered State designations. Some carried the word "Colored" in their designation. Other States gave them a number in sequence without reference to race. Thus the first Negro units were Organized Militia, or National Guard units, initially. As the progress of the Union armies liberated many thousands more of unemployed Colored men, the War Department took a second look at this new source of manpower.

The Federal Military Government of the conquered State of Louisiana was first to create Negro Regiments in an appreciable number. This source organized 29 Colored Regiments of all Arms into a so-called *Corps d'Afrique*. Their White Captains and Lieutenants were top

NCO's selected from neighboring veteran White Regiments who were tendered Federal commissions, of appropriate grade, for such service. Their Field grade officers were, likewise, battle-tested Captains from the same Regiments of State Organized Militia, or National Guardsmen, should we use today's terminology. But the Federal Government stepped in with a Bureau for Colored Troops, Spring of 1863. The State Regiments of Colored men were transferred to custody of the Bureau. The Adjutant General of the Army became responsible for their recruitment and the commissioning of their White officers. The military governments in conquered Counties and States, however, working with nearby field commanders, actually did the job.

The former slaves and their free brethren in the North, who entered the service in State Regiments, thus contributed to the war effort of the North about 150 Regiments, Infantry for the most part, plus some 30 separate Company-and Battery-size units. The aggregate of all Colored units for the war was 187,097 officers and men. The largest number of U.S.C.T. in service at any one time was 123,156 officers and men. This was on July 15, 1865, three months after Appomattox. After that date there were no new Colored Regiments. Some of the earlier Regiments already had been mustered-out.

The Colored Regiment with highest battle casualties was the 79th Infantry, U.S.C.T., with 188 officers and men killed in action. It began its war service as the 1st Kansas Colored Infantry, one of the State Regiments transferred to and officially redesignated by the Bureau for Colored Troops. In the creation of all these purely U.S.C.T. Regiments, regional and State lines in the South were observed; the local Union military government officials were active, and field commanders within the Military Department cooperated. Hence even these Colored Regiments were comparatively free from a centralized management from Washington, which merely wrote directives and sent out occasional inspectors.

The Louisiana term, *Corps d'Afrique,* was unacceptable for many units from non-French areas, these inspectors reported. All Colored Regiments, accordingly, became known as the United States Colored Volunteers, or U.S. Volunteers (Colored). Finally, the War Department settled upon the official phrase, "U.S. Colored Troops." As fast as enlistments expired in the State-organized Colored Regiments, their men were reenlisted and reorganized into Regiments with such designations as the "102nd Infantry, U.S.C.T.," which, incidentally, first entered the Federal service from Detroit as the "1st Michigan Colored Infantry."

Most U.S.C.T. Regiments had been mustered out of Federal service by the end of 1866, though some that were not recruited and organized until 1865 were still in their U.S. Volunteers status at the end of 1867.

The Regular Army's *Lineage Book, Infantry Regiments,* accepts none of these Colored Infantry Regiments from the Union Army as an ancestor for either the well-known 24th or 25th Regular Infantry Regiments of Negro enlistees that appeared in American Troop Lists from 1866 until their desegregation during the Korean War.

## U.S. VOLUNTEERS FOR THE INDIAN FRONTIER

Having developed a formula for creating Regiments of U.S. Volunteers from men and from units that originally entered service as Organized Militia of the States, and further the recruitment of individual Negroes into Regiments that never had had any connection whatsoever with any State of the Union, the U.S. War Department personnel planners soon took recourse to these procedures along other channels. They sought and procured authority for four, and actually organized three, Federal Regiments of friendly Indians for frontier service. The purpose was to pinch from frontier duty some White units for service in the principal theaters of the war. This did not work-out so well. Then someone came up with the bright idea of recruiting Regiments from among the Confederate prisoners for duty restricted to operations against the Indians. Believe it or not, this program got into high gear in late 1864 and actually put six Regiments and one separate Company on the Indian frontiers of the Union States. They simply were designated 1st to 6th Infantry, U.S. Volunteers. They were veterans but from the wrong Army, hence were not authorized that flattering word as a part of their Regimental designations as was being done with other units of seasoned troops.

On July 8, 1864, there appeared in the unit lists of the Department of the Cumberland the "1st Regiment of Engineers, U.S. Veteran Volunteers." Theirs is a long story, but what it amounts to is that Major General George H. Thomas diverted some depleted State units of Infantry to field engineering duties. To keep them in that status and to get them Engineer ratings and pay, he wangled a special law to reorganize them as an Engineer Regiment and give the officers U.S.V. commissions as Engineers. It was a case of stabilizing with a statute what had been done from an off-the-cuff field order.

Meanwhile, March, 1864, the veteran, battle-scarred and depleted I Army Corps was deactivated and its remaining units and men transferred to other Corps, most of them to the V Corps. Soon thereafter the Union War Department decided to reactivate the I Corps, but to do it independently and without any deference or consideration of the States and their recruiting methods or policies. There would be a comparable Federal bounty for veterans who would reenlist. The Regiments, following a new practice of the States, would be listed officially as U.S.V.V. or "Veteran Regiments."

88

The extent, if any, to which the Department planners were indebted to General Thomas and his special Regiment for this idea, the *Rebellion Records* leaves to inference. But all these trends, such as the transitioning of the State, Colored Regiments into the status of Federal, U.S. Volunteers, and particularly the U.S.V.V. idea, strongly indicate the power-grasping Union War Office had plans to phase out of existence as many as possible of the hundreds and hundreds of combat-tested State Regiments of Volunteers (National Guardsmen, in modern terms) and to replace them with a Federal Organized Militia under the name of U.S. Veteran Volunteers.

To get the new project off to a good start, General Hancock, flush with fame since Gettysburg, and as C.G. of Grant's right wing at Petersburg, Va., was brought to Washington, November 28, 1864. He thus became putative commander of this prospective, new I Veteran Corps. A biographer says he was to recruit 50,000 veterans. This was the equivalent of at least four Army Corps of that era. General Hancock's troubles, which garnish the *Rebellion Records,* need not delay us here. It is enough to record that he fielded his Regiment of 1st Infantry, U.S. Veteran Volunteers, March 1, 1865. The 2nd to 9th Infantry Regiments U.S.V.V. followed with slight additional delays, the last not becoming fully operational until June, 1865, almost two months after Appomattox. Hancock's "New I Corps" accordingly never got out of its paper cocoon, notwithstanding the conspicuous need for such a Corps of seasoned troops should the French call America's hand and refuse to get out of Mexico.

While verbose staff papers are of record as to why this personnel project failed, the simple truth is that veterans (men of two or more years of service) readily re-upped in their State Regiment, or one with which their old depleted command was being consolidated. But, notwithstanding a choice of one-, two- or three-year terms in Hancock's U.S. Veteran Volunteer regiments, the same veterans avoided them in droves. Most of those who did enlist took the short term. In July and August of 1866 all nine of the Hancock Regiments of U.S. Veteran Volunteer Infantry were mustered-out. None had gone farther South than the Shenandoah Valley. None fired a shot in anger.

Notwithstanding its signal failure, this one major Civil War effort to implement the professional dream of an "expansible Regular Army" captured the imagination of young Emory Upton, West Point, Class of 1861. At that time he was an Artillery Captain, Regular Army, and a Brevet Major General, U.S.V., commanding a Cavalry Division in the higher temporary rank. Under impact of reduction to permanent rank, he never got over the idea that something was wrong. Staff assignments, an adventurous trip around the World, and inability to find service as a soldier of fortune in the Orient, turned him to writing. When he died by his own hand, 1881, while a Colonel commanding a peacetime Artillery Regiment, the manuscript of his *Military Policy of the United States* had been rejected by his commercial publisher. A later generation, 1903, edited and published the volume, as a War Department document, to serve new purposes. The book's shadow still at times haunts the modern Pentagon.

## STATISTICS ON STATE VOLUNTEER NATIONAL GUARD REGIMENTS IN THE CIVIL WAR

Let us return to the vast majority of the Regiments of the Union armies. While there were about 200 Regiments (nearly 50 of which were clearly of State origin) of all types with U.S. Volunteer designations, they constituted only 10% of the 2,047 Regiments and Regimental equivalents that Captain Phisterer tabulates as having constituted the Union armies between April, 1861, and January 1, 1866. They are, nevertheless, of significance for their trend toward breaking away from any State military connection whatsoever. As such they have a direct relationship with and are definitely the precursors of a Federal Organized Militia, now known as the United States Army Reserve, in contrast with today's Army National Guard formations.

Now, consider Captain Phisterer's tabulation of all other Regiments in the Union Army, April, 1861, to the last Call to the States for short-term troops toward the end of the war. Phisterer credits the States of the Union with having recruited, officered, organized and initially trained no less than 1,877 Regiments, or their equivalents in Companies and Batteries. These units originated in the Organized Militias (National Guardsmen) of the States and Territories whence they were inducted as military units into Federal active duty during the course of the Civil War.

New York led the list with 27 Regiments of Cavalry and 10 separate Companies, and 35 Batteries of Artillery, which, according to Phisterer's equivalents, would be one Battery less than three Regiments of Artillery, and 252 Regiments of New York Infantry with 15 non-regimented Companies of the same. Phisterer thus gives New York a total of 294 Regiments, 25 Companies and 35 Batteries.* Thus, from the Empire State alone came more Organized Militia, or National Guard, units, for fighting the Civil War than were provided by the Regular Army and all the various U.S. Volunteer formations combined. Dakota Territory is at the bottom of Phisterer's list. It had two Companies of Territorial Cavalry that saw Federal service during the Civil War.

---

* Phisterer rates 10 Companies of Infantry as a Regimental equivalent, but for Cavalry and Artillery he considered 12 comparable, separate units necessary for a Regimental equivalency. Civil War Cavalry Captains commanded "Companies." The "Troop" as a unit is post-bellum terminology.

It should be further kept in mind that not all these 1,877 National Guard, or Organized Militia, State Regiments were in active Federal service simultaneously. In the same way that some of the above-described Regiments of U.S. Colored Troops and U.S. Volunteers and U.S.V.V. formations were late-in-the-war short-termers, so were many Regiments of the Northern States.

To get a better picture, let us take a glance at the Regimental Troop Lists of Illinois. Pretty much the same ratio of short- and long-service Regiments will apply to other Union States. The 1st to 6th Illinois, inclusively, were Mexican War State Regiments, hence no such numbers appear in 1861-65 Illinois lists. The 8th, 9th, 10th, 11th and 12th Infantry were "three-months" Regiments under Lincoln's First Call of April, 1861, for 75,000 officers and men. All five Regiments were technically out of service by August 2, 1861. But they were reenlisted almost to a man in the same Companies and under the same officers to continue at the same station (Cairo, Illinois) on Federal active duty as "three-year" Regiments, pursuant to the Second Call. All of these five initial Illinois Regiments finished their war service without change of designation. They did it by recruiting their own replacements and the reenlisting of veterans of the other Illinois Regiments that were discontinued in the Autumn of 1864, when the three-year terms began to expire. Statistically, Phisterer rates such Regiments as "for-three-years-and-over" units.

In Illinois, as a typical Mid-Western State, the five Regiments that served three months and then reenlisted for three years and actually served beyond the war's end were but a fraction of the three-year-Regiments the Illinois Adjutant General sent into Federal service. At the same time he always kept some organized units not in Federal service on home drill status, more-or-less as seed for future Calls and for local security against the Copperheads who were so numerous in Little Egypt. These Home Guard units, as we would call them today, are ignored in the following figures. However, in the summary of the Regiments for Illinois, these first five Regiments, 8th to 12th Illinois Volunteers inclusive, are counted twice in Captain Phisterer's summary below. They were both three-months and "three-years-and-over" Regiments. There appear to be few, if any, other similar duplications in comparing Phisterer's digest with the Illinois A.G.O. list. After 1861, most of the short Calls on all the States were for the Summer of 1864, and for but one year in anticipation of the war's end. By Arms and terms of service, Captain Phisterer credits the Illinois Organized Militia, or National Guard, unit contributions as follows:

"Cavalry—for three years' service and over, 12 regiments; for three years' service, 5 regiments; total 17 regiments.

"Light Artillery—for three years' service and over, 2 regiments and 1 battery; for three years' service, 6 batteries; for three months' service, 1 battery; total, 2 regiments and 8 batteries.

"Infantry—for three years' service and over, 53 regiments; for three years' service, 67 regiments and 1 company; for three years' service, 1 regiment colored troops; for one year's service, 12 regiments; for one hundred days' service, 13 regiments and 2 companies; for three months' service, 11 regiments and 2 companies; for thirty days' service, 1 company; for fifteen days' service, 3 companies; total 157 regiments and 9 companies.

"Total—176 regiments, 9 companies, and 8 batteries."

The comparable totals for the other Union States are:

| | Regiments | Companies | Batteries |
|---|---|---|---|
| Maine | 33 | 25 | 7 |
| New Hampshire | 19 | 4 | 1 |
| Vermont | 19 | 1 | 3 |
| Massachusetts | 77 | 65 | 17 |
| Rhode Island | 14 | 3 | 1 |
| Connecticut | 30 | 0 | 3 |
| New York | 294 | 25 | 35 |
| New Jersey | 41 | 4 | 5 |
| Pennsylvania | 254 | 95 | 19 |
| Delaware | 9 | 13 | 1 |
| Maryland | 24 | 5 | 6 |
| Dist. of Columbia | 3 | 34 | 0 |
| West Virginia | 24 | 4 | 8 |
| Kentucky | 61 | 11 | 7 |
| Ohio | 234 | 29 | 27 |
| Michigan | 50 | 9 | 11 |
| Indiana | 137 | 17 | 26 |
| Illinois | 176 | 9 | 8 |
| Missouri | 94 | 46 | 6 |
| Wisconsin | 58 | 0 | 12 |
| Iowa | 55 | 0 | 4 |
| Minnesota | 14 | 10 | 3 |
| Kansas | 19 | 5 | 3 |
| California | 11 | 0 | 4 |
| Oregon | 2 | 0 | 0 |
| Nevada | 0 | 9 | 0 |
| U.S. Regulars | 30 | 0 | 0 |
| U.S. Volunteers U.S.C.T. included | 135 | 22 | 11 |

NOTE: The remaining Union Regiments with State or Territorial designations came from the Western Territories and from States which were members of the Confederacy. Tennessee, for example, from its Eastern, mountain Counties and from recruiting after the Confederate State Government was disestablished by armies of occupation, contributed 30 Regiments, seven Companies, and five Batteries to the Union forces. One of two Texas Regiments in the Union Army was recruited in

# THE CONFEDERATE ARMY

The Confederate States, as suggested earlier in this chapter, followed the same general patterns in the creation of units to meet the levies of the central government as did those of the Union. Under their States Rights philosophy and concept of State sovereignty they did exercise more freedoms in matters of Tables of Organization and even terms of enlistments. Pressures of conflict and demands of the Richmond Government tended to eliminate many earlier differences. But this was not without considerable resistance from local-minded Governors and others.

It is a long-established fact that in small units, initial officer selections, North and South, were by election, with the South more committed to the principle of election of Field officers than the North. Moreover, the South compounded its officer problem by C.S.A. statutes requiring blind promotion by seniority from among those haphazardly-elected in the beginning, until the Regiment, Battalion or Company went out of existence through casualties, enlistment expirations or other causes. Because of this, Confederate field commanders and the Richmond War Department often complained bitterly. Merit promotions from lower ranks were far more frequent in the Northern armies.

Eliminating from Confederate lists the units of "Militia Reserves," "Home Guards" and comparable home front units that may have participated briefly in joint operations for local defense alongside formations of the P.A.C.S., but which never were committed to extended active duty with the Stars and Bars, the contributions of each Southern State to the field armies of the Confederacy were as follows:

| | Regiments (All Arms) | Battalions (All Arms) | Batteries |
|---|---|---|---|
| Alabama | 63 | 11 | 16 |
| Arkansas | 41 | 14 | 15 |
| Florida | 12 | 3 | 6 |
| Georgia | 80 | 22 | 28 |
| Louisiana | 38 | 11 | 26 |
| Mississippi | 58 | 10 | 20 |
| North Carolina | 70 | 11 | 9 |
| South Carolina | 41 | 4 | 28 |
| Tennessee | 83 | 14 | 32 |
| Texas | 50 | 9 | 16 |
| Virginia | 90 | 21 | 53 |
| Border States | 30 | 9 | 11 |
| Origin Unidentified | 13 | 0 | 1 |

Mexico, late 1862. Likewise, there were many Regiments in the Confederate Army from such Border States as Maryland, Kentucky and Missouri. The ratios for the less-than-three-year units from other Northern States appear to be about the same as for Illinois in the more detailed break-down above. Enlistments in the U.S. Regulars were for three years only. The U.S.C.T. Regiments, excluding 31 credited to States, numbered 119 Colored Regiments of all Arms.

Converting separate Battalions and Batteries to Regimental equivalents, the Confederacy had 764 Regiments, practically all of them of State origin.

Southern war effort did not really begin rolling until three weeks after Bull Run, July 21, 1861. On August 8, an apprehensive Confederate Congress in a poorly-worded statute authorized a Call for 400,000 additional troops. Responding units and/or men could elect one, two, or three years. A subsequent paragraph and an additional statute a few weeks later practically nullified the ceiling of 400,000. The Southern lawmakers were obviously more impressed by the North's manpower build-up than by the easy victory at Bull Run. Response from the States was highly enthusiastic, but too many units elected the shorter terms.

Looking toward a grim 1862 and with the earlier unit service terms of six months expiring, the Confederate Secretary of War, Judah P. Benjamin, wrote the Confederate Governors, citing an amending act of January 23, 1862, calling for obligatory terms of "three years or during the war" (whichever should be the shorter). To activate this, Mr. Benjamin made the Call of February 2, 1862, for troops in Regiments totalling 6% of each State's "total white population." As applied to Alabama, he wrote, the new requirement "would be 15,351; but the State has furnished, in addition to the [prior] troops for the war, 9,970 men for 12 months and it is deemed safe to rely upon the re-enlistment of half that number . . . I have therefore the honor to request Your Excellency to furnish from the State of Alabama twelve [additional] regiments of troops for the war." According to the Secretary's figures, this also called for 11 additional three-year Regiments from Arkansas, 2½ from Florida, 12 from Georgia, 5½ from Louisiana, seven from Mississippi, 26 from North Carolina, five from South Carolina, 32 from Tennessee, 15 from Texas, and 47 from Virginia. A State that already had an extremely large number of early-response six-months Regiments on active duty, as did Virginia with 64,342 officers and men then actually with the Colors, naturally had more of a conversion problem than did some of the States farther removed from the actual theater of fighting. This law, and the Call it authorized, gave the Confederacy, with the three-year Regiments then active in the service, a large, hard core of veteran State Regiments quite comparable to the North's three-year units.

As the fortunes of the Confederacy worsened in the West, particularly at Shiloh, April 6, the Confederate Congress took recourse to the Draft Law, April 16, 1862, which has been described in the preceding chapter. It not only froze existing personnel in their units but it created a pressure factor toward volunteering.

The grand, aggregate, four-years strength of the Provisional Army of the Confederate States is unknown. If there is anyone who likes the present day Pentagon Numbers Game, he could have fun and render history a service by solving this mystery. Until then, 1,100,000 is as good a guess as any for a comparative figure alongside the Union's grand aggregate of 2,324,516 officers and men.

Confederate Provisional Army aggregates for certain dates can be and have been approximated. On or about June 30, 1863, on the eve of Gettysburg and the fall of Vicksburg, the aggregate of Confederate officers and men "present for duty" was 307,364. This figure is from a total strength, "present and absent," of 473,058. The several field head-quarters submitting these figures admitted known omissions of returns from "Ransom's Division and other troops in the Valley" as well as five of Magruder's Texas Cavalry Regiments. An entire Louisiana command under General Taylor, reported by Northern Intelligence sources that Summer to have been four or five thousand effectives, also was omitted from this tabulation. Allowing 25,000 aggregate and 15,000 present for duty as the strength of all omitted units, which is a pretty good guess, the Confederate Provisional Army, June 30, 1863, was carrying 498,058 men on its active duty rolls. Of these, 322,364 were "present for duty."

For those desiring an approximation of the number of Confederate Regimental-size units on duty *as of a given date*, the following are suggested for late 1864: Artillery, 240 Batteries (equivalent of 20 Regiments); Cavalry, 104 Regiments; Infantry, 547 Regiments; Signal, 10 Companies. It was on these figures that the Confederate Quartermaster General, on October 10, 1864, prepared his budget estimates for the first six months of 1865. He obviously expected to pay the equivalent of 672 Confederate Provisional Army Regiments then on active duty, for that coming period. Of course, he padded his estimates just to be safe, but internal evidence suggests the safety factors in his estimates were in unit strengths rather than in numbers of units. He did, in a spirit of pessimism, or optimism, (one wonders which) put in an estimate for 35 "reserve regiments." Presumably he considered these to be maximum potentials from the States that could be called to the Stars and Bars for extended active duty, no matter what happened. In any event, the Quartermaster General's estimates that year, whether padded or not, rested upon far more experience and evidence than we now can summon from fragmentary records.

Most elusive of all are the 13 Confederate Regiments of no identified State origin. One rarely appears on an Order of Battle list. Except for small units operating independently and often behind Union lines, but with commissions directly-issued by Confederate statutes, no Southern units are found comparable to the U.S. Volunteers, U.S. Veteran Volunteers, or the U.S.C.T. The South had a so-called Invalid Corps, but it was not fully comparable to the Regiments and separate Companies of service troops noted in the Union Army. The Confederates did make efforts similar to those of the North to recruit among the Union prisoners-of-war. The Confederates, however, appear to have been more selective. In February, 1865, we find Lieutenant General William J. Hardee, PA.C.S., granting authority to the C.O. of the 1st Foreign Battalion, C.S.A., to recruit from among prisoners-of-war enough men to raise his Companies to 125 men each. But ". . . he will take only men of Irish and French nationality."

Except for such rare units, all Regiments, Battalions and Batteries of the Provisional Army, Confederate States of America, were State-organized and identified as Companies, Batteries and Regiments of and from their several States; i.e., they were National Guardsmen. From April, 1861, to April, 1865, the battle line formations of the North and the South were composed almost entirely of Companies, Batteries, Battalions and Regiments of the States.

Thus, if one looks at the Civil War picture from the viewpoint of an Order of Battle list and Regimental State designations, America's great conflict was not a civil war after all. It was not the "War of the Rebellion." Nor could it have been the "Second American Revolution." The "Irrepressible Conflict" it could have been, but the Order of Battle unit designations definitely proclaim it to have been "The War Between the States."

# Bibliographical Note For Chapter III

*The War of the Rebellion, Official Records* . . . characterized in the bibliographical note for Chapter II is of equal importance as a source for this chapter, particularly Series III and IV. The same is true of most of the other titles in that bibliographical note. Frederick H. Dyer's *A Compendium of the War of the Rebellion* (Yoseloff edition, Bell I. Wiley, ed., 1959) is indispensable for the Union armies. It is to be regretted that there is nothing comparable to it for the South. Nevertheless, see Claude Estes, *List of Field Officers Regiments and Battalions in the Confederate States Army,* 1912. Capt. Frederick Phisterer's *Statistical Record of the Armies of the United States,* 1886, is as good as any, and far better than most works written by those who have been intrigued by the various components of the Northern Army and the proportional contributions of the several States to the preservation of the Union. It has not been equalled by any comparable effort for the South. Basic Union sources, however, are the War Department's contemporary annual *Official Army Registers* and *Directory* (units and officers) *of Volunteers.* Ben La Bree's *The Confederate Soldier in the Civil War,* 1895, and reissued by John S. Blay, 1959, is most convenient for Confederate Order of Battle data. The role of the U.S. Colored Troops has attracted more than passing interest in recent years. T. W. Higginson, *Army Life in a Black Regiment,* 1890, will be of interest to some readers, but has contributed little or nothing to this chapter. Dudley T. Cornish's *The Sable Arm; Negro Troops in the Union Army, 1861-1865,* 1956, gives the big picture. Thomas L. Livermore, *Numbers and Losses in the Civil War,* is a superb supplement to Phisterer's more usable figures for the purposes of this chapter.

CHAPTER IV

# The Guard Survives A
# Difficult Era

AFTER APPOMATTOX Americans were a war-weary people. The surrendering Southern citizen-soldiers went home singly, or in small, informal travel groups, to face a World they never had believed possible. Many Union Regiments participated in the Big Parade in Washington, D.C., thence homeward. Many other Regiments and smaller units quietly returned to their respective States and were mustered-out. There may or may not have been a Regimental or Brigade parade in the State Capital. In the home town of each Battery- or Company-size unit, there was usually some sort of ovation. On the other hand, there is ample evidence that many soldiers in both the North and South arrived home individually, complete with uniform, side accoutrements and rifle. The gun usually was put on a rack over the door, or set in the corner for its souvenir value, if not for future hunting seasons. If the old

99

home town was to have another volunteer, marching and drilling unit of the Organized Militia, or National Guard, as the statutes of the States of New York and New Jersey had proclaimed their units to be, it would be up to the younger generation. With this quiet resolve, the typical citizen-soldier of the North went back into civil life to find an economic order that had changed materially during the three or four years of his absence, but one in which he still knew his way.

The few professional soldiers and Naval officers who had gone South to enter the Regulars of the Confederacy found themselves not only without a profession but further tainted with the label of treason. A few sought and received appointments in the armies and navies of Peru, Mexico or some other Latin-American nation being harassed by overt efforts of Spain to reestablish colonial holdings on the South American continent. The Khedive of Egypt experienced no trouble in recruiting both Northern and Southern officers for the training and leadership of his frontier forces on the upper reaches of the Nile. Those professionals in Blue who declined alluring offers from the North's burgeoning industry to stay with the Service found themselves laying aside the stars of Brigade and Division Commanders to pin on the bars of their permanent Regular Army commissions.*

## DEMOBILIZATION AND REORGANIZATION

On May 1, 1865, three weeks after Appomattox, the strength of the Union Army, officers and men, stood at 1,000,516. Of these, only 22,310 officers and men were Regulars. By January 1, 1866, 800,963 citizen-soldiers had been mustered-out.

It was already fully apparent that Napoleon le Petit, Emperor of the Second French Empire, was withdrawing his challenge to the Monroe Doctrine. Without his support, Emperor Maximilian of Mexico was on the way out. But no one then suspected that, for him, the tinsel regime would end only 17 months later, before a firing squad on the Hill of the Little Bells overlooking Querétaro. There was a strong feeling, however, that 199,553 officers and men on active duty were too many.

The American demobilization continued. By January, 1867, the great Army of Volunteers in State Regiments had vanished. The temporary forces, still being held over from the conflict, numbered only

---

* George A. Custer, for example, commanded a Division at Appomattox. Because of his brilliant record he was one of the last to be mustered out of wartime forces, February, 1866. He thus reverted to his permanent rank of Captain, 5th Cavalry. He was considered quite fortunate to get the permanent rank and assignment of Lieutenant Colonel, 7th Cavalry, in the postwar reorganization of the Regular Army, in July of the same year. That was his rank when he died 10 years later on the banks of the Little Big Horn in the "Last Stand" that bears his name. All his 7th Cavalry Captains bore the courtesy title of Colonel by virtue of their brevet Civil War ranks.

11,043 men. Ten thousand were Negroes in Federally-organized Colored Regiments that had not yet been broken-up. The Regular Army was being reorganized through 1866 into 10 Regiments of Cavalry, five of Artillery and 45 of Infantry, or approximately 60,000 officers and men. But all the enlisted men for these formations never were forthcoming. In August, 1867, the strength of the Regular Army establishment had been built up to 56,815 officers and men. It was the Regular Army's peak strength between Spring of 1865 and June, 1897, by which time its strength had shrunk to 27,532 officers and men.

The trend was inevitable. The Union had been saved at home. The nations of the Old World had been overawed by the amazing strength the New World Republic had demonstrated. Even haughty England was showing a degree of diplomatic courtesy and consideration. She was eager to negotiate damages arising from operations of Confederate warships built in England. What need had America for land forces of 55,000 officers and men, unless it was to win the peace as well as the war?

There were those in the Nation's Congress, and they represented a home front minority but nevertheless one of intense convictions, who saw a need for Union garrisons in the South. They were quite happy that the war had ended, but they sorely feared the North would lose the fruits of victory if the erstwhile rebellious States were treated as other than conquered provinces. And conquered provinces, as a corollary, required loyal, blue-coated garrisons therein. Hence, 60 Regiments of Cavalry, Artillery and foot troops were few enough—perhaps too few, if the Indian frontier was to be patrolled and the Southern States properly garrisoned in order that all war aims be achieved and future treasons stifled in the cradle. In this, the vindictive Congressmen were so much at variance from the principles upon which President Lincoln had waged the war to preserve the Union that these followers of Henry Winter Davis of Maryland, Benjamin F. Wade of Ohio, Charles Sumner of Massachusetts and Thaddeus Stevens of Pennsylvania, quickly became known as the Radical Republicans, or merely "The Radicals."

Many Northerners in public and private life had justified their war for the Union on the theory that the Constitution, and the United States it had created, alike were indestructible. If the Union could not be destroyed, then the Southern States never had been out of the Union. Now that they had put away their guns and admitted their error, it was up to them, within their State Governments, to work-out their own salvation; but, of course, without Slavery. This was disposed of by the Thirteenth Amendment being ratified through 1865. Everyone recognized this as a soft peace and at the other end of the scale from the Conquered Province philosophy.

President Lincoln knew there were stormy politics ahead when he felt the necessity for giving the Wade-Davis Bill, passed July 2, 1864, a pocket veto. The Radicals had written this law with an eye on States already predominantly within Union lines, such as Tennessee and Louisiana. Lincoln never openly commited himself completely to either school of thought. He held that whether the Southern States were in or out of the Union was "a pernicious abstraction." Everyone agreed, Lincoln argued, that the erstwhile Confederate States "were out of their proper, practical relation with the Union" and that it was the duty of the Federal Government, and specifically of the President, to restore that proper, practical relationship.

Lincoln had launched his program as early as December, 1863, by which time ultimate victory was apparent. His formula offered pardon, with certain exceptions, to any Confederates who would swear to support the Constitution and the Union. When citizens of a conquered State, i.e., within Union lines, equal to one-tenth of the State's total vote in the Presidential election of 1860, had qualified under the prescribed oath, and further organized a State Government which abolished Slavery, Lincoln would consider that State in proper relation to the Union and extend to it Executive recognition. Before his death Lincoln had recognized the "Ten Percent Governments" of Louisiana, Tennessee, Arkansas and Virginia. This was the plan the vetoed Wade-Davis Bill of July 2, 1865, was calculated to scuttle in favor of the Conquered Province philosophy.

There was a brief period after Lincoln's assassination, April 14, 1865, during which the Radicals thought the newly-elevated President, Andrew Johnson, was their man. They thought he could be counted upon to adopt their Conquered Province philosophy, lock, stock and barrel. But under the sobering pressures of responsibility, President Johnson embraced the Lincolnian philosophy and Reconstruction formula in every major detail. Though Lincoln's assassination and certain indiscretions by the newly-recognized "Ten Percent" State Governments tremendously strengthened the claims and hands of the Radicals, President Johnson continued the Lincolnian plan.

By January 1, 1866, President Johnson had recognized the provisional, or "Ten Percent Governments," of all former Confederate States except Texas. Under their provisional Governors, these States had held conventions that had voided or repealed their earlier Ordinances of Secession and abolished Slavery within their respective limits. All but South Carolina had repudiated Confederate debts, and all but Mississippi had ratified the Thirteenth Amendment abolishing Slavery throughout the United States. President Johnson's insistence on the repudiation of the treasonable debts and the denial of pardons to all Southerners who were worth $20,000 or more obviously was calculated to put the Southern States under the leadership and control of small landholders,

102

mechanics, tenant farmers, young professional men, and small-town merchants. Most of these, it was presumed, would be unsympathetic toward the deposed plantation economy and aristocracy, with their record of error and disaster, and would have a correspondingly kindly feeling toward the free economy and Republican ideals of the North.

Given a reasonable time factor, it might have worked-out that way. But the Radicals were impatient. If allowed their Conquered Province philosophy, with blue-coated garrisons in every Southern Capital and City, the defeated Southern Whites could be disfranchised indefinitely. With the pliant Freedman simultaneously enfranchised, all future danger of an alliance between Southern and Northern Democrats, to the detriment of the Party that had saved the Union, could be precluded.

Meanwhile, President Johnson's provisional Southern Governors and their subordinates were finding themselves confronted with unprecedented social problems. These came from the sudden liberation of slaves and the lawlessness that naturally had developed following the quick and complete collapse of normal governmental agencies in lands that had been completely ravaged by the flow and counterflow of embattled armies. The restoration of civil authority within the Johnson-recognized Southern States was too much for a few Sheriffs and local police. The citizenry, particularly the returned Confederate soldiers, had been disarmed. President Johnson's provisional Governors sought and received permission to organize and arm Volunteer Militia Companies in sufficient number to apprehend criminals, suppress crime, protect the inhabitants, and bring law and order to the distressed States. This permission was granted.

At the same time, some of the newly-created Southern Legislatures were solving the social problem caused by the suddenly-liberated bondmen with "Black Codes." These new laws broadened the base of vagrancy and increased the range of apprenticeships so that everyone had to go to work. At the same time they kept the Freedmen from voting. And, of course, any massed resistance to these "Black Codes" would result in a riot. That logically meant the calling-out of one or more Companies of the newly-created and armed Organized Militia. Thus the National Guard, in the South, became a part of the melancholy story of Reconstruction. The prestige of the Organized Militia as a defense institution throughout United States suffered accordingly.

This too-early return of the Militia powers to the former Confederate States was perhaps the biggest mistake President Johnson made in his reconstruction program. General Grant, who was not a vindictive man, advised against it. Carl Schurz, who was an idealist but at all times utterly practical, toured the South in 1865. He advised against it. Union Army commanders in the South—and as we have seen, there were still

200,000 Federals in uniform at the end of 1865—did not believe such Organized Militia necessary. They unanimously argued against it.

## USES AND ABUSES OF ORGANIZED MILITIA

The conduct and attitudes of the Southern units of Organized Militia at once made all this adverse, critical advice look extremely good. Members of the Southern Organized Militia units immediately brought out their Confederate gray uniforms and spent most of their drill periods in more-or-less terroristic activities calculated to keep the suddenly-effulgent Freedmen in a quiescent frame of mind. Disarming the Colored population, many of whom were themselves returned soldiers from Union Colored Regiments, was a continuing operation. Dr. Otis A. Singletary, in his superb study of the uses and abuses of the Organized Militia as an institution by both the Johnsonian-inspired State Governments and the regimes of "Scalawags" and "Carpetbaggers" that followed them, considers the disarming of the Freedmen the apparent primary function of these units under the South's provisional State Governments. He believes it was done with genuine relish, and quotes an excerpt from a contemporary letter written late in 1865: "The militia of this county have seized every gun and pistol found in the hands of 'so-called' freedmen of this section of the county. They claim that the Statute Laws of Mississippi do not recognize the Negro as having any right to carry arms." Some National Guard units composed of these recently-returned and certainly unreconstructed ex-Confederates became so arrogant in their pursuit of White supremacy that their own normally sympathetic Governors disbanded some units and restrained the others.

Of course, all these activities made tall headlines. The South in 1865 was a veritable Mecca for starry-eyed reformers, roving journalists, erstwhile war correspondents, and Washington officialdom with a yen for travel and first-hand impressions. All the resulting publicity naturally brought screams of anger from the Abolitionist wing of the Republican Party. To them the war never had been to save the Union; it was to free the slaves. Thus they argued at length and loudly that they had won a war and lost a peace, which seems to be a chronic American lament. Nevertheless, it greatly strengthened the hands of the Radicals. The days through which President Johnson could retain a tenuous control over the explosive situation were numbered.

President Johnson has been severely criticized, North and South, but the record shows that he urged and even begged the Southern Whites controlling the provisional State Governments to act with prudence and to extend the ballot to the more intelligent of the former slaves, and particularly to the returned Negro soldiers from the Northern Regiments. But the Southern Whites, with indisputable citations, reminded President Johnson that many Northern States denied the vote to all Negroes. They offered further convincing evidence that the former slaves were not yet capable of assuming the responsibilities of unabridged participation in local and State government. Subsequent events proved them to be correct in this contention. In any event, instead of offering token voting rights to the Freedmen and otherwise softening the "Black Codes" governing apprenticeship, vagrancy, forced labor, voting and landholding, the Southern Whites made them increasingly severe in Louisiana, Arkansas and Mississippi. Thereupon, the Radicals moved-in with their Congressional policy of Reconstruction in implementation of the Conquered Provinces philosophy.

The Civil Rights Bill of April 9, 1866, one year to a day after Appomattox, was designed to protect the Negro from the "Black Codes." Its running-mate, the Freedmen's Bureau Bill of July 16, extended the life of that institution as the Washington-controlled social agency calculated to protect the Negro, give him economic status and to train him for the responsibilities of citizenship. The President vetoed both Bills on thoroughly sound Constitutional grounds. They were passed over his veto. The same Summer of 1866, the Radical-dominated Joint Committee on Reconstruction reported that the States that once had constituted the so-called Confederacy were not entitled to representation in the Houses of Congress. Reconstruction of the Union was not a function of the President. The elected Congressmen from the provisional governments of the Southern States, most of whom were former General Officers in gray, were not to be seated.

Northern elections in 1866 sustained the Radicals. At long last they were firmly seated in the saddle and without effective opposition. They easily could remain there so long as the Southern States were either out of the Union or administered by pliant Governors and represented by Senators and Representatives chosen by the not-always-unselfish officials of the Freedmen's Bureau and its Union League Clubs for training the Negroes in citizenship and self-government.

Early in the next Congress, the Reconstruction Act of March 2, 1867, translated the Conquered Province philosophy of the Radicals from a theory to a reality. This law, with some subsequent supplementary and related legislation, nullified the "Black Codes" within the Southern States and divided all the former Confederacy, except Tennessee, into five Military Districts. In each of these the authority of the Army commander was supreme. Under him the provisional governments previously recognized by President Johnson were to be disestablished. Former Confederates, civil and military, were to be disfranchised and the Negroes enfranchised. The enforcement of civil rights and the recreation of State, civil governments on this base were the mandates to and the responsibility of each Army commander.

Garrisoning the South on such terms and for such burdensome duties called for a larger Army, hence the figure noted earlier for 1867, which totalled 56,815 officers and men for the peak of the Reconstruction Era. Even so, the strength was less than that provided for in the Fiscal Year Budget for 1867-68. The Army Appropriations Bill, which was passed on March 2, 1867, the same day the Civil Rights Act was passed over President Johnson's veto, contained an obscure rider. It ordered the disbanding of all State Militia forces in the Southern States and prohibited the "further organization, arming, or calling into service of the said militia forces, or any part thereof" until Congress might authorize a restoration of Militia rights to the States in question.

It was a gross infringement upon the authority of the President and thoroughly unconstitutional, but President Johnson felt a compulsion to sign it in order to supply appropriations for the Army. Nevertheless, he at once sent to Congress a communication containing a review of the Militia powers of the States, as provided in the Second Article of the Bill of Rights: "A well-regulated militia being necessary to the security of a free state, the right of the people to keep and bear arms shall not be infringed." But the impetuous Congressional Radicals, with the bit in their teeth, were headed toward an impeachment of the President. They ignored the communication. But with a fearful eye on the Federal courts, legislation to restrain and intimidate the courts into quiescence became an additional order of business.

The rider on the Army Appropriations Bill of 1867 did not take the Organized Militia units out of Congressional and Reconstruction politics. The Military District Commanders disbanded the South's gray-clad Organized Militia units in quick time. They set about creating civil governments under officials presumably of their choosing. In too many instances it was the Freedmen's Bureau officials and the "Union Clubs," under the leadership of the Northern Carpetbaggers and regional, Southern Scalawags who named the appointees for the Army commanders. They also wangled posts for themselves and further controlled the untutored, Colored voters.

Unhindered by any opposition whatsoever and with the visible support of Regular Army bayonets, the Carpetbag regimes quickly went to such rapacious excesses, in greed and public plunder of their conquered provinces, that the possible creation of a White underground of resistance became a mounting fear.

## ORGANIZED MILITIA BECOMES THE FULCRUM OF POWER

The control and containment of such a potential underground throughout 11 States, with a million embittered, militarily-experienced citizens, obviously required an Army of Occupation. Only 60,000 officers and men, contemplated in the Army Budget for 1867, were not enough to implement the Conquered Provinces theory and at the same time control the Indian frontier. But conservatives of both parties in Congress were taking a dim view of the heavy expense. The impending collapse of Emperor Maximilian's Mexican regime removed all arguments predicated upon European encroachments.

Meanwhile, Alabama, Arkansas, Florida, Louisiana, and North and South Carolina had been readmitted to the Union under the program prescribed by the Radical Congressmen. These States had accepted the temporary Governors designated by the Military Commanders, reorganized their governments, repealed their "Black Codes," ratified the Fourteenth Amendment, and, through easily-manipulated, recently-enfranchised Colored votes, had filled the Governors' Mansions and most of the better offices with opportunistic Whites.* There was, however, a substantial sop to the Freedmen in legislative and lesser salaried positions. All this being acceptable to the Congressional Radicals, these six erstwhile Confederate States were readmitted to the Union in 1868—just in time to cast their Electoral College votes for General U. S. Grant, candidate for President.

As it turned-out, Grant most likely would have been elected anyway, but conservative and Democratic gains in Northern State elections in 1866 had frightened the Radicals. They had lost New York and Pennsylvania. In Ohio the wide margin of the War Years had vanished. At the same time Negro suffrage amendments to the Ohio, Kansas, Michigan and Minnesota Constitutions were rejected by popular vote landslides.** Moreover, in the Grant election, the electoral margin for him was wide but the popular vote was far from comforting. Hence Radical desire to retain political control of the South as long as possible was intensified rather than assuaged.

But the newly-elected Governors of these reconstructed and readmitted States felt insecure. Their Sheriffs and municipal police forces were having even less success at law enforcement than had the heads of Johnson's "Ten-Percent Governments" who had been authorized to exercise the Constitutional Militia powers of a State, which they had lost, March 2, 1867, through injudicious abuse. It was natural that the Carpetbag and Scalawag Governors immediately appealed to their Radical proponents in Congress to restore to their States the Constitu-

---

* The White officeholders in the Reconstruction State Governments are known to history as Scalawags and Carpetbaggers. The former were the Southern Whites who cooperated. The latter were, of course, the Northern men who viewed the South as a land of opportunity. Actually there were many Northerners in the postwar South who neither benefited by nor approved what was happening. Moreover, not all the White officeholders in the Reconstructed governments were men of venal intent. A few were honest, starry-eyed idealists of the type that Lincoln Steffens finally decided were more expensively inefficient than were the more competent, crooked politicians who were satisfied with "honest graft."

** In 1867 Northern Negroes could vote only in New York and all of New England except Connecticut. Some of these had literacy requirements.

tional Militia privilege. They held that effective National Guard units were essential to their staying in office and holding the States for their party. Senate Bill 648 proposed repeal of the law prohibiting Organized Militia units in the Carpetbagger-controlled Southern States.

Accordingly, the National Guard, or Organized Militia, in the Southern States, became the subject of acrid Congressional debates. Indiana's Senator Thomas A. Hendricks, who was to become Vice-President under Grover Cleveland, led the attack upon Radical intentions. He hurled the accusation that the only purpose of potential military force in the hands of the Reconstruction Governors was because "you have attempted to reverse the American doctrine and to declare that by force the powers of the States shall be placed in the hands of the minority."

Radical proponents immediately came to the measure's defense. They predicated their arguments upon the necessity for law and order as well as underwriting the fruits of victory. Ben F. Rice, senior Senator from Arkansas, was a Carpetbagger who had resigned from a Captaincy in the 3rd Minnesota, in 1864, to practice law in Little Rock. His Regiment had garrisoned that City since its capture in September of that year. With a pardonable enthusiasm for staying in the Senate, he not only reiterated all the law-and-order arguments but he had an economy plea. He insisted that if Arkansas were permitted to exercise fully its Constitutional Militia rights, every one of the expensive but thinly-deployed Regular Army units in Arkansas could be withdrawn. Other Carpetbag Congressmen agreed for their States. The Bill became a law and went into effect March 2, 1869, exactly two years from the day Militia rights had been taken from the States and provisional Governors whom President Johnson had recognized but whom the Radicals in Congress had rejected.

The day following the passage of the Bill, Congress drastically reduced the Regular Army Budget and authorized strength. The August strength returns for that year reveal the Regular Army had been reduced to 36,774 officers and men. The Congress had taken Senator Rice at his word. The Reconstruction Governors were pretty much on their own thereafter. But the Organized Militia had become an instrument of power politics through a period during which men both White and Black were sordidly and shamelessly exploited. The eminent historian, Claude G. Bowers, has fittingly categorized it with the title of his well-known volume, *The Tragic Era*.

## CHAOS IN DIXIE

Virginia, Texas and Mississippi had not completed their "Reconstruction" in time to benefit by the reversal of the Militia policy, hence were not included in the final form of the measure. Georgia's Reconstruction Governor, Rufus B. Bullock, was in the Radical doghouse. Because his brief political career exemplifies the mechanics of reconstruction within a State, it is worthy of a brief summary.

From New York, Bullock had gone to Augusta, Georgia, in 1859. His immediate success as an express company organizer and telegraph and railroad executive had been interrupted by the Civil War. His talents as well as his small transportation empire immediately became available to the Confederacy. He was paroled at Appomattox as a Confederate Lieutenant Colonel and Assistant Quartermaster. He entered politics in 1868 as a member of the State's convention for rewriting its Constitution to suit the Radicals. He quickly became leader of the Carpetbaggers and Negro Delegates. The convention blended into a nominating convention. Bullock was nominated for Governor. Following a bitter canvass in the Spring of 1868, the new Constitution was ratified. Bullock was declared elected. The ex-Confederates still controlled all the County offices. Bullock encountered far more difficulties than were found in other States. In the Legislature that was elected with him, there was the normal mixture of Negroes and Whites. But reactionists gained control of both chambers and forthwith they unseated the Colored members. Congress ultimately empowered Bullock to reassemble the legislators and to seat the expelled Colored members, but meanwhile the Congressional Radicals were taking a jaundiced view of their Carpetbagger, ex-Confederate officer who apparently did not have a firm hand on the situation.

Their worst fears came true when the duly-reconstructed State of Georgia cast its Electoral College votes against General Grant for President. Bullock's crime was inability "to carry his Ward" for the Radicals. Though Bullock and his Georgia were in the bad graces of Washington, it was deemed necessary to give him and his State their Militia powers in July, 1870. At the same time, Texas, Virginia and Mississippi received the same restoration of Militia rights. They had completed their internal reconstruction by the same procedures summarized above for Georgia.

Though all the erstwhile Confederate States now had full Militia rights for the admitted purpose of providing bayonets to keep minority-elected Governors, legislators and minor officers in power, not all the Governors chose to organize volunteer units for that purpose. Those States were among the more fortunate.

Georgia was one of them. Governor Bullock received the power too late to do him any good. In October of the same year he resigned and fled from the State to avoid criminal indictment. He enriched himself and his followers through pocketing proceeds from bond sales. His general pillage of the public purse by other means was hardly exceeded by New York City's Boss Tweed. This is largely conceded by writers on the subject, other than Bullock himself. His successors declined to use the right to organize and arm Negro Militiamen to perpetuate themselves in office.

Virginia came through the ordeal better than most. Her politicians sent a committee of nine men to Washington to work-out compromises with the Radical leaders of Congress. They achieved a more tolerant Constitution insofar as ex-Confederates were concerned. The first Reconstruction Governor, Gilbert C. Walker, was elected by a fusion of Conservative Republicans and Democrats. He had arrived in Norfolk from Chicago, late 1865. He generally is considered to have enriched himself and compensated pliant legislators, both White and Black, from the State's Treasury. Nevertheless, neither he nor his successors organized Negro Militia Companies. At the same time they did establish and maintain law and order. Modern Virginians write kindly of their bank-promoting Carpetbagger from Chicago. They accept the verdict of a contemporary Walker supporter: He is "not a Yanky; he don't look like one."

Alabama was likewise a fortunate State. Her first Reconstruction Governor, William H. Smith, was a Scalawag who first came into prominence through General George G. Meade's appointing him temporary Governor for calling into existence a convention to rewrite the Alabama Constitution. Smith knew his people. He reasoned the quickest way to create an effective, ex-Confederate underground, with capabilities for real violence, would be an arming of the Negro voters. He enacted elaborate laws for the creation of an Organized Militia. There was some tentative enrolling. At times he threatened their use, but Governor Smith never issued the arms. His successor ordered the State Adjutant General not to enlist Negroes. As in the Smith Administration, too few Whites could, or would, qualify to serve. A belated effort to create an Alabama Negro National Guard in 1874 was abortive. Otherwise, Reconstruction in Alabama followed the normal pattern of public treasury pillage, but without serious violence.

In Florida, Governor Harrison Reed likewise failed to attract enough loyally qualified Whites to create an Organized Militia. He did at once create and arm Negro units, but from fear of starting a race war he consistently refused to use them in efforts for law and order or to intimidate voters at the polls.

While the threat and possibility of a use of National Guard powers was ever-present in the above States, it was within the remaining seven Southern States that it became a hedge-of-bayonets reality. Historians, North and South, who have touched upon the subject, including those who have sought to gloss-over the melancholy events, commonly refer to the military units created by the Reconstruction Governors of the remaining Southern States as the "Negro Militia." Actually, a few units, particularly in Eastern Tennessee and Northern Arkansas, were

110

entirely White. In the latter State one or two such units, reinforced by desperadoes and former guerrillas out of the Missouri Ozarks, were said to have been a greater menace to property, liberty and lives than any comparable all-Negro unit in that State. There were occasional units that were composed of both Negroes and Whites. In the judgment of Dixie, that made them all Black.

Many Companies were completely Black, including the officers. The demobilization of more than 100 Negro Regiments from the Union Army, with the retention of but four Colored Regiments in the Regular Army, had filled every Southern State with five to 15 thousand Colored men with considerable military training. It was inevitable that some of the Carpetbag Governors, who normally left the State at the end of their terms, were bold enough to exploit this available Colored military manpower for prolonging their participation in the spoliation of the State's finances. Native Whites, the Scalawags, were, for the most part, more cautious.*

## ARMED STRIFE ERUPTS IN THE SOUTH

In Arkansas, whence Senator Rice had promised bayonet-supported stability without cost to the War Department, occurred the first example of an abuse of a State's Militia powers. Governor Powell Clayton, who fell in love with Arkansas and a Southern belle while he was a Colonel commanding the 5th Kansas Cavalry, immediately implemented Senator Rice's planned control with Negro Militia. Units promptly were organized and armed. Soon, and for a four-months period, he had the State under martial law. The Militia costs of the operation reached $330,675, a large sum in those days. He had nothing to show for it but more lawlessness and a more deeply-embedded ex-Confederate underground. Governor Clayton did carry the State for Grant; otherwise, Arkansas might have slipped into the Seymour column, as did Georgia.

But the real crisis in Arkansas came when the State's Radicals decided to quarrel among themselves. Governor Clayton eagerly sought elevation to the U.S. Senate, through selection by his pliant Houses of the Arkansas Legislature. At the same time he wanted to make

---

* There were 20 Reconstruction Governors. Eight were Scalawags; two or three were usually honest in money matters, of little ability, narrow-minded and vindictive. Brownlow of Tennessee was among the better Scalawags. The 12 Carpetbaggers were men of greater ability. They were also ruthless promoters and without exception thoroughly money-hungry. Adelbert Ames (Miss.) may have been an idealist, but few conceded him that distinction after 1870, when he became the son-in-law of Maj. Gen. and Senator Benjamin F. Butler of Massachusetts. No Negro became a Governor. A number became Lieutenant Governor, Superintendent of Education, State Auditor, Secretary of State, and Justices in the State Supreme Courts. Fifteen served in the U.S. Congress. Senator Hiram R. Revels (Miss.), who occupied Jefferson Davis's old seat, was as idealistically dedicated to the welfare of his people and State as Mr. Davis had been to the philosophy of John C. Calhoun. Few other Negro officerholders were so exemplary. Most were apt students of their corrupt preceptors.

sure his successor would be subservient to his own future decisions. This situation blended into the Brooks-Baxter war, in which both sides mobilized Battalions of Negro units, but with White natives in some units and in upper command positions. Baxter was Senator Clayton's choice initially. The Conservatives put up no candidate of their own, preferring to back Brooks largely on the theory that since Clayton distrusted him, he could not be as bad as Baxter.

The campaign was tempestuous and, as usual, featured by uniformed and armed Militia units at the polls. Baxter won the bayonet-controlled canvass but lost a subsequent Federal court decision awarding the Governor's office to Brooks. Armed by a court injunction and supported by armed Militia followers, Brooks marched on the State House, occupied the same and relegated Governor Baxter to a temporary military headquarters in a nearby hotel. The growing, opposing forces soon became identified as the "Minstrels" (Baxterites) because their music was sweet to Senator Clayton, and the "Brindle-tails" (Brooks supporters) in memory of a mythical Arkansas brindle-tail bull whose bellow was so loud he frightened the cows to death. For days both factions kept their armed forces in hand. Captain T. E. Rose, U.S. Army, with a Company of the 19th Infantry in Little Rock, tenuously held the balance of power while both sides bombarded Washington with telegrams. They urged President Grant to make up his mind which crowd he wanted to run the State. Both factions shrank from firing the first shot.

But on the sixth day, April 21, 1874, Governor Baxter permitted his field commander, one King White, to parade all his 2,000 officers and men. They wound-up at the Governor's hotel clamoring for a speech. From the balcony he soothed them. When he finished, Colonel White became oratorically-disposed, made a rabble-rousing speech. By the time he finished, the former field hands, mobilized as conflicting Militia formations, were shooting at one another. Marksmanship was bad. Casualties were low. Nevertheless men died and blood flowed from this mixture of tyrannical folly of comedy and tragedy.

The gubernatorial claimants got their respective forces in hand. Hostile Militia units were moved out of Little Rock, pending a special session of the Legislature. But this merely transferred the little war to the countryside, where two additional minor engagements were fought, but with greater casualties. A complaining taxpayer wrote President Grant: "To sustain their lawless, idle vagabondism, they offer their dupes $22 a month and board to enlist on their side. Where, sir, is the money to come from to pay and support these betrayed, poor negroes who leave their crops and families?"

In special session, the second week of May, the Legislature confirmed the original decision as to Baxter's election. An appeal was sent to President Grant that he recognize Baxter. The President complied and paid-off Brooks with the Postmastership of Little Rock. Senator Clayton, in the meantime, had shifted his support and patronage to Brooks from Baxter, because the latter as Governor was too independent. Accordingly, the Brindle-tail bellow of Brooks had become more musical than the discordant minstrelcy of the Baxterites. And that explains the Postmastership. Thus ended the Baxter-Brooks War. The debacle also destroyed Reconstruction government in Arkansas. It broke the power of the creaking political machine created by Carpetbaggers Clayton, of Leavenworth, Kansas, and Rice, of St. Paul, Minnesota.

## STREET WARFARE IN NEW ORLEANS

Competition for political power and plunder often created dissension among the Radicals who sought to exploit the peace that began at Appomattox. As the largest and richest City in the deep South, it was no more than natural that the most rapacious rivalries culminated in New Orleans.

Henry Clay Warmoth was a youthful Missouri attorney who found himself without an Army assignment when his Regiment was consolidated out of existence, following the disastrous Federal failures in the Red River Campaign. He opened a law office in New Orleans. A lucrative practice before military commissions and governmental departments quickly made him a leading citizen. The convention for revision of the State Constitution lowered the age limit for Governor in order that he might become a candidate. He defeated his Negro rival for the nomination by the votes of only two Delegates.

Duly elected in 1868, he proved to be a past master at the old political game of keeping opposition fragmented until he could attack each in turn. He was one of the first Reconstruction Governors to cry for Militia authority. He was quick with enabling legislation and appropriations, but rather slow about actually fielding any units. Came the end of his first term, 1870, and the political road became rougher. Election to a second term, ending in 1872, was achieved, but all opponents were beginning to get together. The resulting Warmoth-Carter Feud was much the same as the Baxter-Brooks War in Arkansas, but with legislative and Bourbon Street variations.

When Speaker of the House George W. Carter was expelled, Jan. 4, 1872, and a Warmoth man was put in his place, the Carter contingent moved to a large hall over the Gem Saloon, on Royal Street, and organized itself into a rival Legislature. It was then that Governor Warmoth bethought himself of the unused volunteer Organized Militia. Meanwhile, he had prevailed upon Lieutenant General

113

James A. Longstreet, lately of the Army of Virginia, Confederate States, to accept the State Adjutant Generalcy at $3,000 a year.

Never a man prone to duck a fray or an awkward argument, Robert E. Lee's old war horse promptly accepted. At last Governor Warmoth had work for him to do. The General received instructions, January 6, to put the Militia units on active duty and to integrate with them the police force of the City of New Orleans. Then it was revealed what few had realized: the State's National Guard included at least 2,500 Whites, all of them ex-Confederates, and 2,500 Negroes. The Governor obviously was prepared to jump in either direction. Also near the City was Major General W. H. Emory, U.S. Army, with several understrength Companies of the Regular Army's far-flung 19th Infantry. His official posture was one of complete neutrality.

Longstreet's local troops made short work of Carter's rival Legislature by dispossessing the members of the Gem Saloon. They adjourned to the Cosmopolitan Club, all the while trying to get General Emory's Federal force on their side. This was the curtain for Carter unless he could conjure a new act, but there was always the black magic. Thousands of circulars incited the Negroes against Warmoth. The Algiers Armory was broken into and the mob was armed. Washington at last took notice and ordered General Emory to back the Governor. Carter rigged in his neck and ate humble pie by leading his gang back to the duly-constituted legislative body.

It was a Warmoth victory, but it left Adjutant General Longstreet rather shaken. He resigned because he preferred to remain "untrammeled in the approaching political canvass." This suggests the General had gubernatorial ambitions, for it was quite apparent that Warmoth was out insofar as a third term was concerned.

But in the November election that followed, not only did two Legislatures emerge but there appeared two allegedly-elected Governors. Before either "Governor" or both could be inaugurated, Warmoth was impeached, December, 1872. This brought a third but highly-temporary Governor on the scene in the person of P. H. S. Pinchback, Warmoth's Negro Lieutenant Governor, who had turned against his political preceptor and patron. Longstreet returned to his post of duty as Adjutant General. His orders from Pinchback were to operate against Warmoth and the incoming Legislature (of the two allegedly elected) more likely to be friendly to Warmoth. It was under the leadership of the putatively-elected but uninaugurated Governor John McEnery. Pinchback had sold-out to the also putatively-elected Governor Kellogg. Both "Governors-Elect" took the same oath of office the same day, January 13, 1873, but, happily, in different places.

To bring order out of such chaos, as if that were possible, General Longstreet again integrated the metropolitan police with his mixed

114

Battalions, which were now predominately Black. His orders were to support the Kellogg Radicals. The rival Governor McEnery called on his people to organize, which they began doing under the auspices of the emerging White League. Their attack upon the Police Station was repulsed by Longstreet's forces. McEnery's Legislature was jailed. For outgoing Governor Warmoth, all this had some virtue: everyone forgot him, including the incomplete impeachment proceedings, which, in the rush of events, suddenly were dropped. The payoff to the disloyal Lieutenant Governor Pinchback was a Congressional seat which he was denied by the Congress. The next year he claimed and received legislative election to the U.S. Senate. On technicalities he again was denied admission to Congress.

The New Orleans strife simmered until Summer of 1874, with McEnery still claiming to be the duly-elected and inaugurated Governor. Actually he was creating a White Militia, under the auspices of the unmasked and quite open White League. The ex-Confederate underground of resistance was coming to the surface in the form of organized and armed resistance. The metropolitan police and General Longstreet's Militia units began intercepting arms known to be en route to the White Leaguers. The cauldron of troubles simmered no longer. It boiled through early 1874.

The clash of arms Monday, September 14, 1874, was precipitated by word that the steamer *Mississippi,* loaded with arms for the White Leaguers, would be seized by the police and Militia under Longstreet's command. This triggered a mass meeting of four or five thousand White Leaguers. The old gubernatorial election claims of McEnery versus Kellogg pushed the arms interception issue into the background.

A delegation was sent to Governor Kellogg demanding that he resign. An immediate answer was made imperative. Kellogg avoided the meeting. The delegation returned, made its report. The mass meeting adjourned, armed itself and reappeared on the streets as a volunteer ex-Confederate Militia accepting orders from Frederick O. Nash, "Provisional General, Louisiana State Militia." He owed this dubious appointment to a General Order No. 1, over the signature of D. B. Penn, "Lieutenant Governor." He had been on the same ticket McEnery was on. Had the McEnery faction been able to steal the last election, instead of the successful Kellogg-Antoine-Pinchback gang, Penn would have been Lieutenant Governor.

The ultimate appeal to arms was at hand. Both the Radicals and the Conservatives now had an army with which to defend or to storm the barricades, which, in good Parisian style, were beginning to appear. General Emory stood by and awaited orders. His was the smallest force in the field.*

---

* At his immediate disposal Emory had less than 400 men of the 19th Infantry. Though famous for an austere sense of duty, his sympathies were not with the Radicals.

By 4:15 in the long Summer afternoon, Longstreet (slow on the attack, the same as at Gettysburg) had deployed 500 to 1,000 troops, composed of Colored Militia units reinforced by the integrated police under command of Police Chief A. S. Badger. The attack upon the White League barricades was to be supported by a Gatling gun and two 12-pound howitzers. Firing broke out immediately.

The White League Militia made a screened counterattack via a side street. Taken on the flank and in the rear, General Longstreet's forces began falling back, abandoning their artillery. "Provisional General" Nash ordered a charge by the main body. General Longstreet is said to have paled when for the first time he was on the receiving end of a Rebel yell. When the smoke cleared away, 27 dead were in the streets, 105 were bleeding from wounds. Longstreet and Badger were among the latter. Governor Kellogg fled to the Customs House, the nearest Federal sanctuary in this storm of violence. "Lieutenant Governor" Penn, McEnery's running-mate, took over the State House pending "Governor" McEnery's return to the State.

Each faction immediately burned the wires to Washington, telling its side of the story and urging Grant's Administration to bless it with the official kiss. The Kellogg telegrams were successful. The White Leaguers were given five days to disband and quietly return to their homes. General Emory was informed that reinforcements, including a Flotilla of the Gulf Squadron, were on the way. McEnery and Penn quietly withdrew. Governor Kellogg, not so quietly, returned to the State House. The pillage of the State's Treasury continued through the uneasy truce that was the remainder of Governor Kellogg's term.

## RECONSTRUCTION VOLUNTEER MILITIA TECHNIQUES

It was only in Arkansas and Louisiana that the chronic undeclared warfare actually saw Artillery in position. But for tense drama, and events leading to the situation, the "treaty" accomplishing the resignation of Governor Ames of Mississippi transcends the miniature battles briefly described above. Texas did not get rid of her Carpetbag regime without seeing a Negro garrison in the State Capitol besieged by forces supporting another candidate. No shooting took place, because President Grant promptly withdrew support from the Radical Governor.

In Tennessee, Governor William G. (Parson) Brownlow was a fearless and honest man in personal, money matters. He was also enough of a politician that he knew he had to "carry his Ward" if he expected to do business with the Washington Radicals. He long had been a Union Whig and as such had opposed Andrew Johnson for Congress. After 1861 he was a fearless editor for the Union until the Confederacy "deported" him North. Hence, in 1865, he had no place to go except to the Radicals. Moreover, he was capable of some rather radical ideas of his

116

own, as every Methodist preacher knew throughout Tennessee and the Carolinas.

Pious and forthright though he was, he hesitated not a moment to create an Organized Militia of more than 1,600 men. To guarantee satisfactory returns on but one election (by deployment of Squads at every ballot box in each doubtful area) he spent $93,000 of the public monies.

Indeed, guaranteeing satisfactory election returns was one of the principal uses of the troops. In this they were far more effective than in policing the countryside or in street fighting. They were literally the shock troops of the political campaigns. Dependent upon the heat of the campaign and how doubtful a County or District might be, units of the "Dark Militia" would be ordered to active duty days or weeks, perhaps a month, prior to the election day. Often the dubious area would be put under martial law. In most States this justified putting a part or all of the Militia cost upon the County or Counties being "policed."

During this state of the election season it was the duty of the State troops to break up unauthorized (opposition) gatherings, dispose of hecklers of chosen candidates, create noise during rejoinders by any opposition speakers, to attend authorized political meetings of the opposition and create confusion while pretending to maintain law and order, and circulate among the Colored Freedmen and give dire threats, up to and including death, to any who might vote in line with a White friend's argument. At the same time they promised ironclad protection to all those who came to the polls and voted the party line.

This last was often of major importance. It goes without saying that such tactics incited the growing ex-Confederate underground to all manner of retaliatory tactics. Freedmen were intimidated from the polls. "Night riding" became common. Whites and Blacks ambushed one another in darkness. Negro troopers often were intimidated into desertion while on active duty. Others were given 75 cents a day, slightly more than their military stipend, to desert or go A.W.O.L. Occasionally one or more quite active, disfranchised ex-Confederates vanished, never to be seen again. The frequent explanation was that he had gone West, although all knew he most likely had been killed. Unusually effective or unduly arrogant Negro Militia officers vanished occasionally and everyone knew they had not gone West, within the literal sense of the term. The casualties and horror of these rural operations far exceeded the flamboyant operations in the cities. Thus the election season was a time of rural terror in most Southern States. The City antics usually took place in the State Capitals after the Reconstruction election officials, guarded and supported by the Militia units, had canvassed the returns and declared their man elected.

How effective was the Negro Militia in carrying elections for the

117

Radicals? Dr. Singletary sought to answer this question. Without going into his more detailed analysis, it is enough here to say they were thoroughly effective. But in time the tinsel of the uniform began to fade or tarnish. And "tinsel" is the right word in view of what many Colored Militiamen did to their issue clothing and accoutrements to give them a personal touch.

In the beginning, the drills in a local horse pasture, frequent parades and sundry calls for local duty had their compensations above and beyond the pay. They usually were accompanied by barbecues, forensics, soirees, music and dancing. The Captain was the biggest man in the community of field hands. But soldiering away from home, for weeks and months at a time, with frequent calls to reinforce the uniformed brethren in an embattled town or City, depressed morale quite rapidly. Moreover, the corrosive effect of the ever-present and growing ex-Confederate underground had its effect. But even so, in the super-heat of the Presidential Campaign of 1876, the City political machines, supported by threats and/or the bayonets of the "Dark Militia," delivered the crucial Electoral College votes of Louisiana, South Carolina and Florida to Rutherford B. Hayes for a final score of 185. Samuel J. Tilden could show but 184 electoral votes, though he had a comfortable majority of the popular vote. But what these three Reconstruction Governors did not know was that Hayes, the man whom they had elected, was far from being a Radical.

Of necessity, historians often simplify. Thus many textbooks mark and attribute the end of the nightmarish Reconstruction Era in the South to the Election of 1876, the terrific, political rumpus created by the Electoral Commission, and the disputed votes of these three Southern States. Actually, the Reconstruction Era in the South was at an end anyway. The Radical-dominated Reconstruction program, 1876, already had fallen of its own weight in most of the former Confederate States. The delivery of the Electoral College votes to Hayes by these three States was merely the death throes of Reconstruction. In most States Radical Reconstruction fell of its own weight before 1876 and would have ceased in 1877 whether President Hayes had turned out to be a Radical or a Conservative.

Moreover, it cannot be shown successfully that the Reconstruction was ended by the triumph of hooded night riders over superstitious Negroes. Matching lawlessness with lawlessness was a factor, but there were many others. The following were of great importance: State Treasuries had been so completely pillaged, refilled with bond issues and plundered again and again, that the credit of the States was destroyed. There was no more money to steal. The motive of Carpetbag and Scalawag leadership had been removed through this exhaustion of funds. Meanwhile, the idealistic and honest Scalawags had turned conservative, taking with

118

them their followers and influence over the Negroes. Old, ex-Confederate leaders were passing from the scene to be replaced by a new generation of White voters who accepted the leadership of men who had worn the Gray, but who were themselves anything but hot-heads and fire-eaters. The Negroes, particularly their responsible leaders, finally realized they were being exploited. They experienced a revulsion against the entire Radical, Reconstruction concept. Mississippi's Colored U.S. Senator Hiram Revels was one of the first among the Negro leaders to realize this and to join the Conservatives in ending the Reconstruction Regime in his State. Even the mercurial Mulatto and opportunistic Pinchback opposed the Radicals in 1876. Finally—and perhaps this was the most important of all—the great mass of American people in the North realized the entire concept and program were wrong and withdrew their support from Radical Congressmen and Senators, not to mention the Presidency. After all, Tilden did get a majority of the popular vote by a good margin, even though he was counted-out of the Electoral College majority by one thin ballot. In short, most Americans everywhere were in agreement that it was not un-American for the majority to resist the vindictive tyranny of a minority, be the prior grievances of the minority ever so great. Reconstruction techniques of the Radicals could not survive such a growing opinion.

## REVIVAL OF HISTORIC SOUTHERN UNITS

As fast as the tide of Radical Reconstruction receded, most of the traditional, independent National Guard units and their supporting voluntary military associations began manifesting signs of revival. This was particularly true of those that owned property. True, where the Armory and club rooms once stood may have been reduced to charred ruins, or a vacant lot, with a barren drill field; but the real estate was still there, and in a common ownership continued. This was often a revival factor.

The spirit of comradeship and nostalgic respect for decreased members also had a cohesive influence. There are Minutes of such associations that reveal meetings of survivors to do honors to departed comrades as early as 1866. Since most present were ineligible to vote, not to mention the bearing of arms, nothing of military character occurred at such rare meetings. But soon the meetings became frequent and periodic. Even so, the tone was no more military than jocular elbow-bending, dances, occasional graveside formations and annual banquets followed by endless toasts to themes such as "To Virginia, Right or Wrong"; "To the Brave Who Have Fallen"; and "To the Lost Cause and the Conquered Banner—Fold It Tenderly!" Ere long some of the volunteer associations were drilling without arms and without status, other than their voided charters and historic reputations.

When the provisional "Ten-Percent State Governments" acquired the right to organize Militia Companies, some of these reviving units appear to have participated in the indiscretions that gave impetus to Radical Congressional triumph over President Johnson. After that error, few, if any, were operating openly, as military Companies, complete with uniforms and arms, prior to 1873. After the inauguration of President Hayes, 1877, there was a revival of the historic, and creation of new, units throughout the region of the erstwhile Confederacy.

Traditional groupings into Battalions, Regiments and Brigades followed. By 1893, a date well in advance of the Spanish War fervor, the strengths of National Guard units of the several States of the Confederacy were as follows: Alabama, 2,719; Arkansas, 911; Florida, 902; Georgia, 3,949; Louisiana, 1,187, Mississippi, 1,712; North Carolina, 1,577; South Carolina, 5,119; Tennessee, 1,029; Texas, 3,229; Virginia, 2,844. Thus the armed and uniformed citizen-soldier volunteers in the National Guard of the former Confederate States reached an aggregate of 25,178 officers and men. Such a showing five years prior to the outbreak of the Spanish-American War is impressive but does not reflect a growth in proportion to the population increases in those States.

This total is less than the comparable figures for the comparatively quiet prewar Summer of 1860. It is certainly less than for the same States as their Secession Conventions began "absolving the bonds" of Union in early 1861. Since all the foregoing States except Virginia* had increased in population from 40 to 110% within the 35-year span, it is quite apparent a smaller percentage of eligible young men were volunteering for National Guard service in 1893 than in ante-bellum days.

But this should not be taken to mean that the sons of the Confederate veterans were not possessed of enthusiasm for service to their Country comparable to that of their Northern brethren. New York's population had risen from 3,880,000 to 6,003,000 within the same three decades. But the aggregate strengths of her uniformed National Guard had declined from 17,756 officers and men in 1859 to 13,500 in 1890. Within the same period, Wisconsin's aggregate for all National Guard units had increased only 34%, though the population had more than doubled. This was in spite of Wisconsin's keen pride in its Civil War record and the sharp stimulus the Franco-Prussian War had given to matters military among her strongly German populace. It becomes quite apparent that, in spite of the Reconstruction turmoil and their late start toward orderly reorganization, the States of the late Confederacy were doing rather well a full five years before the bugles blew for the Spanish-American War.

It is also interesting to note that in recognition of the military interest of their new citizens, the Freedmen and their sons, the forma-

---

* Virginia had a population of 1,596,318 in 1860 and a gain of only 59,662 in 1890. But she had lost the Counties now in West Virginia.

tions of the National Guard of some of the former Confederate States included Negro units. Normally they had White officers. Occasionally their field camps of Summer instruction and range firing were on dates other than those for the White units. But in Florida, one of the White Infantry Battalions had a Colored Band, under the leadership of a Professor Morse. All the Colored musicians could "read and write music," according to the Regular Army inspector, and "played excellent music."

In the Spanish-American War, soon to come, some of the Negro units were activated, accepted into Federal service and saw extended active duty. Reorganized into units of U.S. Volunteers, some saw combat in the Philippines. In his memoirs, the late Lieutenant General Robert Lee Bullard, commander of Pershing's First Army in France, but in 1898 a Lieutenant in the Regular Army, was thoroughly delighted when the Governor of his native Alabama asked that he be detached from his Regular organization that he might accept the command of that State's Colored Battalion. The General always remembered that service with great satisfaction. According to him: "They made me look good. It was my first leg up toward a colonelcy. Few ever hoped to become a brigadier, or higher, in those days."*

## NATIONAL GUARD REORGANIZATION IN THE WEST AND NORTH

Through the North Atlantic and New England States, the move toward reorganization of National Guard units was prompt and on a comparatively wide scale. The old Chartered Companies and military associations were deeply-rooted. They not only were symbols of civic pride and service, but they were rich in tradition. Some were also comparatively rich in money. Urban development, if not encroaching on business centers, had brought soaring prices to real estate adjacent to massive old armories. One-time pasture lands that had been donated or acquired cheaply as a parade ground had attained high value. In the expansion and contraction of organizations with their goings and comings to and from active duty, it was not unusual that the courts occasionally were called upon to determine the right of control, if not the actual ownership, of such properties.

In States dotted with cities and towns in which National Guard units were so deeply embedded, one hardly could say there was any true, or discernible, interruption in the unit's basic history. It was merely a question of how many of the old members desired to con-

---

* Because of unpleasant memories of some 92nd Division units, World War I, Gen. Bullard became opposed to segregated Divisions. Though superb soldiers in small units in the bush operations in the Philippines, he considered it unwise to commit them to action in units of Division size and in the trench warfare of World War I.

tinue their active affiliation. The prescribed participation in all the military duties, as well as the social pleasures and prestige, eliminated many aging members. Others among the returnees were naturally so war-weary that initially they chose to put away all things military, wash the dust of Dixie from their hands, and leave all future "alarums of war" to younger and future generations. Others opined they would, as a civic duty, stay with their unit long enough to see it well established in the new atmosphere of peace, and then would yield to the younger generation. It was inevitable that occasional personalities with complexes that they were indispensable yielded belatedly, reluctantly and perhaps ungraciously. But the records of the large numbers of units examined reveal that yield they ultimately did, and a few by court action.

In the much younger Northern States, such as Wisconsin, Minnesota and Iowa, the war-weariness appears to have been greater, local unit traditions hardly so strong, and military association property owned, if any, was much less a cohesive, continuing factor. But the military flame by no means was reduced to a spark. It was sufficiently healthy and glowing that units in some cities and towns were reorganized as soon as, or sooner, following the end of hostilities in 1865, than was the case following the Spanish-American and World Wars I and II.

In some States and Territories the Indian frontier was still near at hand. Even in Minnesota there remained grim memories of New Ulm and other depredations. California and Oregon still had frontier problems. Generally, along the thinly-settled frontier there was a sigh of relief that the Regulars soon again would be at their posts. But the Westerners could take no chances, particularly through the first year or two of peace while the remaining Veteran Volunteers and Regulars were being deployed in Texas, with an eye on Emperor Maximilian, or in the Deep South to underwrite the peace.

The West, however, had been but little affected by the Civil War, except for the depredations by the unpoliced Indians. Much of their State and Territorial military effort had been required by the restless Indians after the departure of so many of the Regular units. Hence there was little, if any, immediate perceptible change within their Military Departments from what had prevailed since 1861. Until the Regular Army was returned in augmented strength to police the long-neglected and increasingly restless hostiles, the Governors and their Adjutants Generals in the West and Near West were in no position to relax their local safeguards. From their viewpoint, the war had not yet ended.

Colorado Territory, to take a convenient example, had fielded one Cavalry Regiment of Volunteers to Federal service for the full period of the war, one Regiment of Cavalry for three years only and one additional Regiment under the authority for a 100-days Call. The Territory also had created one Battery of Artillery and two Companies of Infantry. When these were demobilized, the Governor and Adjutant General made heroic efforts to keep adequate units in being until the arrival of Regulars. These efforts, under defective Territorial laws, continued until Statehood. At the time of Statehood, August 1, 1876, the National Guard of the passing Territory consisted of two bobtailed Battalions—one each of Infantry and Cavalry. Statehood brought greater freedoms in local and regional affairs with growing population and a greatly-improved military situation.

The Meeker Massacre by the Ute Indians in the last week of September, 1879, aroused the young State. New units came into being, particularly in the exposed, often isolated, mining boom towns. Some of the units thus started continued until the mining boom passed and only ghost towns remained. A brief, unpopular, but serious strike in the Leadville District, Summer, 1880, was a further stimulus to interest in the new State's National Guard. By the end of the year, the Colorado National Guard had been expanded permanently to four Battalions. From these emerged the 1st Colorado Infantry. It went to the Philippines in 1898 as the 1st Colorado Volunteer Infantry and to World Wars I and II as the 157th Infantry.

The basic Colorado statutes of that era stipulated that no Company could sustain its official status with less than 24 active members. The ceiling strength for a unit was 70. This figure was not unusual for most Western States in that era. In the Midwest and East, minimums were 50 to 100% higher. But the organizational structure in Colorado was bigger than the interested manpower could justify, even within the small, lower limit. In 1889 the two Regiments of the Colorado National Guard were reorganized temporarily as two independent Battalions. In 1893, their combined strength with Field and Staff officers was only 901. The population of the State in 1890 was 413,249. Compared to the per capita ratio of the average State of Wisconsin, 1859, Colorado should have had closer to 1,500 officers and men.

Though fighting Indians was a popular activity, being called to frequent strike duty was not. And this was what was happening to the Colorado National Guard. There was increasing sympathy for the miners after the abortive Leadville strike of 1880. True, the tide of sentiment began turning against the strikers when Harry Orchard, the dynamiter, and Steve Adams, both hired killers, blew up a passenger station at Cripple Creek while a train was servicing changing shifts of workers. They thus killed and wounded 37 non-union laborers. Neither Billy the Kid nor Wes Hardin could show that many notches on their pistols, for they had shot at armed men. Orchard and Adams, we now know, were indeed goons in the pay and service of William D. (Big Bill) Haywood's Western Federation of Miners. It was the beginning of the end of the Western Federation's influence in Colorado. But that specific incident was more than a decade, 1904, in the future.

## CITIZEN-SOLDIERS FACE THE BLOODY STRIKES

Citizen-soldiers always have been far more willing to volunteer for service on a battlefield to achieve independence, to preserve the Union or to retain liberties and a way of national life already won, than to engage in what is essentially the work of a State Constabulary or a Provincial police force. That is why some officers and men today are willing to volunteer for or accept an assignment in the U.S. Army Reserve, rather than face the broader implications and responsibilities of the National Guard. But in the Nineteenth Century there was no Federal Organized Militia, or Army Reserve, into which they could find admission. Moreover, there were no States with a Constabulary.

When a problem in law and order became so completely out of hand that the local police or the Sheriff's Office could not cope with it, a posse of law-abiding citizens was deputized and sworn-in. When they failed, as in Billy the Kid's Lincoln County War, the Governor had but the one source whence law and order could be implemented. It was the voluntarily-organized Militia, or National Guard, of his State or Territory. Moreover, the States were sovereign in police responsibilities. If and when the Governor might be willing to concede that the disorders were beyond the might of himself and the State agencies available to him, then, and then only, might he call upon the President to strengthen his feeble hands with the armed might of the Federal Government. Thus the National Guardsman of that era pledged himself first to respond to his Governor, on call to resist invasion, normally by Indians, and to support the maintenance of law and order in the face of any opposition whatsoever. Should the Federal Government invite his services, and if he could possibly make satisfactory arrangements with his creditors and his family, there was the implied obligation to serve the higher government beyond the voluntarily-agreed-upon limits of his State citizenship. This concept, as explained earlier, dated from ancient England via the 13 Colonies.

Thus the citizen-soldiers of the Pacific Coast, Rocky Mountain Territories and States, and those of the Midwest and Northeast, had little toward which to look in 1876 except defensive action against Indian raids, such offensive operations as might be done before the Federal troops arrived and the thankless duty of preserving law and order in mining and industrial disputes. In view of these onerous responsibilities, and with no foreign enemy on the horizon, there is little

124

wonder that the National Guard units of Colorado, and comparable Western States as well as elsewhere, were smaller in proportion to the supporting populations than had prevailed 25 or 30 years earlier.

Industrial strife was a problem that was confrontng Guardsmen everywhere except in the South, and as presented above, they had their own peculiar and far more distressing problems. With no foreign enemies on the horizon, the prospective early service for an interested recruit could be in but one place: the raw, rough, unexplored, bloody industrial frontier within his own State.

## FROM MARTINSBURG, WEST VIRGINIA, TO HAYMARKET SQUARE, CHICAGO

The Great Railroad Strike of 1877 brought this home to the Guardsmen with a jolt. For the Northern National Guardsmen, 1877-1897 was an era filled with almost as many difficulties as those previously noted within the "Conquered States." Inside the former Confederacy, the Organized Militia, or National Guard, was the balance of power (so long as the Regular Army stayed neutral), between the Reconstruction State Governments and the conquered Whites. In the North, the National Guard became the balance of power between ruthless Capital and incendiary labor unions. Once again the Regular Army often held the balance of immediate power. But in the industrial warfare of that era, the Regular Army remained neutral with less frequency than it did in the political wars of the deep South. However, this did not keep the Guardsmen from receiving the more severe abuse.

That these domestic labor wars adversely affected the growth, military horizons and training of both the National Guard and the Regular Army there can be little doubt. They detracted from the opportunity of the professional soldiers to study and grow with the burgeoning strategy, tactics and techniques of the approaching Twentieth Century. The emotions of the era put the Guardsmen on the defensive for being willing to serve their State and Nation in any crisis anywhere at any time.

Muckrakers and other self-appointed custodians of the American conscience have been quick to champion the rights of "free Americans" to picket and promote violence, but they have been reluctant to recognize the rights of other "free Americans" to volunteer in support of orderly, legal procedures and for the protection of property, liberty and life. Whether or not the non-union laborers had a right to work was questioned by no one but the ardent Unionists in that era. The legal principle still prevails in some States. But neither any State nor the Federal Government ever has questioned the right of non-union laborers to live and to be dealt with in a manner compatible with the dignity of Man.

125

The National Guardsman who chose to stand up and be counted on the side of law and human rights was seldom an economic Bourbon or the son of one. He and his comrades were small people from farms, villages and Main Street stores. At times they were so sympathetic toward the strikers, as in the Great Railroad Strike of 1877, that they refused to use their weapons and accepted defeat, occasionally with casualties, rather than fire into the rioters. Such failures resulting from their watering-down their own orders naturally aroused the ire and derision of disgruntled Regulars who were called in to deny the strikers their local victory.

But the cause of Labor between 1877 and 1897 suffered more from its own undisciplined excesses, its identification with bomb-throwers, dynamiters, and anarchistic journalism, than from any repression from either the National Guard units or the Regular Army. The great rank-and-file of industrial laborers through this era rejected the dedicated leadership of Terence V. Powderly, the first practical advocate of the One Big Union. Nor would they harken to the then more practical ideas of Samuel Gompers with his trades unions approach. Instead they defended the murderous gangster tactics of the "Molly McGuires." They took unto their bosom every rabble-rousing orator with a half-baked philosophy. Worse yet, they accepted the infiltrated leadership of such men as Johaan Most, George Engl, Albert R. Parsons, August Spies, Samuel Fielden and Adolph Fischer. All of them were in part, or entirely, devoted to the teachings of the anarchist Mikhail Bakunin.* The popularity of their publicly-avowed purposes and slogans drew off the membership and destroyed the growing power of Terence Powderly's upright Knights of Labor. He knew the proponents of violence for what they were and would have none of them. They destroyed him as a labor leader and set back the cause of the laborer several decades.

The Haymarket Riot and bombing, May 4, 1886, Chicago, at which there were neither Guardsmen nor Regulars present, broke the far-flung and until then popular Pullman Strike. Johaan Most's International Working People's Association, better known as the Black International, disappeared in the smoke of the bombing and the emotional trial of Chicago's Anarchists. But modifications of the Nihilistic philosophy as applied to American free enterprise survived. Hence the

---

* As leader of a Russian school of Nihilists, Bakunin was so far out in left field that at the Hague Conference of the International, 1872, Karl Marx had to expel him. Bakunin wrote, "In a word we object to all legislation, all authority, and all influence, privileged, patented, official and legal, *even when it has proceeded from universal suffrage* . . ." Bakunin's solution was the restoration of the "natural laws" of man through bombings, murder, violence in every form. Such tea was too bitter even for Karl Marx. All he wanted to achieve was the destruction of Capitalism and Democracy in order that he might substitute Communism and the Proletariat's dictatorship.

"Chicago Idea" recurred in such forms as Harry Orchard's mass murder of the non-union workers at Cripple Creek 21 years later. It was a cardinal principle in Big Bill Haywood's "Rocky Mountain Revolution," the bitter fruits of which plagued the Labor Movement until after World War I.

Thus the real enemies of Labor through this difficult era were never those who stood for law, order and justice within the dreams and objectives of true Democracy, as did the National Guard. It was those who exploited laborers and the labor movement to serve their own personal purposes, or the perverted philosophy they had substituted for patriotic instincts.*

Meanwhile, the National Guard, in its dual status, as the National defense institution it had become and as the ultimate in the *posse comitatus* concept for law and order whence it had originated in primitive Saxton times, was caught between the New Era's sociological Titans. From the laborers, temporarily charmed and betrayed by the anarchistic siren songs of class warfare, there came every curse and epithet ever coined to discredit the *bourgeois,* in which the Guardsmen were labeled as the lowest lackeys of Capitalism. From the reactionaries came abuse because the Guardsmen did not give the rioters a "whiff of grapeshot" such as that with which Napoleon was said to have ended the French Revolution.

Nor did the Guardsmen in the strike-ridden Northern States get any sympathy from the unhappy local police or the Regular Army. The police were prone to return to their routine beats once the Governor had hearkened to local pleas to call out the Guard. From these quiet retreats they had nothing to offer willingly but harsh criticism of the newly-arrived Guardsmen. If the disorders reached beyond State boundaries, the Governor called on Washington for help. The Regulars sent to the scene of trouble naturally were irritated. The same was equally true if the President sent in the Army without a gubernatorial request. The Regulars abused the Guardsmen for their lack of utter ruthlessness, and when the nature of their orders permitted, took the attitude that their own duties stopped with protecting Federal property and keeping the mail channels open; the Guardsmen should do the fighting at the embattled industrial plants. Had the National Guard, as an American institution, been less deeply-rooted in the States and the Nation and in less robust health, it could not have survived this harsh era of internal and domestic strife in the North and in the South.

* Johaan Most was father of America's Black International and the most famous of the imported Anarchists of this era. He still is revered in limited circles as the "great apostle of propaganda by deed"; i.e., progress through violence. Yet, Johaan Most never did anything himself other than incite others into killing and getting killed. As an editor and "intellectual" he had some following until his death, 1906, age 70, in Cincinnati. He was there on a lecture tour.

# FALSE INTERPRETATION OF THE GUARD

A recent pseudo-scholarly, quasi-brochure, apparently inspired by superficial knowledge of this era, is further so marred by social myopia and lack of historical perspective that it actually argues that the modern National Guard dates from this era and was created after the Civil War from a moribund Militia concept last in action against the Seminole Indians prior to the Mexican War. Its revival as a military force, the reader is assured, was from Capitalistic pressures on the pliant State Governments for an industrial police. Fortunately the naivete of the writer, a young political science teacher in a Mid-Western college, so betrays his lack of understanding that his thesis is far from convincing. For example, he solemnly wrote that for a "decade or so" after the Civil War "only a few Northern States attempted to maintain a militia organization; and during Reconstruction, Southern States *could not do so.*" This would have been real news throughout the Dixie of this era. Earlier, in establishing to his own satisfaction the complete decadence of the Militia, prior to the need for it as a Capitalistic police force to ride-down Labor, he also assures his readers that the "last significant use by the National Government of the militia organized under the Act of 1792 was the Seminole War (1836-42)." This likewise would have been news to Mr. Lincoln while he was explaining to the ebullient Dan Sickles the legal difficulties inherent in the immediate acceptance of the latter's "Excelsior Brigade" into Federal service without deference to New York and the authorized quota already provided by that State.

The author of this uninformed tract argues that it was the unplanned and spontaneous Railroad Strike of 1877 that put a moribund and decadent Militia back in business to become the National Guard with rapid growth, good appropriations, large armories and Federal subsidies. Concerning the strike itself, he says "credit for breaking the strike probably belongs to the Army and President Hayes, although undoubtedly the militia killed more strikers." According to his figures, there were ultimately 2,000 Regulars and 45,000 State troops engaged in the two weeks that the tumultuous strike lasted. Thus by internal evidence of the brochure's own paragraphs, it would appear that any organization that could, with little or no warning, field no less than 45,000 men practically overnight and for such unpleasant and strenuous duty, was far from being either moribund or decadent. Certainly it must have been somewhat operative before July 19, 1877, the day the strike suddenly started at Martinsburg, West Virginia, and spread like tidal waves of violence to inundate or isolate railroad centers from Baltimore to Chicago and St. Louis.

As for the good appropriations, armories and Federal subsidies the author of the quoted psuedo-brochure indicates to have been the National Guard's reward for loyalty to Capitalism and the cruel States, there was much talk of such being desirable, but statistics do not reveal them as having been forthcoming. Certainly there is nothing in the record that supports his contention that the Federal Government's repeal of the Federal grants-in-aid of 1808 would have "resulted in the complete collapse of the militia and the inheritance by the Army of its police function."

Though such newspapers and magazines as the New York *Times* and *The Nation* did clamor and editorialize for a larger Regular Army and a stronger National Guard for the States, there is little evidence that anyone but the Regulars and the National Guardsmen had much enthusiasm for the idea. As noted earlier, the Regular Army was reorganized and reduced to an actual strength of 25,674 officers and men as of June, 1875. As of the same month for representative following years, the corresponding strength figures are: 25,547 for 1883, 27,544 for 1889, and 27,523 for 1897. Throughout this long, difficult era, the officer strength of the Regular Army fluctuated less than 100 above or below 2,100. Thus, if the Regulars received any reward for strike-breaking, it certainly did not come in the form of expansion and promotions. Indeed, they did not get so much as a campaign ribbon.*

The National Guard appears to have fared but little, if any, better. And in terms of Federal subsidies the State formations fared much worse. As noted above, National Guard strengths through this period did not keep pace with the expanding population base of their States. Such armories as were built were certainly far from adequate. The reports of Regular Army inspectors bristle with criticisms for lack of proper storage and care of Federal ordnance provided and paid for from the Federal appropriations. This aid to the Militia began in 1808, with annual appropriations of $200,000. Seventy-five years later, with a National population increase of 800%, it was still $200,000.

The Hayes-Tilden election controversy and the Great Railroad Strike, the first settled just in time for the second to erupt, caused many thoughtful, responsible citizens in the strife-torn year of 1877 to fear a new Civil War was imminent. Legislation was introduced to improve and better-arm the National Guard. To further improve the Guard and support the legislation, Major General Dabney Maury convened the first gathering of Guard officers in Richmond. "We invited the cooperation of all the States in measures promotive of our military efficiency, and the matter was promptly taken up in New York and

---

* One of the more distinguished Artillery and Ordnance experts of the era, who was graduated from West Point in 1867, was a Lieutenant for 27 years. He was promoted to Captain, October 25, 1894. He transferred to Ordnance in 1898 to become a temporary Major.

followed by the first convention and organization of the National Guard Association of America," Maury wrote.

"We succeeded in procuring from Congress a small increase in the annual appropriation for arming the militia." But what General Maury, Founding Father of the National Guard Association of the United States, did not explain, was the length of time it took to do it.

Mr. William C. Endicott, Secretary of War under President Cleveland, repeated earlier determined efforts to get the amount increased in 1887. In 1893, Secretary Stephen B. Elkins was citing a continuing need. His successor, Daniel S. Lamont, immediately re-echoed the same complaint. He saw the National Guard in its traditional role as an essential part of "national protection" for which "The obligation of the Federal Government to the militia of the States is two-fold—to furnish instruction and inspection and to furnish ordnance supplies . . . The second obligation was recognized by Congress as early as 1808, when an Act was passed allotting $200,000 to the Militia of the States.* In spite of the increase in population, increase of the Militia, and improvements and increased cost of arms, artillery and equipments, the appropriation remained virtually fixed at the original amount, the endeavor of Congress to increase it by the Act of February 12, 1887, failing to accomplish that result."**

In short, a peacetime preparedness appropriation for ordnance originally passed for a Nation of 15 States and 7,000,000 people eight decades later still was being considered by Congress as adequate for a new, growing Union of 38 States and 60,000,000. Can anyone seriously propose this was a Federal aid without which the National Guard of the States could not have survived? To suggest that this static appropriation with its diminishing purchasing power was the life-blood of the National Guard from 1808 to 1886, and at the same time was a reward to the Guard for an ignominious role in the class warfare that erupted in 1877, is amusingly absurd. But of such is the theme of the above-mentioned misinterpreter of the National Guard as a military institution.

The rejections here of the asseverations of this comparatively obscure, quasi-brochure hardly would be worthy of the space given it were it not that its theme represents occasional historical distillations, errone-

---

* This was not a cash subsidy, as the words might imply. It was normally a credit against which each State drew ordnance up to a pro-rated value. In actual practice, it made the Organized Militia, or National Guard, units a legitimate dumping area for weapons ranging from slightly obsolescent to absolutely obsolete, toward the replacement of which for the Regulars the annual allotment of $200,000 could be spent. It was in effect a continuing modernization appropriation to the War Department.

** Actually, President Cleveland's sponsored Act of February 12, 1887, had raised the Federal Aids to $400,000, but had increased the items of equipment that could be issued the Guard so that the situation concerning ordnance items remained little, if any, changed.

130

ous evaluations and careless interpretations of an appreciable amount of ephemeral but venomous class warfare literature of the era that have found their way into a few reputable historical writings.

To be sure, there were events within those melancholy decades, 1877-97, that one may well wish never had happened, just as there were wars that one wishes America might have been spared. But making a whipping boy of the National Guard or the Regular Army to achieve an ultra-liberalistic, gray-zone atmosphere for the lawless excesses of a mobocracy that lent itself to the leadership of such criminalistic destroyers as Albert R. Parsons, August Spies, Johaan Most, Harry Orchard and Big Bill Haywood, does not make sense. Admittedly, the culprits themselves had so outraged the normal agencies of justice that they most likely were not tried in an unprejudiced court.

Likewise, it could be true that the Governor who later pardoned those not hanged was equally prejudiced in their favor and certainly political-minded. But such polemics, with the resultingly wide gray-zone as to what is right and wrong, are luxuries to be indulged in by judges, journalists, academicians and politicians. It was the immediate duty and function of the Regulars and the National Guardsmen to restore law and order, wherever and whenever they were so instructed, thereby making it possible for the judges, journalists and politicians and for us academicians to enjoy our peaceful, speculative luxuries.

That the Regulars and the National Guardsmen ultimately were caught between the Titans and received abuse and journalistic scars from both, should stand as convincing evidence that through these drab decades of class hatreds, the men in military uniform served their Country extremely well and with firm fairness.

## NEW TRENDS BRING RELIEF TO THE GUARD

It did not come in the Nineteenth Century, but early in the Twentieth the Military were to a large extent relieved of strike duty. Incident to the Spanish-American War and the Pacification of the Philippines, Governors and State Legislatures realized that a National Guard that vanished into Federal service as Volunteers the moment a war threatened could not always be counted upon as the ultimate *posse comitatus* for preservation of domestic law and order. Thus was hastened the creation of State Constabularies. Since Cavalry had proved to be most effective in riots, Constabulary details normally were mounted. Mounted detachments became conventional in all metropolitan police forces. At the same time, the laboring men became less gullible. They accepted the advice and leadership of less promising but more productive, resourceful and honest leaders. Except for the Rocky Mountain regions and the Pacific Coast,* industrialism, at the turn of the Century, was becoming of age; reaching maturity. Strikes of a size and nature that required troops became less frequent. When riots did occur, it was the State Constabularies and mounted detachments of the metropolitan police forces that policed the picket lines. They quickly became the target of the soap box epithets and rabble-rousing advocates of violence.

The day of the dynamiters, bomb-throwers and bayonets appears to be displaced by a greater mass appreciation of the blessings of law and order and a willingness to settle matters in the legislative halls and courts rather than in the streets. Both the Regular Army and the National Guard have been disassociated so long from riot duty that service therein is no longer a deterrent to young men contemplating an enlistment or reenlistment. Most labor unions have relinquished earlier bans against their members joining the National Guard.

But this definitely was not true in 1897. The vituperative, emotion-burdened and confused issues were no asset to the National Guard's progress and development. In their way, they were as much a blighting burden in the North as were the Militia use abuses in the South during Reconstruction. That the National Guard survived the malicious propaganda of twisted half-truths that characterized this tragic era speaks eloquently for its long Anglo-American heritage, for its rich traditions and for the confidence the great mass of the citizenry had in it as a defender of the right of the majority to govern at home as well as its ability to serve as a volunteer force capable of standing with the Regular Army in opposition to foreign aggressions.

## THE REGULAR ARMY CONTINUES AN INTEREST IN THE NATIONAL GUARD

In spite of occasional bickerings between Regulars and Guardsmen when distasteful strike duty had tried the patience of both, there is no period in War Department history when more upper-echelon esteem was voiced for the volunteer citizen-soldiers of the States' Organized Militia.

This was natural. Many of the graying Regular Captains had commanded State Regiments in the Civil War. All the Regimental Commanders in 1890 had brevet General Officer titles that stemmed from their having commanded Brigades, Divisions and even Army Corps

---

* In July, 1934, 4,500 California National Guardsmen were called to anti-strike duty in San Francisco by Gov. Frank Merriam on request of Mayor Angelo J. Rossi. The Communist-infiltrated International Longshoremen's Association (Union) had paralyzed transportation to and from the City. Sympathetic strikes by the Teamsters and others aggravated the situation. It marked the leadership emergence of Harry Bridges. He later successfully resisted deportation as a Communist and alien. It was the last major strike supported by all the stage props of a dramatized "class warfare." The Depression, 1931-1940, provided the theme music and backdrop.

132

entirely composed of Volunteer Regiments that had been organized and sent into Federal service by the States. A high percentage of Field Grade officers never had known any military service other than with State Regiments prior to their integration into the Regular Army in 1866, or soon thereafter.

But under such battle-hardened professionals as Generals William T. Sherman (1869-1883) and Philip A. Sheridan (1883-1888) and Lieutenant General John M. Schofield, the West Point career officers ran the Army and held the top Staff and Field command assignments. An exception to this pattern was Nelson A. Miles, who began his military career as a First Lieutenant in the 22nd Massachusetts Volunteer Infantry, September 9, 1861, and became a Brigadier General, Regular Army, 1880.

As tough-minded professionals, these officers naturally felt they needed a larger and better-equipped Army. They knew the temper of the American people. They knew the most they could hope for beyond the small, competent, Regular Army were intelligent and interested civilian volunteers who could and would become the structural framework for future Brigades, Divisions and Field Armies. With no particular enemy on the horizon, there was little basis for specific planning. With no known foreign potential against which to measure strength, there was no basis for budgeting men, equipment, ordnance or supplies.

The Franco-Prussian War had indeed startled Europe and then captured the imagination of soldiers and diplomats of the Old World. For the Americans it offered no more than technical interest. A new doctrine of National security was soothing Americans. At the Naval War College, Newport, R.I., Commander Alfred T. Mahan, U.S.N., was convincing not only America but all the World that when control of the sea lanes was vital to victory, massed armies could become impotent. Hannibal and Napoleon were his exhibits "A" and "B". Anyone with a wall map could see that America was the only major power in the World which could plan defensive wars between two oceans.

As for Helmuth von Moltke's whirlwind campaign through France, ending in the capture of Paris, every veteran of '61-'65 knew that Lee's field fortifications and trench warfare tactics from the Rapidan to Petersburg would have decimated the Prussian Brigades at every river line. World War I was to prove them correct.

It was not until after World War I that English and French staff colleges rediscovered the American Civil War. Many of their teachers and students decided they would have been better prepared for the Marne, Ypres, Passchendale, the Somme and Verdun, had they studied Grant and Lee instead of Marshals von Moltke, MacMahon, Bazaine

133

and Faidherbe. All of which suggests the old saddle-pounding soldiers of the last American frontier were better-informed men-at-arms than subsequent generations of Americans have been willing to concede.

Contrary to general opinion, the Regular Army of this era did interest itself in new weapons, better equipment and modern techniques and their influence on tactics and higher strategy. The concept of postgraduate study for Regular Army officers stemmed from this era, which also witnessed the creation of the Service schools, such as the Engineer School, Artillery School and the school that became the Command and General Staff College at Fort Leavenworth, Kansas.

The top Staff and Field officers of the Regular Army who recognized personnel as a problem in war planning were thoroughly conversant with the conscript systems of Europe. They had seen mass armies fielded and maintained primarily by State-created Regiments of Volunteers. It was their almost unanimous opinion that a willing man made a far better soldier than a Draftee.

The Monroe Doctrine was the American foreign policy. They had seen nations with conscript armies withdraw from Mexico and fall far short of success in Cuba. Moreover, they knew the American people of their day would not have given them a Draft Law and an expensive manpower reserve had they been foolish enough to believe in it, or brash enough to ask for it.

What these Regular Army officers wanted was a good National Guard composed of properly-encouraged and eager volunteers. They badly needed and repeatedly asked for sums sufficient for procurement and development of the most modern equipment and weapons. The procurement they proposed should be in stockpile quantities, adequate to arm immediately the volunteering National Guard formations that would be activated at once upon the outbreak of hostilities. Until then, the National Guardsmen, at their home stations and in Summer camps of instruction, could be issued the older equipment, weapons and ammunition as expendable items for their training.

Moreover, in an era of burgeoning navies of steel and steam, the Regulars and Guardsmen foresaw the clamor of coastal cities for protection against long range, off-shore bombardments. This, they estimated, easily could freeze 90,000 officers and men in static coastal positions. Not only should existing National Guard Regiments of Infantry, Cavalry and Field Artillery be maintained at more than 100,000 men, as the basis for a mobile force, but the coastal needs should be anticipated.

The foregoing was the professional military thinking back of Secretary Endicott's Act of February 12, 1887, expanding the base of aid to the National Guard to include items other than ordnance and raising the total figure to $400,000 annually. Actually the planning

134

Regulars were talking in terms of millions for the National Guard, but the Congress could think only in tens and occasional hundreds of thousands.

In the small and humble beginnings of the National Guard Association, the penny-pinched Regulars saw a ray of hope. If they could transfer obsolescent items to the National Guard to retire appropriation credits, perhaps they might be able to spend the actual funds on themselves. National Guard needs and demands would move old equipment to the State formations and open areas of shortages among the Regulars that could be replaced by modern weapons and supplies. In going to Congress with requests, both the War Department and the Guardsmen naturally and frequently mentioned the current labor strife as reasons why they merited support and aid. These were things within the scope and experience of every Congressman. Even so, their pleas were to little avail.

But there did develop among the Guardsmen, Regulars and the War Department a mutual respect, good will and a commonality of interest.

Soon the Navy Department was taking note. Its leaders thought an Organized Militia of naval crews might be a good idea. Colonial rivalries in Europe could result in a quick need for naval manpower. Suspicions of and friction with England from the Venezuela Boundary Dispute, which began in 1890, were stimuli toward preparedness. The Press magnified the fears from offshore bombardments by fast, phantom fleets. Some States were sure Naval Militia could be valuable warning aid to locally-manned coastal batteries. The tremendous increases in the ranges of seaborne artillery gave considerable credence to the idea. Thus the terminal years of the drab decades 1867 to 1897 witnessed a quickening of the American military pulse that had little or nothing to do with the labor wars. But like all supporters of a budget estimate and request, neither the National Guard Association nor the War Department hesitated to mention those factors which appeared to bulk largest in Congressional imaginations. And some mid-Western Congressmen may have been thinking more strongly of labor unrest in St. Louis than in breaches of the Monroe Doctrine in the Caribbean or possible bombardment of New York by British cruisers, if and when any of them supported military legislation.

But much of the above excitement was after rather than before the statistical year chosen for listing the National Guard strengths of the States of the erstwhile Confederacy. Once again, to show strengths in advance of the growing tensions with Spain over Cuba, the statistics for 1893 are given. That year the aggregate strength of the National Guard of all the States and Territories was 112,507 officers and men.

By individual States and Territories, omitting those previously given for Southern States as of the same year, the returns were: Alaska Territory, 0; Arizona Territory, 293; California, 4,198; Colorado, 901; Connecticut, 2,735; Delaware, 443; District of Columbia, 1,382; Idaho, 229; Illinois, 4,774; Indian Territory, 0; Indiana, 2,654; Iowa, 2,363; Kansas, 1,714; Kentucky, 1,227; Maine, 1,208; Maryland, 2,334; Massachusetts, 6,174; Michigan, 2,934; Minnesota, 1,861; Missouri, 2,355; Montana, 592; Nebraska, 1,366; Nevada, 566; New Hampshire, 1,265; New Jersey, 4,017; New Mexico Territory, 571; New York, 13,500; North Dakota, 513; Ohio, 6,551; Oklahoma Territory, 154; Oregon, 1,406; Pennsylvania, 8,497; Rhode Island, 1,040; South Dakota, 584; Utah Territory, 1,066; Vermont, 706; Washington, 1,388; West Virginia, 864; Wisconsin, 2,676, and Wyoming, 309.

Generally speaking, these figures do not reflect a National Guard growth comparable to that of the Nation. Considering the absence of foreign dangers through most of this era and the trials and tribulations of a domestic character experienced by the National Guard, North and South, through these post-Civil War years, the figures do reveal a strong devotion to the National Guardsman's ideal of willingness to serve his Country at all times in all emergencies in peace as well as war.

# Bibliographical Note For Chapter IV

Concerning Reconstruction in the South, there are a surprisingly large number of extremely well-written historical works. Among them are Claude G. Bowers, *The Tragic Era*, 1929, which is perhaps most widely appreciated from a literary standpoint. George F. Milton, *Age of Hate*, is equally literary, covers pretty much the same ground but has different emphasis and viewpoint. W. A. Dunning, *Essays on the Civil War and Reconstruction*, 1910, and *Reconstruction, Political and Economic*, 1907, is highly scholarly and never has been fully replaced. Written under the general oversight of Professor W. A. Dunning, while a professor at Columbia University, are a number of valuable but seldom-read monographs dealing with Reconstruction in the individual States. Among the more significant are J. A. Garner, *Reconstruction in Mississippi*, 1901; W. L. Fleming, *Civil War and Reconstruction in Alabama*, 1905; James de R. Hamilton, *Reconstruction in North Carolina*, 1914; Charles W. Randall, *Reconstruction in Texas*, 1910; J. S. Reynolds, *Reconstruction in South Carolina*, 1905; in the same vein and carrying out the same tradition also see W. W. Davis, *Civil War and Reconstruction in Florida*, 1913; H. J. Eckenrode, *Political History of Virginia During Reconstruction*, 1904; J. W. Fertig, *Secession and Reconstruction in Tennessee*, 1898; J. R. Ficklen, *History of Reconstruction in Louisiana Through 1868*, 1910; F. B. Simkins and R. H. Woody, *South Carolina During Reconstruction*, 1931; P. S. Staples, *Reconstruction in Arkansas*,

136

1923; and C. Mildred Thompson, *Reconstruction in Georgia*, 1915. Gov. Henry Clay Warmoth of Louisiana offers his own apologia in *War, Politics and Reconstruction: Stormy Days in Louisiana*, 1930. John William DeForest, *A Union Officer in the Reconstruction*, 1948, offers the first-hand observations and opinions of a sensitive New Englander who later became an able if often-overlooked novelist. James S. Pike, *The Prostrate State: South Carolina under Negro Government*, 1874, is a most graphic reaction of a once-famous New York newspaper man. Most pertinent of all, because it confines itself specifically to the activities of the Organized Militia of the several Southern States, is Otis A. Singletary, *The Negro Militia*, 1957.

For those parts of Chapter IV having to do with labor troubles, strikes, etc., the following titles are highly pertinent: John R. Commons and Associates, *History of Labour in the United States*, 4 vols., 1918-35. A more readable and concise review is found in Foster Rhea Dulles, *Labor in America*, 1949. Also recommended is Norman Ware, *The Labor Movement in the United States, 1860-1895*, 1929. Stewart Holbrook, *The Rocky Mountain Revolution*, projects the violence of the Labor movement to the period of World War I. Exceptionally good are books by men who participated in the Labor movement: Terence V. Powderly, *The Path I Trod: An autobiography*, 1940, and Samuel Gompers, *Seventy Years of Life and Labor*, 2 vols., 1925. For detailed accounts of two famous incidents, see Henry David, *The History of the Haymarket Affair*, 1936, and Almont Lindsay, *The Pullman Strike*, 1942. *The Proceedings of the National Guard Association of the United States*, beginning with the St. Louis meeting, 1877, reflect efforts of Guardsmen and Regular Army officers to interest the Federal Government in National Guard improvement. Their professional discussions reflect their experience with some of the labor difficulties of the time. Official publications, such as the *U.S. Statutes at Large* and the *Annual Reports of the Secretary of War*, particularly those sections that constitute the Annual Report of the Inspector General, and the Commanding General of the Army, provide essential statistics and information not available elsewhere.

CHAPTER V

# The National Guardsmen
# Create A Naval Reserve

THE MODERN United States Naval Reserve is a child of the
National Guard. The emergence of the Naval Militia crews from
a number of States in the War with Spain is an interesting by-product
of that "Splendid Little War." Contrary to what often appears to be a
general opinion, the Naval Reserve did not originate as a Federal force.
Likewise, it was not a product of the Spanish-American War. The State
Naval Militia units antedated that War and came into being as a result
of civilian interest in rendering wartime Naval service to the Nation
comparable to that which the Volunteer Militia Companies, or National
Guard, has rendered throughout every American war, Colonial as well
as National. The Naval Reserve originated in the National Guard spirit
and the National Guard concept. Indeed, it was created by National
Guardsmen.

The Nation's need for a Naval Militia was recognized prior to the War of 1812. A Bill providing for such was introduced in Congress during Jefferson's period in office. It failed to pass. During the brief War of 1812, the problem of getting men to go to sea was not so acute as was the need for ships to send to sea. The mercurial maritime policies of both England and France during the Napoleonic Wars, President Jefferson's embargo, the British impressment of seamen and the general disruption of seaborne trade had filled American ports with unemployed sailors. Thus the ships of the small Navy of 1812 competed only with the American privateers in recruiting seagoing personnel.

The maritime aspects of the Mexican War were not so burdensome that any strain was placed upon the Naval resources of the Nation. Came the Civil War, and the situation was quite different. Ninety-day gunboats for blockade duty, tinclads on the rivers and inland waters, merchantmen converted to auxiliary cruisers and hastily-built ironclads created a demand for ship crews such as America never had known. At the same time, Confederate commerce destroyers were driving the tall New England clippers and the New Bedford whaling fleets from the seven seas. Some of the best sailors in the World were on the beach, dreaming of a billet at sea. Expansion of the Union Navy made these dreams come true.

Overnight, unemployed Masters and Mates from the merchant marine began appearing in Naval uniforms and signing their names to official papers as Acting Ensigns, Acting Masters (Lieutenants J.G.), Acting Volunteer Lieutenants and Acting Volunteer Lieutenant Commanders. The crusty sea dogs of the old Navy reserved all higher ranks unto themselves and their Midshipmen disciples. That this resulted in fuzz-featured youngsters, fresh from the Academy, wearing broad stripes as Executive Officers of an ironclad or a high-seas cruiser disturbed them not at all.

In the same manner that the wardrooms became filled with silk-whiskered Lieutenant Commanders and hardy, rough junior officers twice their age from the merchant marine, the forecastles were filled with whalers who had harpooned deep sea leviathans from the South Seas to the Bering Strait, or had clawed at topsail clew-lines in wintry gales off Cape Horn. To these old shell backs a blockade station aboard a steamer off the Southern Coasts, with a chance at prize money, was a yachting trip for which a man might well pay. Accordingly, the Union Navy had few manpower problems during the Civil War. Both officers and men were recruited in Atlantic seaports from Bangor, Maine, to Baltimore, Maryland. They were sent to receiving ships and thence assigned as replacements, or to new ships being commissioned. By the end of the War, many of the ships were commanded by Acting Volunteer Lieutenants. Others, such as Captain John A. Winslow's famous

*Kearsarge,* * in her battle with C.S.S. *Alabama,* were to all practical purposes officered and manned by sailors from the merchant marine.

## THE NAVAL MILITIA IDEA AND ORIGINS

These Civil War veterans from the Union Navy did carry back to civil life a concept that a civilian might well serve his Country, through an emergency, in a Naval rather than a military capacity. Nothing came from this latent spirit until the beginnings of the "New Navy" in the '80's. Civilian Naval enthusiasts in New York sought Federal legislation for a U. S. Naval Reserve, and again in 1888, without success. They then turned to the New York Adjutant General for authority to organize. With National Guard units, under State auspices, demonstrating what might be done, it was natural that this urge toward a Naval Militia should thus manifest itself. Would-be citizen men-of-warsmen in Boston meanwhile were appealing to their Commonwealth for enabling legislation. Massachusetts responded March 17, 1888, with a law providing for not more than four Naval Companies to be known as the Naval Battalion of the Volunteer Militia. The first unit dates from March 28, 1890.

Almost simultaneously New York State was responding to the patriotic Naval interest of its citizens. A basic law was signed July 14, 1889, and a provisional Battalion was organized in New York City October 28, 1889. This has led to the claim, with some validity, that New York was first with a Naval Militia. Since this Battalion was not officially mustered-in until June 28, 1891, the official "birthday" of New York's original unit, and further, in view of the legislative dates, the primary honor appears to belong to the Bay State. The important point to remember is the indifference of most of the professional Naval officers and the Federal Government. Without the initiative of intelligent, interested, spirited citizens and a State Government close enough to them to respond to their will, America's New Navy in 1898 would have entered what promised to be a major war without any trained civilian personnel support plan whatsoever.

## THE SEAGOING MILITIA FIGHTS SPAIN

The expansion of Massachusetts' Militia to Naval crews, closely followed by New York, goaded a tardy Navy Department to a nominal

---

* In this engagement, U. S. S. *Kearsarge* had but three Regular Navy officers aboard. Capt. John A. Winslow, an out-of-age, old Regular, would have been a Commodore, or a temporary Rear Admiral, with the River fleets, or on the blockade, but for his inclination to preach sermons aboard his ship in which he denounced the President and the Administration. Thus he was shelved in permanent grade, commmanding a third-rate wooden cruiser, on a European station. His second in command, a Regular, was likewise in disrepute. As skipper of a light cruiser he had engaged Confederate shore batteries for fun while intoxicated. He thus was considered unqualified for independent command. The third Regular officer aboard the *Kearsarge* was a Midshipman. All other officers and men were from New England's merchant marine.

recognition of what was happening. In 1891, an item of $25,000 was put in the Federal Government's annual Naval appropriations for "arming and equipping naval militia." As the Naval Militia movement grew in these States and spread to other Atlantic, Gulf, Pacific Coast and Great Lakes States, appropriations were increased parsimoniously and ships, obsolete or otherwise inappropriate for high-seas fleet operations, were lent to the Naval Militia organizations, along with necessary material and equipment. An "Office of Naval Militia" appeared in the Navy Department organizational charts. On their part, the States normally appropriated funds for clothing and other items that did not come with the obsolete men-of-war. They also provided the Armories, which often were shared with Army National Guard units. Annual practice cruises became comparable to the National Guard field camps of instruction.

As of the mobilization for the War with Spain in 1898, no less than 15 States of the Union had Naval Militia units that entered the service of the Federal Government for the duration. They were California, Connecticut, Illinois, Louisiana, Maryland, Massachusetts, Michigan, New York, New Jersey, North Carolina, Ohio, Pennsylvania, Rhode Island, South Carolina and Georgia. The District of Columbia, Florida and Virginia belatedly organized and contributed units early enough in 1898 to get their personnel into active duty for the war.

Many fast merchantmen were armed with four-inch and six-inch guns and sent to sea as auxiliary cruisers. Naval Militiamen are found in large numbers among the crews of all, particularly those that saw any action or blockade duty. Six auxiliary cruisers were so completely manned by men from specific State units that their operational histories are associated with those States. Ship Commanders and their Executive Officers were assigned from the Regular Navy. These ships were U.S.S. *Yosemite,* former S. S. *El Sud,* manned by Michigan Naval Militia; U.S.S. *Yankee,* former *El Norte,* by New York; U.S.S. *Dixie,* former *El Rio,* by Maryland; U.S.S. *Prairie,* former *El Sol,* by Massachusetts; U.S.S. *Resolute,* former *Yorktown,* by New Jersey; U.S.S. *Badger,* former *Yumuru,* by Maryland. The four ships with Spanish names were fast Morgan liners. The last two were from the Old Dominion and Ward lines, respectively. The speed with which these and other auxiliary cruisers were manned, outfitted and arrived in Cuban waters is attributed by all sources to the immediate availability of the Naval Militia units of the States that were in being at the time war was declared.

Most of these cruisers performed routine scouting and blockade missions, but for one reason or another, all six came under fire in this short war. Typically, they were of 6,000 tons or more, could steam 16 knots or better, and though completely without armor, their six- to 10-gun batteries had sharp bites. Some saw more action than did the more stately battlewagons. The Michigan Naval Militiamen, for example, aboard U.S.S. *Yosemite,* covered the landing of the Marines at Guantanamo, June 10, 1898. Eighteen days later *Yosemite* and her crew of Michigan sweet-water sailors became a chapter in American Naval history by close pursuit, through rain squalls and low visibility, of S. S. *Antonio Lopez,* attempting to run the blockade into San Juan, Puerto Rico. Spanish light cruisers, *Isabel II* and *General Concha,* sortied from the harbor to aid *Antonio Lopez. Yosemite* accepted the fire of these two intruders to drive *Antonio Lopez* ashore, six miles from the harbor entrance, with her own gunfire. *Yosemite* then engaged the Spanish light cruisers and drove them back into harbor under the protecting coastal batteries of the harbor castle. During the chase of *Lopez* and subsequent engagement with the two Spanish light cruisers, *Yosemite* was repeatedly under gunfire from the cruisers and supporting batteries. Following withdrawal of the Spanish cruisers, *Yosemite* returned to the prize, and with no hopes of her capture, destroyed her with additional rounds of six-inch shells, and with occasional service practice from the six-pounders. During this phase of the operation, the Spanish torpedo boat, *Terror,* appeared on the scene with a rescue mission. She was permitted to pick up the *Lopez* crew, and after darkness may have salvaged sundry items from the abandoned and totally-wrecked *Lopez.* Weather precluded closer action.

The auxiliary cruiser, U.S.S. *Yankee,* likewise was manned by units of the New York Naval Militia. *Yankee* participated in the bombardment that silenced the Spanish forts at the entrance to the harbor of Santiago de Cuba, and joined *Yosemite* and others in covering the landing of the Marines at Guantanamo. In the last days of the war, *Yankee* also had a brush with a Spanish gunboat and a shore battery, while blockading Cienfuegos, in which one of the Militiamen was wounded. U.S.S. *Prairie* and U.S.S. *Badger,* also manned by Naval Militiamen, joined two other auxiliary cruisers in overhauling the Spanish light cruiser *Alfonso XII.* The Spanish cruiser carried six six-inch guns and two three-inch guns, but nevertheless was engaged by the four light blockaders and was driven ashore and destroyed by gunfire near Havana. U.S.S. *Resolute,* manned by Naval Militia, participated in the naval battle off Santiago de Cuba, in which Admiral Cervera's fleet was destroyed. U.S.S. *Dixie,* manned by the Maryland Naval Militia, landed supplies for Cubans, captured a few prizes, and participated in other blockade operations and on convoy service. She and her Maryland crew had the unique distinction of receiving the unconditional surrender of the third and last major seaport captured during this brief war. It was Ponce, Puerto Rico, July 27, 1898.

In addition to manning the foregoing auxiliary cruisers, or converted merchantmen, Naval Militiamen were included in the crews of numerous other ships. It is also worthy of mention that all of the Navy's 36 coastal signal stations during the Spanish-American War were officered and manned entirely by Naval Militiamen from units of the above-mentioned States. All these achievements were in spite of the fact that when the war had started there was no legal machinery set up by the Federal Government for inducting these Naval Militia units into the Federal service. The Governors of the several States solved the problem merely by granting leaves of absence to the personnel who had enlisted under State auspices, thereby permitting them to sign new enlistment papers in the Federal service. Thus, well in advance of the end of the brief war, the Navy Department came to a warm appreciation of the value of Naval units, in being, at the beginning of a crisis.

## NAVAL MILITIA AFTER 1900

Shortly after the Spanish War, the Navy Department began introducing Bills in Congress to create a Federal Naval Militia, or Reserve. It met with no success until February, 1914, when "An Act to Promote the Efficiency of the Naval Militia and for Other Purposes," often referred to as the "Naval Militia Act," was written into Federal statutes. About all it did was to apply the principles of the 1903 Dick Act for the National Guard, fully-reviewed in a later chapter, to the Naval Militia units of the States.

It soon became apparent that the Nation was drifting into World War I, and that sea power might well be a determining factor. Under this stimulus the Navy Department secured the passage of additional legislation, March 3, 1915. It brought into existence the U.S. Naval Reserve Force. Originally, this Act was designed merely to retain in a reserve the men who had been honorably discharged from the Regular Navy. A small retainer pay was established. With expansions and modifications under the Act of August 29, 1916, the U.S. Naval Reserve Force continued alongside the Naval Militia units of the States until the entire structure was completely reorganized in the Naval Reserve Act of 1938.

The self-initiated progress of the Naval Militia of the States was the only volunteer Naval reserve available to the Nation prior to 1916, when the numerically-weak Fleet Reserve began to take shape under the legislation of 1914. Meanwhile, World War I, in Europe, was two years old. The strength and progress of the Naval Militia of the States through these darkening years is best reflected by the table on facing page.

## MARYLAND'S NAVAL MILITIA WAS TYPICAL

Notwithstanding the entry of the Federal Government into the creation of a Federal Naval Militia, the States continued as active partners

144

# ORIGIN AND GROWTH OF STATE NAVAL MILITIAS
## PRIOR TO WORLD WAR I

| State | Date of First Naval Militia Unit | Reported Strength of Returns for Years Shown * | | | | |
|---|---|---|---|---|---|---|
| | | 1891 | 1895 | 1898 | 1906 | Jan. 1 1915 |
| 1. Massachusetts | March 29 1890 | 238 | 409 | 441 | 473 | 638 |
| 2. New York | June 23, 1891 | 342 | 387 | 472 | 583 | 1,462 |
| 3. California | September 3, 1891 | 371 | 313 | 386 | 345 | 791 |
| 4. North Carolina | September 23, 1891 | 101 | 255 | 230 | 110 | 370 |
| 5. Rhode Island | — — 1891 | 54 | 100 | 130 | 172 | 227 |
| 6. South Carolina | November —, 1892 | ... | 165 | 152 | 139 | 111 |
| 7. Pennsylvania | January 6, 1893 | ... | 167 | 216 | 92 | 181 |
| 8. Illinois | September 30, 1893 | ... | 199 | 523 | 629 | 622 |
| 9. Connecticut | November 27, 1893 | ... | 71 | 165 | 188 | 325 |
| 10. Michigan | March 1, 1894 | ... | 187 | 193 | 177 | 433 |
| 11. New Jersey | May 20, 1895 | ... | 216 | 364 | 265 | 443 |
| 12. Louisiana | September 11, 1895 | ... | ... | 262 | 495 | 379 |
| 13. Georgia | — — 1895 | ... | 52 | 225 | 87 | ... |
| 14. Maryland | — — 1895 | ... | 174 | 240 | 211 | 169 |
| 15. Ohio | July 26, 1896 | ... | ... | 216 | 143 | 256 |
| 16. District of Columbia | May 11, 1898 | ... | ... | ... | ... | 252 |
| 17. Florida | — — 1898 | ... | ... | 186 | ... | 74 |
| 18. Virginia | — — 1898 | ... | ... | 44 | ... | ... |
| 19. Maine | December 26, 1899 | ... | ... | ... | 55 | 194 |
| 20. Minnesota | December 15, 1903 | ... | ... | ... | 116 | 225 |
| 21. Missouri | December 18, 1905 | ... | ... | ... | ... | 249 |
| 22. Wisconsin | June 29, 1909 | ... | ... | ... | ... | 126 |
| 23. Washington | January 9, 1910 | ... | ... | ... | ... | 328 |
| 24. Oregon | August 24, 1910 | ... | ... | ... | ... | 213 |
| TOTALS | | 1,106 | 2,695 | 4,445 | 4,280 | 8,068 |

* Absence of returns for a year after date of first unit normally means lack of data for that year. In one or two instances it could mean a suspension of Naval Militia activities in that State since the previous strength return. A few States, Texas, for example, had a unit for such a brief period that data are not included in the above table.

of the Navy Department, and some of them still have Naval Militia units within the terms of the above-cited laws. Maryland is one of the States whose seagoing Militiamen officered and manned auxiliary cruisers in the Spanish-American War and which continued that naval tradition. A brief summary of that State's Naval Militia history may be accepted as a sort of case study for all.

Shortly following the Spanish-American War, the State's "Naval Brigade" was reorganized. In 1902 and 1903, "Naval Divisions" were created at Sparrows Point and Cambridge, respectively. Beginning with December, 1903, the Headquarters of the Maryland Naval Brigade was in Broadway Market Hall, Baltimore. During the great Baltimore fire of 1904, the Naval Brigade assumed the same role as an Army National Guard unit by rendering valuable service to the State and its civil population during the disaster.

Immediately following the Spanish-American War, the Navy Department put at the disposal of the Maryland Naval Militia the small, yacht-like U.S.S. *Sylvia*. In 1906 the growth of the units and training requirements brought U.S.S. *Miantonomoh* into the Maryland Navy. She was a monitor of the *Amphitrite* class. She was slow and had a low freeboard, but her heavy battery in two turrets, and light secondary guns, made her a splendid training ship for the battlewagon man-of-warsmen of that era. In 1909, U.S.S. *Somers*, a 100-ton, two-tube torpedo boat, capable of 18 knots, brought a touch of dash and speed to the Chesapeake. She was replaced in 1913 by U.S.S. *Montgomery*, a light cruiser of 2,000 tons, 17 knots, and nine five-inch guns. She still was assigned to the Maryland Naval Militia when war was declared with Germany April 6, 1917.

On that day the Maryland Military Department received telegraphic orders to mobilize the State's Naval Militia. By midnight, the command was mobilized, and on April 9, the Battalion was entrained for Philadelphia, where it reported for duty aboard Battleship *Missouri*. Upon its integration with the crew of U.S.S. *Missouri*, the Maryland Naval Militia lost its identity, and its personnel served throughout the war as a part of the U. S. Naval forces. This appears to have been the case with the Naval Militiamen of all other States that sent units into World War I.

Following World War I, the Maryland Naval Militia again was reorganized along previous lines and received U.S.S. *Cheyenne* from the Navy Department as a training ship. She was a vintage 1903 monitor of 3,255 tons, capable of 12 knots, with an 11-inch armor belt, mounting two 12-inch guns in a turret, and four-inch guns.

In 1938, the Maryland Naval Militia was reorganized and re-established as a dual force (Federal and State) to conform with new Federal legislation. On the outbreak of World War II, the men of the Naval Militia in that State and others still retaining Naval units went on active duty in their status as U. S. Naval Reservists. In Maryland, this duty began October 18, 1940, and the date is fairly well representative for the units of all other States checked.

The net result of the Naval Reserve Act of 1938 and as amended by subsequent legislation has been the elimination of the crew, or unit, concept from Naval Reserve organization, except as training vehicles. At the same time this new legislation and Naval policy brought the civilian Naval Reservists, in contrast with the Fleet Reserve and Merchant Marine Reserve, into constant supervision, management and training directly under the Navy Department.

While chapter 659 of the U. S. Code, relating to the Naval Militia, continues to recognize State participation therein and sets forth a formula for this participation and coordination, the relation of the Naval Militia of a State to the Navy Department and the Federal

Government is no longer more-or-less the same as that of Army National Guardsmen to the Department of the Army and the Federal Government. Whereas the National Guardsman acquires his Federal recognition as a member of the National Guard of the United States by virtue of his status as a competent member of the organized and recognized Militia of a State, the Naval Militiaman must qualify as a Reservist first and then voluntarily associate himself with a Naval Militia Division, or the Marine Corps Militia Unit, of a given State. No State has continued its Naval Militia tradition under this revised and reversed formula on such an extensive scale as has New York.

## CHANGING CONCEPTS IN NAVAL TRAINING MINIMIZE THE UNIT

To qualify for enlistment in New York's Naval Reserve, or as an officer or enlisted man in New York's Marine Corps component of its Naval Militia, the individual first must qualify in status, grade and rating as a Federal Reservist. Having voluntarily joined the New York Naval Militia, he acquires a status both under the State and the Federal Government. In addition to the training prescribed by the Federal authorities, these Naval Militiamen train in smallarms practice, which is purely for State missions. This is conducted under State supervision and control. Meanwhile, the Navy Department now contributes to and bears a major portion of the State's Naval Militia Armory costs. As of July 31, 1957, the strength of the New York Naval Militia was 4,032 officers and men. Illinois and Connecticut likewise continue Naval Militia units under State laws and auspices. Other States still have authorizing statutes, but apparently do not consider the game worth the candle.

A major factor in the Navy's abandonment of the crew and unit concepts of the State Naval Militia was not a result of dissatisfaction with the cooperation of the States, but was a natural by-product of a revolutionary concept in training needs for service on a modern warship. Except for Marine Corps units of Company size, small vessel crews and Naval Aviation Squadrons, the Navy claims diminishing needs for unit training. A man's value aboard a modern warship is his ability to master the technical skill pertinent to his billet, his battle station assignment. Once aboard the ship and committed to the high seas, the Navy ship commander has no problem of fitting teamwork to a terrain where each component of the team, sometimes down to the lone, individual Rifleman, is separated from his fellows and is expected to coordinate the operation through fire and movement in concert with his teammates. The ship commander has no such individualistic factor in his attack by fire and movement. When he gives the command calculated to close to within 3,000 yards for launching torpedoes, every man aboard is going to go along and do his job. There is no other place to go.*

Thus the emphasis of Navy training is not to train men as members of a combat team, capable of functioning on changing terrain under variable conditions, but to train men for billets, for slots and stations, aboard massive, mechanical monsters. Thus the Naval training units of today, meeting periodically at the Naval Armories throughout the United States, are not units in the normal, Army concept of the term. They are actually night, vocational schools providing training in skills essential to the functioning of a man-of-war and operation of all the scores of appliances and accessories connected therewith.

An application of the Navy's concept of training for billets rather than for *combat skills and constant teamwork* to Army units would be disastrous to American preparedness. Nevertheless, there are many Army professionals today who have become so enamoured of the Navy's success that they have evolved the erroneous idea that an adequate Army reserve of manpower can be reduced to a card index system of military manpower, all properly notched and punched as to individual "Military Occpational Specialty." Comes the crisis, there is nought to do but set the machines purring and throwing into neat stacks of properly addressed summons cards for all of each MOS for a field Division. Those called will presumably arrive at the rendezvous station on the date given; they will receive similarly stockpiled and card-indexed equipment, and a functional Division is theoretically in being.

All field soldiers of any Service recognize this concept as the bureaucratic dream it truly is. Even if the codified card system works 100%, which it never has for the Navy, the result would require four times as long to train into a combat organization as to take a Division of citizen-soldiers who are already functional.

Anyone disposed to challenge this logic should first check the Department of the Army's unhappy and far-from-flattering experience, Autumn 1961, in providing "fillers" for Army National Guard and Army Reserve units by Military Occupational Specialty from machine records. This experience in a quite minor, partial mobilization to support President Kennedy's Berlin diplomacy sustains the old National Guardsman's theory that *there is no such thing as an Army Ready Reservist, irrespective of what a U.S. Statute may term him, who is not a participating member of a unit undergoing regularly-scheduled and periodic*

---

* East Coast Naval Militiamen and Reservists assigned as crewmen of World War II-type destroyers found themselves on active duty in crew status and for maneuvers with NATO naval forces in 1961 as a part of the diplomatic show of strength and state of readiness in the so-called "Berlin Crisis" of that year. This experience of the Navy supports the basic philosophy of the National Guard; i.e., when men are needed suddenly, there is a simultaneous need for teams of men, or tactical units. Unless men know one another and have been working and training together, there is no team; there is no unit.

*training.* In this, most Naval officers will agree, though their vocational school type units necessarily emphasize technical skills rather than the teamwork of the Army's tactical units.

# Bibliographical Note For Chapter V

The most detailed and comprehensive research on State and National policies, as reflected by legislation, concerning the Naval Militia of the States and the resulting U. S. Naval Reserve, is an unpublished Ph.D. thesis: Harold T. Wiand, *History of the Development of the United States Naval Reserve, 1889-1941,* University of Pittsburgh, 1952. There is also a bound ms. copy in the Navy Department Library, Washington, D. C. The *U. S. Statutes at Large* and various session enactments of the several States are widely available. An official Navy Department publication; *Laws and Regulations, State and National, Relating to the Naval Militia,* Washington, 1895, brings into most convenient and comparative form all the pertinent early legislation on this subject. The *Proceedings of the Association of the Naval Militias of the United States for 1895, 1897,* and *1905,* are valuable to the historian. Most of the *Annual Reports of the Secretary of Navy* for the era covered by this chapter take note of the strengths, and obsolete Navy ships on loan to, or otherwise in possession of the States. These *Reports* also reveal the Federal funds expended incident to the Naval Militia Battalions and Brigades of the several States. Since most of the officers and men of the Naval Militia units of the States were scattered through the Fleets and Naval establishments in most mobilizations, there is no Naval Militia literature comparable to the thousands of Company, Battalion and Regimental histories of conventional National Guard units that have followed every war. New York provides a rare exception in the *Yankee Book Committee* (Editors), *U.S.S. Yankee On the Blockade,* 1928. There are many magazine articles, some of them by Naval officers and officials who wrote from first-hand information and professional experience with resulting divergence of opinions. Among these the following are significant: Secretary of Navy Josephus Daniels, "The Naval Reserve—A Great National Asset," *Saturday Evening Post,* May 21, 1921; Rear Adm. C. F. Goodrich, "Newberry's Naval Reforms," *North American Review,* Vol. 191, pp. 155-67 and 340-55; Lt. C. C. Gill, U. S. N., "State Naval Volunteers for the Reserve Fleets of the U. S. Navy," *Naval Institute Proceedings,* Vol. 40, pp. 647-660; J. W. Miller, "A Naval Militia and a Naval Reserve," *Forum,* Vol. 12, p. 262-69; F. H. Potter, "Naval Reserves, A Story of Enthusiasm," *Outlook,* Vol. 118, p. 444-7. Rear Adm. Julius A. Furer's widely-available article, "Naval Reserve," *The Encyclopedia Americana,* Vol. 20, pp. 1-5, tells more and with greater brevity than most.

## CHAPTER VI

# Mr. McKinley Calls The Guard

THE SINKING of the second-class battleship *Maine,* in Havana Harbor February 15, 1898, was not the cause of the Spanish-American War. Had that already-obsolescent man-of-war disintegrated with an explosion in an Italian harbor that same day and year, it would have caused no war—just another investigation. But in a Spanish port, it was a hot blast of salt on an old, international canker sore that was blood-red raw from more than a hundred years of irritation.

From American independence until 1812, volunteer Militia units and a few Regular Companies had policed an uneasy peace along an undefined Spanish Empire border, Florida and Louisiana. The need for a Louisiana Purchase had grown from the mercurial, unneighborly policies of Spain through the decades before Napoleon retrieved the region for France. In the face of a changed situation, Napoleon decided to sell. This purchase in 1803 merely extended the Spanish-American bleeding sore to the Sabine River and beyond, without curing the Spanish Florida problem. Tennessee's Guardsman, Major General

151

Andrew Jackson, led a force of Southern Militia units to pave the way for the Florida Purchase of 1819. It was his highly-controversial Florida Campaign.

## THE SPANISH WAR A RESULT OF
## CENTURY OF IRRITATIONS

Texan independence and the successful secession and freedom of most of Spain's New World colonies did not cure the sore. Spain clung to Cuba, Puerto Rico and other lesser West India holdings. From these Spain continued naval operations against her former colonies, the independence of none of which she was willing to admit. She and possible allies, such as France in the Maximilian venture of 1863-67, were a constant threat to the Monroe Doctrine. Spain's tyranny and inhumane oppressions in Cuba more than once resulted in Americans facing firing squads before traditional stone walls. These medieval tyrannies in remnants of a decadent empire became a stench in the nostrils of the New World.

The sinking of the *Maine* was merely the incident that moved the American people to a firm resolve, as stern as it was at times ebulliently violent, to cure the international sore by amputating Cuba from the Spanish Empire. If the unwilling Empire died under the surgeon's knife, the operation still would be a success. Americans of that vintage knew naught of the Spanish Empire other than 100 years of un-neighborly duplicity.

This firm resolve meant war. Of course, America was but partially prepared. Her Navy was modest in size but reasonably modern. This was largely because the ships retained from the Civil War had literally worn-out or rotted-away. They had to be replaced. Moreover, America was feeling the quickened pulse of steam, industrialization and the new technologies. The long, lean, fast ocean greyhounds under British and German flags, that dominated the North Atlantic trade lanes, at last had convinced even the clipper ship owners that steam had come to stay. Even so, some of the older steam and steel warships Commodore Dewey led into Manila Bay were rigged for auxiliary sails, thanks to traditionalism. On paper, Spain's fleets were equally modern. In some classes—heavy, modern cruisers, for example, and fast, modern destroyers—America was outclassed. But Spanish maintenance was incredibly bad, training was poor, and gunnery a yet-to-be-discovered art. But these were unknown factors as America took the path to war.

The Regular Army in 1898 was better-equipped than it ever had been throughout its entire history. The breech-loading, single shot, .45-caliber, side-hammer Springfield of 1873 had been replaced. For 19 years it had been the official shoulder weapon. It was replaced by the .30-caliber Krag-Jorgensen repeaters. With 53,508 rifles and 14,895 carbines of this excellent new weapon issued and in arsenals, there was obviously more than enough for the war strength of existing mounted and Infantry Regular Regiments. Certainly there were not enough to outfit a force sufficient to underwrite the death knell of an ancient empire that still had holdings as far-flung as the Philippines and the West Indies. The Guard Regiments were the recipients of the old Springfields in lieu of the Civil War muzzle-loaders recently of issue. Other essential items for outfitting an army were also modern, but in quantity were somewhat in proportional shortages to the Krag-Jorgensen rifles and carbines. Clothing had been modernized but there were no patterns or materials for tropical warfare. Shortages were due to parsimonious appropriations, not through lack of knowledge, planning or military-minded desires.

In personnel strength the Regular Army component was weak, also thanks to inadequate budgets. These had been barely sufficient to keep the 2,143 officers and 26,040 enlisted men in the Regular Establishment as of April 1, 1898. Of these, 12,828 enlisted men were distributed among the 25 Infantry Regiments. For war strength Regiments that proposed 12 Companies, grouped in three Battalions, with each Company at a war strength of 106 for a Regimental total of 1,309 enlisted men, one readily realizes that some of the Companies in the professional formations were on paper only. In truth, Regular Regiments of eight Companies, in being, were normal as of 1897. None were at war strength within existing Companies. The same situation applied to other Arms of the Service. It was expected that wartime recruiting would fill them.

## DECISIVE ACTION OFFSETS LACK OF PREPAREDNESS

Much denunciation, criticism and abuse have been heaped upon President McKinley and his Cabinet for the lack of preparedness. Actually, nothing ever has been written of them that could not have been said with equally abusive emphasis of Presidents Lincoln, Polk, and Madison, when they embarked upon major military efforts. It was the McKinley Administration's misfortune to be at the helm when modern news reporting came of age, thanks to a vast telegraph and cable net, rotary presses, unlimited paper and a scoop-hungry public that wanted a new sensation with each breakfast.

Never in the history of warfare have so many high-priced journalists reported with such little restraint and with such profound ignorance upon the military efforts of so few. Moreover, in the naivete of that era, the public had not learned that war is expensive and that emergency-created haste leads to inevitable waste and unavoidable inefficiency. The "scandals" of the Spanish-American War were mere morning dew compared to the torrents of wastage in World Wars I and II that were glossed-over with such soothing, stock phrases as "subject to re-negotiation." Moreover, McKinley and his Cabinet knew no patterns for throttling the Press through classified documents and bureaus of "public information" that manifested themselves in an embryonic way in 1917-18 and reached full bloom in World War II. Actually, for the men they put in the field, for the far-flung operations sustained, and the quick victory achieved at such low costs in lives and money, the Spanish-American War record was a model of immediate, effective, decisive action compared with the extravagant, inefficient gropings of World Wars I and II.

Congress declared war April 24, 1898. By June 23, Major General William R. Shafter's reinforced V Army Corps had a beachhead on a far shore and was in cooperative efforts with the Cuban guerrilla Resistance. In eagerness for more and more American supplies and determination to coordinate effort with no one, the Cuban Insurgents were little better than the French Forces of the Interior, as of 1944-45. By July 10, 1898, Shafter's army nevertheless had besieged and captured a major seaport. Three convoys also were enroute to the Philippines. At home an Army of 200,000 was in being and preparing for service anywhere on any front.

And all of these land achievements, ignoring the aggressive naval operations, were without having to promote a single war bond issue! Such prompt, aggressive vigor is unequalled by the record of any war in American history.

Moreover, the speed with which a large field force was brought into being, and the promptness with which the façade of the Spanish Empire was exposed, deprived Spain of any aid or abetment by any of the colonially-ambitious European powers which, during that era, were fishing eagerly in all troubled waters for their own aggrandizement. These are facts no informed student of the great, imperial game of geopolitics can deny. Too much of the adverse evaluations of the conduct of the Spanish-American War has been by domestic historians with a greater knowledge of back files of the muckraking Press of the day (which they have relied upon as source materials) than they have had of the military problems inherent in the prompt and effective offensive launched by the much-abused Mr. McKinley and his Navy and War Secretaries, John D. Long and Russell A. Alger.

## LEGISLATION FOR U. S. VOLUNTEER REGIMENTS

If McKinley and his Cabinet, following the sinking of the *Maine,* did not unduly concern themselves with manpower planning, it was because they believed the historic American system was fully adequate. And, indeed, it proved to be. They had seen it function to victory through four long, bitter years of strife. Secretary of War Alger had risen from Private to Colonel of a Michigan Regiment, 1861-65. He had served as Governor of Michigan. He understood the system thoroughly. The same could be said of Mr. McKinley, who had ended his Civil War career as a Major in an Ohio Regiment and thereafter had been Governor of his State. Long, as a three-term Governor of Massachusetts, was thoroughly familiar with a State's capabilities in fielding organized military manpower. That they were more than right is evidenced by the fact that they did get more-than-adequate manpower in immediately-constituted units on their initial Call—so much more than the sluggish supply personnel in the Regular Army could cope with, that this became another club of abuse from the headline-hunting, critical Press. They considered legislation quite satisfactory that put recruiting, organizing of Regiments, and designation of their officers upon the States, such as was enacted. There was some immediate agitation for direct Federal recruiting of U. S. Volunteer Regiments. All agreed that the Regular Army could be expanded both in men and units to 64,719 officers and men. In this they would have been correct had the war lasted a few months longer.

Most of the Governors and their Adjutants General were reading the signs of the times and making plans of their own, if and when the military Call might come. Some of them viewed with apprehension and disapproval a direct volunteer measure then being pressed. The protest was made that the Guard units were entitled to a priority of service under any Call and could not be by-passed by Federal legislation creating a direct Federal Militia that might deny them that privilege.

Proponents of the Bill for U. S. Volunteers, who appeared to be speaking with the support of a few young professionals in the War Department bureaucracy, argued that some State laws, and such Federal law as then existed for the governance of the Militia, precluded utilization of National Guard units beyond the limits of their individual States. This, they argued, eliminated the Guardsmen from any participation in hostilities against Spain.

But the Guardsmen had an old and tested formula for meeting this. In the first place, the Federal law could be repealed as easily as the "Volunteer Bill" could be enacted. In the second place, the Guard Regiments could be mustered and given an opportunity to volunteer en masse, take a new oath and individually sign such enlistment papers as the war Call might contemplate. For this the Mexican War offered precedents.

Spain's handing the American Minister his passport, April 21, removed all roadblocks for military legislation, including that for Regulars and direct creation of U. S. Volunteer Regiments. In final form, a ceiling of 3,000 officers and men, to be recruited at large and organized into Troops, Companies, Battalions or Regiments of men possessing special qualifications, temporarily settled the question of U. S. Volunteers. This act promptly was perverted in behalf of a brilliant Assistant Surgeon (Captain) who always had wanted to be a Line officer. He was Leonard Wood, then on duty as White House Physician. He and his good friend, Assistant Secretary of Navy Theodore Roosevelt, thought cowboys from Arizona, New Mexico and Texas, with a few polo players and spirited club men from Harvard and Yale, had the exact "special qualifications" under the law to form a Cavalry Regiment. It became the 1st U. S. Volunteer Cavalry, but better known, thanks to Roose-veltian-inspired publicity, as the "Rough Riders." Two politicians with better service records but less influence, Messrs. J. L. Long and Melvin Grigsby, were given Federal commissions as Colonels of the 2nd and 3rd Regiments of U. S. Volunteer Cavalry. Without the sympathetic publicity and without the subsequent prominence and literary skill* of their senior personnel, these two Regiments have been lost to history.

Nineteen days after the legislation that spawned three Regiments of Cavalry "specialists," Congress was called upon and immediately passed another Bill for three Volunteer Regiments of specialists as Engineers with an aggregate ceiling of 3,500 officers and men. This was probably the intent of the first Bill. This second measure also author-ized a volunteer force of 10,000 enlisted men in 10 Regiments possess-ing immunity from at least one tropical disease. They became known as "The Immunes."

No one Regiment of these additional U. S. Volunteers, not even the Engineers, was allowed more than three Regular officers, normally the Colonel and two Field officers. Four of the "Immune Regiments" were Colored. Most of their Captains and Lieutenants were Sergeants and Corporals from the 9th and 10th Cavalry or 24th and 25th In-fantry Regiments, Colored Regulars from the Reconstruction Era. Similar temporary commissions to outstanding NCO's from Regular Line Regi-ments provided Company-grade officers for the remaining six Regiments of "Immunes." Nearly all the officers for the three Engineer Regiments were direct from civil life.

Thus ended the Federal Militia legislation until after the Spanish-American War finished. Note that these encroachments upon State responsibilities for volunteer military manpower for the duration of a crisis were in the name of specialists, for a special need. The presump-

---

* As a young Army Medic, Leonard Wood had ditched his medicine chest to lead a Platoon-size column in pursuit of Chief Geronimo. Theodore Roosevelt had been a Captain in the New York National Guard. T.R.'s book, *The Rough Riders*, was criticized for its "erroneous title" by one wisecracking contemporary. He held it should be titled *Teddy, Alone in Cuba*. Both T.R. and Wood, of course, brought a touch of genius to every task, whether large or small.

tion was that no one State could turn-out such specialized personnel. At least one of the Regiments was recruited entirely within Georgia.

## THE CALL TO THE STATES

Meanwhile, President McKinley had, pursuant to powers written into the Declaration of War, addressed his Call to the States for 125,000 men on April 23, actually the day before war was officially declared. The Call followed the pattern set by Lincoln, and likewise troop unit allocations were to the States according to their population. The Call was confined first to the Organized Militia, or National Guard, of each State, and in cases where the units thereof fell short of the Regimental quota of that State, then the Call became applicable to the citizens at large within that State. In short, a Governor could not recruit new units until existing unit possibilities were exhausted.

Within a survey of the National Guard as a Nationwide institution, space does not permit a detailed treatment of the impact of this Call upon each State and the manner in which each and every one of them met its quotas. A few, by forehanded promptness, appear to have been able to squeeze-in more than their share of the Call to the handicap of other States that were not quite so handy with the paperwork. But to borrow a term from the stock market, the Call issue was greatly oversubscribed. An examination of a large number of Regimental histories and reference to representative State records reveals minor differences in detail and method, but the general pattern of conditions and procedure was pretty much the same in all States.

Large and thinly-populated Western States such as Wyoming and Nevada were privileged to provide little more than a Battalion, or Squadron, each. At the same time, the four most populous States of that era each made contributions in units well in excess of Division strength for the Tables of Organization of that day. They were as follows: New York, 16,629 officers and men; Pennsylvania, 12,315; Illinois, 10,942, and Ohio, 10,042. The average for the States of the Union as a whole was slightly more than one Brigade; i.e., less than 4,000 officers and men. Thus, were one to pick a typical State, its contribution would be three Regiments of Infantry, a Battalion of Artillery (or Squadron of Cavalry), plus a separate Company, Troop or Battery, if not a Medical unit.

The terms of the Call, however, did not allow the States to provide units larger than Regiments. All Generals and Staff officers for higher headquarters were to be commissioned and assigned by the Federal Government. The Governor of any State was privileged to call on the War Department for the assignment of Regulars to the State's levy, but not to exceed one per Regiment. This practice later was viewed as a mistake. So many of the Company-grade officers of the

157

small, professional, commissioned officer corps of only 1,611 Infantry, Cavalry, and Artillery officers sought and found promotions in the National Guard Regiments of their native or adopted States, or similarly in one of the new Regiments of Federal Militia Volunteers, that the Artillery Battalions, Cavalry and Infantry Regiments of the Regulars suffered sadly in strength, supplies, and training. Indeed, the Spanish-American War was over and the Philippine troubles were well along before the Regular Army formations achieved the strength of 64,719 officers and men that was authorized at the outbreak of the war. This expansion goal was achieved belatedly by permitting mustered-out Guardsmen to enter the Regulars, without loss of rank, or to continue in the service on what is now called extended active duty status.

The Regular Regiments that were sent on the Santiago Expedition and to Puerto Rico were beefed-up to approximate war strength, but at the expense of Regular formations with no immediate, far-shore mission. All this suggests strongly that Regular units did suffer. Some professionals did achieve temporary promotions by assignments in State Regiments, but the number appears to be small, though no precise statistics appear readily available. It is most likely that the Regular Regiments lost far more of their officers to the creation of the numerous Brigade, Divisional and Army Corps Staffs and Headquarters and to the new Regiments of U. S. Volunteers than to the Guard Regiments.

## IMPACT OF THE CALL ON A TYPICAL STATE

While there were minor variations in the impact of the Call and in the manner in which each of the States met its obligation, the major pattern was essentially the same in all. Because Minnesota, in 1898, was quite close to being statistically an average-size State with an average-size National Guard under a typical State administration, it is chosen here as a sort of case study illustrative of the manner in which practically all the States met the same situation.

Shortly after the sinking of the *Maine,* the Governor and the Adjutant General began getting requests looking toward the creation of new Company-size units. Individuals wanted to know how they could serve. The office of the Adjutant General began receiving queries for military manuals and books on tactics. Existing Company-size units began adopting Resolutions requesting, through channels, that the Governor call the President's attention to their immediate availability, if and when he might need some soldiers. This mass of correspondence caused Adjutant General Hermann Muehlberg to prepare for his office, and that of the Governor, a compendium of Minnesota and Federal laws concerning the organized and uniformed units of the National Guard. In some towns that had no National Guard unit, a military

158

society was formed and began drilling in hopes of recognition and a Call if war came.

In 1898 the field units of the National Guard, State of Minnesota, were commanded by Brigadier General William B. Bend, N.G.S.M., who had a small Headquarters and Staff. His command consisted of the 1st, 2nd, and 3rd Minnesota Infantry Regiments, a Medical Detachment, and the 1st Battalion, Minnesota Field Artillery. Prior to the war headlines of early '98, the entire Brigade had a total strength of slightly more than 2,000 officers and men. The 1st and 2nd Regiments had 10 Companies each, conforming to the complete Regimental organization that had prevailed during and since the Civil War. The 3rd Minnesota, following the pattern of peacetime Reduction Tables then prevalent for the Regular Army Infantry Regiments, had in being only eight Companies. The Companies, whether the Regiment had eight or 10 in being, had a strength of not more than 76 men each, the ceiling allowed by the "Peace Footing."

The War Department appears to have avoided any mobilization alert orders, warning instructions, or any hints as to preliminary plans, because it might smack of "jingoism." Alert orders were not necessary anyway. Under the fishbowl conditions of the day, and with every newspaper printing as much of the actions, orders and presumed opinions of all top military, naval and civilian officials as they saw fit, there was not much the War Department could have told either the Minnesota Governor or the Adjutant General that they did not already know. And they knew the Administration was maintaining an attitude of restraint compared to the rising public opinion throughout the Nation. In any event, General Muehlberg, as late as March 31, thought it desirable to restrain the war enthusiasm of his units rather than to excite it—though his personal sentiments were strictly "jingoistic." Some of his units certainly were exceeding the reduced, peace strength Tables.

On April 16, word came from Washington that the President might call on the Militias of the States to provide men for Federal service. The Governor called a conference of his top Guardsmen. An order went out in his name that all units would go to 100 men, but all in excess of 76 of each Company would be carried as "provisional recruits." It also appears that some cognizance was taken of the self-organized units in various towns of the State that had elected officers, were drilling and which had so informed the State authorities with a desire to become integrated with the State's National Guard. The day following the above authorization, Company Commanders of recognized units began reporting strengths in excess of 100. The Captain at Albert Lea apparently was reading the newspapers as to the proposed new Tables of war-strength Infantry Companies. He reported he had enlisted exactly 106.

159

Came President McKinley's Call of April 23. It was handed to the Press rather than sent to the Governors. Not until the 25th did the Governor receive word as to exactly what was expected of his State. It was a telegram from the Secretary of War: "The number of troops from your State . . . will be three regiments of infantry. It is the wish of the President that the regiments of the National Guard, or State Militia, be used as far as their numbers will permit . . . Please wire . . . what equipments, ammunition, arms, blankets, tents, etc., you have and what additional you will require. Please also state when troops will be ready for muster into United States [service]. Details follow by mail."

The same day the Governor issued a Proclamation containing the usual two or three "Whereas" paragraphs and a longer "Now therefore" conclusion that gave notice that Volunteers would be received at the City of St. Paul to the strength of three Regiments of Infantry, of 12 Companies each. The term of service was two years, unless sooner discharged. At the same time the proclamation went to the Press, the Adjutant General, in the name of the Governor, flashed to each of the Unit Commanders, including those of Artillery since one Infantry Regiment was short for muster, a telegram that ended with ". . . as the three National Guard Regiments of infantry of this state have signified their desire of entering the service of the United States as volunteers, The First, Second, and Third Regiments of Infantry, of the National Guard, State of Minnesota, will immediately make preparations to report at these headquarters upon receipt of telegraphic orders . . ."

A conference of Field officers and Staff officers completed details. The State Fair Grounds in St. Paul were redesignated "Camp Ramsey." All Companies would proceed there according to plan, all units to be present in St. Paul by 11:00 Friday morning, April 29, 1898. The State Capitol was the rallying point whence the Companies, properly grouped into their Regiments, were to march to Camp Ramsey, located between St. Paul and Minneapolis. Since Colonel Joseph Bobleter was senior of the three Colonels, and no Brigade Headquarters had been activated, he and his 2nd Minnesota Infantry led the march. It soon took on more of the character of a parade.

## THE REGIMENTS IN THE STATE CAMPS

Camp organization and training were initiated without delay. They were to be at "Camp Ramsey" but 17 days, during which time training was interrupted only by the necessary physical examinations and mustering-in by a board of three Regular Army officers, headed by Surgeon Philip F. Harvey, from nearby Fort Snelling.

Five days after the arrival in camp, the Adjutant General published General Orders renumbering and redesignating all three Regiments. Minnesota had sent into the Civil War Regiments of Volunteer Infantry numbered 1st through 11th inclusive. In the interests of historical clarity, or because the old veterans of the original Civil War 1st, 2nd and 3rd Regiments resented this usurpation of their numbers by new and untested units, or perhaps because the officers and men of the new units preferred distinctive numbers of their own, is not of record. Doubtless the changes were incident to all three considerations. The 2nd Minnesota Infantry, being commanded by the senior Colonel, was considered the senior Regiment, hence it was officially redesignated the "12th Regiment of Infantry, Minnesota Volunteers." The 1st became the 13th, and the 3rd became the 14th.* In the parlance of the day, such Volunteer Regiments in the field became known by the simpler and shorter name of 13th Minnesota, 33rd Michigan, 2nd Wisconsin, 1st Texas Cavalry; 1st Battalion, Ohio Light Artillery, or 1st Massachusetts Heavy Artillery. When no Arm was indicated, the Regiment was Infantry.

Minnesota Regiments, like those of many other States, reported for duty on the assumption that each Company would have a Table of Organization strength of at least 100 men, and from Press reports on new Tables of Organization, most would likely have 106. Thus the three Regiments, as of M-day, were 3,755 officers and men. The Mustering Board, however, came with the word that only 81 enlisted men would be accepted per Company. This cut the strength to 3,096 officers and men. Thus, 659 had to be sent home.

The actual "muster-in ceremony" came on May 6. It was simple but impressive. The Mustering Officer questioned the Company officer as to the character of the men presented, made a personal inspection of the line, and called the roll. Each man responded to his name by moving from the old Company formation to a new, double line facing the Mustering Board. There, with right hands upraised and heads uncovered, the newly-formed Company took the oath en masse, acknowledged their signatures on the mustering papers, and were dismissed. From examination of a large number of Regimental histories, it is quite apparent that substantially the same procedure took place in every State in the Union. In some cases, however, the "muster-in" was by the entire Regiment rather than in Company units.

On Monday, May 16, the Regiments left St. Paul by rail. The 12th Minnesota and the 14th Minnesota went to Camp Thomas in Tennessee, with expectations of seeing Cuba before the War ended. The 13th Minnesota entrained for San Francisco. Dewey's unexpected victory at Manila Bay was expediting the creation of a Philippine expeditionary force.

* Minnesota was not unique in starting Regimental numbers where the Civil War series had ended. Kansas, Indiana and Iowa, for example, independently followed the same rule. Wisconsin, Illinois, and most Southern States, however, are illustrative of the more common practice of starting a new series beginning with one. Some older States activated historic numbers, such as 71st New York.

This Regiment actually joined the 1st California, the 2nd Oregon, the 1st Colorado, the 1st Nebraska, the 10th Pennsylvania, the 1st Idaho, the 1st Wyoming, the 1st North Dakota; two Regular Army Regiments, less two Battalions; two Batteries of Utah Artillery, and New York's Astor Volunteer Battery, along with one Battalion of the 3rd Artillery organized as Infantry, and oddments of Signal Corps, Engineer and hospital units, to constitute Major General Wesley Merritt's Philippine Expedition.

This force, later reinforced by California Batteries A and D, the 51st Iowa Infantry, the 20th Kansas, the 1st Montana, Nevada Cavalry troops, 1st South Dakota, 1st Tennessee, 1st Washington, and Battery A, Wyoming, were the troops that liberated the Philippines and fought the initial and most trying campaigns of the so-called pacification of the Philippines.

The entraining of the three Minnesota Regiments, however, did not take the Governor and his Adjutant General out of the military business. On May 25 President McKinley issued his Second Call for volunteers. Press reports suggested Minnesota's quota would be 1,723 men. The Adjutant General (now more experienced) began thinking in terms of two Regiments.

But he and his Governor were without knowledge of staff intentions in the War Department. At last the size of a Company had been determined at exactly 106 men. Minnesota had sent out three Regiments with only 81 men to a Company. Would not Minnesota recruit these shortages and build-up the Regiments already at Camp Thomas and San Francisco? Having met this objective, would the Governor provide the United States with one additional Regiment of Volunteers?

The Governor, in effect, told the War Department that he wished it would make up its mind, as he already had sent home nearly 1,000 men from the First Call, but in the meantime, Minnesota would do her duty. To bring the 12th and 14th at Chickamauga, Tennessee, and the 13th Minnesota at San Francisco, to war strength, recruiting parties arrived back in the States to enlist men for these units. Their efforts were charged to the Second Call.

The remainder of Minnesota's Second Call quota was made up by the creation of the 15th Minnesota, officered by former National Guardsmen, under a Colonel John C. Shandrew, who previously had commanded the old 3rd Regiment, National Guard of Minnesota. Captain Harry A. Leonhaeuser, a Minnesotan who had gone to West Point and long served in the Regular Army's 25th U. S. Infantry, was commissioned Lieutenant Colonel, from his Regular Army status. He appears to have been the only Regular Army officer that the Governor borrowed for this mobilization.

Since there were more than enough Companies already in existence in the State of Minnesota, drilling without pay in hopes of full recognition prior to the Call, the activation of the 15th Minnesota by the State Adjutant General closely paralleled that of its three predecessors. Actually, this Guard Regiment fared somewhat better in matters of supply, because the Governor and Adjutant General had planned for two Regiments on the Second Call, rather than one. The 15th Minnesota was mobilized July 4 at Camp Ramsey. By August 23, the 15th was en route to Camp Meade, near Middletown, Pennsylvania. Neither the 12th Minnesota, the 14th Minnesota, nor the 15th Minnesota saw combat. The first two were mustered-out the following November. The 15th was kept on active duty until March 27, 1899.

## TYPICAL TERMS OF SERVICE BY GUARD REGIMENTS

The 13th Minnesota Volunteer Infantry and the other National Guard Regiments that had been rushed to the Philippines continued on active duty long after their sister Regiments, which had gone elsewhere, were back home and had been mustered-out. Most of these short-termers were out by September. Some of the Regiments created in the Second Call for volunteers continued on active service after the armistice and well into the following Autumn. A few continued on active duty within the United States, or on occupation service in Puerto Rico or Cuba, as late as March following the Senate's ratification of the peace treaty, February 6, 1899. As noted above, such was the destiny of the 15th Minnesota, which was not back home until the 15th of March following the Senate's ratification of the treaty.

Inasmuch as all the Volunteer Regiments in the Philippines likewise were inducted into Federal service for two years, or the duration of the war, dependent upon the shorter period, the National Guard Regiments under Generals H. W. Lawton and Arthur MacArthur in the Philippines found themselves hotly engaged in suppressing Aguinaldo's Tagalog Rebellion almost a year after their terms of active duty actually had expired. They continued without complaint, however, until Regular Army Regiments, or newly-created Regiments of U. S. Volunteers under the Act of March 2, 1899, had arrived in Luzon to take over their positions. This was in spite of the fact that many newspapers and politicians on the home front were clamoring to "bring the boys home."

It was not until June, 1899 that the American commanders in the Philippines were able to pinch-out these National Guard units for embarkation home. Those officers and men of the 13th Minnesota who desired to remain in the Philippines and continue the fight through the full pacification program were given an opportunity to accept discharge as of the 17th of July, 1899, in Manila. They immediately were reenlisted in grade and absorbed into recently-arrived Regular or Federal Volunteer units. Thus were repeated the replacement practices of the Mexican War.

Most of the officers and men of the 13th Minnesota Infantry who elected to remain were absorbed immediately into the 36th and 37th newly-created Regiments of U. S. Volunteer Infantry. Others preferred the 11th U. S. Volunteer Cavalry. These new Regiments of U. S. Volunteers were pursuant to the Act of March 2, 1899.

Less these losses, the 13th Minnesota Volunteer Infantry embarked in Manila August 10, and returned to the United States under the identical officers, in most instances, with whom they had left their home stations for St. Paul in May, 1898. The Regiment was mustered-out officially at San Francisco October 2, 1899, and the officers and men proceeded to their homes as individuals.

Other National Guard Regiments that had substantially the same record, with slight variations in arrival and departure dates to and from the Philippines, were the 1st California; Batteries A and D, California Artillery; 1st Colorado Infantry, 1st Idaho Infantry, 51st Iowa Infantry, 20th Kansas Infantry, 1st Montana Infantry, 1st Nebraska Infantry; 1st Troop, Nevada Cavalry; 1st North Dakota Infantry, 2nd Oregan Infantry, 10th Pennsylvania Infantry, 1st South Dakota Infantry, 1st Tennessee Infantry; Batteries A and B, Utah Artillery; 1st Washington Infantry, 1st Wyoming Infantry, and the Wyoming Battery, Light Artillery.

All of them appear to have left varying percentages of their personnel in the Philippines as officer and enlisted replacements for Regular Army or U. S. Volunteer Regiments. All rendered dangerous, arduous and debilitating service a full year longer than the hostilities of the war for which they had enlisted. This was without any revision of their original terms of service whatsoever.

In commenting upon it, Secretary of War Elihu Root wrote: "This is an exhibition of sturdy patriotism which it seems to me has never been fully appreciated. No complaint ever came from these soldiers on account of the hardships . . . or for the delay in being returned to their homes after they were entitled to discharge. They yielded to the situation as cheerfully as they endured the great and fatiguing privations . . . The nation indeed owes these noble soldiers a debt . . ."

## STATISTICAL SUMMARY OF ARMY COMPONENTS

In the Spanish-American War the National Guard contributed 8,207 officers and 164,747 enlisted men. Most of the former were of Company and Field grade. A few of the Colonels such as Frederick Funston of Kansas were elevated to General Officer incident to training assignments, or combat. These officers and men were in 139 Regiments of Infantry, two Regiments of Cavalry, one Regiment of Heavy Artillery, 11 separate

Infantry Battalions, 40 separate Companies of Infantry, 41 separate Batteries of light Artillery, and 16 separate Troops of Cavalry.

There were only 763 officers and 16,992 enlisted men in the Federal (U. S. Volunteers) Militia of this mobilization. They were in the units created under the Act of April 22, 1898, and under the Act of May 11, 1898. The first of these two war measures, it will be recalled, made possible the recruiting of the 1st Regiment, U. S. Volunteer Cavalry ("Rough Riders"), which was recruited largely in Arizona, New Mexico and West Texas; and the 2nd and 3rd Regiments, U. S. Volunteer Cavalry, from the Dakotas and Far West, respectively. Of these, only the "Rough Riders," dismounted and less one Squadron, ever fired a hostile shot. The combined aggregate strength of the three Volunteer Cavalry Regiments as of induction was 3,056 officers and men. Under the second of the above laws, the 1st, 2nd and 3rd Regiments, U. S. Volunteer Engineers (Federal Organized Militia), were created. Induction strength of the "Brigade of U. S. Volunteer Engineers" was 3,431 officers and men.

The 9,965 officers and men who constituted the remaining units of U. S. Volunteers represented something of a novelty in American military history. They were distributed among 10 Regiments of U. S. Volunteer Infantry, 1st to 10th inclusive, and are commonly known to history as the "Ten Regiments of Immunes." In theory, no one was allowed to enlist in one of these who was not immune to one or more tropical diseases. In final form, six of these Regiments were of White troops, four were Colored units. They engaged in no combat, but some of them did arrive in Cuba and Puerto Rico as occupation troops after the withdrawal of Shafter's V Corps from Cuba and the return of Major General Nelson A. Miles expedition, the I Corps, from Puerto Rico.

The Regular Army commanders in Cuba and the War Department in Washington found these "Immunes" quite as capable of creating political pressures and headaches as any contingent of State-recruited Regiments were. When the ever-zealous and news-hungry, teeming corps of Press correspondents in Cuba panicked the American people with news of the "Round Robin Incident" arising from the yellow fever epidemic in the V Corps (Regulars)*, the pressure was immediately on to pull those units out of Cuba to Montauk, New York. They should be replaced by fresh troops.

The 3rd Regiment, U.S. Volunteer Infantry (Immunes), was one of those rushed to the much-publicized yellow fever area in eastern Cuba. Senator A. O. Bacon of Georgia at once became vociferous. His

---

* Shooting was still in progress, though surrender of Santiago de Cuba was imminent at the time of this incredible episode. The epidemic in the V Corps was not as severe as was World War I influenza among home and overseas units in 1918.

complaint, written August 5, 1898, from Macon, Georgia, held that this Regiment had been recruited largely in his State. They were "no more immune from yellow fever than any other volunteer regiment . . . No proof was demanded or desired as to their immunity from yellow fever. To send these young men and boys to Santiago at this time . . . is to expose them to the same deadly peril from yellow fever as is now said to confront those who, having reaped honors, are now demanding to be sent to the northern seaside." The Secretary of War reports that Senator Bacon's was but one of many protests concerning the utilization of these "immune volunteers" as occupation troops following the armistice. This is in sharp contrast with the year of uncomplaining extended service rendered by the large task force, approximately an Army Corps of National Guard troops in the Philippines.

There were a few thousand other volunteers in the Spanish-American War who were in neither National Guard nor U.S. Volunteer Regiments. Of these, about 1,000 were officers on direct appointment to the Volunteers by the President. Some were General Officers, such as Major General Joe Wheeler, who had been a youthful and dashing Confederate Cavalry commander in the Civil War. Many other commissions, however, were to sundry rear area staff assignments, supply posts, and doctors to the much-criticized Medical Corps. About 15,000 enlisted men appear to have been permitted to enter various Army units of Regular Volunteers, or National Guard volunteer categories as individuals and enlisted for the duration of the war only.

The remaining troops that saw service in the Spanish-American War may be categorized as Regulars. As of the 1st of April, 1898, the Regulars numbered 2,143 officers and 26,040 enlisted men, largely distributed among the 25 Infantry Regiments and 10 Cavalry Regiments. Under the stimulus of approach to war, recruiting in May, 1898, jumped from less than 1,000 a month to 9,000 for May and June, with a slump to 6,500 in July and but little more than 3,000 in August. This war enthusiasm notwithstanding, the Regular Army never reached its new authorized strength of 64,719 officers and men. As of July, the month in which the shooting in the Caribbean ceased, the Regular Establishment carried on its rolls only 56,258 officers and men. So jealous were the Regulars of the professional commission that the Regular officer increase was but slightly more than that of June's West Point class.

UNMERITED CRITICISM OF REGULAR ARMY'S V CORPS

In Shafter's V Corps, which was the Expeditionary Force against Santiago, the Regulars were, however, in the great majority. Indeed, as constituted at the time it landed on the Cuban beaches East of

166

Santiago, it was the largest command of professional soldiers, Regulars, ever assembled under a single American field commander.

When General Shafter's V Corps sailed from Tampa, the 14th of June, he had 14,412 Regulars and 2,465 citizen-soldiers. These latter consisted of the Federal Militiamen in the "Rough Riders" (1st U.S. Volunteer Cavalry), dismounted and less one Squadron; the 2nd Massachusetts Infantry, and the 71st New York Infantry. The first reinforcements in Cuba consisted of the 9th Massachusetts, the 33rd and 34th Michigan ("Duffield's Brigade"), which arrived in Cuba the 27th of June and the 1st of July. They soon were joined by the 1st District of Columbia Infantry and the 1st Illinois Volunteer Infantry, which arrived at the front the 11th of July. Thus at the end of the campaign General Shafter had commanded in action 14,412 Regulars and 7,443 citizen-soldiers, with most of the latter in the Johnny-come-lately category.

Yes, no other American General ever had before commanded so many Regulars in the field at one time. The Regulars had intended it to be a strictly professional show. It seems a travesty on human affairs that its place in military history should be that of the worst campaign in American history. Actually, it is not the worst; merely the most thoroughly-publicized, criticized and denounced, largely by sensation-seeking reporters who had little knowledge and no experience upon which to predicate an informed critique. Unfortunately, most historians have followed their lead.

With an instinct for handling newspapermen that far exceeded that of his commanding generals, Colonel Theodore Roosevelt, for The Charge at San Juan Hill, reaped for his picturesque command far more publicity for hardships and heroics than they deserved in contrast with Regiments that achieved similar objectives at El Pozo and El Caney.*

The engaged National Guard units mentioned above took their place on the line, moved forward and captured their objectives with no discernible difference from similar operations executed by the Regulars and/or Roosevelt's "Rough Riders." The 9th Massachusetts particularly attracted attention and uninformed criticism from Richard Harding Davis, Beau Ideal of the Press Corps. The 9th Massachusetts also attracted more than its share of the enemy fire. This was not because of lack of training, as compared with neighboring Regiments. Like other National Guard Regiments, it had been issued the obsolete, single-shot, 1873 Springfields, of which there was a surplus from Indian

---

* To the frequent question, did Teddy lead that charge mounted or on foot? the answer is: Both! His men were fighting as Infantry. As Colonel he rode into action. Encountering entanglements, he necessarily dismounted, continued "the Charge" on foot.

wars, but for which only the black powder ammunition was available. The resulting smoke naturally attracted enemy fire, much to the irritation of adjoining units of Regulars as well as men in the 9th Massachusetts.

In deaths from disease on the island of Cuba, 210 Regulars and 206 Volunteers from the foregoing units died from tropical diseases, largely yellow fever. Critical Regulars, who in this and all other wars stayed in the Army and wrote most of the official reports and critiques following the war, saw in this evidence of lack of training among the National Guardsmen, fresh from civil life.

Actually, the comparison is meaningless, even though the ratio for Volunteer Guardsmen appears higher. The early-arriving Regulars were among the first evacuated to Montauk, New York, beginning shortly after the Round Robin episode panicked the Nation on the subject of yellow fever. The later echelons of National Guard Regiments arrived in Cuba just as the fever was manifesting itself, later moving into its peak. It was natural that the last to come were the last to go. Moreover, since none of the troops, including the doctors, in the Santiago Campaign knew there was a relationship between the mosquito and yellow fever, there were no effective training techniques against the disease. It is thus difficult to see significance in these figures. Mosquitos do not check a soldier's training before they bite.

## GUARD UNITS PREDOMINATED IN PUERTO RICO

Since the available Regular Army units had been pretty well committed in the Santiago Campaign, it followed that most of the Puerto Rican operation was composed largely of Guardsmen. General Miles' invasion of Puerto Rico was executed by five convoys. If piecemeal landings on a hostile coast at points beyond supporting distance from one another ever become valid principles of combat, General Miles in Puerto Rico will be proclaimed as their exemplar. Nevertheless, the ever-present Press corps was as commendatory and unrestrained in its praise of this operation as it had been critical of Shafter and his V Corps in Cuba.

On the island's South Coast, at Guanica, July 25, 1898, Miles landed 3,415 officers and men consisting of the 6th Illinois Infantry, 6th Massachusetts Infantry, 275 recruits originally intended as replacements for Shafter's V Corps in Cuba, a Signal unit, a Hospital unit, and four Batteries of light Artillery. Three days later he sent Major General J. H. Wilson ashore at Ponce with 3,571 officers and men distributed among the 16th Pennsylvania Infantry, 2nd Wisconsin Infantry, 3rd Wisconsin Infantry, and Companies D and M of the 6th Illinois Infantry. On July 31 a third force under Major General John R. Brooke went ashore at Arroyo, 45 miles East of Ponce. This command numbered

168

1,272 and consisted of the Philadelphia First City Troop, Pennsylvania Cavalry; Troops A and C, New York Cavalry; Battery B, Pennsylvania Artillery; 27th Indiana Light Battery;* Battery A, Illinois Artillery; Battery A, Missouri Artillery; Troop H, 6th U.S. Cavalry, and Company F, 8th U.S. Infantry. On July 31, Brigadier General Theodore Schwan arrived at Ponce with the 11th and 19th U.S. Infantry; Batteries C and M, 7th U.S. Artillery; Troop B, 2nd U.S. Cavalry, and Battery B, 5th U.S. Artillery, for a total of 80 officers and 2,831 enlisted men. Arriving at Arroyo on August 3, Brigadier General Peter C. Hains landed with 145 officers and 3,581 enlisted men distributed among the 3rd Illinois Infantry, the 4th Ohio Infantry, and the 4th Pennsylvania Infantry. The advance toward the North Coast was in four columns, with necessary troops being assigned to garrison the Southern coastal points.

The 8,233 Spanish Regulars and 9,107 Colonial volunteers, who ultimately surrendered upon news of the armistice at Santiago de Cuba, did not get concentrated for sufficient resistance to test the combat mettle of but one column, that of General Wilson moving from Ponce to Coamo to Aibonito along the old military road. In this movement, all agreed that the Pennsylvania and Wisconsin Guardsmen handled themselves extremely well. Colonel William J. Hulings of the 16th Pennsylvania Infantry conducted the flank movement and facilitated the advance at slight cost. American casualties for the entire campaign were three enlisted men killed; four officers and 36 enlisted men wounded. Most of them were Guardsmen, apparently for the very good reason that the only Infantry Regiments to come under fire were citizen-soldiers. Two of the officers were Regulars; one was a General's Aide, and the other was with a light Battery of Artillery in a supporting action. The operation was in truth a realistic field maneuver against opposition in which the Guard Regiments fully demonstrated their powers to live in the field, move, and shoot.

News of the cessation of hostilities reached the American troops in Puerto Rico at the termination of a brief Artillery duel in the vicinity of Aibonito. General Wilson suggests the success of the campaign was thanks to the smaller number of "newspaper men at hand to spread exaggerated reports about it for glorification of popular favorites."

## PEACE AND POSTWAR CRITIQUES

Actually, the wholly-unexpected decadence of the Spanish Empire, the complete failure of the Spanish Navy, and the comparatively easy triumph of American forces in Cuba and Puerto Rico, combined

---

* Indiana put 25 Batteries of light Artillery in Federal service, 1861-65. Spanish-American War Batteries continued designation by numbers and extended the series.

with the effervescence of the "Yellow Press" of that era, caused American historians to view the Spanish-American War as a comic opera. In truth, President McKinley and his Secretaries of War and Navy deserve far more credit than they have received. Spain's Navy a year before the war was rated powerful and fast enough, not only for high-seas actions, but for hit-and-run bombardments of American defenseless coastal cities. Spanish troops in Cuba numbered 155,302 Regulars in famous, old European Regiments. They were supported by 41,518 Colonial volunteers. Puerto Rico's garrison of 17,340 has been noted. All Spanish troops in both islands reportedly were seasoned in tropical warfare. Against these the Administration acted with a quick decisiveness that never has been achieved before or since by any American War President and Cabinet. If more men were mobilized than were needed, 289,923 all told, the criticism is from hindsight rather than foresight. The same hindsight criticism can be and has been made with more damning evidence, of General George C. Marshall's disastrous over-estimate of the need for Russian aid to help crush Japan. McKinley's Administration did dispatch, within a matter of weeks (not months or years), expeditions to Cuba, Puerto Rico and the Philippines. This promptness, combined with aggressive naval action, chilled European opportunism. Otherwise, Spain might have acquired one or more powerful allies seeking to be present at the division of the remnants of an old empire.

It was McKinley's misfortune to have this mobilization at a time when there were no scientific checks upon typhoid fever, yellow fever and many other kindred tropical and subtropical diseases. Mobilization reached its peak in the Summer when such diseases in that era were normally near epidemic stage along the Gulf Coast every Summer. The "Yellow Press," hungering for news, and with operations often providing them with insufficient copy, made the most of these sick-nesses. Actually, the medical services were superior to what was generally prevalent *throughout the World armies of that day.*

Lest we in our modern and superior environment and opportunities look back upon American war effort against Spain with disdain, let us forget neither the ravages of influenza in World War I nor the 50,000 American soldiers, unknown numbers of whom died or suffered permanent disabilities, 1941-42, from improper yellow fever vaccines. This blundering, man-made epidemic in World War II mobilization created far more casualties than President McKinley and his allegedly incompetent Secretaries lost by gunfire and disease throughout their entire war. Indeed, these vaccine casualties of 1941-42* exceed the

---

* ". . . the peak of the epidemic among the troops in the continental United States was reached in late June (1942) and in overseas contingents about a month later. A total of over 50,000 cases of jaundice believed to have occurred in relation to yellow fever vaccination were reported." *Preventive Medicine in World War II,* Vol. 3, p. 312.

entire strengths of Shafter's Santiago command and Miles' forces in Puerto Rico. Had the forces mobilized in 1898 suffered similar casualties *from their own Medical Corps,* McKinley and his Secretaries would have been lucky to settle for an impeachment. The Press of that day would have whipped the public into a mob-like frenzy.

In 1941-42, it was the Army Medical Corps' good fortune that the man in the White House was a Press and public relations expert and that a more educated public accepted censorship and the principle of a bridled wartime Press.* But this is small comfort to victims and their families of modern blunders that pale those of Shafter, Miles, Alger and McKinley.

If there is a major lesson to be derived from the Spanish-American War, it may well be summed-up with this concept: There are times when prompt, aggressive and decisive action and a willingness to fight quickly with what a nation has, saves far more lives than months and years of preparation in order that a campaign may be launched under perfect auspices.

This was the situation in 1898. After all, McKinley, a former Ohio Guardsman, himself, did not risk more than 17,000 men in his first tentative operation, and he knew it would be well-supported by insurgents, though he had no right to expect the Spanish forces of nearly 200,000 men in Cuba (36,582 in Western Cuba, Province of Santiago) to accept defeat so readily. It was the quick capitulation by homesick Spanish troops and the breaking of the cocoon of red tape in which the Regulars had encased their little army of 28,000 that created the comic opera atmosphere, much more than the alleged bungling on the part of the Administration and zealous volunteer Guardsmen of that day. The war is also significant for its brilliant success in bringing into Federal service, fully-constituted and with a competence fully equal to the professional competence of the Regulars of their day, such an imposing Army of effective citizen-soldiers.

The shortage of modern combat equipment was clearly due to the pacifistic penury of the American people as reflected by a long succession of inadequate Congressional appropriations. The clashes within the little bureaucracy empire that was the War Department of that day were clashes of career personalities. Generally it was the Army Commanding General versus the entrenched bureaucrats such as the Adjutant General, the Chief Quartermaster and their respective henchmen. The troop embarkation chaos at Tampa, Florida, and such

---

* The epidemic news was suppressed until the peak was well past, situation under control and corrected. When it was admitted officially to the Press, figures were scaled-down to 56% of the number finally conceded. *Time* Magazine, August 3, 1942, p. 312, and *Science,* August 7, 1942, p. 12, both admit they and the press services had known of and had suppressed news of the epidemic "at the request of the Army authorities." *Ibid.,* p. 12.

tactical oddities as the piecemeal landings on Puerto Rico and the insubordinate "Round Robin" among the Regulars and U.S. Volunteers (Colonel Roosevelt played a leading role) before Santiago were results of the fortunate haste that characterized this war. Few Regulars had seen a full Regimental formation since final withdrawal of occupation troops from the South in 1877. Few had experience in staff planning. Even so, the Regular Army had many able officers, but the dead hand of promotion by seniority was heavy upon them.

The war was won by decisive political action, aggressive naval operations, the ability of the States in prompt fielding of high-morale, complete Army units of willing citizen-soldiers, plus the unknown factor of Spain's weak Navy and her war-weariness from fruitless colonial campaigns. But as usual the citizen-soldiers went home to civilian pursuits while the Regulars remained on duty with opportunity and time to write reports and professional papers and occasional books. Criticisms created recriminations and explanations. As with most professions, they arrived at the unoriginal, professional conclusion that their own profession should be larger, stronger, better-equipped, better-financed. It was the "amateurs" who received the shifted blame.

There came the new concept, typical of most professions, that, ideally, all non-professionals should be eliminated. When not feasible, the citizen-soldiers were a burden and a danger unless kept subordinate to all professionals. Complete military units resulting from Calls to the States continued a long-standing historical barrier to this professional principle. How could civilians function satisfactorily as Majors, Colonels, even Generals, when it took professionals until their graying 50's to qualify for such ranks with corresponding responsibilities? The professionals must protect the profession and the Nation, they consistently concluded, by capturing the manpower policies of the Nation. There should be no sharing of manpower responsibilities and ranks within the profession, with the States.

Major William H. Carter, a palace soldier in the Adjutant General's office, personified this professional scheme of things. He early found the ear of that genius for organization, Elihu Root, who became War Secretary July 26, 1899. Before Mr. Root left that office, February 1, 1904, Major Carter had become an officer marked for the stars, which he achieved in 1911 as Chief of Artillery, thereby jumping the single star. He had no prior service in Artillery!

For him it was a good day when he found a copy of Brevet Major General Emory Upton's little-known *The Armies of Europe and Asia,* in a second-hand book store. He presented it to the mentally-omniverous, fast reading, new Secretary of War. Emory Upton, in his permanent grade of Colonel, had been dead by his own hand since March 15, 1881, but this simple present led to the resurrection of a dusty manuscript

on American military affairs that Upton's publisher had rejected. It
was made to order for the professional school of thought. Root saw in
it arguments for some Staff reforms dear to his own heart. He had
Upton's *Military Policy of the United States* printed as a public
document. To the ambitious, professional-minded, military Regulars it
became a military Bible. But the posthumous influence of the energetic,
data-collecting, frustrated Upton upon America's military personnel
policies properly belongs to future chapters on military legislation.

# Bibliographical Note For Chapter VI

Any student of this controversial little war should at all times check
secondary materials against official statistics, records, and reports. Most
indispensable among these are the Government Printing Office editions
of *Annual Reports of the War Department for 1898,* Vol. I, Parts 1
and 2; followed by the corresponding volumes and parts of the same
*Annual Reports for 1899, 1900, and 1901.* For pertinent legislation see
*Statutes at Large,* Vol. 30, particularly Chaps. 187-89. *The Congressional
Record,* April, May, June and July, 1898, contains much pertinent
ephemera, and is correspondingly less rewarding. Sen. Doc. 230, 55th
Congress, 2nd sess., entitled *Cuban Correspondence and Correspondence
Relating to the War with Spain* (2 vols.) merits attention. The 3rd
volume of *Message from the President of the United States to the Two
Houses of Congress* takes the form of "Report of the Major General
Commanding the Army," 1898, and is particularly fruitful to those interested in operations as well as personnel. Sen. Doc. 221, 56th Congress,
1st sess., being the *Report of the Commission Appointed by the President to Investigate the Conduct of the War Department in the War
with Spain* (8 vols.), frequently referred to as the *Dodge Commission
Report,* is an essential source.

In proportion to its duration, few wars have produced a more voluminous literature of conflicting personal memoirs and polemic secondary accounts. Russell A. Alger, *The Spanish-American War* (1901),
suffers the stigma that attaches itself to all apologias. The harsh facts
and figures, nevertheless, show his book to be the most authentic of
those written by political participants. Its accuracy is in sharp contrast
with the irresponsible flamboyancy of Theodore Roosevelt, *The Rough
Riders* (1899), the principal value of which is its intimate picture of a
Regiment of Federal Militia in process of organization and training.
Lt. Col. J. D. Miley, *In Cuba with Shafter* (1899); Lt. Gen. Nelson A.
Miles, *Serving the Republic* (1911); Maj. Gen. Hugh L. Scott, *Some
Memories of a Soldier* (1928), and Maj. Gen. Joseph Wheeler, *The Santi-
ago Campaign* (1898) are less irresponsible than Col. Theodore Roose-
velt. Nevertheless, they are not always in agreement as to facts.

Stephen Bonsal, *The Fight for Santiago* (1899), is good on contemporary rumors. His fellow reporter, Richard Harding Davis, *The Cuban
and Porto Rican Campaigns* (1898), leaves one wondering whence came
his reputation as a great war correspondent. Back files of the *New York*

*Tribune, New York World* and *New York Journal,* supplemented by Press extracts in contemporary issues of the *Literary Digest,* typify the hasty, rumor-mongering superficialities of correspondents less famous than Bonsal and Davis.

Among writings by non-participants, Walter Millis, *The Martial Spirit* (1931), captures the irresponsibilities and superficial effervescence of the contemporary Press better than does any other secondary account. Franklin F. Holbrook, *Minnesota in the Spanish-American War* (1923), is one of the more scholarly of many similar volumes for other States of the American Republic. J. A. LeRoy, *The Americans in the Philippines* (2 vols., 1914) is adequate for initial phases of operations. A number of good biographies have been helpful, such as Hermann Hagedorn, *Leonard Wood: A Biography* (2 vols., 1931); Joseph B. Bishop, *Theodore Roosevelt and His Time* (2 vols., 1920); Phillip C. Jessup, *Elhu Root* (2 vols., 1938); and Maj. Gen. William H. Carter, *Life and Public Service of Lt. Gen. Adna R. Chaffee* (1917).

For an overview of Regular Army professional opinions as to the lessons in personnel to be learned from the war, see Capt. Charles D. Rhodes, "The Experiences of our Army since the Outbreak of the War with Spain," *Journal of Military Service* Institute, March-April, 1905; Maj. Gen. William H. Carter, *Creation of the American General Staff* (Sen. Doc. 119, 68th Cong., 1st Sess., 1924), and *The American Army* (1915). In their chapter on the Spanish-American War, Lt. Col. Marvin A. Kreidberg and Lt. Merton G. Henry, *History of the Military Mobilization of the United States Army, 1775-1945,* provide a superb tabulation of pertinent statistics. They also mirror with extreme fidelity the traditional writings and viewpoints of professional soldiers.

CHAPTER VII

# From the Spanish War to the
# Dick Act

NATIONAL GUARD participation in the postwar policing of Cuba
and the suppression of the Philippine Insurrection officially
ended in the late Summer of 1899. Not until this late season were
the Guardsmen from California, Colorado, Idaho, Iowa, Kansas, Minnesota, Montana, Nebraska, Nevada, North Dakota, Oregon, Pennsylvania, South Dakota, Tennessee, Utah, Washington and Wyoming
returned to the States. It will be recalled that they had gone to Manila
as the major portion of the VIII Army Corps to fight the Spaniards,
but willingly remained a year beyond their term of service to meet
the initial crisis of native insurrection. Their place was taken by Regiments and Batteries of Regulars, or by units of a newly created
"Volunteer Army."

This latter force had come into existence under hasty legislation enacted March 2, 1899, following news of the outbreak of fighting between American troops and Emilio Aguinaldo's Philippine Insurgents 30 days earlier. The law was conspicuously designed to eliminate the National Guard units of the States from further participation as units, but was carefully designed to attract Guardsmen as individuals. It continued the strength of the Regular Army at substantially the same figure to which it had been authorized to expand at the outset of the Spanish-American War, approximately 65,000 enlisted men. To take the place of the outgoing Guard Regiments, a force of "not more than 35,000 volunteers to be recruited . . . from the country at large, or from localities where their services are needed," was authorized in addition to the Regular Army. The phrase "from localities where their services are needed," though vague, actually meant "in the Philippines." The idea back of it was not the recruitment of Philippinos but to attract Guardsmen from the above States to change of status as individuals, in grade, to the new Volunteer Army.

## GUARDSMEN AS U.S. VOLUNTEERS
## REPLACE THE GUARD REGIMENTS

This Volunteer force (actually a Federal Organized Militia patterned on State practices) was to be organized into "not more than twenty-seven Regiments organized as are Infantry Regiments of war strength in the Regular Army, and three Regiments to be composed of men of special qualifications in horsemanship and marksmanship, to be organized as Cavalry for service mounted or dismounted." Enlistments in these Volunteer Regiments were to be for only two years and four months, unless sooner discharged. Obviously, it should have been for the duration. In prescribing the short-term active duty limit for its own Organized Militia, the War Department and the Congress were underwriting a recurrence of all the short-term evils for which all Guard units, including the three-year Regiments of the Civil War, have been so lustily abused by the professional military planners.

There was one provision by which a Guard formation could become U.S. Volunteers as a unit. An outgoing Guard unit could be accepted into a Volunteer Regiment as a unit, should it so elect, but with the loss of its identity as such. The emphasis, however, was to recruit individual officers and men, in grade, from among outgoing Guard units, particularly those in the Philippines and those Guardsmen recently from active duty in Cuba or elsewhere. That they could retain their prior N.C.O. or commissioned rating was important. Moreover, pay and allowances were improved in this Act of March 2, 1899, for both Regulars and the new Volunteers. Within six months all 30 of these Volunteer Regiments were in being with a strength of 1,524 officers and 33,050 enlisted men. Practically all of them eventually reached the Philippines for a major share in the fighting that broke the rebellion's back. Indeed, two full Regiments of the Volunteer Army and some Troops of Volunteer Cavalry were created in the Philippines largely of Guardsmen who elected to stay to the end of the Pacification.

By the end of 1899, there were 51,167 officers and enlisted men, Regulars and Volunteers, deployed in the Philippines and active in operations against the Insurgents. On May 5, 1900, Arthur MacArthur, a Brigadier General U.S.A., but at the time in temporary rank as a Major General U.S.V., superseded Harrison G. Otis, Major General U.S.V. and a California citizen-soldier. At that time, the strength returns show 2,225 officers and 61,059 enlisted men, Regulars and Volunteers, in the Philippine Theater. By the following November 30, the aggregate of both components had risen to 74,094 officers and men. A majority were former Guardsmen and citizen-soldiers from the Spanish-American War mobilization.

## EX-GUARDSMEN PLAY A LEADING ROLE IN PACIFICATION

Thus, the contributions of the National Guard to the aftermath of the Spanish-American War were indirect, but nevertheless patent. It may well be doubted if the Federal Government could have created the U.S. Volunteer Regiments readily enough to have met the emergency had not the recent active duty of all the Guard Regiments of the States filled the Nation with restless, adventure-minded and trained men who had experienced a tinge of disappointment that they had not been able longer to serve their Country than through the brief hostilities with Spain. It is significant that the crowning event in ending hostilities, the daring, commando-like raid and capture of Emilio Aguinaldo, March 1901, was exclusively by five former Guard officers, in company with 78 Macabebe Scouts, who willingly posed as Insurgents with the former Guard officers as their presumed prisoners.

These former Guardsmen were led by General Funston, who had gone to the Philippines as Colonel commanding the 20th Kansas Infantry, from which he had been promoted to star rank in the Volunteers. He later was integrated into the Regular Army in grade. Captain Russell T. Hazzard and First Lieutenant O. P. M. Hazzard had accepted U.S. Volunteer commissions in the 11th U.S. Volunteer Cavalry from the old 1st Washington Infantry, one of the first Regiments to arrive in the Philippines in 1898. Captain Harry W. Newton had accepted his commission in the 34th Volunteer Infantry from prior service in the 3rd Wisconsin Infantry, in which he had served and had been under fire briefly in the Puerto Rican campaign. The junior member of this daring party of former Guardsmen, then serving under

U.S. Volunteer commissions, was Lieutenant Burton J. Mitchell, who, like the commander of the raid, was from the old 20th Kansas. These officers, as were many other former Guardsmen, were tendered commissions in the Regular Army with the expansion authorized in 1901.

All-in-all, the Pacification of the Philippines was not a big war, though it was expensive, did draw into action many thousands of men and included 2,811 exchanges of gunfire, ranging from obscure skirmishes to battles of some significance. Anyone who cares to examine the reports of all these operations will be sufficiently impressed by the constant presence of former Guardsmen in such a large percentage of the incidents that he will utterly reject the oft-stated theory that this was one war the professionals were able to handle without having to call on the National Guard for help.

It is quite true, however, that the professionals were deeply seated in the saddle after 1901. Elihu Root had become Secretary of War early in 1899. He was a brilliant attorney who, having gained great wealth, all-but made a career of contributing his talents to Cabinet-level services to America. He was thus a man who responded to the professional approach by professional soldiers; but Root made it easy for competent citizen-soldiers to enter the growing fraternity of professionalism with little or no reduction in grade. He made it easy for enlisted men to rise from the ranks if they could prove a thorough, basic education by passing written comprehensives. Any physically-fit young man under 28 with a diploma from a State Military Institute, such as The Citadel and Virginia Military Institute or a Land Grant college requiring military training along with the baccalaureate curriculum, could have a Second Lieutenancy for the asking. Thus it was that the young George Catlett Marshall, Jr., put his V.M.I. diploma on file in 1900 to begin his long march to the five-star grade under an initial commission dated February 2, 1901. He was but one of the many "outsiders" to enter the Army, with or without rank prejudicial to the vested Regimental and/or seniority interests of those already ensconced in the Old Army lists.

Root, with some reluctance, retained the principle of seniority, but he removed it from the Regimental lists. At the same time, he founded an Army War College and modernized all Service schools for officers. His General Staff assignments and General Staff Eligibility Lists brought the Army considerable flexibility in personnel matters, in spite of the fixed seniority rule that Root reluctantly accepted. Because of all these changes and by reason of so many "outsiders" being integrated as Company Commanders or higher, as late as 1930 the aging and graying, passed-over Regular Colonels still were talking darkly of the "Crime of '99." To them, it became what "the Hump" was to the Regulars of 1940.

But when Root followed Secretary Alger in 1899, the Army was feeling the quickening pulse of new weapons, new techniques and youth. There was much loose talk of Empire responsibilities making essential an ever-expanding professional Army, much of which always would be overseas and large enough at all times to meet any contingency. Sober advocates of a "Colonial Army" were getting a serious hearing. Their plans usually called for native Regiments with their Company officers being recruited from among the cream of the Sergeants in the American Regular Infantry Regiments. Field and General grade officers of these "Colonial Forces" would come, of course, from the professional list of American Regulars. The Philippine Constabulary, with the Philippine Scouts and the Puerto Rico Regiment of Infantry, were as far as this proposed imitation of the British Indian Army was carried. The pendulum of public opinion already was swinging the other way in the face of mounting costs within the American Republic's Empire, with a corresponding slump in enthusiasm for helping England "bear the White man's burden."

## THE GUARDSMEN RE-ASSERT THEIR MISSION

This was the status of affairs in the Army and the War Department when the Governors and Adjutant Generals of the 45 States, not to mention the Territories of Arizona, New Mexico and Oklahoma, with the National Guard Association of the United States as a catalytic agent, confronted Secretary Root with reminders that the Regular Army never had won a war without the active assistance of the National Guard. Some boldly suggested it most likely never would.

The States and their Regiments had shared in the abuse from the Press that had resulted in Secretary Alger's resignation and the elevation of Mr. Root. They rightly felt they had done more than the Federal Government had asked of them and in many instances with more mobilization competence. The poor sanitation of the Spanish War training camps, the heavy clothing for the tropical duty and the allegedly embalmed beef were not of their doing. They were merely the understanding, informed victims. They did resent such items as the single-shot, 1873 rifles with black powder, the smoke from which pin-pointed their positions to draw hostile fire, while Regular Regiments firing on the same objectives had repeaters with smokeless powder. Moreover, with the vanishing of the frontier and the Indian menace, combined with the trends toward overseas and frontiers of Empire scope should not the rising cost of the militarily-organized peacetime National Guard units be shifted, in part, toward the Federal Treasury? They insisted Mr. Root had not finished his job of correcting the errors of the Alger regime until the growing gulf between the Military Departments of the States and the War Department was closed, or properly bridged.

To infer that Mr. Root had any desire to sidestep the issue or that he had been so busy with the Regular Army and Philippine revolt that he was unaware of the National Guard, would not only be unfair, but it would be untrue. He was never a man to duck an issue or to let one come upon him unawares. Moreover, a War Department professional, Lieutenant Colonel William Harding Carter, from his post as Assistant Adjutant General of the Army, was there with ready advice. A five-year graduate of West Point in 1873, it had taken Carter 24 years to become a Major and to discover comforts of palace soldiering where one might indulge in high-level, ivory tower planning for others. His first efforts at such planning were toward expediting promotions for professionals. He may or may not have fathered the concept of the 30 United States Volunteer Regiments, largely recruited and officered at the Company level from the disbanding National Guard Regiments with all Field grade and higher ranks, when possible, reserved for the Regulars. But Carter certainly was enthusiastic about the system. He had the Secretary's ear at all times. It is not surprising that Mr. Root initially took a quite dim view of the National Guard Regiments and Brigades of the United States and Territories as they immediately began their own self-initiated reorganization early in 1899.

## THE SECRETARY OF WAR UNDER THE INFLUENCE
## OF THE UPTONIANS

In his report for that year, the new and unseasoned Secretary of War signed his name to concepts that he later saw fit to reject, and further to express pride in his rejection thereof. He did begin with the historically obvious, conventional and inescapable concept that the Regulars never could be more than a small part of any wartime Army. The major part of any such Army necessarily would be composed of citizen-soldiers. With a particularly hostile eye on the old Militia Act of 1792, which so long had confused the organized State units of National Guardsmen with the unorganized, militarily-obligated male citizenry within arms-bearing ages, Mr. Root struck boldly at this basic law. If the Regular Army was to remain small and wartime Armies were to be expanded by military-minded citizenry, a uniformity in training and skill must exist between the Regulars and the willing National Guardsmen. Some new approach should be made toward utilizing military talent in the less willing but large military manpower pool.

He thought the National Guardsmen should be privileged to benefit from the new trends in military education and training. The records of good Guard officers should be kept on file to insure basis for their selection for United States Volunteer commissions in time of war. It will be noted that the officer selection was to be by the Federal Government. The Governors of the States were not to participate. To emphasize this point, Mr. Root erroneously said that this was the manner in which all the officers had been selected under the March 2 Act of 1899 for the Volunteer Regiments sent to the Philippines. It had worked so well that it should be the permanent plan.

Nowhere in this Report of 1899 is there any indication that Mr. Root wanted to use the National Guard as units in time of war. He was interested only in the skill and efficiency of its members as a sort of special recruiting preserve for temporary expansion of the Regular Army or for the Federal creation, from the ground up, of new temporary Regiments under Volunteer designations. Guardsmen, if used at all, would be accepted only as individuals, be they for enlisted or commissioned status.

It apparently took time, discussion and even negotiations to wean Secretary Root from the idea that the National Guard ever could be more than a training school and recruiting preserve for wartime, individual volunteers for Federal service of known or unknown duration. It could be argued that Mr. Root never was entirely weaned from this idea. As late as 1916, in a letter to a Mr. Robert Bacon, he opined that the National Guard never could be developed into a functional force. But by that time Mr. Root's party was out of office and a Democratic President, with an ex-Mayor of Cleveland in his old War Department seat, was sending National Guard Regiments, Brigades and even two Divisions to the Mexican Border. It could be that it was merely Mr. Root's turn to be critical. Certainly Mr. Root withdrew from his Uptonian position when he accepted, worked toward the passage, and later expressed pride in the Dick Bill of 1903.

In his War Department Report for 1900, Mr. Root reveals himself still under the magic spell of the Assistant Adjutant General, Carter, and others of his professional philosophy. In this report, Mr. Root believed that for a wartime Army "the entire body of Troops . . . will be composed of U.S. Volunteers." He did not want the National Guard to be a balanced force. Engineers, Cavalry and Artillery, he thought, should be Regulars. The Regulars should have surplus officers, both of the Line and of the Staff, so as to permit their being detailed to every part of the combined Army of Regulars and Volunteers because the officers from civil life, in Root's then signed opinion, "must necessarily have but a small part of the knowledge, experience and training" requisite at the outset of any campaign.

The following 12 months brought but little change in the official thoughts of Mr. Root. But the National Guard units back in the States were growing so fast in their self-initiated progress that time was approaching for him clearly to adopt them or offer a better alternative. Mr. Root returned to his basic and valid concept that some provisions should be made in advance for the selection of officers for volunteering citizen-soldiers if and when war should come.

He had nothing better to offer than the pattern of the Volunteer Army created for the Philippine service under the Act of March 2, 1899. By the time of his Report of 1902 it appears to have occurred to him, and even to some of his professional advisers in the War Department, that the "Volunteer Army" that had been so quickly raised and expedited to the Philippines could not have been possible without the great pool of service-minded and trained individuals created by the premature deactivation and demobilization of the equivalent of 155-State-inducted Regiments of all Arms immediately following the Spanish War Peace and prior to the Aguinaldo-led Philippine Insurrection. In speaking of the National Guard in 1902, Mr. Root thought Guard units should be given weapons of the new type; they should have instructors from the Regular Army detailed to them. Guard units from time to time should go to joint encampments with the Regulars, as if this was not already being done. Guard officers should have the privilege of some benefits from Mr. Root's newly-created, or refurbished, schools for higher military professional education. Guard officers could be encouraged to such studies to and including the school at Fort Leavenworth.

But the official position of the War Department careerists continued to be that the National Guard never should be more than a recruiting preserve whence prior-trained officers and men could be accepted individually into the Federal Organized Militia, to be euphoniously and legally designated as the U.S. Volunteer Army. To further this end, however, the Department shifted its position slightly. The Guard could be called into the Federal service, as in 1861, *for three months only*. There was the obvious concept that on their deactivation at the end of the three months, a vast new pool of individuals thus would be created for luring into expanding units of the Regular Army or for the creation of at least 30, and if need be perhaps many more, Regiments for a new Volunteer Army. Through the entire document it is quite clear that neither Mr. Root nor his advisers, who were creating the official position, had yet gained the scope of horizon or evolved the necessary constructive imagination to view the National Guard as a National force in peace as well as war.

But the foregoing was something of a shift in official position. The Guard, through the National Guard Association, through political channels to the Congress and by work in the field, was calling attention vigorously to itself on a Nationwide basis. Guard units in strength, and at no expense to the Federal Government, voluntarily participated with credit in the Army's joint maneuvers at Fort Riley. Mr. Root spoke well of these units. He also took a kindly view and agreed to the manning of coast defense fortifications near their homes by National Guard units in Massachusetts, Connecticut and New York. Notwithstanding these minor key changes in the same old music, the basic words of the Departmental song remained the same. Mr. Root summarized the National Guard as he saw it in the following words:

"The National Guard contains two widely different elements. One is composed of men who wish to perform their duty to the State as members of the Militia, but do not wish, or do not feel at liberty to leave their homes or their business interests and become soldiers for all purposes, liable to be sent away for distant military operations. The other element wish to go wherever there is adventure and a chance to fight. The amount of strictly *local* military work of the highest importance to be done in case of war is so great that the whole National Guard force, of the seacoast States, at all events, can be made just as useful as if they all became volunteers for all purposes."

In other words, he would leave the Guard units at home to do home duties. He would welcome the adventurous volunteers from the Guard to become enlisted men and junior officers in the professionally-commanded formation of the Volunteer Army. Be it said for Mr. Root that opinions voiced from within the Guard gave some support to Mr. Root's views. Nevertheless, in this Report for 1902, Mr. Root gave evidence of a reappraisal of the manpower situation and allowed himself marginal room for maneuver in the legislative battle for which the lines were being drawn.

## THE SECRETARY OF WAR SHIFTS POSITION

Later, in his book, *"Military and Colonial Policy of the United States,"* Mr. Root tacitly concedes the coming showdown with the States. He took the offensive with a Bill of his own setting forth his views on the future of the National Guard. The appropriate Senate and House Committees were given copies. A convention of the officers of the National Guard Association which, in January of that year, met in Washington, likewise received copies. The Guard officers went to work on the Bill. Congressman Charles W. Dick of Ohio provided the necessary liaison between the National Guard officers and the House committee.

The Guard officers, with their clean-cut knowledge of the grass-roots difference between the mass, Unorganized Militia idea and their units of the Organized Militia that had gone voluntarily to every war, gave Mr. Root's Bill a complete overhauling. Smarting from having been entirely bypassed as State units in the suppression of the Philippine Insurrection and confident in their merits and potential for the future, in the Indianapolis Convention of 1899 the Guard leaders had determined to contact Governors and members of both houses of the National Congress with proposals of their own. Under the leadership of Colonel Edward Britton of New York, who was Chairman of their Executive Committee, they conducted an active and ambitious promotional campaign. Accordingly, before they ever saw Mr. Root's Bill, their program was thoroughly formulated and actually contained most of the essential modifications they attached to the measure in the form in which it eventually went through Congress. Far from originating the Act of 1903, commonly called the Dick Bill, Mr. Root appears to have been convinced by the Guardsmen of their own strength and he modified his own position, and that of the War Department, to a willingness to go along with them. Mr. Root was being no less than honest when he later declared that the final Bill did not "fully represent anyone's view" but did include "many provisions upon which a general agreement [was] reached."

## THE NATIONAL GUARD'S POSTWAR REVIVAL

Lest it appear that this was a purely political victory for the National Guardsmen, it should be noted that their success rested upon the solid basis of self-initiated achievements in the field. Without their demonstrated unselfish contributions toward National defense, they would have failed.

The Guardsmen did not await political success before breathing new life into their cherished institution. Immediately upon the disbanding of their Regiments as State Volunteers in Federal service, 1898-99, they underwrote their perpetuation in the defense scheme of the future by reorganizing at once from the grass-roots up. The history of the 1st Vermont Infantry is illustrative of what happened in most States of the Union. As a National Guard Regiment, purely in its long-standing State status, the officers and men of this Regiment had volunteered to a man to qualify the Regiment as such for Federal status as the 1st Vermont Volunteer Infantry. When the Regiment returned for the muster-out from Federal status, each local unit was reconstituted and reinstituted to form the 1st Regiment of Infantry, Vermont National Guard; a true successor of the original Regiment. The issue even became the basis of a court decision. The Vermont Supreme Court held the reorganized Regiment to be a true, continuing, institutional successor to the original Regiment. Other courts of other States most likely would have held the same had they been called upon to rule on a similar point at issue with reference to the reorganized units in their States.

Moreover, the numbers that these reorganized units, throughout the Nation, had enlisted and were turning-out for regular drills, were impressive. In 1903, Texas, though still the biggest in size, was about average for population. Their local Company-size units were reconstituted immediately and at once brigaded into the nearest approach to a balanced force of all Arms that the Texas Guard's strength permitted. It consisted of two Brigades of two Infantry Regiments each, a separate Battalion of Colored Infantry, a separate Squadron of Cavalry, a Battalion of Field Artillery and a Signal Corps Company. With an overall strength of 3,266 officers and men, these Regiments and Brigades were far closer to war strength and more functional than the comparable Regular Army Brigades and Regiments stationed in the Continental United States. The latter had been skeletonized for replacements to beef-up the formations in the Philippines.

With a strength of 1,294, the little District of Columbia did even better than Texas on a percentage basis. This figure accounted for no less than 2% of its potential for all-out military manpower. Kentucky, with more Armory troubles than most and with a large, mountainous rural area, was turning out 1,251 officers and men for approximately three-tenths of 1% of its Militia-obligated population. New York, of course, by virtue of its wide margin of population, with excellent armories and a rich military tradition going back to the Dutch West India Company's garrison that posted sentries along the line of modern Wall Street, led all the States in Guard strength as of 1903, with 13,869 officers and men. These were organized into a balanced force of Infantry, Engineers, Light Artillery, Heavy Artillery, Cavalry and Signal Companies. At this time, New York also had no less than 41 separate Companies awaiting assignment to Battalions and Regiments.

As one might assume, Nevada had the smallest National Guard, as of 1903, with two Companies of Infantry. But the combined strength of all the National Guard units of all the States was no less than 116,542 officers and men, all voluntarily enrolled without promise of drill pay and most of them paying dues and/or buying their own uniforms in order to belong.

These achievements, so promptly after returning from active duty, were the factors and the figures that no doubt convinced Mr. Root that the National Guardsmen and the Unorganized Militia, with which he too long had confused them, were two entirely different items in the American defense picture. He could well afford to go along with the Guardsmen. He was having trouble enough getting appropriations for a Regular Army of only 66,000. His Volunteer Army that had borne the brunt of the Philippine field fighting had vanished in 1901, with the first breath of peace, though the Islands were still somewhat less than actually "pacified." The Dick Act was not a political victory for the Guardsmen as much as it was a reluctant Federal recognition of the National Guard's demonstration of its inherent vitality by fielding so many militarily-valuable men and units so soon after their complete demobilization.

The highly-important and significant Dick Act of 1903 cannot be studied in a vacuum. It accordingly has been necessary to give all the foregoing tide of events for its fullest understanding. Against this background, it is possible to review the Bill as a whole and present its legal impact and effect.

## THE DICK ACT

The Dick Act was, first and last, new legislation to take the place of the aged, much-abused and nearly-always-misunderstood Militia Acts of May 2 and May 8, 1792, with their amending or cognate measures, that long had been vital statutory precedents for Federal procurement of emergency military strength. There were new things in the Dick Act, to be sure, but there were also many old ones. This is easily understood because the Guardsmen naturally wrote into the new Bill all those constructive practices permitted under the old laws that they had been doing all along. In their contributions to the Dick Act, the Guardsmen quite naturally made the most of this opportunity to have blanketed by Federal law those practices they had been following within laws of their several States that they considered good, as well as the measures they considered essential. Their plan quite naturally called for some Federal aid and support in matters of modern equipment, and in keeping units organized in the same manner as corresponding units of the Regular Army. They wanted skilled instructors from the professional force to improve training, and opportunities for Guard officers to benefit by attendance in the Army schools for higher military education.

But first of all, the Guardsmen sought a clearly-defined Federal legal differentiation between themselves with their units and the unorganized, militarily-obligated manpower within statutory ages. There always had been a difference even before Colonel Benjamin Franklin publicized the voluntary "military associations" as a device, for non-Quakers with irate Quakers weak in the faith, to organize for the defense of their Colony in the French-and-Indian War.

Mr. Root, of course, was thoroughly familiar with exactly what the new law did and did not do. He was at the friction point between his professional advisers, such as the now Brigadier General William H. Carter and other disciples of Emory Upton, and the legislative-minded Guardsmen. In his address before the National Guard Convention of 1903, Mr. Root talked in measured phrases for an audience that knew exactly what he was saying and for professionals in the War Department who undoubtedly were viewing much of the new law with dissatisfaction.*

---

* Emory Upton's *The Military Policy of the United States* was in the process of being completed, edited and revised for its posthumous publication by Brig. Gen. Joseph P. Sanger and George A. Forsyth, assisted by Maj. William D. Beach and Capt. Charles D. Rhodes, at the time this Bill was passed.

A year later, at Presidential election time, Mr. Root was less restrained. It is for this that he may be charged with some of the misconceptions of the law that have existed in uniformed circles unto our own day. In this election year Mr. Root went all-out for the law's absolute newness. In fact, in gloating over the virtues of the new law, for political purposes, he pushed his points so hard as to overemphasize the faulty impressions. But he was extolling the achievements of his Party and the Administration under whom the law was passed for campaign year consumption. Hence, he should be excused for any boastful exaggerations that suggest an enthusiasm for the law that hardly is consistent with some other prior and subsequent utterances.

## THE GUARD IS RECOGNIZED AS A FEDERAL FORCE

The Dick Act belatedly declared that the National Guard should constitute the "Organized Militia" and that all other able-bodied manpower of the States should constitute the "Reserve Militia." This last was name, and name only, but it is the forerunner of the present Selective Service phrase, "military manpower pool." All the old provisions for enrolling all citizens between ages 18 and 45, for keeping personal weapons on hand, for registering in paper organizations and general musters, were wiped-out. While the term "Reserve Militia" was indeed a name only, it is worth emphasizing that the connotation of the term is in line with the basic Common Law concepts. The Draft Law of World War I and Selective Service legislation for World War II and after were predicated upon this reiterated concept in the Dick Act.

The Dick Act further stipulated that within five years after the signing of the law, "the organization, armament, and discipline of the organized Militia . . . shall be the same as that which is now, or may hereafter be prescribed, for the Regular and Volunteer Armies of the United States." Mr. Root and his advisers obviously had plans, which

---

From the preface written Jan. 12, 1904, Mr. Root's obvious purpose in presenting the book as a public document was to justify and *further reforms he was insisting upon within the tradition-bound and seniority-minded Regular Army*. It was not his intention that it be used against the National Guard. In his short preface, Mr. Root specifically states: "Many of the mistaken practices which General Upton points out have already been abandoned. We no longer feel obliged to have recourse to short enlistments to obtain enlisted men . . . Provision has been made by the Militia Act of 1903 for furnishing the discipline and training, upon which he is so insistent, to that part of the Militia which is now known as the 'Organized Militia,' and for the training of many citizens in the knowledge and practice which will make them competent to serve as officers in the larger body of citizen soliders, upon whom we must chiefly rely in time of war."

Mr. Root thus made it clear that in his opinion Upton's manpower criticisms had been met. But the book became practically required reading for all Regulars until well after World War I, and it is still drawn upon, directly or indirectly, by all who seek to indict military personnel who are not of the profession. Upton's book has been the source of much needless discord among patriotic men who sought a common good.

a later provision of the Act revealed, for salvaging their U.S. Volunteer Army plan.

To implement uniformity between the National Guard and the corresponding elements of the Regulars, the United States should issue arms and equipment to the Guard without charge. Furthermore, any annual appropriations, such as previously had been restricted to arms and specific equipment, now could be used by the National Guard for other military stores and professional publications. Guardsmen could get Federal pay and subsistence, but only when on joint maneuvers with the Regular Army, or while in attendance at Fort Leavenworth or the Army War College. There was no provision for a weekly drill pay, but a unit had to have at least 24 drills, or target practice periods a year, plus a Summer encampment of not less than five days in the field, to continue its status as a National Guard unit. Instructors were to be provided the States by detail from the Regular Army. Inspections by Regulars and Guardsmen were required. Ammunition for target practice should be provided by the Federal Government at Summer camps only, and if the practice were held at a Regular Army Post.

Several old provisions of the statutes, although technically repealed, actually were embodied into the new law. One of them related to apportioning Militia Calls to the States according to population. Other stipulations subjected Guardsmen and others called in this manner to the same punitive Articles of War as prevailed in the Regular Army; to having their courts-martial composed of Guard officers only, and extending to them, while on active service, the same pay as the Regular Army. The old provisions guarding the special privileges of the "ancient corps" of Artillery, Cavalry and Infantry that had existed, many of them long before 1792, were repeated from the otherwise generally-repudiated organic Militia Acts of that year.

It was in the law's proposals for a future use of the National Guard that the War Department tipped its hand as to the manner in which the concept of the Volunteer Army, as designed in the Act of March 2, 1899, was to be preserved. The National Guard was to serve again as its recruiting preserve for individual officers and men. The Guardsmen, with an eye to the integrity of their Regiments, naturally favored a Call for the duration of hostilities, or three years. They predicated this upon the distinguished service of so many of the three-year Regiments the States had sent into the Civil War, many of which were reorganized and consolidated at the end of that period, 1864, to go the full duration. But it will be recalled that the Report of the Secretary of War for 1902, with rare inconsistency, endorsed the three-months Call limit found in the much-criticized Militia Act of February 28, 1795. The purpose of the Uptonians in proposing a three-months maximum Call was, of course, to destroy the National Guard units quickly and thereby create the neces-

188

sary pool whence could be drawn the desired Company officers and enlisted men for new U.S. Volunteer Regiments. In this manner could be reserved all desirable Field grade and Staff slots to be filled with professionals enjoying higher ranks and assignments under wartime commissions in the Volunteers.

The purpose is even more obvious when one finds in the other sections of the Dick Act all the details for again creating a Volunteer Army in the style of the Regiments sent to the Philippines in 1899, even though this was presumed to be strictly a Militia Bill designed to give the National Guard a significant role in the Nation's defense. But the Guardsmen had won their big battle when they achieved the recognition and aid they had sought. It was not too hard for them to compromise on the highly-inconsistent nine-months Call that was written in the final draft of the Dick Bill.

But they were able to safeguard their units with significantly protective clauses. The transition from State status to Federal active duty for the nine months would be pursuant to the practices followed in the Act of April 22, 1898, for the Spanish War. It further was stated expressly that appointments of officers from the lists of persons examined and found qualified to hold Volunteer commissions should not include appointments to organizations of the National Guard which volunteered as a body, or the officers of which were appointed by the Governor of a State or Territory. In other words, should a National Guard unit, at the end of its nine months, elect to volunteer into the Volunteer Army as a unit, it was to be accepted on an "as-is" basis. It could not be thrown into the pool of individual officers and men whence the new Volunteer Army was to be created.

In this manner the Guardsmen had written themselves into any future Call and had saved themselves an opportunity for longer Federal service than nine months. But in return they had to let Mr. Root, and his top advisers in the War Department, retain a blueprint for a continuation of the Volunteer Army concept which was calculated to eliminate the National Guard, or Organized Militia of the States, from the entire scheme of things as soon as practicable—and that in a Bill allegedly originally conceived to recognize the National Guard, or organized units of the Militia of the States, in the great scheme of things.

The National Guard had won its long battle for legal recognition by the Federal Government and for the aid in arms, equipment, instruction, and a balanced force of combat units for duty far beyond and above mere strike calls from apprehensive Governors. The Dick Bill rightly is considered a landmark in the evolution of America's National defense program. But the Guardsmen had won their battle on terms that were most challenging.

# Bibliographical Note For Chapter VII

Many of the sources and bibliographical materials previously cited at the end of Chapter VI are equally applicable to this period immediately following the Spanish-American War. *The Annual Reports of the War Department* for the years 1902 and 1903, not previously listed, are, of course, vital to an understanding of the Department's views as it approached the Dick Bill. Volume 32 of the *Statutes at Large* contains the vital legislation of the period. The *Congressional Record* offers some rewarding reflections on the legislative temper of the times, but little else not found in a more convenient form elsewhere. *The Proceedings of the National Guard Association, 1903-05,* reflect objectives of Guardsmen. Eilene Galloway, *History of United States Military Policy on Reserve Forces, 1775-1957,* (prepared at the request of the Hon. Overton Brooks, Chairman, Subcommittee, No. 1, Committee on Armed Services, House of Representatives), Government Printing Office, Washington, 1957, probably packs more documentary and legislative information into less space than most writings. Its emphasis is naturally upon the period of World War II and after, with some emphasis on the Dick Bill as the legislative landmark it truly was.

Maj. Gen. William H. Carter's two books (see bibliographical notes for Chapter VI) are vital to an understanding of this era. Frederick Louis Huidekoper, *The Military Unpreparedness of the United States,* New York, 1915, is a not-always-understanding compilation and impassioned interpretation of sundry facts and figures, some of which are important and many of which are ephemeral. As founder of the Army League, he often extends himself to accomplish a predetermined mission. Huidekoper is a partisan of Maj. Gen. Leonard Wood and Secretary of War (May 22, 1911-March 4, 1913) Henry L. Stimson in the attacks upon the Wilsonian Military policies after the outbreak of war in Europe, 1914. Philip C. Jessup, *Elihu Root,* 2 vols., New York, 1938, and Mr. Root's own *Military and Colonial Policy of the United States: Addresses and Reports,* Cambridge, 1916, are equally indispensable to a study of the military affairs of this era. Brevet Maj. Gen. Emory Upton, *The Military Policy of the United States,* first edition, 1904, with reprints by the War Department as late as 1916. See remarks in text and notes, Chapter VI and in this Chapter. Many of Upton's ideas were obsolete when Mr. Root published the book as a public document to further his program for a General Staff and other reforms in the Regular Army. Brig. Gen. John McA. Palmer, a most astute student of military affairs, thought Root's adoption of the incomplete and revised-for-publication manuscript of the long-dead Upton actually defeated the full completion of the Root program by creating the Upton-minded General Staff which precipitated the later crises from 1912 to 1916. Also see Brig. Gen. (U.S.V.) Peter S. Michie, *Life and Letters of General Upton,* 1885.

There are certain articles vital to an understanding of the legal evolution of the organized units of the several States to the peacetime dual-status of the National Guard that came into existence with the Dick Bill of 1903. Most significant are: Maj. S. T. Ansell, "Legal and Historical Aspects of the Militia," *Yale Law Journal,* XXVI, pp. 471-80; Col. Elbridge Colby and Lt. Col. James F. Glass, "The Legal Status of the National Guard," *Virginia Law Review,* XXIX, pp. 839-856.

CHAPTER VIII

# The Guard Accepts the Challenge

## --1903-1912

CAME THE SUMMER training season of 1903 and Mr. Root, through special inspections and visitations, checked to see if the Guardsmen could and would meet the challenge he had written into the Dick Bill of January 21, 1903. In his Annual Report he indicated a thorough canvass; "of the 1,943 separate units in the Organized Militia, the men of 1,486 had a thorough understanding of their obligations under the Statute; 250 organizations had no such idea, and 57 had a partial idea." Returns apparently were not in from the remaining 150. Root added that, of the 116,542 officers and men then in the Guard, 100,345 had declared themselves "ready to respond to a sudden call of the President."

To modern statisticians and poll-takers accustomed to the present-day, rapid, wide and detailed transmission of information, the fact

191

that 250 units did not appear to know what it was all about, is hardly impressive. But it must be kept in mind that the Statute had been on the books less than six months. It was quite new to the thinking of the public, whence came the enlisted men. In many States, sweeping redesignations and reorganizations were in progress because of the full implications of the Dick Act. In any event, Secretary Root seemed to think it was pretty good. There can be no doubt but that he took comfort from the fact that 100,345 officers and men were being properly equipped and that they would respond immediately "to a sudden call of the President."

Mr. Root's Volunteer Army of '99 was gone. A third or more of the Regular Army was overseas. Instead of approaching the 100,000 ceiling established in the 1901 legislation, it was shrinking to less than 60,000. In that situation it was gratifying to know exactly where he could lay his hands on 100,000 eager and willing officers and men who had new guns in their hands and new equipment flowing to their Supply Rooms each month.

Mr. Root nevertheless was quick to remind the Guard of the limited character of his prior recognition and left it in no doubt as to the challenge ahead, in peace or war—particularly in war. Once again he admitted the Regular Army would be insufficient for "immediate and special exigencies." The Country necessarily relied upon the Organized Militia not only "for instant service," but "for service going beyond the proper limits of [State] Militia duty." A possible transition to Regiments of U.S. Volunteers was clearly indicated. He further emphasized the need for not only a trained force, but for "a large number of citizens sufficiently instructed and exercised in the art of war to organize, train and command Volunteer Forces." He insisted that in time of peace the Guard would be rendering "immediate service as the School of the Volunteer Soldier." Though apparently comforted, the Secretary of War was re-stating his challenge—and the foregoing threats to the Guard's existence.

But, before Mr. Root had occasion to write his Report of 1903, he had appeared before the National Guard Association in May, while the ink was still wet on the Dick Bill, to tell it of the steps he was taking to make the Guard the "great school of the volunteer soldier," but he was not "doing everything for nothing." He appreciated the fact that there would be wide varieties of conditions, that some of the stricter requirements could not be imposed immediately before all the States had sufficient notice. He promised arms and equipment without charge against a new million-dollar appropriation. There would be appropriations for Summer camps and field exercises. He promised money from the Regular Army funds for Guard troops going to joint maneuvers with the Regulars. He further promised Regular Army officers as instructors, and if such were not available from the Active List, he would recall to duty officers from the Retired List. The Guard units were to have "instruction and inspection." He warned that States would have to do their share. Under no circumstances would he substitute Federal funds for State money. The War Department was willing only to supplement the latter. Meanwhile, Mr. Root called upon all units, even those in the rural communities, to achieve the "greatest efficiency in discipline and strength."

## MR. ROOT KEEPS HIS WORD

Right while he was talking to the National Guard Association, Mr. Root's special inspection teams of Regular officers were visiting 1,196 Towns and Cities. Their reports were not flattering. Nevertheless, the Dick Bill had provided for joint maneuvers, the Guard units with the Regular Army, and Mr. Root obviously was prepared to comply with the full measure of the law. There was nothing novel about the idea. It was one of those things the Guardsmen had done before, more-or-less on their own. They had found it good and had wanted it written into the new law.

Late in the 1880's, without any authorization by Federal or State laws, the War Department began permitting Regular Army units to participate in Summer instruction encampments with the State troops. The practice was informal, often local and without any great co-ordinated effort. By 1901 and under the stimulus in military interests incident to the Spanish and Philippine wars, Congress even took cognizance of the practice. The Congress directed the selection of four permanent camp sites "for instruction of Troops of the Regular Army and the National Guard." During the Fall of 1902 the Regulars and the Guardsmen from Kansas and Colorado participated in joint field exercises at Fort Riley. They were of such quality, and so satisfactory to all, that Mr. Root mentioned them favorably in his Annual Report for that year. With joint encampments, maneuvers, and field exercises so high in the area of mutual agreement between the Guardsmen and the Regulars, combined with Congress already being well-indoctrinated on the subject, the Army Appropriation Act of March 2, 1903, earmarked ample funds for joint field instruction of the two military components.

Thus, in five designated areas, from Portland, Maine, to the Hawaiian Islands, there were combined training, maneuvers and field exercises. It is axiomatic among men of any appreciable military service that all reports on all training are normally far more critical than otherwise. Those sampled on these field activities for the Summer of 1903 were far less critical than normal. The two components of the Army appear to have gotten off to a good start. It is perhaps worth noting that incident to this Summer of joint training, the first National Rifle Match under a Federal grant was fired at Sea Girt, New Jersey, September 8 and 9, 1903. It was declared to be "eminently successful." Six prizes were awarded. The first prize was won by "a team from the New York National Guard." The Army Rifle Team was fifth and the Marine Corps sixth, "but the latter was disbarred from the cash prizes owing to the oversight of Congress in failing to include the Navy and Marines among the contestants."

Under authority of the Dick Bill, there was also prompt action with regard to rearmament. By the time Mr. Root wrote his Annual Report in the Fall of 1903, the Chief of Ordnance already had issued 88,301 magazine rifles and carbines to the Guard. He also had credited back to the States the Territories' $336,893, which had been charged to them for similar issues since December 1, 1901. "All the States and Territories but three," Mr. Root's report said, "have been fully supplied."

In addition, money had been set aside to replace the old 3.2-inch field guns in 14 Batteries of National Guard Artillery. This was not enough to finish the full replacement of Field Artillery pieces, but it was a strong start in the right direction. On the smallarms, it was indeed fast work.

To the best of his ability, Mr. Root also kept his word on the detailing of Regular Army Instructors. Actually he was hard-pressed for Regular officers. The demands for full units in Cuba and the Philippines were causing many Regular Army Companies and Batteries in the Continental United States to be commanded by Second Lieutenants. Only the year before, Mr. Root necessarily had reported that of the 2,900 Line officers of the Regular Army, 1,818 had been appointed since the beginning of the Spanish War. Of these only 276 had been supplied from West Point. Of the remaining 1,542, no less than 616 were integrated, some in rather high grades, from the Volunteer Army; 512 were from civil life, and 414 were from the ranks.

Thus was created the "hump" in the seniority promotion lists that old-timers of 1925 vintage often criticized as the "Crime of '99"; but, actually, 2,900 was a rather small officer corps for an Army of 66,000 from which there were constant demands for details to the Philippine Scouts, Philippine Constabulary and sundry assignments, both in the distant islands and in Cuba, for what would be described today as "military government." Even so, and gratified by the enthusiasm of the State units for Regular Instructors, Mr. Root sought and received from Congress permission to recall and assign 20 officers from the Retired List for duty as National Guard Instructors.

Meanwhile, the War Department already had drawn-up Regulations concerning muster of the Guard into Federal service, should there be a mobilization. There were also examinations to qualify active Guardsmen for appropriate commissions in the ultimately-prospective U.S. Volunteer Regiments of a new Volunteer Army that Mr. Root and his professional advisors were determined to have, should an emergency arise.

In this, the modern Guardsman recognizes the seeds of what everyone today knows as "Federal recognition." Though Mr. Root and his Regulars never planned details to materialize the way they have, all now accept the result as a splendid thing. But it is a principle on which there has been general agreement from the beginning.

The War Department planners also prepared for the consideration of the State Legislatures a model Military Code for individual States and Territories. The purpose was to articulate better their Organized Militia units with the Federal provisions of the Dick Bill. The military chapters of most State Codes needed an overhauling anyway, hence they, in time, accepted the suggested Code in principle, and quite often in duplicated terminology.

Under Mr. Root's drive, it can be said the Department was doing all within its power to make the compromise Dick Bill both workable at the National level and fully acceptable to the Governments of the States. It may well be regretted that Mr. Root left the Department the following January 31, 1904. Though not always consistent in public utterances, he at all times saw things clearly, accepted the cooperative spirit of compromise and implemented such decisions with the same incisive action that he did for those policies that were his very own. It is not unreasonable to assume that had Mr. Root been associated with the Guard in its new status longer than the single, short year following the Dick Bill, he would have come to an even greater appreciation of the National Guard and its potential. Basically he strongly stood for those things in National defense that so strongly motivated the Guardsmen. They were drawing closer together as he left office.

## SECRETARY TAFT CARRIES ON

Mr. Root was followed in the War Department by William Howard Taft, then recognized as an eminent administrator and later to achieve even greater fame as Chief Justice of the United States. But between these two stages of his long public life, he was to become a President embattled within his own party. The acrimony of the party battles has detracted from an appreciation of his great worth as an administrator and jurist in non-elective assignments.

Mr. Taft served as Secretary of War from February 1, 1904, to June 30, 1908, when he resigned to receive from outgoing President Theodore Roosevelt the mantle of succession to the White House. Mr. Taft was followed in the War Department by Mr. Luke E. Wright of Tennessee. After a brief tour of duty there, July 1, 1908, to March 11, 1909, Mr. Wright was followed by Mr. Jacob M. Dickinson, likewise from Tennessee, who served for slightly more than two years, March 12, 1909, to May 21, 1911.

On the day following the latter date, Mr. Henry L. Stimson, age 44, accepted the War portfolio as a consolation prize following his defeat, on the Republican ticket, for the Governorship of New York. Mr. Stimson served until the inauguration of Woodrow Wilson on March 4, 1913. He saw active duty as a Colonel commanding the 31st Field Artillery through World War I, returned to the War Department as Secretary under President Franklin D. Roosevelt July 1, 1940, and filled that office until September 21, 1945. Mr. Stimson nevertheless will be best known to future historians for his diplomatic missions to Latin-America, for his service as Governor General of the Philippines and as Secretary of State under Republican Presidents Coolidge and Hoover. Mr. Stimson was 73 when he began his second tour as Secretary of War. Some will say that as an elder statesman he then allowed himself to be eclipsed by the brilliant and aggressive Chief of Staff, General Marshall. Others will say Secretary Stimson constantly was bypassed by his Democratic Presidential Chief, Roosevelt, whose primary interest in Mr. Stimson's return to and retention in Cabinet status was to give the impending hostilities and subsequent war effort a unifying, bipartisan complexion. There could be truth in both theories. But the Stimson the Guardsmen and the War Department knew for two years beginning in the Spring of 1911 was in the full vigor of his life, moving into his first high-level assignment. He was both dynamic and ambitious to become another Elihu Root.

Until the arrival of Mr. Stimson in the War Department, none of Mr. Root's successors showed any marked inclination to reject any basic laws or substitute any sweeping revisions insofar as the National Guard was concerned. The attitude of Messrs. Taft, Wright and Dickinson toward the Guard appears to have been one of remedial approaches through Regulations and administrative orders accompanied by as much supervision as available personnel and appropriations permitted. Indeed, all three of these gentlemen were burdened primarily with getting adequate funds for a shrinking Regular Army from a succession of Congresses that increasingly were lulled by the so-called piping times of peace.

At the same time, they had inherited Regular Army reforms from Mr. Root that burdened them heavily. The Bureau Chiefs and comfortably-ensconced dons of the Old Army, as personified by Lieutenant General Nelson A. Miles, would have no part of the concept of a European-style General Staff for the American Army. The issues were fought in the halls of Congress and in the Press of the Nation. The heat of the friction arising from conflicting policies and personalities often seared the souls of all concerned and tested the Solomonic wisdom of Mr. Taft long before he ever dreamed of a distinguished career as the Chief Justice of the United States.

Mr. Root had retired Miles, smothered with honors, shortly before the arrival of Mr. Taft. But when it came to in-fighting and official sabotage, the old bureaucrats of the Regular Army, who took up the cudgels Miles had laid down, knew more than the old Indian-fighter ever could have learned. Brigadier General Frederick C. Ainsworth, as The Adjutant General of the Army, became the focal point of vested resistance. Mr. Taft quite smoothly kept this Regular Army rumpus under wraps. His successors from Tennessee were less successful, and it finally was left for the Chief of Staff, Leonard Wood, and Mr. Stimson to squelch the die-hards ruthlessly in a well-timed and coordinated effort. It was to their advantage that an already thoroughly-irked Mr. Taft was in the White House.

## THE GUARD DOES ITS SHARE FOR PREPAREDNESS

Meanwhile, the National Guardsmen were making the most of their new opportunities to qualify fully for emergency National service under the Dick Act. Armed with the heavy Federal property responsibilities inherent in the law, each unit according to the pattern of its State, City or community lifted up loud voices for adequate Armories. The necessity for unit club rooms, drill floor and facilities for festive occasions, long had been recognized as essential in urban areas with a rigorous climate. They were necessary to the social solidarity and commonality of interests inherent in any voluntary association. Thus, the addition of space to existing, extensive drill floor facilities was quite simple in the expanding urban areas that were dotting the map from Portland, Maine, to Denver, Colorado. But from Baltimore, with some shining exceptions, to San Diego, California, where seasons are more kindly to the open-air enthusiasts, there often had been no pressure for drill floors or riding halls. Moreover, from Kansas City West, at the Turn of the Century, many rural Towns and Counties were having trouble enough floating bond issues for schools, jails and courthouses. Pleadings from the gun-happy week-end warriors fell upon deaf ears. But those units that met the local housing challenge flourished, quite often at the expense of rival, local units that showed less initiative.

In New Orleans, for example, there was the Louisiana Field Artillery, consisting of a Band and two Batteries. Its housing was no more than an "old, small and dilapidated structure." Drills were in the adjacent yard. Likewise, in the Crescent City, there was an old marching society

197

which was light on service of crew-manned weapons but rich in its knowledge of the *code duello* and its right to serve as the escort guard of the Governor, or any other dignitary whom the membership might consider worthy of a turn-out. It was known as the "Washington Artillery." Its leadership at this time viewed the Dick Act as an opportunity to vest the "Washington Artillery" with a true military status commensurate with its long social and military record. They met fully the housing challenge inherent with the large amount of equipment required by their mission. Their facilities began attracting more men and a more military-minded type of men, "an excellent class of men," as the chronicler recorded.

The "Washington Artillery" qualified fully for State and Federal support. It grew to a Battalion of three firing Batteries. Some of the new officers and men in this gradual expansion were from the poorly-housed "Louisiana Artillery." By 1912 the latter had to be disbanded, while the "Washington Artillery" rode on a crest wave of consistently high ratings to mobilizations and enviable records in World Wars I and II.

This is illustrative of what housing so often has meant to the Guard and is suggestive of the essential value of the housing contributions of the States, Cities, communities, and local "Armory associations." The last-named were often local non-profit associations of unit members who assessed themselves and/or borrowed money to pick up local distressed property that might be converted to their use. They then would seek, and often achieve, anything from a token to a bona fide, adequate rental from their State's Military Department to service the debt in part or entirely. Building maintenance and a part or all the principal had to be found through future assessments, Armory rentals or local projects. Consequently, by sundry and varied means, ranging from direct, single or joint appropriations of States, Cities, Towns and Counties to private efforts of voluntary associations, there was a rash of Armory expansions, new Armories, and Armory improvisations throughout the United States immediately following the Dick Act. With the temper of the times what it was, dissenting economic historians and left-wing journalists occasionally have interpreted all new Armories of this era as a part of the domestic "class warfare." Many Guardsmen of that era were misunderstood and abused accordingly. All through these years, with constant reorganizations, shuffles, and changing equipment, the Guard maintained an overall strength of well over 100,000 officers and men.

Notwithstanding the heroic efforts of many large and small Unit Commanders, each working within a pattern that he and his officers thought the most likely to achieve success, the Regular Army inspection reports of this era all-but call upon the saints to witness the horrible manner in which the irresponsible States and their Guardsmen were dissipating, misusing, and failing to care for the obsolescent, heavy Krag rifles and other more-or-less war surplus guns and uniforms from the Spanish War.

The inspectors often conceded the splendid facilities often complemented a corresponding degree of high responsibility in the Armories at Louisville, Knoxville, Chattanooga; in Maryland, Minnesota, Wisconsin and the traditionally military-minded States of Pennsylvania, New York, Ohio and Illinois; but there are accusations ranging from arms stored in a damp Capitol basement, to no rifle racks at all, arms and equipment kept in homes of Guard enlisted men, and inadequate storage in rented rooms in many of the States. While the inspectors denounced the provinces for their property irresponsibility and lack of Armories in some areas and States, the War Department was having even less luck getting decent Armory facilities in the large and growing Federal City of Washington for its own District of Columbia National Guard.

When one views the entire picture, the States and the Guardsmen were not doing badly by the War Department and the Federal Government. In 1909, for instance, the Federal Government was issuing obsolescent arms and equipment listed at $2,053,316.82, and providing $807,286.45 under Section 1661 of the Revised Statutes, and $1,246,030.37 under Section 14 of the Act of 1903. For the same year and also according to Federal reports, the States were doing much better. Their Legislatures provided a total of $9,438,286.49 in various forms of National Guard support.

The equipment normally sent the Guard was not the latest, notwithstanding the implications of the Dick Act. It was not until 1905 that all the Guard units had the Krag magazine rifle. By then it was actually out of date. The famed 1903 Springfield was already in production. Nor was the other equipment up to the mark, as intended by the law. In 1905 only 1,169 of the Guard's 2,151 units were considered "fully armed, uniformed, and equipped for field service at any season of the year," but progress continued throughout this period.

The obsolescent and obvious war surplus character of much of this equipment, combined with the long feeling of local autonomy within the units, made property accountability a slow, educational process. Though the States of New York, West Virginia and Wisconsin were, by 1912, especially cited as excellent in this respect, the situation was so bad in one State that the Secretary of War temporarily denied it any additional funds or supplies. As a way out, he suggested that the State Adjutant General be made a property and disbursing officer with a Federal salary and thereby accountable to Washington. Others for some years had been suggesting paid "Care-takers." Here we find the origins of ideas that reached fruition in the legislation of 1916 and after.

It is axiomatic that attendance and training improved between 1903 and 1912. They follow improvements in housing and equipment with the certainty that the stars move in their courses. For the highly-important Federal visitations of 1903, absenteeism averaged 23.4%. By 1907, the percentage had been reduced to 14.48. Rhode Island and New York were tops with percentages of absences for Federal inspections of only 1.05 and 2.55, respectively. The Territory of Arizona, standing hat in hand for Statehood, looked extremely bad with 48.9% absent. But Nevada, a larger-than-average State with then less than 75,000 population, spared Arizona a blush from being at the bottom. Nevada had 60% absent, and from sheer disgust thereby went out of the National Guard business for many years.

The Dick Act did not call for more than 24 drills, or target practices, a year at home stations, and five days in the field, normally during the Summer months. In 1907 no less than 97 of the 2,094 units had failed to comply with the full measure of five days in the Summer. Some of these, perhaps most, were undergoing reorganization or redesignation in the War Department's constant shifts in efforts to achieve the General Staff's mercurial ideas of a balanced force. But some Guard units just failed. Worse yet, 155 units, for various reasons, had not made their 24 drills. Widely-scattered and rural situations reflected by the attendance reports from Nevada and Arizona are partially explanatory. But these shortcomings were more than offset by voluntary drills in more populous areas far in excess of the minimums under the Dick Act of 1903.

Many Regiments prescribed weekly drills except during the five to 15 days of the Summer encampment. While few States joined New Mexico in requiring 15 days, few took the minimum as a satisfactory figure. Some States prescribed different periods for different Arms. North Carolina thought seven days enough for Infantrymen, but apparently thought 10 days none too much for her Coast Artillery Batteries. Ohio required eight to 15 days, whereas a New York Guardsman could get by on eight, nine or 10 days, dependent upon his Regiment and Arm.

## EFFORTS FOR A BALANCED FORCE

The struggle toward a balanced force of all Arms was then, and apparently still is, a chronic problem. The Regular Army never has solved this problem for itself, but since 1903 has been quite articulate as to what the Guard should be. The Guardsmen, however, brought it upon themselves and even today seem even more pleased with their original demands for a balanced force of all Arms, though occasionally there are dark suspicions that some of the Pentagon's reorganization and redesignation ideas for the Guard occasionally have been related to motives independent of the balanced, combat force concept. Be that as it may, the basic fact remains that the Guardsmen in 1903 demanded and received the right to be organized into units of Infantry, Artillery, Cavalry, Engineers, Signal Corps and such other elements of a fighting Army as normally would constitute a balanced force.

This term implies specifics to the mind of every educated soldier, but few agree as to the precise details for achieving the perfect balance. And nothing will upset the balance in the thinking of everyone like the suddenly-revealed obsoleteness of one weapon or the devastating power of a new one. In 1903, the machine gun was one of the great unknowns. A few bold dreamers were saying the horse and saber were on the way out. Thus, reorganization into properly-balanced teams of the Combat Arms was almost as much of a problem in the era 1903-12 as it is today. Accordingly, while the Regular Army was pulling and hauling over the General Staff concept, the Guardsmen were up to their eyes in arguments as to how they could conform to the requirement that they be organized on the same identical patterns as the Regular Army.

This means the decade following the Dick Act was a time of argument and turmoil within the Guard. Much was done, however. In those years, a total of 792 units were disbanded and 902 new units created on the new patterns. Though the letter of the law that all this reorganization should be complete within five years had not been met, the War Department extended praise for the achievements. By 1909, all but Delaware and Pennsylvania and a few stray units in 11 other States were in conformity with comparable Regular Army Tables of Organization.

This had been expedited in no small degree by the meeting of the National Guard Association in Boston, 1908. At this session the word was given out for a new, overall organization of the Regulars and Guard jointly. Throughout, they would be integrated into 17 combat Divisions, with the Guard furnishing two-thirds of the Regiments in each Brigade, two-thirds of the Batteries in each Artillery Battalion, and two-thirds of the Squadrons in each Cavalry Regiment.

This plan was further announced in detail in 1910, along with sharp criticism of the Guard Battalions of less than four Companies in being. Deficiencies also were cited in special units in the five States, Illinois, New Jersey, Ohio, New York and Pennsylvania, which already were maintaining Divisions. Some historic Regiments with units in overlapping localities also were bringing headaches to the paper planners of the blossoming General Staff in Washington.

But ideas were coming from the field. Though these early Staff planners rejected them, they were accepted eagerly by later planners. Guardsmen from North Carolina and Michigan for example, arrived at the simultaneous conclusion in 1910 that all National Guard Regiments should be renumbered from 100 upwards. This would avoid the confusion inherent in 40 or more different Regiments of Infantry having the word "1st . . . Infantry" in their official designation. Seven years later, under the pressure of World War I reorganizations, the idea was adopted and prevails unto this day.

By 1912 much progress had been made, but not enough to satisfy the War Department. The Guard, by that time, had nearly all the Infantry and Signal units needed for the new 17-Division pattern, but of Cavalry Squadrons only 75% of the required number were in being. Guard Artillery and Engineer units were short 50% for the proposed 17 integrated Divisions plans. The Guardsmen denounced the General Staff's failure to issue horses, artillery pieces and other technical equipment. The General Staff maundered about the Guard's inflexibility. The scheme was dumped as impractical. This brought little or no visible unhappiness among the Guardsmen, particularly within those States that had, or could show, a potential for a complete Division within their own boundaries.

Actually, the regional flexibility of the Guard organization, inherent in decentralization of authority and freedom from departmental red tape, allowed the Guard to do some forward-looking planning and reorganization that were denied the Regular Army. For example, Congress had specified by law exactly what should be the composition of units of the Regular Army. But the applicable statute did not make any provision for machine gun units, though they had been used in the Spanish War and their value was fully recognized. But by legal default, the best the Army could do was to buy some experimental models of the weapon and issue them to "special duty" details from Rifle Companies. These details often bore a striking similarity to Machine Gun Platoons. The military literature of the day continued to advocate the need for Machine Gun Companies.

Nebraska had taken considerable abuse, since the Dick Act, in military matters, which may or may not be the reason for a National Guard Machine Gun Company being organized at Beatrice, Nebraska, January 25, 1910. At first the War Department offered encouragement; thought it could furnish the Benet-Mercier model to the Guard, but later hedged with the warning that since Machine Gun Companies did not "conform" to any existing, legal Regular Army pattern, a Machine Gun Company never could be brought into the Federal service as such.

This did not bother the Guardsmen too much. By 1911 there were two Machine Gun Platoons in Illinois and one in Oklahoma, and a

202

Machine Gun Company in Minnesota. More units were added, there and elsewhere. When Congress, in 1915, under the impetus of the successful use of the weapon in the Balkan wars and the first year of fighting in France, still was being asked to authorize Machine Gun units for the Regular Army, there were no less than 35 Machine Gun Companies in the National Guard.

Meanwhile, the long-deceased Upton's book on the alleged failures of all past military policies, and insisting, among other things, upon a General Staff along European lines, had been in print eight years as a public document. It had gone through two or three printings to become the all-but Holy Writ of the American General Staff Corps it supposedly had created. General Ainsworth, the last of the recalcitrant old dons in open opposition to the Staff, was taking his whipping (not lying down, but nevertheless taking it) from Secretary of War Stimson, and Leonard Wood. The complete triumph of the Staff was imminent. A result of all these factors, as John McA. Palmer has written, was a completely Uptonian-minded General Staff on personnel matters, which was not the thought Mr. Root had in mind when he had the book printed in support of the General Staff concept.

Nevertheless, under the Uptonian impulse, the War Department's newly-born General Staff was turning away from both the Guard as a balanced force and the Root concept of a new Army of U. S. Volunteer Regiments. It was becoming captivated by Upton's vague but oft-reiterated insistence for an "expansible Regular Army." Of course, it often was playing with words, as had Upton, but the attractive term, "expansible Regular Army," has intrigued and confused planners even unto our own day. In any event, it was this and an Attorney General's opinion in 1912 that caused some officers in key positions to become blind to the idea of building constructively upon known institutions. Like all planners of little experience, they had the high urge to rub-out and begin over, as if three centuries of historical evolution could be ignored.

But while the burgeoning General Staff first was being charmed by the Uptonian phrase "expansible Regular Army," the Guardsmen in 1908 had sought and received, on the strength of the progress, an Amendment to the Dick Act which materially strengthened their position. These Amendments are dated May 27, 1908, 34 days before Secretary of War Taft vacated the office to begin his successful candidacy for the Presidency. They provided that in an emergency, the Organized Militia, or National Guard, was to be called-up before the Volunteers; the nine-months tour of duty was dropped in favor of a clause whereby the President could specify the time to be served, though this action of the President could not automatically extend the term of an individual

Guardsman's enlistment. The Amendment further stated the Organized Militia, or National Guard, could be called into Federal service "either within or without the Territory of the United States."

This must have been a shock to such stalwart, early Uptonian disciples as Carter, the War Department's Staff expert who had been most instrumental in unearthing the long-buried Upton manuscript and who had done all in his power to discredit the Guard while Mr. Root was Secretary. But the erstwhile Colonel was not doing badly. Mr. Root had made him a Brigadier General before leaving the War Department. He was soon (November 13, 1909) to demonstrate the adeptness one learns through years of palace soldiering. He wangled a second star as Chief of Artillery, notwithstanding the brutal fact that not a day of his 36 years of service was in the Artillery Branch. Yes, the discoverer of Upton's philosophical greatness was finding the General Staff idea personally advantageous. But Carter was consistent to the end, as all will note who care to study his book, *The American Army*, published in 1915. It stands as a major exhibit of the General Staff effort, backed by the young, unseasoned Secretary Stimson, to destroy the National Guard as a National defense institution.

### THE GUARDSMEN RECEIVE A RUDE SURPRISE

Incidentally, it was the revival of interst in things military that made General Carter's book, *The American Army*, an attractive trade title for a commercial publisher. By 1912 it had become apparent that the troubles in Mexico, beginning the Summer of 1910, (Madero versus Diaz) were much more than a Latin-American election with bullets instead of ballots. Hard on the heels of this realization came the Balkan wars, precursors of the World War I chaos of 1914. Though America was enjoying the apparent splendid isolation underwritten by two large oceans, she could well afford to check her weapons and forces.

By 1912 the National Guardsmen considered themselves fully a part of these forces. They had met Mr. Root's challenge. They had done and were doing far more than had been asked of them. The per capita disbursements on them and their units by the Federal Government had been negligible compared to the per capita costs of the Regular Army. If they were not better-outfitted and better-trained, it was hardly their fault. Through their National Guard Association they had made constructive suggestions to this end. They had done about all that could be done without "Caretakers" or Armorers for their issued equipment. They were clamoring for more and better Regular Army Instructors to be available at all times to all units, at least to the Battalion and Squadron level. For Armories and additional drills and additional Summer camp time, they had procured about all that could be drawn from the States.

204

All the foregoing and some form of drill pay seemed in order if the Federal Government was going to call upon the Guard to pipe a longer and stronger tune. Certainly the Guardsmen had shown their willingness in the Amendment to the Dick Act of May 27, 1908, when they sought and received additional responsibilities to the Federal Government. Indeed, many felt comfort in the assurance that they had guaranteed themselves a place in the forces by getting these additions to the law. Any smugness some Guardsmen may have felt under this legal guarantee for full participation in America's defense was rudely shattered in February, 1912. Against the possible need for an intervening Army of Occupation to police Mexico, such as went to Cuba, 1906-1909, a Constitutional question was raised. Could the National Guard be used beyond the limits of the United States to serve in, or as a part of, such an occupation force?

President Taft's Attorney General, George W. Wickersham, of Pennsylvania and New York, answered the question in a written opinion that gave the Guardsmen of that era a severe jolt. He held (29 *Opinions of the Attorney General,* 322, 1912), that the Federal Government had no Constitutional authority to send State Militia, of which the National Guard was the organized elements, outside the United States. He reluctantly conceded that hot pursuit across the Border might well be part of any action to repel invasion, but service in an army of invasion or on extended occupation and police duty was unconstitutional.

The dual status of the National Guard, hovering as the units did between State and Federal authority, still awaited a solution. The Guardsmen had met Mr. Root's challenge. His successors in office had conceded their worth by expanding their scope of usefulness. But this legal opinion by Mr. Wickersham put them right back to 1902, and where they were before the Dick Act. But it was not against Wickersham that the Guardsmen vented their bitterness. It was against Leonard Wood and his growing General Staff of palace soldiers. It was they and their Judge Advocate's Section who had inspired and written the opinion to their own purposes from its inception.

# Bibliographical Note For Chapter VIII

The most remunerative sources concerning the National Guard immediately following the passage of the Dick Act are in the *Annual Reports of the War Department,* most particularly those of the *Division of Militia Affairs,* which, by 1910, had become one of the four coordinate branches of the General Staff of the War Department. Maj. Gen. William H. Carter, *The American Army,* 1915, epitomizes the views and objectives of the younger post-Spanish War professionals. Uptonianism and the influences of European professionalism are quite apparent. The *Proceedings of the National Guard Association of the United States* naturally reflect the opinions of the citizen-soldiers. Lt. Col. Marvin A. Kreidberg and Lt. Merton G. Henry, *History of the Military Mobilization in the United States Army, 1775-1945,* an official publication of the Department of the Army, 1955, Chapter VI, summarizes well the problems of the era and gropings toward a policy. The magazines of the day sounded strong notes in behalf of professionalism within the Services. This was in part due to the Army's having a number of officers who were both articulate in print and persuasive. Secretary of War Stimson ably assisted them. Most significant was a coordinated, far-reaching series of articles, in which Stimson as Secretary of War wrote the concluding article. The articles appeared originally in the highly-influential *Independent,* Vol. 72, (1912), but they were brought together later and published as an official document. They were: Maj. Gen. Leonard Wood, U.S.A., "What is the Matter with our Army? It Lacks Concentration," *Independent,* Vol. 72, pp. 301-4; Brig. Gen. Clarence Edwards, U.S.A., "What is the Matter with our Army? It Lacks Organization," *Independent,* Vol. 72, pp. 408-11; Col. Hunter Liggett, U.S.A., "What is the Matter with our Army? Its Alienation from the People," *Independent,* Vol. 72, pp. 460-64; Maj. George H. Shelton, "What is the Matter with our Army? Its Piecemeal Development and Divided Control," *Independent,* Vol. 72, pp. 619-23; Brig. Gen. Robert K. Evans, "What is the Matter with our Army? The National Failure to realize its Purpose," *Independent,* Vol. 72, pp. 777-80; and, Henry L. Stimson, "What is the Matter with our Army?" *Independent,* Vol. 72, pp. 827-28. Herman Hagedorn, *Leonard Wood: A Biography,* 2 vols., 1931, is the most rewarding biographical study of this era. The recent biography of Stimson, Elting E. Morison, *Turmoil and Tradition: A Study of the Life and Times of Henry L. Stimson,* 1960, naturally places its emphasis upon the more dramatic era of World War II. For reasons given as to unconstitutionality of Militia use for planned invasion and foreign occupation duty, see 29, *Opinions of the U.S. Attorney General,* 322.

CHAPTER IX

# The Guard Fights for Its Life
## --1912-1916

THE OPINION of Attorney General Wickersham that the Federal Government had no Constitutional authority to send units of the Organized Militia, or National Guard, to service beyond the limits of the United States, caught the Guard leaders surprised and unprepared.

The question had often been raised and favorably answered. It had attracted the attention of some of the best legal minds in and out of Congress. The Congress twice had debated and accepted the complete flexibility in use of such a force as the Dick Act and its amendments of 1908 had contemplated. Moreover, every Guard officer with any memory of the Spanish War, then but 14 years in the past, knew the War Department had found no unsurmountable legal barrier keeping National Guard Regiments from service in Cuba when President McKinley had turned to the Governors and State Adjutants General in 1898. Some

207

Regiments had gone to the Philippines, fought battles and performed occupation duties long after the Peace Treaty with Spain was signed! The legal authority for such foreign service existed within the Dick Act.

It still provided the possibility for their Call and perhaps ultimate absorption into Mr. Root's Volunteer Army, the retention of which in the Act the Guardsmen had viewed initially as both a challenge and a threat. Furthermore, all men with legal training and a sense of military history, of whom the Guard always had attracted an appreciable number, knew the War Department had found prompt and ready means in the Mexican War for the utilization of State-created combat formations of Organized Militia units. Likewise, they knew the War Department seldom before had quibbled over thin Constitutional implications, and during the Civil War on more than one occasion cavalierly had ignored some of the Constitution's most conspicuous clauses. Why the War Department's sudden warmth for some of its thinly-drawn Constitutional implications in 1912? The War Department may or may not have realized it, but almost any answer could only bring the malodorous aroma of bad faith to the nostrils of the volunteer Guardsmen.

## POLITICAL WARRIORS CHALLENGE THE GUARD

Be that as it may, the answer was that the Judge Advocate of the Army had prepared a brief citing the unconstitutionality of the vital provision of the Dick Act. He had laid it on the desk of Secretary Stimson, who had been from his New York law office six months, or less, when he first saw the brief. Of course, Mr. Stimson could have ignored this staff paper, as many Secretaries have done before and since, but big-league lawyers do not ignore legal opinions, particularly when they come from within their own firm, so to speak; and Mr. Stimson most likely viewed this as such a document. Since it seemed persuasive to his legal mind, it is quite apparent that he passed the buck to Mr. Wickersham, the Attorney General. He had agreed with the Army's Judge Advocate. This saddled Mr. Stimson with an opinion he could not ignore had he desired. With Leonard Wood his Chief of Staff and source of guidance, he could have had no such desire. The remaining alternatives were a new law or new plans for the National Guardsmen.

If the Army's Judge Advocate had a legal draft and brief for the former alternative, it was not revealed. But the Uptonian-minded General Staff, led by General Wood, was prompt with an elaborate personnel blueprint for disposing of the National Guard as a component of the American Army.

Wood had followed Major General J. Franklin Bell as Chief of Staff, April 22, 1910. General Wood was one of those rare soldiers who had the unusual quality of bringing more prestige to his rank than his rank brought to him. That he was energetic, versatile and carried the spark of genius, courage and imagination to every task that challenged him, his most severe critics never have denied. With those sparks flashed a flair for publicity and cold, endless ambition.

On an M.D. degree from Harvard, he entered the Army Medical Corps as an Assistant Surgeon, January 5, 1886. That Summer he made news with Lawton's thin Cavalry column riding hard on the heels of the Old West's last great hostile, the aging Chief Geronimo. In March, 1898, he was leaving his post as White House Physician to President McKinley to command the legally-authorized but non-extant 1st Regiment, U. S. Volunteer Cavalry ("Rough Riders"). Someone in Washington belatedly remembered those hard-riding deeds of 12 Summers past. He was awarded the Medal of Honor. It was timely if belated. It could embellish the blouse of a Colonel, U.S.V., if and when he and the prospective Lieutenant Colonel Theodore Roosevelt, then vacating his duties as Assistant Secretary of the Navy, had organized their proposed Regiment. Colonel Wood's battlefield promotions to Brigadier General and Major General of Volunteers, his proconsulship as Military Governor of Cuba, and subsequent integration into the Regular Army as a Brigadier General, U.S.A., in 1901, and thence to Major General and Chief of Staff, constitute a well-known and brilliant record. With such a man quarterbacking the General Staff and presenting the plans for the Guard's destruction to the inexperienced but forceful Mr. Stimson, the Guardsmen knew they had a fight on their hands.

It was a fight for which the Guardsmen were unprepared. Senator Dick, who had fathered their Bill in the House of Representatives in 1903, had moved in 1904 to the Upper House, where he had been a pillar of strength for the Amendments of 1908. But in 1911 he had returned to his private law practice in Ohio.

## THE DIVISION OF MILITIA AFFAIRS UNDER HOSTILE LEADERSHIP

There was, to be sure, a Division of Militia Affairs in the office of the Chief of Staff, pursuant to the Departmental reorganization in 1903. But it had been caught in the squeeze created by the power plays of the Chief of Staff versus the recalcitrants in the Army Adjutant General's Department. The latter's office had continued to prepare instructions and digest and arrange reports for encampments, training and sundry other important details. In 1908 Mr. Taft, as the Secretary of War, clarified the situation by putting the Division of Militia Affairs in the office of the Secretary of War and vesting it with overall supervision of the Guard, including all the functions previously retained by The Adjutant General. All records and work pertinent to the Organized Militia, or National Guard, formerly under General Ainsworth thus were transferred to the Secretary's Office.

In 1910 the Division of Militia Affairs was switched to the Chief of Staff, but as one of the four coordinate Divisions of the War Department General Staff, its head reported directly to the Chief of Staff. In 1911, Congress first mentioned the Division of Militia Affairs by placing a General Officer at its head and making him an additional member of the General Staff Corps. Under Brigadier General Albert L. Mills, a rugged, forthright old Cavalry Regular with a recent, distinguished record as Superintendent of West Point, the Division came to life. It quickly distributed to the Guard more than a million publications and forms, handled 24,804 pieces of incoming correspondence and 127,049 papers relating to disbursements.

It served as an information clearing house for all National Guard, or Organized Militia, matters. The Division was staffed by competent Regulars with a devotion to detail that gave them an understanding of the Guard. Most of them later achieved enviable records in the field through World War I. Consequently, while General Mills, schooled in the rigid disciplines of the Service, was not a man to argue with Leonard Wood on matters of policy, an area in which he was prepared to take orders, he and his Division were an agency whence full and accurate figures and facts existed. Their availability, interpretation, release and use were in the hands of Mills and Wood.

The Guardsmen and their proponents had one entree into the halls of the Department. It was a thin reed upon which to lean, but better than nothing. A so-called National Militia Board had been created in the legislation of 1908. It was intended to provide representation in official circles for the National Guardsmen of the several States to advise the Secretary of War on the "condition, status and needs" of the Guard. Its members met annually in Washington. They made recommendations on all sorts of details concerning allowances, ammunition, inspections, field training, and such other minor items as a distinctive insigne to indicate both the U. S. and the State affiliations of the units.

An extra and special meeting was called in 1912 to hear officially the bad news inherent in the Attorney General's opinion and to consider the new Army plan of that year. About all that was accomplished was that the members left Washington as a delegation of self-appointed Paul Reveres, spreading the alarm. But to finish the story of this "advisory body," we can add here that the year following the Secretary of War had a tight agenda awaiting it. In this 1913 meeting the group went far beyond the agenda with some uninvited and unwelcome recommendations of its own. The meeting of 1914 was called again to deal with minor matters, but its members were in constant after-hours conferences with the Association of the State Adjutants General, who were in session in Washington through the same dates.

Smarting under the restricted agenda, and, no doubt, encouraged by their Adjutants General, the Advisory Board members proposed that their own Chairman be authorized to call meetings instead of waiting for the Secretary of War to give the nod. But for this they promptly were rebuked by the Chief of the Militia Division. The Secretary, Mr. Garrison, whom President Wilson brought to the Department, made the tactical error of asking them for advice as to how they could be more effective as an Advisory Board. They responded that the Board should have all peacetime Regulations pertaining to the Guard referred to it before being issued. They further presented him with the draft of a law calculated to get that result. The Guardsmen wanted to protect themselves against peacetime arrogance through Regulations prepared by a General Staff, which were often contrary to the letter and spirit of a law. But the Division Chief, General Mills, gave them the answer they had every right to expect: "Impractical and hampering of routine"— rejected!

The idea was not resurrected until the National Guardsmen got something to the same effect inserted into the National Defense Act of 1916. Nevertheless, the Board met again in annual session in 1915. The Department kept the meeting on strictly routine matters, but in the Fall of that year there was a special meeting called by Mr. Garrison to announce his newest and final plan. It would have completely relegated the Guard to a home front force—the last thing it wanted. The Guardsmen refused to go along.

Mr. Garrison considered no meeting necessary in 1916, and there was none. Thus, the final future of the Guard passed from the planning rooms of the War Department to the Halls of Congress. There the Guardsmen fought one of their greatest legislative battles against Secretaries Stimson and Garrison, the General Staff, and their "Continental Army Plan." But in the shuffle of events, the National Militia Board members briefly found themselves out of existence as an "advisory body."

## THE ISSUES ARE JOINED

But let us return to Mr. Stimson and February, 1912, when he found himself confronted by the Attorney General's opinion that had been inspired by the General Staff and legally briefed by his own Judge Advocate General. Mr. Stimson's attitude toward the National Guard changed almost overnight. A short time prior to the adverse opinion, he had been pleading for more money for the Guard as constituted when he took office the preceding May. Within days after Attorney General Wickersham's opinion saying the Guard troops could not serve outside the United States as part of an army of planned invasion and occupation, Mr. Stimson, with dubious legality, was more than willing to switch

211

funds from the Guard allotments to other Departmental purposes. To the astounded Guardsmen, this was stealing from the Guard units to fatten the Regulars. That Mr. Stimson may have been within the strict letter of the Appropriation Law and was indeed hard-pressed for funds with which to concentrate the weight of the home front Regulars along and near the Mexican Border, did not assuage their dismay. With irrefutable logic, the Guardsmen argued that when the Regulars encountered additional fiscal burdens, they should go to the Congress and ask for additional funds.

As they approached a showdown with General Wood and his General Staff, Mr. Stimson's attitude convinced them they were without a civilian friend in a War Department that had capitulated to those who would deny them a complete soldier's role in the wars of their Country. The future of the National Guard could be determined only in Congress, with the concurrence of the President.

The National Guardsmen necessarily were slow in learning the details of the opposition's plan, but they had full reason to believe the General Staff already had organized a special and active lobby in the halls of Congress, with or without the tacit consent of the new Secretary of War.

On May 25, 1911, only three days after Mr. Stimson had moved in, Senator Henry F. du Pont had introduced a Bill to "provide for the raising of Volunteer Forces of the United States in time of actual or threatened war." By the very nature of his State's and family's interests in munitions, he was known to be quite close to the professionals of both the Army and the Navy. The measure was considered a child of the Palace Regulars. It was not a Bill that gave the Guard initial concern, though Mr. Stimson enthusiastically endorsed it in his report for that year. After the usual trips back and forth to committees, such legislation as finally emerged on the subject, August 22, 1912, merely provided a scale of bonuses for men with prior honorable and creditable service in the Regular Army who would "reenlist" into an on-call status in an Army Reserve. Senator du Pont's law further lengthened the Regular Army enlistment period to seven years, the first four of which would be with the Colors and the last three on furlough to the new Army Reserve, from which the soldier would be subject to immediate recall to active duty. Mr. Stimson publicly thought the time with the Colors was longer than necessary, in the light of "experience of nations in Europe," but was sure the new measure was a step in the right direction. Privately he did not think much of it; he considered it too much a professional theory. Two years and three months later, Secretary Garrison was to write into his 1914 Annual Report: "We have a Reserve—that is, men who have been trained in the Army and under the terms of their enlist-

212

ment are subject to be called back to the colors in time of war—consisting of sixteen men."

Accordingly, this preliminary legislation looking toward an "expansible Regular Army" not only left the Guard untouched but its patent failure ultimately strengthened the Guard's hand. But the Guardsmen in the Summer of 1912, as the Act was being debated and passed, did not know such legislation could fail so dismally. They only knew they had a fight on their hands and that Bills hostile to them were being poured into the Congressional hopper. Ten days before the foregoing Army Reserve measure became a law, the War Department issued a new plan, entitled *Organization of the Land Forces of the United States.* This plan of August 12, 1912, abolished the "17 Integrated Divisions" plan of 1910, of which Guard units in being were a part, and actually proposed cutting officers and men out of the National Guard, or units of the Organized Militia, and collecting them into a new Federal Reserve, whence they would be available as individuals for beefing-up the depleted units and nominal cadres of the Regular Army. At last the Guard knew the full implication of the "expansible" concept.

The Guard had a long tradition, antedating George Washington and his tattered Continental Line, of being "expendable" rather than "expansible." But the Guard's tradition contemplated expendability in units of its own initial origin and not as an aggregation of warm bodies to facilitate the "expansibility" of Regular Army Regiments.

At basic issue was, and still is, the ages-old question with which Flavius Vegetius, the old Roman advisor to Theodosius the Great, and many others since, have wrestled. How much of what kind of training does a soldier need before he is prepared for combat? How small can a highly-trained professional cadre be and, at the same time, absorb recruits to war strength and, as a unit, be ready how soon? When should basic training end and military specialties within unit training begin? Confronted by a sudden crisis, what does a nation that is committed to a small, professional force, need most urgently? For a powerful, ready reserve, is the best investment in large numbers of highly-functional units organized into fully-equipped, battlefield teams of the associated Arms but composed of volunteer, part-time avocational soldiers, such as the citizenry in the National Guard? Or can the nation best trust its final security to a manpower reserve consisting of a vast pool of chosen civilians in which each man is trained as an individual to the few limited but highly-perfected skills of a predetermined military assignment slot in a paper Company, Battalion, Division, all to be activated by punch card and machine records processes?

In theory, the latter is perfect. Comes the emergency, the sorting machines and cards begin to purr, down to the last automatically—

Addressographed call to duty for each man, rank and rating, who proceed to rendezvous without delay to the assigned training cantonment, whose uniforms, arms and equipment await their arrival. But it is a Prussian General Staff officers' dream predicated upon a completely regimented society. But how functional is a Division created overnight in this manner for a major emergency? Is it not a misapplication of the Navy's technique of training for aboard-ship billets? But soldiers do not fight from built-in billets. They fight from teamwork formations—units. Without functional units in being, there is no emergency force. Such was and is Guard doctrine.

Of course, neither National Guardsmen nor Regulars of experience will completely accept the full adverse implications of either extreme. However, proponents of emphasis toward either extreme could then and can today be found within the ranks of both Regulars and Guardsmen. But generally speaking, the great mass of Guardsmen argued in 1912, and still do, that every soldier must quickly acquire the essential skills of his slot, or "billet" to borrow the Navy's term, but he is best motivated to do this and acquire necessary interchangeable skills with teammates through sustained association with members of a unit and all its equipment at home station and in the field. Teamwork, unit *esprit*, and unified understanding of purpose with confidence and mutual appreciation are achieved but slowly at best, but without which "slot perfection" becomes ineffective. Moreover, the Guardsmen of every era have demonstrated that individual technical skills and teamwork can be achieved within the Guard unit structure if the Government is willing to provide the equipment, instructors, Armories and drill pay comparable to the prospective demands. The Air National Guard is a living demonstration of this truth. Moreover, the per capita manpower cost will be far less than that of the Regulars for comparable skills and fully-functional teamwork.

But too often, when Guardsmen and Regulars get into a legislative hassle, neither pauses to indulge in these basic philosophies. At least, such was the case from 1912 to 1916. It immediately became a game of mutual recrimination (a technique that the General Staff boldly and blatantly initiated) and a question as to which could field the larger number of votes in the Houses of Congress.

An appendix to the Secretary's Annual Report for 1912 contained inaccurate, unjustified recriminations against the Guard as an institution. Moreover, at Norfolk, Virginia, the following October, a representative of the War Department told the Delegates attending the National Guard Association session that:

"Militia as such took practically no part in the Mexican War, the Civil War, or the Spanish-American. . . . We are again involved in war, the Armies which we will employ will be national armies. . . . We must avoid the confusion, embarrassment, and delay which characterized the breaking up of the Guard in 1898 in an effort to organize volunteers."

It is not likely that a Guardsman was present who did not recognize these statements as the basic, libelous lies that they were. They indicted the intelligence as well as the integrity of the speaker.

## THE GENERAL STAFF PROPAGANDIZES THE PUBLIC

Synchronized with all these showings of the General Staff's hand, General Wood personally, and coordinating with friendly journalists such as Richard Harding Davis, and the newly-founded and burgeoning Army League under its first President, Frederic L. Huidekoper, began a brilliant campaign for preparedness with emphasis on personnel. Citizens' Military Training Camps, each and every Summer, and the "Plattsburg Movement" for Officer Candidate Summer schools and training, were the salient features of General Wood's publicity throughout the Winter of 1912-13. As early as the Summer of 1913, two such camps were held for college undergraduates. From that year onward the camps grew and multiplied. General Wood and his General Staff were conspicuously looking for sources completely outside the Guard, and in no way associated with it, for a pool of individuals with superficial military knowledge and training to provide "fillers" for an "expansible," professional Army.

Meanwhile, the Army's Staff sections were busily engaged in new plans and new projects which finally jelled in the "Continental Army" idea. The very title of their plan was a theft from Organized Militia history. Also, a new political tide was bringing into office a resurgent Democratic party under the leadership of President Woodrow Wilson. He was inaugurated March 4, 1913. His War Secretary, Lindley Miller Garrison, took over Mr. Stimson's prior duties the day following. Messrs. Stimson and Garrison had much in common, notwithstanding their different party labels. Both were eminent attorneys with metropolitan clients. From Jersey City, Mr. Garrison served that side of the river, but his reputation as an able attorney extended the length of New Jersey with strong professional contacts in Philadelphia. He was a friend of Mr. Wilson and a warm supporter from the days when Wilson was progressing from the leadership of Princeton University to the Governorship of New Jersey, and thence to the White House.

Mr. Garrison, though critical of Stimson's long-enlistment Army Reserve Bill, found little to change in the War Department. Personnel for any impending crisis continued to be the major subject. Pilot models of effective field artillery and lack of ammunition stocks received comparatively slight attention. The flying machine was viewed as a mere novelty, but a review of the War Department activities and publicity of that era suggests little less than a phobia on the subject of personnel. Where men would be trained, how they would be clothed, fed, paid and deployed, with operational details for meeting threats or combinations of threats, could be ignored until a plan was found for filling the ranks of an "expansible Regular Army." Certainly the chaos of the subsequent 1916 mobilization of the National Guard to Mexican Border service revealed an utter absence of planning for the birds and problems in hand. General Wood and his Staff appear to have been expending all their efforts on the birds in the bush.

Mr. Garrison's arrival diminished in no way General Wood's free-wheeling publicity for citizens' military camps and civilian Officer Candidate Schools to create an unorganized mass of superficially-trained young men from a month in Summer camp.

The Guardsmen offered no opposition to these ideas and activities. Most viewed them with positive and warm approval. The more citizens who were interested in military training as a form of war preparedness, the better. It was good for Guard recruiting. The strength of their organized units was increasing. By June 30, 1912, strength was up to 122,000 officers and men without a corresponding or substantial increase in the numbers of units. The Regular Army at 82,305 officers and men was still about 5% under the numbers budgeted for that year. Though more new Second Lieutenants were commissioned from the ranks and direct from civil life that year than came into the Army from West Point, 134 vacancies remained unfilled.

All the while the General Staff continued its labors, invoking the assistance of the War College to solve the big question as to how the Uptonian dream of an "expansible Regular Army" could be achieved. Mr. Garrison gave these studies his blessing with even more enthusiasm than had Mr. Stimson. Both Secretaries equally accepted the General Staff's major assumption and thesis: The National Guard could not be used, merely because of an Attorney General's rejection of just one of the many provisions of the Dick Act. That this rejection might be cured by any one of several suggested legal formulas did not interest either the General Staff or Mr. Garrison. But the overall, hopelessly worthless character of the Guard units was propagandized continuously.

## PROGRAM OF GUARD HARASSMENT IS INITIATED

The virtue of the Regulars was extolled equally. Criticisms of the Guard were underscored in all manner of critical reports from the field. The anti-Guard propaganda also took the form of harassing tactics on items that the War Department itself alone could provide to the Guard, and were supposed to have taken care of under provisions of the Dick Act, but which never had been complied with.

216

It is worth noting that in 1913 Federal appropriations to the Guard totalled only $4,288,552.83. The same year the States collectively over-matched this with $5,834,140.77, and this for forces far in excess of what the States ever could need for maintenance of internal law and order. The General Staff's inspectors and balanced force studies nevertheless kept continually knocking the Guard for insufficient Cavalry and Artillery units; and further for inadequate riding and draft training in the existing units. But the Department would do nothing about horses. Many Guardsmen necessarily furnished, cared for and fed their own. A few crack Troops of proud States were able to wangle a few mounts from State or even municipal treasuries. Chicago's Black Horse Troop shared 55 publicly-owned horses with four other Troops. Pennsylvania's famous First City Troop could turn-out but 12 nags as State-owned organizational property. Its other mounts were privately-owned.

This was in the bitter European War years of 1914 and 1915, that the War Department General Staff was damning the Guard as worthless for not taking care of Mounted Service deficiencies that were the patent responsibility of the Federal Government. It was not until 1916, when the legislative triumph of the Guard appeared assured, and the war in Europe had accentuated the role of Artillery, that the War Department finally admitted that if it wanted much more than standing gun drill and service of the piece, it was up to the Department to give the Guard Batteries more than dummy rounds for obsolescent cannon. Forage and Caretaker funds for organization-owned horses were genuinely sought for the first time. Both General Wood and Mr. Garrison were then no longer in the Department.

Mercurial attitudes in the War Department with reference to funds was another form of unjustified Guard harassment in this period. Carping about storage and leather that was brittle with age from lack of care when issued was stepped-up. Shipments to Guard units were cancelled on sundry pretexts, usually that the State in question owed the War Department some money. Nothing short of an Act of Congress could get anything surveyed during this period. All these conditions were blamed on the Guard and swelled into a new, rising crescendo of anti-Guard ballyhoo.

## LEGISLATIVE SKIRMISHES

In the Spring of 1913 the Comptroller of the Treasury came in with an assist. He upset War Department fiscal practices in such a way that the Department threatened to abandon the entire Summer encampment program that year. A special action of Congress saved the encampments for the Guard by putting supervisory control over funds for the Guard units in other hands. From this incident and from the crystallizing attitudes of certain Governors and their powerful friends in both Houses of

Congress, General Wood and his Staff planners should have known the Guard would not take its dismemberment, or relegation to a home front Constabulary, lying down. Nevertheless, the Staff planning went forward as if certain that an Attorney General's opinion sustaining a legal flaw, turned-up and magnified by their own Army Judge Advocate, had forever defeated the full potential for wartime service of patriotic Guardsmen.

The first real test of strength between the General Staff planners and the Guardsmen, under the leadership of their State Adjutants General and the National Guard Association, was over the so-called New Volunteer Act in the Spring of 1914. In its initial form the Bill was an attack upon those parts of the Dick Act favorable to the Guard. Through changes and reemphasis of that Act's clauses retaining Mr. Root's original concept of nothing but U. S. Volunteer Regiments, it was calculated to let the Guard, as constituted and nurtured since 1903, wither on the vine.

The Guardsmen marshaled their strength and successfully amended every clause that they thought did not best serve the interest of National defense and the Guard. In doing so, they touched nothing that would be a barrier to a quick expansion of the Regular Army by utilization of any Reserves it had or could create under either the Dick Bill or Mr. Stimson's later plan for long enlistments with only a comparatively short period "with the Colors." They accepted, even endorsed, provisions to create a pool of Reserve officers from existing Departmental lists or from graduates of Land Grant and military colleges. What the Guardsmen did get into the Bill, with the warm assistance of Congressman James Hay, Chairman of the House Military Affairs Committee, was that the "land forces of the United States of America shall consist of the Regular Army, the Organized Land Militia while in the service of the United States, and such Volunteer Forces as Congress may authorize." In effect, it again recognized the Guard as a component of the Army of the United States.

The Act further stated that Congressional approval must precede the Call. Prior to the Call of volunteers at large, the potential of the National Guard should be exhausted by acceptance of all Organized Militia units, of which three-fourths of their minimum enlisted strength might volunteer as units. The General Staff immediately complained. How could it plan without prophetic minds as to how many Guard units would volunteer at a given time under speculative situations? Of course, the Guardsmen's answer was that all of them would volunteer as units. How could they miss on a three-fourths decision of the minimum authorized strength of each unit? The Hay Bill of April 2, 1914, was a signal victory for the Guard. At the same time it was significant as the first faltering step of an inept War Department, that so long had overlooked

218

the potential of the Land Grant colleges and the State-owned military colleges such as V.M.I., the Citadel and Texas A. & M., toward tapping a vast potential source for Reserve officer material. The Guardsmen warmly supported this feaure of the law.

As this minor legislative victory was being won, the Guardsmen also came into a bit of luck. The conspicuous and personal publicity efforts of their implacable foe, General Wood, in the name of preparedness on land as well as at sea, not only had helped recruiting for the Guard, but his continuity in the public eye as a man determined to save a nation in spite of its incompetent political leadership, gave him the appearance of a Regular Army General with White House ambitions. The Republicans were known to be looking for a man without a party fight record whose neutrality between factions could heal the wounds of the 1912, Bull Moose split. General Wood could be their man! President Wilson was a political science professor before he was a politician. He knew the dangers to his own party inherent in either aggrandizing or discriminating against an ambitious military leader who might well achieve the top of the opposition ticket, come the next Presidential election year, 1916.

Accordingly, General Wood was quietly permitted to finish a four-year tour as Chief of Staff, April 20, 1914. Then, as if it were a routine matter, he was assigned to a command appropriate to his rank and seniority, where he could get publicity with great ease but also where he was fully insulated from the worsening Mexican situation and from the policy levels of the War Department. This put General Wood on Governor's Island, New York. General Funston, commanding the Mexican frontier from San Antonio, Texas, soon was to become the center of a shifting spotlight of public military interest. These events and Brigadier General John J. Pershing's getting the nod in 1917 for the top assignment in Europe, embittered General Wood and at the same time fanned his always-glowing ambition. His strong bid for the Republican nomination in 1920 helped to deadlock the convention and make a President of Senator Warren G. Harding.

## NEW CHIEFS OF STAFF

General Wood's successor in the Chief of Staff's office was Major General W. W. Wotherspoon. He was not the Staff type and hardly a year short of statutory retirement. Seven months later, November 14, 1914, he was followed by Major General Hugh L. Scott, an extremely able, scholarly type who was, among other things, the recognized authority on the Plains Indians, their languages, customs and mores. His was a mind that would irrevocably marry no single school of thought or formula in human affairs. With Wood's departure, the General Staff and Palace Regulars lost their uncompromising leader and best publicity man; and this just before their unveiling of their "Continental Army" plan in its final form. But Mr. Garrison was still with them and for their plan, hence initially there was no evidence of a change in pace whatsoever following General Wood's departure. Indeed, from his Governor's Island Headquarters, he continued to beat the tom-toms of publicity but without such an effective sounding board as he had found in the Washington Chief of Staff office.

The unveiling of the General Staff's ultimate, the "Continental Army" plan, hardly was done with a single gesture. It was eased-out with a series of studies, dignified by the War College imprint, under the title of *Statement of a Proper Military Policy for the United States.* There were 30 supplementary documents.

The attack upon the National Guard was from every conceivable angle, but conformed so conventionally to the prevailing pattern that there is no point in examining it further. While the studies had a tremendous impact in the newspapers and magazines, they also had the effect of convincing the Guard's friendly Representatives and Senators that the National Guard Association and the Governors were not merely crying wolf in the face of imaginary fears of extinction. Moreover, with a war in Europe and troubles South of the Border, it was refreshing to find citizens organized into the best military units that the parsimony of an uncooperative War Department permitted. At the same time, they were having to lobby for the opportunity to serve their Country in battle, subject to call any day and for the duration or a stated length of time. To Congressmen this was a refreshing experience. The Guard was gaining friends who would continue to fight its battles in Congress.

Moreover, Mr. Garrison and the Staff Regulars to whom he was a willing prisoner had labored and brought forth a military mouse. Their "Continental Army" was an embellished throwback to Mr. Stimson's idea that in more than two years had yielded but 16 Army Reservists. The scales, however, were weighted differently. The Regular Army would be approximately doubled to 141,843 officers and men. Active duty "with the Colors" would be greatly reduced to expedite rapid furloughing of 133,000 men per year into the "Continental Army" until the aggregate of active personnel and those "furloughed," but immediately available, Army Reservists underwrote an immediately-available Federal land force of 500,000 men. Those Guardsmen not lured into the "Continental Army" as individual Reservists could continue strictly as a Constabulary and local security force of their several States. To assuage them in this home front category, they would get more Federal money and aid than they had been getting as a component of the Nation's land forces under the Dick Act. This was viewed by many Guardsmen as a palpably sordid effort toward a buy-off.

# NATIONAL DEFENSE ACT OF 1916

The Guardsmen stood firm and united. They offered no opposition to college R.O.T.C. and readily accepted the concept of a Federal Officers' Reserve Corps and other significant provisions. But they had no intention of being relegated to second-class citizen-soldiers with home and fireside missions within their State boundaries. The basic issue was joined.

The Press and the public took sides with equally partisan heat. The Pacifists, Splendid Isolationists, Anti-Imperialists and escapists-in-general lifted up their voices in pious protests against such a vast, burdensome, armed host. ExPresident Theodore Roosevelt was sure a mere 500,000 men were ridiculously inadequate. In Europe millions were locked in stalemates on both Eastern and Western Fronts. General Wood, now that he was no longer Chief of Staff, had grave mental reservations. Messrs. Stimson, Root, and many others plopped for Mr. Garrison's plan exactly as written by the General Staff. They would change neither a comma nor a period.

Out of this turmoil the Guardsmen's legislators got exactly what the Guard had stood for all along: the complete Nationalization of the National Guards of the several States, as the favored phrase had it.

The National Defense Act of June 3, 1916, as it finally became a law, turned out to be the most comprehensive military measure in American history up to that date. Many of its principles remain. Even so, most likely no measure in any form would have been passed but for new troubles between the Navy and irresponsible Mexican revolutionists at Tampico. Then, March 3, 1916, General Pancho Villa staged his infamous raid on Columbus, New Mexico. It resulted in General Pershing's punitive, Cavalry column going deep into Mexico in a pursuit that was something less than hot. More and effective forces were needed.

These were the events that passed the Bill. The President and Garrison had disagreed so thoroughly on the War Secretary's personnel policies that the Secretary and the Assistant Secretary resigned in protest, of which there is more in the chapter that follows. Thus, the Defense Act of 1916 was essentially a Congressional Bill that finally faced-up to the entire problem. It increased the size of the Regular Army to 175,000 for a period of five years and authorized an Army Reserve similar to that proposed. But neither the new strength of the Regular Army nor its Reserve ever became recruited realities. It was the plan to utilize for the National defense the Militias of the States, both Organized and Unorganized, for which the Guardsmen had lobbied; thereby saving the Guard and paving the way for a modern Draft Law. These were, and still, are the most significant aspects of the 1916 legislation.

In the foregoing vital area of Militia Nationalization the law specifically said, "The Militia of the United States shall consist of all able-bodied citizens of the United States and all other able bodied males who have or shall have declared their intentions to become citizens of the United States, who shall be more than 18 years of age and younger than 45, and said Militia shall be divided into three classes: the National Guard, the Naval Militia, and the Unorganized Militia." It was this "Unorganized Militia" that soon was to be fingered for the Draft. The initial registrations and selections by lot, however, were initially from the 21-to-30 age group of hale-and-hearty males. Thus, the Guardsmen had builded better than they knew. In demanding their own Nationalization they highlighted and led to the establishment at the National level of a responsibility for service to which they always had been obligated, more or less by Common Law, to their Colonies and later to the several individual States of the American Republic.

As for the immediate future of the National Guard, right while the law was being passed, units of the Border States of Texas, New Mexico and Arizona were being activated under the old Dick Act of 1903, as amended. They were being assigned patrol missions. The Brigades, Regiments, Battalions and Batteries of the other States were soon to follow. In pinching-out sufficient Regular Army units for Pershing's Punitive Expedition, the military cordon along the Border was left so thin as to invite more incidents and raids. The President and his Pacifistically-inclined new Secretary of War, Newton D. Baker, felt the need for a Rooseveltian "Big Stick." The genuinely Pacifistic Secretary of State, Mr. William Jennings Bryan, already had turned-in his portfolio and checked out of diplomacy rather than sign his name to a tough note to the Kaiser on the sinking of the unarmed passenger liner *Lusitania,* thereby wantonly taking American lives. The Guardsmen were on the verge of having their enthusiasm for service thoroughly tested.

222

# Bibliographical Note For Chapter IX

Most of the authors and titles mentioned in the bibliographical notes for Chapters VII and VIII are equally applicable to this chapter. This is particularly true of the biographies of such men as Elihu Root, Leonard Wood and Henry L. Stimson and the articles in criticism of the National Guard. Likewise the *War Department Annual Reports* and *U.S. Statutes* for the period 1905-1916, contain the usual indispensable official documents and enactments for a study of this era of clamor for an "expansible army." *The Hearings on H. 14,483* (sometimes called the second Dick Act), 60th Congress, 1908, by the Committee on the Militia, is highly pertinent. Even more important is the House Committee on Military Affairs document, *To Increase the Efficiency of the Military Establishment of the United States* (National Defense Act of 1916), 2 vols., 64th Congress, 1916. *The Annual Proceedings of the National Guard Association of the United States*, 1907-1915, continue to be the most convenient reflector of the views and purposes of the Guardsmen through this period. In addition to the Huidekoper volume, previously cited, the public interest and often partisan writings on the military manpower are exemplified by the following: Henry Breckinridge, *Preparedness,* 1917; Ralph B. Perry, *The Plattsburg Movement,* 1921; Ira L. Reeves, *Military Education in the United States,* 1914; Maj. Gen. Leonard Wood, *The Military Obligation of Citizenship,* 1915. The following more-or-less typical magazine articles are also representative of news and views of the day: Eric Fisher Wood, "The New Army Act and the Militia," *Century Magazine,* Vol. 92, pp. 801-12, 1916; Leonard Wood, "The Army's New and Bigger Job," *World's Work,* Vol. 28, pp. 75-84, 1914; A. W. Page, "Garrison of the War Department." *World's Work,* Vol. 26, pp. 293-301, 1913; J. Bigelow, Jr., "If the United States Should Go to War," *Atlantic Monthly,* Vol. 107, pp. 833-44, 1911; William H. Carter, "The Militia Not a National Force," *North American Review,* Vol. 196, pp. 130-5, 1912; and, Henry L. Stimson, "Needs of Our Army," *Harper's Weekly,* Vol. 56, p. 12, August 31 issue, 1912. The *Readers' Guide to Periodical Literature* for years, 1910-1916, lists more than 100 additional articles and editorials in the above and similar magazines concerning military manpower, training and legislation. Many of them are by active duty Army officers and civilians in the War Department. Their interest in the tactics, strategy, equipment, materiel, artillery and scientific progress of their profession in America and elsewhere, is strangely lacking compared to that reflected by the writings of contemporary Naval officers.

## CHAPTER X

# Mr. Wilson Calls the Guard

THE NATIONAL DEFENSE Act of June 3, 1916, was not an Administration measure. As of his inauguration, March 4, 1913, President Wilson was a Pacifistic idealist to a degree of being unrealistic. The Mexican Revolution, with its irresponsible, regional warlords; its kaleidoscopic changes in the nominal Presidency of that unhappy country, the wanton murder of unarmed Americans in Mexico, and the Border incidents resulting in American deaths North of the Border, became Mr. Wilson's grim school of experience. In it he learned to discriminate between a theory and a condition.

He backed Rear Admiral Henry T. Mayo to the limit in the Tampico incident that quickly led to the capture of Vera Cruz, April 21, 1914. A Brigade of Regulars and a Regiment of Marines under General Funston, briefly occupied a perimeter about the City as a potential lodgment area for further operations. Offers of mediation by Argentina, Brazil and Chile, combined with the fall of the unrecognized usurper, President Victoriano Huerta, took the Pacifistic Mr. Wilson out of the dilemma of further invasion or withdrawal under pressure. Funston's forces were recalled to Texas City, on Galveston Bay. There Funston's command continued as elements of the Regular Army's badly-skeletonized, "reinforced" 2d Division. Its 15,000 men, distributed among units designed for a "war strength" of 25,000, represented the most potent "striking force" of United States troops in the Western Hemisphere.

The mild-mannered Mr. Wilson hardly had breathed a sigh of relief from this close brush with Mars when the war clouds over Europe let loose their torrents of men, steel and fire. Through the late Summer and following Fall of 1914, all the best military minds in Europe and America agreed it would be a short war—perhaps the shortest major war in history. The devastating firepower from long-range repeating rifles, from massed machine guns, from the fast fire-rate of the famed French '75, from the heavy but mobile siege guns, combined with the absolutely-certain intelligence inherent in air observation, had made all battlefields utterly untenable—so the experts said! Hence the war absolutely could not last through more than a few months.*

## DEFENSE BECOMES A MAJOR POLITICAL ISSUE

The President apparently believed them. But military, critical men like Teddy Roosevelt and Leonard Wood continued shouting for men, money and means for disciplining and "pacifying" unhappy Mexico and, further, to make sure of getting into the European act on the best possible terms, should the World situation demand it. Meanwhile, Mr. Wilson was planning quietly to be the neutral umpire, the peaceful moderator, perhaps chairman of the conference; or, at least, the "honest broker" when the spoils were distributed following the short European War. These Wilsonian thoughts were not foolish in Autumn, 1914. Had not President Theodore Roosevelt been awarded a Nobel Peace Prize in 1906 for doing exactly that at the end of the Russo-Japanese War? Thus the benign President frowned when told his Secretary of War

---

* Horatio H. Kitchener, Field Marshal and Earl of Khartum, was the one significant exception. He urged preparedness for a long, bitter war. At normal retirement age in 1914, his voice was considered that of a dotard who had learned nothing new, forgotten nothing old. His dramatic death in the sinking of H.M.S. *Hampshire,* June 1916, right while the stalemated Western Front and collapsing Russia were proving him to be so eminently and prophetically correct, greatly augmented the prestige and fame of his twilight years.

was becoming a prisoner of the General Staff professionals and was playing footsie with such blatant militarists as the publicity-minded General Wood, ex-President Roosevelt, war correspondent Richard Harding Davis and preparedness propagandist Frederic L. Huidekoper* along with their associates and affiliates in the National Security League and the American Defense Society. Their attacks upon the Wilson Administration's Pacifistic lack of realism created concern in the White House.

At the same time, the stalemated fronts through the cold Winter months, the wet Spring and the incredible Summer toll of trench warfare revealed the short-war theory as the idle mouthings of false prophets. The Eastern Seaboard's clamor for immediate preparedness was rising. Preparedness parades, naval and military, were becoming popular. Five-weeks Summer camps in the Plattsburg style became stylish for all masculine ages.

Preparedness had become a National issue. Mr. Joseph P. Tumulty, Wilson's White House Secretary, had a simple political philosophy of "count 'em carefully and if they seem to have a majority, join 'em." Consequently, in November, 1915, Tumulty rewrote a Wilson speech to include *immediate preparedness*. He arranged for the President to lead a Washington Preparedness parade on foot. Seldom, if ever, has a plank from the opposition's political platform been more artfully purloined.

But the President's War Department apparently did not know politics from policy, for it was this that emboldened the General Staff and Mr. Garrison to go all-out for their Continental Army plan. The Secretary of War even unveiled his complete plan, (though he knew Mr. Wilson was not in agreement) as if it were the fully-endorsed military program of the Administration. Mr. Wilson personally, and as an historian, viewed the Navy as the Nation's first line of defense. Likewise, Mr. Wilson knew there was a vast difference between the Organized Militia, or National Guard, and the unorganized Militia, or military manpower within the limits of each State. As an historian and professor of political science, he had written one of the better biographies (published 1897) of George Washington. His four-volume *History of*

---

* Mr. Huidekoper had been agitating for more preparedness since 1906. The General Staff had made a convert of him long before he witnessed in Europe the opening months of World War I. He returned to America late 1914. He lectured and wrote more than articles and impassioned pamphlets. He is said to have dashed-off his 717-page book, *The Military Unpreparedness of the United States,* in five months. This surprising time factor could easily be true. The first 15 chapters, in organization, style and viewpoint are nothing but an embellishment, paraphrasing, duplication, and expansion of Upton's *Military Policy of the United States,* which the author frankly admits in the preface. Like his preceptor, Mr. Huidekoper never achieves a working definition or a clean-cut differentiation between the National Guardsmen and the unorganized civilian manpower within military ages. Leonard Wood kissed the book with a eulogistic introduction.

*the American People* had been accepted as one of the more readable and scholarly reference works since its publication in 1902. His highly-interpretative *Division and Reunion* had required a depth of reading and profound knowledge of the Civil War. Expecting a scholar of that breadth of reading, research and writing to accept the Emory Upton propaganda myth that George Washington and his Continental Line were Regular Army was, of course, absurd. Mr. Wilson knew them to be the Organized Militia, or National Guardsmen, (as Lafayette later saw fit to call them) of their day. Mr. Wilson further knew State-organized Regiments of Volunteers the States sent into the Mexican War and into both armies of the Civil War to be the Organized Militiamen, or National Guardsmen of their day. Furthermore, as author of the even more widely-known *Constitutional Government of the United States,* Mr. Wilson was not likely to be a President who readily would accept an Attorney General's opinion on a Constitutional question without looking back of it. A Regular Army Judge Advocate's professional-soldier-serving legal opinion that an unsurmountable barrier precluded a full and effective use of National Guard units in a future foreign war, notwithstanding their use in all previous conflicts, was sure to arouse his suspicions.

## WILSON AND GARRISON DISAGREE

Certainly the President was not satisfied with Secretary Garrison's "Continental Army" plan when it first was shown him shortly prior to its surprisingly premature publication. Wilson had urged more attention and a greater role be given to the existing National Guard. He doubted if an expansible feature for the Regulars required such a large standing army as Garrison and the General Staff insisted was essential to the creation of the filler Reserves. Mr. Wilson also thought a brief period of training each Summer for three-year volunteer Reservists might be enough. Anyway, he could not see Mr. Garrison's maximum figures.

Mr. Garrison first took alarm over the draft of the President's speech to the Manhattan Club, New York, November 4, 1915. He protested passages about the Guard. He particularly took alarm over a phrase, "would not be organized as a standing force," with reference to the "Continental Army." Mr. Wilson said it was too late for him to change the speech, hence Mr. Garrison found himself stuck with the high administrative utterance. Garrison plunged ahead anyway with the plans he had inherited from Mr. Stimson and the palace soldiers. His attitude was unyielding. He hoped to win in the Congressional committees. There he encountered increasing resistance. He considered the Congressmen ignorant on military matters and needful of Presidential pressure.

On this, Mr. Wilson disagreed and refused. Garrison's friction with Congressmen blossomed into a feud.

In a final effort to patch the rupture between his War Secretary and Representative James Hay's Military Affairs Committee, Mr. Wilson did write Congressman Hay to give Garrison's plan serious consideration. Out of its context one of Wilson's paragraph's reads like a full endorsement, and a desire to sacrifice the Guard, but it was purely in the nature of oil on troubled waters. At the same time, Wilson was telling Garrison the Congressmen were not ignorant on military affairs and that he, as President, was irrevocably committed to no specific finality and "am willing to discuss alternative proposals." But this was not enough for Garrison. For him and his General Staff it was the entire "Continental Army" with its "expansibility" built-in with Reservists of its own creation, or nothing. Mr. Hay made it clear that they would probably get nothing, as he saw no major military legislation in the immediate future. By February 4, 1916, Mr. Garrison was shifting his positions, but still farther from that of the Congress than his original stand. Then came Garrison's wholly-unnecessary hassle with Speaker of the House, Champ Clark, over a Resolution concerning the Philippines. Mr. Garrison and his Assistant Secretary of War, Henry Breckinridge, dramatically tendered resignations. Mr. Wilson's acceptance was polite, regretful, warm in personal esteem; but between the lines and in later communications to others one detects a heavy sigh of Presidential relief that Garrison was gone.

## PANCHO VILLA EXPEDITES LEGISLATION

As noted in the preceding chapter and predicted by Mr. Hay, sweeping military legislation on personnel was not likely in 1916 until Mexican Border difficulties recurred. Mr. Wilson had evidenced no sense of urgency. The new Secretary, Newton D. Baker, was saying he knew nothing about the Army and all were taking him at his word. Congressman Hay and his House committeemen, not to mention some Senators, were ostentatiously refusing to be rushed. The more they saw of the General Staff's plans, the more suspicious they became. Mr. Hay openly told all and sundry to expect nothing that year. It was a Presidential election year with nominating conventions in the fast-approaching Summer.

Had Mr. Hay known Francisco (Pancho) Villa he might have been more cautious with prophetic remarks. The American State Department, having contributed to the fall of El Presidente Victoriano Huerta, gave its smiling blessing to the rapid rise and election of what appeared to be one of the more civilized of the Mexican regional warlords, one Venustiano Carranza. It quickly developed that North Mexican warlord Pancho Villa had more bullets than Carranza had ballots. The Revolution continued. Villa resented America's support to his principal opponent. To prove to the *Gringos* they had backed a man who could not bring peace to a troubled Mexico, he deliberately created Border incidents. He further found that constant defiance of the *Yanquis* increased his support within Mexico.

On the night of March 9, the end of Mr. Baker's first day in his new office, Pancho Villa raided Columbus, New Mexico, base of the 13th U.S. Cavalry. Villa's column is said by some to have numbered 1,500. It was most likely much smaller. In the night-shrouded confusion, they killed eight American Troopers, some still asleep, and nine civilians. Local pursuit was brief and unsustained, though it is said to have yielded some compensatory retribution. But whatever the local punishment may have been, it was not enough to suit the long-harassed Washington officialdom and the aroused citizenry of the West and Southwest. Public opinion was divided elsewhere.

In a spirit of "bring in Villa, dead-or-alive," General Pershing, commanding the Southwestern Department's Cavalry elements, was ordered to mount a "punitive expedition" capable of penetrating deeply enough into Mexico to accomplish the mission. There was the time lag for concentration, which in turn created wide, unguarded sectors of the Border.

Such mobile striking force as existed at the time of the raid consisted largely of the 2nd Infantry Division, which was on or near the Gulf of Mexico. As Pershing's dusty columns of Troopers moved Southward to Parral, his "Provisional Division" of two Cavalry Brigades, one of Infantry and a few auxiliaries, soon numbered more than 12,000. Civilian truck drivers, often seen in the S.O.S., were not included in this total. The American pursuit meanwhile was consolidating all Mexican factions on one point of agreement: all should fight *Los Americanos*.

Carranza became more obstreperous than Huerta ever had been before the Vera Cruz affair. To force Pershing's withdrawal, Mexican forces belonging to both Villa and Carranza began moving toward the thinly-patrolled Border with its many wide, unguarded sectors. Congressman Hay reacted to all this with a listing of hearings on the military Bills which had been pigeonholed in his Committee. He reported-out a Bill without delay. Meanwhile, all the field Headquarters of the Regulars, from Texas City, San Antonio, El Paso to San Diego, were hollering for help. But this, as shown in the preceding chapter, did not keep the Regulars from their last desperate lobbying against the National Defense Act of 1916.

## NEED FOR GUARD COULD NOT AWAIT LEGISLATION

On May 5, two months after the raid and with the strain of Pershing's long, thin column approaching its break-point, there were raids on

Glen Springs and Boquillas, Texas. Mr. Wilson hearkened unto the alarums of both his State and War Departments to ask the Governors of Texas, New Mexico and Arizona to call-out all units of their National Guard, with their commanders to report to designated Regular Headquarters. The Call was dated May 9. Two days later the Guardsmen of these three States were in movement toward San Antonio, Columbus and Douglas within their respective States. The field Regulars apparently were so happy to see them that if there was any technical criticism whatsoever of this surprise, minor mobilization, it did not slop over into the Press.

Shortly all Guard units of these three States were on or within support distance of patrolled sectors. As of the date of the Call, Texas had a strength of 3,381 officers and men, New Mexico 972, Arizona 907. Numbers grew with immediate recruiting. The 5,260 citizen-soldiers, accustomed to the local conditions and terrain and already organized into functional teams, were indeed welcomed by the regional Regulars.

But the problems arising from Pershing's deepening penetration into Mexico multiplied. Carranza served notice that Pershing could advance no further—East, South or West. The omission of the supply road North was suggestive. At the same time, Pershing was groping. Air observation, though crude, was available but not being used. Blinded by alkali dust and lack of information, Pershing was planless, poorly supported. His ground patrols found nought but cactus and occasional hovels. Villa and his raiders had vanished into the folds of the distant, pale blue and phantom-like mountain ranges.

Militarily the "Punitive Expedition" had become an abortion, but diplomatically it remained a potential power play. Mexico should put her house in order, abate the nuisance to her neighbors and keep marauders from the Border, or Pershing could and would continue his advance. But right while Generals Pershing and Funston conferred with Carranza's General Treviño, bandits and troops of all Mexican warlords were edging toward the thinly-patrolled, vast frontier extending from Brownsville, Texas, to San Diego, California. When Treviño had the effrontery to give his "no movements East, South, or West" ultimatum on June 16, it appears to have triggered Mr. Wilson's decision to call out the Guardsmen of the remaining States. This he did under date of June 18.

Congressman Hay's National Defense Act of June 3, 1916 was just 15 days old. The Call of the Southwestern States Guard units five weeks earlier had demonstrated what the Guard leaders had argued from the beginning; i.e., *when there is an emergency, it is not individuals, even though they be highly-trained and their specialties indexed, that are most needed. It is military teams of men, organized into units that can*

231

*function without delay.* Skills in specialties can be perfected even under stress if the understanding teamwork in units accustomed to working together is present. The Companies, Troops, Batteries, Battalions and Regiments of Texas, New Mexico and Arizona were proving it while Mr. Hay's Bill was in stages of final passage. The units of the remaining States soon were to demonstrate it further on this quick and unexpected Call of June 18, 1916. It is worth noting here, however, that all units were activated initially under the terms of the Dick Act of 1903. The mission was purely defensive, and Guardsmen were not yet under the dual oath stipulated by the new law.

Enough correspondence and other evidence now are available that Mr. Wilson's intentions were quite clear. It was never his plan to invade Mexico with sufficient forces to "pacify" through conquest. To him, sending the Guard to the Border was merely further implementation of his established policy of "watchful waiting." But he was insistent upon watching and waiting on terms that protected Americans and gave weight to his firm diplomacy calling for a responsible Mexican Government that would have to live-up to its international covenants. From some source he had the highly-cautious and pessimistic estimate that "pacification" of Mexico would require a force of 500,000 men. To him, this was a cost in excess of America's responsibility for Mexican law and order. He wanted no such Kiplingesque "White Man's burden." Moreover, as a political scientist of his era, he believed the salvation of Mexico could be achieved only by the Mexicans—but they were to do it within their own borders, and with as much respect for American lives South of the Border as might be exacted without actual and formal warfare.

## ACTIVATED MANPOWER WAS NOT IN EXCESS OF NEED

With modern roads, motorized forces, with direct and photographic air observation, it is easy for an historian today to assume that nearly 170,000 Regulars and Guardsmen in the Southwest for frontier security against the Mexican hit-and-run raids of that day were an excessive number. It is thus quite common for the claim to be made that Wilson's real purpose was not protection against Mexico but was a preparedness measure for the coming World War I. Much of this is *ex post facto* rationalization. Sending the Guard to the Border in 1916 did have this happy result for creating new Divisions rapidly in 1917. But Mr. Wilson's Call did not activate manpower in excess of the mission. Actually, for an era of wagon ruts and a Regular Army still committed to horses and justly distrustful of the few motor vehicles and airplanes it did have, 200,000 men were quite few enough for the job. With nearly 100,000 Guardsmen already in the Southwest within a matter of days, the Department Commander still voiced a crying need for many more—

at least 65,000 more. For this reason, in late August and early September, 25,000 Guardsmen, principally from Vermont, Kentucky and Ohio, who had been held in Northern stations through lack of facilities in the Southwest, were put in motion Southwestward as reinforcements.

As every military man readily realizes, not each and every unit and man was posted on, or immediately at, the exact boundary. The Border was indeed tightly-patrolled for initial light resistance and prompt intelligence. General Funston then followed the conventional pattern of close supports, supports, tactical reserves, strategic reserves, and a strategic striking force. The disposition pattern near the boundary, or immediately along the Rio Grande, necessarily was dictated by local trails and County roads for animal movements. The farther-removed strategic elements naturally were concentrated in areas best served by highway, rail, and water communications. As a result, except for the 12,000 or more horsemen and foot-slogging Doughboys deep in Mexico with General Pershing, the numerical preponderance of General Funston's field command of Regulars and Guardsmen had no immediate military mission. This left them concentrated in areas as far removed from the actual boundary as Galveston Bay area and San Antonio. General Funston made the most of this golden opportunity for reequipment, training and perfecting of reorganization. From the worm's-eye view of the average high Private in the rear rank, all of this added-up to what an English Tommy once mildly described as a bloody bit of busy work. But the force was where the Mexican warlords understood it.

## LACK OF PLANS AND EQUIPMENT

Indeed, reorganization was the *bete noir* and principal morale depressant from the very outset. Although there had been strife South of the Border for six years and there had been two years of shooting in the greatest of all European wars, as of that date, the President's decision to call the Guard caught the General Staff flat-footed and far out in left field. It had been so busy with Uptonian expansibility planning that it had no operational plans for the Guard units. Indeed, in its efforts to discredit the Guard formations in being, and with a mere legal opinion as the excuse, it had denied the Guard Regiments sufficient uniforms, weapons, equipment and animals to execute a smooth mobilization and movement, had an effective plan for such been available. If there ever was a lesson suggestive that America's General Staff should subordinate interest in politics and give first priority to tactics, strategy, arms, scientific progress and to planning the utilization of what is in hand and what can be had within a foreseeable future, that lesson is found in the personnel fixations that discredited Staff Chiefs Wood and Wotherspoon. Their gross errors quite naturally hamstrung the first year or more of General Scott's tour as Chief of Staff.

But the most ghastly mistake that arose to haunt the War Department in this hour of need was the past efforts to discredit the Guard by the withholding of equipment needed for the balanced force contemplated under the Dick Act of 1903. Many Guard units in sundry States were more-than willing to be converted to Cavalry or Artillery, if the Government would provide the horses and their upkeep. In an earlier chapter it has been shown that the General Staff, more-than willing to see the Guard discredited, consistently refused to go along. There was the obvious hope that a discredited Organized Militia would be a stepping-stone to their schemes for a Federal Militia of individual Reservists to be fed into Regular Army formations for an expansible Army. We further have seen how many Guardsmen in the too-few mounted units that did exist met the horse shortage by lending or providing their own mounts. But on a Call to active duty on the Border, such self-mounted National Guard Artillerymen and Cavalrymen put their privately-owned steeds back in the barn or coach house for family or farm use. They joined in the local clamor that horses and harness should be forthcoming without delay if the War Department wanted Cavalry and cannon in the Southwest immediately.

Horses and mules were already at a premium in the Southwest, thanks to the needs of the American Regulars and Canadian buyers for the British army. The Washington planners accordingly elected to convert an appropriate number of Infantry units to Artillery and Cavalry at Northern training camps before entraining them for the Southwest. The service record of Virginia's famed Richmond Light Infantry Blues is illustrative of how this decision worked-out.

## A TYPICAL UNIT IN TRANSITION

In existence since Richmond was a village of log cabins in 1792, the Blues had served in a Federal or Confederate status in every subsequently declared war, except that with Mexico, 1846. Came Mr. Wilson's Call to Virginia, June 16, 1916, for two Regiments of Infantry immediately for the Mexican Border, the Blues feared they might miss the boat again; and in the same direction, because the Blues were a separate Battalion. Washington, D.C., was near at hand. In the Militia Affairs office the Battalion's committee was told that Coast Artillery Batteries were being left at home near their immobile coastal guns. Adequate Infantry units already were available. Would the Blues take the Federal oath as Cavalrymen? The answer was yes.

By a stroke of the State Adjutant General's pen at the bottom of State General Order No. 13, dated June 21, 1916, the "Richmond Light Infantry Blues, Separate Battalion, National Guard, State of Virginia," became "1st Squadron, Virginia Cavalry." As such it immediately was included within the Presidential Call.

Pending further movement orders from the War Department, the Squadron Headquarters, with its four Troops, A, B, C, and D, went into training, internal reorganization and further recruiting to war strength at the Battalion Armory in Richmond. The next big worry was physical examinations for Federal active duty. "Thanks to the wisdom, the judgment and the independence of mind of Colonel Alexander N. Starke, of the United States Army Medical Corps, a Virginian by birth, who was the senior medical examining officer," everybody who really wanted to pass was rated physically fit in every respect, including one eager Guardsman, who, to the best knowledge of all in the Squadron, could not have read the designated line of the letter chart without a telescope. So wrote Colonel John A. Cutchins in 1934. Meanwhile, Virginia's 1st and 2nd Infantry Regiments, which had within their formations the great majority of the Old Dominion's 2,936 Guardsmen, had boarded the War Department's troop trains to disappear toward the setting sun.

But the late Light Infantry Blues, reborn as the 1st Squadron, Virginia Cavalry, was destined for dismal days. The 1st Squadron lingered in its Armory until July 5, when it was sworn into Federal Service and left the Armory to join other miscellaneous units at Camp Stuart, near the local Fair Grounds. During this first month at Camp Stuart there was much "strenuous dismounted drill, and such training in mounted work as an accomplished officer of the Regular Cavalry, Captain Joseph F. Taulbee, could give with the aid of a wooden horse . . . Later a small number of condemned horses was issued the Squadron. These, with the arrival of several tons of horse shoes and many boxes of saddles and bridles and other equipment, afforded some slight justification for the yellow hat cords, the spurs and the cavalry designation."

By October 18, 1916, the Border was quiet, and America was looking with increasingly anxious eyes toward Europe. Pershing's Punitive Expedition was stalemated deep in Mexico by terrain, lack of an S.O.S. and diplomacy. The new Cavalry Troopers of the late "Richmond Light Infantry Blues" were giving up hopes of ever getting outside the City limits. Morale was low. But on the above date came the word: Virginia's 1st Cavalry Squadron would entrain for Brownsville, Texas. Five days later it was there.

By virtue of the seniority of its own Major Edgar W. Bowles, Virginia National Guard, it became 1st Squadron, 1st Provisional Regiment. Its commander was Lieutenant Colonel John D. L. Hartman of the 3rd Cavalry, United States Army. The Regiment's 2nd Squadron consisted of three Troops of Colorado Cavalry and one Troop of New Hampshire Cavalry. The Regiment's 3rd Squadron was detached from a Regular Regiment, the 3rd U.S. Cavalry. Meanwhile the Virginia

235

Squadron had arrived in Brownsville with but two horses. Both were privately-owned mounts. The thin, equine cadre of old, condemned Cavalry plugs had been left at the Virginia Fair Grounds.

Nevertheless, upon arrival of 1st Squadron, the C.O. was told to be prepared for a mounted review for Brigadier General James (Gallopin' Jim) Parker, U.S.A. This soon was modified in favor of full participation in a 10-day maneuver by the 23,000 men, Guardsmen for the most part, under General Parker's command in the Brownsville area. The 1st Illinois Cavalry had been in the camp and had been scheduled for the maneuvers. But since it had been one of the first to arrive on the Border, it had been rotated homeward. Horses, many that never had been ridden, became available.

Of the maneuver, which began November 16, General Parker later officially reported that they "showed the troops of this command ready to take the field in active campaign. The cavalry and field artillery made long marches . . . increased gaits . . . maintained their animals in good condition . . . Two hundred and seventy-eight men, out of a total of nearly twenty-three thousand engaged, were removed to the hospital, or about a total of about twelve men per thousand . . . The work of the cavalry reconnaissance was really remarkable when it is considered that only two and one-half weeks had elapsed since the receipt of new horses by new men." He appears to be referring specifically to the erstwhile Richmond Light Infantry Blues.

The record of the 1st Squadron, Virginia Cavalry, is thus illustrative of the depths of depression and low morale experienced by scores of Guard units that encountered long delays in movement, equipment and faltering reorganization, but which later were to feel the lift that comes with achievement and commendation in the field. The Guardsmen were back in Richmond for reversion to civil life, March 18, 1917. It was on a Sunday and the storied old City made a gala day of it. "The sight of former Blues, in the old full-dress uniforms, forming a 'guard of honor' was a most welcome one, while the feast which had been spread and the speeches of welcome at the Armory made the whole border experience seem well worthwhile." America declared war on Germany 18 days later.

It had indeed been well-worthwhile for them and all other Guard units that their experience exemplifies. It was also a highly worthwhile experience for old field Regulars like Gallopin' Jim Parker, austere Colonel John D. L. Hartman and the command professionals that they typify. With formal declaration of hostilities with Germany but 18 days away when the return of the Blues was celebrated in Richmond, it was inevitable that they soon would be back in uniform and that Hartman soon would command citizen-soldiers with a star on his shoulder. And, of course, such officers as old Gallopin' Jim soon were called upon

236

to organize and command the 17 National Guard Divisions that soon were to go to France. Major General James S. Parker, late Summer of 1917, took command of the Wisconsin and Michigan National Guard units at Waco, Texas. They, too, were recently from the Border service. He quickly organized them into the famed 32nd Infantry Division, the record of which in both World Wars I and II is quite comparable to that of the Richmond Blues, C.S.A., from Bull Run to Appomattox through the Civil War.

## THE UNPLANNED MOVEMENT "WITHOUT DELAY"

But let us return to the main body of National Guard units that did leave more-or-less immediately for the Southwest without undue detention at or near their home cities. Many of them also experienced throes of immediate reorganization. In Iowa, for example, Cavalry and Artillery Regiments were organized anew and four old Infantry Regiments were reconstituted into three. All this was done before the movement of troops between July 20 and 25. All such last-minute shuffles notwithstanding, and on an impetus of movement initiated by the Adjutants General of the several States (each usually working in his own individualistic way), much of the Guard did get rolling in good time. Indeed, more often than otherwise, the delay was for rolling stock. The Presidential Call came during a busy shipping season. The planless General Staff in the War Department was forced to "commandeer" (as one officer expressed it) cars and coaches in a haphazard style wheresoever they might be found.

On July 1 there were 122 troop trains in motion laden with 36,042 Guardsmen. Four days later there were 101 troop trains rolling. By this date there was an aggregate of 56,681 Guardsmen on Border stations or en route thereto. By July 31, 112,000 had been transported there. The principal areas of concentration were the vicinities of Douglas, Arizona; El Paso, San Antonio and Brownsville, Texas. There were no barracks, seldom any mess halls or headquarters shacks. Arriving Regiments of Guardsmen normally had to create their own encampments from the ground up.

Many of the units were under war strength and continued receiving recruits from home throughout their tour of active duty. This caused the General Staff in Washington to maunder heavily and publicly of the failure of the Guard to field its war strength immediately. All of which came with poor grace and may be classified as diversionary publicity to detract attention from its own failures. The Regulars had been conducting frantic recruiting campaigns since the Vera Cruz incident and had stepped it up after the outbreak of the war in Europe. Right while they were criticizing the Guard, the Regulars were 20,292 officers and men below their own authorized and budgeted strength. Being much smaller numerically than the National Guard, this represented a percentage about which inquisitive Congressmen and publishers could have asked some embarrassing questions.

Actually, for the National Guard of that day, neglected as it had been by the War Department for the preceding four years, the fielding of 112,000 men in the Southwest by July 31, 1916, and with an additional 40,138 as of the same date still in the mobilization camps of the States, was a tremendous achievement. Coast Artillery units, as we have noted, were not called. And all the foregoing was accomplished by National Guard units, including the coastal units, that had numbered but 132,194 officers and men as of June 18, two days after the Call. Thus it safely can be assumed that the General Staff was merely attracting attention away from its own, far more significant personnel failures by criticizing the already much-abused Guardsmen.

## THE PRESS VIEWS MOBILIZATION WITH MIXED OPINIONS

And the National Guard units had indeed received much abuse during the haphazard, hurry-scurry movements toward the Southwest. Viewed from thousands of curbstones by millions of inexperienced eyes, the entrainment and movements of the Guard units were unmitigated chaos. After all, the typical American's concept of things military was conditioned by the neat, straight, colorful lines found in the Currier and Ives chromos of Regimental dress parades. There also lingered in the public's mind the muckraking news and magazine articles from 1898 and recent professional criticisms by advocates of the "Continental Army." Thus the readers of the daily newspapers were prepared to believe anything about the citizen-soldiers that might be militarily uncomplimentary. Moreover, the General Staff's proximity to the opinion-forming Washington and East Coast Press, and as the source of high-level, quasi-official news, placed it in position to blame the Guardsmen for almost anything that was not as pleasing to the eye as the Currier and Ives chromos. There were, also, the normal number of eager-beaver, provincial reporters with more than a mild yen to follow in the footsteps of such renowned war correspondents as Stephen Bonsal, Ralph D. Paine, Stephen Crane and Richard Harding Davis. Adverse criticism and Monday morning second-guessing had been a sure-fire technique for them. Accordingly there were plenty who were more than willing to go forth and write caustic criticisms rather than try to locate and explain the cause.

Of these, Floyd Gibbons not only proved to be the most apt in the use of the old technique, but he most nearly approximated success.

Floyd Gibbons' pace-setting, critical comments are worth passing notice. At that time Gibbons was by no means the experienced correspondent and commentator he later became, but he was on the way. He was 29 years of age. For the Minneapolis *Tribune* he early had achieved regional recognition for covering (and monopolizing the one wire out of Hayward, Wisconsin) a lamentable, one-man, swamp war, waged by an unbalanced trapper. Thence Gibbons had gone to the Chicago *Tribune*. That paper's bitterly anti-Wilson Editor thought young Gibbons just the man to go Southwestward to interview Mexican warlords. He had met Villa before the Columbus raid. He had followed Pershing to Parral, Mexico. Accordingly, Mr. Gibbons in 1916 wrote hastily from a wealth of sophisticated ignorance and inexperience, but with a born reporter's flair for creating tall headlines.

Gibbons bemoaned the "dingy overloaded day coaches" arriving in the Southwest laden with "weary, sleepless, unwashed human freight." He sought not the cause for a New York Regiment on Federal duty being on a diet of "hardtack and water," but he thought it extremely poor discipline when at train halts men would "raid" or "storm" any nearby restaurants or grocery stores. "Riot" was his climactic word.

Mr. Gibbons, for his Republican Editor, easily discovered and quoted unnamed Regular Army officers who criticized the whole concept of the movement as a "disheartening spectacle" of "untrained troops," thrown into the field unwarrantedly. They further told Gibbons that the General Staff had not planned or wanted this mobilization this way. Except for small caretaking details, the Northern posts had been empty since the Vera Cruz episode had caused most of the Regulars to concentrate in the Southwesst. It had been the desire of the higher staffs to concentrate and train the Guardsmen in the Northern barracks normally occupied by Regular units. Thence they would be committed to the Border piecemeal. This seemed plausible, but ignored what Generals Pershing, Funston and other field commanders in the Southwest insisted their needs to be for the mission assigned. Gibbons revealed further that the new civilian Secretary of War, Mr. Baker, had arrogantly overruled the informed professionals, thereby keeping the General Staff from doing a good job.

Young Mr. Gibbons' sources remain unidentified. In any event, his "revelations" constitute a further indictment rather than a defense of the General Staff. Moreover, the worst place in the World for the training of units of citizen-soldiers is in barracks that are near their homes and far removed from the climate, vegetation and terrain where they are most likely to be utilized. For the purpose of training and conditioning the Guard, Mr. Baker, wittingly or unwittingly, made the right decision in getting the majority of the Guard units into the Southwest as quickly as the absence of proper General Staff planning permitted.

Most likely Mr. Baker's motives were more diplomatic than guided by training considerations. From his viewpoint, there was a threat of more Border incidents, raids, even invasion. Pershing was deep in Mexico. Carranza and Villa were equally hostile to Pershing's presence. Their joint action could create situations in which functional teams of armed men would be needed on the Border immediately. They did not have to be the best in the World. They just had to be better than the Mexicans, and would naturally improve rapidly with concurrent training and seasoning in the region where they would be used. Above all this, the very nature of the situation and the legal basis of the Call required at least 100,000 Guardsmen in the Southwest within the shortest time possible. The complaints and excuses of the Regulars, as revealed by youthful journalist Floyd Gibbons, reflect no credit upon him and even less upon those Regulars who fed him their alibis for chaos through lack of top-level plans.

The Guardsmen did have some embarrassing episodes of which the General Staff and other critics quite naturally made the most. The dual oath in the new legislation was but two weeks old when Mr. Wilson called the Guard. It had not been administered. Hence the Call and induction rules of the old Dick Act of 1903, as amended, still prevailed. Keokuk's Company L, Iowa National Guard, became confused and chose to finesse the Call trick by declining the oath. Iowa's impatient Adjutant General summarily disbanded the unit and created a new Company L. But Bostonians were even more embarrassed when it developed their Cavalrymen of the 1st Squadron "were recusant." But when a more patient Adjutant General explained the oath to the misinformed Troopers, they "swore in with a whoop."

These untoward incidents notwithstanding, many of the Press and most of the publications were complimentary and understanding. The Indianapolis *News* considered such episodes as full justification for the dual oath and other reforms so recently written into law by Congressman Hay with his National Defense Act of June 3, 1916.

The New York *Sun* was complimentary. "The gain in efficiency and morale has been marked. To say the Guard has improved 100 per cent since the Spanish War period would not be an exaggeration; but there is a good deal of room for improvement, and when $25,000,000 a year is expended upon the Guard by the Federal Government, in place of a present average of $4,000,000, we ought to have a force of citizen soldiers worthy to be brigaded with regular troops, if not equally efficient and dependable." This suggests the *Sun* Editor thought that in the Guard the Nation had been getting a lot for its defense dollar.

Unlike the arch-Republican Chicago *Tribune,* some influential newspapers took a strictly non-partisan view of the Guard and the "blunders" connected therewith. The Des Moines *Register and Leader,* likewise

240

Republican and anti-Wilson, viewed the situation with more than passing discernment. Its Editor was positive the National Guard "has measured up to the mark in the matters over which the State and individual Guardsmen have control." Critics of the National Guard had been predicting, so the Editor said, that the Guard would be found deficient in physical standards, discipline, drill and rifle practice, that it was not properly balanced among the various branches of the Service, that it would not respond to the Federal Call and that it would take six months to mobilize. Now, continued the *Register and Leader,* the mobilization had disproved all these old charges but the clamor continues: "The Guard is not equipped . . . has failed to supply it with uniforms . . . worn out rifles marked 'repaired' but with useless barrels . . . the cavalry and artillery are short of horses . . . The same men who were denouncing the Guard a year ago are still denouncing it, not for its own crimes but for the weaknesses which are directly chargeable to the War Department." The General Staff's errant chickens had indeed come home to roost.

## PROFESSIONAL OPINIONS OF THE MOBILIZATION

New York State's officialdom became so excited over such reports as Floyd Gibbons authored that they hustled a former Commissioner of Health for New York City, Dr. T. Darlington, to the Southwest to see if the boys were healthy. He found all well and good. All were eating regularly, sheltered, and sanitary, with "no contagious diseases." And not all the approval came from sympathetic, regional editors and the civilian Health Commissioner. Two junior General Staff officers who, each in his own way, were to become distinguished, viewed the Guard mobilization with satisfaction and approval. And both, at this time, were Majors but held assignments that made their opinions significant. One was the late Brigadier General John McA. Palmer. As a middle-aged Captain, 20 years out of the Point, in 1912, he had drawn a personnel study assignment while on his first General Staff duty tour. The planning was preparatory to the subsequent "Continental Army" scheme for which Secretary Garrison had broken his sword. Palmer early had come to the independent conclusion that Upton was wrong and that his own staff colleagues were influenced erroneously by his book on American military policy. He not only thoroughly approved of the new law, and its refreshing attitude toward the Guard that came with Mr. Wilson and his new Secretary, Mr. Baker, but in his ultimately-published *America in Arms,* General Palmer boldly reveals Upton's complete lack of scholarship that led to errors in Upton's major premise and conclusions. For this and other writing, General Palmer, too old for World War II active duty, achieved a quiet but increasing fame of his own as the Regular Army's most scholarly student of military personnel policies.

The other General Staff Major, younger and less reserved than Palmer, was publicly bold and loud in his approval of the National Guard mobilization in 1916. He immediately rushed into print with: "When one considers the number of men moved and distances they were moved, the recent mobilization . . . on the Mexican border was the best job of its kind done by any country." It was the beginning of a mutual confidence that soon was to reach fruition by this young Major's becoming Chief of Staff, and later a Brigade Commander, in one of the first Guard Divisions to land in France, the "Rainbow Division." The young Major quoted above was Douglas MacArthur.

## THE MOBILIZATION IN REVIEW

Taking it all-in-all, 1916 was indeed a big year for the National Guard. In the halls of Congress the Guardsmen had triumphed over a General Staff that had sought to relegate them to an internal, home front, Constabulary status. Their own-devised, dual-oath formula had disposed of the General Staff-inspired, Wickersham myth that constitutionally the Guard could not be used beyond the territorial limits of the United States.* They had written into National policy a definite priority for themselves in their sense of duty and in their right to serve their Country any time, anywhere, through any armed threat or crisis. And before the ink was dry on this legislation, Mexico and Mr. Wilson had given them an opportunity to show their worth in the field.

It was also a big year for America in terms of preparedness. It is an often-overlooked fact that about two-fifths of the Guard units and Guardsmen who were called-out by Mr. Wilson for Border duty in the Summer of 1916 were still on active duty when war with Germany was declared April 6, 1917. As of April 1, 1917, the American Army numbered 199,705 officers and men. Of these 127,588 were Regulars, 5,523 were Philippine Scouts and 66,594 were National Guardsmen in Federal service. Back in civil life, but still sun-tanned by Border service, were 117,500 National Guardsmen immediately available in home-drilling, seasoned units.

That part of the National Defense Act of June 3, 1916, which had implemented the General Staff's dream of a Regular Army Reserve of individuals, produced little within the same length of time. Notwithstanding the publicity and ballyhoo of Wood and his civilian associates in the National Security League, the declaration of World War I

---

* In the mobilization for Border Service only one National Guard Regiment performed duties South of the Border. It was the 2nd Mass. Inf., based at Columbus, New Mexico.

found hardly 4,000 men in the Enlisted Reserve Corps and an additional 3,000 in the Officers' Reserve Corps, most of whom were former Guardsmen. These were the "filler" availables for an "expansible" Regular Army that the General Staff's most-favored section of the law had yielded within the same 10 months.

The departure of the National Guard units for the Border without a single Regiment of U.S. Volunteers, in the style of Leonard Wood's and Theodore Roosevelt's Spanish-American War "Rough Riders," was of the bitterness of gall and wormwood to the ex-President and other critics of the Guard and proponents of the Federal Volunteer Militia that they exemplified. In July, 1916, the New York *Times* broke a story that "on a call for volunteers, Colonel Theodore Roosevelt will become a Major General and command more than 20,000 soldiers." It was to be the "T. R. Division."

The Colonel's New York office was "attending to the flood of letters that pours in by every mail." He had been "rounding up a few of the boys" since the sinking of the *Lusitania*. His Brigade and Regimental commanders as well as higher Staff officers already were selected. Most of them were Regulars the ex-President had known favorably. But oddly enough, one Brigade Commander was to be a retired Rear Admiral. The Chief Quartermaster was to be ex-Secretary of War Stimson. Soon thereafter some journalistic wag was quoted as saying the position for *intelligence* was still vacant. By and large, the old ex-Guardsman and Volunteer Rough Rider did not get as good Press as he deserved. His motives were patriotic and honorable. His efforts to imitate the Guard under a U.S.V. label were a most convincing form of flattery to the Guardsmen.

# Bibliographical Note For Chapter X

*The Annual Reports of the War Department* for 1916 and 1917, and most particularly *Report on Mobilization of the Organized Militia and National Guard of the United States,* initially released as a separate pamphlet by the War Department, late 1916, are the essential sources. Newspaper and magazine treatments are voluminous and occasionally rewarding for their contemporary views and flavor of the times. Some are mentioned in the chapter text. The contemporary official views and the periodical accounts do have one general pattern in common. The closer the writer was to New York and to Washington, D.C., and the farther he was removed from the operation, the more certain he is likely to be that the mobilization is a complete abortion. Those closest and most deeply involved in the actual operation generally were convinced of its worthiness and success. Everyone today recognizes it as having been most fortuitous from a preparedness standpoint, independent of its relation to Mexico. Meanwhile, the Mexican Border Mobilization has become so completely entwined with Wilsonian diplomacy that the following titles are not only helpful but necessary: J. Fred Rippy, *United States and Mexico,* 1931; Chapter XXX of Samuel F. Bemis, *A Diplomatic History of the United States,* 4th ed., 1955, and the same author's *Latin American Policy of the United States,* 1943; Arthur S. Link, *Woodrow Wilson and the Progressive Era, 1910-17,* 1954; and *Wilson the Diplomatist,* 1957. Even greater detail may be found in Ray Stanard Baker, *Woodrow Wilson, Life and Letters,* 8 vols., 1927-39. Brig. Gen. John McA. Palmer, *Washington, Lincoln and Wilson,* 1930, is an informed military man's estimate of political greatness, and also in connection with this era see his *America in Arms,* 1941. Barbara W. Tuchman, a literary historian of unusual perception and dramatic skill, underscores the importance of Mexico in the tangled diplomatic web of the era in her *The Zimmermann Telegram,* 1958. To her, Carranza and Pancho Villa were part and parcel of the German threat. Russell F. Weigley, *Towards an American Army; Military Thought from Washington to Marshall,* is a long-range, biographical and philosophical approach. It is excellent.

## CHAPTER XI

# Origins Of The Draft

WHILE THE NATIONAL GUARD formations were on the Border, or elsewhere on active duty pursuant to that Call, America's great Preparedness debate continued. And what was happening in Mexico and along the Border had little to do with it. The rising crescendo of the debate was stimulated by the War in Europe. What the military experts had proclaimed would be of necessity a short war was well into its third year with costs in lives and treasure measured in astronomical figures. Each major power, except England, had entered the war with conscripted standing armies and trained reserves tabulated in millions. These were being doubled and occasionally tripled as the war progressed, notwithstanding the staggering and ever-higher casualty statistics. Little Belgium had fought her brief delaying action in late Summer of 1914 with an army as large as that of the United States as of the same year.

England, like America, had put her faith in salt water and powerful fleets for complete security. Accordingly, she had entered the war with an ally's commitment to France of but six Divisions of Infantry and one of Cavalry to the Western Front; and that only in case of grave emergency. But before the end of 1915, to keep France in the war, England had to send an army of Territorials and other volunteers of more than a million men to France alone. If the Western Front was to be held, another million Englishmen would have to be forthcoming. In early 1916, England reluctantly adopted her new Military Service Act, which was another name for systematic and selective conscription. It came as no surprise. The grim necessity for the measure was painfully apparent.

Simultaneously, increasing numbers of American leaders, journalists, statesmen and politicians were becoming convinced America could not, or would not, maintain her neutrality. This suggested an initial land force of at least a million men, if an involved America was to influence materially the ultimately favorable outcome. Would volunteers into the National Guard and Regular Army formations yield such a number soon enough? The General Staff's and Secretary of War Garrison's Continental Army Plan, being pushed by them through the first half of 1916, promised a yield of only 500,000 trained men within three years—and few believed that without the National Guard in the picture they could achieve any reasonable approach to that figure.

## AMERICA DRIFTS TOWARD A DRAFT LAW

Meanwhile, the situation in Europe and particularly in England caused more and more thoughtful Americans to wonder if their Country could enter the war and restrict her participation to so few as a million soldiers. They were constantly being reminded of the Duke of Wellington's oft-cited theory that it is utterly impossible for a great nation to fight a small, or limited-liability war. If America should get into a shooting war in which both friends and foes were playing the numbers game to fill the ranks of their embattled armies by conscription techniques, how could America avoid doing likewise? This is the impression one gets today from examining the mass of news comment, ephemeral periodical literature, editorials and public speeches of that era. These and the subsequent speed with which the Draft Law was passed, clearly indicate the public was ahead of their President, the War Department and most of the General Staff planners.

Be it said, however, there were Regulars and Guardsmen who saw the necessity, if a role in the European War was in the list of assumptions. As early as late 1915, while Mr. Garrison was still Secretary of War and working hard for his Continental Army Plan, an able and alert Regular Army officer, Captain George V. H. Moseley, then on General Staff duty but soon to command a Brigade of Artillery in Europe, sat down and wrote a Draft Law to fit his personal philosophy. Never a man to hide a bright candle under a bushel, he incorporated it into a memorandum and circulated it.

The rapidly growing National Association for Universal Military Training, with the help of the *Army and Navy Journal,* read the memorandum and adopted it as its very own. Republicans Henry Stimson, Elihu Root, and Robert R. McCormick of the Chicago *Tribune,* had given up all hope that their Democratic friend and disciple, Mr. Garrison, could get the Continental Army program through the Democratic Congress and past Mr. Wilson, hence they already had plopped for a Draft Law and were members of the Association's Advisory Board. Other prominent proponents of Preparedness, including General Wood, had done likewise. But Captain Moseley's immediate reward was a dark frown for muddying the water around the official General Staff line with its Continental Army bait; and from the cautious and scholarly Chief of Staff, Hugh L. Scott, the growl was little less than a reprimand. But the Moseley memorandum proved to be a trial balloon indicative of favorable minds. The public response was good. Accordingly, few of the cognoscenti at the War College, where most of the heavy personnel planning then was done, were surprised the following January 10, 1916, when General Scott cautiously said he personally favored compulsory military training. He emphasized this was not an official view.

Thereafter, however, the idea really began to roll. The concept came up often in the hearings before Congressman James Hay's House Committee on Military Affairs incident to the passage of the National Defense Act of June 3, 1916. The National Guardsmen, in their arguments for the nationalization of their organized military State units, also pointed out that the Unorganized Militias of the States, collectively the military manpower of the Nation, likewise should be nationalized. Perhaps not all, but certainly many of them knew this to be an essential preliminary step toward a successful National selective service statute. Its inclusion in Congressman Hay's Defense Act of June 3, 1916, has been noted in an earlier chapter as one of the most important provisions of that law. This is particularly true in the light of what followed, though it did not seem so vital to many at the time.

The departure of the National Guardsmen for the Border the same Summer gave impetus to the idea. In every City and Town where there was a Guard Company, there was a demonstration of one or more prominent, busy, civic leaders in that small community pushing aside family, business and civic affairs to serve as an enlisted man in response to a patriotic urge, while others with no responsibilities and less sense of duty sat at home to finesse the trick.

This reaction on the home front was contemporaneous with the occasional successes of German saboteurs, as climaxed by the $50,000,000 Black Tom explosion and holocaust. Then came the crass, if unrealistic, effrontery of the decoded Zimmerman note. All these events served to underscore America's unrestrainable drift toward the maelstrom, with the inevitability of a military draft.

## THE PHILOSOPHY OF DUTY

Most National Guardsmen, moreover, believed in the validity of a military responsibility to one's Country. They had faith in the concept that when the manpower need of the Nation exceeded those willing to volunteer, the sluggards should be needled to a sense of responsibility. A Draft Law would have this effect. Moreover, it would give substance to the threat in case there were slackers sufficiently thick-skinned to resist local public opinion.

Indeed, the National Guard and the practice of selective service, as we have seen in earlier chapters, had a common heritage from early England and the most primitive days of the Thirteen American Colonies. In the American Colonial wars, when the communities of New England and New York that were far removed from danger failed to contribute to the needed manpower by sufficient volunteers in organized formations, the Colonial Governor told the local authorities to strengthen their units for active duty by a designated number of bodies. It is regrettably true, as we have seen, that the jail was often the first place visited in the local search for available military manpower, but since the English prison was then the best recruiting agent for the crack Regiments of British Regulars being sent to America, little criticism can be visited upon the civilian Colonial fathers. Indeed, many of them, and/or their fathers, had left English jails to come to America; hence, who could criticize?

The extent to which the individual officers and men in the National Guard units on the Border and returning therefrom were fully aware of these principles upon which their institution rested could easily be underestimated, particularly by professional military men accustomed to dealing primarily with men in Regular Army barracks or drill formations. Hence, the Chief of Staff, General Scott, and the planners he assembled following the departure of General Wotherspoon, hardly can be criticized for the reluctance with which they approached the Draft problem. The historical enormity of the Civil War Draft debacle naturally dominated their thinking. But in National Guard circles at all echelons there was no such reluctance.

Irrespective of how much or how little military experience they may have had, the officers of the National Guard units still on active duty, or recently reverted to civil life, were informed men and normally were civic leaders. They and most of their men knew in a general way, and often quite specifically, the basic relationship between Militia duty as a civilian and the civic duty to respond to service in the common welfare. It was all as simple as jury duty. And if a Guardsman did not know these essential facts when he enlisted, he hardly could avoid learning them later.

Many of the National Guard units had a known and traced heritage back to Colonial days when Colonies and States had drafted reluctant citizens. But whether the traditions of the unit were long or short, it was common community knowledge that National Guardsmen were vulnerable to immediate call in cases of great fires or floods, not only for rescue purposes but to prevent thievery and looting. Likewise, they knew themselves to be subject to immediate call not only for such military duty as the Governor might proclaim, but for the suppression of insurrections, riots and disorders in areas where order could not be restored by local officers and the posse summons process.

Against these concepts and background, it was natural that every informed Guardsman in early 1917 favored a Draft Law that would become operative the moment lack of volunteering to their own National Guard units, or to the other Armed Forces, demonstrated an imperative need for more men sooner. To the Guardsmen, the idea was as simple as a summons to any other civic, legal duty, and it was in these terms that they talked to their neighbors. And since returnees and furloughed visitors from active duty units were the local experts on military affairs to the people in their home towns, their opinions carried weight.

Consequently, the Guard, and its service on the Border, became a potent agency in a normally Pacifistic-minded America toward conditioning the minds of the people at large for a ready acceptance of military conscription—a practice many considered wholly foreign to the American way of life and the most odious requirement of an otherwise civilized Europe. Indeed, many Pacifists had argued conscription was the principal instrument of an Old World militarism and thereby the cause of the holocaust of the war then raging. Confusing a symptom with cause rather than effect seems to be a weakness of most Pacifists.

Such ideas were difficult to denounce successfully through 1915 and early 1916, but thanks to the follies of German diplomacy, the rising tide of propaganda for Preparedness and the impact of the National Guard activities upon the personal lives of men and families in almost every County of the home front, the renunciation of these earlier concepts was readily forthcoming when the President decided a Draft Law was necessary.

## PROGRESS OF DRAFT PLANNING

Meanwhile, though the War Department, under Secretary Garrison, had frowned upon Captain Moseley for his unwitting trial balloon upon the subject; and in spite of Hugh L. Scott's being extremely cautious and restrictive with his personal views, the War College was making confidential studies. The areas of interest were the Draft practices in Europe, America's own laws, North and South, during the Civil War, and how these lessons could be applied to the current American picture. But it was not until December 12, 1916, that General Scott directed the War College Division to prepare a specific proposal, as a basis for legislation, that would include a system of compulsory training and service. These belated instructions were confidential. Severance of diplomatic relations with Germany the following February 2 was only 47 days in the future!

Just when President Woodrow Wilson came to an acceptance of an implementation of the Draft concept is not known. It is of record, however, that on February 4, at 4:00 P. M., Mr. Wilson, unattended and without previous appointment, entered the office of Secretary of War Baker. He and Mr. Baker were in conference for about 30 minutes. Immediately thereafter, Mr. Baker sent for Enoch H. Crowder, a Brigadier General and then Judge Advocate of the Army. He told General Crowder: "The President, as a war measure, had decided upon a draft as an auxiliary means of recruiting and maintaining the Regular Army and the National Guard at their war strength and as the exclusive means of recruiting and maintaining a national army."

Mr. Baker, in those few words, had built better than he knew. He had joined the man, the time and the mission: the trinity of success. General Crowder was 57 years of age; out of West Point, Class of '81, with an LL.B., University of Missouri, '86. He previously had read sufficiently in law to be admitted to the Missouri Bar, but took advantage of a tour as Professor of Military Science and Tactics in the University of his home State to earn the degree. On the last Indian frontier, he quickly became *de facto* defense counsel for all "gentlemen of the guardhouse." He cleared Lieutenant Matthew F. Steele* for knocking down Private Dell P. Wild, and all concerned acquired Coast-to-Coast publicity. Young Crowder was on his way to a brilliant career in public law and military government assignments in the Army. He did, however, see considerable Line service and some combat during

---

* Lt. Col. Matthew F. Steele, West Point '83 and retired 1912, is best known for his widely read *American Campaigns,* which has been through several editions since its publication as a public document in 1901.

the fighting against the forces of the Philippino insurgent, Emiliaño Aguinaldo.

As an avid student of military history in both its literary and documentary forms, Crowder always read everything of this character that came his way. While a Lieutenant on lonely duty at Fort Yates, Dakota Territory, he came across the now-famous and critical treatise by Major General James B. Fry, U.S.V., on the centralized character and abject failures of the Civil War Draft.* Crowder followed-up this interest with a study of Lieutenant Colonel James Oakes' far more constructive critique. As an Army officer with a trained legal mind, Crowder had been intrigued by the problem from those early days. The clash of the conscript armies of Europe and America's manpower problems as relations with Germany worsened, naturally renewed Crowder's interest in the subject. Whether Mr. Baker knew it or not, he most likely was calling-in America's one and only completely-informed mind on the subject of a citizen's military obligations to his country and the possible approaches to a workable legal and administrative machinery for its modern implementation within this Democracy. When General Crowder asked Mr. Baker what the President's views were on the subject, Baker told him none had been expressed, but a draft of such a law was expected tomorrow forenoon—at 10 o'clock!**

Since a score or more of planners on the General Staff and in the War College for days and weeks had been pondering ideas, memoranda, and preliminary drafts of this and that pertinent to manpower and the desirability of compulsory service, it is natural that from their sources varying stories have arisen as to the basic influence of various persons upon the creation of this all-important legislation. Moreover, sundry biographers of this General or that statesman have seen the hand of their subject as essential to the law. Certainly, General Crowder and his four assistants, Colonel Walter A. Bethel, Lieutenant Colonel Samuel T. Ansell, Captain Hugh S. Johnson and Lieutenant E. K. Massee, were undoubtedly beneficiaries, directly and indirectly, from reading and/or conversational knowledge of various prior and recent studies and ideas, official and otherwise, on the subject. Never-

---

* Lt. Col. Fry, U.S. Army, had been a part of the failure. He was on Staff duty in Washington, D.C., throughout the War, and most of the time as Provost Marshal General.

** A widely repeated story of that era gave the impression that Crowder's prior interest in the question of compulsory military service was because his father was drafted under a Missouri State law for Union service during the Civil War. The impression seems to be untrue. John Crowder, of Edinburgh, Missouri, voluntarily enlisted in "Perry's Volunteers," a locally-organized unit of the State's Organized Militia, then on active duty as Company K, 1st Missouri (Union) Cavalry. He enlisted March 1, 1862, presumably for three years, or the duration, whichever might be the shorter. He was discharged April 7, 1865, at Warrensburg, Missouri, and arrived home April 11, which young Enoch later said he could remember because it was on his sixth birthday.

theless, it was these five men who produced the basic document in legal phraseology by 10 o'clock the following morning.

General Crowder met with the above-mentioned assistants in his office at 5 P. M. He went over the problem briefly; asked them to return at 8. Ansell was unable to comply because of an earlier commitment he could not break. The other three were back ahead of time and found Crowder had utilized the interim to block-out in longhand what he considered the basic sections. He handed Bethel, Johnson and Massee each a page of his longhand script, told them to go to their desks and return to him with the best they could do by 11. At that hour there was another conference reinforced with coffee. Thence they worked far into the night. General Crowder's scholarly, meticulous and exhaustive biographer, Dr. David A. Lockmiller, historian and President, University of Chattanooga, who enjoyed complete access to all of his subject's papers, thinks Crowder borrowed more of Captain Hugh S. Johnson's exact phraseology than from any other member of the team. But early the following morning, Crowder was back at his desk and "on the basis of his own notes and the written and oral suggestions of his assistants, he wrote in almost final form on legal cap paper the law which was subsequently presented to Congress and which, with a few changes and additions, became the Selective Service Act . . . Before and while the law was being typed, its terms were scrutinized by all who had participated . . . At exactly three minutes before 10 o'clock, the Judge Advocate General handed the completed draft to Secretary Baker."

It was hardly as great a feat as it seems, considering Crowder's having been so well grounded in the subject from purely academic interests. Crowder's long association with administrative law held him to the fundamentals. The study and recommendations of James Oakes had left a blueprint with which General Crowder was thoroughly familiar. The time factor was so short that neither he nor any member of his team could pause to ponder and be led astray by any of the myriads of speculative "assumptions" that accompany the "staffing" of any minor matter of petty policy in today's Pentagon.

## THE DRAFT BILL GOES TO CONGRESS

It is impossible today for anyone to reconstruct all the thinking and argumentation that went into those brief hours of creative effort, but from the results it is conspicuous that under Crowder's leadership was recognized the traditional and historic relationship between the National Guard, or Organized Militia, and the Unorganized Militia, or military manpower pool, of the individual States of the Union. Fortunately for Crowder, the Militia-nationalizing amendments the

Guardsmen had written into the National Defense Act of June 3, 1916, had cleared the ground as to military obligations directly to the Federal Government as well as to the several States.

Crowder's basic job was to create a law that would produce a National Army and at the same time recognize the military partnership the Constitution had created between the Federal and State Governments in which all had assets and duties. No one had to research the project to tell Crowder that the Northern Draft had been an even more dismal failure than that of the South (actually *both* laws had failed) because the Union had more flagrantly ignored this basic partnership principle.

He knew that the Draft had to be selective; that it could not be entrusted to a military bureaucracy that would require more soldiers to attempt its enforcement than it would put in the ranks; that a house-to-house check as in a Federal census was too slow, too expensive and too personal to attract grass-roots support, and that area units of administration could not be based upon Congressional Districts with their constantly-shifting boundaries and lack of regional, administrative heritage. These were known errors from 1863. From the start, Crowder further most certainly instructed his assistants that Draftees should be credited to their permanent residence, Town, County and State; that allotments of quotas should be made to States instead of to Congressional Districts, that medical advisers and lawyers should assist the Governors of the States and presumably their Adjutants General, they being the chiefs of Military Departments in most States; and the responsibility of selecting those who would be compelled to serve would be that of Local Boards created by the State authorities. Moreover, Crowder must have been insistent that "bounties and employment of substitutes should be prohibited . . . that military service be for the duration of the war; and justice decreed the basic liability of all male citizens to defend the Nation in time of peril." Without such immediate principles and guidelines as these, predetermined in his mind by a rich background of reading and thoughtful study, General Crowder could not have forged in one night, not even with a team's assistance, the document they brought forth by 10 o'clock the next forenoon.

The initial draft naturally was kept under wraps. Mr. Baker and President Wilson were pleased by the draft's clarity of language, its decentralization, recognition of existing institutions, and democratic spirit. Scott and his extremely able assistant, Major General Tasker H. Bliss, were early shown the document by Secretary Baker. Various members of the General Staff and Brigadier General Joseph E. Kuhn, Director of the War College, were asked to give it close scrutiny. Except for some penal clauses added by Colonel Ansell, the initial draft remained but little changed.

With a superb sense of timing, President Wilson and Secretary Baker threw the measure into the Congressional legislative hopper April 7, 1917, the day following the Declaration of War. They knew it was in for an emotional and bitter tempest through the committee hearings and floor debates.*

The six weeks of hearings, amendments and joint conferences of House and Senate Committees provided a National sounding board for the denunciations of orators representing such divergent constituencies as Senators Vardaman of Mississippi, LaFollette of Wisconsin, Borah of Idaho, and Gronna of North Dakota. Debates in the House were almost equally bitter. Champ Clark of Missouri, Speaker of the House, hotly opposed the Bill, for in his thinking a "conscript" and a "convict" were essentially the same. He would not make convicts of American patriots. The Pacifists, newspapers, clergymen, publicists, lecturers, opinion magazines, Preparedness proponents, Governors, and local and State politicians joined in the pro and con clamor.

The Guardsmen and the Governors were at first suspicious of the Bill because of President Wilson's initial stipulation that the Draft Law should provide the "exclusive means of recruiting and maintaining a National Army." They also feared the new Bill was a return to the disastrous centralized plan that had failed so ignominiously in 1863. This last point became clarified as hearings progressed. Also, as a part of the campaign to educate the Governors and their Adjutants General, under date of April 30, General Crowder—most likely on orders from Baker and indirectly from the President—sent a long, confidential letter to each of the Governors. In it he not only briefly reviewed the law's purposes, but he went into considerable detail as to how it would work through their own channels and down to the communities. Their responses, almost without exception, were prompt and favorable. This, along with the debate, disposed of the fears of overcentralization.

But on the right to volunteer, the Guardsmen, joined by many others such as Theodore Roosevelt, Leonard Wood, and other proponents of the Volunteer Army idea, stimulated such Congressional sentiment that added amendments protected the rights of men to serve their Country voluntarily and also greatly strengthened the law by thus making it more flexible. But motivated by some absurd idea that Draftees would feel better about service to their Country if all others likewise legally were classed as Draftees, Wilson later inducted the

---

* General Peyton C. March, who became Chief of Staff, February, 1918, wrote in his memoirs, *The Nation at War*, published in 1932, that Crowder "was steadily opposed to the introduction of such a Bill in Congress . . ." The preponderance of evidence is against March's memory on this and sundry other points; but unfortunately some writers have taken them at face value, with resulting confusion and uncertainty.

National Guard by Draft Order after all the Guardsmen had volunteered as individuals. But this playing with legalistic semantics deceived no one, least of all the Draftees.

## THE SELECTIVE DRAFT LAW OF MAY 18, 1917

The law provided that the Regular Army would be given manpower, in addition to its then strength and immediate volunteers, to give its units and increments the strength provided for in the National Defense Act of 1916. The National Guard and National Guard Reserves were to be called into Federal service, automatically and immediately, on the same terms as the Draftees, *but retaining, insofar as practicable, their State units and designations.* This was calculated to keep them on active duty for the duration, the same as Draftees, to which the Guardsmen offered no objection, as they were asking for no favors in terms of service to their Nation, but they did make a major issue of the right to serve with their fellow-citizens from home towns and from within their States and in units they themselves often had created or nurtured long before the emergency. The law also provided for the immediate drafting of 500,000 men, within the required enrollment ages, 21 to 30 inclusive, to be *selected* in the manner prescribed; and further, at the President's discretion, an additional 500,000 would be selected and ordered to the Colors, in the same manner as the first half-million.

The President further was authorized to accept into the Army as many as four Divisions of United States Volunteers to be composed of men over 25 years of age. This was a further concession of the right of free citizens to volunteer, for which the Guardsmen had insisted but which in this instance was a concession to the Army Reserve provisions of the National Defense Act of 1916. It was a recrudescence of the old idea for Regiments of United States Volunteers that had been originated toward the end of the Civil War, and which paved the way for the three Regiments of Volunteer Cavalry (including the "Rough Riders") and the 10 Regiments of "Immunes" in 1898. These, we have seen, were forebears of the entire Volunteer Army of 1899 that had been created largely from disbanding National Guard Regiments for the subjugation, or pacification, of the Philippines. Under this provision of the law the President could have activated ex-President Theodore Roosevelt's Volunteer Division, in which there had been a sharp revival of interest, had the President so desired. But he did not so desire. Mr. Wilson perhaps felt he had had enough off-stage interruptions from ex-President Roosevelt and his former comrade-in-arms, Leonard Wood, without aggrandizing them with a magnified "Rough Rider" command and the publicity of an overseas mission of high priority. Nothing came of this provision of the law.

255

The foregoing are the essentials of the Selective Draft Act of 1917. There was, of course, the basic provision that substitutes and bounties, the major abuse of the Civil War law, were absolutely prohibited. There was also included a list of exemptions, automatic and discretionary, for the guidance of local Selection Boards, State Adjutants General and Governors. The President was left with a wide range of freedom in the making of rules and regulations; and once again, out of deference to the traditions of the National Guard, there was the provision that all "persons enlisted or drafted under any of the provisions of this Act shall as far as practicable be grouped into units by States and the political subdivisions of the same." This section of the law explains why the subsequent 77th (Statue of Liberty) Infantry Division of Draftees in the National Army came from New York City and immediate communities, and the 90th (T superimposed on O) Infantry Division, National Army, came from Texas and Oklahoma, and similarly why later National Army Divisions of Draftees were regimented, brigaded and often assigned to regional Divisions. It proved to be a good practice and should have been followed more closely through World War II and the subsequent Korean Police Action.

The law also contained the conventional and undebatable provision that officers and men of all components—Regulars, National Guardsmen and National Army men (Draftees)—should draw the same pay and allowances while in the service. It also provided a new pay scale for the enlisted men. Existing restrictions upon the detail of Regular Army personnel were removed for the duration of the emergency. This was an echo from Upton's complaint that during the Civil War, Regulars were held down to low ranks in Company-level assignments within their own professional Regiments, while non-professionals moved into the Army and over their heads in rank as commanders of activated Organized Militia, or National Guard, Regiments from the States. More-or-less as a rider to the Bill, and out of deference to the cresting wave for Nationwide prohibition of alcoholic beverages, the law also put a limit on how close a saloon or brothel might be to a military camp and stipulated severe penalties for anyone selling liquor to men in uniform.

Of course, not all of these items were in the original draft of the law as prepared by General Crowder and his assistants that long night of February 4-5, but all the basic elements of compulsory service by selection and draft as we understand the term and as it operated, were in the document that Crowder handed to Mr. Baker.

It was inevitable, of course, that riders and amendments would be written-in such as those noted; and, further, there would be additional minor and perfecting legislation after the Act had been in operation for a time. On May 16, 1918, almost exactly a year after the basic law, there was a special law adjusting the quota basis to total population of Class I registrants rather than total population. This was a concession to States with large foreign, or alien populations. Four days later, May 20, a minor law clarified the registration status of persons who had become 21 since the first enrollment. The third supplementary law was dated August 31, 1918, and placed the Navy and Marine Corps personnel procurement under operation of the Draft. They had been omitted in the original law's restrictions on voluntary enlistments, and by the above date had begun "stockpiling" volunteer enlistees faster than they could be put on active duty and in training.

## THE DRAFT EXPEDITES VOLUNTEERING

Meanwhile, the Declaration of War and compulsory military service were swelling the volunteer lists of the National Guard, the Regular Army, Officers Reserve Corps and the Enlisted Reserve Corps. This last component, as we have seen, was only a few thousand and strictly in the paper stage when war was declared. But it quickly was recognized as a channel for entering the Army for no more than the duration, whereas the old term enlistment law for the Regulars was not changed until after unexplainable delay. Thus, the Enlisted Reserve Corps and Officers Reserve Corps eventually numbered 183,797 before voluntary enlistments were terminated for men with Draft status in December, 1917. These men, of course, immediately went on active duty, in ranks or to Officers Training Camps.* At the same time the National Guard was picking up thousands of recruits for a war aggregate of 433,478.

These Guardsmen were for the most part early birds. Their units were soon back to active duty and scheduled for departures to one of the 16 tent-type training cantonments being built in the South and Southwest. A National Guard Division was scheduled for each camp. Meanwhile, an equal number of frame, barracks-type cantonments were under construction for the subsequent National Army, or Draft, Divisions and supporting troops. The average cost for each of the National Guard cantonments was only $4,500,000, and for each of the 16 camps

* The Officers Reserve Corps, as envisioned in the National Defense Act of 1916, remained pretty much a paper proposition until the series of three 90-day Nationwide Officers Training Camps. The first 16 camps opened near the middle of May, 1917. By approximately the same date a year later, there had been commissioned into the Army Reserve no less than 56,237; most of them, naturally, as Lieutenants and Captains; however, some initial commissions ranged as high as Colonel for men of greater maturity and experience in administrative and managerial positions, in addition to their Training Camp record. These wartime officers created an Officer Reserve Corps, which, with ROTC and CMTC postwar replacements for the inevitable attrition in turn gave the Army an effective pool of Reserve officers until the Mobilization of 1940-42. The Regular Army Reserve and Enlisted Reserve Corps, as envisioned in the Defense Act of 1916 and earlier legislation, did not survive the patriotic fervor of the War years.

for National Army troops the average cost was $12,500,000. Not all of this was due to a greater solicitude for the welfare and comfort of the Selectees as compared to the Guardsmen. The Guard camps were, for the most part, in areas of mild weather; the Guardsmen admittedly were better-organized and trained for taking care of themselves under more adverse circumstances, and it further was expected that many of them would be in Europe, or en route, before the hardest part of the coming Winter would be at hand. And this was true of many. The Guard leaders made no complaint concerning the above logic and arrangements, but to the contrary argued the same assumptions themselves and cooperated fully with the cheaper, less comfortable and perhaps less healthful arrangements. The Regular units, for the most part, were augmented and trained at their traditional permanent posts, which often were temporarily and greatly expanded.*

In conclusion, it should be emphasized that Selective Service is historically a part of America's Militia heritage with its arms-bearing responsibilities reaching back to English Common Law. Inasmuch as the National Guard is a voluntarily-organized aspect of that same heritage, the two cannot logically be separated. The Act of May 18, 1917, was the first effective effort at gearing all the Unorganized Militia of all the States and coordinating these pools of obligated, military-age manpower to a simultaneous, National purpose.

America was also fortunate that the man to whom the legal task fell was an officer who knew and appreciated the Guard and saw the necessity for utilizing the States, with their Military Departments, in the operation of a selective service. Finally, without the whole-hearted understanding, sympathy and support of the Organized Militia, or National Guard, at the grass roots and through State Governments, it is not likely that the Law would have weathered the tumultuous and emotional assaults that came from the Pacifists, Isolationists and various small but intense and compact minority groups who saw no reason for America becoming involved in Europe's maelstrom in the first instance; and, granting the essential involvement, thought only in terms of a limited-liability participation. The role of the Guard and Guardsmen through those crucial months of transition from peace to war should not be overlooked, though it often is.

---

* During World War I, the Regular Army reached an aggregate of 545,773. A goodly percentage were comparatively late enlistees. The peak month was December, 1918, the last month in which a man between the vulnerable age limits was permitted to volunteer. That month the Regular Army enlisted 141,931. Men outside the vulnerable age limits still had the right to enlist in the Regular Army until the following August, by which time an additional 199,109 had joined the Army. Thus, 341,040 of the Regular Army's men were being issued their first uniforms on, or after, the dates that the National Guard Divisions were enroute to or landing in Europe.

# Bibliographical Note For Chapter XI

The compulsory military service legislation of 1917 is best identified as the Selective Draft Act in distinction from the Selective Service and Training Act of September 16, 1940, a peacetime measure, but under which, as amended, compulsory manpower was provided for World War II. The heritage and need for both measures are almost identical, hence the literature and source materials of both Acts are largely the same. J. C. Duggan, *Legislative and Statutory Development of the Federal Concept of Conscription for Military Service,* 1946; Edward A. Fitzpatrick, *Universal Military Training,* 1945, and Jack F. Leach, *Conscription in the United States,* 1952, are among the most convenient sources of detailed information. Maj. Gen. Enoch Crowder, *The Spirit of Selective Service,* 1920, and David A. Lockmiller, *Enoch H. Crowder: Soldier, Lawyer, Statesman,* 1955, are as vital to this chapter as the Statute itself, which is most readily found in the appropriate biennial volumes of the *United States Statutes at Large. Selective Service Regulations,* 1917, as the title suggests, is also an important, contemporary Government publication. Gilman G. Udell, *Selective Service Act as Amended,* is an excellent public document. It is more than a compilation of cognate legislation on compulsory military service from the 65th to the 86th Congress, inclusive (18 May 1917–18 July 1962). It includes legislative history and appropriations. The Selective Service System, under Lt. Gen. Lewis B. Hershey, began publishing in 1946, as public documents, a series of 19 scholarly studies entitled *Special Monographs.* Their detailed scrutiny of the entire theory and practice of compulsory military service in America since 1607 is both legalistic and microscopic. These *Special Monographs* are not only rich in source materials, such as the pertinent military laws of the Thirteen Colonies, but in their entirety they constitute field manuals for coping with Draft problems. These individual Special *Monographs* have such titles as *Backgrounds of Selective Service* (No. 1): *Military Obligations: The American Tradition, a Compilation of the Enactments of Compulsion from the Earliest Settlements of the Original Thirteen Colonies in 1607 Through the Articles of Confederation, 1789;* (this title is in 14 parts); *Conscientious Objection* (No. 11); and, *The Operation of Selective Service* (No. 17).

## CHAPTER XII

# The Guard Goes To Europe--
# 1917-1918

THE WAR DEPARTMENT began recalling National Guard units into Federal service two weeks prior to the Declaration of War, April 6, 1917. As previously noted, however, no less than 66,594 Guard officers and men were still on active duty as of that date from the Mexican Border Call. They were, of course, continued in Federal status without

261

missing a day of active duty or experiencing a change of station. Some, awaiting the formal muster-out, found that last formation cancelled. They were deployed back to the field, with various missions, which, more often than otherwise, were local security missions for some railroad bridge, waterfront installation, or industrial plant considered vital to the war effort.

The units that had been completely mustered-out began getting recalls to active duty as early as March 20, 1917, and likewise were deployed to sundry security missions, given training assignments in State camps or temporarily attached to some Regular Army formation or station. Security was the prevalent mission, for it was feared the German sabotage apparatus might be far greater than anyone could possibly know and that the Declaration of War would be the signal for a veritable series of explosions similar to the Black Tom affair.

Notwithstanding the drab character of such security duty, many units managed to get in some good training above and beyond mere guard duty. Many found opportunity for pistol and rifle practice, considerable close order drill, conditioning exercises, short marches, and the on-the-job training that comes with a small unit being responsible for its own supplies, messing arrangements and living in the field. Even so, it was indeed a lucky Company Commander as well as one of more than average initiative who was able to get in much, if any, small unit tactical training while on such missions. Recruiting was the top priority. A favorite play was to refuse anyone a long weekend pass home or a furlough unless he promised to return with a recruit.

When a reasonable length of time after the Declaration of War had brought an easing of fears as to possible damage to the Nation by sabotage, most of the security missions were cancelled. By the end of June, or early July, the typical Guard unit of the typical State found itself back with its parent Regiment or Battalion within its home State for more complete equipping, reorganization and additional training. All the Guard units of the State might be present in a State-owned camp, but in those States with limited camp facilities, all the units could not be sheltered at the same time and various improvisations were conventional. Normally, they thus were concentrated sufficiently close for ease of administration and supply.

Once again, recruiting was the top priority, but frustrations began to occur. About the time the Selective Draft Act was passed, or when its passage appeared certain, down came an order to suspend recruiting. By the time the word was disseminated to every City, Town, village and farm that it was too late for the boys to join-up with the home-town crowd, down came another order to resume recruiting, posthaste, and with unabated vigor. Notwithstanding these red- and green-light frustrations, by August 5 the Guard units awaiting movement to Federal tent cantonments in the South and Southwest had a reported strength of 379,071 officers and men.

This was an important date in the memories of those Guardsmen. It was the day of their official induction into the National Army pursuant to the Selective Service Act. Previously they had gone on active duty as State soldiers in Federal service and as members of units of the National Guard of their States. After August 5, 1917, they were in the United States Army as individuals. Off came the bronze discs with the abbreviations for the National Guard of their States. These were replaced by the regulation collar ornaments for all enlisted men—similar discs with the letters "U.S."

The State pride of the officers was assuaged to some extent. They were allowed to buy the regulation "U.S." for officers but with the abbreviations of their States superimposed thereon. A year later, July 31, 1918, the new Chief of Staff, General Peyton C. March, decided there should be just one big Army without any reference to, or visible evidence of, its basic components. It was thought the stroke of a pen at the bottom of an order would do it. By that time the Guardsmen were battle-seasoned and their *esprit* was extremely high. All sorts of excuses were given by Guard officers as to why they were unable to buy new collar ornaments. And officers and men of all Divisions continued to refer to themselves and to their outfits as Regular Army, National Guard, or National Army. Nevertheless, August 5, 1917, gave all ranks a new feeling of status. They were in for the duration and on an equalitarian basis with everyone of like rank and pay. There remained but the two questions wartime citizen-soldiers always are asking: What's our outfit going to look like after we get reorganized? Where do we go from here?

## REORGANIZATION INTO "SQUARE DIVISIONS"

Meanwhile, General Pershing and his Staff had left for Europe shortly after the passage of the Selective Draft Act. The tactics of defensive position warfare on wide, static fronts of trenches and barbed wire dominated most thoughts. Some English and French Generals had ceased thinking in other terms. The problem was how to break through; to create flanks and a war of movement supported by mobile firepower for a conceded victory through maneuver.

Pershing quickly decided upon powerful "Square Divisions" built around four massive Infantry Regiments of 3,720 enlisted men each. There would be only two Regiments in a Brigade to be supported by a Regiment of light Artillery (the famous French 75mm when it could be made available), with a third Regiment of 155mm Schneider howitzers in general support completing the Division's Brigade of Artillery.

Three Machine Gun Battalions and a Trench Mortar Battery further increased the normal firepower of the "Square Division." A Regiment of Combat Engineers could be pulled from its usual field construction and repair duties to create the full and fair equivalent of a Rifle Battalion in Divisional reserve, should a hostile breakthrough appear imminent. A Signal Battalion, like the Machine Gun Battalions, was commanded by a Major; and a Division Train, consisting of Military Police, an Ammunition Train, a Supply Train, an Engineer Train and a Sanitary Train, provided the Divisional communications, supply and medical support. In attack situations, powerful reinforcing fires came from Corps and Army Artillery. Attachments of additional Machine Gun Battalions, Chemical Warfare units, and perhaps some primitive tanks of the era, further beefed a Division for a breakthrough. On the line with full sector responsibility, but without attachments, the American Army Division, at Table of Organization strength, had 991 officers and 27,114 men. Beefed-up for an assault, attachments from the rear boundary forward could easily bring the number under a Divisional command to more than 35,000.* In that wagon soldier era, with every French 75mm gun drawn by six horses, and all Divisions in narrow sectors, this was a thoroughly cumbersome and complicated command, but it had a frontal attack, breakthrough power unknown to any army until the advent of full motorization of Divisions and the creation of large units of fast, armored vehicles, self-propelled guns and tanks.

The new, Pershing concept threw out all prior General Staff planning for three Regiments, in "Triangular" Infantry Brigades with three such Brigades in each Division. The "Triangular" formations were also weaker in organic Artillery and support troops. The most immediately apparent effect was that the Guard had a surplus of Regimental and Brigade Commanders (Colonels and Brigadier Generals) and a comparable shortage of command slots in any switch that might take place from the old planning and tentative organizations to the new Pershing Divisions. Thus the question as to what their outfits would look like after full reorganization was highly pertinent in early August, 1917. Nevertheless, exact Tables of Organization for the new "Square Divisions" were not available, even to the Regular Army Major Generals under assignments to command them, until August 14, or later.**

---

* Table of Organization totals varied during war, but not excessively. Figures above are for Autumn, 1918. Divisions in action were seldom at full strength. Likewise they were seldom under 24,000.

** A number of the National Guard Divisions, World War I, are credited officially with having been activated in July, 1917, but most of their commanders were not credited with having been in command until the last week of August, or later. The one notable exception was New York's 27th Division, activated with Maj. Gen. John F. O'Ryan, N.Y.N.G., commanding July 16, 1917. The 27th had functioned as a full Division on the Border and in State status prior to the World War I Call. Hence O'Ryan went on active duty with it as a Major General and commanded it through-

The question—where do we go from here—already had been answered by the time the new Tables of Organization were at hand. Every latrine orderly in the Illinois National Guard knew that the units disappearing daily were headed for Camp Logan, Houston, Texas, where they were to become the 33rd Division commanded by Major General George (Ding-Dong) Bell, Regular Army.*

Likewise, everyone in the Texas and Oklahoma National Guard units knew he was scheduled for Camp Bowie, at Fort Worth, to form a Division to be known as the 36th under Major General Edwin St. John Greble, and the Guardsmen of Michigan and Wisconsin knew that at Camp MacArthur, Waco, Texas, they would be merged into a 32nd Division under command of Major General James (Galloping Jim) Parker; and so on across the Nation.

## THE GUARD UNITS ARE RE-NUMBERED

Before the war, as we have seen in an earlier chapter, there had been a suggestion from the National Guardsmen themselves that since the designations "1st North Carolina Infantry" and the "1st South Carolina Infantry" were easily confused, not to mention 46 other possible "1st infantries" in a future Army, all National Guard Regiments should begin with the number 100. Within the General Staff, notwithstanding the specific language of the National Defense Act of 1916 and the Selective Service Act of 1917, there was still a strong feeling that the sooner the regional background and historic heritage of citizen-soldier units were obscured or obliterated, the better it would be for the Regular Army, and presumably for National defense—hence the idea of re-numbering the Guard Regiments without any reference to the home State was completely adopted for the impending grand reorganization for the American Expeditionary Force to Europe. Likewise, the resulting Divisions and Brigades should bear no designations indicative of State or region. There would be no "Wisconsin Iron Brigade," no "Hood's Texans," nor "Roosevelt's Rough Riders," as in the Civil and Spanish Wars, the very names and regional associations of which would steal publicity and public esteem from more deserving Regulars and less conspicuous Selective Draft formations.

---

out its active duty period, which ended April, 1919. The Division's distinguished combat record is noted elsewhere.

In at least 44 of the States there was no National Guard rank higher than Brigadier General. Pennsylvania fielded a full Division, the 28th, commanded by Maj. Gen. Charles M. Clement, Pa.N.G. He had passed his 62nd birthday and was honorably released from active duty for physical disabilities December 11, 1917. Several Regular Army officers of like rank and assignment likewise were retired from their Divisional commands for reasons of age and health before their commands embarked for France.

* There were two Regular Army Generals Bell of that era. Maj. Gen. J. Franklin Bell, then organizing the 77th National Army Division at Camp Upton, was a smallish man with a high voice. He was known as "Ting-a-Ling" Bell.

For orderly bookkeeping, however, the numbers 1 to 25 inclusive for Divisions, and all Regimental numbers to 100 inclusive, would be reserved for the Regular Army. Divisional numbers 26 to 75, inclusive, would be reserved for then-current and future National Guard Divisions, and the Divisions of Draft Selectees would have numbers beginning with the 76th.

Regimental numbers within Divisions would be equally orderly. The four Infantry Regiments of the squared 26th (Yankee) Division, for example, would be the 101st Infantry to 104th, inclusive. With two Regiments to a Brigade, it followed as a corollary that National Guard Brigade numbers should start with the 51st Infantry Brigade composed of the first two of the above Regiments. The three Field Artillery Regiments of the 26th Infantry Division likewise would be numbered 101st, 102nd and 103rd, to be organized into the 51st F.A. Brigade. Spare parts such as the Division Train and Signal Battalion were numbered the 101st, etc.

Following through this system of staggered, mental arithmetic, it may or not be seen readily that the numerical structure of the 36th Infantry Division would be, and was, the 71st and 72nd Infantry Brigades, composed of the 141st to 144th Infantry Regiments, inclusive; with the 61st F.A. Brigade, consisting of 131st, 132nd and 133rd Field Artillery Regiments with Division Trains and other spare parts numbered the 111th Signal Battalion, etc. This bland, orderly numbering for all Divisions and their internal units would minimize the individuality of all units. The Army would be one big magnificent, orderly machine. All Divisions would be called "National Army Divisions."

But all this General Staff planning was without deference to the personalities of men and the instincts of good soldiers. They always think of their outfit as something different. The 1st Infantry Division Headquarters immediately inserted a parenthetical "Regular Army" in its letterheads, and so captioned its Division orders. The 2nd Infantry Division did likewise and adopted the slogan: "Second to None." Other low-numbered, Regular Army Divisions followed suit until ordered to cease and desist—which they did until they wrote their Divisional histories.

The Divisions of National Guard origins began to accentuate their regional background and historical military heritage with appropriate shoulder patches, slogans and nicknames, such as "The Blue and the Gray" for the 29th from Maryland, New Jersey, Washington, D.C., and Virginia; the "Buckeye" and "Keystone" for the 37th of Ohio and the 28th of Pennsylvania. Within weeks, all who could read letters and news stories knew that the National Guard was very much in the War and that Divisions numbered 26th to 42nd inclusive were of that origin.

Meanwhile, General Crowder's Draftees were being organized with greater regard for the spirit of the law and the merits of regional and State pride. Draftees who were sent to Guard Divisions as fillers were normally from the States whence came the Division receiving them.

In official practice and public parlance it was only the Divisions of Draftees from the ground up that acquired the designation of National Army Divisions. They were, however, constituted along regional lines. Hence, what was more natural than that the 77th Division, composed largely of New York City Draftees, should adopt the Statue of Liberty as a shoulder patch and refer to itself as the "Liberty Division?" Its men also sneeringly referred to older and rival volunteer Divisions as "Draft-dodgers." Thus the asinine assumption that State, regional and unit origin pride could be smothered with a cloak of anonymity very early fell by the wayside.

## REORGANIZATION PAINS OF A TYPICAL GUARD DIVISION

With volunteering into National Guard units booming as departure time for the Southern camps neared, it should not have been necessary to send fillers to any of the Guard Divisions had General Staff planning been adequate and fully cooperative. In the first place, there would have been many more volunteers into the Guard had it not been for the vagaries of War Department policies and mercurial instructions relative to recruiting. Moreover, many of the States and regions providing National Guard formations for merging into the new Pershing-size Divisions found themselves dumping surplus men and units into Depot Brigades at a time when other Guard Divisions were receiving drafted fillers.

The concentration of New England units for merger into a giant-size Pershing Division for later movement to Camp Greene, North Carolina, is illustrative. Camp Greene was slow in being made available. Major General Clarence R. Edwards, U.S.A., was in command of the Army's Department of the Northeast, with Headquarters near Boston, when war was declared. In early June he was scheduled to command a Division. Meanwhile, as C.G. of the Northeast, he was concentrating the National Guard units of New England in comparatively large but more-or-less temporary Connecticut, Rhode Island and Massachusetts installations between Newburyport, near the New Hampshire boundary, and New Haven. In a telegram dated August 13, with Camp Greene still unready, he was authorized to take command of the newly-designated 26th Infantry Division and to organize the New England National Guard troops available into a Pershing-type Division, tables for which were being hand-carried to him by a Staff officer.

General Edwards, with his Aide, a Major who was to become a temporary Colonel and Chief of Staff for the Division, and a small nucleus Staff, composed of both Regular and Guard officers, immediately opened his 26th Division Headquarters in Boston. He reorganized and redesignated units in their then positions, but with shifting of some personnel. Thus all the New England troops immediately were tabulated into a Square Division. From Boston, General Edwards soon issued his Divisional General Order No. 1, assuming command of the Division. General Order No. 2, dated August 22, declared it duly organized in position, and General Order No. 3, dated August 30, created the 51st Depot Brigade, into which he dumped 217 officers, most of them surplus in grade for the new Divisional tables,* and 3,674 enlisted men, all of whom became available for individual or group assignments elsewhere.

General Edwards was also conventional, and in line with the practice in creation of the other National Guard Divisions then in progress, in that he retained and assigned National Guard Colonels to command each of the four enormous Infantry Regiments, each of the three Artillery Regiments, the Regiment of Engineers and the Division Train. Lesser Divisional spare parts all were commanded by National Guard officers of grade appropriate to the assignment. One 26th Division National Guard Brigadier General was retained. He, like most of the Colonels and lower Field Grade officers commanding Divisional units, went all the way through the Division's 210 days of subsequent European combat with distinction and credit to themselves and their component of the Army.

A study of other Divisional histories of the National Guard component shows clearly that the story of the 26th Division's National Guard Colonels was normal rather than unusual. General Edwards did pass-over a New England Infantry Brigadier General to fill the other Infantry Brigade command slot with Colonel Peter A. Traub, U.S.A., a distinguished Regular who but recently had been promoted to temporary Brigadier General in the National Army. Likewise, a Brigadier General from the Regulars came to the Division to command the Artillery Brigade. This was the case in practically all the National Guard Divisions then being created. Through the failure of the General Staff to plan, and the War Department to provide Artillery equipment to the States by way of implementing the Dick Act of 1903, few, if any, of the States had a National Guard Brigadier General with Artillery service or train-

---

* An officer from Maine, Brig. Gen. Albert Greenlaw, the State's former Adjutant General, was so intent upon going out with the boys of his State, and sensing that he had too much rank for inclusion in a combat formation in that grade, previously had resigned to take a Captaincy in a Maine Regiment. Thanks to his foresight, he stayed in the Division and came home as Lt. Col. and Assistant C. of S., G-1. This formula was repeated, in modified form or otherwise, by one or more organization-minded and eager Guard officers from almost every State of the Nation, thereby unfairly giving color to early rumors of demotions for incompetence incident to Divisional organizations—rumors that some Regulars happily repeated rather than explained.

ing. Except for these two Brigadier Generals from the Regulars, his Aide, and six or seven Majors and Lieutenant Colonels as nucleus for his General and Special Staff slots, General Edwards' entire command was composed of citizen-soldiers. And this, too, was conventional for the other 16 National Guard Infantry Divisions then being activated from Coast to Coast.

### THE RACE TO BE FIRST IN FRANCE

Simultaneous with these activations of National Guard Divisions, the War Department was busily engaged in creating Regular Army Divisions for service in Europe. The 1st Infantry (Regular Army) Division had been activated under earlier tables the preceding June 8. It quickly was transitioned to the "Square" tables. The 2nd, 3rd, 4th, 5th, 6th and 7th Divisions were phased for activations through October to January 1, 1918. It was apparent immediately to the militarily-minded cognoscenti that the one Regular Army Division was being groomed for the first landing in Europe by American combat formations, and well ahead of the almost equally old National Guard Divisions.

The Press made much of it. The martial spirit and pride, Nationwide, asserted itself. Military and Marine formations everywhere under the American Colors wanted a part, or all, of the eminent honor. Secretary of War Baker was greatly harassed. Confirmation of the intended role for the Regular Army's 1st Division on a purely numerical basis did not get the War Secretary off the hook. The question remained: What State, or group of States, would be honored by having its citizen-soldiers first ashore in Europe to make the World safe for Democracy?

At this juncture, Major Douglas MacArthur, whose enthusiasm for spirited Guardsmen has been noted previously, thought of all the surplus Guardsmen and Guard units that had been and were being dumped in much the same manner General Edwards had disposed of his surplus of 217 officers and 3,674 men from the New England Guard formations. Why not an additional National Guard Division to be moulded from units and men not being absorbed into the 16 Guard Divisions (26th to 41st, inclusive) that had been planned? He proposed that such a Division would cover America "like a rainbow" and if sent to France first it would give honor to all the States and regions of the United States by being the first Division of citizen-soldiers to land in France. The harassed Mr. Baker knew a good idea when he heard one and proceeded to get off the hook by adopting it. Furthermore, it pleased President Wilson. MacArthur's reward, the desire for which he did not bother to conceal, was a temporary Lieutenant Colonelcy and acting Chief of Staff. He came home a Brigadier General and commanding the "Rainbow's" 84th Infantry Brigade. A great military record had been launched.

But young MacArthur and Messrs. Baker and Wilson had failed to consult General Edwards, C.G. of the "Yankee" Division. And at this point the New England Guard units ceased to have a training history more-or-less identical with that of most of the other Guard Divisions.

In short, instead of taking his command to Camp Greene, North Carolina, from its New England stations, and for which orders actually were issued, the wily General Edwards finessed the trick. He moved his units direct to Ports of Embarkation from their State stations, scattered though they were from the New Hampshire border to New Haven, Connecticut. So engrossed did he and his Division Headquarters become in this stealthy and somewhat secret overseas movement operation, that only a last-minute thought kept them from inadvertently leaving an advance detachment then at Camp Greene, for the purpose of opening the Division's Headquarters there.

The 26th Division's covert movement originated through direct liaison with and more-or-less connivance between the New York Port of Embarkation Commander and General Edwards. Any time the former had immediate need for human cargo to effect a quick turn-around of empty troop ships, the latter would have the desired number, duly processed for overseas movement, right on the dock. Some Staff officer for transportation in Washington undoubtedly procured Departmental clearance in the interest of keeping the ships moving.

It worked so well and rapidly that General Edwards made a similar deal with the Canadians in Montreal! His senior New England officers included high-level business executives who experienced no trouble in getting full and secret cooperation from the regional railroad officials and in promoting the Canadian deal. Thus, for a month or more, thousands of fond fathers, mothers, and sweethearts throughout New England were sending letters, boxed goodies and home-knitted socks to their boys at Camp Greene, North Carolina. Never have so many hundreds of Yankees been the victim of such a slick, Yankee trick—though General Edwards was from Ohio. The Yankee volunteers never saw Camp Greene. Most were in Europe before even the Plans Section of the War Department General Staff knew about it.

But the backlash of the operation cut the General, when the secrecy caught the War Department General Staff by surprise. It is an old Army rule that one should always surprise the enemy, but never a higher headquarters. Edwards had surprised them all except the transportation channels. By the time the rest of the War Department General Staff and Special Staff world had learned what was happening, the flow of the 26th Infantry Division could not be stopped without unexplainable harm. But more unpardonable than all this, enough of the "Yankee" Division reached France simultaneously with, or ahead of, the Regular Army's 1st Infantry Division that it was a matter of bookkeeping as to which Division merited the coveted honor. Both Divisions have statistics that satisfy each but not one another.

In any event, both of them were slightly ahead of the widely heralded 42nd Infantry (Rainbow) Division composed of National Guard oddments from 26 States. But the hastily-activated 2nd Infantry Division, one Brigade of which were Marines, was hard upon the heels of all three. Although many old Regulars and most of the General Staff long viewed General Edwards as a sort of warmed-over Benedict Arnold, willing to sell West Point down the river for the citizen-soldiers, almost everyone else was quite happy—most particularly the Secretary of War. He was off the pride priority hook, and even the Marines had been given a chance to land; but they hardly had the situation well in hand. Russia was folding like an Arab's tent and the Germans were building for a long-remembered offensive in the West.

## FLOW OF DIVISIONS CONTINUES

Meanwhile, through August and the following Autumn, most of the remaining 17* National Guard Infantry Divisions were moving from their State concentration areas to the newly-prepared tent camps in the South and Southwest. In addition to the 26th, 27th, 28th, 29th, 33rd, 36th, 37th, and 42nd Divisions, previously mentioned and their origins earlier identified, the remaining World War I National Guard Divisions were created as follows:

The 30th Infantry (Old Hickory) Division came from the Carolinas and Tennessee; the 31st Infantry (Dixie) Division was created from the Guard units of Alabama, Florida and Georgia. The 32nd Infantry (Red Arrow) Division came from Michigan and Wisconsin. The 34th (Red Bull) Division was composed of National Guardsmen of Minnesota, Nebraska and Iowa.** The troops in the 35th (Santa Fe) Division were from Kansas and Missouri. Its shoulder patch signified the region of the Santa Fe Trail, but many of the wheat belt volunteers said their name came from the Santa Fe Railroad, which was a legitimate application of modernity to an historic suggestion. The 38th (Cyclone) Division was constituted from Guard units of Kentucky, Indiana, and West Virginia. The forming units of this Division became involved in a

---

* It is conventional to say, and it often appears in print, that there were 17 National Guard Divisions in World War I. There were 18. Note subsequent mention of the misnumbered 93rd Infantry Division. Also in France were non-divisional units of National Guard origin consisting of First Army Headquarters Regiment, two separate Brigade Headquarters Companies, two Field Signal Battalions and 14 Regiments of Pioneer Infantry. These were enough to compensate for the missing Artillery Brigade in the 93rd Division, with enough units remaining to be the equivalent of two additional National Guard Divisions. In other words, the war strength units of the National Guard in Europe were equivalent to 20 World War I Divisions.

** North and South Dakota contributed a unit each to the 34th, but most Dakota Guardsmen were assigned to the 41st Division.

tornado and decided to join-up with the idea of organized destruction; thus, they capitalized on the bad luck. The 39th Infantry (Delta) Division was composed of Guard units of Louisiana, Arkansas and Mississippi. The 40th (Sunshine) Division was, of course, dominated by California National Guardsmen, though it contained units from Utah, New Mexico, Arizona and Colorado. The 41st Division was created from National Guard units of Oregon, Washington, Idaho, Montana, the Dakotas, Wyoming, and Colorado. Its shoulder patch suggested "Sunset," but the nickname seldom was received with enthusiasm. It emerged from the South Pacific, World War II, as the "Jungleers," a tribute to an enviable South Pacific record.

The "Rainbow" Division, as we have seen, was something of an afterthought, but because of its high priority for overseas, its units, from 26 States and the District of Columbia, went direct to the staging camps in the immediate vicinity of the Ports of Embarkation. Camp Mills, on Long Island, for the Port of New York, staged most of them. Hence, this Division, like New England's 26th, was spared the organizational and training pains in one of the Southern tent camps.

## THE 33RD DIVISION TYPIFIES TRAINING CAMP SHAKEDOWNS

Since most of the Regular Army, National Guard and National Army Divisions organized for World War I did go through a barracks cantonment, or a tent camp, for their organizational and training phase before going to the Ports of Embarkation, a brief survey of the vicissitudes of such a Division is appropriate. To this end the 33rd Division, also quite properly known as the "Prairie" Division, is selected to reveal the conventional experiences of most National Guard Divisions. The 33rd appears to have had all the troubles any of them experienced and some special troubles of its own unknown to some others. In short, notwithstanding its ultimately magnificent combat record and sacrifices on the fields of France, the Division acquired something of a hard-luck record from the outset.

On Monday, August 27, Major General George Bell, Jr., issued his General Order No. 1, activating the 33rd Infantry Division at Camp Logan, Houston, Texas. The General and his small party had just arrived. The camp was far from completed. Present for duty was the normal and small advance detail from Illinois. The General was accompanied by Brigadier General Henry D. Todd, assigned to command the yet-unformed and unarrived 58th Field Artillery Brigade, and five or six Captains and Majors, in temporary National Army ranks from the Regular Army's permanent list. They were to be assigned to key positions in the Division Headquarters.

The General, a permanent B.G., had been a temporary National Army Major General less than three weeks. He was a sturdy, bearded

Infantryman, 58 years of age, out of West Point, Class of '80, with an LL.B. from Cornell, '94, acquired while on duty at that University as Professor of Military Science and Tactics. As an Infantry officer he had an excellent record in Cuba and the Philippines; obviously a carefully-selected officer for the new command. Brigadier General Todd, National Army, was a Colonel on the permanent list, a thorough Artilleryman, graduate of the War College, and had done a long tour of duty on the General Staff. Three weeks later, with increments from Illinois still not arriving as rapidly as expected or hoped, General Bell took off for Europe for a first-hand look at the war, leaving Todd, the hardly aggressive but able book soldier, to do the work of two men until the following December 7.*

Liaison, cooperation and a mutual understanding of problems among the Division Headquarters, the Army's Central Department Head-quarters in Chicago, and the Illinois State Adjutant General's Office, appear to have been only nominal at best and normally non-existent. It was October 26, 1917, before the last arriving units closed their columns at Camp Logan.

When all had arrived, General Todd continued to be a far from happy man. Among them was Chicago's South Side pride; and in more than full strength, the 8th Illinois Infantry (Colored). Race riots in the Houston area and at Brownsville involving Colored troops were fresh in the minds of the Military. There were rumors of a plan for one or more Colored Divisions to accommodate the induction of Colored, volunteer Guardsmen, of which there were a number of Regiments, separate Battalions and separate Companies in Southern as well as Northern States. After considerable letter writing and telegrams, the 8th Illinois was eliminated from the 33rd Division's Troop List. This and other evidences of poor Staff work in Washington and at Camp Logan left the Division with an initial manpower shortage, if it was to go to a Square Division with a strength of 28,000.

Apparently weary of dealing with the State of Illinois for personnel, the Division Headquarters sought replacements through the Central Department Headquarters, Chicago, U. S. Army. It was known that the Draft was pouring selected, or drafted, recruits into new Divisions at Camp Grant, Rockford, Illinois, and Fort Dodge, Des Moines, Iowa. In due time, 5,600 Draftees arrived in Houston. Most of them were from Camp Grant. Upon their arrival, the 33rd Division Headquarters at Camp Logan, Houston, Texas, thought somewhat better of the National Guard as a source of military manpower. On the first screening of the Draftees, 433 were found physically unfit; 103

---

* This is not specifically in criticism of General Bell. All new Division Commanders apparently were given the opportunity. Some accepted. Of those who did, some returned sooner than others. Bell left early and lingered long.

were "unsuited," 118 were ticketed "worthless," 328 could not speak English, 256 were illiterate, and 87 were venereal cases! Thus were 1,325 of the 5,600 peremptorily challenged and rejected. By February, 1918, the Division had discharged 2,189 enlisted men on the Surgeon's certificate of disability, most of them from this contingent.

Stiff physicals were invoked also on a comparatively short list of National Guard officers, particularly those of rather high rank and all others who might become surplus in grade. Such superfluity was inherent in the smallness of the pre-Pershing Regiments compared with the 3,700 officers and men in the new Pershing Regiments. A few extra Colonels and Lieutenant Colonels and a number of Majors and Captains normally would be left unassigned and without billets. But of Lieutenants there was a shortage, for the 250-man Rifle Companies of the Pershing-type Regiment called for six Lieutenants instead of two, as in the earlier prewar Tables of Organization. Tough physical examinations not only eliminated a few Field officers but achieved the ultimate discharge of one of the Illinois Infantry Brigadiers. Other officers surplus in grade went to Arms or Branch schools and thence to new assignments. Others went to Depot Brigades and from there were assigned elsewhere. Some surplus National Guard personnel (though apparently no enlisted personnel from the 33rd Division), both officers and men who went to Depot Brigades, later were given billets in one of the new non-divisional Regiments of Pioneer Infantry, a euphonious name for Labor Battalions. When the manpower pinch fell upon America's share of the French Front, Regiments of Colored Draftees took over their duties and the earlier Pioneer Infantry Regiments became replacement pools for Line Divisions. Thus, some Guardsmen, officers and men, who were surplus initially, found themselves back with combat troops before the Armistice was signed.

But, by-and-large, General Todd gave the upper ranks in the Guard the benefit of a forthright trial, once he had decided who should be retained, and the great majority of them went all the way with complete competence and without official criticism. One Regular Colonel was brought in to command an Infantry Regiment. In March, 1918, just before leaving for the Port of Embarkation, something went wrong and he promptly was relieved and replaced by another Regular. The other three Infantry Regiments continued to be commanded by Guardsmen all the way. A temporary Brigadier General, Major on the permanent list of Regulars, came into the Division to replace the National Guard Brigadier, who was disqualified for overseas by the physical. The other Brigade Commander, a National Guardsman, arrived in France, but in July was summarily relieved and sent rearward for reclassification. He accepted reduction in grade, conditioned on subsequent command of an Infantry Battalion in another National Guard Division. He was killed by enemy smallarms fire while directing elements of his new command in the elimination of a German strongpoint. One other similar demotion was noted from among the upper National Guard ranks that went overseas in 1917-1918; it affected a former Regular, who reverted to Colonel.

At war's end, only one Infantry Regiment and one Artillery Regiment of the 33rd were commanded by Regulars. The other National Guard Colonels in the Division had gone "all the way and back"; moreover, General Bell was reputed to be a man with a quick finger on the relief trigger, hence most Guard Divisions had an even better record with reference to the overseas and combat service of their upper-ranking Guard officers. As noted earlier, only two States sent National Guard officers to Federal duty as Major Generals. One was 62 and in poor health. The other, General O'Ryan of New York's 27th Division, commanded that outfit all the way out and back, and saw it through an enviable combat record.

All-in-all, the occasional suggestion that the Army suffered through the inability of National Guard upper ranks to pull their weight is not borne-out by the record. Indeed, the War proved their capacity for Field Grade and General Officer assignments to field commands. While it is true that a few were relieved, the same is true of some of the professionals. A Regular Army General who commanded the 26th Infantry Division, after General Edwards' transfer, was summarily relieved by his Corps Commander. The same happened to other Regulars in less conspicuous assignments. The crucible of combat is no respecter of ranks, persons or Army components.

Meanwhile, General Todd's troubles with the hard-luck 33rd continued while his chief was visiting the embattled armies of the Allies in Europe. The next higher headquarters kept wanting to know if the "Prairie" Division was sufficiently trained, hardened physically and equipped for overseas movement. Each time the answer was a reluctant negative.

Then came the worst news of all. The 32nd Infantry Division, Wisconsin and Michigan National Guardsmen, had been activated about the same time at Camp MacArthur, Waco, Texas. Its temporary commander, William G. (Bunker) Haan, was a supply and fortifications expert out of the Artillery. Under him the Division was shaking-down in such great shape that he was promoted early from its Artillery Brigade to permanent command. "Galloping Jim" Parker, its first commander, had been retired compulsorily for age immediately following his return from the educational tour of the Western Front. In short, the 32nd received the priority for overseas intended for the 33rd. Thus, General

Todd's troubles were compounded when the 32nd dumped 414 of their undesirable enlisted men on the 33rd, by way of purging their own ranks for overseas. Injury was added to insult when 32nd Division Supply Officers appeared with an order and requisition for the 33rd to turn over to the 32nd sundry essential supplies, down to and including woolen uniforms. Spring would be well advanced before the 33rd Infantry Division was afloat, whereas the 32nd would make the Winter passage.

## ABSENCE OF PLANS FOR COLORED REGIMENTS

The foregoing is sufficient to give a Division-level view of the National Guard units as they girded for war and left for the Ports of Embarkation through the Winter, Spring and Summer of 1917-18. But the story would be incomplete without some mention of the destiny of the Colored units, such as the 8th Illinois Infantry, which General Todd had declined to integrate—pursuant to War Department policy, of course.

The War Department General Staff apparently had neither plans nor policy for these 15 or 20 thousand National Guardsmen. But there they were; the 8th Illinois (Colored) Infantry at Camp Logan, Houston, Texas, and the 15th New York (Colored) Infantry hoping to become a part of New York's 27th Division, at Camp Wadsworth, South Carolina, and so on across the Nation to a lesser degree because the other units were usually smaller. In Selective Draft channels the philosophy gradually and slowly evolved that Colored men should be given a role in the war's combat phase by the creation of a complete Division of Negro Draftees from throughout the Nation. This thought led to the belated creation of the 92nd Infantry (National Army) Division.

But the National Guard units of Colored citizen-soldiers were in being. They were arriving in the training cantonments. Recent riots, involving the presumably well-disciplined troops of the Regular Army's Colored Regiments, gave basis for serious concern. Thus events tended to make policy rather than policy creating events. Today, the great concern about the riot potential of the Colored units of the World War I National Guardsmen appears to have been groundless. They were more amenable to military discipline and had better and more understanding leadership than had the Colored Regulars of the 25th Infantry, credited with the regrettable riots mentioned above. But, be that as it may, someone in authority had to make a quick decision. The emergent philosophy and logic apparently took the very practical slant that if there were to be riots, the place for them was in No-Man's Land, France, with the German Army as the focal point of resentment. Ergo, Colored National Guard units should embark for Europe without delay!

The adventures of the 15th New York Infantry (Colored), is illustrative of what happened to other Regiments and comparable smaller units of the Colored National Guardsmen from New York, Illinois, Connecticut, Massachusetts, Maryland, Tennessee, Ohio and the District of Columbia, before they ultimately became consolidated into the 93rd Infantry (National Guard) Division.

The 15th New York Infantry (Colored) was a rather new Regiment recruited in Harlem. Its officers were of New York City's socially elite, and some were men of considerable political influence. Its creator and commander was Colonel William Hayward, a Nebraska lawyer and National Guardsman (Captain, 2nd Nebraska Infantry, Spanish-American War), who had moved to Manhattan and made good. When he failed to get his Regiment—often styled by himself and his officers as "the 15th New York Heavy Foot"—included in the "Rainbow" Division, he wangled an attachment to New York's 27th Infantry Division, then well-organized at Camp Wadsworth, Spartansburg, South Carolina. This did not work-out. By October 26, the 15th New York was on troop trains rolling back to New York, with a high embarkation priority. It arrived in France unheralded and unexpected. The Colonel, said to have been a warm personal friend of Pershing's from University of Nebraska law school days, would not settle for a Labor Battalion status.

The Regiment was, late March, 1918, dumped into the lap of the 16th Division of the French Army, where it learned its new designation was 369th Infantry, U.S. National Army, but was detached and assigned to the French Army. The 16th French Division issued it French helmets and French arms, reorganized the Regiment pursuant to French specifications, and assigned missions on the line alongside the veteran French formations.

That was the last the American Army saw of the 15th until after the Armistice. By that time it had suffered 172 killed in action and 679 wounded in action. At the time, in France, it was said to be one of the most-decorated Regiments in the American Expeditionary Force. Its ranks were indeed well-garnished with the Croix de Guerre. There were at least two American Medals of honor: Major G. Franklin Sheils, Medical Corps, and First Lieutenant George S. Robb. The record of the 369th is one of which any Regiment of any army should be justly proud. It is a record that exceeds that of any one of the four, storied, Colored Regiments of the old Regular Army, the 9th and 10th Cavalry and the 24th and 25th Infantry, which were not desegregated until 1951, during the Korean affair. The adventures of the 370th and 372nd Regiments of American National Guard Colored Infantry were as varied, but with less combat, as those of the 369th Infantry.

Meanwhile, there were belated plans in the General Staff mill for retrieving these Colored units from the French and Labor Battalion assignments, to constitute a Square Division of Colored National Guardsmen to be put on the line as the 93rd Infantry Division. It would be the volunteer counterpart of the drafted 92nd Infantry Division of Negro Draftees. This latter Division had arrived in France as scheduled and had taken its place on the American sector of the Front with results that were somewhat less than satisfactory.

This could have delayed the final groupment of the Colored National Guard units until after the Armistice. Certainly Major General Roy Hoffman, Oklahoma National Guard, the 93rd's commander, was in Europe with his Headquarters and all other Divisional elements (less Division Artillery, which was to be assigned from one of the White Divisions being broken-up for replacements), and he was making every effort to retrieve the 369th Infantry from the French. The determination of the French to retain it is further evidence of the high esteem in which they held these troops. The total combat casualties of the National Guard elements later brought together into the 93rd Infantry Division totaled 3,534, of whom 591 were killed in action. The casualties of New York's 369th were the highest of any single Colored unit.

## ARMY AND CORPS NATIONAL GUARD UNITS

There were other National Guard Divisions and separate units that landed in France, the men of which saw considerable action, but not in their original, or Divisional, organizations.* Though conspicuously clear to all that American Divisions could not serve long overseas without a flow of replacements, the General Staff had elaborate plans for handling Draftees in America, but details for moving some to combat-depleted Divisions as replacements were unduly delayed. The War Department's Baker Board stimulated hurried study and a program of replacements that delivered too little too late. Meanwhile, General Pershing's initially-small overseas staff and early-arriving units had expanded his command establishment to GHQ, American Expeditionary Force. From its on-the-ground observations, exchange of professional opinions with the English and reviewing Allied tables of experience, Pershing arrived at a replacement decision of his own. The best that can be said is that the result was a magnificent, stupendous and sometimes disjointed improvisation that often appeared on the verge of collapse, but which worked.

Though GHQ of AEF welcomed the Stateside simultaneous plan and effort of the Operations Division of the General Staff to predict monthly overseas needs by automatic personnel shipments, it was early denounced

* Delaware was represented in no Division. The old 1st Delaware Infantry Regiment became the 59th Pioneer Infantry assigned as Army Troops.

as unsatisfactory. Basically, Pershing's solution was the redesignation of certain arriving Divisions as "Depot Divisions." Two such redesignated Divisions would be under control of each of his Army Corps Headquarters. Normally the Army Corps would consist of four fully-functional combat Divisions and the two Depot Divisions. Divisions redesignated as Depot installations would provide immediate replacements from their own ranks to the Line Divisions of their own Corps. They likewise would become receiving and further training agents of additional replacements where found; i.e., returnees from hospitals, reclassification centers, broken-up Regiments of Pioneer Infantry already in the Theater, and such unassigned personnel as might come directly from America under the War Department's plan for automatic shipments, or pursuant to special requisitions sent to the War Department from GHQ, AEF. Subsequent complaints both as to quantity and quality centered primarily on replacements received in the General Staff's automatic monthly shipments direct from America. Thus, in May, 1918, GHQ of AEF requested that the automatic replacement system of personnel shipments be discontinued.

Thereafter, Pershing's Headquarters cabled monthly requisitions for replacements, officers and men, with total numbers for each Branch, Arm, and Service. Meanwhile, the stripping of men and units from newly-arriving Divisions to provide Corps Troops and Divisional replacements continued right up to the Armistice. And be it said, the shooting ceased in good time. The entire system was facing its most severe test. As of November 13, 1918, most of Pershing's 30 combat Divisions could muster less than 25,000 officers and men each. A number including the 5th, 26th, 27th, 29th, 30th, 42nd, 78th and 90th, were down to less than 21,000 each. With a shortage of more than 50,000 replacements requested for July, August and September, the authorized strength of Divisions had been reduced in October. The principal reductions were in the size of the Infantry Rifle Companies.

The replacement practices through 1917-18 are a phase of the war effort in Europe upon which there is little unanimity of opinion. The primary concern here is the impact of this system upon the National Guard Divisions. Pershing's major plan for 1917 called for five Army Corps of six Divisions each. Each Army Corps at all times would have four Divisions in combat, and two Replacement Divisions. From the latter would be detached sufficient of their Artillery Brigades to become Corps Artillery and other oddments for Corps and rear area use. Of course, the contingencies of combat upset the tidy plan. Some Divisions were in and out of the replacement mechanism, while others got into it and never got out.

# THE TYPICAL REPLACEMENT DIVISION

The 41st Infantry Division best illustrates one that served its entire time in France in this non-glamorous but essential role. It was arriving in France, December, 1917, when it immediately was redesignated the Replacement Division, I Corps. A month later the official name changed to Base and Training Division, I Corps. On March 5, 1918, is was given a new official letterhead, "Depot Division, I Corps." Meanwhile, from its installations in the St. Aignan and Noyers area it immediately had sent 2,800 of its Infantry to other units, many of them to the 1st Division, which had arrived in France well under the 28,000 called for in the Tables of Organization. The Infantry Brigades of the former 41st also furnished units for duty at schools and for work in the Line of Communications, the early name for the S.O.S., or Service of Supply. One Regiment of the Field Artillery Brigade became Artillery school units. The other two Regiments became Corps Artillery, and the Ammunition Train was set up as a Remount outfit. In Angers, the Division's 116th Engineers became an Engineer Replacement Depot, and the Headquarters personnel and elements of the 66th Field Artillery Brigade opened-up shop at La Courtine as an Artillery Replacement Center. Enough Infantry unit Headquarters were retrieved from working in the S.O.S. to provide Infantry training Battalions, a salvage camp, and a school for training specialists.

In July, 1918, the erstwhile 41st Infantry Division had its official name changed again. It became the 1st Depot Division, AEF. This apparently reflected a change in policy. Army Corps Headquarters and areas moved about too much to carry out the idea that each Corps Commander would handle his own replacement machinery. Depot Divisions would remain in one position and would feed men to such combat Divisions and units as came within their zones of personnel supply. After the Armistice, the former 41st Division continued in business, but merely reversed the flow. The procedure was to receive casuals, many of them men whose wounds or prolonged sickness had separated them from their original units. They were formed into Casual Companies for shipment home. The 41st Infantry Division was reconstituted as such December 26, 1918, and its original units likewise designated and returned to it. The officers and men of the Division had made a great contribution, both in service and in battlefield sacrifices, but the latter wore the shoulder patches of other Divisions and of Corps Artillery troops.

Other National Guard Divisions that became completely committed to replacement functions were the 31st, 34th, 38th, 39th, and 40th. The 32nd and 35th Divisions briefly functioned in the replacement system. The 32nd initially joined the 41st as the other Replacement Division for the I Army Corps. It immediately was ordered to select-out 7,000 of its own men, including all of Wisconsin's 128th Infantry Regiment up to but excluding the grade of Major and above, to go to the 1st Infantry (Regular Army) Division. Remaining units worked briefly in the S.O.S. until the contingencies of warfare required the restoration of the 32nd to combat strength and an assignment to the Front. It, in turn, received many of its incoming replacements from other less fortunate National Guard Divisions. Its splendid record in combat retained it in that status, and General Haan moved on to the command of an Army Corps. He was a beloved commander and, upon retirement, moved to Wisconsin, though he was not a native of that State.

## REPLACEMENT PRACTICES CREATED RESENTMENT

Many officers and men of some of these Replacement Divisions from the National Guard were resentful for decades because of the manner in which their units had been destroyed. This was particularly true of the proud and exceptionally well-trained 40th, from California and the Mountain States. Its record is quite similar to that of the earlier-arriving 41st. An oft-told story held that out of long-standing personal antipathy, General Pershing had no intentions of entrusting a high combat command to the 40th's commander, Major General F. S. Strong. The impression is hardly worth running to earth here or elsewhere. Had General Pershing wanted to get General Strong off the European horizon, all he had to do was to give him a Distinguished Service Medal (which Pershing failed to do at war's end) and send him home to train another Division. Of course, he had sent Peyton C. March home, to become Chief of Staff. There is reason to believe Pershing early lived to regret this. And it is possible he did decide to leave General Strong, a good training man, in a top administrative and training slot, right there in Europe.

If, in the replacement policy, one were looking for a National Guard Division that *did* become the object of professional disagreement at the top-brass level, a better choice would be the 31st Division. Pershing's Headquarters set it up to be a Depot Division in October, 1918. General March, in Washington, D.C., vetoed it. The 31st was completely broken-up anyway, except for one officer from each Company or comparable unit to become custodian of records. All other personnel became available as replacements. The incipient breakdown of the replacement system appears to have been sufficient reason. A like fate befell the 34th and 38th Divisions, and to a large extent the same can be recorded concerning the 39th Division.

The Guardsmen had no legal basis for complaint. The stipulations of the Draft Law and the manner of their mass induction as of

August 5, 1917, had given the Army a blank check as to their future for the duration of the war. Thus, no informed complaint ever has been made on these grounds by Guardsmen. Many Guardsmen long have argued, with forceful logic and facts, that the Army would have received much more for the investment had the integrity of more, if not all, Guard Divisions been preserved in Europe.

By November 2, 1918, nine days before the Armistice, it is quite apparent that General Pershing and his AEF, GHQ, as students in the grim school of trial, error and experience inherent in every Theater of Operations, had arrived at the same professional opinion. On the above date AEF, GHQ, cabled the War Department a reminder that 140,000 replacements were expected by the end of that month and added the following: "To send over entire divisions, which must be broken up on their arrival in France so we may obtain replacements that have not been sent as called for, is a wasteful method, and one that makes for inefficiency; but as replacements are not otherwise available, there is no other course open to us."

Accordingly, when looking at the big picture, it appears to have been a case of the General Staff in the War Department not providing Pershing's Headquarters the replacement manpower with which to preserve the integrity of units essential to the front. The AEF was in dire need of good officers and men as immediate replacements. From initial experience it had been learned that such officers and men were in the arriving National Guard Divisions.

At the same time, it hardly can be argued that in the avid search for replacements the National Guard Divisions exclusively were selected for breaking-up or diversion to Depot Division duties. Of Pershing's eight Regular Army Divisions, only six fought as Divisions, and one of the six was but partially and lightly engaged. The 7th and 8th Divisions became involved in the replacement hassle and neither received Divisional combat missions. The 8th arrived in France late and badly-fragmented by creation of the Siberian Expeditionary Force.

From among the National Army Divisions, of which only 18 reached France, the 76th, 83rd, 84th, 85th and 86th became involved in the replacement problem. Two of them were completely broken-up. Likewise, the 10 or 11 thousand officers and men in the 4th, 55th and 57th Pioneer Infantry Regiments (formerly the 6th Massachusetts, 74th New York and 1st Vermont, respectively) were put in the replacement pipeline when they landed in France. Moreover, two additional National Army Divisions, the 87th and 88th, were not committed to action, even in the Meuse-Argonne offensive. They represented a strategic reserve as well as conspicuous sources for replacements should this last, big Allied push of 1918 fail and, at the same time, create exorbitant casualties.

We can be reasonably sure that all Divisions of all components served and fought to the fullest measure of their capacities. It is regretted that neither the space nor the scope of this work permits the full tribute merited by all the National Guard units individually, as well as to pay tribute to outstanding units of all components of the Army. In the final analysis it was then, and still is, a case of one for all and all for one. Hence, a listing of all Divisions by components and showing campaigns and casualties not only gives recognition to all that went overseas in 1917-18, but fits the National Guard Divisions into the AEF Order of Battle. The list of Divisions also is followed by the officially-recognized campaigns of World War I in which American Divisions participated. These, with the campaign dates, will enable the reader to approximate the location and activity of a given Division at a stated time. There are detailed histories of practically all Divisions of all components mentioned in this chapter, the more outstanding of which are mentioned in the note on historical sources following this chapter.

The table on pages 285, 286 lists the American Divisions that had an overseas status of major and minor degree through America's phase of World War I. And America's role was not minor—it was decisive!

That decisive role was not that of the thin child who tips the teeterboard. It was that of a giant coming to the rescue of democracies that had been bled white. When America's first troops timidly took over a quiet sector for indoctrination and training, in late January, 1918, the frontage was six miles. On October 10 of the same year the American-manned frontage was 101 miles. Within the same period the British frontage had shrunk from 116 miles to 70; that of the French from 323 miles to 244; and that of tiny Belgium from 23 to 15. True, the Western Front had been shortened to some extent by the elimination of hostile salients. But it was the force of America's powerhouse, land offensives that took the German-created kinks out of the long, hard line from the Alps to the North Sea that was the Western Front when the Americans first arrived.

The Army did not do it alone. The Navy did not do it alone. The Service of Supply and the bond-buying industrial home front were necessary but less sacrificial factors in the great operation. The final instrument, with its hard cutting edge and its sacrificial wearing-down, consisted of the above Army Divisions on the line and the replacements from broken-up Divisions made necessary through lack of General Staff competence. The 433,478 National Guardsmen who voluntarily served between April 6, 1917, and January, 1919, were no small part of that sharp-edged battle instrument.

There were Divisions of record in World War I not listed on page

286. Once in the war, President Wilson, his Secretary of War and the Congress virtually gave the new Chief of Staff, General March, and his General Staff, a blank check against the Treasury, the industrial resources and manpower of America to win the war. The plan, when the Armistice cancelled everything, was for 80 Divisions, including the 43 listed, to be overseas by July, 1919. By the end of the Calendar Year, 1919, the number was to be 100 Divisions.

Actually, only 12 additional Divisions were in being at sundry American training cantonments, and four others were being organized when news of the Armistice reached America. The role of the National Guardsmen in these Divisions was relatively unimportant in terms of volunteer manpower. Nevertheless, it was the work, understanding, and know-how of the Military Departments of the States, headed by their Adjutants General, who ran the decentralized Draft Law machinery within their States. Thus, it was they who worked with poise, understanding, diligence and skill, under General Enoch Crowder's directives, to keep the pipeline of military manpower full and flowing from the home towns to the Western Front. This phase of the National Guard's contribution to the war effort too often has been overlooked and not fully appreciated, because it has become merged with the story of the Home Front where industrial efforts enjoyed the spotlight.

## RETENTION OF THE GUARD FULLY VINDICATED

From the viewpoint of the National Guardsmen, the basic principles for which they had stood throughout American military history had been vindicated. The military responsibility of every citizen had become an article of National faith and as applicable to the Unorganized Militia of a State as it had been assumed voluntarily by themselves. The value of and the necessity for citizens of States to have and exercise a volunteer military interest with a self-imposed, joint responsibility to their State and to their Nation, with both sharing the costs as advocated in the Dick Act, 1903, also had been fully vindicated. And, finally, World War I had proved the value of the National Guard as written into the National Defense Act of 1916.

As summarized in the *Army Almanac,* an official publication of the Department of the Army, 1950: "How well the National Defense Act of 1916 accomplished its mission is demonstrated by the ease and speed with which the National Guard Regiments were redistributed into the Combat Divisions for the American Expeditionary Forces of 1917 and 1918. Two-fifths of the Divisions in the AEF were National Guard Divisions, and the total combat days of these Divisions exceeded that of either the Regular Army Divisions or the National Army Divisions."

And the foregoing quotation constitutes a fitting tribute and citation of merit to those Guardsmen of all States and status who, following the

Spanish-American War, refused to see their local and State institutions, so rich in their traditional and historical service to America in times of crisis, relegated to the functions of local police reserves in order to make way for a Federal Militia of enlisted men and Company-grade officers to be called the U. S. Volunteer Army.

Again, the Guardsmen had proved their institution was not obsolete, but could grow with a changing America and could render front line duty under changing tactics and techniques with ever more modern and scientific weapons. World War I was not only a victory over a foreign foe; it was a renaissance of America's oldest and most often-tested defense institution: the Volunteer Colonial Militia, or the Continental Line, or the State Volunteer Regiments, or the Organized Militia, or the National Guard. Various Colonies and sundry States had preferred the one term or the other in changing times, but they all were and are one and the same continuing institution.

## CAMPAIGNS AND CASUALTIES BY DIVISIONS

| | Killed in Action | Wounded in Action | Total |
|---|---|---|---|
| *National Guard* | | | |
| 26th Infantry Division: Champagne-Marne; Aisne-Marne; St. Mihiel; Meuse-Argonne | 2,281 | 11,383 | 13,664 |
| 27th Infantry Division; Somme-Offensive; Ypres-Lys; Meuse-Argonne (F.A. only) | 1,829 | 6,505 | 8,334 |
| 28th Infantry Division; Champagne-Marne; Aisne-Marne; Oise-Aisne; Ypres-Lys (F.A. only); Meuse-Argonne | 2,874 | 11,265 | 14,139 |
| 29th Infantry Division: Meuse-Argonne | 1,053 | 4,517 | 5,570 |
| 30th Infantry Division: Somme Offensive; Ypres-Lys; St. Mihiel; Meuse-Argonne | 1,641 | 6,774 | 8,415 |
| 31st Infantry Division: No campaigns; replacements to other units; casualties credited elsewhere. | | | |
| 32nd Infantry Division; Aisne-Marne; Oise-Aisne; Meuse-Argonne | 3,028 | 10,233 | 13,261 |
| 33rd Infantry Division: Somme Offensive; St. Mihiel (F.A. only); Meuse-Argonne | 993 | 5,871 | 6,864 |
| 34th Infantry Division: No campaigns; replacements to other units; casualties credited elsewhere | | | |
| 35th Infantry Division: Meuse-Argonne | 1,298 | 5,998 | 7,296 |
| 36th Infantry Division: Meuse-Argonne | 591 | 1,993 | 2,584 |
| 37th Infantry Division: Ypres-Lys; Meuse-Argonne | 1,066 | 4,321 | 5,387 |
| 38th Infantry Division: No campaigns; replacements to other units; casualties credited elsewhere. | | | |
| 39th Infantry Division: No campaigns; replacements to other units; casualties credited elsewhere. | | | |
| 40th Infantry Division: No campaigns; replacements to other units; casualties credited elsewhere. | | | |
| 41st Infantry Division: No campaigns; replacements to other units; casualties credited elsewhere. | | | |
| 42nd Infantry (Rainbow) Division; Champagne-Marne; Aisne-Marne; St. Mihiel; Meuse-Argonne | 2,810 | 11,873 | 14,683 |
| 93rd Infantry Division: (See remarks in foregoing text) 369th Infantry Regiment; 370th Infantry Regiment; Oise-Aisne; St. Mihiel. 371st and 372nd Infantry Regiments; Meuse-Argonne | 591 | 2,943 | 3,534 |
| National Guard Divisions Total | | | 103,731 |

285

| | Killed in Action | Wounded in Action | Total |
|---|---|---|---|
| **Regular Army** | | | |
| 1st Infantry Division: Montdidier-Noyon; Aisne-Marne; St. Mihiel; Meuse-Argonne | 4,996 | 17,324 | 22,320 |
| 2nd Infantry Division: Aisne; Aisne-Marne; St. Mihiel; Meuse-Argonne | 2,683 | 9,063 | 11,746 |
| 3rd Infantry Division: Aisne; Champagne-Marne; Aisne-Marne; St. Mihiel; Meuse-Argonne | 3,401 | 12,000 | 15,401 |
| 4th Infantry Division: Aisne-Marne; St. Mihiel; Meuse-Argonne | 2,903 | 9,917 | 12,820 |
| 5th Infantry Division: St. Mihiel; Meuse-Argonne | 2,120 | 6,996 | 9,116 |
| 6th Infantry Division: Meuse-Argonne | 68 | 318 | 386 |
| 7th Infantry Division: No campaigns | 287 | 1,422 | 1,709 |
| Casualties were in units attached to other combat formations | | | |
| 8th Infantry Division: No campaigns | none | none | |
| Regular Army Divisions　　　　　　　　　Total | | | 73,498 |
| **National Army** | | | |
| 76th Infantry Division: St. Mihiel (2 regiments of F.A. only). Became a Replacement Division; casualties credited elsewhere. | | | |
| 77th Infantry Division: Oise-Aisne; Meuse-Argonne | 2,110 | 8,084 | 10,194 |
| 78th Infantry Division: St. Mihiel; Meuse-Argonne | 1,530 | 5,614 | 7,144 |
| 79th Infantry Division: Meuse-Argonne | 1,517 | 5,357 | 6,874 |
| 80th Infantry Division: Somme Offensive; Meuse-Argonne | 1,241 | 4,788 | 6,029 |
| 81st Infantry Division: Meuse-Argonne | 248 | 856 | 1,104 |
| 82nd Infantry Division: St. Mihiel; Meuse-Argonne | 1,413 | 6,664 | 8,077 |
| 83rd Infantry Division: Elements credited with Aisne-Marne; Vittorio-Veneto. Only American Division to serve on latter front. Not credited with any battle casualties. | | | |
| 84th Infantry Division: No campaigns; replacements to other units; casualties credited elsewhere. | | | |
| 85th Infantry Division: No campaigns; replacements to other units; casualties credited elsewhere. | | | |
| 86th Infantry Division: No campaigns; replacements to other units; casualties credited elsewhere. | | | |
| 87th Infantry Division: No campaigns; replacements to other units; casualties credited elsewhere. | | | |
| 88th Infantry Division: No campaigns; replacements to other units; casualties credited elsewhere. | | | |
| 89th Infantry Division: St. Mihiel; Meuse-Argonne | 1,466 | 5,625 | 7,091 |
| 90th Infantry Division: St. Mihiel; Meuse-Argonne | 1,496 | 6,053 | 7,549 |
| 91st Infantry Division: Ypres-Lys (less F.A.); Meuse-Argonne (less F.A.) | 1,454 | 4,654 | 6,108 |
| 92nd Infantry Division: Meuse-Argonne (less F.A.) | 182 | 1,465 | 1,647 |
| (See remarks in foregoing text) | | | |
| National Army Divisions　　　　　　　　　Total | | | 61,817 |

The offically-recognized World War I Western Front campaigns in which American troops participated and in which most of their casualties occurred were:

Aisne ......................................................27 May to 5 June, 1918
Montdidier-Noyon ...................................................9-13 June
Champagne-Marne .................................................15-18 July
Aisne-Marne ...............................................18 July-6 August
Somme Offensive ....................................8 August-11 November
Oise-Aisne ...............................................7 August-11 November
Ypres-Lys ...............................................19 August-11 November
St. Mihiel ...............................................12-16 September
Meuse-Argonne .........................................26 September-11 November
Vittorio-Veneto ........................................24 October-11 November

# Bibliographical Note For Chapter XII

Previously-mentioned biographies and memoirs of conspicuous personages of the World War I era such as Woodrow Wilson, Newton D. Baker, Gen. Peyton C. March and others, are directly or indirectly pertinent to this chapter. To them should be added Lt. Gen. Robert L. Bullard, *Personalities and Reminiscences of the War*, 1925; Maj. Gen. Johnson Hagood, *The Services of Supply*, 1927; Maj. Gen. James G. Harbord, *America in the World War*, 1933, and *The American Army in France*, 1936; Lt. Gen. Hunter Liggett, *Commanding an American Army*, 1925; Maj. Gen. John A. Lejeune, *The Reminiscences of a Marine*, 1930; Gen. Charles P. Summerall, *Annual Report of the Chief of Staff, U.S. Army*, a public document, 1930; and *Final Report of General John J. Pershing*, a public document, 1920. Pershing's *My Experience in the World War*, 2 vols., 1931, is better reading and often more informative. Most of the statistics and particularly battle casualties credited to Divisions are from *The Army Almanac*, a public document, 1950. Unit histories tell the stories of most, but not of all, of the World War I Divisions. They are written with varying degrees of literary skill and accuracy of minor detail. Official records and final reports had not been published, and sometimes were not available in any form, when some of them were published. But all are quite accurate as to time, place, operations and major adversities both in and out of combat. Some Divisions, the 26th "Yankee" Division, for example, have been the subject to two or more histories. A few others that had no combat record, such as the Regular Army's 8th Division, and the National Guard's 39th, appear to have attracted no historian for the World War I record. The following titles are representative: Emerson G. Taylor, *New England in France, 1917-1919, A History of the Twenty-Sixth Division*, 1920; Maj. Gen. John F. O'Ryan, *The Story of the 27th Division*, 1921; Col. Edward Martin, *The Twenty-Eighth Division, Pennsylvania's Guard in the World War*, 1924; John A. Cutchins, *History of the "Blue and the Gray" Twenty-Ninth Division, 1917-1919*, 1921; Elmer A. Murphy, *The Thirtieth Division in the World War*, 1936; Michigan-Wisconsin Joint History Commission, *The 32nd Division in the World War, 1917-1919*, 1920; Frederick L. Huidekoper, *The History of the 33rd Division, A.E.F.*, 1921; Ben H. Chastaine, *Story of the 36th*, 1920; Ralph D. Cole, *The Thirty-Seventh Division in the World War, 1917-1918*, 1929; Raymond S. Tomkins. *The Story of the Rainbow Division*, 1919. Often Regimental and lesser unit histories will reflect the record of a Division that attracted no historian, but of which the lesser unit was a part. For example, Arthur W. Little, *From Harlem to the Rhine: The Story of New York's Colored Volunteers*, 1936, is actually a Regimental history of the 369th infantry and is the best from any unit of the 93rd Division. For brief mentions, dates, statistics, charts of Division sectors in combat campaigns, maps, etc., *American Armies and Battlefields in Europe*, prepared as a public document by the American Battle Monuments Commission, 1938, is not only in compact and convenient, one-volume format, but it is little less than indispensable. The same Commission's *Summary of Operations in World War*, 1944, is a 28-volume series. Each volume is devoted to one of the Divisions that fought in one or more campaigns as a Division. The maps are superb. The compact and factual text of each seldom exceeds a hundred pages.

CHAPTER XIII

# The National Defense Act of 1920

THROUGH the long months of the Winter, Summer and early Autumn of 1918-19 the troop ships and merchantmen of the victors and the vanquished impatiently steamed Westward. Outbound from Brest, St. Nazaire and Bordeaux, the topsides of all ships were a blend of leathery faces; old, faded khaki and bright, new olive drabs. The mass of military color concealed the weird camouflage paint patterns of the promenade decks and cabin superstructures. The homeward-bound manpower spilled onto the lifeboats, often festooned the standing rigging, and always decorated the horizontally-lashed cargo booms above the fore and after decks.

The American Expeditionary Force of 1917-18 was headed West. The "Bridge of Ships" was bringing the boys home. There they were to experience a whirlwind demobilization, the speed of which was rivaled only by the rapidity of their mobilization. The war "to make the World safe for Democracy" had been won. More wisely than he knew, Will Rogers, the wit of the day, was quipping: "Anyway, it had been made safe for the Democrats." Most of those returning soldiers were to live long enough to wonder if they had accomplished even so little as Rogers then suggested.

But the America of those victory months of the Armistice was still happily naive and enjoyed the pleasant mental glow that went with it. There were a few Jeremiahs in the streets. They were the few realistic history and political science professors with a major interest in diplomacy, but their voices were lost in the hosannahs of idealism. There were also the Preparedness professionals, who either made sinews of war or made a living exercising or expending them on maneuvers, cross-country flights, or on target ranges. Any remarks they made were frowned upon as bad taste commercials for the "merchants of death." There were also the hard-core National Guardsmen. Many of them were avid readers of history in general and military chronicles in particular. All of them had a justified pride in the traditions and achievements of their organizations. That the war just ended had added luster to the long and enviable records of their units they knew full well.

In the most modern of wars, making use of the most technical equipment then known to science, they had broken German offensives launched and fought by the best Army ever fielded in Europe. Their own units, exclusively composed of Guardsmen and replacements of citizen-soldiers of even less experience and training than themselves, had borne their full share in making shreds of the Hindenburg Line. They then had converted the Western Front into a war of movement and maneuver. With all this in mind, and eager to profit by experience, the Guardsmen naturally were articulate and loudly vocal in favor of a sound and sustained program of Preparedness.

As citizens with far less to gain than to lose in any major call to active duty, the Guardsmen naturally had the ears of an appreciative public both in and out of office. They were not always able to carry the mass of their idealistic neighbors with them. Too often local civic leaders viewed the Guardsmen as just another group of fraternal order devotees who happened to join the local volunteer Militia unit instead of the Elks. But when a public question arose concerning the spending of defense dollars that most likely were going to be spent by the State or the Nation anyway, even the civic skeptics queried the local Guardsmen as to how Uncle Sam could get the most for his Defense Budget. The service-seasoned Guardsmen had seen some things extremely well done, other things poorly done, and things done that were entirely wrong. They were quite ready to talk.

## "LOBBYING" IS A MATTER OF VIEWPOINT

These simple and obvious truths are reiterated here because the bitter charge of "lobbying" soon was to be lodged against Guardsmen in connection with the National Defense Act of 1920. Almost everyone knows that the word, "lobbyist," is quite flexible in its meaning. It is a word of opprobrium normally reserved for use against the most effective of one's opponents in legislative hearings and Congressional contacts incident to the passage of controversial legislation. A forceful person in agreement is never a "lobbyist;" he is either a dedicated and dutiful public servant or an unselfish civic leader motivated only by the compulsive desire that Congressmen be properly informed as to the vital needs of the Nation. Conversely, a dynamic, argumentative, well-informed, persuasive, convincing opponent quickly becomes a selfish public employe unworthy of his trust or a vile "lobbyist" who would sell his Country short for immediate, or distant, unrevealed gain. Thus, as always, the question as to whether or not there was lobbying incident to the National Defense Act of 1920 necessarily depends upon who is talking and what concepts he has chosen to espouse.

As we have seen, Elihu Root had accepted the desirability of a War Department General Staff. To that end he had printed and distributed as a public document the long-forgotten manuscript of Upton's book on military policy as indoctrination for the creation of such a group of military specialists. To the General Staff thus created, the belatedly-published writings of Upton became little less than a Biblical directive for things that ought to be. Since Upton had lifted his ideas from the Europe that shortly followed the Franco-Prussian War, this meant his advocacy included not only an all-powerful General Staff, but a large professional Army backed by a bureaucratically-administered Reserve of militarily-trained Draftees. They necessarily would receive that training through some form of compulsory universal military service.

Moreover, under Chief of Staff Leonard Wood, the War Department Staff developed rather complete plans for the regimentation of all American youth. Wood's Staff, as noted earlier, also developed extremely effective, if not always visible, techniques for getting its ideas before the public and Congress. The entry of America into World War I had given the War Department General Staff, in its role as the detail planners for the war effort, little less than a blank check on the Nation's resources.

Came the Armistice, there was the institutional and instinctive desire to retain that blank check. Many, but not all, professional soldiers were in more-or-less natural agreement. Moreover, one can hardly be critical of a young and war-tested temporary Brigadier General like Lesley J.

McNair or an imaginative, brilliant young Colonel, such as George C. Marshall, for taking a dim view of a military system that at once would put them back in low-seniority Promotion List ranks, just as if no war ever had been fought and won. In any event, it was the Regular Establishment that had the greater vested interest to protect in the forthcoming legislation.

And since there is a strong correlation between the degree of vested interest and true lobbying, it safely may be assumed that the War Department General Staff, backed by its civilian following from the previous legislative campaigns, indulged in strong lobbying that was both subtle and forceful. The General Staff's promptness in hurling the charge at the Guardsmen, and other proponents salvaging as much as possible of the traditional volunteer system, suggests the counterattacking accusation was actually a defensive measure.

## NOT ALL REGULARS AGREED WITH THE STAFF

Before going further with details, another point should be clarified and emphasized. Not all Regulars were for the War Department Bill that had been prepared for the Secretary of War under the direction of the Chief of Staff, General March.* Many of those in disagreement were sure that war-tested officers of merit should not revert to the prewar static promotion lists as if no war had been fought. But they saw a remedy in a new promotion system for Regulars rather than in the overall structure of the American land forces. Similarly, there were returned Guardsmen who joined the U.S. Army League and professionals in urging a large Regular Army, supported by a Federal Militia and Universal Military Training. National Guard officers of no less distinction than General O'Ryan of New York and Brigadier General Charles T. Boardman of Wisconsin, both of whom held commands appropriate to their rank throughout the War, were supporters of much of the General Staff plan.

On the other hand there were command-type Regulars, such as Douglas MacArthur, former Chief of Staff, Brigade Commander and Division Commander of the all-National Guard Rainbow Division, who were sure a continuance of the volunteer system was vital to America. In this MacArthur was joined by Generals Edwards, Haan and others who had commanded National Guard Divisions in America and in France.

There was one point, however, on which practically all Guardsmen

---

* Gen. March was temporarily in the full four-star rank and considered himself as having been promoted, by assignment, over Gen. Pershing's head. Within the General Staff concept and philosophy, March was right. Both history and Congress failed to support the idea. March was honorably discharged as "Gen. (emerg.) 30 June 1920" and retired three months later in his permanent rank of Major General. In 1930, he was given the permanent rank of four-star General on the Retired List.

and many other citizen-soldiers, not to mention some Regulars, were agreed. It was their built-in hostility to the War Department General Staff and against its Chief, General March. There were also a few unkind words for the preceding Chiefs, Major Generals Hugh L. Scott and the political-minded former surgeon, Leonard Wood, who had allied themselves solidly with March. General Tasker H. Bliss had recognized the merits of the Guard. He, more than any other Regular, was responsible for the splendid recognition given the Guard in the National Defense Act of 1916.

## THE GUARDSMEN AIR THEIR COMPLAINTS

But the War Department agency and the men for whom the Guardsmen reserved their greatest scorn were the Militia Bureau Regulars and the successive Chiefs following the enactment of the 1916 reorganization. The passage of this law, it will be recalled, was almost simultaneous with the President's Call that sent the Guard units to the Mexican Border. The Guardsmen were able to brief a solid case of administrative bad faith within the General Staff and the Militia Bureau from 1916.

Secretary of War Baker was a man of great integrity and stern qualities. He, like all the truly great war ministers, entrusted details of broad policies to experienced subordinates, accepted errors they might make as his own and backed them heartily through resulting criticism and strife. Thus, Mr. Baker was a man who believed and practiced the philosophy that loyalty began at the top. But in the legislative war that erupted following the first postwar convention of the National Guard Association, in St. Louis, Mr. Baker found himself increasingly embarrassed. Before it had finished, General March and his stay-at-home War Department General Staff were pretty much on their own, though General Pershing and his returning top commanders and Staff did come to March's assistance on the issue of Universal Military Training. In this the Guardsmen concurred, as they had in the passage of the Draft Law in 1917. But the Guardsmen did not propose to remain quiet while General March and the General Staff made UMT an instrument for the destruction of the National Guard and for completely supplanting the traditional volunteers with a Federal Organized Militia under another name.

The Guardsmen were not opposed to the Reserve Corps as a co-existing, volunteer agency, but its use for the absorption or complete destruction of the Guard, contrary to the terms of the Defense Act of 1916, they proposed to resist firmly. To this end it was necessary to reveal the bad faith of the General Staff in the administration of that law. It was for this that some of the Old Regulars of that era never forgave the Guard. In their eyes it was little short of mutiny. But the Guardsmen held that the Regular Army code of military customs, regulations, Articles of War and laws applicable to professionals applied to Guardsmen only when they were on active duty in time of war, incident to a peacetime assignment, or for training at Federal expense; on all other occasions they were citizens. The fact that they had volunteered and served once and were prepared to volunteer and serve anytime, anywhere, again, did not subtract from their treasured privileges of citizenship. If anything, their volunteer status had added to their responsibilities and privileges of a fuller citizenship. They proposed to exercise their informed citizenship to the hilt insofar as the War Department, the General Staff and the Militia Bureau were concerned.

With the zeal of reformers, the Guardsmen utilized every forum available: the home town newspapers, letters to friends, complaints to their State Military Departments, interviews for metropolitan newspapers and finally and most effectively in the legislative hearings, which were widely publicized.

## THE MILITIA BUREAU ON THE DEFENSIVE

Most of the charges of the Guardsmen may be catalogued under a comparatively few headings. First and foremost were the transparent efforts of the General Staff after the Defense Act of 1916 to discredit the National Guard as a component of the Army of the United States. To this end the General Staff had utilized its access to the Press and public by means of official statements and press releases to blame the Guard for General Staff shortcomings. At the same time, reports of the Guard's conspicuous successes were so garbled with the achievements of other agencies that the credit was unduly shared-in, or completely diverted to others.

In support of the foregoing, the Guardsmen, with the National Guard Association as its own mobilizer of facts, went back to the first days of the Mexican Border Call. They admitted the Mexican Border mobilization left much to be desired. But the Guard units had been far more ready than the General Staff had been. The Staff had no detailed plans for such a mobilization, though the Army's own field commander in San Antonio had been showing the need for reinforcements and had been begging for additional troops long before Villa's raid triggered the Administration to such action.

The inference was clear that had the General Staff through 1915-16 been engaged in its proper field of planning military operations instead of fighting a legislative war with its own and only volunteer reserve, the troop movement could have been above criticism. Moreover, the War Department's official report on the Mexican Border mobilization

294

had been little more than an amazing collection of critical remarks. All explanatory reports by Guard officers and their constructive suggestions had been ignored. Favorable and complimentary reports upon the Guard units, in the field and on maneuvers, that had been written by Regular Army field commanders in the Southwest, had been pigeonholed in the Militia Bureau or elsewhere.

Not all the National Guard units in being as of the Call had been activated. Some of those called to the Colors never had been sent to the Border or elsewhere for thorough field training. Some units called and sent to the Border were kept on active duty longer than necessary. They could have been ordered back home into State status, thus rotating the opportunity for complete field training of all Guard units.

With reference to the National Guard Divisions and lesser units mobilized for service in France, the Guardsmen correctly insisted that this decision had been made at levels higher than the General Staff. In its implementation the General Staff in many minor ways had ignored the spirit and at times the letter of the law and directives under which these units were activated, reorganized, trained and ultimately sent to France.

They further showed conclusively that on active duty, the Guard units were sent to inferior tent camps, whereas the Reserve officers, coming out of the officer training camps, and the Draftees they normally commanded, were quartered in hastily-built but fully-timbered barracks with recreational facilities. The Guardsmen made no special point of this. At the time they had volunteered for early service and were prepared to accept such as might be available. Nevertheless, the contrast was there. Conditions could have been and no doubt would have been better had the General Staff been less interested in its own aggrandizement and more interested in its proper sphere: logistics, supply, training, and operational plans.

The Guardsmen also called attention to the far less consideration given their officers as compared with Regulars and recently-commissioned Reservists. The Chief of the Militia Bureau, Brigadier General J. McI. Carter, refused to take this. But in rising to his own defense he was forced to make such admissions, particularly concerning National Guard Medical Officers, that he would have fared just as well, or better, had he remained silent. Indeed, even in his final report, he had to admit that a brief law, *designed especially to put the Guard Medical Officers on the same equitable basis as doctors commissioned direct from civil life into the Medical Reserve Corps, had been of little or no benefit to the Guard Medics. They continued to be held down by unit assignments. But that very law had been used to promote Regular Army Doctors, Dentists and Veterinarians without regard for Tables of*

*Organization stipulations as to rank in assignment.* General Carter reluctantly admitted that more than 1,200 National Guard Medics were victims of an administrative failure to comply with a law passed for their relief. That the same law was used to favor further the Regulars and Medical Reserve Corps Doctors compounded the inequities.

Not so numerous but more conspicuous, and thereby more hurtful to the individual, were the cases of the National Guard officers who were inducted and then rejected. For some it was because they were surplus in grade under the revised Tables of Organization. Some accepted reductions in grade for lesser assignments. Others resigned and accepted a ticket home but had a hard time explaining. This group numbered only 648. Only 50 were above the grade of Captain, but it included three Brigadier Generals, nine Colonels and five Lieutenant Colonels. Many of the 648 subsequently were urged to re-enter the wartime National Army, particularly for duty in the United States Guard, a Federal, anti-sabotage, security service for guarding docks, munitions plants and other essential industries. A few accepted; most declined. Had these officers been U.S. Reservists or Regulars, some effort would have been made to find assignments for them appropriate to their grade before they initially were sent home. No such effort was made for these surplus Guard officers. Nevertheless, at the same time, Field Grade, spot commissions were being issued in the Reserve. Practically all Regulars had been upped two or three grades right while these officers were being declared surplus in their ranks. That the War Department General Staff so soon felt an unforeseen and unplanned need for their service within a matter of weeks and months of their rejection for duty with their men, and then expected them again to interrupt civilian pursuits to render voluntary service, was viewed by some of these Guardsmen as an insult rather than an apologetic palliative.

General Carter eagerly explained that 24 of the 648 officers resigned to avoid facing efficiency boards. Thereafter he confirmed suspicions as to prejudice by clearly showing that almost any resignation by any Guard officer would in his opinion be for the good of the Service. His final plea: "Any error can be attributed to error in judgment, or decision to which all are liable."

The Guardsmen also viewed the medical examination practices of the Regular Army with a jaundiced eye. Eleven National Guard General Officers, 18 Colonels and 17 Lieutenant Colonels, physically fit for recent active duty on the Mexican Border, were found to be physically unfit but little more than a year later. Guardsmen darkly thought the General Staff had upped the physical requirements for high-ranking Guardsmen compared with men of the same age in the two favored components. In any event, every Guardsman washed-out in this manner created a vacancy for the rank-hungry professionals, because such vacancies were not being filled by the promotion of Guardsmen. But on this the complaining Guardsmen could prove nothing. The medical records could not be opened. They accordingly hinged all complaints upon lack of planning that permitted men to be fully inducted into active duty only to have the Army Medics decide within a month or more that the officer never was physically fit to begin with. It was no way to treat an officer, they argued, who volunteered to serve his Country for the duration of the War.

With reference to inefficiency, disciplinary actions and courts martial, the protesting Guardsmen were comparatively silent. Some of them undoubtedly knew that on officer strength ratios the Judge Advocate General could show that court-martial cases involving officers in the Regular Army were almost identical with those for the Guard. On this score, the record of tolerance was in favor of the Reserves.

Another thing that irritated the Guardsmen, though they could not blame this entirely upon the General Staff, was their induction in 1917 under the Draft Law. Their leaders knew this was largely political and calculated to put ointment upon the thin feelings of the Draftees in the National Army Divisions. But the fact remained that the Guardsmen were volunteers and they wanted the World to know it and recognize it. White House policy though it was, they still retained a dark suspicion that the fine, Italian hand of the General Staff was in it somewhere. In this, they were perhaps correct, but it was a minor, technical point at best. All America knew then and history has recorded that they were volunteer units of officers and men. That some of them may have signed the volunteer enlistment papers with the hot breath of a Draft Board on their necks was immaterial. This had been true of some of the men in Washington's Continental Line, for most of the erstwhile Colonies had compulsory military laws in their statutes. On this one of the National Army Regiments of Draftees had already voiced their advance alibi. While marching at route step past a National Guard outfit the men had shouted joyously: "Draft dodgers!"

Far more serious to the Guardsmen was the conviction that the Militia Bureau was not their friend and brotherly advisor-in-arms, as originally conceived, but was their avowed enemy. With some justice, they felt its Regular Army leadership and Staff were as rank-hungry and as indifferent in planning for the welfare and future utilization of the National Guard as was the remainder of the War Department General Staff. True, the Chief of the Bureau, when the War started, Brigadier General William A. Mann, had been enthusiastic about young Douglas MacArthur's idea of an All-America "Rainbow" Division composed of surplus Guard units not needed for the World War I Divisions. Moreover, when time came for a commander, General Mann could think of no one better than himself, with an appropriate advance in rank to Major General. His second in the Bureau, Colonel Jesse McI. Carter, stepped up to a star as the new Chief of the Bureau. Within a matter of months Carter was likewise off to the Headquarters of the newly-activated 11th Division, where he posted his flag as Division Commander and temporary Major General. Colonel John W. Heavy moved up and pinned on a temporary star.

The Armistice found Carter and his 11th Division still in America. It was Carter's misfortune to be ordered back to the Bureau, reverting to the grade of Brigadier with corresponding adverse effect on General Heavy, just in time for them to pick up the pieces of their little staff empire that had been shattered by extremely high turnover with repeated shifts up and down at all levels. Carter was also back in the Bureau just in time to face the well-informed, highly-articulate and irate National Guardsmen who were home from European battlefields and wondering what their future was to be in the Nation's defense picture.

## THE GUARDSMEN SENSE AN UNCERTAIN FUTURE

There was ample evidence that the Guard's future was most uncertain, even prior to the Armistice. In paragraph 1, General Orders No. 73, War Department, August 7, 1918, General March promulgated his famous One Army manifesto. Without so much as a glance at existing laws, he had declared all the land forces, however raised, then on active duty, to be the United States Army—the conventional as well as legal designation of the Regular Army. All appellations such as Reserve Corps, National Guard and National Army, forthwith were abolished. Officers and men were to be transferred back and forth as best served the interests of the Nation, explained the order, as if in self-justification. Such transfers were being done anyway. As we have seen, entire Divisions from all three components already had been broken-up and converted into Depot Brigades of replacements.

This strange order, without legal base, created much talk at that time. But fighting was in progress and all assumed there must be some legal or moral reason for it. Came the Armistice and the return home. Guard leaders in retrospect decided the purpose was to confuse the American people as to who was doing most of the fighting in Europe. Hence the purpose back of this illegal General Staff fiat over the signature of the Chief of Staff was to make the United States Army—the Regular Army—smell sweeter at the expense of the 37 National Guard and National Army Divisions (compared to the eight Regular Army Divisions) that had gone overseas in 1917-18.

But be it said in behalf of the combat Regulars in Europe that this rather specious order was even more unpopular with them than it was within the Guard and National Army Divisions. Under its terms they were expected to delete such designations as "1st (Regular Army) Division" from their official letterheads. As a proud veteran of the "Big Red One" afterward explained, "We were so busy fighting we forgot to make any such silly change."

After the Armistice the word was abroad throughout the A.E.F. that all Guardsmen and Reservists with creditable records would be offered a promotion in the Officers Reserve Corps upon release from active duty. Such a terminal promotion would mean almost any officer could go home in the next higher rank, but *not* if the officer retained National Guard status. The inference was clear that no sensible Guardsman would worry about a Guard status with such an opportunity available within the Reserve.

But the lowest blow of all came upon arrival back in the States. There was the natural desire of all units to return to their home States, Cities and Towns as units. They had marched away as such. Johnny Guardsman wanted to come marching home—literally as well as figuratively. New York's 27th Infantry Division did get the hosanna treatment up Fifth Avenue. Here and there, in a few of the other larger cities, there were bobtail parades by units, or fragments of units, from regional Divisions. But most of the Guard Divisions, Regiments, Battalions and lesser units were demobilized at various cantonments or Army Posts most convenient to the logistics of the moment. The Guardsmen straggled home, each with uniform, barracks bag, terminal separation "bonus," and the stub from a one-way railroad ticket.

But no matter how they reached home, they also had another important document about which the National Guard leaders had much to say through the years ahead. *The Army's discharge was a complete release from all duty, State as well as Federal.* Many men from sundry States had enlisted for two, three or four years of State status, much of which had not expired when the duration-of-war Federal service had ended. Guard leaders argued that these men undoubtedly rated their honorable releases from Federal service, but each man should have been given orders simultaneously to report to his State's basic unit Armory within a designated period of time. This would have given the reorganizing National Guard units an automatic cadre of seasoned men in each Armory around whom to reconstitute the town's Company, Troop and Battery-size units for a new, postwar Guard.

As it was, there was no cadre, not even of officers, most of whom had accepted Reserve commissions as a sort of ace in the hole. All the officers were in doubt as to what their status might be upon arrival back at the home town Armory. To the Guardsmen and in the think-

ing of most communities, States and Governors, this was proof positive
that the Militia Bureau had collaborated with the War Department
General Staff not only to bury the Guard with the war dead, but
further, to do it in a potter's field without the dignity of a funeral
under their own honored Colors. Their banners, with the heritage
they represented, were to be transferred to a Federal Organized Militia
under the Johnny-come-lately name of the Organized Reserve Corps.

## THE STATES VIEW THE SITUATION WITH ALARM

Less sentimental but more practical, some of the Governors, particularly of those States that as yet had no Constabulary, sat up and
took notice. It came to their individual minds that their State Constitutions and statutes called for an Organized Militia that had become
known as the State's National Guard. Moreover, their Attorneys General,
when consulted, referred them likewise to Article II of the Bill of
Rights. Too many times it had been interpreted as a guarantee to
the States of the necessity for a Militia and sovereign right of the State.
Some Governors instructed their Adjutants General to proceed with the
reorganization of their State's Militia from the ground up.

From the War Department there came nothing but obstructions.
Shortly after the Armistice, for example, a Company-size unit was recruited quickly to 80 men. Local pride was high. Twenty-seven of the
prewar Company had become officers. When the State authorities
notified the Militia Bureau and requisitioned the usual ordnance, the
Bureau rejected it, though all the World knew American arsenals and
warehouses were bulging with war surplus arms and equipment. Since
the Company-size unit did not have a strength of 100, it would have
to disband and leave its Armory vacant, the War Department General
Staff ruled. To Generals March and Carter, the funeral arrangements
must have seemed complete.

But had they paused in these funeral arrangements for the Guard
long enough to read their own statistics for June 30, 1919, they would
have realized they had a rather lively corpse on the slab. As of that
date, and in spite of such administrative obstructions, no less than
19 States* and the District of Columbia had organized units with an
aggregate of 36,018 enlisted men. Accordingly, only seven and a half
months after the Armistice and before a peace treaty had been signed,
the National Guard was back to more than a fourth of its enlisted

---

* The States were Maine, Vermont, New York, New Jersey, South Carolina,
Tennessee, Arkansas, Colorado, Iowa, Kansas, Minnesota, Ohio, Missouri, Oklahoma,
Texas, Utah, Washington, Oregon and California. Some of these had "State Guard,"
or "Home Guard" units for local and internal security during the absence of the
National Guard units. In such States, the temporary, emergency units (often filled
with men out-of-age or physically unfit for field service) "are being disbanded by
the States as the units of the National Guard are formed," to borrow the words of
the Army Headquarters for the Northeastern Department.

strength as of the activation for Mexican Border service. The ratio of officers was still higher.

But, by the above date ending Fiscal Year 1918-19, it was apparent to the Guard leaders that the future of their institution was most uncertain. Through the following Autumn and Winter, National Guard strengths remained little changed. Few if any additional States began reorganizing. Indeed, at least a dozen States with distinguished Volunteer Militia records, including Illinois, Indiana, Massachusetts and Louisiana, did nothing toward creating any units or enlisting any personnel until after the enactment of the National Defense Act of June 4, 1920. When it became apparent, early Summer of 1920, that a satisfactory Bill would be approved, most of the States again became active. By June 30, 1920, the enlisted strength of the reorganizing Guard units had reached an aggregate of 1,866 officers and 54,017 enlisted men. Such was the measure of importance the Governors and their Adjutants General attached to some sort of definite Federal legislation.

## GENERAL MARCH BEGINS THE LEGISLATIVE BATTLE

It was in January, 1919, while most Guardsmen of all ranks and ratings were still in Europe, that the word came that the General Staff had plans for dumping the long, hard-fought compromises that had gone into the National Defense Act of 1916. It was the outgoing, Democratic-controlled Congress in its last session ending March, 1919, that uncovered the War Department's official and professionally-prepared position. General March presented Secretary Baker with an Army Reorganization Bill calling for well over 500,000 officers and men. This was in the postwar peace. At the moment all enemies were crushed and allies were disarming.

To the Congressmen it looked like a section lifted from the old, misnamed Continental Army plan that had launched the fervid publicity and debates before and during the passage of the National Defense Act of 1916. Thus, with little or no concerted prompting by Guard leaders or Governors, interested Congressmen of both parties began asking searching questions. Some frankly feared they were not talking about a temporary, or stopgap, situation until the arrival of the next Congress (Republican-controlled), but might be committing the Nation to a long-time policy.

The same searching questions arose in connection with Army appropriations. When Mr. Baker was testifying, Representatives Anthony (Republican) of Kansas and Quin (Democrat) of Mississippi raised the question as to how so large a Regular Army would affect the future of the National Guard. Mr. Baker said, "There is no possible objection to having a National Guard": and the law of 1916 should be carried out. Further, the idea of having the two was "not antagonistic." He was, however, pressed into admitting that plans for the National Guard through the coming peace had not been discussed with him by the General Staff. He did not know the extent to which it had taken the Guard into consideration; if, indeed, it had done so. He readily admitted that funds asked for the Guard were "probably insufficient."

If the Secretary of War was disappointing to the War Department General Staff, its Chief, General March, must have been even more distressing. He admitted the Guard financial support requested was purely of a token character. He ducked the direct question as to whether he and the General Staff had any plan for the Guard's reorganization. Under pressure he fell back on the lame excuse that the Federal Government would have to wait for the States to do something. If he knew that 15 or more States and the District of Columbia, right under his nose, already were reorganizing under the 1916 statute, March did not reveal or admit it. Instead, he became confused in implications that a law required the States to act and that the Governors were remiss for not having decided in their last conference what they wanted.

Baker rescued him from this confusion. He further took his Chief of Staff off the hook with a promise that the National Guard would be taken care of under existing laws, and furnished arms and equipment from existing stocks, even if he had to overrule his own Judge Advocate General to do it. A new appropriation would be requested for the Guard when it had become sufficiently reorganized to need it.

The entire tone of General March's testimony clearly revealed that he and his General Staff had forgotten nothing and learned nothing since taking the teachings of Brevet Major General Emory Upton unto their hearts and souls as the Biblical word in personnel matters. It does not appear to have occurred to either March or his Staff that within the immediately past 18 months the National Guard Divisions and the Colored Infantry Regiments of a bob-tailed Guard Division had conclusively proved Upton to be a false prophet. It merely remained for a scholarly Regular Army Colonel from Pershing's Staff to publicize that Upton was also a most unscholarly and inaccurate author.

The new Republican Congress began its First Session in June of that year, 1919. When it started working on appropriations it early stumbled upon the same issues. But now the General Staff faced a Congress dominated by the party of Theodore Roosevelt, who had passed away but five months previously. His views favoring a 100% Federally-organized Militia backed by Universal Military Training camps were fresh in the memory of all. Likewise, Leonard Wood, mellow in voice but vigorous in ideas, again was reaching ears of men in key positions. His penalty for being the military favorite of the Republican Party had been retention to wartime assignments in the States. He still was in Chicago, sitting-out his non-repentant exile from the planning tables. He still was assigned as C.G. of the Central Department of the Army. Though circumscribed by directives dedicated to administrative routines, he still was articulate and his influence reached far. His views on militaryy manpower concurred with those of March, but he considered a half-loaf better than none. He eventually settled on 250,000 as an absolute minimum for the Regular Army, supported by a large Federal Reserve screened from Universal Military Training.

These factors and a more adroit and better-planned legislative campaign by the War Department resulted in a House Committee Bill for funds sufficient for a Regular Army of 400,000. On the floor of the House it was slashed to 300,000. The Senate accepted the higher figure. A joint conference committee compromised on 350,000 for the coming, single year only. Even this figure experienced a turbulent passage. It attracted the opposition of the peacetime Universal Military Training *aficionados* who sought a more ambitious pattern.

Equally opposed were those with faith in and an admiration for the voluntarily-organized citizen-soldiers such as the National Guard and the Officers Reserve Corps. America never had needed a large and burdensome Military Establishment. In their opinion none was needed in 1920. All current questions had been debated and settled in 1916. That law had stood the test of a World War in which the Guard Divisions had been thrown into action against the best troops of Europe, alongside our own Regulars and the combat-seasoned units of the French and English Armies. What immediate need could there be for a standing Army of 350,000? With new warships afloat and building, by 1922 Britannia's vaunted fleets would be second-rate in quality, speed, guns and numbers compared with corresponding American Flotillas, Squadrons and Fleets. If defense dollars were to be appropriated lavishly, they should go to the Navy—the Nation's truly first line! To a generation and in an era for which such a phrase as "anti-missile missile" could have meant no more than nonsensical doubletalk, the foregoing was solid, overpowering logic.

But the attitude of the new, Republican-dominated 66th Congress filled thoughtful Governors, Adjutants General and returning Guardsmen with alarm and concern. Appropriations for a standing Army of 350,000 and little more than the assurance of an outgoing Secretary of War that the Guard would be cared for, struck them as being an impressive victory for the War Department General Staff. There were also the pressures of fact.

As noted above, some of the States already were organizing units at home stations. The Treaty of Versailles had been signed in June, 1919. A host of more than 120,000 wartime officers were arriving back in civil life. Many were combat-tested potential leaders of larger units in any future emergency. If the Organized Militia was to become exclusively a Federal force, it should be decided without delay. If the Guard was to be preserved, there should be policy and funds whereby its course could be charted. Provision had to be made for its further training, promotion, and replacement. Wastage is high at best as veterans outlive their fundamental military obligations. It is a wise nation that encourages and provides facilities and opportunities for professional knowledge to those with inclinations, interests and functional patriotism for service beyond the essential requirement of laws. Accordingly, the Congress in the humid heat of Washington in the August of 1919, expressed a willingness to face the fundamental issues.

## THE GUARDSMEN VIEW TRENDS WITH CONCERN

Meanwhile, the National Guard Association had held its annual meeting in St. Louis, May, 1919. It was still a comparatively small assemblage of higher-ranking Line officers and Adjutants General. To say that they were sufficiently in full agreement to constitute a good and effective lobby would be crediting them with more singleness of purpose and political acumen than was actually the case.

General O'Ryan of New York's 27th Infantry Division led an imposing faction who honestly believed the National Guard would be better served if reorganized exclusively as a Federal force under the broad military powers given the Federal Union in the Constitution. Another appreciable faction, under the leadership of Brigadier General Milton A. Reckord,* believed the dual enlistment oath had the virtue of meeting not only the Bill of Rights stipulation concerning the Militia of the States but the delegated war powers of the Federal

---

* Few modern, living soldiers, whether professionals or gifted amateurs, have records of service comparable to that of Gen. Reckord. He enlisted in the Maryland National Guard, 1901; commissioned Captain, 1903; entered Federal service as a Major, 1917; Colonel and Regimental Commander, 29th Division, overseas; as a Colonel and senior officer present, he commanded a Brigade in combat; Adjutant General, State of Maryland, 1919-1940; Maj. Gen. commanding 29th Division, 1934; re-entered Federal service, Feb., 1941, as Div. C.G.; transferred to C.G., III Corps Area, 1942; Provost Marshal General, European Theater, Dec., 1943, to June, 1945; Adjutant General, Maryland, 1945, to present, 1963. Decorations include Distinguished Service Medal, two oak leaf clusters; Croix de Guerre with palm, WW I; second Croix de Guerre with palm, WW II; Bronze Star; Order Commander of Bath (England) and sundry lesser citations and decorations. As a civic leader in other fields, he became equally distinguished, but all Governors of his State, of all changing administrations and political complexions, have drafted him back to duty as Maryland's Adjutant General each time he has sought to shift military burdens to other shoulders.

Government under the Constitution. It had worked satisfactorily in the recall to active duty of all Guard units in 1917.

Some rejected this theory on the technicality that the Guardsmen, though volunteers, actually had been drafted by virtue of their earlier acceptance of a State military status. Thus the situation became one of constitutional hair-splitting whereby men hoped to achieve the same satisfactory result through different channels. But on certain things there was uniformity of opinion. The National Guard, or its full, fair equivalent, should be preserved as an American defense institution in which the volunteer citizen-soldier could be organized into functional units for future first-line service. They were further in agreement that the National Guardsmen had been dealt with unfairly by the War Department General Staff and that the Militia Bureau had been unfaithful to its statutory trust for helping the Guard. Some changes had to be made.

In this the National Guardsmen had the forthright support of none other than General John J. Pershing himself. The commander of the victorious A.E.F. put the facts on the line in a cold-blooded, blunt statement that could leave no one in doubt. "The National Guard," Pershing declared, "never received the whole-hearted support of the Regular Army during the World War. There was always more or less prejudice against them, and our Regular Army officers failed to perform their full duty as component instructors, and often criticized when they should have instructed. The National Guard people resented this and properly so."

The National Guard Association's newly-elected President, Colonel Bennett C. Clark, of Missouri's 140th Infantry, brought inflammatory articulation to long-smouldering thoughts. As a U.S. Senator, 1933-45, and as an able, admiring biographer of John Quincy Adams, Colonel Clark was to prove himself a master of better-advised phrases than some he used in his inaugural address at this convention. His promise that the Guard "would smash the Regular Army" became the tocsin of strife that gladdened the hearts of the headline writers. To General March and his War Department General Staff, it was the gage of battle.

In more calm, collected and experienced minds present in St. Louis was the grim realization that the gauntlet had been thrown. Though originally they might have willed it otherwise, such zones of compromise as might have existed were present no longer. That Guardsmen had to win the coming legislative battle or cease to exist was the point at issue.

Largely under the leadership of General Reckord, key members of the Association became a sort of *de facto* board of strategy for legislative operations in behalf of the National Guard as a defense institution.

They outlined their major and minor objectives. They knew that some of the key legislators who had been towers of strength in 1916 were present no longer. Some still in Congress were no longer in key committee assignments. But they also knew that many Regulars, from General Pershing down, had acquired a fuller understanding of the volunteer soldiers and their potential when organized into properly-equipped and functional units up to and including Divisions. In short, they did not believe Generals March, Carter, and their desk-bound palace soldier associates represented the full opinions of the Regular Army, not to mention the Congress and the Nation.

## THE BATTLE OF THE MILITARY BILLS

For greater clarity from the outset, though with the need for some subsequent repetition, it is best to list and briefly characterize the several major Bills around which the conflicting concepts became centered.

(1) The "Baker-March Bill" originally proposed a Regular Army of 750,000 men to provide a minimum force of one Field Army of five Corps, skeletonized to about 50% of the strength of all units. It would be immediately "expansible" with peacetime, trained civilians. They were to be secured by compulsory methods. It was just another revival of the Emory Upton dream. Indeed, March says his Staff called for 11 months of *service* by all youth, but he personally rewrote the plan for only three months' *training* of all draftable 19-year-olds. He was proud of having pruned away his Staff's prewar ideas and ambitions.

(2) The "Frelinghuysen Bill" was introduced at the request of the National Guard Association. It left the Act of 1916 practically unchanged with respect to the citizen-soldiers, National Guard and Army Reserve, but it shook the Guard free of the Chief of Staff and the War Department General Staff. It left the Militia Bureau in being but staffed and manned it from the Guard and under a National Guard General Officer who always would have the ear of the Secretary of War.

(3) The "Kahn Bill" came out of the House Committee. It eschewed compulsory training, pegged the Regular Army at 300,000, subject to future appropriations, of course. The National Guard was left in its 1916 status.

(4) The "Wadsworth Bill" came out of the Senate Committee, largely as a result of the views of Generals Pershing and O'Ryan, and Pershing's brilliant personnel expert, John McA. Palmer.* The Wads-

* A few weeks after the Armistice, Nov. 11, 1918, Col. Palmer was relieved of command of a Brigade of the 29th (Md.-Va.) Division and sent by Pershing as an "uninstructed delegate" to assist the War Department General Staff in personnel planning in the light of European Theater experiences. Years later Palmer wrote: "On my way across the Atlantic our proper military program seemed very clear to me. During the recent war we had created a great citizen army. This army should

worth Bill would have perpetuated the citizen-soldier units of the National Guard and augmented their number and strength by including volunteers from the rapidly-demobilizing National Army Divisions. These Divisions would be officered by Reserves who presumably would volunteer for peace service and future emergencies if given a constructive program. All would be exclusively under Federal control. They would be relieved of internal responsibilities such as strike duty. The measure contemplated a mild form of short-term universal military *training* (not service) whence volunteers would move into the former National Guard and National Army formations. Thus Pershing and Palmer had concurred in the National Guard philosophy but not in the method of achievement. Moreover, the battle between the General Staff and Guardsmen already was joined before this Bill was offered. Neither March's General Staff nor the Guardsmen would accept it.

## VIEWS ON THE MILITARY BILLS

The Frelinghuysen Bill, as noted above, was the Guard Association Bill. Its legislative sponsor was Senator Joseph S. Frelinghuysen, of Raritan, New Jersey. He was a Republican wheelhorse of vast experience ranging from County Chairman, to the Senate, to the Governor's office, and back to the Senate. His measure included the one feature in which the Guardsmen took the offensive. Most of their positions on other Bills were defensive, but always clinging to the line of the Defense Act of 1916.

The most aggressive feature of the Bill took the control of the National Guard entirely out of the hands of the Regular Army. The existing Militia Bureau was too much dominated by the Regular Army and the War Department General Staff. A new National Guard Bureau should be created. The Frelinghuysen Bill proposed that it should consist solely of Guard officers. It should function directly under the Secretary of War. It would not be subject to the Chief of Staff, or any other Regular Army officer whosoever he might be. Chief of the Bureau should be appointed by the President on the recommendation of a National Guard Council. In turn, this Council would be composed of one officer from each of the 48 States. This Council was to meet twice a year and would determine all policies and prepare all regulations concerning the Guard—its organization, discipline, and government.

This proposal in its entirety was bound to fail. More than one of the planning committees for the Guard knew it would fail, but it was

---

be perpetuated . . ." But upon arrival in Washington he found the War Department already fully committed to the March plan. "This measure proposed a standing army of more than half a million men. It frankly discarded our traditional citizen army as an element in our national defense. Hereafter military leadership was to be a monopoly of the professional soldier. At the close of a war against German militarism we were to have a militaristic system in the United States." Palmer, *America in Arms*, pp. 153-54.

offered as a springboard for the indictment of the bad faith of the War Department General Staff throughout the War. It offered a chance to denounce thoroughly the Militia Bureau as administered under Generals March and Carter while the Guardsmen were embattled in Europe.* Moreover, they were confident that they would emerge from the legislative hassle with at least a voice within the War Department. In this, they were partially successful, and the resulting enclave in the Bureau was expanded later to achieve most of their initial purpose.

The Guard's Frelinghuysen Bill was more conventional in other respects. It accepted short-term Universal Military Training with the hope that it would be of benefit not only to the National Guard but to the Regulars and Reserves. But in the hearings there was some divergence of opinions. Some revealed mild skepticism concerning a peacetime Draft. Others wanted to go all-out and give the Guard a phase in training the young men. The Guardsmen also argued for the Bill's decentralized features with Guard officers nominated by the Military Departments of the States, but subject to Regular Army boards and specifications for Federal recognition. In their opinion the Militia Amendment in the Bill of Rights and the Military Clauses in the Constitution were not in conflict. That gap had been bridged by the dual oath.

Generals March and Carter and their supporters did not apathetically accept all the indictments and arguments. In the Senate they fought back, venomously at times. Carter accused the States of "pernicious meddling." He viewed with alarm this splitting of the Army. Cooperation could not be possible. For the most part he confirmed the Guardsmen's charges of wanton prejudice. Nevertheless, Generals March and Carter were sufficiently strong in the Senate that the Frelinghuysen measure failed.

Through the long and wordy debates and hearings that extended from the Summer of 1919 to late Spring of 1920, the Guardsmen continued their fight for representation. Their tactics took the form of amendments to the Defense Act of 1916. At the same time they adopted and supported some of the specific proposals of Palmer, O'Ryan and Pershing, but not on their divergent theories as written into the Wads-

---

* For example: *The Army Almanac*, an official War Department publication dated 1950, credits the National Guard with having contributed 433,478 officers and men to the military manpower effort of World War I. But in the Annual Report of the Chief of the Militia Bureau, 1918, Appendix C, the role of the National Guard in the war effort is minimized to 12,115 officers and 366,959 enlisted men "drafted into Federal service, August 5, 1917." What the Bureau appears to have been deliberately concealing, or had lost track of through incompetence, were approximately 55,000 enlisted Guardsmen, most of whom apparently were released to attend the Officer Training Camps and who were commissioned therefrom into the Officer Reserve Corps. Thereby and in other channels those 55,000 Guardsmen became merged temporarily with other components. The Guardsmen of 1919 had just cause to distrust thoroughly the Militia Bureau as of that era, as further evidenced by the confessed maladministration of the Medical Corps promotions.

worth Bill. Exclusive application of the Army Clause of the Constitution and all other ideas that looked like hang-over concepts of Secretary Garrison as of 1913-16 were challenged, even when some of the features were endorsed by Generals Pershing and O'Ryan. The overall result was a completely confused Senate, which finally passed a measure still designated as the Wadsworth Bill, but which made so many concessions to the Guardsmen, particularly in giving them a voice in the Militia Bureau, that Carter and March had a foretaste of defeat. The Wadsworth Bill failed even in name when it reached the House.

In the House of Representatives, the Committee on Military Affairs emerged with the measure named for Congressman Julius Kahn of California. From the beginning it had powerful support. It represented the National Guard point of view, but did not follow the details of the measure Senator Frelinghuysen had introduced in the Senate for them. The Kahn Bill was simpler, more conservative and better reflected the opinion of the general public on the question of Universal Military Training. In short, it ducked the issue. It authorized a Regular Army of roughly 300,000 officers and men. It left the National Guard pretty much as it was under the National Defense Act of 1916. There were also alterations in the organization of the War Department which made permanent some temporary war measures. Most notable among them were the new Staff Sections, and Arms or Services such as Finance, Chemical Warfare Service and Air Service. These affected the Guard very little but did open the door for the other Departmental and Bureau changes the Guardsmen had in mind. Thus they turned again to their amending techniques.

The Guardsmen offered no material objections to that part of the Bill that more fully recognized and expanded the Organized Reserve though all knew it had the makings of a rival, Federal Organized Militia. They did ask for and get: (1) the rate of pay for Armory drill attendance was increased; (2) upon discharge from any Federal service, National Guard units should revert automatically to their previous State status; (3) minimum strength of units would be 50 enlisted men; (4) the Chief of the Militia Bureau should be a National Guard officer, and (5) the Guard was given further voice in planning through a permanent committee and a limited number of officers on active duty within the Department. The Kahn Bill passed the House, February 27, 1920, and was sent to the Senate March 18.

Meanwhile, in the Senate, the wrangling over the merits of the Frelinghuysen Bill, with some of its features written into the Wadsworth Bill, had completely sunk the Baker-March Bill. In this the statements of General Pershing and Colonel Palmer were paramount. As a result General March, when he wrote his memoirs years later, still was bitter against these fellow-Regulars. Likewise, 20 years later, a few Guardsmen with long memories still were critical of New York's General O'Ryan. In their eyes he was a compromiser who sought favor with all factions. Not even Pershing's prestige could keep Universal Military Training in the Wadsworth Bill. To get it out of the Senate, this provision was deleted and some of the Guard amendments were attached. It came out of the Senate, a much-battered measure, April 20. The Senate declined acceptance of the Kahn Bill as a substitute and the two Bills went to a joint conference committee for consideration.

In final analysis, the two measures were not too far apart. The principal differences related to the National Guard, but there are some basic variations. The Senate Bill stood pat on use of National Guard units under the Army, or military powers, Clause of the Constitution; the House stood for the Militia Clause status recognized in the Act of 1916. On the other hand, the Senate did provide for National Guard representation on the General Staff; otherwise, the House Bill more nearly followed the desires of the National Guard Association and further stipulated that the Chief of the Militia Bureau should be a National Guardsman. The Senate Bill, though void of compulsory military training, did provide for voluntary training in Summer military camps. The House Bill was silent on the subject. In general, it was the Senate that gave up most in the legislative conference. The Act, as finally agreed upon, passed both houses and was signed by the President on June 4, 1920. Basically, the final result was a modified Kahn Bill, which in turn was a series of amendments to the National Defense Act of 1916.

The National Guard, thanks to its friends in both houses of Congress and the ability of its leaders, through their Association, to crystallize a high degree of unanimity in thought and action, won another victory over those who would destroy it as a defense institution. At the same time they had accepted searching and supervisory conditions by the Federal Government in exchange for Federal monetary support and training. Governors could continue to "appoint" or to "commission" Guard officers, but only those capable of meeting War Department specifications and standards in military knowledge, experience and leadership could achieve *Federal recognition* for receiving funds for themselves and their units. Few Guard officers objected to this. Most thought it good and proper and for the long-range welfare of the Guard. No responsible Guardsmen today would have it otherwise, but one still meets occasional Regular Army officers, both young and old, who in their ignorance complain that the Guard is a mere area of patronage for Governors of the States. In such ignorance they are doing no more than indicting the integrity of their fellow-Regulars charged with the responsibility for professional and legal compliance with the law with reference to Federal recognition of National Guard officers.* The Army certainly has at its disposal means for exacting the same or higher standards of military proficiency among Guard officers than it does for the Army Reserve. Should it fail to do so, it has no one to indict but itself.

Other features of this law are of such importance that the sections affecting the National Guard merit a review by sections.

Sec. 1. When in the service of the United States, the National Guard would be a part of the Army of the United States.

Sec. 3. The organized peace establishment would have three components: the Regular Army, the National Guard and the Organized Reserve, forerunner of the present U. S. Army Reserve.

Sec. 3a. In the reorganization of the National Guard, the names, numbers, flags, and records of the Divisions and subordinate units that served in the World War should be preserved as far as practicable. And in this initial reorganization by a committee of the War Plans Division, General Staff, half the committee were to be citizen-soldiers with World War service.

Sec. 5a. Admitted to the General Staff Eligibility List all Guard officers who prior to July 1, 1917, had been graduated from either the Army War College or the Staff School and all others who since April 6, 1917 had demonstrated their fitness for General Staff assignment by actual service.

Sec. 5b. All policies and regulations affecting the organization, distribution, and training of the National Guard would be determined by committees of the War Department General Staff, which should include an equal number of National Guardsmen. While so serving, such officers should be regarded as additional members of the General Staff.

Sec. 24. Not less than half the vacancies caused by the reorganization of the Regular Army to its peacetime basis were to be filled by appointment of persons, other than officers of the Regular Army, who had served as officers between April 6, 1917, and the passage of the Act of 1920.**

---

* The author can find but one instance in which a Federal Recognition Board for a National Guard Line officer experienced any political pressure. It came not from a Governor but from the White House and at the insistence of the officer himself. He was a National Guard Colonel with a superior World War II staff record, but not as a combat Line officer commanding the type of units, Arms and equipment his promotion to Brigadier General in the Guard would have given him. The Board, including National Guard members, denied Federal recognition. The candidate for promotion appeared before a subsequent board, a majority of whom were National Guard General Officers. Again Federal recognition was disallowed. A memorandum, Secretary of Defense to Secretary of the Army, said to have been prompted by the White House (Truman), directed that the Colonel be Federally-recognized for a Brigadier Generalcy. The latter sent his name to the Senate for confirmation with the next list of General Officers for the Army and the Guard. As usual, confirmation of the full list was *pro forma*. He is said to have been an effective Line Brigadier until his transfer to the Guard inactive list a few years later.

** This provision was calculated to prevent filling all vacancies by promotion of time-serving, Seniority List Regulars to all upper rank vacancies, irrespective of war records, and to provide opportunity for professional service by Guardsmen and Re-

Sec. 37. Any officer then on active duty could be appointed as a Reserve officer in his then or lower rank, and any Reserve officer might hold a commission in the National Guard without vacating his Reserve commission.

Sec. 43. Enlisted personnel were divided into seven grades and six classes of Specialists for pay purposes, i.e., the same as in comparable formations, or units, of the Regular Army.

Sec. 60. Organization of the National Guard units was to be the same as prescribed for the Regular Army, but Company-size units might receive Federal recognition with a minimum enlisted strength of 50.

Sec. 69. First enlistments were to be for three years, except that any person who served in the Army for not less than six months and had been honorably discharged might enlist within two years in the National Guard for a one-year period. Reenlistments were to be for one year.

Sec. 78. This section provided for a National Guard Reserve.

Sec. 81. After January, 1921, the Chief of the Militia Bureau was to be a present or former National Guard officer of 10 or more years of commissioned service in the National Guard, at least five of them in the Line.* (b) Appropriations permitting and with the consent of the officers, the President might assign up to 500 officers of the National Guard and Reserve Corps to active duty for limited periods of time. Reduced appropriations greatly restricted and often nullified this obviously-sound provision.

Sec. 109. Company officers in the National Guard were to receive one day's base pay of their grade, for not exceeding five days per month, for each attendance at regular drills, providing not less than 50% of the officers and not less than 60% of the enlisted men of the Company received instructions for the full drill period. In addition, Captains commanding Companies could receive $240 per year additional as adminis-

---

servists who might desire a career in the uniform. Nearly 3,000 Guardsmen and Reservists were integrated into the Regulars under this provision. None were integrated as General Officers, as was the case following all previous wars and World War II. Many became professionals with initial Field Grade ranks, but only a few as Colonels. The great majority thus began their careers as professional soldiers in the grade of Captain.

* Since an Adjutant General for a State often bears much the same relationship to his Governor that a Secretary of Defense does to the President, the War Department already had accepted the concept that the best judge of who best could do the job during the specific administration of a specific Governor was the Governor himself. Hence Federal recognition to Adjutants General, as General Officers for their terms of office only, early became automatic. Meanwhile, responsible Guardsmen in most States were restricting patronage-minded Governors with State statutory long terms for that office, some of them to age 64, and with specifications as to prior military service, military rank, and experience for initial appointment thereto. Accordingly, most State Adjutants General could qualify today, but the few from States that still treat the office as gubernatorial patronage cannot, barring an exceptionally good appointment by the current Governor. All Line General Officers, Army National Guard and Air National Guard, easily can qualify for Chief of the Bureau.

trative pay. This also served as a "cushion" for property responsibility. Few Guard Captains, because of petty property loss, ever were the personal beneficiary of this full amount. An Artillery Battery Commander, for example, easily could have a property responsibility into the hundreds of thousands of dollars. Except by pranksters, cannon seldom were misplaced, though machine guns were to become a lure for gangsters. But it was keeping tab on attractively expensive pistols, clothing (especially shoes), tools, field glasses and radio tubes that has caused more than one National Guard Captain to become a Reservist rather than stay in the Guard.

Also under this section, Field Grade and General Officer ranks were like virtue in that they were largely their own reward. All Majors, Lieutenant Colonels, Colonels and Generals were to draw the same Armory drill pay—$125 each three months, except for the quarter in which the two-weeks field camp of Summer instruction fell. There was a pro-rated reduction for that quarter, for during the field camp, these officers, like Company Commanders and their Lieutenants, drew the *base* pay of their grade. Thus a Company Commander with top administrative pay often drew as much pay in a year as did a General Officer and almost always more than his Major and Colonel.* This section of the Act also authorized National Guard and Reserve officers to buy uniforms and other personal military equipment from the Signal Corps, Quartermaster, and Ordnance Departments.

Sec. 110. Enlisted men in the National Guard were to receive one day's pay of their grade for each full participation at drills duly ordered, but for not more than eight drills in any one month nor more than 60 in one year, provided they should receive no pay for any month in which they failed to attend 60% of all drills or approved equivalent duty ordered in that month. But under no circumstances could the pay of an enlisted man be forfeited by the absence of others, as could happen easily in the case of an officer.

Sec. 112 stipulated that the National Guard was subject to draft into the United States service in time of war (the dual oath provision in the Act of 1916 actually took care of this, but it seems to have been reiterated for emphasis.) Furthermore, while in such service all such soldiers became part of the Army. On termination of the emergency, such men should be discharged from the Army and revert to the status of Militia (civilian, military manpower pool, answerable only to a Draft Board)

---

* This suggests that as selfish lobbyists the National Guard Association and top officers of the Guard were uniquely unsuccessful in serving self. All of them were Field Grade officers or higher. Actually it was their idea, for they realized the Company-size Unit Commander, with his property responsibility and local leadership for keeping the unit functional and in being, was indeed the backbone of the Guard. This unusual pay scale for Field and General Officers continued until 1948, but was seldom a basis of complaint among the responsible Guardsmen.

but if State laws so provided, such men would resume an active status in the National Guard until expiration of their State enlistment. Service in the United States Army under these conditions was to run concurrently with their National Guard enlistments.

The Act was of further significance in that it set a ceiling on the Regular Army at 17,700 officers and 280,000 men. It envisioned a maximum strength for the National Guard of 450,000. It also authorized a vast pool of Reserve officers and enlisted Reservists in ambitious numbers. These figures would not prevail, of course, unless subsequent Congressmen voted the necessary funds. This was not done. The natural result is reviewed in a later chapter.

The National Defense Act of 1920 has been reviewed in considerable detail because it continued with but minor changes until the mobilization of 1940-41. It is the framework within which the Guard exists today. A knowledgeable National Guard First Sergeant, or competent Battery Clerk, of 1930, could join his old unit as of today and within a short time would feel thoroughly at home except for the new weapons and training techniques. The big picture is little changed except for proliferation of red tape and paperwork flowing from the Washington Wonderland of Bureaucracy.

Moreover, this legislation wrote *finis* to the Uptonian dreams of a mass Army of rotated, citizen, Draftee Reservists, in the European style, who would be officered and led only by professional soldiers in all ranks above that of Captain. It ended the compromise idea of a Volunteer Federal Force that augmented the Regulars in the Philippine Insurrection, and as envisioned by Mr. Root and his early Staff advisors. It even ended the fanciful play on words, conjured-up by Secretary Garrison, for the creation of a "Continental Army" that George Washington never would have recognized as such. It disposed of the Leonard Wood-Peyton C. March concept of a large professional Army, excessively heavy in its ratio of officers in proportion to enlisted Regulars, who would have a monopoly on the training and in time of war all the leadership posts above the grade of Captain, with enlisted Regulars holding Reserve commissions who would have been ready to fill many of the Company-grade slots.

All-in-all, the National Defense Act of 1920 was a triumph for the National Guard. It is easy for some to aver that it was Congressmen Kahn and Anthony who won for the Guardsmen. Old Regulars have argued that it was the schism between Pershing and the inept Peyton C. March that lost the legislative battle for Uptonian dreams. Others have said it was due to the masterful lobbying of the National Guard Association. All statements are slightly true, but they are mere froth at the top of the cup. The real source of the triumph of the National Guard over its detractors through this long legislative battle was the battlefield records of the 18

National Guard Divisions in Europe plus those of the 17 non-divisional Regiments of Guardsmen, the existence of which made possible the prompt fielding of a great American Army in Europe. These were the men and the units whose military aptitudes and valor underwrote the National Guard for a place in the future military history of America.

# Bibliographical Note For Chapter XIII

Few, if any, single and purely military legislative measures have created more printed words than did the National Defense Act of 1920. Edward Brooke Lee, *Politics of our Military National Defense,* published as Senate Document 274, 76th Cong., 3rd Session, 1950, is a conventional and often-cited, comparatively brief and compact work. Its rather complete bibliography offers a good springboard for those interested in the minutiae. The digests of conflicting opinions in the comparatively thin volume are excellent in view of the author having written the book merely as a baccalaureate thesis at Princeton University, but they are less than adequate in both content and mature evaluation. The contemporary issues of the *Army and Navy Journal,* Parts I and II, Vol. 57, Sept. 1919 to Aug. 31, 1920, provide the best and most accurate digest of the overly-verbose, question-and-answer testimony of those who appeared. The U. S. Congress, *National Defense Hearings . . . Relating to the Reorganization Plans of the War Department and to the Present National Defense Act,* U. S. Government Printing Office, 1927, is the basic source, aside from the resulting legislation itself (*Statutes of the U. S.,* 66th Cong., 2nd Sess., 1919-20, 759-812). *The Congressional Record,* vol. LIX, pp. 5182-96, 5238-51, 5275-91 and 5824-50, is valuable for intentions of Congress. The contemporary issues of New York *Times* not only yield news stories of conflicting opinions, including attitudes and activities of various groups, such as the National Guard Association, but it offers occasional and pertinent editorial opinion. The *Times* supported the Wadsworth Bill. *The Proceedings of the National Guard Association of the United States* for this period are to be found in the Washington Headquarters of that organization. See bibliographical note for Chapter XIV. Howard White, *Executive Influence in Determining Military Policy in the United States,* 1925, is an often-overlooked study of more than passing significance. Biographies and memoirs of actors in the legislative drama normally offer sidelights, but usually they are more interesting than significant.

CHAPTER XIV

# Spokesmen For The Guard

IN PREVIOUS CHAPTERS occasional reference necessarily has been made to the National Guard Association of the United States. During and after the passage of the Defense Act of 1920, this organization played an increasingly important role in National Guard history. Its annual conventions, or conferences; the meetings of its standing committees, followed by their circularized reports or findings; the constant interchanges of voluminous correspondence, all combined to make of this Association an important agency in the unification of thoughts, purposes, and concerted action.

For the first time, since the individualistic and often divergent laws and practices of the 13 Colonies and their successor States, there had come into existence a self-initiated, voluntary, continuing influence toward improvement of military principles and practices among the several States. Through the Association, Guardsmen learned they had common problems. A solution that had worked well in the State of an Association acquaintance often could be counted upon to solve a more-or-less identical problem in one's home State. More and more, the military statutes of the States began to reflect converging rather than diverging patterns.

The hasty expansion of the Guard for World War I and the prolonged legislative hearings of 1919-20 convinced responsible and thoughtful citizen-soldiers that the National Guard had far outgrown the scope of individual States, in peace as well as in war. If the National Guard was to continue as an agency for American war effort, its strength in each State would at all times necessarily exceed requirements of any foreseeable domestic or internal emergency that might arise within the boundaries of the typical, individual State. At the same time, the acceptance of a status as a purely Federal Army Reserve would leave the individual States with no force at all with which their governments could come to the aid of a State citizenry, who might be distressed by lawlessness, floods, fires, hurricanes, blizzards, tornadoes, and other violences of either Man or Nature.

## NEED FOR CONCERTED ACTION

The duality features of the Act of 1916, the magnitude and speed of Guard expansion for World War I, and the continuing legislation of 1920, convinced the Guardsmen that at last they had demonstrated clearly the feasibility and desirability of complete military cooperation between the individual States and the Federal Government in all matters of Guard policy. Moreover, such an arrangement was vital to the welfare of both the individual States and the Nation. These dual needs and objectives could be achieved at a minimum expense to each. Such self-evident truths became articles of faith within the National Guard after 1920. Though Guardsmen, in and out of the Association, and holding ranks both high and low, often disagreed with one another as to means and methods, the foregoing certainly became a unifying philosophy as to major objectives.

The Guardsmen often brought to military policy discussions, combat experience comparable with that of their most rugged Regular Army contemporaries. They also often were endowed with superior avocational skills, enthusiasms, and knowledge in military matters as well as in civil affairs. The Guardsmen, like officers in the Organized Reserve, enjoyed another advantage not available to their professional contemporaries in the Regular Army. The former were citizens first and soldiers secondarily. They enjoyed an unfettered right to voice opinions for military welfare (in behalf of the Regular Army as well as for the two Civilian Components), which was not a privilege enjoyed by the censored, or officially frowned-upon Regulars serving in Staff and planning assignments.

One often is impressed by these conspicuously recurring factors as one goes through legislative hearings or peruses the vast amount of controversial literature (often ephemeral) concerning military personnel, organization, retention and training techniques. These subjects increasingly have characterized military writing contemporaneously with the advancing techniques arising from new weapons. Because of the forceful role of the National Guard officers through the agency of the National Guard Association, a brief survey of the Association is essential to any history of the Guard.

## EARLY BEGINNINGS OF INTERSTATE COOPERATION

Associations and publications devoted to the welfare and professional improvement of the Organized Militia, Volunteer Militia, or Uniformed Companies, were not a novelty in America prior to the Civil War. Normally, however, they were along State lines. In the era between the Mexican War and the Civil War, the State of New York had a highly professional military association that met regularly, published proceedings that bristled with informed discussions of weapons, military engineering tactics and techniques; personnel procurement and training. There were similar associations in a few other States prior to 1860.

Regional conferences between two or more adjoining States were not uncommon. When they did occur, more likely than otherwise, they were at the behest, or instigation, of one or more of the Governors of adjacent States. Ex-Governor James Barbour of Virginia, who became Senator and Chairman of the Military Affairs Committee and later accepted the War Department portfolio under President John Quincy Adams, appears to have been the first Secretary of War who appreciated the need for greater military cooperation among the States and with the Federal Government. He urged the President to make military improvements along these lines one of the principal policy aims of that Administration. In this he was not successful. He did convene a voluntary Board consisting of Regular Army and National Guard officers from several representative States. Its purpose was to study the Volunteer Militia units; provide for their professional betterment; activate the distribution of manuals and textbooks, and, further, to integrate their organization and tactics with those of the small Regular Army. Citizen-soldiers on the Board were

Major General Thomas Cadwallader of Pennsylvania; William H. Sumner, Adjutant General of Massachusetts, and Beverly Daniel, Adjutant General of North Carolina. They sat with three Regulars under the Chairmanship of Major General Winfield Scott. Through correspondence and questionnaires the Board assembled a vast amount of information and interchanged considerable opinion, but little came of its deliberations. President John Quincy Adams gave the subject but little more than passing mention in his Presidential Message of 1826. It was far short of the firm, policy-making statement the Board and its sponsors had sought.

## FOUNDERS OF THE ASSOCIATION

Historical knowledge of these antebellum associations, publications, official and semi-official conferences, appears to be the only historical link between them and the origins of the National Guard Association of the United States in 1878, and in the year that immediately followed. Following the Civil War, Major General Dabney H. Maury, C.S.A., concerned himself with Southern military history in general and Virginia history in particular. His fame as founder, 1868, of the Southern Historical Society, transcends that of his enviable record as a soldier. From his mind apparently came the spark that activated the National Guard Association of the United States. To this extent he may be acclaimed the Founding Father.

General Maury was a native of Virginia and a nephew of the famous Naval officer and scientist, Matthew Fontaine Maury. He was graduated from West Point just in time for full service through the Mexican War, in which he served with distinction. He left a Captaincy in the Regular Army to accept a Captaincy on the Regular Army list of the Confederate States of America, but with much higher rank in the Provisional Army of the Confederate States. Most of his campaigns were in Missouri, Arkansas, and along the lower Mississippi River. At War's end he was Major General and Commander of the Confederacy's Military Department of the Gulf. As soon as home rule was returned to the reconstructed States, General Maury, like many other former officers of the Confederacy, took an active part in the Organized Militia affairs of his State. Though impoverished by the War, he refused $30,000 a year as Supervisor of Drawings for the Louisiana Lottery, a temptation that not all of his fellow General Officers of the late Confederacy were able to resist.

When some of the officers and units of the Organized Militia of the war-born State of West Virginia failed to perform their duty in the turbulent railroad strike of 1877, many soldiers and ex-service men, North and South, were shocked. The War Department was filled with apprehensions that policing of riots and domestic disturbances within the States might become a part of its normal peacetime duty. Congressmen were thoroughly alarmed. Hence it is not surprising that legislation vitally affecting the voluntarily-organized Militia units of the States was introduced in Congress.

It was this that stimulated General Maury to action. On his invitation, groups of officers from both the North and South met in Richmond, Virginia, in 1878. Not only were they interested in the legislation, but their agenda included such measures of practical reform and improvement as might arise from their discussions. General Maury's primary area of personal interest appears to have been the very areas of discussion with which the Barbour Board of 50 years earlier had concerned itself.

If any minutes were kept of the Richmond meeting they were not considered sufficiently important to reproduce and give wide distribution. The Conference adjourned to meet again, the following January, in New York. This proved to be a two-day meeting, January 16-17. The principal decision made at this time was to meet again the following September 30 in St. Louis. For reasons not explained, the Call to Order, in the Armory of the 1st Missouri Infantry, was not until October 1. This was the first meeting in which a definite Constitution and By-Laws were adopted and for which the Proceedings were printed. Even after the adoption of the Constitution and By-Laws, there remained some confusion as to nomenclature. These Proceedings are captioned:

"The Volunteers of America"
"Proceedings of the Convention of the National Guards"
"St. Louis"
"October 1, 1879"

Pending the adoption of a Constitution and By-Laws, the Convention was addressed by the Mayor of St. Louis, with a response by General L. F. Hunt of Ohio. Following this there was a temporary organization, with the selection of Brigadier General J. W. Denver, Ohio, as Temporary Chairman, and General William L. Alexander of Iowa, Secretary. For convenience of parliamentary procedure, it was decided that each State should be entitled to cast six votes upon all questions brought up for consideration. The States represented in the convention were Massachusetts, New York, Virginia, Mississippi, Louisiana, Tennessee, Kentucky, Ohio, Indiana, Illinois, Iowa, Missouri, Kansas and Michigan.

The most distinguished soldier in the St. Louis of that day appears to have been General Pierre Gustave Toutant Beauregard, late Confederate States Army. His opening of the War and masterful concentration of lesser forces for a victory at First Bull Run and subsequent classic defense of Charleston, through the last years of the War, had given him a high place in Confederate military annals. Since the War he had been serving as President of the New Orleans, Jackson and Mississippi Railroad, Adjutant General of Louisiana, and at that time drawing the annual salary

321

of $30,000 that General Maury had declined from the Louisiana State Lottery. But among those present, his record as a soldier for the Lost Cause was unblemished. Had he not declined commissions as Commanding General of the Armies of Roumania and of Egypt?

The most colorful personality, the most outstanding politician, and withal a first-class fighting man, was the gentleman they elected temporary Chairman, General Denver. He had just reached 60 but already had the Capital of a new State named for him—Denver, Colorado. Out of the Mexican War as a Missouri Captain of Volunteeers, he had moved to California. Challenged by Congressman Edward Gilbert of California to a duel, he elected rifles. Gilbert was killed on the second shot. Such weapons for settling minor quarrels were frowned-upon even in the robust California of that era, but in this instance not sufficiently to preclude Denver's election to the Congressional seat once occupied by the deceased challenger. After a single term in Congress, Denver accepted an appointment from President Buchanan as Commissioner of Indian Affairs, which he resigned to become Governor of the Territory of Kansas, just before Statehood. On active duty through the Civil War he was a Brigadier General, following which he settled-down to a rather prosaic practice of law in Washington, D.C., but maintained an active role in Volunteer Militia affairs. Like many Washington lawyers of that era, he identified himself with the State of his birth—and of his wealthiest clients—Ohio.

When time came to elect permanent officers, however, neither the illustrious Beauregard nor the colorful Denver was selected as permanent President under the newly-adopted Constitution. The top honor went to Brigadier General George W. Wingate of New York. He had emerged from active duty in the Civil War as a Captain, 22nd New York Infantry. In 1878 he was only 38 years of age but already had achieved wide distinction and a Brigadier Generalcy, thanks to a law practice that enabled him to give a great amount of time to military studies in general and to riflery in particular. General Wingate was to live until 1928, by which time his principal claim to fame was authorship of "Wingate's Manual of Rifle Practice," 1872, and his role as a founder and long-time President of the National Rifle Association.

General Beauregard graciously accepted the Vice-Presidency of the burgeoning Association, with General William L. Alexander of Iowa becoming Recording Secretary. Brigadier General A. H. Berry of Massachusetts was elected Treasurer. Virginia's Maury accepted a place on the Executive Council. He continued active in National Guard affairs until President Grover Cleveland appointed him Minister to Colombia. Following that four-year tour, he returned to Virginia and resumed an active role in the affairs of the State's Organized Militia until his retirement a few years before his death in 1900.

As is normal in such organizations in the formative stage, most of the early, routine work of the Association fell upon the Secretary, William L. Alexander of Iowa. He continued active in the organization until 1889, when he accepted an appointment as Captain, Commissary of Subsistence, in the Regular Army. He retired as a Brigadier General, U.S. Army, 1903. Such were the caliber, military interests and backgrounds of the founders of the National Guard Association of the United States.

## EARLY ISSUES AND ATTITUDES

The St. Louis Convention also set a pattern for areas of interest and methods of procedure for subsequent conferences and conventions. There were addresses by informed and distinguished citizens and civic leaders. Very early in the session, however, they abandoned generalities and got down to specific facts and figures. Since the Delegates were comparatively few in number, the newly-elected President, General Wingate, sought to review the pending legislation by reading it paragraph by paragraph for discussion by the Delegates assembled. With so much articulate military talent present, he apparently lost control of the parliamentary situation. He early took refuge in the appointment of a Special Committee for studying, digesting and recommending, while the remainder of the Delegates went about other business, or recessed.

The subsequent report of the Committee and the action of the Delegates upon it so well reflect the continuing philosophy of Guardsmen and the National Guard Association that it merits more than a passing glance. It also adequately reflects the parsimonious terms of the Bill then being considered by Congress. The Special Committee concurred in Federal legislation for a sharper differentiation between volunteer citizen-soldiers in the Uniformed Companies, Active Militia, Organized Militia, or National Guard, and the merely obligated military manpower in the Militia mass of men within the 18-45 age group. In return for Federal aid, Guard units should become available immediately to the Federal Government for war service. The Federal military aid to the States should be increased from the $200,000 per year, strictly for arms, that had prevailed since 1808, and broadened to include other items of military equipment.

On this point there was some dissent. With the Federal Government spending $40,000,000 annually on a Regular Army of 26,000 officers and men, it seemed to at least one articulate Guardsman present that the Federal Government would be getting a rich return in value received were as much as $4,000,000 spent on improving the arms, equipment, training and efficiency of the States' volunteer units. With such aid the Guard strength easily could exceed a normal peace strength of 100,000 men. All Guardsmen then and now would have heartily accepted that idea, but the Committee was modest. It dissented only to the extent of recommending the $1,000,000 in the Bill be doubled and allowed to be expended for a wide range of military equipment as well as for ordnance.*

There was further dissent on the Bill's stipulations for allocating Federal aid on strength of the Organized Militia units of a State (with a ceiling of 700 Volunteer Guardsmen for each Congressional District), rather than distribution based on the total population of a State. This resulted in a minority report from within the Committee. But the Committee was in full agreement that rules and regulations for discipline of the Guardsmen, when not on active Federal duty, necessarily should be approved by the Governors and Legislatures of the respective States and Territories.

With these modifications, the Committee reported, the Bill could result in an excellent law. The Convention accepted the report of the Special Committee. On the minority report from the Committee there was lively discussion, with the majority vote, nine to four, supporting the distribution of Federal funds by population rather than by size of National Guard units in being. Mississippi and Michigan joined Massachusetts and New York in support of the distribution as stipulated in the Bill.

The Special Committee further recommended that a committee of five be appointed by the President of the Association to act in conjunction with a committee created in the New York Conference on the subject of Federal legislation. It would become the duty of this expanded committee to present the Association's views to the Congress. Thus began legislative principles and practices that have characterized the views and actions of the National Guard Association unto the present day, with the necessary changes in details and outlook inherent in advancing military technologies and the vastly broader base for potential and immediate hostilities.

Having more-or-less unwittingly created a highly influential agency in future military personnel affairs and disposed of its own immediate interest in legislation, the Association went into the subject of officer improvement. This brought General Maury to the platform with a report from his Committee on that problem. He insisted that the military schools of the States, such as V.M.I., the Citadel and the Land Grant colleges, should be used more and more as sources of officer procurement. He thought West Point should acquire more of the character of

---

* As noted in an earlier chapter, the Regular Army was equally, if not more, enthusiastic about expanding the historic allotment of only $200,000 for ordnance than were the Guardsmen. Passing old and obsolete arms and equipment on to the Guard and utilizing the Guard appropriation for the replacement with new ordnance for issue to the Regular formations was often their only channel for modernization. It is interesting to note the warm cooperation and collaboration the Guardsmen of this era enjoyed from the Chief of Ordnance, then Brig. Gen. Stephen Vincent Benét, U.S.A., and grandsire of the literary Benéts so prominent in our own century.

324

a graduate school in the arts and sciences of war. On this last opinion the revered Virginian, who had taught at West Point before the Civil War, was years ahead of many other educators who have proposed the same general idea. But West Pointers long have resisted such change. They rightly argue that America has many graduate schools open to intellectually-inclined officers, but there is but one West Point.

In subsequent conventions of the National Guard Association, there were to be many similar, professional-betterment discussions. They still prevail, but not on the floor of the modern and vastly larger conferences; one must attend the long and argumentative sessions of the highly-vocal Resolutions Committee to hear them. Hence they no longer become a part of the published Proceedings; but for unfettered imagination and opulence of originality one hardly can predict when a new high may be achieved. It can be safely assumed that some of the ideas in the Resolutions Committee's deliberations are as far in advance of this generation as General Maury was ahead of his.

## FEDERAL LEGISLATION LANGUISHES

Hopeful though the Guardsmen were at St. Louis, and later at Philadelphia, 1881; Cincinnati, 1884, and Washington, D.C., 1885, little came of their efforts to achieve an overhauling and refitting of their forces through Federal support, supervision and instruction. The records fully reveal they were as eager for the last as for the other two. But with the Indian frontier all-but obliterated, with a cooperative Dictator-President, Porfirio Diaz, South of the Border, and with oceanic barriers East and West, and not so much as a prairie revolt in Canada, the Federal lawmakers were unable to rise above the idea that the peacetime volunteer citizen-soldiers of the States needed any more than the $200,000 subsidy for arms. That this sum had been established eight decades earlier for an infant Nation with a population of only 4,000,000 did not impress them. This failure left the Guardsmen more and more dependent upon private means, such as unit dues, Armory rentals, local community and City subsidies plus the State appropriations, if any. This meant a continuance of divergence in standards, equipment and organization to a minimization of the value of the National Guard to the Nation's immediate war effort, should war unexpectedly come—as indeed it always has come to America.

But another wave of domestic riots, a near-war with distant Chile, a war ultimatum to Britain because of an overly-aggressive English Colonial Office that had not heard of the Monroe Doctrine, and the bleeding sore of an unemancipated Cuba, soon were to improve Federal appropriations beyond the original and static $200,000 annually. The Guardsmen eventually did begin receiving some Federal equipment other than ordnance. On an informal inter-professional basis, Regular

Army officers did begin accepting invitations to visit, inspect and instruct at National Guard Summer encampments. Guard rifle teams, stimulated by General Wingate's writings and Rifle Association connections, did compete on more-than-even terms with teams from Regular Army and Marine Corps units. The Association thus contributed materially to the progress of the Guard, notwithstanding the lethargy of Congress and of some State Legislatures.

But without burning and recurring Preparedness issues to stimulate the Guard leaders, it was natural that some years there were less-than-full convention gatherings, if any at all; and certainly there is found a frequent hiatus in the publication and distribution of the session *Proceedings,* or their equivalent. But sufficient records and correspondence are available to identify 1890 as the closing year of General Wingate's almost quarter-century of service to the Association.

He was followed in the Presidency by Colonel Fred Bennitt of Illinois. He was to command the 3rd Illinois Volunteer Infantry in the Guard mobilization for the Spanish War, but he appears to have had little time for Association affairs. At what appears to have been the earliest opportunity, he passed on the office and its duties to his colleague, Colonel William Clendennin of Illinois. Both of these gentlemen were somewhat less than vigorous in behalf of the Association; as a result, it lapsed into innocuous desuetude until 1896. Caribbean tensions in general and bleeding Cuba in particular appear to have had more to do with the revival in Association affairs than any revitalization of the leadership. Be it said in defense of the leadership through these early years that there was little help and no money with which to sustain an effort toward betterment. Actually, it was not until the second or third Presidential administration of Major General Ellard A. Walsh of Minnesota, and after World War II, that the Association became really organized and on a sound financial basis. The Association had no Headquarters during the early decades. Though Pacifists and strike leaders occasionally were vociferous in accusations of lobbying, there was no paid staff, or lobbyist, within any remote sense of the modern term. On one of his trips to Washington, at his own expense and to contact Congressmen, General Wingate had trouble convincing some of them he was not hiding a big arms deal, or munitions contract, somewhere in his altruism for National defense. That men would "lobby" for the privilege of serving their Country on a field of battle was little less than startling to the cynical Congressional imaginations of that era.*

---

* The infant National Guard Association learned early that no matter what legislative proposal it might publicly make, sundry persons both in and out of Congress, (often through sheer ignorance of things military in general and of the dual structure of the National Guard in particular) inevitably manifested dark suspicions as to the hidden desires and ulterior motives of those volunteer citizen-soldiers who made the proposal. General Wingate lamented to the 1881 convention that its efforts

The Association's only funds accrued from the $15 collected from the delegation of each State upon arrival at a Convention City. This was normally inadequate, following Convention expenses, to pay postage and stationery bills for the Call of the next Conference. Petitions, personal letters and self-financed trips to Washington were about the only instruments available to an officer of the Association, or anyone else interested primarily in military personnel and organizational legislation. General Albert W. Ordway, senior officer for the District of Columbia National Guard, did maintain a more-or-less official open house in behalf of the Guard's proponents and probably did more through these lapsed years for the Guard than did some of its nominal Presidents.

## THE SPANISH WAR REVIVES THE ASSOCIATION

The Association came out of its coma at a General Conference of the Association in St. Louis, in 1897, but under a slightly different name: The Interstate National Guard Association. Incidentally, its Proceedings appear under that masthead through the next 20 years or more, but to avoid confusion, the Association, in this book has been and will continue to be referred to by its original and present name.

In the revival meeting in St. Louis, General M. F. Bell of Missouri was elected President. A year later, in the Chicago Conference, General J. N. Reese, Illinois, became his successor and served from 1898 until 1902. This period was characterized by a complaint against the War Department. In quickly mustering-out the National Guard Regiments, 1898, and then offering the suddenly "at liberty" and unemployed officers and men their corresponding ranks and ratings, particularly to Captains or under, to form the Infantry and Cavalry Regiments of U.S. Volunteers for the "pacification" of the Philippines, was a shabby device for promotion of rank-hungry Regulars, some Guardsmen argued. The War Department, they felt, was stealing the National Guard from the States, along with their brilliant Civil War traditions, to reflect greater credit upon the Washington Government.

Actually, the brief Spanish War had ended before any appreciable

---

in behalf of legislation to bring some cohesiveness and uniformity to the Guard resulted, on the one hand, in "the fear that the reform we propose contemplates an attack on the liberties of the Country, by organizing and arming some blood-thirsty and mysterious organizations for the purpose of enabling the States to defy the authority of National Government. On the other, we find the same measure denounced as an attempt to place the Militia of the States under the absolute control of the President, and create a new Federal Army of 150,000 men, to enable the General Government to trample on the rights of the States." Congress seemed to feel, "that there was a job of some kind—a great gun contract—or something of that description, concealed, somewhere in our proposed law. It apparently seemed almost incredible to members of Congress that there could be a number of gentlemen in the various States who would put themselves to any inconvenience solely from a desire to advance the military strength of the Country, and without any idea of personal benefit, and it has been difficult to disabuse their minds of this impression."

weight of the National Guard Regiments was committed. Even so, the Guard had come out of the War with little if any less credit than had the Regular Army units that had formed the major portion of Shafter's V Corps in the brief, limited-objective campaign for Santiago de Cuba. The only reputations to emerge from that war were journalistic. The irresponsible war correspondents, with Richard Harding Davis, Stephen Crane, Stephen Bonsal, Ralph D. Paine and John Fox, Jr., as the pace-setters, have been cited elsewhere. Their writing created a post-Spanish War cacophony of conflicting public opinions that briefly impaired the unity of thought and action by the Guardsmen.

Some normally sound thinkers among the citizen-soldiers became confused. There was never a greater lack of unity of thought among them. Generally speaking, the Western, Southern and Midwestern Guard leaders clung to the traditional concept that a proper role for the Guard was alongside the Regular Army, in offensive operations, wheresoever the fortunes of war might require. But in the industrial East, there was the instinctive fear that riots and domestic strife, while Guardsmen were at some distant war front, might leave the home State without the means for maintaining law and order.

The election of Major General Charles Dick, Ohio National Guard, to the Association Presidency in 1902 settled these transitory schisms within the ranks of the Guardsmen. The Dick Act of 1903, fully reviewed in an earlier chapter, not only reflected his views but it charted the future of the National Guard as an agency in the Nation's first line of defense. It also restored unity of purpose and objectives to the Association. Accordingly, General Dick's tour of duty as the Association's President, 1902-09, rightly is considered one of progress and achievement.

General Dick, of Akron, Ohio, was born November 3, 1858. He served in the Ohio National Guard from 1876, but his only active duty in Federal service was Lieutenant Colonel, 8th Ohio Volunteers, in 1898. He entered Congress from that service. In 1904 he was elected to the Senate, in which he served until 1911. Few men so conspicuous in public life for such a long period of time have been so quietly modest. His elevation to the Senate had been in the days of election by joint sessions of both houses of the Legislatures of the States. He had little aptitude and less taste for Statewide campaigns for election by popular vote as required by the 17th Amendment to the Constitution, adopted in 1913. His years after withdrawal from public life were in the comparatively quiet practice of law in Akron. He died March 13, 1945. Thus he lived to see his faith in the volunteer units of citizen-soldiers fully sustained in two World Wars.

General Dick was followed in the Presidency of the Association by Major General Thomas J. Stewart of Pennsylvania. He served in this office from 1909 to 1916. He appears to have been the last General

Officer with a Civil War, Union combat record to withdraw from an active military status. The Regular Army's Major General John L. Clem, who retired August 29, 1916, appears to have been the last such Regular to leave the active duty list. Pennsylvania's Stewart was Adjutant General of his State from 1895 until his death September 11, 1917, thus extending beyond General Clem's record by slightly more than a year. Both Generals Clem and Stewart had enlisted as drummer boys, 1862, Clem in the 22nd Michigan Infantry and Stewart in the 135th Pennsylvania Infantry. Though General Stewart could show the later active status record, the Regular Army's Major General Clem outlived him 20 years.

The period of General Stewart's Presidency of the Association was characterized by amendments to the Dick Act, increasing Federal support in appropriations, and the adverse ruling by the Attorney General of the United States concerning the use of the National Guard beyond the limits of the United States. These and the efforts to supplant the National Guard by the Continental Army plan of the General Staff have been reviewed elsewhere. It is sufficient here to note that General Stewart and his appropriate Committees functioned effectively in behalf of the National Guard.

The Mexican Border mobilization, followed immediately by declaration of war on Germany, took most of the membership of the National Guard Association to active duty. These were fallow years in Association affairs. Brigadier General E. LeRoy Sweetser of Massachusetts, 1916-1917, and Brigadier General Harvey J. Moss of Washington, 1917-18, bridged the gap of War years. As noted elsewhere, the highly-articulate and politically potent Colonel Bennett C. Clark, Missouri, returned from the battlefields to spark the fire of political strife that characterized the passage of the National Defense Act of 1920. Colonel Clark served two years, 1919-21. Though it was Colonel Clark who provided the sound and the fury, it was the then Colonel Milton A. Reckord who mobilized Guard opinion back of those who defeated the Peyton March and Wadsworth Bills designed to destroy the Guard as a defense force.

## ERA OF PRESIDENTIAL ROTATION

After 1922, the National Guard Association leaders fell into the habit of honoring fellow members by passing the Association Presidency around. Until 1940, with but one exception, no member served longer than a year, and Brigadier General J. Clifford R. Foster of Florida, elected in 1926, did not complete his brief annual term. The Presidents of the Association through this era were: Colonel Guy M. Wilson, Michigan, 1921-22; Major General Edward L. Logan, Massachusetts,

1922-23; Brigadier General Milton A. Reckord, Maryland, 1923-25; Brigadier General J. Clifford R. Foster, Florida, 1926; Major General William G. Price, Pennsylvania, 1926-27; Colonel G. Angus Fraser, North Dakota, 1927-28; Brigadier General Ellard A. Walsh, Minnesota, 1928-29; Major General Alfred F. Foote, Massachusetts, 1929-30; Brigadier General Dudley A. Hard, Ohio, 1930-31; Brigadier General Robert J. Travis, Georgia, 1931-32; Brigadier General Claude V. Birkhead, Texas, 1932-33; Major General Matthew A. Tinley, Iowa, 1933-34; Major General Roy D. Keehn, Illinois, 1934-35; Brigadier General Thomas E. Rilea, Oregon, 1935-36; Brigadier General S. Gardner Waller, Virginia, 1936-37; Major General George E. Leach, Minnesota, 1937-38; Brigadier General James C. Dozier, South Carolina, 1938-39; Brigadier General Walter A. DeLamater, New York, 1939-40, and Major General Edward Martin, Pennsylvania, 1940-43.

Like most lists of citizen-soldiers, it would be difficult to categorize the foregoing as a group. Their only common meeting ground was an enthusiasm for the National Guard, its drills, riflery and gunnery contests, Summer field camps, and friendly contacts with kindred spirits in essentially a man's World and finally the opportunity for service, should the Nation be confronted with a major emergency. With all it was an avocational interest in the beginning. With some it became vocational, with the prior civilian vocation becoming avocational. This was normally the case with those who accepted appointments as Adjutants General of their respective States. Some, such as Martin, Leach and Reckord, were sufficiently versatile that they met with marked success in one or more lines of endeavor in addition to their fulltime responsibility to the State's Military Department. Among those who accepted appointments for short or long terms in a State Adjutant Generalcy, law was perhaps the most frequently associated profession.

Others, such as Clark, Wilson, Birkhead, Tinley, Hard and DeLamater, were strictly Line officers who never permitted the Military to become more than avocational, though at times they necessarily worked at it harder than they did their business or profession. But all of them, whether occasional fulltime Adjutants General of their States or avocational officers in Line assignments, had served through World War I. Almost without exception, they were overseas and in combat assignments. Leach wore both the D.S.C. for valor and the D.S.M. for outstanding command in the presence of the enemy. These decorations came to him while commanding an Artillery Regiment of the "Rainbow" Division. Purple Hearts and Silver Stars were comparatively common in the above list of officers. Dozier was privileged to wear, but seldom did, the coveted and highest decoration of all, the Medal of Honor.

As might well be expected in any association that annually rotates its top honor by a *pro forma* election that elevates the previous year's Vice-President, various Presidents gave varying degrees of attention to the one-year tour of duty. Some exercised forceful leadership, as did Generals Leach, Reckord, Walsh and Martin. Others relied heavily upon the Executive Council, Chairmen of the Standing Committees, the Secretary and the Treasurer. These two positions were elected annually but were not rotated. From shortly after World War I, the Secretary was Colonel and later Major General Walsh. When as a Brigadier General he served his first term as President, 1928-29, he was followed in the Secretaryship by Lieutenant Colonel and later Brigadier General Frederick M. Waterbury, New York. He served in that position until 1951. The perennial Treasurer, who served even longer continuing terms through annual reelections, but who handled little money until after World War II, was Brigadier General Milton R. McLean of Kansas. Neither General Waterbury nor General McLean drew any remuneration for these important and prolonged services. General McLean died in 1950, still functioning as Treasurer.

The dynamics of the Association actually flowed from the Executive Council. Past Presidents enjoyed ex-officio memberships. Some Past Presidents saw fit to continue active in its deliberations. Others accepted the end of their annual term as a time to become little more than occasionally critical elders. The Council, however, drew sustaining vitality from those who did choose to continue their activity within the Association. It was augmented by nine "Additional Members on the Executive Council." This allowed one active officer to be elected from each of the nine regional commands, or Corps Areas, of the Army. For the most part these Additional Members were carefully-selected Colonels and Brigadier Generals on the way up.

## THE TYPICAL CONVENTION

The annual Conferences were not large. In 1926, to take a sample year of that decade, no less than 10 States and Territories, including the great and military-minded State of California, did not bother to send any representation whatsoever. Several States sent but one officer, normally a Brigadier General. Texas sent but four officers, two Line Brigadiers and two Colonels, one of the latter from the State Staff, and most likely representing the Adjutant General. Though the meeting was in Louisville, Kentucky's Delegation of only five was headed by a Colonel, and included three Majors and two Captains. New York, with 26 Delegates and Pennsylvania with 21, provided nearly a fourth of all Delegates on the floor. But on most issues, balloting was by States, with an assigned voting strength of accredited Delegates for each State. Thus, except for reasons of home front morale, there was little premium on a State having a full Delegation in attendance. The four Texans with 17 votes had almost the same voting power as the four-times-larger Illinois Delegation who rated a count of 18 ballots.

Conference registration fees, dues and sale of Annual Proceedings of the previous meeting, constituted the principal sources of revenue. The Association began that Fiscal Year with $4,328.43. Though the Chair graciously balked on the idea that States partially delinquent in dues proportional to their voting strength be read into the Proceedings, the situation did improve. The balance on hand at the end of the year was $5,695.03. Twelve years later, at San Francisco, California, September 26, 1938, the liabilities were none; due the Association, $46.50, and cash in bank, $6,386.47, for net assets of $6,432.97. But attendance had improved materially. Only six States, including Wisconsin and Georgia, were not represented. Guests and Delegates from California and neighboring States exceeded the number of ballots allocated. Some of the more distant States had Delegates present in strengths that approximated the ballot strength. On the whole, it was, except for the preponderance of rank and distinguished names on the program, an unimpressive gathering of less than 350 officers.

The typical Conference of this era featured the Association President's Report. It traditionally summarized progress and status reports on the Association's objectives as established by Resolutions of prior years. Committee Reports were always of interest, particularly those having to do with War Department policies, budgets, new equipment, new types of military units, allocations of such units, if any, and legislation in which the Guardsmen, present or at home, might be interested.

The Governor of the State in which the Conference was being held always was invited to address the group. The Secretary of War, or his representative, normally attended and appeared on the program. The same was occasionally true of the current Chief of Staff of the Army. The Regular Army Commanding General of the Corps Area in which the Association was in session was present almost invariably, as was the Chief of the Militia Bureau or National Guard Bureau, as it was redesignated in 1933.

It is quite clear from the verbatim stenographic Proceedings that everyone from Secretaries of War down, Regulars and Guardsmen, appear to have said pretty much anything they pleased about everything. They did occasionally preface their remarks with the customary statement that they spoke only for themselves and not for the Government, or Department, or military component of which they were members. The Association occasionally drew on its own membership, other than Officers and Committee Chairman, for appropriate addresses on military trends and events. A notable example of this was the address by Major General David P. Barrows, a National Guard Line officer and for a number of years commander of California's 40th Infantry Division. He was better known as the President of the great State University at Berkeley, and later became the first Chancellor of the State's expanding university system.

## THE ASSOCIATION'S RAPPORT WITH THE REGULAR ARMY

The Association's record of achievement during the era between the Wars was more impressive than any of its Conferences. True, the end result of the National Defense Act of 1920 had been a settlement of the major issues and the plotting of a definite future for the National Guard, but there were sundry minor items with which the Guardsmen were somewhat less than satisfied. These continued to be minor areas of friction. They are reflected by recurring Resolutions, progress reports, and ultimate corrective action, occasionally by legislation, sometimes by cooperative action within the Guard and sometimes by directives and policies within the War Department that the Guardsmen insisted were for the welfare and progress of National defense.

Among these was the motorization of the National Guard Artillery Regiments, over Regular Army opposition because of a professional firm belief in horses for the rugged Southwest along the Mexican frontier. Where else could one think of Americans fighting a war in 1935? As late as Spring, 1940, while the German blitzkrieg was rolling across France toward Cherbourg and Brest, the map maneuvers in the Command and General Staff College at Fort Leavenworth were played with "Square" Infantry Divisions that had one Regiment of horse-drawn light Artillery and one Regiment motorized. Then Brigadier General Lesley J. McNair, the Commandant, explained the Artillery Regiments. He said it would be folly to forget or to underestimate the long-proven and splendid capabilities of the horse by an over-emphasis of this noble animal's apparent limitations on the modern field of battle. Good pedagogy, perhaps, but the proved limitations of the horse had been extremely well-emphasized in World War I. Unfortunately, Artilleryman McNair had fought that war as a temporary Brigadier and in high-level Staff assignment.

The National Defense Act of 1920 had given the Guard leaders a listening post within the War Department. This was in the Militia Bureau, which was charged with the issuance of supplies, uniforms and equipment to the States for their Guard units. There were also a few short-term General Staff slots available to Guard officers who could qualify and at the same time escape from civilian pursuits long enough to accept the assignment.

The objectives of the Association through this era included a consolidation of footholds within the Bureau and an increase in its freedom from the General Staff's uninformed bungling in routine Guard affairs. There was never any desire to dabble in strategic war plans or anything specifically pertinent to the Regular Army or the Officers Reserve Corps.

The General Staff, nevertheless, resented this "encroachment." The Association countered with a Bill that would have increased the Bureau's independence and written its detailed functions into law. The War Department assuaged the Guard in 1926 with a "charter" for the Bureau from within the Department. Incidentally, this "charter" was one of the first casualties of World War II mobilization. Nevertheless, the Guardsmen continued to strengthen the Bureau and among other things achieved its name change to "National Guard Bureau" in 1933.

Moreover, there continued to be resentment against the legal technicality that Guardsmen were drafted men rather than volunteers for World War I. And how to be a State force in time of peace and at the same time a component of the Armed Forces of the United States, automatically, the moment there should be need for a partial or complete mobilization, continued to bother the legal-minded gentry in both the Regular Army and the Guard. This point was refined further with appropriate legislation in 1933. In the same way that in America each person has two citizenships, the National Guard was recognized as having a dual legal and institutional status. In a nut-shell, the New York units, for example, continued to constitute the Armed Forces of the State of New York under the historic Article II of the Bill of Rights, or Second Amendment to the Constitution. Upon summons to Federal duty, the same units became elements of the National Guard of the United States. Such legislation, with sundry directives and regulations from within the War Department, did much to clarify the relationship between the two citizen-soldier, volunteer components of the Army of the United States (the National Guard and Organized Reserve Corps) and to facilitate the transfer of qualified officers and men from one to the other.

The Guard Association members also were insisting constantly upon more "slots" for Guardsmen in all levels of the Army schools, such as the Field Artillery School at Fort Sill; Infantry, at Fort Benning; Command and General Staff, and the War College. Additional assignments, both for service and training, in the General Staff, were sought constantly. As one officer enthusiastically argued: "Let's not fight them; let's join 'em."

Rapport between the professional and volunteer soldiers was generally good throughout this period, notwithstanding the minor friction areas. When the Army said "no," there was usually a pricetag explanation. Thus did the Guard Association find itself in the role of a military lobbyist for funds not only for itself but for the Regular Army. The Great Economic Depression of the '30's was drying-up the thinning stream of tax dollars to all Governmental agencies. Relief was competing with increasing success for the limited funds that were available. In the name of Peace, Pacifism and Isolation, catastrophic Budget cuts were attempted on the Regular Army. Chiefs of Staff and War Department Secretaries more than once appealed to the Guardsmen and the Association for help. Through Congressmen and their Governors, the Guardsmen fought as stoutly for the entire Army Budget, as prepared by the General Staff, as they ever did for the accounts specifically earmarked for their own military component. General Douglas MacArthur, as Chief of Staff, was particularly appreciative.

Other legislative achievements of the National Guard Association in behalf of its own members and future preservation include the Act of April 3, 1939, which provided for the same treatment as to care and pay for National Guardsmen who incurred disabilities, or who died, or were killed during an active duty period in excess of 30 days, that was accorded all other soldiers of like rank then on active duty. Since the Civil War, volunteer citizen-soldiers in these matters had been victims of discrimination.

In the interest of American preparedness, following the outbreak of Hitler's War, 1939, the Association warmly supported and lobbied for passage of Public Resolution No. 96, 76th Congress, and approved by the President, August 27, 1940, under which members and units of the National Guard and Reserves would be called to active duty for 12 months. The Guard Association further lobbied for the passage of the Selective Training and Service Act of 1940. The promise that the National Guard exacted in return for its support of this, America's first peacetime compulsory military service Bill, was the stipulation within the law that "the strength and organization of the National Guard, as an integral part of the first-line defenses of this Nation, be at all times maintained and assured." Accustomed to so many and constantly selfish pressures, it must have been refreshing to the Congress to find "lobbyists" for a group of public-spirited, volunteer citizen-soldiers, demanding the prior right to serve in the front lines; and that their historic position not be usurped by War Department war planners who might prefer to use almost juvenile, drafted Selectees, as more pliant "bodies" in preference to the Guardsmen. It was, indeed, evidence of a pressure group with a difference.

Without these provisions, America would have found herself bombed into the European War at Pearl Harbor utterly unprepared, instead of merely partially prepared, had the tidal wave of Pacifism through the '30's engulfed America in the guise of "good will" and "splendid isolation." The civilian Reservists, officers and enlisted men, of the Army, Navy and Marine Corps, most of them civic leaders within their respective age groups, were also conspicuous among the architects of the slowly-growing, realistic opinion that held back the wave of passivity, Pacifism and the increasing lack of faith in America as a champion of freedoms in a World headed toward tyrannies and totalitarianism. No one can be more convincing to the public than a man who is willing to serve and sacrifice as well as to talk. First, foremost and most conspicuous among these Americans who had obligated themselves voluntarily to such service, were the National Guardsmen and their Company-size units scattered among most of the Towns, Cities and Counties of the Nation. Moreover, their National Guard Association of the United States was the exemplar for the corresponding Reserve Officers associations of the Navy and the Officers Reserve Corps of the Army.

Since the days when the old Anti-Saloon League demonstrated to the fullest the ulterior and devious abuses that could be achieved by the tightly-woven, single-purpose association, political scientists have been writing books and articles in denunciation of government by pressure and citing all organizations of which they do not personally approve as illustrative of "pressure groups." Since success attracts attention and creates critics, it is inevitable that this shotgun accusation occasionally has been aimed toward the National Guard Association and Reserve Officer associations for the other Services, not to mention the American Legion and Veterans of Foreign Wars, who have taken similar stands.

## ARTICULATE GUARDSMEN

It is true that during those long, lean years of the Depression-ridden '30's, the Association did develop some rather stellar performers in making logical and convincing headlines in public hearings of the Military Affairs Committees of the Congress. Actually, this does not appear to be difficult if one keeps cool, calm, collected, knows all the facts instantly, and is brutally honest with them and permits them to add themselves up to one unalterable conclusion. But the foregoing is a hard formula to follow. Nevertheless, General Walsh mastered it thoroughly. One critical but admiring Regular of the World War II era remarked, more or less, as follows: "I always cringe when Walsh makes an appearance and drops into that low, gravelly, analytical voice and begins citing statutes and regulations by chapter and verse. Our slightest departures from the letter of the law—and he knows them all—sound like conspiracies rather than good intentions for the

Service. But I can't argue with him. He is always loaded with more facts and figures." Actually, the Regular Army of that period had but one officer who could hold his own with Walsh. He was a somewhat unconventional, military personnel expert now widely known as Lieutenant General Lewis B. Hershey, Director of Selective Service. To the dismay and irritation of most of the free-wheeling and uninhibited personnel planners in the War Department G-1 section of that era, Hershey and Walsh were, more frequently than otherwise, in complete agreement. This was hardly strange, inasmuch as Hershey began his military career in the Indiana National Guard.

But Walsh was far from being alone. Indeed, the perennial Chairman, *de facto* or otherwise, of the Association's Legislative Committee was the earlier-mentioned General Reckord. His instinctive techniques were just the reverse of those that came naturally to Walsh. Though far from timid or inarticulate when on his feet in public, Reckord's approach was that of the softly-speaking, gentlemanly, Baltimore cavalier. One of his quick, verbal rapier thrusts often would be administered with such deft, smiling touch and keen charm that his opponent did not feel it until the next day, and then without anger. General Reckord's nearness to Washington and first-name friendship with everyone in the War Department made his Annapolis office the receiving point for every Guard complaint from Sacramento, California, to Augusta, Maine. His advice was sought by Regulars as well as Guardsmen. His differences of opinion with other Guardsmen never became public property when they did occur. This caused some critics of the Walsh-Reckord teamwork to aver that the latter "moulded all the snowballs that Walsh threw." This was not true—Walsh moulded his own. But if Reckord thought one Walsh had moulded might miss the mark from being a bit lop-sided, he did not hesitate to round it off with a personal touch.

General Martin, who commanded Pennsylvania's 28th Infantry Division, is the Association leader of that era who normally is considered the outright politician among the Guardsmen. This impression stems from his phenomenal success in politics overshadowing an equal success as a Guard officer and in the practice of law. He was elected Governor of Pennsylvania, 1943-47, whence he went to the U.S. Senate for two terms until his voluntary retirement in 1958.

Back home from the Spanish War and the Philippines as a Sergeant, Edward Martin had reentered college and was admitted to the Bar where in the practice of law he met with marked success in Washington, Pennsylvania. He immediately sought and received a commission as a Lieutenant of Infantry, 1901, and, by 1917, was a Major. He returned from World War I a Lieutenant Colonel with two wound

337

stripes and a D.S.C. with Oak Leaf Cluster. Came induction of the 28th Infantry Division February 17, 1941, and for the fourth time Guardsman Martin went into Federal service, but he knew, or soon learned, that Regular Army Major Generals younger in years were being denied field commands. He would have to sit it out on the home front. Thanks to fortuitous circumstances, the Republicans were short of immediate talent for the Governor's Mansion. General Martin accepted and began a fulltime political career in the Governor's Mansion, January, 1943.

To General Walsh, Senator Martin was in the character of an elder statesman. But this was hardly true of General Reckord who, almost as old, once alleged that he had missed the Spanish War largely through the misfortune of not having been a premature baby. That General Martin's presence in the Senate, 1947-58, was a bit of luck for the National Guard, cannot be denied. Moreover, it was Martin who, as President, and soon with the aid of Walsh, kept the torch burning while other outstanding leaders of the Association were on active duty, beginning with the First Call to the First Division, September 16, 1940.

There are other names, some not previously mentioned here, that occur so frequently in the exceptionally well-recorded and published Proceedings of the Association from 1920 until the present, that they merit equal space and comment here, but for whom available information and records are inadequate. Moreover, some are still so active in the National Guard and affairs of the Association that a brief profile here would be both presumptuous and premature. Mention of a few others by name, however, is appropriate. General Leach has been mentioned briefly as President of the Association, 1937-38. He also served as Chief of the National Guard Bureau, 1931-35. Few soldiers, professionals or gifted amateurs, ever have equalled his ability for long-range planning along practical lines and getting satisfactory results with a minimum of friction. It was he who equipped the Guard Artillery Regiments with the then thoroughly modern equipment, such as high-speed, rubber-tired, French 75's and motorized equipment. And all the while he was smiling to his friends and with prophetic vision saying that if America did not have better than that, come *der Tag*, there was need for God's help. Meanwhile, the professional soldiers still were buying horses, all of which made Leach's job of motorizing the National Guard Field Artillery Regiments much easier.

There are many others, such as Raymond H. Fleming of Louisiana, who, when told he had been the senior Brigadier General in the Army for some time and that scores had been promoted over his head, retorted that he knew it and was so happy to be wherever he might serve best that he did not care who was promoted over his head to what. He later served as Chief of the National Guard Bureau through a most difficult period. There were also Major General Heber L.

Edwards, who was always apprehensive that his "fur-bearing Swedes in North Dakota" might be neglected; Major General H. Miller Ainsworth of the "Lone Star State's" 36th Infantry Division, who served on the National Guard General Staff Committee and said little but voted right every time; Major General Edward J. Stackpole, who retired from the Guard in time to find a new vocation as a battlefield historian of the Civil War; Major General Edward D. Sirois, Massachusetts, whose dedication to the Guard and the Association, following an enviable World War II record, rendered inestimable service to the Association in the transition of its financial affairs from its small prewar status to its postwar expansion and the financing of the construction of its Memorial Building in Washington, D.C.

Also in the transition period certain younger officers representing a new aspect of the modern National Guard merit special mention. They are among the fathers of the Air National Guard. In fostering this new area of military service for the citizen-volunteer, they have worked within the traditional framework of the National Guard and at the same time met the increasingly exacting, technical demands of the Federal Government. First among these were the late Major Generals Earl T. Ricks of Arkansas and Ray Miller of Minnesota, and Brigadier General Louis E. Boutwell of Massachusetts. Contemporaneous and equally forceful were Errol H. Zistel, Ohio; Stanford W. Gregory, Colorado; Winston P. Wilson, Arkansas, and Clarence A. Shoop, California. These officers and their scores of younger subordinates are demonstrating the falsity of the myth that modern warfare is too technical for the layman, or the so-called civilian amateur. Dedicated civilians in the Organized Militia of 1775-82 proved to the British in Boston and elsewhere that muzzle-loaded artillery was not, after all, too technical for the ingenious American civilians to learn to maintain, operate and shoot. Modern Guardsmen, reaching maturity in a far more technical age but endowed with the same spirit, are encountering no more difficulties in the maintenance and operation of missiles and in launching from supersonic aircraft.

Every generation of Americans thus has contributed its testimony and evidence that so long as there are men in America willing to dedicate their spare time and enthusiasm, and in instances where and when it can be arranged, an occasional short tour of fulltime training and instruction, there always will be an Organized Volunteer Militia— a National Guard.

Not for a moment would any Guardsman—not even the most superlative-minded member of the National Guard Association—so much as suggest that the National Guard has a monopoly on such American, volunteer citizenry. They occasionally are found among the professionals. The Army was no livelihood to General and Mrs. George S. Patton. Both had material wealth beyond heart's desire. To General Patton, military service was a sacrificial way of life. There are many other professional soldiers, sailors and marines who have not comparable material wealth but who have talents that could bring them a more luxurious livelihood with less confining, regimented effort. This is particularly true in the Medical Corps, but the same applies, if less frequently and conspicuously so, in the other Arms and Branches of the professional Armed Services. The Army Reserve and the Naval Reserve are part and parcel of the same philosophy of service as the National Guard; indeed, the National Guard is the parent of both. But the purely Federalized Reservists enjoy a greater degree of flexibility and official tolerance in the dedication of the spare time than is permitted the National Guard. Hence there appear to be wider ranges in the degree of dedication to the practice and philosophy among the purely Federal Reservists than among the Guardsmen.

The guiding principle of the National Guard Association always has been one of sympathy and cooperation toward all the Armed Services, National Defense in general, and reserve programs in particular. Likewise, the National Guard Association has enjoyed harmonious relations with the Associations of the Army, Navy and Air Force Reservists. It has been only when attacked by uninformed, rank-covetous professionals and star-studded empire-builders in the old War Department, or the more recent Pentagon, that the Guardsmen, through their Association, occasionally have bared their teeth and reminded the Regulars that the Guard was in National defense first, has borne its full share in all the wars, is today far from being obsolete, and still has a specific place in the United States Constitution and the Nation's defenses.

## THE ASSOCIATION IN TRANSITION

The National Guard Association, as do the associations of Reservists for all the Armed Services, has one readily recognized and fundamental weakness. Comes a major mobilization, and all the membership still in age for grade that can pass an induction physical examination is swallowed-up by the Armed Forces. When the World War mobilization began for the National Guard, Fall of 1940, the Association's bank balance was in the customary zone of five to ten thousand dollars—$6,363.61, to be exact. Other assets consisted of the account books, blank receipts for dues if and when paid and a stack of unsold *Proceedings* from past Conferences. There was no Headquarters, no home office; not so much as a parttime stenographer to mail out Mimeographed notices that all bills were paid and until further notice the Association was in a state of suspended animation. Indeed, except for the offices of the State Adjutants General, which necessarily were retained in active status on the home front in order to operate the Draft machinery, there were few Guardsmen who could have spared time from their units or obtained leave to attend a Conference had one been called.

In the Summer of 1940, a student of military legislation, Edward Brooke Lee, was interviewing two of the Nation's top columnists and commentators of that era, Frank R. Kent of the Baltimore *Sun* and Turner Catledge of the New York *Times*. From them he gathered—and he saw no reason to disagree—that the National Guard was a negligible factor in future military planning. They reckoned without Generals Martin, Reckord, Walsh and a few other Guard leaders who became available for keeping the torch burning.

All three answered the Call and went into Federal service as commanders of their respective Divisions: Martin of the 28th, Reckord of the 29th and Walsh of the 34th. Reckord and Martin, though past their sixtieth birthdays, proved to be as healthy and hearty as the traditional oak. They were able to laugh at the grim-faced Regular Army Medics who adjusted stethoscopes, thumped chests and scowled knowingly and eagerly at the X-rays of the final type physicals. But it was to General Walsh, 10 years younger, to whom the Medics kept returning.* Their final verdict on General Walsh was disqualification for field command. There was the farewell party in the 34th Division Headquarters at Camp Claiborne, La. Russell P. Hartle, a low-ranking Colonel on the Army's Regular list but recently accorded the temporary rank of Major General, soon arrived as his successor; and an exceptionally fine commander he proved to be. General Walsh could have had administrative duties at a desk and in an assignment suitable. The Chief of Staff, General Marshall, personally urged that he accept such. But Walsh counselled with himself and came to the conclusion that if such was to be his contribution to America's War effort, he could do as much, or more, for the welfare of the Republic as Adjutant General, State of Minnesota, as he could at a desk in Federal service.

Their excellent induction physicals notwithstanding, the age-in-grade directive for field assignment, or overseas service, from the War Department in 1941, lowered the boom on Martin and Reckord. The latter accepted transfer to C.G., Third Corps Area, January 1942. In terms

---

* All officers who went through these physicals will bear witness as to their repetitious thoroughness, which increased with the rank of the examinee. As the saying then went, all Field Grade Guardsmen got the "double whammy" and a star was a guarantee of the "triple treatment." This gave credibility to the idea that the Regular Army Medical Corps, that year before Pearl Harbor, was motivated by the belief that every time they "found" a Guardsman of rank, an opportunity for the promotion of a more deserving professional soldier was being created. The Medical Corps officers justified their unusual thoroughness on the National Guard-fostered law that gave Guardsmen and Reservists, on active duty more than 30 days, the same sickness, disability, hospitalization and death benefits accorded the Regulars of corresponding rank, should the sickness, etc., occur while on that tour of active duty.

of assignment it was a promotion, but it was calculated to keep him on the home front. Then came mounting troubles in England, December 4, 1943, which caused General Marshall to make an exception of his own age-in-grade directive and send Reckord overseas as European Theater Provost Marshal. General Reckord was two years beyond the statutory retirement age, 64, for Regular Army Generals, before the war ended, and General Marshall at last released General Reckord to civil life.

It was much the same story with Edward Martin, the oldest of the three, except that he, like Walsh, declined an Army administrative assignment for the duration to become Governor of Pennsylvania. Moreover, in the last pre-Mobilization Conference of the Guard Association, General Martin had been elected President. It was now 1943 and no successor had been elected. He felt that, as Governor, he could not give the National Guard Association the attention it deserved. Out of Washington, D.C., were coming well-authenticated reports, and from the field many incidents, that clearly showed Lieutenant General Lesley J. McNair, Commanding General, Army Ground Forces, and sundry members of the War Department General Staff, had decided the time was ripe for killing the National Guard so adroitly and thoroughly that not even the traditional *coup de grace* would be necessary.

Against this background, which is more fully set forth in a subsequent chapter, Governor Martin called a conference of available Guard leaders in Harrisburg, Pa., State Capitol, April 1, 1943. Only 16 States and the District of Columbia were represented. Delegates and guests numbered less than 65. The guest list was comparatively modest, compared with prewar years. It primarily consisted of General Reckord (apparently because he was still on active duty and on 48-hour pass from his command Headquarters); the then Major General Lewis B. Hershey, U.S. Army, Director of Selective Service; Brigadier General John McA. Palmer, U.S. Army, recalled from the Retired List to serve as General Marshall's research man and advisor on civilian and military personnel planning;* Brigadier General Miller White, U.S. Army, (G-1, Person-

---

* Gen. Palmer appears in an earlier chapter as the scholarly Regular Army Colonel who handed up the ammunition with which Gen. Pershing and Gen. O'Ryan of New York's 27th Inf. Div., battered-down the War Department General Staff's March-Baker Bill. Palmer then took the stand and fired a few telling salvos of his own. Afterward he was Senior Aide to Gen. Pershing at the time George C. Marshall was Junior Aide. Critical Old Army gossips held that Palmer's job was to keep Black Jack primed on enough history and policy views to commend him as Presidential caliber, should a "draft" for the White House shape-up. Marshall's job was to remember names, faces, incidents back when, where and how, and to "humanize" the austere, erstwhile Commander of the A.E.F. of World War I. Old Army gossips are seldom correct and are always too colorful for historians, but their view is offered here as a within-the-profession compliment to both Palmer and Marshall—two extremely able soldiers, but each in his own way. Actually, there is ample evidence that Gen. Pershing had as little interest in the White House as did Gen. Sherman when he rejected all considerations. Meanwhile, it was Maj. Gen. Leonard Wood who then had the post-World War I Presidential fever.

nel) General Staff; Colonel Walter F. Adams, U.S. Army, Executive Officer, National Guard Bureau, and the Hon. J. Buell Snyder, Chairman, House Subcommittee on Military Appropriations. A Colonel and two Majors from relatively unimportant assignments completed the guest list.

There were justified views with alarm, but the salient result was the thrusting of the Presidency, until the end of the war, upon ex-President Ellard A. Walsh. He accepted upon his own terms. There would be a Washington Headquarters for the Association. There would be a permanent office with secretariat. It would cost money. A spade would be called a spade, and not a gardening instrument. From informal and formal historical sources, there appears to have been no dissent. The Association gave him a blank check on the small funds available and general mandates to proceed in behalf of the Guard.

Few, if any, (most likely not Walsh himself) were prepared for what happened. What really had irked Walsh and aroused his Irish ire was not his physical examination,* as critics in the Regular Army quickly and with malicious logic later assumed, but it was the unnecessary and unjustified abuse the National Guard Battalions, Regiments and Divisions had received from Army Ground Force Headquarters. Moreover, he was convinced the abuse had been fed to the Press through Army Information channels. At the time many officers, Guardsmen and others considered it a mere publicity cover for the chaos through lack of adequate plans for such a Call. The later documented attitudes by General McNair and in his Headquarters did give it a more sinister significance.

But after his assumption of the Presidency, there flowed to General Walsh's desk and over his phone unending complaints of discriminations against Guardsmen in behalf of Regulars, including old Line Sergeants in temporary commissions and Reservists whom Ground Force Headquarters apparently had adopted as their very own, as compared with Guard officers.

In the War Department, Walsh could find no channel for adjudication or even discussion. The "Charter" given the National Guard Bureau in lieu of a National Guard Association-proposed law, had been set aside. The Bureau was transferred to the Service of Supply. Its Chief, Major General John F. Williams, found himself little more than head of a caretaking detachment in charge of National Guard personnel records, sundry out-of-date status reports and thousands of vouchers covering past disbursements, some of which still were unaudited because of the War. No longer was there a direct contact with the Secretary of War as stipulated in the Bureau's Charter. Nor did there appear to be a channel to anyone else.

---

* Now in apparently good health at age 74, Gen. Walsh is a retired resident of Minnesota. Insurance actuarial figures suggest he has outlived the Regular Army Medical Corps Colonels who found him afflicted with an "incurable ailment."

General Walsh spent most of his first year writing his Presidential Report for the May 3-6, 1944, Conference scheduled for Baltimore. In published form (but condensed for reading) it was 145 pages of tightly-printed indictments of the Regular Army "Samurai" who sought self-aggrandizement through vilification, persecution and otherwise down-grading the Guardsmen and their units. Among the 17 guests of the otherwise lightly-attended Conference, the War Department was well represented. The *Proceedings* carried the indictment in full. It was distributed widely within the United States. Within the War Department it was read extensively and with deep concern.

There is evidence that the War Department already had sensed a certain and unwanted political warfare with the Guard, and, persuaded by General Palmer, already had circulated confidential Staff papers re-jecting the philosophy and purposes of the Army Ground Forces Head-quarters under General McNair. Be that as it may, from that day for-ward, the War Department was on the defensive. Oddly enough, how-ever, the great mass of Guardsmen, scattered among the embattled fronts of the Great War, knew nothing of it and heard little of it until during and after September, 1946, in the Buffalo, New York, Conference. With-out so much as reading the Walsh Philippic against America's military caste of "Samurai," they almost unanimously accepted his philosophy and purpose. Nor was this confined to Guardsmen. Throughout America there were tens of thousands of citizen-soldier returnees who had served in embattled Companies, Battalions and Regiments in which there was not a single professional soldier present, enlisted or commissioned. Quite naturally they readily embraced the idea that if battles to save a govern-ment of, for and by the people are to be fought almost exclusively by the amateurish people, then representatives of those people should have a place in the peacetime personnel programming and planning. And, in a nutshell, the Walsh thesis was just that simple. Few, if any, found it necessary to read his brief to arrive at that opinion.

The final outcome is a part of the history of the National Guard's reorganization following World War II. Here it is sufficient to say that General Walsh continued in the Presidency of the Association until 1957. Thanks to his genius for organization and the enthusiasm of Guardsmen returnees, and many former Reserve officers who came into the Guard at this time, by 1949 the National Guard Association of the United States was no longer a small convocation of General Officers and Colonels. It had reached down to include the Company and Battery offi-cers. Only the larger cities had auditoriums large enough to accommo-date the plenary sessions. A flourishing Washington Headquarters had a burgeoning staff. A monthly magazine was being published upon which the Association was able to lose $4,500 that year and still show an organ-izational cash on hand and total net worth of $57,000. As of 1961, the

Association had financed a modest but attractive National Guard Memorial Building, 1 Massachusetts Avenue Northwest, Washington, D.C. It houses the Association Headquarters and library. The Association's audited net worth was just short of a million dollars. This growth is mute testimony of the loyalty, confidence and continuing volunteer spirit of the modern National Guard officers throughout America. Major General William H. Harrison, Jr., Massachusetts, has been President since 1957. He and his staff continue the traditions and objectives of the founders.

Such success and solidarity of purpose demonstrated by the Guardsmen naturally have stimulated some flattering imitation and the inevitable, cynical critcism. Be that as it may, the National Guard spokesmen and their predecessors in the Association, beginning in 1876, appear to be the first Americans who, in pride of voluntary military service to the Nation, have lobbied so long and vigorously to guarantee their being among the first on the front line against a foreign foe. It is not a minor distinction.

# Bibliographical Note For Chapter XIV

The only exhaustive bibliography on the National Guard Association of the United States is contained in a Ph.D. thesis, Harvard, 1961, by Dr. Martha Derthick. Her work is highly pertinent to this chapter, but is hardly a history in that it is a political science study, largely concerned with the National Guard Association as a single-purpose organization with a legislative program. She was not interested in the National Guard as a defense institution or even the National Guard Association as a public-spirited organization sustaining traditions of service to the Nation and a continuance of a volunteer, avocational, semi-professional military force. Her findings and views are narrowly restricted to politics, legislation and associational methodology incident thereto. Within these limits she demonstrated herself to be a tireless researcher and generated some penetrating if provocative opinions. The *Proceedings* of the National Guard Association's conventions and conferences (the terms are used interchangeably) are the primary sources in Dr. Derthick's study, and in this chapter. No complete, non-broken file is available. The nearest approach thereto is in the Headquarters of the National Guard Association, 1 Massachusetts Avenue N.W., Washington, D.C. An almost equally complete file is available in the Wisconsin State Historical Library, Madison. Most large libraries and depositories have rather complete holdings beginning about 1940. Available in Washington, D.C., are *Proceedings* for 1879, 1881, 1897, 1903-15, 1917-19, 1922-24; 1926 (there being two conventions in that year and none in 1925); 1927-40; and 1943 to present date without hiatus. Conventions or conferences appear to have been held in 1884, 1885, 1890, and

1902, with the possibility of a few in other years, but, if so, they have not been dignified by existing formal records. A bound scrapbook of newspaper clippings and sundry manuscripts, kept by Gen. George W. Wingate, supplements extant *Proceedings* through 1890. The National Guard Association of the United States also has published a monthly magazine, *The National Guardsman,* without interruption since 1947. The Association also has published an attractive and informative work, *The Nation's Nation Guard,* 1954, the principal text of which consists of War College addresses by Maj. Gens. Ellard A. Walsh and Edgar C. Erickson. Dabney H. Maury, Maj. Gen., C.S.A., *Recollections of a Virginian, 1894,* touches lightly upon the organization of the Guard Association. Some contemporary magazine articles contribute more than passing bits of information and evidence of views held by Guard spokesmen. Major W. Boerum Wetmore, "The National Guard Bill in Congress," *United Service,* Vol. VI, (1882) pp. 337-42, is most important. Major Wetmore, West Point, 1867, was in the New York National Guard and for a time was the Association's Corresponding Secretary. Views of early spokesmen for the Guard, prior to World War I, are rather well reflected in a few articles in semi-official periodicals as well as in general interest magazines such as the *Nineteenth Century* and *Forum.* Maj. Gen. George W. Wingate, "Army Organization," *Journal of the Military Institution,* Vol. XV, (1894) p. 119; Lloyd S. Bryce, "A Service of Love," *North American Review,* Vol. CXI, (1887) p. 285; A. W. A. Pollock, "The National Guard: A Hint to the United States," *Nineteenth Century,* Vol. XVI, (1909) pp. 910-20; Theophilus F. Rodenbough, "The Militia of the United States," *United Service,* Vol. XI, (1897) pp. 283-89, and the same author, "Militia Reform Without Legislation," *Journal of the Military Institution,* Vol. II, (1881) pp. 388-420, are such sources. No National Guard leaders were consulted or interviewed incident to this chapter. The author became acquainted with most of them during and after World War II. Dates and personal statistics concerning those mentioned are from the conventional sources such as *Who's Who in America* and the *Official National Guard Register,* Department of the Army. The author has sought to abstain from personal opinion as to men and issues and to include only facts of record and the pertinent opinions of others that can be documented. The historical interpretations are, of course, those of the author. They are a right and a duty of all historians, handed down by Thucydides from the Peloponnesian War.

CHAPTER XV

# Between The Wars

IN THE IMMEDIATE, postwar hearings and debates incident to the passage of the National Defense Act of 1920, there was general agreement that America should have a strong Army. The concepts of being "too proud to fight" and living in "splendid isolation" had not worked. In its final form, the military legislation contemplated a highly-competent professional Regular Army of approximately 300,000; i.e., 17,700 officers and 280,000 men including the Philippine Scouts. The National Guard, with 60 drill periods a year and 15-days Summer field camp, was to number 486,000. The Reserve Corps, of as many as would volunteer, was to provide a vast source of officers and enlisted men. These veterans and trainees from World War I would bring to war strength all units of the Regular Army, with enough remaining to provide Regimental and Divisional cadres to train and lead future Draftees, should an all-out military effort be required. Officer replacements were to come from college R.O.T.C. units and from Citizens Military Training Camps.

With nearly 800,000 Regulars and Guardsmen organized into functional units and fully-armed with World War I surplus equipment, not only could America adequately defend the land frontiers, but a punitive expedition could readily be mounted in sufficient strength to help World War I allies police the World and thereby make the scheme of things safe for Democracy.

But out of the mass disillusionment that came out of the peace negotiations, America had a sudden change of mind. There was an emphatic balk on joining a League of Nations. Did America have an obligation, through a so-called League of Nations, to police an evil, avaricious Old World? America's future was in the bright, new, Western Hemisphere. "Splendid Isolation" appeared to be more splendid than ever. Pacifism through "disarmament" (euphony for arms limitations) offered both a philosophy and an idealistic implementation for a "spiritual triumph" over evils in the Old World and for rectification, by example, of any despotic evils that might be thriving in Central America and the Caribbean. Hand-in-hand with these blue-sky dreams came a most natural urge toward retrenchment in expenditures, for a return to an economic "normalcy." In short, successive sessions, Congress voted sufficient funds for neither a Regular Army of the proposed size, nor for National Guard units in adequate number or size to approximate the proposed manpower figures. The promised 60 drills a year soon became a myth. In practice the number leveled-off at 48 for the greatly-reduced Guard that did emerge from the hardly-ambitious intentions.

## RECESSION FROM WORLD WAR I

Because of these economies and the new philosophy of Pacifistic isolation and arms limitations, instead of the Regular Army going upward to nearly 300,000 from its 1920 strength of 200,367, it rapidly slumped to 134,624 in 1925. America's military posture through these drab years of Pacifistic idealism and unrealistic follies can be most briefly revealed by a short table of statistics.

| June 30 | Regular Army Strengths Total | National Guard Strengths Total | Reserve Corps Strengths Total | Total Military Expenditures | Federal Appropriations To The National Guard |
|---|---|---|---|---|---|
| 1920 | 200,367 | 56,090 | 107,083 | $1,610,587,381 | $13,177,750 |
| 1925 | 134,624 | 177,525 | 94,013 | 254,914,783 | 31,104,642 |
| 1930 | 137,472 | 182,715 | 106,638 | 323,291,496 | 32,619,798 |
| 1935 | 137,960 | 185,915 | 116,913 | 268,619,653 | 29,527,575 |
| 1936 | 166,114 | 189,173 | 119,066 | 377,345,249 | 34,130,866 |
| 1937 | 178,101 | 192,161 | 114,358 | 352,734,943 | 38,004,559 |
| 1938 | 183,447 | 197,188 | 116,175 | 416,529,159 | 41,109,187 |
| 1939 | 187,886 | 199,491 | 119,773 | 435,634,219 | 43,477,133 |

The above War Department expenditures, exclusive of 1920, represent actual disbursements for military purposes. They do not include outlays for rivers, harbors and other non-military purposes for which the War Department was responsible.

Note that the column for National Guard is *appropriations* rather than actual expenditures, largely because such figures reveal in full the degree of responsibility for the Guard the Federal Government was willing to assume. Actual disbursements were $100,000 or more, annually, less than appropriations. The dollar expenditure figures for the Guard are included in the total expenditures column. No breakdown was obtained differentiating between Regular Army costs and expenditures on the Reserves. Note that Federal funds appropriated to the Guard were 10 to 12% of the total military expenditures for the typical Fiscal Year. In 1936, the year the figures first took an upward trend, but with little increase in Guard strength, the average per capita cost, in Federal tax dollars, all disbursements across-the-board, for the 189,173 Guardsmen, was only $180. Of course, the Guardsman was the beneficiary of some State tax dollars, local donations, occasional endowments, donations, benefit functions and at times local tax funds. An effort to ascertain a comparable figure of per capita costs per year from non-Federal funds quickly becomes a statistical game that is hardly worth the candle. Getting State budgets and local receipts and expenditures on a common denominator for States and units would be an unending task. From sampling a few States and local units, a non-Federal per capita cost of $80 per Guardsman as an average throughout the United States is offered as a more-or-less educated guess.

In any event, it is doubtful if modern, Twentieth Century America ever has received so much civic-minded, voluntarily-organized, military manpower at such little expense in time of peace. It is admitted readily that New York's General Nicholas Herkimer and Vermont's General John Stark achieved a greater fiscal miracle when they put their National Guardsmen, or Organized Militiamen, on the battle lines at Oriskaney and Bennington, with the requirement that each man provide his own rifle, complete with personally-owned balls, powder and expendable flints. But that was war, with Burgoyne's Red Indians and Red Coats ravaging the frontier!

## MILITARY LOW TIDE

But through the Twittering 'Twenties and the Thrifty 'Thirties of this Century, a man had to have a degree of dedication to and an inborn belief in the need for such service or he could not have been a good Regular, Guardsman or Reservist. The tide of opinion was against the Military. Pay and allowances were exemplars of parsimony. For the Regular Army to achieve its 1936 enlisted level of 147,103 Americans and

6,386 enlisted Philippine Scouts, it was necessary to recruit and reenlist 77,397 men. Of these, 46,906 were original enlistments of raw recruits, 4,242 were prior service men, and only 26,249 were reenlistments. For the Regulars, the economic Depression had blown a few favorable winds. The curse of the one-year enlistments, of which there had been an astounding 34,381 in the rising economic tide of 1923, had declined to only 299 in 1936. The Army, by 1936, was once again a three-year institution for the enlisted personnel, thanks to hard times. Moreover, losses by desertion in 1936 were down to a comparatively modest 3,556 among the American Regiments, and only one deserter from the Philippine Scouts.*

Compared with the enlisted turnover, the Regular officer corps of these two decades represented a truly dedicated group of well-educated men; particularly when one considers the many, far more favorable opportunities most of them had rejected during the prosperous and flourishing 10 years immediately following World War I. The officer list included scores of West Pointers who served as Lieutenants for 17 years. There were also a few thousand graying Captains who began wearing the bars of a Company-grade officer in 1917-18 but who were to wait until 1935-40 before savoring the minimum field grade perquisites inherent in a permanent oak leaf—with a tincture of gold. At Fort Leavenworth, Spring of 1940, the 'teen-age son of a well-matured Captain returned from school much depressed and upset. His sad-eyed explanation: "The teacher says Dad's name is on the next Promotion List. He can't be a Captain and command a Battery any more. From now on he can't be anything but a damned, frosty, old Major."

Notwithstanding the slow promotion lists that had been stagnated by the heavy hand of seniority to the grade of Colonel (with that rank the normal, eligibility requirement for selection to Brigadier General), the officer corps of the Regular Army stayed rather closely to the annually budgeted strengths of 12 to 13 thousand. From the 12,036 officers with which the Fiscal Year 1935-36 started, there was an attrition of only 316 officers. Of these, 220 were lost by retirement, 18 resigned, one was discharged, one was "dropped," four were dismissed, 39 died from illnesses, 25 were killed in accidents and eight committed suicide. Replacement of Line officers was by commissioning new Second Lieutenants from that year's graduating West Point class. Doctors, Dentists, Chaplains and

---

* The Philippine Scouts are not to be confused with the Philippine Constabulary, an arm of the civil government as well as a quasi-military organization originally officered by American soldiers, most of whom, who so desired, had been integrated into the Regular Army by 1923, as replacements by Philippine officers became available. The Scouts and the Constabulary are the parent organizations of the present Regular Army of the Republic of the Philippines.

other specialists in the "Non-Promotion List Services" * were appointed direct from civil life. Such new appointments raised the Regular Officer Corps to 12,125, as of June 30, 1936.

Between 1940 and 1945, America was to become deeply indebted to these 12 to 13 thousand Regular officers. They and the avocational National Guard and Reserve officer enthusiasts provided the Field Grade and higher leadership for America's ground forces through all the bitter land fighting between the Elbe in central Europe and Papua to Tokyo in the far-distant reaches of the misnamed Pacific. It was natural that the Regulars were found most frequently in key Staff positions of the higher Headquarters in Washington, for Theaters of War, Army Groups and Armies.

## THE OFFICERS RESERVE CORPS

The Reserve Corps, throughout the two decades of the above abbreviated table of strengths and military price tags, was referred to most frequently, officially and otherwise, as the Officers Reserve Corps. That is exactly what it was. Admittedly there were in 1936, to continue the same statistical year, 3,897 Enlisted Reservists in the 119,066 included in the table. These few Enlisted Reservists were not, however, armed or equipped or otherwise organized into functional units. For the most part they were minimum service-time, enlisted retirees from Regular Army noncommissioned grades on whom there continued to be a recall obligation. The remaining 115,169 Reservists were commissioned officers. Only 12 to 15% of them had an unbroken and continuing military status from World War I. For the most part they were young men in Company officer grades, more-or-less recently from college and university R.O.T.C. units and Citizens Military Training Camps, with the former source greatly predominating.

The Reserve officer lists were sub-divided further into two separate groups: (a) those assignable in time of peace for two or more weeks of Summer training, usually with Regular formations, or grouped into officer schools at sundry Army Posts, or given duty as instructors at Citizens Military Training Camps, and (b) those Reserve officers who were "nonassignable." A Reserve officer moved from an assignable status to nonassignable when he had gone five years without doing 200 hours of Army extension courses in correspondence courses appropriate to his grade, or who had failed to do at least two tours of 15 days each in one of the forms of active duty training described above for officers in

---

* This official term was a misnomer. Promotions were available on time-in-grade basis, but with ceilings beyond which one could not be promoted. Line officers on the Seniority Promotion List could rise higher, but through this era rose more slowly to the grade of Colonel on the official Promotion List than did specialists on the Non-Promotion List.

the assignable status. Five additional years in a nonassignable status and he was dropped automatically from the Officers Reserve Corps. On the other hand, as soon as he might, within the five years on the non-assignable list, make up his deficit in active duty and/or home study courses by additional correspondence courses, he was returned to the list of Reserve officers assignable to active duty for training.

In 1936 the Officers Reserve Corps included one Major General. He was assignable. But of the 30 Brigadier Generals, only 14 were assignable The assignable list, for example, included the highly active and distinguished Brigadier General Leigh R. Gignilliat, for many years Superintendent of Culver Military Academy. Old Culver men still identify one another by whether the stranger correctly pronounces the Superintendent's name.

Of 1,085 Reserve Colonels, only 691 were assignable. Only 2,109 of the 2,941 Lieutenant Colonels were eligible for training tour orders and the same was true of no more than 4,726 of the 6,480 Majors. Company-grade officers had a better score: Captains, 12,680 out of 15,430; First Lieutenants were best of all with 34,796 out of 39,204; and of Second Lieutenants there were available for assignment 40,602 out of 49,998. In summary, there were 115,169 Reserve officers, about 12% of whom were above the grade of Captain. Moreover, of the entire total, no less than 19,550 had given insufficient evidence of interest to remain eligible for Summer training in minimum dosages of only 15 days for two out of five Summers.

At Reserve Officer Association meetings through this era, the complaint frequently was voiced that rank-envious Regulars on the General Staff Eligibility Lists, who ran the details of the Reserve program from their assignments to the War Department and the nine Corps Area Headquarters, were trying to cancel-out as many Field Grade and General Officers by deliberate withholding of training opportunities to the higher grades. Moreover, for Field Grades the validating correspondence courses were far more time-consuming and frequently most difficult to arrange, it was alleged. The objective of the General Staff, some senior Reservists argued, was to reduce the Officer Reserve Corps to a great availability pool of Captains and Lieutenants, thereby making sure of immediate Field Grade opportunities to deserving Regulars should a major mobilization occur. The statistical trends through this era give some credence to the complaint and the charge. But there appears to be no conclusive proof. Moreover, advancing years and increasing civilian responsibilities naturally diminished the avocational military enthusiasms and time availability of many older and higher-ranking Reserve officers.

At the same time, it is remarkable that such high percentages of officers, most of them proud veterans from World War I, would nurse their military enthusiasms to Lieutenant Colonelcies, Colonelcies, and Brigadier Generalcies, and then quietly lapse their commissions when apparently so little was required of them to retain an assignable status. Indeed, some of them were not so quiet about it. It was from these grades that most of the complaints and charges were made. They noted with rising concern a lack of training assignment slots above Company and Battery levels. In 1936, of the 22,175 Reserve officers who received 15-day, or longer, tours, one was a Brigadier and only 218 were Colonels. Of the 543 who had longer tours, only 38 were above the rank of Captain. Ten of the 38 were student officers in the Command and General Staff College. Thus the statistics tend to sustain the complaint.

## DISTRIBUTION OF THE FORCES

As rapidly as it became apparent in the bright new World of post-war hopes and idealisms that the Military was to be sacrificed upon the twin altars of Pacifism and parsimony, War Department General Staff planners ran through a series of improvisations calculated to adjust the situation and at the same time provide the framework of another A.E.F., should there ever be a repetition of World War I. The problem was to get the largest potential from the available men and money. World War I stocks seemed sufficient to solve the equipment problem for the time being. Costs of storage and wastage from non-use largely nullified this dream, but there remained a broad horizon for numerous units. Planning was big indeed, with the result that both the Regular Army and National Guard formations became rather thinly-spread and with barely enough authorized strength to keep units in being. Many Regular Army units went out of existence. Others became little more than administrative and caretaking cadres.

Within this concept it naturally followed that each of the nine Corps Areas in the Continental United States should have the framework of units in being and cadres whence would be created quickly one war-strength Regular Army Infantry Division, and two war-strength National Guard Infantry Divisions, for a quick total of 27 Divisions soon after M-Day. Of course, within the Continental United States and distributed among the nine Corps Areas, there would be the necessarily prompt makings of two Regular Army Cavalry Divisions; an adequate, if small, essential GHQ Reserve, harbor defense troops, and a proportion of the necessary Communications Zone and Zone of the Interior Service of Supply and other support units. The Officers Reserve Corps and a Draft machinery from a compulsory service law, in the face of the approaching danger, would be expected to provide the major man-power portion of these non-divisional elements, many of which could be delayed until as late as M + 4 months. At the same time, there would be prorated among the nine Corps Areas sufficient National Guard Cavalry units to constitute four mounted Divisions, plus Corps Artillery, a small contribution to an early GHQ Reserve, and a maximum of the harbor defense Artillerymen and supporting coastal defense troops.

Such an ambitious scheme of things placed unprecedented burdens upon both the Regular Army and the National Guard. It represented a most amazing but apparently necessary dispersal of effort. For example, the commander of the I Corps Area, consisting of the six New England States, with Headquarters at Boston, had only 153 Regular officers, 49 warrant officers and 4,769 enlisted men, with which to meet his responsibilities. Only in the sense that they were thinly distributed among every Arm and Service known to ground and air could one think of them as the nucleus of a Regular Army Division. A Squadron Headquarters and two Troops of Cavalry were the associated Arm for four motorized Batteries of light Artillery at Fort Ethan Allen. A Regiment of two abbreviated Battalions of Infantry was divided between Forts Devens and Adams. The former Post also had two or three Companies of light tanks. Another abbreviated Regiment of Infantry was scattered along the coast of Maine, some of it in harbor defense assignments. A coast defense Brigade "garrisoned" 23 harbor defense installations with little more than caretaking detachments. A few additional coast defense forts simply were listed "not garrisoned." For this far-flung, thinly-manned empire, the C.G., I Army Corps Area, had to provide the essential detachments of Signal, Ordnance, Finance, Medical, Veterinary, Quartermaster, Engineer supplies and services, not to mention the Port of Boston and Corps Area Headquarters overhead, similar overhead of the many lesser Headquarters, recruiting stations all over New England and the Air Corps Detachment at Boston Airport.

When one visualizes less than 5,000 officers and men deployed over such an area and scattered through so many installations, urban, rural and coastal, meeting so many static and/or non-combatant responsibilities, he readily realizes that any potential the I Corps Area Commander had for turning out a war strength, functional, M-Day, Regular Army Division was strictly on paper rather than *de facto*. Army planning or talk of an early-ready Regular Army Division from such meager and miscellaneous personnel so thinly deployed was an indulgence in fanciful daydreams. The fielding of two reinforced National Guard Divisions, equipped and functional in the field by M + 1 month, was easily within his capabilities. They were the 26th Division, entirely from Massachusetts, and the 43rd, composed of units from the remaining five New England States.

Pursuant to the ultimate objective of three early-ready Divisions from each of the Corps Areas, backed-up by a reasonable ratio of non-divisional combat units to insure a balanced and powerful force, the 27th and 44th Infantry Divisions became the major units in being within the II Corps Area. The States within this command were New York, New Jersey and Delaware. From his Headquarters on Governor's Island, New York Harbor, the C.G. of this command in 1936 wrote orders for the 15,822 officers and men of the Regular Army within these States. They were scattered from Fort Dix to Plattsburg and Niagara, with the great majority pinned-down in the Second Coast Artillery District, Brooklyn Port of Embarkation, and within the New York City complex. Their potential for the creation of a Regular Army Division was as little as that of the Regular troops in the I Corps Area.

From a Regular Army viewpoint, essentially the same problems prevailed in the III Corps Area, which consisted of Pennsylvania, Maryland and Virginia, and the District of Columbia. The presence of the Nation's Capital in the middle of his command did not simplify the problem of the Regular Army General commanding the III Corps Area from Baltimore. He, too, had myriads of coastal Batteries, Anti-aircraft installations and old, historic Army Posts for which the house-keeping was interminable. They absorbed his 14,468 Regulars. Thus, faced by a sudden mobilization, the only two Divisions of functional formations he could put on the line immediately were his two National Guard Divisions, the 28th of Pennsylvania and the 29th of Virginia, Pennsylvania, District of Columbia and Maryland.

The IV Corps Area was composed of the two Carolinas, Tennessee, Arkansas, Georgia, Florida, Alabama, Mississippi and Louisiana. Since this vast domain was comparatively removed from the heart of the Nation, and had a coastline of shallow harbors and off-shore sand bars, its Commanding General normally was assigned as many, or more, Regulars than in any of the Atlantic Corps Areas. In 1936 there were 16,515 Regulars assigned, but they were divided as elsewhere among under-strength units, caretakers and custodians, service units and Head-quarters personnel. There were at Fort Benning, near Columbus, Georgia, two most impressive demonstration Battalions. They were part of the Infantry School troops. Their units were maintained at full war strength. They were probably the only fully-equipped, war-strength, firing units in the entire United States Army. Excellent though these Battalions were, they fell far short of being a Division. Thus the commander of the IV Corps Area primarily had at his disposal, come a major emergency, the conventional two National Guard Divisions, assigned to be recruited, organized and created within the above-listed States. The 30th Infantry Division (National Guard) was composed of units from Georgia, Tennessee, North Carolina, and South Carolina. The 31st Infantry Division (National Guard) was composed of units from Alabama, Florida, Mississippi, Louisiana and Tennessee.

Ohio, West Virginia, Kentucky and Indiana were grouped together to constitute the V Corps Area, with Headquarters at Indianapolis. With reference to the troops from which could be created a Regular Army Division, the situation in these four States was little different from what has been noted elsewhere. The V Corps Area commander seldom had more than 6,000 to 8,000 men (6,783 in 1936) for the administrative work, training cadres, recruiting stations and house-keeping in his comparatively large and populous empire. At Fort Knox, Kentucky, despite the blue grass and horses, was stationed the Army's first Regiment of Mechanized Cavalry, which Douglas MacArthur, as Chief of Staff, 1930-35, had insisted upon. It was being expanded into an experimental Armored Brigade. It was the Army's first low rumble of modernity. Once again, the only Divisions actually in being were the 37th from Ohio and the 38th from Indiana, West Virginia and Kentucky.

## DISHEARTENING CONDITIONS IN REGULAR FORMATIONS

The VI Corps Area consisted of the States of Michigan, Wisconsin and Illinois, and Jefferson Barracks, just West of the river in Missouri, with Headquarters in Chicago. Though Chicago was the Nation's second largest City, this command in the heart of the Continent, with comparatively few Army Posts and installations, likewise was considered of lesser importance. The C.G. in Chicago seldom had more than the 7,563 officers and men assigned from the Regulars in 1936. Accordingly, in the VI Corps Area, it was the same old story, of administration, housekeeping, custodial responsibility and some Summer training, always coordinated with the National Guard and the Reserves. In 1927-28, when the author was briefly in training at Fort Sheridan, the Infantry component of the "garrison" consisted of a Regimental Headquarters Detachment, in lieu of a Company, and a Battalion of the 2nd Infantry Regiment. The remaining units of the Regiment were in Upper and Lower Michigan. Two-thirds of the Howitzer Company were on paper. One-third of the Machine Gun Company and of each of the Rifle Companies were non-extant except for more paper. Post guard details, rifle range detachments, absences with leave, kitchens, quarters, stables for draft animals and mounts for Field and Staff, along with grass-cutting, absorbed so many men that the personnel available from the entire Post for a formal Retreat formation seldom reached the equivalent of a war-strength Platoon. Turning out a first-class, full-size honor guard for a Cabinet-level V.I.P. required drastic orders and little less than heroic effort.

An Infantry Regimental tactical exercise staged for the final "dry run" for the tactical inspection of that year would have been farcical to the point of mirth, had it not been so dishearteningly pathetic. In those days the principal military activity around Fort Sheridan seemed to be the constant sitting of a court-martial for the trial of deserters from all over the United States who were apprehended in Chicago by City police (reward about $50 per arrest resulting in conviction) and maintaining an extremely well-conducted guardhouse. It had to be good. It was the receiving station for such deserters until trial and a departure point to the Disciplinary Barracks for those who were convicted and given the usual short-term "imprisonment and a bobtail discharge."

It would not be so bad could one report that the proud, old 2nd Infantry Regiment was abnormally emaciated, but such would be untrue. Twenty-six of the Regular Army's 65 Infantry Regiments had been deactivated entirely by 1923. Thus were cancelled-out, until the eve of World War II, all those numbered higher than the 31st Infantry except the "native Regiments," composed of Philippine Scouts, and the 65th Infantry, recruited entirely, except officers from the Continental U.S., in Puerto Rico. In time, 14 of the remaining 38 Regiments were cut to two Battalions each. "Nor was the whole reduction yet complete," to quote *The Army Lineage Book: Infantry*. "Next it was necessary to modify the tables of organization so that in peacetime all but two regiments had headquarters detachments instead of companies, while only one had a howitzer company, the rest having howitzer platoons. Also rifle and machine gun companies had two instead of three platoons. Thus reduced, they were hard pressed to turn out one warstrength platoon for purposes of training." Other combatant Arms—Artillery, Cavalry, Engineers, etc.—likewise had suffered, but this brief overview of Infantry is offered because this Arm normally constitutes 50% of the thoroughly-disciplined and trained cutting edge of an army. But in the drab two decades between the wars, it sank to slightly less than 25% of the manpower in America's Regular Army.

Thus the situation in the VI Corps Area with reference to the combatant formations assigned to it was not materially different from elsewhere within the Continental United States. For a balanced force of combatant units, the C.G. of the VI Corps Area was almost entirely dependent upon the capabilities of the 32nd Division, National Guard (Michigan and Wisconsin) and the 33rd Division, entirely from Illinois. As in most other Corps Areas, there were some non-divisional National Guard units that will be reviewed later.

The VII Corps Area was commanded from the Major General's Headquarters in Omaha. It consisted of the two Dakotas, Minnesota,

Iowa, Missouri, Nebraska and Kansas. This large inland area had no hostile frontiers, but it was dotted with traditional and historic Army Posts from Indian days, such as Fort Leavenworth, Fort Des Moines, Fort Snelling, Fort Crook and Fort Riley. Those responsible for Regular Army manpower in Washington normally felt that 10,000 Regulars were adequate for this command. In 1936, 9,968 were so assigned. Their duties and composition were essentially no different from those discussed elsewhere. The Corps Area did contain two significant Army posts. The Cavalry School (horse) at Fort Riley was the mounted counterpart to the Infantry School at Fort Benning. The Command and General Staff School at Fort Leavenworth was becoming famous in military circles throughout the World as the Western Hemisphere's equivalent to the English Staff College at Camberley, the French Ecole de Guerre, and the German General Staff College,. The operation of these schools, however, was like that at Fort Benning. They were under command of Brigadier Generals who were directly responsible to the Operations Section of the War Department for their teachings, techniques and doctrines. Administrative and supply details, however, came under the Corps Area Commander.

Accordingly, except for the school troops at Fort Riley, the most significant formations at the disposal of the VII Corps Area Commander were the 34th Division, composed of Regiments, Battalions, Batteries and Companies of Iowa, Minnesota, North Dakota and South Dakota, and the 35th Division, likewise composed of the National Guard units of Nebraska, Kansas and Missouri.

The 36th (Texas) and 45th (Oklahoma, Colorado, New Mexico, Arizona) National Guard Infantry Divisions were organized and functional in the VIII Corps Area, which consisted of the above parenthetically-mentioned States. A thin bite of Wyoming, to include Fort Francis E. Warren, was also a part of the VIII Corps Area. With reference to Regular Army troops, the VIII Corps Area was distinctly different from the other commands. With a jaundiced eye toward still-turbulent Mexico, the famous 2nd Infantry Division (less one reinforced Infantry Brigade garrisoning Fort Francis E. Warren) was stationed at Fort Sam Houston, San Antonio, Texas. As elsewhere, its Regiments, Batteries and Companies were bobtailed with paper Battalions and Platoons, and with units in being functional but sadly understrength. Likewise, the Regular Army's 1st Cavalry Division (horse) was kept at weak but functional strength at Fort Bliss and in satellite Posts along the Rio Grande to Brownsville. Its two Brigades of two mounted Regiments, each with light Artillery, were indeed a thin cordon.

But since the VIII Corps Area included the Army's only two continental Divisions, it was considered the most important field command available to a Major General, Regular Army, of that era. In addition to his National Guard component and Reserve officer training activities, he normally commanded 25,000 to 30,000 Regular Army troops, most of them in functional, tactical formations. In 1936 VIII Corps Area Regular Army rosters totalled 27,237 officers and men.

The States of California, Nevada, Utah, Wyoming, Idaho, Oregon, Washington and Montana constituted the IX Corps Area with Headquarters at San Francisco. With the far-flung coastal installation and mountainous distances, the Commanding General of this largest of the Corps Areas, in 1936, was assigned 15,932 Regulars. Once again he was unable to organize them into a semblance of a functional Division. His main reliance rested upon two National Guard Divisions, the 40th, from California, Nevada and Utah, and the 41st, composed of volunteer citizen-soldiers from Washington, Oregon, Wyoming, Montana and Idaho. Alaska, which was attached to the IX Corps Area, was considered of little military significance during the two decades between the two World Wars. Of Regulars, it rated only 11 officers and 378 enlisted men, many of them Signal Corpsmen, for communications that were not commercially feasible. Alaska had no National Guard units until the end of this era.

## OVERSEAS TROOPS

During these two decades between the World Wars America's heaviest military commitment beyond the continental limits of the United States was to Hawaii. Following Japanese aggression against China, Hawaii rapidly became America's most important off-shore bastion. In authority and importance it was considered second only to the VIII Corps Area, and as tensions mounted and the situation in Mexico quieted-down, the command of the Hawaiian Division came to be considered even more important than that of the VIII Corps Area. Army troops in Hawaii as of 1936 totalled 18,702. They were organized into the defensive-type "Square" Division, that was further reinforced by coastal defense Batteries, air Squadrons, Marines at the Naval Base, and other defense agencies in the Islands. Actually the defensive forces were concentrated on Oahu. The defense of the other islands, it was considered, depended upon seapower. This in turn depended upon Honolulu and Pearl Harbor always being firmly within the American grasp. Of National Guard units, the Hawaiian Department Commander could integrate but two Territorial National Guard Infantry Regiments with his defense plans. Their initial missions were anti-sabotage and internal security.

A comparable task force, and considered but slightly less important than that in Hawaii, was organized into a defensive garrison of the Panama Canal Zone. Defense of the Canal was the joint responsibility of the Army and Navy, the latter providing the air units for the Army task force of 12,759 Regular officers and men stationed in the Zone, 1936. There were constant maneuvers by the Infantry and light Artillery elements of this task force to control the jungle approaches to Panama and at the same time man the enormous coastal Batteries, which included 16-inch guns, largest that the American Army ever has emplaced in a static position. Also at top priority for the troops at the Panama Canal was internal security against acts of sabotage by a hostile power.

In the Philippines, since America was already committed to curtailment of empire by promised independence, the importance of this command had declined steadily following World War I. As late as 1939 the Regular Army commitment to the Philippines was only 4,514 American officers and men. Army Air Corps Squadrons, Coast Artillery, and service units accounted for most of them. The principal Infantry force in the islands was the Philippine Scouts, which numbered that year 6,406 officers and men for a U.S. Regular Army total of 10,920—substantially the same as for 1936. The defense plans were coordinated with the Philippine Constabulary and the fast-growing Philippine Army, looking toward independence. General Douglas MacArthur (Retired) went from his tour as Chief of Staff, U.S. Army, to serve the Commonwealth as Field Marshal and director and organizer of the dominion's little burgeoning Army for two years beginning in 1935. He was not called from retirement until 1941.

The Puerto Rico Regiment (65th Infantry) of 800 to 900 officers and men was the Army's garrison for that island. It was matched, in 1936, by one Regiment and one Battalion of Puerto Rico National Guard Infantry. In Tientsin, China, through this period, the storied 15th ("Can Do") U.S. Infantry sustained a mission that dated from the Boxer Rebellion. In 1936 this show-piece Regiment numbered only 841 officers and men. To keep its units in being at functional field strength, the 15th Infantry's 1st Battalion and Rifle Companies G and L of the two remaining actual Battalions were non-extant, in that they were carried on paper only.

From the foregoing it is seen readily that economies between the wars burdened the Regular Army with so many housekeeping, administrative, training and Army school responsibilities, that all the ambitious planning notwithstanding, there was no Regular Army striking force larger than the VIII Corps Area's under-strength 2nd Infantry Division, divided between Texas and Wyoming, plus the Regular Army's far-flung (El Paso to Brownsville) 1st Cavalry Division. Otherwise, commitments at home and overseas were strictly of an administrative, custodial, small training cadres and garrison character. For all practical purposes the organized and equipped ground forces of the United States between the wars were vested largely in 18 National Guard Infantry Divisions, two in each Corps Area, and in four National Guard Cavalry (horse) Divisions.

## ARMY AREAS AND CORPS TROOPS

It will be recalled also that the National Guard was expected further to provide sundry units of Corps Troops, Harbor Defense troops, and some General Headquarters Reserves. That is where the Cavalry Divisions came into the picture. Since the Infantry Divisions had top priority, the Cavalry units and non-divisional Regiments, Battalions and Company-size units for the Corps Troops and the General Headquarters Reserve were, for the most part, organized after the National Guard Divisions progressed well toward completion in the early '20's.

In the same way that a Field Army Corps, with supporting troops, could be organized from two or more, but usually at least three Divisions, a Field Army could be organized from two or more Army Corps, with additional Army supporting troops. Inasmuch as at least Nine Army Corps were anticipated from the nine Corps Areas of the Continental United States, each with at least two functional National Guard Divisions immediately available, it was natural that in the light of World War I experiences plans should be made for Field Armies.*

In line with this thinking, I, II, and III Corps Areas were termed the First Army Area; V and VI Corps Areas, the Second Army Area; IV and VIII Corps Areas, the Third Army Area; and VII and IX became the Fourth Army Area. It was not until the eve of World War II that actual Feld Army Headquarters were created. Normally, one of the Corps Area commanders in each of the four Army Areas was assigned the more-or-less mythical duties of Army Commander in addition to responsibilities of himself and Staff for their Corps Area. This "doubling in brass" for at least four of the Corps Area Commanders did not end until after 1940. Nevertheless, the organizing of non-divisional combat units of National Guardsmen to give depth and substance to Army Corps and Field Armies almost kept pace with the creation of National Guard Infantry Divisions.

Within the Army and Corps combat and support units there was considerable shifting about, redesignation and reequipping of Battalions, Regiments and even Brigades of National Guard formations, as various plans were made and modified. At the end of the 20 years between the wars the National Guard's four horse Cavalry Divisions, and sundry other combatant formations, had become categorized as General Headquarters Reserves. A brief listing and characterization of the major

---

* Pre-1940 planning in detail and units did not progress to the next higher field commands to include Army Groups and Theaters of Operations. At such high levels of field command, the administration and tactical military cloth must be tailored to fit the scope of the operations and the nature of the embattled Theater.

units of the G.H.Q. Reserves and designated Corps troops are essential to an appreciation of the National Guard just prior to the Mobilization Call of 1940-41.

The National Guard Cavalry Divisions were the 21st, 22nd, 23rd and 24th. Two of the four were for years without a Division Headquarters. Some were similarly short organic supporting units, such as Quartermaster Squadrons. Complete organization was authorized as hostilities erupted in Europe, Summer of 1939. By Autumn, 1940, they were quite complete except for the usual, low authorized strengths for Troop- and Battery-size units. The eight Brigades and four Horse Artillery Regiments in General Headquarters Reserve were as follows:

21st Cavalry Division, National Guard
    51st Cavalry Brigade, New York
    59th Cavalry Brigade, New Jersey, Connecticut, Massachusetts
    165th Field Artillery Regiment, New Jersey
22nd Cavalry Division, National Guard, Headquarters, Harrisburg, Pennsylvania
    52nd Cavalry Brigade, Pennsylvania
    54th Cavalry Brigade, Ohio, Kentucky
    166th Field Artillery Regiment, Pennsylvania
23rd Cavalry Division, National Guard, Headquarters, New Orleans, Louisiana
    53rd Cavalry Brigade, Wisconsin, Illinois, Michigan
    55th Cavalry Brigade, Louisiana, Georgia, Tennessee
    141st Field Artillery Regiment, Louisiana
24th Cavalry Division, National Guard, Headquarters, Topeka, Kansas
    57th Cavalry Brigade, Kansas, Iowa
    58th Cavalry Brigade, Idaho, Wyoming
    168th Field Artillery Regiment, Colorado

Other major Cavalry units in G.H.Q. Reserve included:
    56th Cavalry Brigade, Texas
    111th Cavalry Regiment, New Mexico
    122nd Cavalry Regiment, incomplete in 1939, Alabama

National Guard Infantry and Artillery assigned to G.H.Q. Reserve as of early 1939 were as follows:

165th Infantry, New York City
201st Infantry, West Virginia
369th Infantry (Colored), New York City
372nd Infantry (Colored), Ohio, 3rd Bn. in Boston, Massachusetts
128th Field Artillery Regiment, Missouri
147th Field Artillery Regiment, South Dakota
179th Field Artillery Regiment, Atlanta, Georgia
144th Field Artillery (155mm Gun) Regiment, California
197th Coast Artillery (Antiaircraft) Regiment, New Hampshire
198th Coast Artillery (Antiaircraft) Regiment, Delaware

202nd Coast Artillery (Antiaircraft) Regiment, Chicago, Illinois
203rd Coast Artillery (Antiaircraft) Regiment, Missouri
206th Coast Artillery (Antiaircraft) Regiment, Arkansas
211th Coast Artillery (Antiaircraft) Regiment, Boston, Massachusetts
212th Coast Artillery (Antiaircraft) Regiment, New York City
213th Coast Artillery (Antiaircraft) Regiment, Pennsylvania
214th Coast Artillery (Antiaircraft) Regiment, Georgia
251st Coast Artillery (Antiaircraft) Regiment, San Diego, California
260th Coast Artillery (Antiaircraft) Regiment, Washington, D. C.
250th Coast Artillery (Tractor-Drawn) Regiment, San Francisco, California
242nd Coast Artillery (Harbor Defense) Regiment, Connecticut
261st Coast Artillery (Harbor Defense) Battalion, Delaware
265th Coast Artillery (Harbor Defense) Regiment, Florida
264th Coast Artillery (Harbor Defense) Battalion, Georgia
240th Coast Artillery (Harbor Defense) Regiment, Maine
241st Coast Artillery (Harbor Defense) Regiment, Massachusetts
245th Coast Artillery (Harbor Defense) Regiment, Brooklyn, New York
244th Coast Artillery (Tractor-Drawn) Regiment, New York City*
252nd Coast Artillery (Tractor-Drawn) Regiment, North Carolina
249th Coast Artillery (Harbor Defense) Regiment, Oregon
243rd Coast Artillery (Harbor Defense) Regiment, Rhode Island
263rd Coast Artillery (Harbor Defense) Regiment, South Carolina
246th Coast Artillery (Harbor Defense) Regiment, Virginia
248th Coast Artillery (Harbor Defense) Regiment, incomplete in 1939, Olympia, Washington

Each of the four Armies, the regional and Divisional composition of which has been mentioned earlier, also had non-divisional National Guard units earmarked for each of them. These non-divisional units for each Army tabulate as follows:

FIRST ARMY
    93rd Infantry Brigade
        Headquarters and Headquarters Co.
        10th Infantry Regiment,** Upstate New York
        14th Infantry Regiment,** Brooklyn
    1st Infantry Company (Colored), Baltimore, Maryland
    Medical Company (Colored), Baltimore, Maryland
SECOND ARMY
    8th Infantry Regiment** (Colored), Chicago, Illinois

* The 245th and 244th Coast Artillery Regiments were joined with the 212th Coast Artillery (Antiaircraft), listed earlier, to constitute the New York Harbor Defense Brigade.
** A few National Guard units, upon return to State status following World War I, protested surrender of their historic low numbers for non-historic numerals higher than 100, as of the World War I pattern. Some were allowed to keep their lower numbers through the two decades between the wars. Among them were the 1st Infantry (Virginia), dating from 1652; the 10th Infantry (New York), from 1860; the 14th Infantry (New York), from 1848, and the 8th Infantry (Illinois), from 1895. Such Regiments were given new, or their old World War I, numbers, upon induction into Federal service 1940-41.

THIRD ARMY
178th Field Artillery (155mm Howitzer) Regiment, South Carolina
FOURTH ARMY
153rd Infantry Regiment, Arkansas
92nd Infantry Brigade, Minnesota
205th Infantry Regiment, Minnesota
206th Infantry Regiment, Minnesota

Five Guard Regiments and four Corps Aviation Squadrons were earmarked for immediate service as elements of an Army Corps.
I Corps, assigned units and Corps Aviation:
172nd Field Artillery (155mm Howitzer) Regiment, Manchester, New Hampshire
152nd Observation Squadron, Photo Section and Medical Detachment, Hillsgrove, Rhode Island
II Corps, assigned units:
258th Field Artillery (155mm Gun) Regiment, New York City
101st Signal Battalion, New York City
III Corps
None
IV Corps, Corps Aviation, only
153rd Observation Squadron, Photo Section and Medical Detachment, Meridian, Mississippi
V Corps
None
VI Corps and Corps Medical Service
182nd Field Artillery (155mm Howitzer) Regiment, Detroit, Michigan
135th Medical Regiment, Wisconsin
VII Corps, no ground units assigned, Corps Aviation only
154th Observation Squadron, Photo Section and Medical Detachment, Little Rock, Arkansas
VIII Corps, Corps Medical Service only and organization incomplete as of early 1939.
IX Corps
None

In addition to the non-divisional Brigades, Regiments, Battalions and Aviation Squadrons in the G.H.Q. Reserve, Army, and Corps lists above, there were the four Regiments of Infantry in Hawaii and Puerto Rico. Theirs was a Territorial status and outside the Corps Area limits of the Continental United States. Thus they came within the military responsibility of their respective overseas Departmental Commanders. The Regiments were:

295th Infantry Regiment, Puerto Rico
296th Infantry Regiment, Puerto Rico
297th Infantry was reserved for Alaska but not organized in early 1940.
298th Infantry Regiment, Honolulu, Hawaii
299th Infantry Regiment, Maui and other islands, Hawaii

## REORGANIZATION OF NON-DIVISIONAL
## GUARD REGIMENTS

The fame of the National Guard Divisions on the battlefields of World War II has led many to the logical opinion that the 18 Divisions, numbered 26th to the 45th, inclusive, and the Americal Division, organized in the South Pacific from surplus units from "triangularized" Guard Divisions, represent the full measure of the Guardsmen's contribution to the armies of that War. It is to explode this logical myth that the foregoing Troop List of non-divisional National Guard Cavalry Divisions, Brigades, Regiments and Army Air Corps Squadrons is given in full as of 1939. It reveals that there were half-again as many combatant Guardsmen not in Infantry Divisions as there were in those justly-famous larger units.

But that is not the only reason for presenting the full list. It offers other and more astounding surprises. Insofar as the profession of Arms is concerned, it reveals a General Staff that was predominantly obsolescent in its thinking and planning.* The large ratio of commitment to horse Cavalry is reminiscent of the Polish Army just before Hitler's Panzer Divisions struck in the late Summer of 1939.

Came the following Winter of 1939-41. The Polish formations quickly were broken and bleeding in the black, gumbo-mud that was supposed to render immobile Hitler's mechanized Divisions for a return to the 1916 trench warfare of Flanders' fields. The American General Staff apparently decided the tank had come to stay. An almost-frenetic madness for "redesignations and conversions" struck the above-listed monuments to two decades of obsolescent military thought. There was a clamor for Tank Battalions, Anti-Tank separate Companies and Battalions, Mechanized Reconnaissance Squadrons, Regiments and Brigades of non-divisional medium and 155mm gun Field Artillery and massive conversions to Anti-Aircraft and Harbor Defense Regiments and to creation of Regular and Guard Air Corps Squadrons.

Without an apparent thought of a future need for additional Infantry, Minnesota's 92nd Infantry Brigade (separate) suddenly was redesig-

---

* Gen. Douglas MacArthur, as Chief of Staff, Nov. 1930-Oct. 1935, was shackled by the darkest days of the Depression, but he did achieve a sharp urge toward modernity. Under Gen. Malin Craig, Oct. 1935-Aug. 1939, the General Staff quietly reverted to old, routine habits and comfortably-canalized World War I thinking. Brig. Gen. George C. Marshall joined the War Department General Staff as Chief of War Plans, July, 1938. He became Deputy C. of S., October, 1938. Whether it was Munich or Marshall that jolted the General Staff from erstwhile complacency may well be debated, but it appears to have been Munich, Sept. 30, 1938. In a momentous White House conference, Nov. 14, 1938, which included Craig, Marshall, the Secretaries for War, Treasury, W.P.A. Chief Harry L. Hopkins, and Maj. Gen. H. H. Arnold, Chief of Air Corps, the President called for an Army of 20,000 planes, with an industrial, annual productive capacity of 24,000. Craig and Marshall immediately hitched modernization of all Arms to this sudden executive interest in aircraft.

nated the 101st Coast Artillery Brigade. Its erstwhile 205th Infantry Regiment became Anti-Aircraft Coast Artillery, and the 206th Infantry became a Harbor Defense Regiment. Just why anyone would have gone to the heart of the Continent, a thousand miles or more from the nearest salt-water-splashed coastal gun emplacement, for a quick Regiment of traditional Harbor Defense Coast Artillery National Guardsmen, is one of the as-yet unrevealed mysteries of this era's Washington chairborne planning. In time, someone thought there might be an easier way. Thus the Mimeograph machines purred once again and the entire organization was redesignated the 215th Coast Artillery (Anti-Aircraft) Brigade, without the ultimate expense of shipping a coastal Battery, complete with concrete barbette, to the heart of the Continent for training purposes.

Sweeping changes likewise went into effect to a major or minor degree in every State. For example, New York's 14th Infantry Regiment, organic in the 93rd Infantry Brigade (separate) forfeited its pride in the low number to which it had clung, by becoming the 187th Field Artillery, 155mm Howitzer. Brigaded with other suddenly-redesignated New York units, it became a part of the 71st Field Artillery Brigade of Corps Artillery. Under then-current Tables, such a Corps Artillery Brigade was to consist of a Headquarters and Headquarters Battery, a Field Observation (Flash and Sound) Battalion, two Howitzer Regiments and one Regiment, 155mm Gun. Initially redesignations were for three Battalions in each Regiment with only two firing Batteries to a Battalion. This was changed. Shortly new Mimeographed Tables came down from above calling for only two Battalions, with three firing Batteries each.

Similar redesignations and reorganizations befell the Cavalry Divisions. Beginning, early Autumn, 1940, they too belatedly experienced the obvious lessons of the Polish campaign. In Pennsylvania, for example, the 52nd Cavalry Brigade was called upon to stow its 30-ounce light sabres and sign property responsibility receipts for obsolete, World War I, French G.P.F. 155mm guns which, with their eight-mile an hour, caterpillar-tread prime movers, weighed exactly 30 tons. The 52nd Cavalry Brigade Headquarters Troop* was reorganized as Headquarters Battery of the 73rd Field Artillery Brigade, while elements in the 103rd and 104th Cavalry provided Battery-size units of the 190th Field Artillery Regiment. From the erstwhile 166th Field Artillery (horse) there emerged a 155mm Howitzer Regiment. Though there were ample units available in Pennsylvania to have completed the Artillery Brigade in that State, the haphazard planning of the General Staff in this era is further demonstrated by the source of the third and last Regiment for this Brigade. In New Orleans, the 141st Field Artillery (separate) Battalion, better known since 1839 as the "Washington Artil-

---

* The Philadelphia First City Troop, a continuous, voluntary military formation since 1774.

366

lery," recently had been authorized expansion to Regimental size by creating new Batteries within the Louisiana National Guard. Rearmed with 155mm howitzers, it became the third and last Regiment of Pennsylvania's 73rd Field Artillery Brigade.

The National Guard Infantry Divisions were not entirely free of this sudden reorganizational impact. With somewhat better planning than going to Louisiana to get an Artillery Regiment for a Pennsylvania Artillery Brigade, it was decided to absorb Wisconsin's elements of the 105th Cavalry Regiment into the 32nd Division and free a Michigan light Artillery Regiment, the 119th, for the formation of a Michigan Artillery Brigade. Thus the troops of the 105th Cavalry Regiment became Batteries of a newly-authorized 125th Field Artillery, giving to Wisconsin the entire Artillery elements of the 32nd Division Brigade. At the same time the 32nd Tank Company was removed from the Division, as was the corresponding unit in all other Divisions, for its immediate expansion to the 192nd Tank Battalion. Likewise the Division's 107th Air Observation Squadron, with all other similar Divisional Observation Squadrons, became non-divisional and available for Corps and Army assignments. Thus 18 badly-needed Armored Battalions and a like augmentation of 18 vital Army Air Corps Squadrons became available from the National Guard.

At the same time there was frenetic haste in authorization for the immediate organization of new and similar aviation Observation Squadrons anywhere in almost any State that a State's Adjutant General was willing to propose or accept. Thus in addition to the air Observation Squadrons pinched from the Divisions and those National Guard Air Corps Squadrons already organized with Corps designations, new Squadrons from the ground up were authorized for the National Guard of the District of Columbia, Georgia, Iowa, Kansas, Louisiana, Oregon, Oklahoma and Wisconsin. They were numbered 121st to 128th, inclusive. The speed with which the Guardsmen met the challenge of creating these new aviation units in time to respond to the active duty Federalization Call that came in early 1941, is a tribute to the enthusiasm and capability of the volunteer who senses his Country's need.

With Hitler's Divisions in Norway and the highly-touted French Army broken, disarmed and demobilized, and England under threat of invasion, the spirit of the Guard was never higher. The challenges and creation of new units were met with unabated enthusiasm within the Divisions and non-divisional Regiments, Squadrons, Battalions and separate Companies. Those mentioned above are purely for illustrative purposes. There was not a State that did not feel the reorganizational impact to a major or minor degree. Though occasionally dismayed by a unit going through two or three redesignations, thanks to the General Staff's

367

frequent vagaries, reorganization and redesignation missions were accomplished on schedule.

## GENERAL STAFF PLANS FOR ARMY STRENGTH

The above-mentioned reorganizations, redesignations, conversions and new units involved more than 700 Battery- and Company-size units and Air Corps Squadrons of the National Guard. Nevertheless, they were hardly a part of what might be called the General Staff's master plan for personnel. They were merely belated adjustments toward a balanced force of volunteer, citizen-soldier units they already had. The big personnel picture then normally was referred to as the Protective Mobilization Plan, or PMP. In 1936 PMP had contemplated 1,000,000 to 1,250,000 officers and men.

Since 1920 the General Staff actually had contributed no imagination and very little constructive thought to the basic ideas that emerged from the debates and results of the National Defense Act of that year. The Congressional figure, as a ceiling for the Regular Army, was roughly 300,000 officers and men. The same Congress had thought a National Guard of 486,000 officers and men as being within reason, should subsequent Congressmen vote the money. Thus as late as 1936 the General Staff was cherishing the comfortable thought of a PMP of 1,000,000 to 1,250,000 officers and men that, in the face of growing danger, might be easily reached in advance of actual hostilities by CVE—Civilian Volunteer Effort. Actual hostilities could be counted upon to give the Army another Draft Law, exactly like that of 1917, which would provide manpower in proportion to the enemy threat. Along with this was a major premise, which General Marshall, as Chief of Staff, appears to have accepted also as late as the Summer of 1940. This premise held that no United States compulsory military service law was possible in time of peace.

But when the "Phony War" phase ended in Europe with Hitler's slashing conquest of Norway, quickly followed by the collapse of France, General Marshall already was thinking of a PMP of 2,000,000 with first priority to a Regular Army of 400,000. This was hardly out of line with the Presidential mandate, shortly after Hitler's triumph over England's Prime Minister Chamberlain at Munich, September, 1938, that the Army should include an Air Corps of 20,000 planes. Prior estimates for PMP never had accorded the Air Corps such emphasis.

Meanwhile, Congressional authorizations and appropriations had increased the Regular Army to 280,000 by early Summer of 1940 and the National Guard to 242,000. The latter figure was mainly through slightly higher enlisted ceilings on existing units and a few new, but small, units. The Regular Army's additional manpower muscle was making possible the old dream of one Regular Army Division for each of the nine Corps

Areas. Thus, in early 1940, General Marshall was able to show nine raw and green Regular Army "triangularized" Infantry Divisions, numbered 1st to 9th inclusive, and two, the 1st and 2nd, Armored Divisions. Most of their junior officers were Reservists who volunteered for extended active duty. Not all of the nine Infantry Divisions were stationed according to the number of each within the nine Corps Areas.

But with the Regular Establishment enjoying such prosperity, thanks largely to the Civilian Conservation Corps, or "Tree Army"—a relief project for salvaging thousands of unemployed City youth and which largely had been staffed and officered by Reservists who welcomed transfer to troop duty with the Regulars—General Marshall began having increasing doubts concerning the National Guard. Its jump from 199,491 officers and men in 1939 to 242,000 in the first half of 1940 suggested to his General Staff that the Guard had so many recruits to digest that it could not be trusted to attempt so much as a training mission. Perhaps this should be left entirely to the Regulars. Certainly the Guard could not be entrusted with a vital overseas mission, and it was doubtful if it could execute satisfactorily a simple training mission.*

On May 20, 1940, General Marshall asked his G-1 and G-4: "Assuming Congress gave us a Selective Service Act, how long would it take to procure 750,000 men?" There is every reason to believe it was a purely hypothetical query with an eye on the ultimate utilization of the 100,000 Reserve officers still on the inactive lists. The Administration was busy then trimming sails for the forthcoming National election, with the Third Term Tradition a serious handicap. The President was busy assuring anxious mothers that no sons would be sent overseas to fight wars for foreigners. Not since the failure of Universal Military Training to become a law in 1920 did the General Staff premise that no peacetime Draft Law could be passed, seem more valid. In any event the resulting study of the War Department G-1 and G-4 hardly could have been comforting. They decided it would require 45 days after receiving legal authority, merely to procure the bodies. Induction, clothing, equipment and training presumably would start after a month and a half. And who would train them? Could it be Reserve officers, a goodly percentage of whom had defaulted on as little as 15-day Summer camps for only two out of five years, or had

---

* Immediately following Pearl Harbor, Dec. 7, 1941, the first three Divisions alerted for overseas movement were the 32nd (Wisconsin, Michigan), 34th (Minnesota, Iowa, North and South Dakota) and 37th (Ohio); even though they had not yet been "triangularized" or trained in the most recent equipment, then widely available but still limited in some items. In two World Wars it was the odd role of the National Guard to be viewed by the General Staff as military amateurs of dubious value until time for an overseas movement. The Spanish-American War, 1898, and the Korean "Police Action" initially were strictly professional shows. Military history suggests the General Staff was instinctively, if illogically, right in World Wars I and II.

declined completion of only 200 hours of correspondence courses in five years? The General Staff was sure the training should be by Regulars, but if they were dispersed into training cadres for this Continental chore, whence could General Marshall find one or more powerful Army task forces for implementing Rainbow Plans 1, 2, 3, 4, and 5 or a simultaneous combination of two or more of them?* The General and his Staff apparently decided they would have to hope for the first priority of a Regular Army of 400,000 from which necessarily would be pinched a potential task force of at least 60,000 Regulars for one or more of the five Rainbow plans.

Meanwhile, the election-year Congressional session appeared to be dragging its feet on some highly important Preparedness requests. The Isolationists and Pacifists were as vocally rampant as ever. The Autumn elections hovered like a threatening cloud. It seemed the War Department would have to mark time until the end of the Fiscal Year, June 30, 1941. Pressing for an immediate expansion of the Regulars to 400,000 in order to avoid or delay the necessity for calling into Federal service all or a part of the National Guard seemed to the General Staff and General Marshall the proper decision as of May, 1940. Moreover, rumors held that a new Secretary of War, Republican Henry L. Stimson, the old veteran citizen-soldier and recurring Cabinet officer, was about to take over from the Acting Secretary, Louis A. Johnson, who had served outgoing Mr. Harry H. Woodring as Assistant Secretary. Consequently, the General Staff marked-time and apparently planned little or nothing specifically for what was about to happen.

## PREPAREDNESS-MINDED CIVILIANS AND CONGRESS TAKE THE INITIATIVE

At the same time Guardsmen throughout America, their Commanding Officers and State Adjutants General were asking when somebody was going to make a military decision. With Hitler's star always climbing higher, and England being bombed daily and under the threat of invasion, the potential of the National Guard was being ignored by the planning professionals. All the ghastly errors of World War I appeared to be compounded. There was rising concern everywhere

---

* These were joint plans with the Navy. Number 1 was to hold overseas possessions, control sea lanes and sustain the Monroe Doctrine; 2, sustain authority of democratic powers in Pacific Ocean zones; 3, to secure control of the Western Pacific; 4, task forces to South American and Eastern Atlantic areas or governments; and 5, to achieve purposes of 1 and 4 by sending forces to Africa and Europe, contemplating cooperation from England and France. All or parts of all these plans soon were to become highly pertinent. They were not, however, constantly kept up to date, because of the speed of events. It was perhaps just as well, for both the Japanese and the English gaily and blithely interfered with all American assumptions and preconceptions. Their principal difference was the element of violence in their respective protests. But both were quite effective at writing off the books much of the General Staff's prewar plans.

except in Washington, where everything seemed to be on dead center pending the all-important Third Term issue and the coming November election.

At this stage of affairs John McAuley Palmer, retired for disabilities incident to the service since 1926 but who still knew more than the General Staff concerning the potentials of willing civilian, military manpower, called on General Marshall. There had been a Preparedness dinner in New York. Mr. Stimson and other members of the Military Training Camps Association had been present. The time was ripe for compulsory legislation. There were Congressmen in both houses who would introduce such a measure independent of Administration policies. General Marshall sent three officers to assist the civilians in writing a Bill that New York's Republican James W. Wadsworth, the former Senator but in the Lower House since 1933, would be willing to introduce. After a number of influential but cagey Senators had shied-away from the idea, Senator Edward R. Burke (Democrat) from the presumably Isolationist and Pacifistic-ridden Midwest, Nebraska, embraced the measure. Meanwhile, Julius Ochs Adler, of the New York *Times* and an active Reservist, not to mention others, called on General Marshall urging that he press the Administration to get back of a peacetime Selective Service Act. General Marshall refused. But Administration support was not necessary. The public and the Congress were a year ahead of the War Department General Staff planners and the President. On September 16, 1940, less than four months after General Palmer's call on General Marshall, the first Federal, peacetime compulsory military service Act became a law.

Some National Guard leaders, though warmly enthusiastic for any measure that would make America stronger, took a dim view of the measure as being unnecessary at that time. They knew that through Civilian Voluntary Effort an equivalent or greater military manpower yield could be achieved than the highly-selective, one-year compulsory service measure was intended to bring to the Colors. Recruiting rates and waiting lists in hundreds of unit Armories convinced them that little more was necessary than merely to remove the peace strength ceilings on the existing units followed by an activation schedule of the entire National Guard. Such procedure would give the Nation earlier and more willing manpower. Maryland's General Reckord was initially most critical of what he considered hasty and unnecessary, stopgap legislation.

But Congress had the Preparedness bit in its teeth. A Joint Resolution of both Houses, under date of August 27, called for Federalizing the entire National Guard for 12 consecutive months of active duty. General Marshall suddenly decided that if he could get the Guard, though there were no immediate plans as to where it could be sent or its immediate utilization, he most certainly could use it. He felt an acute need for an increment of at least 60,000 men without delay. They could fill a void that might be created by a sudden need for that number of Regulars for a Rainbow mission. Assured by his G-4 that there was sufficient tentage from World War I stocks to shelter the Guardsmen until infirmaries, kitchens, mess halls and housed latrines with plumbing could be built and covered sewers installed, General Marshall executed an about-face to insist that all the Guard should be phased-in through the following Winter. The Guard leaders further were promised that sufficient Selectees for the one year of service would be ordered to Guard units from their States to bring them to full war strength, thereby making unnecessary their immediate recruitment beyond the existing, low peace strength Tables. Moreover, the time lag for Selectees would enable camp construction for their reception.

It naturally followed that such Selectees could continue with those Guard units at the end of their year of active duty. The law stipulated that they would continue to have a military responsibility, if needed, to the age of 45. Actually, General Reckord was correct. It was indeed hasty, stop-gap legislation. Without Pearl Harbor and all-out war effort, such a limited number of men could not have been held vulnerable to recall for so many years. But, as it worked-out, hostilities prolonged their active duty for the duration of the War that followed. At its end they were given quit-claim, honorable discharges, pursuant to subsequent legislation. In short, it was Pearl Harbor and the initial chaos that followed, that made the hasty legislation look extremely good indeed.

But now that the War Department unexpectedly had come into possession of the National Guard by the Joint Resolution of August 27 and a peacetime Selective Service Act of September 16, the next question was how and where to get it into early training. As in the Mexican Border Mobilization, the General Staff was caught unprepared. It merely knew it had the tentage and where some likely camp sites might be had. History was repeating itself in sing-song routines. Meanwhile the baneful Third Term election, that had kept the Staff sitting on its hands, was still two months in the future. The first increment of Guardsmen, hardly home from the three weeks of Army maneuvers of that Summer, would be rendezvousing at their Armories September 16 for movement to camp facilities, much of which did not exist.

## THE GUARD MOBILIZES

The movement from home stations to the assigned camp sites was made by motor march serials of organic vehicles laden with both personnel and Federal items of issue, by private autos of individual officers and Guardsmen and by railway movements. The Infantry Regiments, with practically no organic vehicles, were principally the beneficiaries of the rail travel.

The mobilization of the entire National Guard was in 22 increments. The First Increment went on active duty and began its movement to training areas September 16, 1940. It consisted of the 30th, 41st, 44th, and 45th Infantry Divisions and sundry units of Coast Artillery and Air Corps. They totaled 63,646 officers and men. General Marshall thus fortuitiously had his 60,000 officers and men already equipped and in functional units.

No subsequent increment was so large. The nearest approach thereto was the Second Increment of October 15, 1940, consisting of the 27th, 32nd and 37th Infantry Divisions plus other units. The aggregate of this increment was 38,578. Increments grew steadily smaller thereafter, 'though it was March 5, 1941, before Illinois' 33rd, the last Division to be Federalized, constituted the major portion of the 17th increment. The 22nd and last increment was June 23, 1941. It consisted solely of the 38 officers and 324 men of the 121st Coast Artillery Battalion. In this manner and between these dates the National Guard fielded 19,795 officers, 221 warrant officers and 277,738 enlisted men.

Slightly more than a third, 6,800, of the officers were graduates of one or more of the Army Service schools, i.e., the Infantry School, Command and General Staff School, etc. Had funds and "slots" in the schools been available through these drab decades, there could have been many more than 6,800. Every State normally had waiting lists of eligible officers who had completed the prerequisite correspondence courses for admission. Even so, the 6,800 graduates included practically all the Captains, Field Grade and General officers, as well as some of the more military-minded Lieutenants. No other army of volunteer citizen-soldiers ever had fielded a more competent, hard core of informed and trained officers and noncommissioned officers. If the 1940-41 quality record has been broken (and it most likely has been), it was by the National Guard units inducted for Korea and the minor mobilization for the Berlin Crisis of 1961-62.

For the first time since 1919, the American Army had the capability of setting up a large, balanced task force of functional units representing all Arms and Services, Divisional and non-divisional. That initially they were deficient both in training and modern equipment all conceded. But, even so, they could have functioned immediately and rendered a good account of themselves in any major emergency within the Western Hemisphere, and such, with concurrent training, was their only prospective mission as of the date of their Call. General Marshall's revised Protective Mobilization Plan was suddenly a full year ahead of his own planning.

The National Guard units, strengths, dates of Federalization and training are listed below.

FIRST INCREMENT, SEPT. 16, 1940

| Unit | Home States | Training Stations | Total Strength |
|---|---|---|---|
| 30th Div., less 30th Tank Co. | S.C., Ga., Tenn., N.C. | Fort Jackson, S.C. | 9,918 |
| 41st Div., less 41st Tank Co. | Wyo., Wash., Mont., Ore., Idaho | Camp Murray, Wash. | 12,372 |
| 44th Div., less 44th Tank Co. | N.J., N.Y. | Fort Dix, N.J. | 10,822 |
| 45th Div., less 45th Tank Co. | Colo., Ariz., Okla., N.Mex. | Camp Barkeley, Tex. | 9,499 |
| 197th CA (AA) | N.H. | Camp Hulen, Tex. | 1,297 |
| 198th CA (AA) | Del. | Camp Edwards, Mass. | 946 |
| 202d CA (AA) | Ill. | Fort Bliss, Tex. | 1,455 |
| 203d CA (AA) | Mo. | Camp Hulen, Tex. | 1,343 |
| 211th CA (AA) | Mass. | do | 1,337 |
| 213th CA (AA) | Pa. | Camp Stewart, Ga. | 1,185 |
| 251st CA (AA) | Calif. | Malakole, T.H. | 1,220 |
| 244th CA (155mm Gun) | N.Y. | Camp Pendleton, Va. | 1,012 |
| 250th CA (155mm Gun) | Calif. | Camp McQuaide, Calif. | 998 |
| 252d CA (155mm Gun) | N.C. | Fort Screven, Ga. | 1,079 |
| 240th CA (HD) | Maine | Fort Williams, Maine, H.D. of Portland | 997 |
| 241st CA (HD) | Mass. | Fort Banks, Mass., H.D. of Boston | 1,397 |
| 242d CA (HD) | Conn. | Fort H. G. Wright, N.Y., H.D. of Long Island Sound | 873 |
| 243d CA (HD) | R.I. | Fort Adams, R.I., H.D. of Narragansett Bay | 966 |
| 245th CA (HD) | N.Y. | Fort Hancock, N.J., H.D. of Sandy Hook | 1,363 |
| 246th CA (HD) | Va. | Fort Monroe, Va., H.D. of Chesapeake Bay | 955 |
| 248th CA (HD) | Wash. | Fort Worden, Wash., H.D. of Puget Sound | 937 |
| 249th CA (HD) | Ore. | Fort Stevens, Ore., H.D. of Columbia | 1,007 |
| 105th Obs. Sq. | Tenn. | Columbia, S.C. | 165 |
| 119th Obs. Sq. | N.J. | Fort Dix, N.J. | 169 |
| 154th Obs. Sq. | Ark. | Abilene, Tex. | 147 |
| 116th Obs. Sq. | Wash. | Fort Lewis, Wash. | 187 |

Total strength of units inducted Sept. 16, 1940      63,646

## SECOND INCREMENT, OCT. 15, 1940

| Unit | Home States | Training Stations | Total Strength |
|---|---|---|---|
| 27th Div., less 27th Tank Co. | N.Y. | Fort McClellan, Ala. | 11,389 |
| 37th Div., less 37th Tank Co. and Cos. F and I, 112th Med. Regt. | Ohio | Camp Shelby, Miss. | 9,632 |
| 32d Div., less 32d Tank Co. | Mich., Wis. | Camp Livingston, La. | 11,602 |
| 102d Obs. Sq. | N.Y. | Fort McClellan, Ala. | 149 |
| 153d Obs. Sq. | Miss. | Key Field, Meridian, Miss. | 130 |
| 107th Obs. Sq. | Mich. | Camp Beauregard, La. | 163 |
| 295th Inf. | P.R. | Camp Tortuguero, P.R. | 1,359 |
| 296th Inf. | do | do | 1,363 |
| 92d Inf. Brig., Hq. & Hq. Co. | do | do | 47 |
| 253d CA (155mm Gun) (1st Bn.) | do | Fort Buchanan, P.R. | 175 |
| 162d FA (75mm Gun) (Trk.-D) (1st Bn.) | do | Henry Barracks, P.R. | 274 |
| 201st CA (AA) (1st Bn.) redesignated 123d CA (Sep. Bn.) (AA) | do | Borinquen Field, P.R. | 323 |
| 130th Engrs. (C) (1st Bn.) | do | Camp Tortuguero, P.R. | 193 |
| 298th Inf. | Hawaii | Schofield Barracks, T.H. | 646 |
| 299th Inf. | do | do | 1,133 |
| Total strength of units inducted Oct. 15, 1940 | | | 38,578 |

## THIRD INCREMENT, NOV. 18, 1940

| | | | |
|---|---|---|---|
| 56th Cav. Brig. | Tex. | Fort McIntosh, Tex. | 2,564 |

## FOURTH INCREMENT, NOV. 25, 1940

| Unit | Home States | Training Stations | Total Strength |
|---|---|---|---|
| 31st Div. | Fla., Ala., Miss., La. | Camp Blanding, Fla. | 12,484 |
| 36th Div. | Tex. | Camp Bowie, Tex. | 12,362 |
| 106th Obs. Sq. | Ala. | Jacksonville, Fla. | 158 |
| 111th Obs. Sq. | Tex. | Camp Bowie, Tex. | 164 |
| 112th Obs. Sq. | Ohio | Fort Bragg, N.C. | 135 |
| 128th FA (75mm Gun) | Mo. | Fort Jackson, S.C. | 1,127 |
| 106th Cav. (H-Mecz) | Ill. | Camp Livingston, La. | 1,203 |
| 147th FA (75mm Gun) | S.D. | Fort Ord, Calif. | 1,008 |
| 102d Rad. Int. Co. | Calif. | do | 98 |
| 214th CA (AA) | Ga. | Camp Stewart, Ga. | 1,322 |
| 192d Tank Bn. | Wis., Ill., Ohio, Ky. | Fort Knox, Ky. | 377 |
| 101st Obs. Sq. | Mass. | Camp Edwards, Mass. | 160 |
| 152d Obs. Sq. | R.I. | Fort Devens, Mass. | 160 |
| Total strength of units inducted Nov. 25, 1940 | | | 30,758 |

## FIFTH INCREMENT, DEC. 23, 1940

| 35th Div., less 35th Tank Co. | Neb., Kans., Mo. | Camp J. T. Robinson, Ark. | 12,059 |
|---|---|---|---|
| 153d Inf. | Ark. | do | 1,831 |
| 110th Obs. Sq. | Mo. | Little Rock, Ark., Adams Field | 164 |

Total strength of units inducted Dec. 23, 1940        14,054

## SIXTH INCREMENT, JAN. 6, 1941

| Unit | Home States | Training Stations | Total Strength |
|---|---|---|---|
| 101st CA Brig., Hq. & Hq. Btry. | Minn. | Camp Haan, Calif. | 84 |
| 200th CA (AA) | N.Mex. | Fort Bliss, Tex. | 907 |
| 204th CA (AA) | La. | Camp Hulen, Tex. | 1,287 |
| 206th CA (AA) | Ark. | Fort Bliss, Tex. | 1,440 |
| 208th CA (AA) | Conn. | Camp Edwards, Mass. | 778 |
| 215th CA (AA) | Minn. | Camp Haan, Calif. | 1,461 |
| 216th CA (AA) | do | do | 192 |
| 260th CA (AA) | D.C. | Fort Bliss, Tex. | 861 |
| 265th CA (HS) | Fla. | Fort Crockett, Tex., H.D. of Galveston | 897 |
| 102d CA Bn. (AA) | N.Y. | Camp Edwards, Mass. | 412 |
| 105th CA Bn. (AA) | La. | Camp Hulen, Tex. | 463 |
| 106th CA Bn. (AA) | Ky. | do | 332 |
| 142d FA | Ark. | Fort Sill, Okla. | 1,046 |
| 184th FA | Ill. | Fort Custer, Mich. | 892 |
| 102d Cav. | N.J. | Fort Jackson, S.C. | 1,013 |
| 201st Inf., less 3d Bn. | W.Va. | Fort Benjamin Harrison, Ind. | 1,114 |
| 101st AT Bn. | N.Y. | Fort Benning, Ga. | 424 |
| 104th AT Bn. | Ga., Ala., Tex., Colo. | do | 393 |
| 193d Tank Bn. | N.Mex. | Fort Sam Houston, Tex. | 400 |
| 151st Med. Bn. | Ohio | Fort McClellan, Ala. | 319 |
| 120th Obs. Sq. | Colo. | Fort Bliss, Tex. | 138 |

Total strength of units inducted Jan. 6, 1941       *16,017

* War Dept. total did not balance-out precisely with its own enlisted returns in breakdown by units. War Dept. total shown here.

## SEVENTH INCREMENT, JAN. 13, 1941

| Unit | Home States | Training Stations | Total Strength |
|---|---|---|---|
| 73d FA Brig., Hq. & Hq. Btry. | Pa. | Camp Shelby, Miss. | 85 |
| 141st FA | La. | do | 802 |
| 166th FA | Pa. | do | 1,010 |
| 190th FA | do | do | 921 |
| 263d CA (HD) | S.C. | Fort Moultrie, S.C., H.D. of Charleston | 823 |
| 369th CA (AA) | N.Y. | Fort Ontario, N.Y. | 1,397 |
| 113th Cav. | Iowa | Camp Bowie, Tex. | 1,106 |
| 135th Med. Regt. | Wis. | Camp Shelby, Wis. | 474 |
| 102d AT Bn. | N.Y. | do | 424 |
| 101st Sig. Bn. | do | do | 300 |
| 101st Rad. Int. Co. | Pa. | do | 97 |

Total strength of units inducted Jan. 13, 1941      7,439

## EIGHTH INCREMENT, JAN. 16, 1941

| | | | |
|---|---|---|---|
| 26th Div. | Mass. | Camp Edwards, Mass. | 9,081 |

## NINTH INCREMENT, JAN. 17, 1941

| | | | |
|---|---|---|---|
| 38th Div. | Ky., W.Va., Ind. | Camp Shelby, Miss. | 9,054 |
| 113th Obs. Sq. | Ind. | Key Field, Meridian, Miss. | 145 |

Total strength of units inducted Jan. 17, 1941      9,199

## TENTH INCREMENT, JAN. 22, 1941

| | | | |
|---|---|---|---|
| Serv. Co., Co. F, and 2d Bn., 103d QM Regt., 28th Div. | Pa. | Indiantown Gap, Pa. | 181 |

## ELEVENTH INCREMENT, JAN. 27, 1941

| Unit | Home States | Training Stations | Total Strength |
|---|---|---|---|
| 112th FA | N.J. | Fort Bragg, N.C. | 825 |
| 178th FA | S.C. | do | 1,070 |
| 186th FA | N.Y. | Madison Barracks, N.Y. | 991 |
| 101st Cav. | do | Fort Devens, Mass. | 1,183 |
| 151st Engr. Regt. (C) | Ala. | Camp Claiborne, La. | 752 |
| 261st CA (HD, Type B) | Del. | Fort DuPont, Del., H.D. of Delaware | 334 |
| 134th Med. Regt. | N.Y. | Fort Bragg, N.C. | 451 |
| 122d CA Bn. (AA) (Sep). | N.J. | Fort DuPont, Del. | 358 |

Total strength of units inducted Jan. 27, 1941      5,964

## TWELFTH INCREMENT, FEB. 3, 1941

| Unit | Home States | Training Stations | Total Strength |
|---|---|---|---|
| 191st Tank Bn. | N.Y., Mass., Va., Conn. | Fort George G. Meade, Md. | 409 |
| 71st FA Brig., Hq. & Hq. Btry. | N.Y. | Fort Ethan Allen, Vt. | 87 |
| 187th FA (155mm How.) | do | do | 1,010 |
| 258th FA (155mm Gun) | do | do | 1,481 |
| 29th Div. | Md., Va., D.C., Pa. | Fort George G. Meade, Md. | 9,865 |
| 105th AT Bn. | Pa. | do | 304 |
| 104th Obs. Sq. | Md. | Frederick, Md. | 188 |
| 108th Obs. Sq. | Ill. | Battle Creek, Mich. | 173 |
| 144th FA (155mm Gun) | Calif. | Fort Lewis, Wash. | 941 |
| 205th CA (AA) | Wash. | do | 1,105 |

Total strength of units inducted Feb. 3, 1941    15,563

## THIRTEENTH INCREMENT, FEB. 10, 1941

| Unit | Home States | Training Stations | Total Strength |
|---|---|---|---|
| 102d CA Brig. (AA) Hq. & Hq. Btry. | N.Y. | Camp Stewart, Ga. | 81 |
| 207th CA (AA) | do | do | 1,646 |
| 209th CA (AA) | do | do | 1,529 |
| 212th CA (AA) | do | do | 1,257 |
| 104th CA Bn. (AA) (Sep) (37mm Gun) | Ala. | do | 589 |
| 101st CA Bn. (AA) (Sep) (37mm Gun) | Ga. | do | 404 |
| 107th CA Bn. (AA) (Sep) (37mm Gun) | S.C. | do | 488 |
| 34th Div. | Iowa, Minn., N. Dak., S. Dak. | Camp Claiborne, La. | 12,279 |
| 217th CA (AA) | Minn. | | 1,427 |
| 109th Obs. Sq. | do | Camp Beauregard, La. | 170 |
| 194th Tank Bn. (less 1 Co.) | Minn., Mo., Calif. | Fort Lewis, Wash. | 348 |
| 103d AT Bn. | Wash. | do | 348 |

Total strength of units inducted Feb. 10, 1941    20,566

## FOURTEENTH INCREMENT, FEB. 17, 1941

| Unit | Home States | Training Stations | Total Strength |
|---|---|---|---|
| 28th Div., Less 2d Bn., Serv. Co., Co. F, 103d QM Regt. | Pa. | Indiantown Gap, Pa. | 11,318 |
| 104th Cav. | do | do | 1,057 |
| 103d Obs. Sq. | do | Harrisburg Airport, New Cumberland, Pa. | 165 |

Total strength of units inducted Feb. 17, 1941    12,540

378

## FIFTEENTH INCREMENT, FEB. 24, 1941

| Unit | Home States | Training Stations | Total Strength |
|---|---|---|---|
| 43d Div. | Conn., Maine, Vt., R.I. | Camp Blanding, Fla. | 12,092 |
| 115th Cav. | Wyo. | Fort Lewis, Wash. | 1,051 |
| 74th FA Brig., Hq. & Hq. Btry. | Ga. | Camp Blanding, Fla. | 53 |
| 75th FA Brig., Hq. & Hq. Btry. | Tenn. | Camp Forrest, Tenn. | 73 |
| 168th FA | Colo. | do | 1,084 |
| 172d FA | N.H. | Camp Blanding, Fla. | 996 |
| 179th FA | Ga. | do | 941 |
| 181st FA | Tenn. | Camp Forrest, Tenn. | 1,086 |
| 191st FA | Tenn. | do | 953 |
| 210th CA (AA) | Mich. | Fort Sheridan, Ill. | 854 |
| 103d CA Bn. (AA) | Ky. | do | 354 |
| 118th Obs. Sq. | Conn. | Jacksonville, Fla. | 168 |

Total strength of units inducted Feb. 24, 1941     19,705

## SIXTEENTH INCREMENT, MAR. 3, 1941

| Unit | Home States | Training Stations | Total Strength |
|---|---|---|---|
| 40th Div. | Calif., Utah | Camp San Luis Obispo, Calif. | 10,873 |
| 115th Obs. Sq. | Calif. | Paso Robles, Calif. | 165 |

Total strength of units inducted Mar. 3, 1941     11,038

## SEVENTEENTH INCREMENT, MAR. 5, 1941

| Unit | Home States | Training Stations | Total Strength |
|---|---|---|---|
| 33d Div. | Ill. | Camp Forrest, Tenn. | 11,716 |
| 107th Cav. (H-Mecz) | Ohio | do | 1,201 |

Total strength of units inducted Mar. 5, 1941     12,917

## EIGHTEENTH INCREMENT, MAR. 10, 1941

| Unit | Home States | Training Stations | Total Strength |
|---|---|---|---|
| 101st MP Bn. | N.Y. | Fort Dix, N.J. | 466 |
| 372d Inf. | D.C., Mass., Md., Ohio, N.J. | do | 1,723 |

Total strength of units inducted Mar. 10, 1941     2,189

## NINETEENTH INCREMENT, APR. 1, 1941

| Unit | Home States | Training Stations | Total Strength |
|---|---|---|---|
| 183d FA | Idaho | Fort F. E. Warren, Wyo. | 919 |
| 188th FA | N. Dak. | do | 1,337 |
| 76th FA Brig., Hq. & Hq. Btry. | Calif. | do | 61 |

Total strength of units inducted Apr. 1, 1941     2,317

| 72d FA Brig., Hq. & Hq. Btry. | Mich. | Fort Leonard Wood, Mo. | 62 |
|---|---|---|---|
| 182d FA | do | do | 985 |
| 177th FA | do | do | 952 |
| 119th FA | do | do | 911 |

Total strength of units inducted Apr. 7, 1941     2,910

TWENTY-FIRST INCREMENT, JUNE 2, 1941

| 126th Obs. Sq. | Wis. | Fort Dix, N.J. | 166 |
|---|---|---|---|

TWENTY-SECOND INCREMENT, JUNE 23, 1941

| 121st CA Bn. (AA) | Nev. | Camp Haan, Calif. | 362 |
|---|---|---|---|

# Bibliographical Note For Chapter XV

In the public affairs literature of the era 1919-1939, there was a greater review of war guilt than of war. Writers, both the lightly popular and heavily intellectual, concerned themselves with war prevention and soothing, international pacts against war and to outlaw war, rather than to prepare a people to cope with war when confronted by that unwanted and grim turn of events. A Coast Guard cutter chasing a rum runner made more headlines and news magazine comment than did major naval maneuvers. America's newest and most modern naval tonnage in the world was being scrapped short of completion. The era produced a spate of books and hundreds of articles on disarmament, but comparatively little print on armament. The military tank as a weapon initially created more immediate interest than did Brig. Gen. Billy Mitchell's publicity crescendo for the military airplane. The tank's battlefield appearance in the twilight of World War I excited a few military imaginations and some writing, particularly in England. But when an American invented a high speed tank the War Department General Staff evidenced little or no interest. When the inventor sold his tank to Russia, there was no journalistic or public outcry, least of all from the "merchants-of-death" school of writers and lecturers who so delighted and entertained the Pacifists of the era. Accordingly, the foregoing chapter rests almost exclusively upon Government publications, most particularly the *Annual Reports of the War Department*. The *Reports* of the Secretary of War, the Chief of Staff and the Chief of the Militia Bureau (the National Guard Bureau after 1933) were most rewarding. *The Army Lineage Book*, Vol. 2, Infantry, 1953, provides facts on Regular Army Regiments of the era. The semi-annual *Army Directory* with the Troop Lists, and the intermittent editions of the *National Guard Register* with its Troop and Station Lists, were equally indispensable. Mark S. Watson, *Chief of Staff: Prewar Plans and Preparations*, 1950, in the History of the War Department Series, *History of the Army in World War II*, from the Office of the Chief of Military History, Department of the Army, is splendid and was followed when applicable.

CHAPTER XVI

# Two Unprepared Armies
# Separated By Misconceptions

FROM INDUCTION, pursuant to the Federalization for 12 consecutive months of active duty, until Pearl Harbor, the National Guardsmen of all ranks and ratings found themselves in a most unenviable situation. Though to serve their Country they had interrupted their business pursuits, closed professional offices, laid down the tools of their trade for an enlisted man's pay and often uprooted their families, they heard no shouts of welcome or words of appreciation other than from the Chambers of Commerce, businessmen and property owners, in the cities nearest the new training camps.

To such citizenry, glancing backward at a decade of economic recessions, it appeared the much-talked-of prosperity, that was said to be lurking just around some unidentified corner, might actually be there.

The arriving Division of Guardsmen might prove to be the corner. For the local City, they were right in every instance. And most of the City folk greeted the arriving citizen-soldiers with a friendly, cooperative warmth that merited the arriving prosperity. Most Guardsmen, after 20 years, express little other than pleasant memories of those welcoming townspeople.

Back in their home stations the Guardsmen were both missed and esteemed, but normally in a quiet sort of way. It was more within their own homes and among immediate associates than elsewhere. America was not at war. Both candidates for President were vociferously opposed to any American manpower participation in Europe's war. Neither could have been elected had he spoken otherwise. Hence friends and neighbors brushed-off their Guardsmen's departures with observations that the uniforms, *camaraderie* of the camps, outdoor living and the guns always had appealed to their departing friends. Hence it was hoped they could financially afford the extended interruption of civil pursuits and reductions in income. In the case of a skilled laborer, friends carried the thought a step further with the opinion that the Guardsmen's departures might create some vacancies for other craftsmen who had been unemployed and on the extra call-board too long. And for the younger Guardsmen called from college classrooms, or just out of high school, there was the friendly hope that the temporary Army status would prove to be a healthful, profitable year in their progress toward maturity. And mature many of them most certainly did. More than 75,000 of these youthful National Guard Privates and fuzz-featured N.C.O.'s were to return five years later as decorated Lieutenants, Captains, and some in Field Grades.

On the other hand, a tremendous percentage of the American civilian population, most of whom had little or no direct contact with so much as one Guardsman, viewed the entire Federalization of the National Guard as nothing more than another gigantic, election-year boondoggle. To them it was no more than another New Deal idea to get more money in circulation faster in the interest of another temporary, if false, prosperity from lavish economic "pump-priming," to borrow the then-current phrase. The Presidential election then in progress tended to underscore the idea.

Actually the Guardsmen were an almost perfect cross-section of their many home towns, the sections of their cities, and the traditions of their units. But the longer they had been in the local Guard unit, the greater the likelihood that they were leaders among their pay-group peers. Their comparative wages, salaries and incomes reflected such leadership. It naturally followed that the most recent enlistees, of whom there were many incident to the increased strength authorizations and reorganizations, were adventurous-minded youngsters, unmarried and

382

still under 21. They were the young men on the path to maturity. They had no economic status other than that of their parents. More often than otherwise, parental consent for enlistment in the local Guard unit was predicated upon the young man being associated with one or more friends of long standing, and with active duty, should it come, initially under officers who hardly could avoid being thoroughly acquainted with civilian as well as military minds.

Only a comparatively small percentage of these young enlistees were eligible for any form of Federal or State social relief. The Civilian Conservation Corps had been and was doing an extremely good job in that realm of social welfare. By 1939 it was largely in the hands of Reserve officers on extended active duty. They and the ranks from the "Tree Army" had done much, as noted earlier, toward the quick expansion and creation of the new Regular formations motivated by the outbreak of hostilities in Europe in late August of that year. Thus relief personnel in that age group had vanished from many communities. Indeed, many National Guard Unit Commanders, with waiting lists to select from in practically every Armory, bluntly made a relief status a *prima facie* cause for a rejection. That such personnel could stay at home and talk to their Draft Boards was their quite logical and often instinctive reaction. Some Colonels so directed their Company and Battery Commanders, just in case there might be some loose, local thinking on the subject. Hence the percentage of relief "clients" who showed-up in the ranks of the Federalized Guard units in the Autumn of 1940 and the following Winter was thoroughly negligible. The "clients" could do better, economically, on relief.

## IMPACT OF DEPRESSION UPON THE ARMY

Meanwhile, the core, or long-term, Regular Army professionals, commissioned and enlisted, had experienced but two brief but highly unpleasant brushes with the devastating Depression of 1930-40. Early in the Franklin D. Roosevelt First Administration, the salaries of all Federal employes, except those of Judges and a few other exceptions, had been reduced as a temporary Budget-balancing measure. Within the cloistered, country-club life of the sleepy Army Posts and among officers, men and families who had foregone every opportunity for fast civilian advancement in exchange for predictable Army incomes for the remainder of their lives, this salary reduction was viewed as a mass breach of contracts and a wanton betrayal of the Military by unsympathetic and unappreciative civilian politicians. Since Emory Upton's harmful opus had been required reading for most of them, the word "Militia" and everything associated therewith was synonymous with "politicians." That the National Guardsmen consistently had exerted every effort in behalf of Military budgets and were among the first to clamor for the restoration of the old pay rates, was either unknown by the rank-and-file of the Regulars or had become buried in the dark resentment from finding that not even the Armed Services were Depression-proof. The Roosevelt Administration's first act, after embracing the "pump-priming" economic philosophy, was an immediate restoration of all Federal salaries.

The other unpleasant but somewhat longer brush the Army had with the Depression was none other than the "Three C's," or the "Tree Army" itself. The diversion of precious and diminishing stocks of tentage, tools, mess equipment and vehicles to a social experiment in youthful manpower, when military manpower was needed, was, to the professionals, nothing short of appalling. Many of these items then were considered irreplaceable, and with considerable justice. Certainly the Administration was showing no disposition to buy anything new for the Army, except a few, precursor type airplanes. But worse yet was the diversion of Army personnel to the organization and initial operation of the social experiment for the young men of military age who should be doing, according to their philosophy, a compulsory training tour in the Army. In this the Regulars had the sympathy and support of most Guardsmen.

The Civilian Conservation Corps was indeed a para-military compromise between social service and post-juvenile Boy Scouting. Had the Companies of the Tree Army been allowed a distinctive uniform, some degree of military courtesy and a modicum of the discipline normally associated with a first-class, well-organized, Boy Scout Jamboree, or, better still, an R.O.T.C. unit, the Regulars might well have taken to the task with warmth and enthusiasm. But in 1934 the Disarmament and Pacifist claques were in full cry. An Army was being created covertly in the name of Conservation, they accused. Moreover, the high-level social worker leadership that dominated the Three C's often was hand-in-glove with the claques. In any event, they hearkened hastily to the Pacifistic plaints. The young men were not to be marched from mess shacks to their tasks in cadenced strides in close formations. There was to be no assimilated military manual of arms with picks or shovels. There were to be no uniforms of the day or inspections as to attire before going out on an evening pass. Company punishment was taboo. And when one zealous officer combined his evening roll call with Stand-To, field music, and a lowering of the flag, he was all-but reprimanded for conducting unauthorized Retreat formations. A directive on the subject was rushed to all other possible offenders.

Catapulting an Army officer of that era from the quiet security of an Army Post, with its known regulations, techniques of command and terms of reference, into a cut-over wilderness with command responsi-

384

bilities over an unskilled and undisciplined Labor Battalion, was a shock to more than one grim-faced, professional soldier. There were often no training cadres, no utilities, no formal health service, no familiar channels of supply, and only the most vague and uncertain means of discipline. It was almost comparable to throwing an officer into immediate battle, leading strange, untrained troops, without intelligence estimate, without reconnaisance, without maps and without a plan of maneuver. Moreover, for the Government to waste time and money on such splendid potential military manpower was to the careerists little short of nauseating. Though one Field Grade officer, fresh out of the Command and General Staff College, committed suicide from sheer frustration from such an assignment, most Regulars did a creditable job, at building and organizing. Gradually they happily turned the lower echelons of the job over to junior Reserve officers who considered the pay and allowances of their military rank to be more attractive than their current earnings in civil life. Many Regulars considered these incoming young officers from the Reserve as being in no military service, but merely as social workers masquerading in military status for pay scale purposes.

Except for the hunting and fishing potential in some areas, few professional soldiers left the C.C.C. with kind memories. They were sure that a Draft Law, turning the unemployed young men over to the Army, as in Europe, for a period of time, was the only valid solution. It increased their apprehensions concerning and suspicion of any civilian volunteer effort. Calling the Guard into Federal service without a specific enemy on the horizon could be another political boondoggle and waste of money and equipment that the Regulars needed, it was suggested quietly on at least one Army Post of the era. As noted earlier, mobilizing the Guard so soon was not in the General Staff planning.

Confronted by these facts and recognizable trends, two Guard Brigadiers in casual conference in Alexandria, Louisiana, October, 1940, arrived at the joint prophecy that the Guard was in for some hard days of misunderstanding and much abuse.

"It is not like the Mexican Border mobilization," said one. "There we had a tangible, weak but aggressive, prospective foe near at hand. Today, neither National Party leader has come forth with statements that give purpose to our being here. The War and State Departments cannot publicly review their fears and war contingency plans.

"Too many people, in and out of uniform, think our being here is all domestic politics and not a result of international tensions and dangers. We are not today viewed as patriotic sons of our States. We are merely the subject of National controversy," he concluded.

"Worse than that," the other Brigadier retorted, "my old friends among the Regulars think we are another Tree Army and all of us are highly fortunate refugees from the Depression."

The former was Brigadier General Paul B. Clemens, Assistant Superintendent of Schools in one of America's largest cities, where his income had been higher than that of a Brigadier General for many years, and which he was forfeiting while on military leave.

The latter was Brigadier General William S. Wood, a West Pointer with nine years' active Army service whence he had resigned for a highly-successful career as an industrial engineer. The monthly salary differential his company was paying him to make sure he returned at the end of the "12 consecutive months" was more than his active duty pay as a Brigadier.

## PROFESSIONAL STAGNATION THROUGH SENIORITY

Notwithstanding the perceptive quality of the foregoing highly accurate analysis and prophecy by the two Brigadiers, they had not foreseen another highly important, unfavorable factor. It was indeed obscure but quickly manifested itself. It was the difference between the comparative results of promotion practices within the Regular Army and the National Guard.

The Regular Army had a near-catastrophic officer personnel situation. Unlike the Navy, the War Department General Staff had been utterly unwilling to face-up to it. Early, following World War I, the Navy refused to let the dead hand of seniority dry-up promotion opportunities for sharp, competent, intellectually alert Line officers. The Navy adopted an orderly "selection-up" system for all grades, Junior Grade Lieutenant to Admiral. When a Line officer had been in grade sufficiently long that panels of officers of like grade, but junior to him in date of rank, came under review for promotion and were "selected-up," that officer appropriately was said to have been "passed-over." His career as an active duty Naval officer was automatically in jeopardy. One more pass-over from additionally-considered panels within his rank, but junior to him, and he was forced into retired status without deference to age—provided he had enough total commissioned service to merit some form of retirement benefits. In that case, his much lower fractional pay on the Retired List was more in the nature of a retainer, for he became subject to recall in grade and with active duty full pay and allowances should the Navy need him in a future expansion. Lacking enough years of active duty commissioned service for the minimal retirement, the twice-passed-over Naval officer was just another ex-Naval officer, looking for a job. Periodic professional examinations and tours of school duty further sharpened professional minds, embellished service records and stepped-up competition.

The personnel planners in the Army's General Staff were thoroughly aware that they had the same problem in an even more aggravated form, because of the nature of peacetime soldiering. What chance did an Infantry or horse Cavalry officer have for demonstrating his actual incompetence such as often came to inept Naval officers? Ship handling in stormy weather and narrow seas was the same in peace as in war. At any moment a Naval officer might ruin an evaporator, wreck a condenser, bash-in a bow or clip the end from a municipal pleasure dock, and thereby conclusively give tangible proof of incompetence. Only the Army Air Corps fliers faced frequently a full proficiency test. Funerals were the hazard of failure for them, rather than the more-or-less subjective report of a Board of Inquiry.

The General Staff personnel planners also were fully aware of the Navy's plan for loosening the dead grip of seniority. But the Army would have none of it. Through the '20's and early '30's they smugly noted and repetitiously opined the Navy was neither a happy nor a dedicated Service. It had become a self-seeking, cut-throat Service. Such was not for the Army. Meanwhile, it was increasingly admitted that the Army's "B-boards," calculated to rid the Service of incompetence by putting the Class B label on an officer, were failures. But those very failures fostered a sense of security with a corresponding uplift to happiness in the Service, if not to dedication, one pseudo-defender of the Army's Seniority List facetiously suggested as late as 1938.

By that date, unhappiness among the Army Line officers over lack of promotion, after 12 to 17 years in one rank, was somewhat higher than were the earlier naval displeasures from adoption of the selections-up-two-pass-overs-and-out policy. Indeed, by that time, those still left in the Navy decided theirs to be a splendid, professional personnel plan.

But the War Department General Staff officers preferred working on civilian, military age manpower personnel problems, to guarantee a mass of enlisted men for the next emergency, rather than putting their own house in order. Thus they chose the easy solution for unhappiness over non-promotion within the Army Line. What could promote more happiness, and perhaps dedication, than promoting everybody except the newest of the Second Lieutenants? The professional experience rule for promotion resulting from time-in-grade and total length of commissioned service seemed to be keeping the Army Medics, Dentists, Veterinarians, Nurses and Chaplains happy. Why not apply seniority and the same principle to the promotions of the Line officers?

A number of classical diehards among the Regulars, who still harbored the old-fashioned idea that Platoons were commanded by Lieutenants, Companies and Batteries by Captains, Battalions by Majors and Regiments by Colonels, arched their eyebrows. If all the officers in "the Hump" were promoted on a basis of time-in-grade, or total service as a commissioned officer, there would be too many Chiefs and not enough Indians; too many commanders and not enough units to command. The rank structure soon would resemble that of the Mexican Army through the era of Pancho Villa, in which Colonels commanded Platoons of 50, and it was a potent *general de brigada* who could sound a bugle and put 250 *soldados* on the line. In the American Army, could Colonels and Lieutenant Colonels be assigned as Battery Commanders? the classical diehards asked. Was that making for a happy Army?

The answer to that was a unanimous negative, especially among the classicists. But the next question was not so easily answered. If the Chiefs do not command Indians in proportion to the relative numbers of each, then what will the enormous excess of Field Grade Chiefs do? There is an old Army axiom that nothing is more danger-ous than an ambitious officer with substantial rank without enough duties to keep it exercised. He has enough authority to foul-up an operation for others; enough experience and cunning to protect himself in doing it, but not enough rank to keep his immediate Chief out of trouble or to protect officers in subordinate assignments. The con-servative diehards pondered this ancient concept and asked again what all the surplus rank could be doing.

The promoters of happiness and contentment within the War Department General Staff pointed out that in the light of World War I experience, all the Captains in "the Hump" would be jumped two to three ranks in the next mobilization of any size anyway, so why not promote them at least one rank, without delay and with a guaranteed, additional rank within the near and easily-foreseeable future? Mean-while, there were increasing numbers of assignments arising in which rank was immaterial. The demands of the Tree Army had demon-strated as much. Moreover, instead of Lieutenants and Captains to the colleges and universities as R.O.T.C. Instructors, why not Colonels, Lieutenant Colonels and Majors? The same policy could be applied to Instructors assigned to the National Guard and Officers Reserve Corps, to teaching slots at West Point, and to desks in sundry Head-quarters and in supply base assignments where rank and basic Arm could be listed as immaterial. Moreover, in most armies Lieutenant Colonels commanded Battalions. Adoption of that practice could help.

These arguments prevailed and the time-in-grade principle as basis for promotion became the approved philosophy. Under date of July 31, 1935, Congress enacted a War Department-designed statute under the grandiloquent, if dubious, title of "An Act to Promote the Efficiency of the National Defense." Its sole purpose was to achieve wholesale promotions of Regular Army officers without disturbing by so much as an eyelash the sacred and existing seniority structure, Second Lieutenant to Colonel. It was thought to be so rigged with high percentages in Field Grades, with stipulated years in lower ranks for eligibility, that any officer commissioned before or during World War I might be promoted. But the estimates were shoehorn tight. It brought the West Point class of 1915, who had been Captains and Majors for 18 years, within one year of a Lieutenant Colonelcy. Lieutenants of 17 years' standing began pinning on Captain's bars. But there was happiness within the Army Posts. It suggested strongly that any officer who could escape the admittedly ineffective and impotent B-Boards to age 64, if not already too far above average age-in-grade, stood a good chance of retiring as a Colonel.

The result, however, was just another personnel logjam. It was not broken until a new statute, July 13, 1940, by which time the Army already was flexing its muscles. Regular officer strength had been raised earlier, 12,000 to nearly 15,000. All newcomers were Lieutenants. The lockstep seniority principle with time-in-grade for promotion, without regard to percentages in each grade below Colonel, was adopted boldly. A numerical ceiling was, however, put on full Colonels at 705. Three years as a Second, 10 as a First made all Lieutenants Captains on the Promotion List. They in turn became Majors within, or at the end of, seven more years, and Lieutenant Colonels within or not later than six more years. This merely moved all the logjam, or "the Hump," into Field Grade status with 5,352 Lieutenant Colonels and Majors,* more than a third of the commissioned strength of the Regular Army. Most of these new Lieutenant Colonels were carefully scoring the annual deaths and retirements within the authorized list of 705 full Colonels. For these the new retirement age was pushed down to 60, and to 62 for Brigadier Generals. Promotion List Major Generals could continue active to the traditional age of 64. While this legislation was in the mill, another statute authorized *temporary* promotions *by selection* to General Officer grades and to full Colonelcies for Lieutenant Colonels. Similar *temporary* promotions became available *by selection* for lower-ranking Regulars of appropriate years of commissioned service. This was disconcerting to many. Sacred seniority was being threatened.

## THE SCOPE OF "THE HUMP"

"The Hump" in the Promotion List for Line officers, the reader no doubt has detected, was the direct result of an overwhelming majority of the Line officers in the Army, as reorganized to peace basis in 1920,

---

* Figures are as of October 20, 1940.

having begun their commissioned service within the four years that bracketed the prewar Preparedness surge and the World War I years, namely June, 1915, to June, 1919. By the former date, steps were being taken to recruit Line Second Lieutenants direct from civil life without the normal, solid requirement that the candidate for appointment be a graduate of a military college. The vast majority of the "Hump" officers, however, first were commissioned between the middle of August, 1917, and November 11, 1918, when battlefield commissions ceased and Officer Candidate Schools in America and Europe were closed incident to demobilization.

The scope of "the Hump" may best be illustrated by two familiar names, neither of whom was under fire in World War I. Dwight D. Eisenhower was graduated from West Point and was appointed Second Lieutenant of Infantry, June, 1915. He was on the forward edge of "the Hump." Alfred M. Gruenther was commissioned into the Field Artillery out of West Point, November 1, 1918. Upon reorganization of the Army, in which General of the Armies John J. Pershing quite naturally received O-1 as his serial number, Major Eisenhower was assigned serial number O-3822. But Second Lieutenant Gruenther drew O-12242, though he had only three and-a-half years' less commissioned service than Eisenhower. Gruenther did not become a permanent Promotion List First Lieutenant until 1923. And "permanent" almost proved to be the right adjective. Pursuant to the age-in-grade policy, he became a Captain in 1935, after nearly 18 years as a Lieutenant; a Major in 1940, and a Promotion List Lieutenant Colonel December 11, 1942, by which time he already was a war-made temporary Brigadier General. With equal permanence, Eisenhower continued as a Major until his Lieutenant Colonelcy as of July 1, 1936.* Before he acquired enough Permanent List seniority to rate an automatic Colonelcy, Eisenhower, by special legislation, had been promoted to permanent Brigadier General, August 30, 1943, to give him permanent status above such Permanent List Colonels as George S. Patton and others whom he then commanded but who outranked him on the Permanent Promotion List.

The complete imbalance of the Line officer structure of the Regular Army as a result of "the Hump" and application of the above policy in an effort to solve the problem is revealed by the officer distribution by ranks as of October 20, 1940. According to the Army Directory of that date, there were 21 Major Generals, 45 Brigadier Generals, 705 Colonels, 2,883 Lieutenant Colonels, 2,469 Majors, 1,877 Captains, 2,017 First Lieutenants and 2,219 Second Lieutenants. The upper-bracket First

---

* The above-mentioned serial numbers are not to be confused with the Promotion List numbers and Relative List numbers of this era. One's serial number never changed. Experienced clerks could glance at it and guess within nine months of the date of an officer's first commission.

Lieutenants on this list were in their early '30's and had been out of West Point nine years. But the senior Second Lieutenants were thought to be still wet behind the ears. They were out of West Point with the June class of 1938.*

The foregoing is sufficient to reflect the disparity in speed of advancement, comparative ranks and pay among career soldiers in the same uniform, so nearly the same ages, and with negligible calendar differences in lengths of service. It was thus inevitable that when an expansion of the Army gave promise of breaking the rigid lock-step of seniority through the channel of selections-up to temporary commissions, long-dampened ambitions were fired. "The Hump" became a volcano of erupting military ambitions, notwithstanding restrained dignity and highly ethical attitudes of hundreds of fine officers whose Excellent to Superior records in every situation, such as those of Eisenhower and Gruenther, gave them complete confidence as to their professional futures. The favorite *modus operandi* of the mediocre and less competent "Hump" officers who were correspondingly less certain of their future was soon to become the hurling of sizzling rocks and spewing of lava at the mobilizing National Guardsmen and such Reservists as might have enough rank to become a "block file" to a promotion for themselves. Since it was the Guard formations that had the most rank and the greater potential for assignment slots requiring stipulated ranks, there was the natural attempt to convert their units into stepping stones for soaring ambitions, and further to function as the scapegoats for old professionals who had become experts at passing the buck by way of glossing their own performance, or glossing-over the lack of it.

## AMBITIONS IN HIGHER ECHELONS

Furthermore, the folly of the Regular Army's seniority Promotion Lists had left its mark on some senior officers who had outranked "the Hump" all their professional lives. Lieutenant General (Temporary) Ben Lear, for example, was up from the ranks, via the Spanish War

---

* The totals of these numbers by ranks do not represent the aggregate of the officer corps of the Regular Army as of that date. Doctors, Dentists, etc., were not included in Promotion Lists because they were not Line officers. Likewise, three short lists totaling 116 Colonels and General Officers, temporarily serving in assignments and ranks higher than their permanent commissions are ignored above as duplicative. The same is true of Gen. George C. Marshall, then a low-ranking Major General by permanent appointment but a four-star General by virtue of assignment as Chief of Staff. Routinely, he would have retired as a Major General, but with the courtesy title of General, as had his immediate precedessors, Malin Craig and Douglas MacArthur. The War changed that and brought about MacArthur's recall to command assignments. Also omitted were several thousand Reserve officers, Lieutenants and Captains for the most part, then on extended active duty. Their names and numbers do not appear on the Regular Army lists, published in the *Army Directory*.

and the Philippines, from which he had emerged as a Regular Army Cavalry Lieutenant December 1901. World War I had seen him through to a comparatively quick, temporary Colonelcy. But some officers junior to him similarly had achieved at least a single star. The cup of World War I resentment was filled further by his reversion to Permanent List status as a Lieutenant Colonel. Duty with troops no longer seemed to him to be the path to promotion. Most of the years that followed were in Army Service schools, ending with the War College, Staff assignments and duty in the Inspector General's Department. May, 1936, had brought him the long-awaited single star. The second star came two years later but just in time to see George C. Marshall, an erstwhile, far junior Colonel, jumped over his head to four stars and the assignment as Chief of Staff. In 1940 General Lear was hale, hearty, formal and somewhat pompous, and nearly four years short of statutory retirement at age 64. But the Army again was expanding. Old ambitions took fire. Had not Pershing turned 60 in France? With the National Guard again called to active duty, another overseas force again could be in the making. Obviously it was a situation that called for decisive and professional vigor.

Quite naturally the ambitious old warhorse became even more decisive than vigorous. Because a few effervescent young Guardsmen yoo-hooed at pretty girls on a golf course in sports attire, who most likely wanted to be yoo-hooed at, the old General present and in civilian clothes himself, arbitrarily punished the entire unit. His prompt reward was the widely-proclaimed nickname that clung to him thereafter— "Yoo-Hoo Ben Lear." But vigorous and decisive Generals often have the last word. From his Headquarters as C.G., Second Army, he spent the mobilization and training months of 1940-41 blaming all the faults and shortcomings of his command upon the alleged shortcomings of the Guard and Guardsmen. Actually, the splendid and normally charming old gentleman was too form-fitted and rigid for a fast-changing situation. As Commanding General in Hawaii he would have been of far greater value to the Service. He most likely would have been more vigorous and hardly could have been less alert than was Lieutenant General Walter C. Short on Pearl Harbor Day.

Brigadier General Lesley J. McNair, who became Number Two on a list of 29 temporary Major Generals in September, 1940, was another officer whose spirit harbored dammed-up resentments against the Army reorganization scheme of 1920 and the seniority policies thereafter. Out of West Point in 1904, and four years younger than Ben Lear, McNair had a wider margin of time in his favor. But he had an increasing physical disability. His hearing was greatly-impaired. In a rank-hungry Army such as then prevailed, any conspicuous physical handicap made a senior officer highly vulnerable to compulsory retirement. Indeed, had

392

General McNair been a National Guard officer of any grade in 1940, he would have been rejected for active duty in the rather cursory, pre-mobilization physicals before the rendezvous of the units for movement to the training camps.

When the author first knew McNair, however, in early 1940, the General had learned to live with the hearing handicap. But even after 20 years, he made no effort to conceal resentment against a system that had reduced him from a temporary Brigadier General, at age 35, to a Permanent List Major in 1920. He had achieved a brilliant Staff record in France under Pershing. He was Chief of Artillery in the A.E.F. Staff Section for training within the overseas Theater. McNair made more than one conversational remark that clearly indicated he thought he might have fared better as to rank in the postwar reorganization, had he commanded troops in battle.

General McNair's lack of field command experience both in peace and in combat was indeed his greatest handicap. A close scrutiny of some directives and the official history of his Headquarters readily reveals as much. After a conference in North Africa with General Patton, who differed on organizational concepts, McNair, in his notes, assured himself that though lacking in combat experience himself, his judgment (presumably through sheer scholarship) was better than that of General Officers then actually in combat. However, with the great Second and Third Army maneuvers of 1941 behind him, which he observed fully and for which he conducted the critiques, he had learned little about motor transport and maintenance in the field. In April of 1942 we find him in argumentation with Lieutenant General Brehon G. Somerville, C.G., Services of Supply. McNair wrote ".... not more than five years ago, it was found . . . that motor maintenance could be effected properly with a ½-ton pick up truck of parts and tools for each 64 vehicles to be maintained."

Had McNair sprung that proposition on Patton, he would not have received the courtesy of laughter behind his back; it would have been to his face. Somerville was more polite. From the wealth of his experience as an officer of Engineers on many large non-military and civilian projects, Somerville knew what he had to have for his Supply Services. He settled with a joint committee from his own and McNair's staffs for approximately *one ton of rolling maintenance per 13 vehicles!* And this was for rear area supply units. McNair might well have fainted had he ever accurately envisioned the real and vastly greater ratio of maintenance overhead required by the personnel and ammunition carriers, signal equipment, trucks, tanks and Artillery prime movers that were organic to the combat formations operating within the beaten zones of enemy gunfire.

393

Personally, McNair was gentlemanly but hardly easy to know. A conversation had to interest him or he gave it nothing. When he did participate, he was openly forthright and usually brief. Socially he could reveal a charming, frank personality and become quite talkative and informative when with a good listener. His interest in and mastery of weapons appeared to be as inexhaustible as it was pedantic.

His service as a Major, Lieutenant Colonel and Colonel, 1920-37, was almost exclusively on upper echelon staffs interspersed with student tours in advanced Service schools, including the War College, and teaching in the Artillery School or the Staff College. At no time did he serve as an Instructor for either Guard units or for the Officers Reserve Corps. His only civilian tours were as Professor of Military Science and Tactics, Purdue University, in the late '20's, which he liked, and a brief civilian year or so, in Louisiana, with the C.C.C., 1934-35. For the latter his disdain was complete. He was a much better book soldier than most. He occasionally revealed the professional's low esteem for amateurs, be they Guardsmen or Reservists. The former he viewed with the greater suspicion, for he appeared to be reasonably sure all were transitory State or municipal politicians.

General McNair's battlefield death near St. Lo in Normandy was doubly tragic, not only because it came from American weapons but because he had no business being there. For the benefit of German Intelligence, he had been taken to England as the announced Commander of FUSAG—First United States Army Group—the Intelligence cover for a mythical force that existed only in poorly-camouflaged, artificial installations and ostentatious radio activity immediately across the English Channel from Calais. It was calculated to screen the real, silent and massive concentrations in West England opposite Normandy. FUSAG, at the same time, could freeze in position a German Army Group in the Calais area in expectation of a main cross-channel effort there. The *ruse de guerre* was working. General McNair should have continued being discreetly conspicuous in England. Being seen in Normandy, not to mention attendant publicity from getting killed at an observation post overlooking St. Lo, was no way to perpetuate the ruse.* For this reason there was an initial effort to keep his death a secret, but too many people who knew him had seen him. Indeed, there were newsmen with him at the time.

The assignments of Generals Lear and McNair to C.G., Second Army, and C.G. of Army Ground Forces, were not among General Mar-

---

* It is realized that friends of both the author and McNair may charge bad taste for this critique of a loyal, dedicated soldier who died for his Country on a foreign field. But the heroic, dying words of Capt. James Lawrence, "Don't Give Up the Ship," have not kept discerning historians from truthfully recording that Lawrence, with his ship, had no business being where he was that day.

shall's better appointments.* That of McNair was particularly unfortunate. His temperament and instincts were those of the meticulous scholar and Staff officer; not those of a commander of armies. When an answer was in a regulation, Intelligence report, a blueprint or in the military literature, his reaction to a problem was usually prompt and right. But in 1940-42, the reports, literature and the blueprints were not keeping abreast of essential command decisions. And in creating civilian armies there are scores of non-military command decisions. The official historian of his Headquarters proclaims him to have been a great, decisive organizer. But why the Guard Divisions were not "triangularized" until after Pearl Harbor and more than a year of active duty is not discussed. The same is true of many other shortcomings of Ground Forces GHQ that may not have been apparent from its own ivory towers but which were obvious to every Field Grade officer in command of Battalions and Regiments, not to mention Divisions and higher field commands.

Moreover, these shortcomings of Ground Forces H.Q. and its Commander's reflected jaundiced view of the Guard units were not necessary. Other high-level commanders such as Lieutenant Generals Hugh A. Drum, First Army; Walter Krueger, Third Army, and Jacob L. Devers, from his sprawling complex at Fort Bragg, and many of the Corps Commanders, certainly demonstrated the effectiveness of constructive attitudes. They thereby did much through local training initiative to offset the shortcomings of McNair's Headquarters. Indeed, most of the senior professional officers who had any appreciable field service in France under Pershing were highly pleased by having Guard units under their command. They treated them and welcomed them as units of great potential and as collaborators in a common enterprise toward excellence.

But such was not the attitude of either McNair or Lear. And they are reviewed here, not only for their important roles, but because they typified others of the same vintage in similar or lesser roles. Their preconceptions were reflected early in the spirit of their respective Headquarters and Staffs. Their attitudes were an encouragement to the erupting ambitions of the mediocrities in "the Hump." These were also among the crosses of professional narrowness and lack of Regular Army experience and far-sighted Staff planning that the Guard had to bear from every unit's induction date until Pearl Harbor Day.

---

* The assignments of Gens. Lear and McNair were not Gen. Marshall's biggest errors in personnel judgment. The dubious distinction of being the worst selection belongs to McNair's classmate, Joseph W. (Vinegar Joe) Stilwell, of China and Burma. McNair was enough of a canny Scot that he would have done far better in China than did Stilwell.

# GUBERNATORIAL ECCENTRICITIES WITH
## HONORARY COMMISSIONS

Many professional officers who never had been detached to Guard Instructorship tours of three to six years entertained most bizarre ideas as to how the recently-mobilized Field Grade Guard officers had acquired their ranks. The myth that Captains and Lieutenants were elected by their own men apparently satisfied most curiosities concerning these grades, but the question remained as to who elected the Majors, the Colonels and the Generals. Regulars who were former Guardsmen from World War I could say what had happened in their State in 1916-17, before their own integration, but were justifiably sure things might be different under new statutes and perhaps different in some or all the other States of the Union. Officers back to Army assignments from Instructorships with Guard units did not always reveal similar practices within adjacent States. But since the Guard's Field Grade officers, not to mention an occasional youthful-appearing Brigadier in his middle '40's, were somewhat younger than their opposite numbers among the Regulars, many ambitious professionals instinctively were sure that all the worst they ever had heard about Guard promotions must be indisputably true.

It was not a good basis for unrestrained and enthusiastic collaboration in a major training mission for both Guardsmen and the new, modernizing Regular formations. Moreover, the Guardsmen did not always do a good job in orienting their new military colleagues as to the facts concerning the Guard under the National Defense Act of 1920. Indeed, too many of them were not too fully-informed as to the history and evolution of their own component of the Army of the United States. Moreover, they often assumed that the Regulars, being professionals, must be more fully-informed on the subject than they, so why bother?

And there was the confusion caused by Gubnernatorial Honorary Colonelcies. One of Kentucky's Governors, eager to spread the fame of his State as a land of Colonels, issued so many honorary commissions in that historic rank that a hostile legislative committee threatened to investigate his waste of public funds for expensive, ornate and unnecessary printing and stationery. Actress Mae ("Come up 'n' see me sometime") West was one of the several thousand beneficiaries of his military effulgence. Other Governors occasionally got into the game. Governor Ma Ferguson of Texas, and her immediate successors, trumped the mint julep Governors with a few commissions as Admiral in the Texas Navy. Not to be outdone, the Governor of Nebraska began issuing commissions in the Nebraska Navy. The masthead of his commission was embellished by oxen-powered prairie schooners cruising sedately in a "line ahead" formation past sun-bleached skulls of long-deceased buffalo.

Wisconsin's Julius (the Just) Heil found himself Governor in 1939. He noted the rising tide of honorary, military interest. He quietly got into the act with a few discreet commissions to old Milwaukee friends, as Honorary Colonels, on his equally honorary Staff. Before he could turn off the flow of parchment and tell the public that no emoluments or duties were involved, his Executive Secretary had issued well over 100 Honorary Colonelcies. Each was complete with silver, spread eagle, lapel button. The relative rank was said, by the derisive Democratic opposition, to be stamped on the reverse side of each insignia button, but this never was fully validated. Nevertheless, the Lieutenant Colonel of Wisconsin's 120th Field Artillery, upon being routinely promoted, Federally recognized by Army board action and duly commissioned as Colonel of the Regiment, was mildly amused to see his picture in the Press of the State over the caption: "Upstate Democrat is Colonel No. 120 on the Governor's Staff." The Governor was much less amused. It took him 24 hours, the Adjutant General being out of town, to find out how such a thing could happen without the knowledge of anyone in his office. By that time he had been forced to promise additional Colonelcies to sundry snubbed or slighted Republicans to underpin his protests that he was denying his friends nothing to curry favor with any Democrat, upstate or elsewhere.

All such courtesy commissions in the above and other States* not only were confusing to the more serious-minded professional soldiers, but to some it was sacrilege. There should be no such cavalier-like horseplay with titles they hoped to achieve at the end of a long and dedicated career of duty and service. At the same time such careless use of the States' neatly-embossed stationery bothered the National Guardsmen of those States little or not at all. Indeed, many thought it good, clean fun, particularly when they knew the specific situation and the personalities involved. It was indeed a rare Honorary Colonel who went to the expense of buying a uniform for either formal or informal occasions. When one was pompous enough to do so, it made the joke all the better. But to some serious-minded Regulars, it was an illegal act, covered by a spurious document—a clear case of fraudulent impersonation of an officer of the United States Armed Services.

In the workaday life of their own home towns, most Guard officers carried their own military titles rather lightly—perhaps too lightly. But after all, it was a strictly avocational activity—an activity that was both military and civic. A local lawyer or merchant might well be the Com-

---

* A Louisiana Governor once commissioned three friends into the rank of "Buck Private." His alleged purpose was so there would be some Privates at State functions to salute all the Honorary Colonels on his Staff. Since they at once claimed to be the only "Commissioned Privates" in American military history, their embossed parchments were said to be documents of true distinction.

mander of the local Field Artillery Battery and a few Doctors and dentists could be officers in local Medical Detachments, but except in Armory drills and periods of instruction at camp, in Summer training or otherwise actually in uniform, they seldom, and some never, were addressed by their military titles. The capacity of the Captain for leadership of the local Battery, Troop or Company did not reside in a title, or even in the framed commission on the Orderly Room wall, nearly so much as it came from his civic leadership, his own interest in matters military and his willingness to assume the full responsibilities for all the property, Armory supervision, raising and supervision of unit funds, and recruiting and maintenance of interest through an active training program. There was normally just enough social activity to keep the organizational ball rolling. It was these qualities, combined with enough study on his part to know the answers when his officers and men asked questions—and if he did not know, readily admit it and make it a point to know at the next Armory training period—that not only kept the unit functional and in being at the home Armory but caused the men to play the game with prompt response to all orders in a spirit of teamwork for the unit.

Invoking a law or regulation to achieve prompt compliance was seldom, and for many Guard officers, never necessary. Why should there be when all were members voluntarily? These qualities gave most units many of the characteristics of a civic welfare organization and a fraternal order. A self-analytical Guard officer once described his own local status more or less as follows: "In my own town I am just another lawyer until Decoration Day ceremonies remind everyone that I am Captain and Commander of Battery C. In that capacity, I rank with but junior to the Captain of the Shrine Patrol and one file higher than the High School Bandmaster. But our Scoutmaster has salvaged so many youngsters from juvenile delinquency that in our town he outranks all three of us."

This self-description would not now be remembered had it not so thoroughly irked a recently-arrived, slightly pompous, new Regular Captain of Artillery, assigned to the Regiment as instructor. That a properly-uniformed, Federally-recognized Captain in America's Armed Services, which the Guardsman most certainly was, could concede himself outranked in public esteem or in any other way by the local Scoutmaster, was shocking. And in his state of shock, the middle-aged West Pointer was quite articulate. But within a year or more he became thoroughly acclimatized to the Guard and realized the most effective Guard officers often rejected the slightest degree of anything that savored of ostentation as one of their techniques of community leadership and unit command. In the Guard, particularly through those Pacifistic years, a Guard officer's capacity for leadership and command had to rest upon something higher and less tangible than the framed commission on the Orderly Room wall or a handbook of military statutes and a set of Regulations on the shelf.

The casual, deceptive quality of such leadership often concealed a forceful, dynamic, highly-informed personality of unusual judgment that nothing short of a real emergency was likely to reveal. Moreover, in a society of machines, both mobile and stationary, the case of transfer of skills from civilian radio and telephone services, garages, road-building equipment and farm machinery to firing ranges, gunnery teamwork, motor maintenance, and Army field wire and switchboards, was so natural that the techniques of Army equipment and its use offered no difficulty to Guard officers and their men. Hence there often was demonstrated an official casualness toward those matters which the more narrowly-trained Regulars, accustomed to conventional, peacetime, untrained Army enlistees, always approached with ostentatious emphasis, textbook formality and parade ground precision. Because of the informally deceptive qualities of the avocational citizen-soldiers, many Regulars, including some who did tours of duty with the Guard and Reserves, never penetrated the veil to discover the essential military qualities of the officers and men. They saw only the civic side of the Guard as a City or community institution. They naturally and gravely fell into the repeated error that Guardsmen and Reserve officers never could be real soldiers "under the demands of modern warfare"—as if all warfare has not been modern within the era in which it was fought, and that American military history has been little more than a history of citizen-soldiery!

Most Regular Army officers who completed a full four or more years of duty as Battalion or Regimental Instructors came to some appreciation of the inherent difference between Reserve officers, Guard units and their counterparts in the Regular Establishment. Many became firm believers in and warm admirers of the Guard as an inexpensive and highly-effective defense agency as well as civic institution. Of equal importance, they learned that what is avocational to a mass of men has vastly different terms of reference than does the same activity when it is 100% a man's livelihood, a profession, or a vocation; and that quite often the truly zealous or gifted amateur can and may transcend the professional in knowledge and skills. But most other Regular Army officers could not be convinced that the Guard was anything but a strange, civilian jungle of high ranks based on political friendships, and local marching societies in which the men elected the Company officers and Governors used Colonelcies purely as political patronage.

The Guardsmen themselves would have been the first to concede that the always-zealous and the gifted amateurs in the Guard were not always the first to be promoted. But the situation was far from being as deadening as the lock-step of the Regular Army's seniority Promotion Lists. All fixed concepts of promotion by seniority, or by time-in-grade, as among the Regulars, would have collapsed in the face of the essential geographical distribution and unit structure of the National Guard of the several States. Promotion practices that could have prevailed in an urban area, boasting of two or more complete Regiments or Combat Teams, could not possibly be applied to promotions in two other Regiments of the same Arm in the same State, but which were scattered through 30 or more market towns and County Seats of an agricultural area.

The localized character of the Guard units was both a strength and a handicap (with the strengths far outweighing the handicaps), but officer personnel handicaps there truly were and always will be. Batteries A and B of the Hundred and Humpteenth Field Artillery, for example, might be in a college or university town too small to support more than the two units, but nevertheless might be rich in talent in both commissioned and non-commissioned grades. Six of the eight Battery officers easily could be young faculty members of the university's engineering school; all NCO's might be college graduates, and most of the Privates were often upperclassmen in the university. Battery C of the same Regiment and only 40 miles distant easily could be in a County Seat in which military talent was scarce and the four officers weaker than average for their rank. Obviously it was, and in similar circumstances still is, impossible to equalize the situation by transferring talented officers and NCO's from Batteries A and B to the less-fortunate Battery C, and dropping the latter's less-competent personnel from the roster. It was not that the Battery C personnel might have stood on their tenure rights, because they had none. Moreover, the remuneration was not worth an embarrassing public argument. At best the gross remuneration was then less than a maximum of $650 a year for the Captain and less than $400 for the Lieutenants—not worth even a protest, particularly since transfer to the Officers Reserve Corps was available. Transfer of two Lieutenants to Battery C from A or B was impractical because their professions held them in their university town. Likewise, the officers in Battery C had to be from that local community, in which no better military talent was available.

But the surplus of good officers and men in the two university town Batteries was not necessarily lost from the Guard. Came a mobilization, redistribution of personnel within the Battalion became possible.

Moreover, many of the enlisted students were graduated to the towns and cities of the State to become Guard officer material in those communities.

Recent R.O.T.C. graduates and other Reserve officers who might move into a community often were taken into Guard units directly as officers. It was not unusual for a Guard unit Captain to find his military duties conflicting so severely with his profession or business, that he would notify his Colonel and the State Adjutant General of his intention to transfer to the less demanding Officers Reserve Corps. The military qualifications certified by examining boards Chairmanned by a Regular Army officer were identical for Guardsmen as for Reserve officers, hence no more than application and transfer was involved.

When a Guard Captain in a one-unit town thus resigned, it occasionally happened that no local Lieutenant was willing to accept promotion because of the property responsibility and pressures of his own civilian job or profession. In such a case the Regiment's Colonel and/or the State Adjutant General would visit the town and prevail upon a local O.R.C. officer to accept command. Failing this, the unit might be broken-up and reorganized elsewhere. Because of Armory considerations and other attendant costs, little short of heroic efforts were made to avoid such a solution. For example, in a Midwest town of about 6,000, the Captain was killed in an accident. Both Lieutenants refused promotion to the vacant Captaincy because of property responsibility and demands of their own civil occupations. It so happened that the First Sergeant was an O.R.C. Lieutenant. The First Sergeant was designated Captain, on orders from the State Adjutant General. He was "boarded" for physical and military qualifications, which specifications were identical with those for a Captain of the same Arm in the O.R.C. Thus the erstwhile First Sergeant was Federally-recognized as a Captain. Both the Lieutenants continued in their grades and happily served under their former First Sergeant.

Such suggested flexibility within a small unit was often a surprise to rank-conscious Regulars who cherished the seniority concept that nothing short of a war could get an enlisted man promoted over one's head, and in time of peace a self-respecting Lieutenant would resign rather than accept it.

Of course, the more typical and normal promotion within a local Infantry Company or Battery was for two Lieutenants to move up a grade, and the most alert and best-qualified Sergeant, often the holder of a Reserve commission, to move into the vacant Second Lieutenancy. But in the Guard of this era no Second Lieutenant ever became a First merely by serving time-in-grade, nor did any other Guard officer of any

401

other rank or assignment. Until there was a vacancy in the War Department's prescribed Table of Organization for the Arm and unit concerned, there was no promotion for anyone. The same Table was applicable to noncommissioned ranks and ratings. All officer promotions had to be validated by a Federal Recognition Board presided over by an officer of the Regular Army.

Nevertheless, the idea was widely current in 1940 that in many States, perhaps all, Company officers were elected by the enlisted men of the local unit. There is a tradition-encrusted, East Coast unit, proud of its comparatively ancient, original Charter, that uses an election stipulation as an excuse for a periodic major social event. But the election is strictly ritualistic and thoroughly in accord with the spirit of the social event. The incumbent officers always are reelected to the tune of after-dinner speeches and a refilling of the flowing bowls. But such an election was as meaningless as the ancient Charter which long since had been completely abridged and invalidated by subsequent laws and regulations by both the State and the Federal Governments.

In cities large enough to sustain a full Regiment, Brigade, or even a Division, as in the case of New York City, the contiguity of units, often in the same Armory, made for greater flexibility with reference to Company and Battery-level officers. A vacancy in Company D could be filled readily by transfer and promotion of any one of 12 or 15 alert and promising First Lieutenants from one of the other units or Headquarters of the Regiment. Seniority could be and often was a factor in the selection for promotion, but never seems to have been the only factor in a representative number of regimental-size local units that were checked.

Indeed, First Lieutenant was a popular rank. By declining a promotion to Captain, an officer could have a maximum of fun and a minimum of responsibility. As a Captain he had property responsibility for rifles, pistols, machine guns, ammunition, clothing, blankets, bedding, binoculars, range-finders, trucks and cannon. No one ever stole a $15,000 cannon, but the other items were quite attractive to juvenile delinquents and some who were not juvenile. The Captain paid for all shortages he could not survey as a result of fair wear and tear, or loss by a broken lock or other evidence of forced entry. Out of a gross income for the year of but $640 he stood to lose much and gain little. Some part of almost every day, he had to visit the Armory. For a carefree First Lieutenant, such an assignment was no promotion. Thus in many Regiments, in both urban and small town areas, the average age of Captains and higher gradually became lower than that of their Regular counterparts, while the Guard Lieutenants were often well into their '40's and losing no sleep over lack of promotion.

Promotion to Major was the big jump for the enthusiatic, alert

Guardsmen. It had neither the tight, geographical restrictions nor the property responsibilities of a Captain. Because of the lower, if not complete absence of the $250 annual Administrative Pay of the Captain, the Major could and often did take a small cut in annual pay. Nevertheless, it was a sought-for rank among the Captains who really liked to work at their hobby. Promotion to Major by merit within the same Regiment was a common practice in most States. Others ignored the Regimental restrictions and promoted to Field Grade within the Arm.

Merit was established sometimes by written competitive examinations lasting a day or more. In Wisconsin, while Brigadier General Ralph M. Immell was Adjutant General, any Captain might take the written examinations. Time-in-grade and accumulative efficiency ratings counted for 30% of the total competitive score of each. The same rule prevailed for Majors who aspired to a vacant Lieutenant Colonelcy. The Artillery Brigade Commander and his Colonels scored the non-written 30% value of the rating. The Infantry Brigade C.G. and his Colonels did likewise for that Arm. The questions and answers, map exercises and/or field problem of the written, professional 70% all were graded by a board of Regular Army officers, convened from among the assigned Instructors.

Since the Army and Guard Regiments prior to 1940 had but one Lieutenant Colonel, the next promotion for a Wisconsin Lieutenant Colonel was contingent largely upon his staying active in the Guard longer than his Colonel. Right of succession seems to have taken over at that point. As with the Regulars, a Colonelcy was the end of the rainbow in the minds of the most avid Guardsmen. Active Guard service, same as for Regulars, ended at age 64. Federal recognition was withdrawn at that age. Relatively few Guard Colonels, who could expect nought but their civilian savings to count upon for retirement, actually remained active to that age, unless the word was dripped about that the Brigade Commander was having trouble with his annual physical.

With seniority playing a relatively minor role in all Guard promotions, as compared to "the Hump" grades and lower ranks in the Regular Army, it naturally followed that Field Grade officers in the Guard were most frequently one to 10 years younger than professional Field Grade officers in the Regular Army's rank-hungry "Hump." Guard Major Generals, of whom there were 21 in 1940, more frequently than otherwise approximated the ages of the 21 Major Generals on the Regular Army's Permanent Promotion List. But the mobilizing Guard in 1940 did have a few surprisingly young Brigadiers and two or three Major Generals who appeared to be about the right age for a Lieutenant Colonelcy or a Majority in the Regular Army.

403

TO SUMMARIZE:

1. Congress was instinctively right in triggering the Guard's mobilization without delay, to give force to a diplomacy for neutrality.

2. For political reasons neither major political party nor its candidate for President would concede a probable utilization of American citizen-soldier volunteers or Selectees outside the continental limits of America, which raised the cogent and unanswered question of why the mobilization at all.

3. Thus robbed of purpose and specific training objective and appearing to many as just another pump-priming boondoggle, the Guard on active duty immediately became an object of doubt and controversy.

4. The War Department General Staff had no workable plans, not even realistic estimates, for immediate Guard mobilization, in terms of shelter, for camp grounds organized to meet bare minimums of sanitation, or for leasing lands adequate for training so many large bodies of troops in modern warfare.

5. The Administration's diplomatic policy of being an arsenal for the forces opposing Fascistic and Nazi totalitarianism gave top priority of land and air warfare equipment to future allies, leaving the Regular Army a second priority and the Guard in a badly-trailing third and last position, and top performance in training hardly can be separated from availability of equipment.

6. The Officer Corps of the Regular Army, cloistered for two decades in the quiet security of seniority and on scores of small, country club-like Army Posts, had only a confused and sometimes jealous, and usually a deprecatory impression of the Guard. Their terms of reference from fixed seniority had little relationship to or afforded a knowledge of the ethics commonly applicable to civil life competition for professional and business advancement.

7. The Guard officers, primarily being a vocational and professional cross-section of American civil life and secondarily soldiers as an avocational hobby combined with a sense of service, naturally represented a set of values, terms of reference, and viewpoint different from those of the Regulars. Thus the sudden merger of these two components of the Army of the United States into one active duty Army for a prospective 12 months resulted in what one might call a clash of military cultures, both in the same uniform and devoutly looking toward the same objectives, but separated by misconceptions.

8. At the same time, events in Europe were filling the public and the Press with ever-mounting concern, and even alarm, because of lack of preparedness. In such situations, the American public begins looking for a scapegoat. The Secretary of War and the General Staff

were quite willing that the Guardsmen be that scapegoat. From a standpoint of diplomacy of the day and National policy it was an almost criminally silly thing to do. When a nation is mobilizing and arming in an embattled World to give force to a diplomacy of neutrality, it is hardly intelligent to advertise impotence in its largest military component in being—in this instance, the National Guard. A better-informed policy would have presented them as being far more potent than they really were, and then, in a quiet, unselfish way to have sought to make them as fully potent with filler manpower, top-priority equipment and training as they were advertised initially. Doing otherwise was disarming American diplomacy and inviting the aggressions from two fronts that came December 7, 1941. As of that date, both friends and foes were greatly underestimating America's actual military strength and early potential. Deceiving friends and foes as to America's true strength was no way to implement a forceful diplomacy in a strife-ridden World. An Administration more experienced in foreign affairs would not have allowed it.

These comparable background factors within the two most active components of the Army of the United States, as of the mobilization and Army buildup that took on momentum in 1940, have been reviewed at considerable length, not because they are considered interesting, but because they are essential to an understanding of the lack of appreciation, unsympathetic treatment, officially-inspired adverse publicity, and occasional evidences of bad faith that characterized the National Guard's relations with the Regular Army's highest echelons through active duty training prior to Pearl Harbor Day, December 7, 1941. For any Guardsman who had neither an eye for analytical understanding nor a rugged sense of humor, and who had only a keen sense of duty to his Country and of proud loyalty to his Company, Regiment, Brigade and Division, it was a year of pettifogging critiques, inadequate equipment, unwarranted delays in obvious need for reorganization, occasional insults, unappreciated improvisations to overcome shortages and lack of General Staff planning.

# Bibliographical Note For Chapter XVI

This chapter is drawn not so much from the conventional, historical sources as it is from the author's notes and experience through the Mobilization and World War II years as a Regimental and Artillery Group Commander. Throughout the training period, he was impressed by the sincerity of purpose of Regulars, Guardsmen and volunteer Reservists toward giving the American people the finest Army possible with the funds and materials then available. Jealousies, lack of mutual appreciation and needless disharmony often retarded progress toward this common goal; and the higher the Headquarters, the more pronounced this situation seemed to be, most particularly in a high Headquarters, the Commanding General of which was most imbued with the Uptonian myth of a mass, military professionalism being essential to America. Staff officers, moreover, almost always over-accentuated the known views and attitudes of their commanders. After all, in the American Army it is the Staff officer's duty to implement the decisions and purposes of the commander, hence this tendency is not noted in criticism but in explanation of some over-emphasized conditions that prevailed. Fortunately, there were some Regulars at the Division, Corps and Field Army levels, such as Walter Krueger, Omar N. Bradley, Jacob L. Devers, Clarence R. Heubner and Leonard T. Gerow, who reflected little or absolutely no evidence of Uptonian indoctrination. Under such leadership rapid progress was always in contrast to recrimination, alibis, distrust and confusion elsewhere. It was from experience with these contrasts that the author then hoped he might find time some day to write something that would create a greater understanding and appreciation among the military-minded components that necessarily constitute the whole of an American Army. For the stultifying effects of the dead hand of "the Hump" and seniority upon a high percentage of the Regulars between the World Wars, one has but to consult the successive annual editions of the *Official Army Register* and the Relative Rank lists in the semi-annual editions of *The Army Directory*, in conjunction with the contemporary *U.S. Statutes* calculated to alleviate the situation. Maj. Gen. Otto L. Nelson, Jr., *National Security and the General Staff*, 1946, is perhaps the best study of that institution and the War Department organization from 1900.

## CHAPTER XVII

# Training and the Great Maneuvers Prior to Pearl Harbor

THOUGH conditions were different, and presumably America was endowed with General Staff officers who had learned much since their less experienced predecessors had fouled-up the Mexican Border mobilization of 1916, in many respects military history merely repeated itself. The camp sites to which the Guard units reported were locations rather than facilities. In September of 1940, the 45th Division, Major General William S. Key of Oklahoma commanding, was scheduled for Camp Barkeley at Abilene, Texas. As of that date Barkeley was merely a dry prairie bounded on the South by a series of low mesas and on the North by quick gusts of increasingly cold windstorms. Side trackage for a railhead was under construction. The mobilizing 45th found temporary refuge on Fort Sill's Artillery reservation. Preparations for its arrival at Sill consisted of stakes on the brown, dry meadows to define streets and tent rows. In March, 1941, the Division displaced to still-incomplete Camp Barkeley.

The 44th Division, with Major General Clifford R. Powell of New Jersey commanding, concentrated within the home State of most of the units at the old familiar Summer training areas around Fort Dix, New Jersey. It was adequate for such a number of troops through a brief, hot Summer season. Getting it habitable for a Winter already near at hand was something else. Learning to take care of themselves under adverse conditions was good training within itself, but hardly conducive to immediate and effective schedules in weapons and minor tactics pursuant to the 13-weeks initial training plan that had been handed-down from a distant General Staff Section, which had planned peering outward through the shutters of a remote ivory tower rather than from the field. At the same time the National Guard troops arriving at stations everywhere were having to cope with lamentable shortages of supplies, including medicine. Moreover, a better-informed and more practical-minded group of planners would not have assigned the 44th Division to a training camp and area within its own State in the first instance. With most officers and men at Camp Dix within commuting distance of their homes and erstwhile work, a quick and clean break with civilian business and professional obligations was impossible. Thus the 44th was off to an unlucky start. Though endowed with less facilities in distant Abilene, Texas, the 45th was the more fortunate. Abilene and Sill were so far from Washington, D.C., that the visitations of sundry War Department General Staff officers who merely wanted an official excuse to get out of the swivel chair for a day were conspicuously less than at Dix. The 45th's Unit Commanders had more time in which to get their essential work done.

The 41st Division (Wyoming, Washington, Montana, Oregon and Idaho) at Camp Murray, Washington, had much the same experience of the other three Divisions in the First Increment, September 16, 1940. Camp facilities were more limited than at Dix, but what there were of them were better than the 45th's undrained tent city and open sewers. The 41st Division also was benefited proportionally by its even greater distance from Washington, D.C. Thus, from a comparison of unit histories and contacts with officers who were there, the 41st, commanded by Major General George A. White of Oregon, appears to have been the most fortunate. All, however, had much the same experiences. The only difference was in varying degrees and details of the same adverse factors.

The 30th Division, from the Carolinas, Tennessee and Georgia, commanded by Major General Henry D. Russell of Georgia, went into training at Camp Jackson, South Carolina. It, too, was one of the four Divisions in the increment activated September 16, 1940. General Russell soon found himself experiencing all the difficulties of his National Guard colleagues at Camps Barkeley, Murray and Dix, with emphasis upon the disadvantages of proximity to homes of many units, and the nearness of Washington. Camp Jackson was just an overnight sleeping car ride from Washington. For the benefit of posterity, General Russell has recorded: "There were all kinds of visitors, some intelligent and some not so very wise. They came from every section of the staff in Washington. They brought along with them some memorandum, or a checklist, which was followed in going about in the Division, looking and collecting data. All asserted they wanted to help us."

And not all the visitors were routine Staff snoopers. The Brass rapidly appeared in force. "Everybody in Washington came to see us . . . When the Chief of Staff, Marshall, came to see us and went away, I remarked to the Divisional Chief of Staff that we had seen them all except the President. Shortly thereafter, the Chief of Staff came into my office with a very secret radiogram, saying that now the President is on his way, and our list of visitors is complete."

## UNPROFESSIONAL ETHICS BY PROFESSIONALS

Later, according to General Russell, he was to be heavily-visited by Artillery officers of less rank but with a more specific purpose. They came, for the most part, from General McNair's Ground Forces GHQ and General Lear's Second Army Headquarters in Memphis, Tennessee. When Brigadier General Robert J. Travis, commanding the Division's Artillery Brigade, along with a few other Field Grade officers, were "found" physically unfit soon after their arrival at Camp Jackson, General Russell had to make some prompt and important decisions. Should he call in Regulars of lower rank to fill these key assignments for the 12 months of training, or should he insist upon promoting Guard officers within the Division? These were decisions, in major or minor degrees, that sooner or later confronted every commander of National Guard Divisions, separate Brigades and non-divisional Regiments, thanks to the extremely thorough final physicals on upper-grade Guardsmen and the subsequently-invoked age-in-grade policy. Hence, the 30th Division case is reviewed in slightly more than passing detail by way of bringing out the pros and cons at issue.

Were the decision in favor of the Regulars assigned to the Division as Instructors, Russell, as Commander, would have professional officers who presumably knew all the answers, who also knew the Division and its strengths, weaknesses and equipment shortages. He would be the full beneficiary of their experience, professional education and overall wisdom. They likewise would be the beneficiaries of immediate temporary promotions to the level stipulated in the Tables of Organization.

409

For such a professional lift, they would be appreciative and presumably do their utmost.

On the other hand, at the end of the 12 months,* the 30th Division Guardsmen would return to home stations in their several Southern States and the temporarily-promoted Regulars would be reassigned to duties elsewhere. The vacancies would still be there. The officers then promoted at home stations to fill the vacancies would be without experience except in their lower ranks and responsibilities while in the 12 months of training. If the purpose of the 12 months of active duty was to turn-out fully-trained units, staffs and commanders at all levels, and in all assignments within a reconstructed and modernized Division that could be recalled immediately for any emergency anywhere without delay, it behooved the Division Commander to fill such vacancies in his citizen-soldier Division with the best available avocational officers of long-known merit and enthusiasm for such service. As for the Regulars, were they not already with the Division as Instructors? As such, were not the Division and its Commander entitled to their wisdom and utmost efforts anyway?

Since the purpose of the Guard mobilization was to train Guardsmen under Regular Army tutelage, the logic of the situation called for the promotion of Guardsmen and keeping the Regulars around to dispense their wisdom and guidance from whatever rank they might then hold. If the War Department wanted these specific Instructors to be experienced in a higher, temporary grade, was it not plausible that the Department would so promote them and send them to such assignments?

Confronted by these pros and cons, General Russell followed the logic of the situation, as did practically all other Guard Commanders *when they considered adequate Guard talent available.* Russell decided in favor of promotions within the Division of Guard officers to provide for the future contingencies that readily could follow the 12 months of active duty training. He chose Godfrey Cheshire. At 47 he had been a Guardsman and Reserve officer since 1910 with creditable World War I service as an officer. He had been a Colonel commanding North Carolina's 113th Field Artillery Regiment for the preceding eight years. He was "boarded," declared professionally-qualified by Regular Army examiners who signed the Board's reports, and Federally commissioned as a Brigadier General.

If Russell was wrong as to War Department policy or as to the candidate and his alleged merits, this was the time and duty for adverse professional action by the Regular officers on the Board. *Actually, the decisions to promote Guardsmen when available were in line with published War Department policy and repeated pronouncements by the*

---

* Extended to 18 months by law, September, 1941, and to nearly six years by what happened Pearl Harbor Day, and after.

410

*Army Chief of Staff, Marshall.* But many of the ambitious and rank-hungry, middle-aged Majors and graying Lieutenant Colonels in the Regular Army's stagnated Promotion List either did not know it or did not want to know it. Moreover, it was neither the policy of General McNair nor of one or more of the four Army Commanders, specifically of Ben Lear.

The situation in the 30th Division continues to be illustrative of what happened elsewhere, sooner or later, and in more-or-less the same degree of overtness, in most of the larger Guard units in the mobilization. It developed that even before the vacancy created by General Travis's physical disability, three or four of the National Guard Instructors from the Regular Army were already in cabal as to ways and means whereby each of them might convert any high-ranking vacancies that might occur into stepping stones to promotions for all of them. They were, according to General Russell's account, A. L. P. Sands, Field Artillery; Colonel Reginald H. Kelley, Infantry; Lieutenant Colonel Frank E. Brokaw, Infantry, and Major Hugh G. Elliott, Field Artillery. On the outskirts of the alliance Lieutenant Colonel William Hones, Infantry, was more of a lone wolf Regular, but was playing a more deft game for the glittering quarry others might flush through awkward or untimely error.

It was Brokaw who made the error. In an effort to get General Russell on his side, he spilled the entire story to the Division Commander. Sands was to get a star by becoming successor to Travis, the promotion that actually went to Cheshire. As soon as they could stack-up enough adverse reports to dump the Division's Chief of Staff, that full Colonelcy would go to Brokaw. Colonel Kelley was scheduled by the cabal to get the slot and rank of the first of the two National Guard Infantry Brigadiers who might let his lance sag, and so on. General Russell summarily shipped the Sands-Kelley-Brokaw combination and asked for replacements. Such abrupt reliefs embellish no one's record. General Russell soon acquired deep regrets for not having also dumped Lieutenant Colonel William Hones into the same shipment.*

---

* The 32nd Division Guardsmen (Wisconsin and Michigan) long retained even deeper regrets. Their Chief of Staff was a casualty in the home station physical examination. Maj. Gen. Irving A. Fish, of Wisconsin, quietly canvassed individually those of his Line Colonels who had been graduated from the Command and General Staff College, with the thought that one of them might happily relinquish his Regimental command for the vacancy. None volunteered. Two Michigan Colonels recommended Col. Hones, who recently had appeared at Camp Beauregard and already had commended himself most favorably to Gen Fish. Hones became the cunningly-ambitious and conniving Bugbear of the 32nd Inf. Div. from late 1940 until his relief by Maj. Gen. Edwin F. Harding, U.S.A., just as the Division was about to launch the Army's first offensive—the Papuan Campaign, Summer of 1942. It is interesting to note that none of the four, though in ages and grades with the professional experience whence high commanders were selected, became General Officers.

That a National Guard Division Commander on active duty could so readily rid his command of three Regular Army officers of such long service for what he considered unethical conniving for their own promotion, must have been little less than appalling to them, their friends and all other professionals who had knowledge of it. And no electronic device has yet been achieved that could relay gossip faster than the Army camp grapevine of 1940-41. One who fully understands these officers and their viewpoint can almost sympathize with them. The fact remains that by their own conduct, in the light of the Division Commander's ethical code, they had destroyed his confidence in them. But this early experience of three senior, career soldiers did not deter others afflicted with a lust for rank; it merely made them more cautious.

Thus the 30th Division, according to General Russell, was thereafter the beneficiary of many, many visitors in Regular Army ranks of Colonel and under. They came from McNair's GHQ, Ground Forces; from Lear's Second Army, and from the Corps Headquarters. Their specialty was finding something wrong with Brigadier General Godfrey Cheshire and his Field Artillery Brigade. In barracks and in the field, gunnery practice and in maneuvers, it was always the Division's Artillery Brigade that was in the doghouse. General Cheshire brought a Regular Army Artillery Lieutenant Colonel, Albert C. Stanford, to command one of the three Regiments, thereby elevating him to a Colonelcy, with the expectation that he and his Regiment might become an exemplar model and pace-setter for the Brigade. But there was no surcease of compiling skin sheets on the Artillery Brigade and its Commander by visiting Staff officers of all senior Regular Headquarters. Colonel Stanford's units apparently were no better than the others.

While the Division was going through its long-overdue "triangularization," late Winter and early Spring, 1942, the skin-sheet dossier was complete. The National Guard Brigadier was ordered before a Reclassification Board. The charge was that units under his command had not progressed adequately in training. When the accused National Guard B.G. suggested to Colonel Stanford that under this specification, he should initiate reclassification proceedings against the subordinate Commanders in direct command of the deficient Battalions, the Regular Colonel became frantic, declared he had no other profession, it would be ruinous, and he must be spared. Following a phone call to a War Department friend he was, the next morning, more at peace with the World. Five days later Colonel Stanford was transferred from the Division, and before either the National Guard Artillery Brigadier or the Division Commander could have executed any such proceedings had they truly intended to do so.

The foregoing brief review of personnel decisions in one Division of the First Increment of the Guard mobilization in 1940-41 not only illus-

412

trates similar occurrences, though no two identical in detail, that confronted all Division and higher unit Guard commanders through the mobilization and training that followed. It further gives the tactics and techniques the ambitious Regulars used, in a game that professionals of true Service dedication did not play.

They did not have to. Regular officers who had long-standing records and reputations for excellence in military theory and practice with known qualities for sound judgment, were getting temporary promotions anyway, just as fast as the expanding needs of a rearming America created the demand. Officers of their type in the professional Service were in the majority. When they did appear within a National Guard station, pursuant to command inspections, Headquarters umpiring, as Instructors or by assignment to a vacancy, they quietly proved to be natural leaders and most helpful. But they and their good work so often were obscured by the chronic carping, needling and undercutting of the arrogantly ambitious that the truly dedicated and ethically-minded professionals too seldom were noted, and the other category seemed to the harassed Guardsmen to be far the more numerous.

## ANNOUNCED PERSONNEL POLICY OFTEN IGNORED

One would like to insist that the rank-hungry professionals of the Regular Army's promotion list "Hump" were unaware of the published War Department policy. It would be untrue. Except for the occasional lone wolf operator, most of them normally reflected the attitude of their own Army or Corps Commanding General. General Krueger's Third Army Headquarters and its representatives, including Krueger himself, were vastly different from those of General Lear's Second Army. V Corps, endowed with a brilliant G-3, Colonel (later Lieutenant General) Ray E. Porter, was exemplary through the pre-Pearl Harbor training period. But General McNair's Ground Forces Headquarters was over all. His minions often by-passed all intervening commands to Guard Divisions, Brigades and Regiments. There is no doubt as to McNair's views and policies.

General McNair, of course, knew the *announced* policy, but he did not agree with it. He sought through training details and controls to create what he considered a better policy of his own. Moreover, he quickly found that publicity, for Press and magazines starved for defense news and articles, also could be a potent instrument. He gave free reign to personnel ambitions. He apparently surrounded himself with an official family of non-command Staff types who had Service school records far more brilliant than their World War I combat records—if any such records at all. The visitors from his Headquarters consistently brought less understanding, mouthed more vague training cliches, wrote

413

the most inconsistent reports (yes, many of them were sent back through channels for unit review, study and remedial action) and withal proved to be the worst hatchet men with whom the Guard field commanders had to deal. Lieutenant Colonel Lloyd D. Brown (Inf., G.S.C.), was one of the worst, though he impressed one initially as being the mild, indecisive, gentlemanly type, but whose reports were viciously uninformed and inaccurate. If he ever made a practical, constructive training suggestion, it was not circularized among the Commanders and Staffs of the 32nd Division.

Now, in the postwar writings of General Russell of the 30th Division, it is found that Brown, who immediately was promoted to Colonel in McNair's burgeoning Staff empire, did give confidential and what he considered constructive advice to his University of Georgia classmate, General Russell. Brown insisted that if Russell was to survive the exactions of the Regular Army, it would be necessary for him to sack as many Field Grade Guard officers as practicable, most particularly Colonels and Brigadier Generals, and call in Regulars to perform these highly technical duties and exercise the presumably occult leadership qualities known only to professionals.

Colonel Brown, though a Phi Beta Kappa himself (as was Russell), was of the Army type who was quite sure that no ordinary civilian, in just his spare time within a short 25 years, possibly could master all those techniques and abstract intuitions required to command such a gigantic operation as a war strength Regiment of 3,000 officers and men.

But General Russell was not impressed by this advice. He already had crossed that bridge in the promotion of Colonel Cheshire to Brigadier General. Moreover, in civil life Russell was a widely-and favorably-known attorney of strong convictions and a militant manner of voicing them. Like most lawyers, he held free advice in low esteem, and Brown was a non-fee classmate, University of Georgia, 1912. But his conversations with "Class Mate Brown," as he termed him, receive considerable emphasis in Russell's resentful memoirs of those unpleasant months. Some of Brown's dire warnings came true, but not entirely. Russell finished the war as a Major General in an appropriate Staff assignment, and thence to reorganize and command the Deep South's new 48th Infantry Division. But he continued to be an angry man.*

---

* Maj. Gen. Henry Dozier Russell was born December 28, 1889; began law practice, 1914; became officer, Georgia National Guard, 1916; ended World War I active duty as a Major. In Guard reorganization after 1920, he rose rapidly, to Federal recognition as a Major General, Line, commanding 30th Division September 20, 1932. He had a militant devotion to and a possessive attitude toward the Division in 1940 that unimaginative Regulars easily could have misinterpreted as an uncooperative spirit. From writing hastily and while still in anger, Russell damaged his published, personal narrative. (See citation in Bibliographical Note at the end of this chapter). It lacks discrimination and restraint. No one, however, who knows Russell will doubt his word as to facts and incidents that happened in his presence. Indeed, similar incidents elsewhere, some involving the same personalities, lend

Brown rose rapidly to temporary Major General commanding the 28th Infantry Division (Pennsylvania National Guard) which he took to Europe. In Normandy, following a few days in combat, he was relieved summarily, reduced to Colonel, the rank he was to hold in his last active duty assignment before his final retirement in 1948. There appears to have been no publicity then or later.

As will be shown in some subsequent figures, the Regulars were prompt in dealing with their own who let down the professional officer corps; sometimes more readily than with Guardsmen and Reserve officers. But it was the Guardsmen who most frequently received the embarrassing adverse publicity. Relief, reclassification and demotion of Regulars was always a quiet operation, unless there was a debacle, as in Lieutenant General Walter C. Short's case at Pearl Harbor. The Pearl Harbor attack publicly reclassified, demoted and retired Short from active duty in one brief forenoon.

## A PUBLIC RELATIONS PROBLEM CONFRONTS THE ARMY

Political scientists and sociologists occasionally have voiced the theory that when an institution, governmental agency or a bureaucracy finds itself the subject of public controversy and bitter denunciations so severe that the critical outcry cannot safely be ignored, it normally and instinctively takes on protective coloring and defensive action in conformity with one or more of three typical formulas. This is because agencies and bureaucracies have the same vital urge to survive as do human beings. All of which is quite natural, because human beings are the principal component of many such institutions. Each institution has the composite personality and collective views and reactions of its membership and most particularly of its leadership. The leadership may and usually does consciously choose the defensive formula and guides procedures in the chosen channels. On the other hand, they may instinctively react and act in such simultaneous harmony to the situation that it has every appearance of planned coordination.

The three choices normally are: (1) counter-publicity playing-down shortcomings and accentuating past and present virtues with emphasis on constructive, recent and contemporary services; (2) counter-publicity

strong supporting credibility. So long as the 30th Division was scheduled to return to home stations at the end of 12, and then 18 months, Russell was completely in line with published policies, public and private written directives. Moreover, he ran a good training program and a tight Division, according to competent witnesses. The unexpected hostilities changed the original purpose and intent. Thereafter, Gen. Russell appears to have erred in some judgments, thanks, perhaps to a sense of persecution Gens. Lear and McNair unwittingly had planted and nurtured. The author disagrees completely with some of Russell's absentee criticisms, most particularly those of his successor, Maj. Gen. Leland S. Hobbs, U.S.A., and his few Regulars who happily found themselves inheritors of a fine Division. All who saw and worked with the 30th Division, from England to the Elbe River, rated it one of the best and considered Gen. Hobbs an outstanding field commander.

upon cognate or similar institutions that will spread the blame and make the initially-attacked institution look good by comparison, which at the same time diverts the attention of critics and the public to other factors and perhaps graver dangers; and (3) finally, and most dreaded of all, short of outright extinction, is a partial or complete reformation to regain public and political confidence. This last has salvaged many ancient institutions—including the National Guard. Witness the Dick Act of 1903.

When the Congress proved to be more defense-minded than the War Department, the Executive Branch of the Government, and both candidates for the Presidency, by calling for the mobilization of the Guard and operation of a peacetime Selective Service, it was the General Staff in particular and the Army in general that were caught flat-footed and daydreaming on second base. An increasingly aware public was not long in finding it out. The Press and public rapidly passed from watchful waiting to carping criticism, to distress and thence to alarm.* Congress took note. A lavish appropriation of $466 million was made for the expansion of existing camps, forts and stations and the creation of new facilities. The activation of the Guard was the prime reason for the appropriation. In the costs and budgets of that Depression-ridden era, it was considered a stupendous sum of money to spend merely for emergency, transitory training purposes. In any event, the Army had the money requested, but not enough had happened soon enough. What was happening did not look good. Hundreds of Guardsmen were in sick lines and often necessarily sent to civilian hospitals each morning with respiratory illnesses. Doctors said it was from living weeks and months under no better than field bivouac conditions. All kinds of other gross inefficiencies immediately appeared. The Army was in deep trouble before its leadership knew it. Curious Congressmen, silently looking for issues, began visiting the camps.

Representative Albert J. Engel of Michigan did the grand tour and returned to the Capitol in April with bitterness and some astounding estimates. He had a flair for figures. Without benefit of Univac, he estimated the Army's impending deficit in the camp construction account at 330 million dollars. The War Department accountants and Budget Bureau sadly agreed Mr. Engel was off only $8.5 million and soon accepted a deficit appropriation of $338.5 million. Being short 72% for range on initial sight settings is extremely bad shooting. Something

---

* The public and its Press were, of course, the true cause of the unpreparedness of both the Regular Army and the Guard in 1940. Two decades of Pacifistic idealism and a passive public attitude toward defense were the true causes. But no institution ever survived by sweeping indictments of its own public, which is sovereign and never can be wrong. Indeed, by 1940 some of the more articulate of the Pacifist claque were loudest in their screams for immediate and complete security.

must be wrong in our Army, was the natural Congressional and public reaction.

Congressman Engel had a lot to tell that was wrong. Original estimates for Fort Meade's expansion were $9,053,187. With plans slightly altered to accommodate only 1% more troops, the revised estimated cost was $23,117,000. Contrary to local advice that the old, World War I expansion site be used, the sewers and roads of which were said to be still extant and usable, the higher-level planners in Washington insisted upon a new site, and new facilities. Estimates at Meade and elsewhere suggested the Army never had heard of overtime pay for extra hours and weekend work! This was within a two-hour auto drive, during bad traffic hours, from General and Special Staff Headquarters, War Department, Washington, D.C. If it was so bad at Meade, what must it be at distant camps and forts?

But of all the camps and installations, it was Camp Blanding, Florida, that blew the lid. Nearly half of Blanding's 117,000 acres were lower than the level of a nearby lake. There was an immediate outlay of $740,000 for unanticipated drainage, dredging and replacement of muck with sand fills. Getting a temporary tent spread for immediate reception of troops out of the mud cost mere chicken feed money at $10,000. Crushed rock for roads at Blanding cost $1.25 million, according to Army specifications. Local engineers insisted nearly half of this could have been saved through use of readily-available sand, and oil with a clay binder. The new but aging War Secretary, Mr. Stimson, normally was indifferent to details, but he had visited Blanding, made a speech to all warm with congratulations on progress, but he was hardly back in his office before there was a shake-up and replacements at that station.

But the angry and critical Congressman Engel was hardly satisfied. He loudly insisted, on which he was widely quoted, that: "The officers in the United States Army who . . . are responsible for this willful, extravagant and outrageous waste of the taxpayers' money ought to be court-martialed and kicked out of the Government Service." It was the beginning of a vast and rising tide of Congressional queries and criticisms that created special Senatorial investigations. Its revelations of defense planning inefficiencies made a Vice-President and later a President of its Chairman, Senator Harry S. Truman of Missouri.

The institutional reaction of the Army toward protective coloring was immediate and instinctively in line with the first and least painful of the three normal choices, i.e., improvement of the public image through counter-publicity. There was an immediate spate of feature stories and articles in that vein.

From the Chief of Staff, General Marshall, it was learned that he had just received "more exact data than we have previously had as to the employment of German armored and motorized forces . . ." When fully digested it would be the basis for changes in the combat doctrines in America's fast-burgeoning Armored Force. The fast progress of the Force was reviewed. The top commanders were named. Their records were reviewed briefly in laudatory and forceful military terms. Lists of new General Officers, most of them temporary and selected from the list of Line Colonels, were featured. Mentioned specifically among them were the grandsons of two famous battle names. They were Thomas Jonathan Jackson Christian, grandson of the great "Stonewall" Jackson, and Ulysses S. Grant III, a direct grandchild of Appomattox. How could the public better be reminded that the German Army was not alone in having a heritage of brilliant operations and victory?

The defense problems of the Caribbean were reviewed. The "tall and resplendent" Lieutenant General Daniel Van Voorhis was in command, with Headquarters in the Canal Zone. The "Caribbean Defense Command . . . which up to now [May 12, 1941] had existed largely on paper" was shaping-up into bastions of defense. At San Juan, Puerto Rico, Major General James Lawton Collins was converting that island "eggshell" into a Gibraltar. Collins, older brother of the confusingly-named Joseph Lawton Collins who was to establish one of the truly great combat records in World War II, was a fine soldier, but when he left Puerto Rico it was still an eggshell. There was no reason for it to be otherwise. Puerto Rico was in the wrong ocean for Japan to strike. Hitler was finding more eggs in Europe, with and without shells, than he could eat. Such fanciful strategic blather was recognizable even then as being worthless except for its favorable publicity value.

Similar stories blossomed in sundry sheets. There were also many humanizing short squibs such as that of a Private of the Regular Army, who handed his Mess Sergeant $8 in cash because he had eaten more than his share of the Company food. Most likely, he had lost the eight clams to the Mess Sergeant in the Company's floating crap game, but it made a good story at a time when there was a need to cheer-up the Country and make its Army look better.

At the same time a rather natural, oral alibi began to circulate among the Regulars on most Posts and stations that everything would be all right had not the politicians in Washington dumped the Guard on their hands without warning. All they needed was a Selective Service that would give them the raw recruits in a steady, orderly stream for quick conversion into topflight combat soldiers in the proper and professional way. Sending recruits to the Guardsmen to train was asking the blind to lead the blind. In time it was to appear quasi-officially in print with General McNair's austere approval.

418

From this oral alibi phase there was easy progression to supplementation of the normal first choice for a better Army image to one with the second possible defensive action; i.e., diversion of public attention to a cognate institution as being a bigger and more serious problem. The Guard must have seemed truly Heaven-sent for the role of a whipping boy riding into the desert astride a dejected scapegoat. Thus, at the same time that every release and public relations news feature of the Regular Army took on the tone of soaring efficiency by hardened professionals merely awaiting more men, munitions and equipment from American industry, anything and everything that concerned the National Guard had the demanding tone of drastic corrective action.

An adverse interpretative twist against the entire Guard was even given a news story of a Guard General's compulsory retirement for having reached the statutory age of 64. At the same time, the news release was slanted into another journalistic propaganda nose-gay for the Regular Army. Within the preceding 12 months, and for decades prior thereto, Regular Army General Officers, and frequently Master Sergeants of long, honored service, had been retiring at age 64 to the tune of blaring brass bands and Regimental, Brigade, or even Divisional reviews. In May, following Congressman Engel's attack upon the Army, and interspersed among the sudden spate of upgrading and humanizing releases for the Regulars, Major General Robert H. Tyndall, Indiana, commanding the 38th Division at Camp Shelby, reached 64. There was, of course, the usual camp courtesy.

From Washington, however, there appears to have been no conventional War Department release honoring the retirement and past services of a Federally-recognized Major General who voluntarily had given the Nation an immediate claim check on his military talents (which were not small) since the age of 20. In lieu thereof was the Washington news tip as to the name of his successor. He would be a Regular, who would, with sharp military precision, immediately rectify all shortcomings the 38th Division was presumed to be afflicted with. *Time* Magazine snapped at the scoop lure and swallowed it, hook, line and sinker. Under the caption, "Sultan of the Guard," that widely-influential news periodical reported:

> Last week there was a small but hopeful sign that the U.S. Army might be on the way to getting tough—tough enough to face modern military competition. Major General Daniel Isom Sultan was ordered to command the 38th (National Guard) Division at Camp Shelby, Miss. He was the first Regular Army officer in this emergency to replace the National Guard commander of a Guard division. He will not be the last. Of the 17 National Guard divisions that went to France with the A.E.F., only one (the 27th) had its original commander (Major General John F. O'Ryan) at the war's end . . .

419

The story trailed off into a 200-word wreath of rhetoric for the revered elderly "Black Jack" Pershing who, it was implied, had won the 1917-18 War in Europe largely by breaking incompetent Division Commanders, at least 16 of whom were incompetent National Guardsmen. Splendid "Pershing men," such as Chief of Staff George C. Marshall, still were running the Army, *Time* noted hopefully, and they too might ultimately win a war by adhering "to the rigorous Pershing standards of World War I." In much less space, *Time* could have noted the simple truth as to why the Division was getting a new Commander. If an interesting dip into history was desired, greater economy in words also would have been found in the truth. Only one National Guard Major General was on extended active duty through World War I, and he was John F. O'Ryan and he did indeed command a great Division with distinction throughout its World War I service.

At this late date it is impossible to center the responsibility of such a story upon any official. *Time* quite properly would assume full responsibility anyway. Its Editors did not have to print it. But the publishers of a splendid periodical of its character never would have run such a story had not their field men been imposed upon by some officer in a military post of high responsibility and who was presumed to be a completely reliable source. It is also noteworthy that no disclaimer or correction came from either the War Department, the General Staff, or General McNair's Headquarters. Officially pulling the props from under such a story would have fouled-up the pipeline to one of the Public Relations Section's best outlets, the entire *Time-Life-Fortune* group. At the same time, all the informed and articulate Guardsmen were on active duty and thereby hushed from seeking connections. Thus the imposition upon the editors was highly successful. They remained ripe for future impositions and use.

Most Regulars and Guardsmen in the field of that era naturally noted the news story and many commented upon it. All agreed unanimously with its sentiment that no greater liability existed than a dumb General. But in V Corps Headquarters, at Camp Beauregard, Louisiana, where most were hard-working, field Regulars and to which the 38th then was assigned, they knew General Tyndall was the man being subjected to indirect libel. There the only comment was a wish that the 38th Division's Old Man might have had better luck. Those who expressed themselves thought he had done a magnificent job until high noon of his birthday and had gone to the final parade with everything shipshape and a clean desk for his successor.*

---

* Maj. Gen. Robert H. Tyndall, born 1877, enlisted as a Private in a National Guard Battery, Nov., 1897. His service was continuous from that date in either the Guard or the Officers Reserve Corps, the latter during the brief period the Guard was not fully organized following World War I. Commissioned 2nd Lt., F.A.,

With the foregoing story, the Public Relations Sections in the War Department and Ground Forces GHQ found their stride. Thereafter the new image of the Army began to take definite shape. Under its dynamic and highly-trained, hard-headed, realistic and ruthless (the politicians permitting) leadership, America's great new Army was all-but achieving the impossible ahead of any reasonable schedule. But, being handicapped by the deadweight of the National Guard and its politicians disguised as officers, it hardly was possible to guarantee anything prior to any specific date. There was also an occasional pot shot at the Reserve officers, apparently just to keep the Guard officers from feeling lonely. "No longer could the synthetic fire-breathers of the Organized Reserves leapfrog lightly over their Regular brethren," was the explanation in one news story for the Regular Army's adopting a more liberal policy for fast promotion of Regulars in all grades without deference to seniority.

## THE PROPAGANDA PURGE AND THE REAL PURGE

In June another high note was struck on military reform to lighten the Regular Army of the heavy burden of having to carry so many substandard Field Grade active duty officers from civil life, most particularly in the Guard units. The Associated Press and United Press announced new emergency legislation being introduced in Congress at the request of the War Department. It authorized a far-reaching purge of incompetents from the officer lists of all components, but the officers of the National Guard would be the most adversely affected because of their appointments, which had rested purely on State politics, and because there had been a complete failure within the Guard to keep up-to-date on techniques, tactics and strategy.* This impending purge aimed at the Guard received a big publicity

---

in 1902, following Spanish War service, as a Private in the 27th Indiana, he rose to Col. in 1917 and commanded the 150th F.A. ("Rainbow" Division) throughout its service in France. Maj. Gen. Douglas MacArthur cited him and he was awarded the D.S.M. He had commanded the 38th Division 16 years. He knew he could not serve the full 12 months, but being in superb health he went on active duty to see the Division well started on its year of training. Home from Camp Shelby in 1941, his fellow-citizens drafted him back into public service as Mayor of Indianapolis, January 1, 1943. It was his first and only political office. In civil life he was a banker and corporation official. Why senior professionals who had nothing to lose, should resent such gifted amateurs as Tyndall represented, and were so reluctant to concede the value of their voluntarily-donated military obligation to serve through so many years, is most difficult to explain. They naturally wanted to reward loyal subordinates through many earlier tours of duty and they must have accepted without a challenging thought the self-serving adverse reports their rank-hungry Lieutenant Colonels were writing.

* More than one informed Guardsman remarked at the time that there was something phony about this news release, because legal authority and prompt procedures already existed for immediate purging of incompetent Guard officers. Guard senior officers had used it on their own subordinates who were not pulling the weight of their ranks.

play from Coast to Coast with favorable editorial comments from sundry newspapers. Once again, no Guardsman was in position to challenge it publicly without giving validity to the charge by virtue of that very act of public challenge. There was nought to do but to carry on with the hope that ultimately truth might triumph.

Today, thanks to the discerning and selective research and able authorship of the splendid journalist and historian, Mark S. Watson, the truth is indeed available to all who wish to read. In his book, *Chief of Staff: Prewar Plans and Preparations,* one of the best of the official *United States Army in World War II* series, Mr. Watson devotes all of Chapter VIII to "Officer Selection, Promotion and Rejection." He reveals clearly that the resulting law (Public, 190, 29 July 1941) had no application to either the National Guard or the Reserve, but specifically was drafted to make possible the purging from active duty of an incompetent Regular as easily as a Guard or Reserve officer could be returned to civil life under already-existing laws. Mr. Watson goes further and reviews the comparative results of putting the Regulars on the same active duty tenure status as were Guard and Reserve officers:

> A summation of final action by reclassification during the summer and autumn of 1941 reveals that from June to November 195 Regular Army officers were in fact removed from the active list by discharge or forced retirement. This represented . . . 1.3 per cent of all Regular Army officers . . . Nearly all were field officers, 31 colonels, 117 lieutenant colonels (a part of the promotion list's embarrassing "hump" in that category resulting from World War I additions to the corps) 31 majors, and 16 captains. In the same period 269 National Guard and Reserve Officers had been similarly reclassified . . . Of these 33 National Guard officers had been reclassified and 94 had resigned . . . The 127 National Guard officers thus dropped represented three-fourths of 1 per cent of the Guard's officer total . . ."

The Officers Reserve Corps, with but 142 compulsory separations by reclassification, or forced resignations, had an even better percentage score, only one-fourth of 1%. There are obvious reasons, however, for the O.R.C.'s extremely low rate. The ratio of older, Field Grade Reservists was much lower than for either the Guard or the Regular Army. At the same time, many low-ranking and younger Reserve officers actually were enlisted men serving in their Reserve status and grade, or were vulnerable to Selective Service. The normal formula for them was not complete separation from active duty, but reversion to their enlisted status or continuation by enlistment. Reclassification was not punishment, but a review of capabilities in efforts to arrive at options. It was absence of options for the age and grade that forced the complete separation, or, in the case of Regulars, retirement from active duty with such pay as rank and longevity of service might warrant.

Mr. Watson concedes that this purge score was somewhat unexpected. What the General Staff did expect was acute political pressure in behalf of adversely-affected Regular officers. To overawe and preclude such political maneuvers, individual wire-pulling and Congressional conniving for retention of Regulars, the preceding Chief of Staff, General Malin Craig, temporarily was called from retirement to become Chairman of the "Removal Board," as it was called initially. But Craig and Marshall feared the very political heat such a Board title might engender. Accordingly, to minimize further heat and to confuse inquiring reporters, the title of the Board cleverly was changed from "Removal Board" to the "Appointments Board." It was under this caption that General Craig's temporary recall from retirement was given to the public. It was clever, but was it honest? In any event, from all the foregoing facts, it becomes apparent that the Regular Army's concept of a politics-riddled National Guard officer corps may well have come from two decades of chagrined contemplation of its own backyard.*

## FIELD TRAINING AND MORALE

Meanwhile, most Guard Divisions and lesser units were well past their initial 13 weeks of refresher training on fundamentals and rapidly had become physically hardened by exposure to long hours of exercises under vigorous leadership. Expansion of camps for the Guard was catching up with the soldier population on most locations by February and March of 1941. Range firing was behind most Riflemen. Squads and gun crews were going through their paces with precision on improvised Infantry combat fields and in Artillery service practice. Artillery range facilities were utterly inadequate at or near most installations, but General McNair's GHQ Ground Forces appeared to lose little sleep over the absence of this vital facility, which continued to the eve of Pearl Harbor in most locations and until much longer in others. To many field Regulars and non-Regulars, this was thought to be another manifestation of a McNair theory that was said to have revealed itself as early as his gunnery instructorship days in the Artillery School at Fort Sill; i.e., very little service ammunition and actual range gunnery were needed to produce fast and superbly accurate fire from trench mortars, French 75's and larger crew-served weapons. His reputation was one of being a relentless exponent of surveys and map problems, Bishop Trainers, sub-calibers, ex-calibers, miniature ranges, simulated

---

* According to Eltinge E. Morison (see bibliographical note at end of this chapter), Robert M. Lovett, then Special Assistant to Secretary of War Stimson, considered the War Department General Staff so full of deadwood "that the place was a positive fire hazard." Maj. Gen. Joseph W. (Vinegar Joe) Stilwell was more pungently analytical. He agreed with a friend that the War Department was "just like the alimentary canal. You feed it at one end and nothing comes out of the other but crap."—*Stilwell Papers*, p. 19.

bursts, large terrain tables with chemical smoke gadgets and other training aids.

But through most of 1941, requisitions for such brought only laughter. No imaginative blueprints or practical guidelines for such came down from McNair's Training Staff sections. No funds with which lower units could improvise their own became available until the year of training was approaching its end. Even then, funds were inadequate. Furthermore, most Guard units already had improvised their own, some of which were brilliantly imaginative and highly effective within their essential limitations. They often were designed and built by the highly-skilled labor from within the units, of materials paid for by donations or improper diversions from Company or Battery funds. In latter cases some Guard officer, usually the Captain, often received a skin-sheet, which his Colonel usually refused to take seriously in a counter-endorsement that occasionally was more sarcastically explanatory than were the models illustrative of proper correspondence printed in the manuals of that day. Some of the more ingenious and artistic of the home-made devices, however, were flatteringly photographed. Scale drawings with specifications of simulation devices were made for referral to Ground Forces GHQ. Service journals and future Regiments of Selectees after Pearl Harbor appear to have been the immediate beneficiaries of some of the better ideas. Moreover, such devices often were left in original locations by outgoing Guard units when they left for overseas staging areas, beginning in December of 1941.

Be it further of record here that all Guard units found some intervening higher Headquarters normally were most encouraging and helpful with constructive suggestions and procurement of additional training areas and their utilization. This was particularly true of General Krueger's Third Army, Fort Sam Houston in San Antonio, and V Corps, at Camp Beauregard, Louisiana. They also rendered splendid and practical guidance rules for large unit field exercises, controlled and free maneuvers, and in the meaningful as well as practical training of field Umpires. Their warm willingness to assist in sundry administrative mysteries of the old peacetime Army, many of which were slow in breaking-down even under the stress of the subsequent hostilities, was nothing short of indispensable in many instances.

But if the occasional field team of two or more Colonels or Lieutenant Colonels from McNair's GHQ Ground Forces ever did more than help themselves to ideas for training aids that they found in a field unit, and unrealistically carp, orally or in subsequent reports, about the lack of realism in the field work of the visited Brigades and Divisions, it was seldom of record. Their normal solution to a criticized situation was a suggestion of immediate relief and reclassification.

424

The favorite and most hackneyed, nagging carp was lack of combat realism. When one was asked bluntly what was unrealistic, the typical response was the threadbare complaint about road-bound Infantry, the necessity to work across country—a practice everyone knew and recognized thoroughly in every Field Manual. "But, Colonel," a Guard officer in substance once remonstrated, "I know it and the men know it, but there is no Umpire marker that this road is under fire. Moreover, right up to the Line of Departure and beyond there is nothing but plantations and pecan orchards. They are mapped as 'off limits' for maneuver. Between an adverse written critique from you and having to talk for stenographic record for hours to the Corps I.G. on a damage-of-property claim, I elect your adverse critique—but please quote me on the choice and the reasons for it."

He eventually received a copy of the adverse report, but without the facts and the explanation. With such field visitations and constant emphasis upon reliefs and reclassifications as the solution of all and sundry complaints, there is little wonder that visitors for McNair's GHQ quickly became known as "book soldiers" at best and "hatchet men" in the less tolerant parlance.

But somewhere in Ground Forces GHQ there appears to have been an anonymous noble spirit with an inspiration to render help toward combat realism. He would bring a modicum of the real thing to peacetime training with appropriate battle noises, mounted on a sound truck with an unknown number of turntables, squawk boxes, horns and platter records. When it was demonstrated proudly in a back area of Camp Livingston, Louisiana, an astounded, decorated veteran of the First World War listened and contemplated it, with jaws ajar in amazement. When the grand cacaphony of assorted screams, whimpers, explosions, metallic clangings, groans and rumbles came to an intermission, he wanted to know what it was for.

An adventurous-minded Infantry Colonel thought he might use it as a surprise package in a Regimental maneuver. Two of his Battalions, reinforced, were in an attack problem against their third Battalion Combat Team in a delaying action situation. In darkness the "battle sounds" vehicle was camouflaged between the lines of impending contact. As the assault Battalion crossed the Line of Departure and the conventional flash crackers, cherry bombs and rifle blanks began to boom and pop, the cacaphonic delirium went into action. The smallarms sputtered into silence. The simulated gunfire and movement ceased completely while the noise machine ran through two cycles.

Brigadier General Paul B. Clemens, Wisconsin, was attracted to the machine's horrendous crashing crescendoes. He noted the defenders laughing in their foxholes and the attackers lying on their arms under concealment of the tall grass. He rather cautically wanted to know, from

425

a young Captain, why the war had bogged-down. The Captain had the answer. "The Umpires have not agreed as to which side the mobile juke boxes are fighting for. If all that noise is us killing them, we'll capture the objective standing up. If it is them killing us, the Umpires will soon flag all of us survivors into a running retreat that will not stop short of the river."

That was the end of mechanized noise in the 32nd Division war games. Nevertheless, someone in Ground Forces GHQ deserved a kudo or at least a kind word. That abortive inspiration long stood as conclusive evidence that at least one officer in that Headquarters was truly trying, thinking constructively and wanting to be helpful. It is hoped that no exhaustive future research brings forth the disillusioning discovery that the noise realism idea actually originated elsewhere.*

## PROGRESSIVE TRAINING AND THE SELECTEES

The command post exercises, field exercises and war games followed rapidly on the heels of the individual, the Squads, the gun and communications crews and range training. After that it was Companies against Battalions, Battalions defending against attacking Regiments, Brigades attacking defending Combat Teams, and Brigades defending against Divisions. There were maneuvers designed to develop into free deployments from meeting engagements, for delaying actions, forcing of river crossings, defense of river lines and complete organization of defensive positions against prolonged attacks. Scouting, patrolling and screening were emphasized. All problems were written locally and fitted to the terrain, and supervised by the Divisional Staffs or a designated lower Headquarters and its Staff. Army and Army Corps Headquarters took over all supervision when any unit larger than an Infantry Brigade was involved.

These activities kept officers and men almost continually in the field, except those detailed to set up basic training schools for the incoming Selectees. They began arriving, all from the home States of the units to which they were assigned, as fast as sufficient camp facilities were finished to accommodate them. This proved to be a wise decision. Had young men, ordered to compulsory active service for one year, been forced into the static bivouac situations for the months that the volunteering Guardsmen initially accepted willingly, the abusive recrimina-

---

* Some Oklahoma Indian machine gunners in the 45th Division are said to have been more realistically convincing. Each time the gunner gave a short burst of blanks toward the closing-in opposition, all others in the strong point would let fly BB bullets from long, rubber-band sling shots. With the pellets rattling among the twigs and leaves overhead, the attackers (an East Coast Regiment) and the Umpires beat an unorthodox retreat to spread the general alarm that "those damned Indians think this is a real war!" The campaign was suspended long enough for neutrals, wearing white brassards, to search the alleged hostiles for live ammunition.

tions the Army was receiving from Congress in general and the Truman Committee in particular would have multiplied many-fold. Actually the Selectees were generally quite happy to find themselves among others of their age group who were from their own home State and who knew their home towns, and more often than otherwise, found friends of long standing already in the Division.

It has been almost an article of faith among the professional soldiers that a preponderance of all the officers and men being from one State is bad enough, but for a Regiment, Battalion, Company or Battery to be entirely from one City or rural market town is most reprehensible. They shudder at the thought of the bitter, anti-militaristic reaction of that town or City should its unit be wiped-out and vanish in one unfortunate campaign. That logic is as spurious as it is plausible. In the course of World War II, that happened to at least one National Guard unit in many States of the Union. The Bataan surrender alone accounted for a dozen tank units from almost as many States. Instead of the predicted bitterness there crystallized a fierce, militaristic pride for the unit and those who had suffered in its service. Younger brothers and sons of the men who suffered were often among the most eager to continue the family's proud record of service. Certainly, those who reorganized the Guard Divisions after World War II consistently considered it much easier to re-create a unit in such a town than it was to organize a unit *de novo* in a City or town that never had had a National Guard unit.

Notwithstanding their favorable initial reactions to home State units, for the Guard and for the Army as a whole, if the Congressional debates have validity, the Selectees were largely at the root of the great morale problem that the Press generally viewed with such rising alarm through the long, hot Summer of 1941. The Selectees began unit soldiering in their Companies, Troops and Batteries just as the constant living in the field through the wet Spring was mounting toward the climax of major maneuvers. Simultaneously, the Guard Divisions were being stripped of Lend-Lease items for shipments to distressed England and to give the first ripples of military assistance to hard-pressed Russia. Some Guard Artillery Regiments were even stripped of their guns. They had to maneuver with improvised dummies and borrow French 75's and fire control equipment and instruments from more fortunate sister Regiments for standing gun drills and service practice. With shrinking materiel and increasing personnel, all of whom, including Selectees, being tossed suddenly into constant and arduous field service, a slump in morale in all units, Guard and Regular formations, was to be expected and did occur.

But the morale problem did not really floriate until Congress began

427

its long debates on whether or not to extend the period of all concerned from one year to two, three, or to an indefinite emergency period. When it was scaled-down to an additional six months in September, the measure passed by the thin margin of one vote in the House of Representatives. When the long and much-debated question thus was answered in specific terms, and individual plans could be made, the morale of the Selectees took an upturn. Meanwhile, Major General John F. Williams, Chief of the National Guard Bureau, had caused a survey to be made as to morale and attitudes of Guardsmen. He reported morale substantially the same as of date of Call, with most having plans sufficiently flexible that extension of active duty a year or more would cause no great concern. But his remarks were ignored in the great debate. And the Press, still relying on the handouts and planted stories from the War Department and GHQ, Ground Forces, continued to give the Guard a black eye.

General Marshall, at the same time, bluntly blamed Congress for the morale problem. He publicly proclaimed that postcard writers to Congressmen would be dealt with by their commanders. He darkly hinted that Congressmen who sent postcards to Servicemen soliciting complaints and criticisms in the guise of learning legitimate desires of constituents were approaching treasonable activities. It was a justified criticism, but there were other basic factors on the home front of the Selectees.

In the absence of a "shooting war" as of September 16, 1940-December 7, 1941, and even during and since Korea, the great majority of Selectees inevitably have gone on active duty with the internal plaint of "Why Me?" and "Why My Boy?" and "Why My Man?" Given the public sympathy of a rabble-rousing minority, the secret "Why . . .?" becomes the anguished cries of young, expectant fathers and other exuberantly-youthful but fireside indispensables.

Resultant reluctance in performance of necessarily team-like duties often prevails. This happened in some of the equipment-stripped Guard units in the closing gigantic maneuvers, late Summer of 1941. It also happened in some of the Regular Army units heaviest with recent Selectees for whom the best available equipment had been reserved and issued. It happened to sufficient degree in the Korean calls that new Selectees and the machine records-recalled Reservists were let off with two years of active duty and a "rotation policy" that was both disastrously expensive and on the whole harmful to the efficiency of all overseas units in combat and support missions. It will happen again when there is a partial Call of an appreciable number of Selectees, or a recall, by machine records procedures, of a large number of "Obligors" from among the trained Selectees in Reserve status.

Meanwhile, history and modern Guard experience and figures, not to mention the recent brilliant postwar records of the Air National Guard, show conclusively that 1.5 to 3% of America's military manpower pool, in ages and ranks appropriate to their potential will organize themselves voluntarily into State-associated Companies and Batteries, air Squadrons and Wings, Battalions and Divisions, if fully and modernly equipped and provided with adequate fulltime Technicians and facilities. With paid training programs; fair, nondiscriminatory professional treatment, and opportunities to attend short-term Service schools, such units can and do result in a competent and constant stand-by force for cold war and diplomatic emergencies, as well as the "early-ready" force for a shooting war with conventional weapons.*

Selective Service is another problem and should be disassociated as much as practicable. This is the lesson in the Army's great morale problem of 1941 and the post-World War II partial mobilizations. It thus may be reasonably concluded that America could have had as large an Army, and a much more willing and better-trained force, had the 1940 personnel procurement been exclusively through the Staff-proposed and professionally-much-talked-of, but not attempted, CVE, Civilian Voluntary Effort. The very Reserve officers and young R.O.T.C. graduates that the Army did receive were volunteers. The voluntary flow of young men diverted from the C.C.C. camps to the Regular Army would have continued just as it did and might have been stepped-up. The Guard Divisions and lesser units certainly could have gone to war strength by voluntary recruiting before leaving their home stations. And Generals Marshall and McNair would have been spared the nightmare of what would happen to their trained Divisions and lesser units had Congress hearkened in September, 1941, unto the parents of Selectees and the letter-written gripes of minds still in the military nursery, and sent them all home, thereby wrecking all functional units on the eve of the overt hostilities that actually did come.

Demobilization is exactly what would have been in full swing at the time of Pearl Harbor except for the one-vote majority in the House of Representatives. Had Japan delayed Pearl Harbor until the follow-

---

* The truth of this was exemplified not only during the stress of war and after Pearl Harbor, but through the Korean emergency and into the present. Many of the Army National Guard's Antiaircraft Artillery Battalions that accepted the "on-site" mission of active participation in the defense of the United States when still armed with artillery, smoothly underwent the transition to the NIKE-AJAX, and as of 1963 were "converting" again to take over from the Active Army a large segment of NIKE-HERCULES defense of the Continental United States and Hawaii. Certain Air Guard Squadrons assigned to the Air Defense Command for some years have been rotating air and ground crews on "runway alert," and Aircraft Control and Warning units have been on watch around the clock at radar scopes in Colorado, Utah and Hawaii. And with evolution, former Fighter-Interceptor Squadrons have learned to accept as "routine," trans-Atlantic and trans-Pacific flights in giant C97 heavy transports, combining training missions with payload-hauling for the Military Air Transport Service.

ing Summer, the expensively-trained field formations would have been melting away even under the Military Service Extension Act that was passed. Thus General Reckord and other Guard leaders may have been instinctively right in early 1940 in proposing that the Guard get its military manpower in the historic manner before going on active duty, rather than accepting the General Staff deal that they immediately could be brought to war strength through assignment of early Selectees from their respective States.

## THE GREAT MANEUVERS

The Civilian Volunteer Effort did not do badly even within the compulsory service plan adopted. Between July of 1939 and August 31, 1940, the Active Army of the United States had risen from 188,565 officers and men to 326,946. In the latter year nearly half of the 23,921 officers included in the second gross figure were from the Officers Reserve Corps who had volunteered their services, or who had responded voluntarily to a specific call to fill a certain slot for which they were known to have special talents. The number also included a few thousand enlisted Reservists who were in that status of their own volition. By January 31, 1941, with 93,196 officers and men of the National Guard still in home stations awaiting camp construction and facilities before being phased into active duty, the Active Army of the United States had risen to 732,946, of whom about 200,000 were Guardsmen volunteers. The Selective Service pipeline began to approach a full flow by March of 1941. By the end of September it had pumped into the Active Army nearly 800,000 Selectees for a total Active Army of 1,601,013, of whom 109,456 were officers, including the 6,578 women in the Army Nurse Corps.

The pressure upon the Guard units for officer material quotas to fill the expanding Officer Candidate Schools for all Arms and Services, became terrific, because the Guard formations were rich in such talent. The Army Air Corps was particularly solicitous to the point of pressure for Flight Cadet talent. At the same time the Guard units were training their assigned Selectees, rotating many senior officers to refresher courses, sending even higher quotas of junior officers to the Infantry School, Field Artillery School and those of the other Arms and Services. Finally, the Guard units were participating fully in a series of the most grandiose field exercises and full maneuvers ever staged any time, anywhere, before or since, by American troops. Indeed, it was said by more than one old pro that General McNair was excessively enthusiastic on the subject. His thinking and force, assuming he did not write every word of it himself, was back of the not-always-effective official document for Umpires and other controls for the so-called free maneuvers.

It is significant that the fielding of 460,000 men in two opposing

430

Armies with a contact front of 60 miles never has been repeated. Though it was not mentioned in the critiques, most of the Line and lower Headquarters Staff officers who were there would have agreed that a good idea had been expanded far beyond the point where the Law of Diminishing Return obviously had taken-over. Moreover, it should be noted that the morale problem, sparked by the Congressional debates on extension of involuntary military service, was at its most acute stage as these field maneuvers built-up from Divisions against Divisions, and Army Corps against Army Corps, to the grand finale of Lieutenant General Ben Lear's Second Army defending and Lieutenant General Walter Krueger's Third Army on the offensive. The troop morale hassle and the highest August and September dust and heat records Louisiana had known in years did not add to the *elan*.*

Lear's Second Army (Red) Order of Battle included three "square" Infantry Divisions (Guard), two "triangular" Infantry Divisions, two Armored and one Cavalry Division. Krueger's Third Army (Blue) consisted of eight "square" Infantry Divisions (Guard), two "triangular" Infantry Divisions, one Tank Group of only 60 light tanks, three Anti-Tank Battalions, one Cavalry Division and one Cavalry Brigade. Each Army Commander had 300 Air Corps planes at his disposal. A Company of Paratroopers was present and operational for the first time in American history. Note that Lear with 130,000 officers and men was comparatively light and nimble with a tremendous preponderance in Armor and enjoyed all the advantages inherent in being on the defense in most difficult terrain. The opposing Third Army was heavy with 330,000 officers and men, weak on proportional motor vehicles and short on Armor and modernity of Divisional organization and equipment.

Initial deployment for Krueger's Blues, with Headquarters at Lake Charles, was from Beaumont, Texas, to Bayou Teche, Louisiana. Lear's Red Second Army initially was deployed North and East of the Red River from Alexandria Northwesterly to Shreveport and Caddo Lake on the Texas border. The river line and its terrain were unfavorable to tank tactics, hence Lear with some logic crossed the river on a wide front for a strong thrust forward to seize the comparatively open Peason Ridge country where the preponderance of Red Armor would be most advantageous. Red Cavalry swept wide from the Northwest flank to help foreclose the mortgage on Peason Ridge country and threaten Blue's flank from the line of the Sabine River. But the Red Cavalry did not sweep wide enough and started its flanking movement too soon. Krueger's Third Army Blue Cavalry successfully screened its own Army's open flank but also used its weight and mobility to sweep still

* A homesick Selectee from the Paul Bunyan country of Northern Wisconsin sadly told the author that his own morale was so low he could "get on stilts with my morale on my back and walk under a sleeping snake's belly without waking him up." No lower morale appears to be of record, but he lived over it.

431

more widely and cut deep into Red's rear North and East of Mansfield, Louisiana. While the horse Cavalry war was proceeding along a line that would have met with the warm approval of both Phil Sheridan and Jeb Stuart, Blue Army's eight "square" Guard Divisions were proving to be far less cumbersome and awkward than their obsolete organization and shortage of equipment had appeared to dictate. By temporarily "grounding" a part of each Division while all vehicles did fast shuttle movements, Blue Infantry from the Guard Divisions appeared amazingly soon in areas where time and space factors had suggested an impossibility.

Fast shuttle motor movements reconcentrated the "square" Divisions for coordinated attacks upon specified objectives on their fronts. Thus each Division fought its own little war within its zone of action. Lear's Red Armor was denied the ownership of Peason Ridge with its potential for a quick defensive victory through offensive tactics.

The Red Air Force was either less lucky or not so well-handled. Moreover, it had been beefed-up with some Navy fliers who knew not the terrain and who had no opportunity to become integrated into an instinctively-reacting membership of their entire team. The 300 Blue planes were credited with more successful missions. A Blue paratroop drop of 127 officers and men, as rear area raiders and saboteurs, wrecked General Lear's Red communications. They stank-up Lear's own Headquarters with smoke bombs simulating complete destruction, which could have claimed Lear as a casualty. "A re-e-edicu-u-lous performance!" General Lear sputtered in the lobby of the Camp Polk movie theater shortly prior to the grand critique.

The Umpires must have partially thought likewise. The Squad that pulled the stunt was ruled-out because its only hostile identification was a short, thin strand of blue baby ribbon. This notwithstanding, the tide of battle forced Lear to displace his Headquarters to the rear. But it was the Cavalry that ended the long, hot, dusty campaign. With the Guard Cavalry Brigade screening and thus containing the entire Red Cavalry Division, the Blue Division of horse Cavalry swept far to Westward and came in behind the Red forward positions to capture and destroy supplies. These included the Red gasoline depot. There could be but one Umpire ruling. The Red tanks and other mobile vehicles were declared immobile as their fuel tanks became empty.

The maneuver war was over except for the equally-grandiose critique. In it there was almost as much yapping about improperly-policed, vacated bivouac areas as there was about tactics and strategy. This fell alike upon all units, Regulars and Reservists in the "triangular" Divisions and Guardsmen in the "square" Divisions. This situation was indeed bad throughout the maneuvers for the simple reason that the thrifty Louisiana farmers broke out their shovels and opened all the marked and dated kitchen refuse pits as fast as the sites were vacated so that their hogs could get at the garbage. Maneuver Headquarters, largely composed of McNair and his Staff, must have been aware of this, for one of the Guard Regimental Executive Officers sought a measure of remedial action by switching the markings upon otherwise properly-covered kitchen pits and the latrine trenches. There appears to have been a civilian complaint. In any event, the Guard officer received a written rebuke for having displayed an unsanitary sense of humor.

The Great War Games in Louisiana, with smaller editions of the same in First and Fourth Army Zones (but not against one another) were the crowning events in the training efforts of McNair and his Ground Forces GHQ Staff. As a finale thereto he made a characteristic statement to the Press. in which he seemed always eager to oblige with eye-catching copy: "A lot of these Generals who want to fire their Chiefs of Staff ought to fire themselves. We're going to start at the top and work down. We've got some bum Generals, and maybe I'm one of them, but we are going to weed them out. Have we the bright young Majors and Captains to replace them? Yes."

Actually, the maneuvers did reveal Krueger to be a fast-reacting, sound and masterful strategist and tactician. Of the 21 Regular Army officers on the Permanent Promotion List of Major Generals on October 20, 1940,* when the Guard was going on active duty, none but Krueger was to command troops overseas and in operations against the enemy. This statement, of course, ignores General Short, of Hawaii and Pearl Harbor. He hardly commanded in that situation; he merely contemplated the havoc being wrought by the Japanese sneak attack. But Krueger's assignment to the South Pacific allegedly was not McNair's idea. General MacArthur asked for Krueger from Australia in May of 1942.

It thus appears that McNair meant exactly what he said. But he was also drawing a bead on many officers who were Captains and Lieutenants. The Reclassification Boards were not achieving the desired purge.

## THE AGE-IN-GRADE POLICY

In anticipation of such a purge of civilian officers on active duty and the transfer of all presumably sluggish Regulars to desk jobs without the necessity of argumentation from any source, a new age-in-grade

---

* The list also included the names of Gen. (temporary) George C. Marshall, who held the higher rank by assignment, and six Lt. Gens. (temporary) who likewise held their higher ranks by virtue of assignment to major commands. Lear was then in that temporary grade as C.G., Second Army. Krueger soon was to join the short list of temporary Lt. Gens., vice Herbert J. Breese, former Commander of Third Army.

policy had been announced two weeks before the Great Maneuvers in Louisiana ended. Second Lieutenants were disqualified for field assignment at age 30; First Lieutenants at 35; Captains, 42; Majors, 47; Lieutenant Colonels, 52; Colonels 55; Brigadier Generals 60, and Major Generals commanding Divisions, 62. Since the Air Corps was so bitterly short of experienced men, the policy was not applicable to its officers.

It was a meat-axe operation that clearly called for a scalpel. The very nature of the policy meant that those adversely affected would be convinced the remainder of their lives that the measure was designed specifically for discrimination against and for the embarrassment of their age groups and ranks. Many of the 705 Seniority List Regular Colonels were already over 55. For practically all of them who had not already wangled, or soon could wangle, a temporary star, it was from the paths of promotion and to a desk exile for them. Moreover, the figure 52 for Lieutenant Colonels was neatly chosen to shear-off about half of the "Hump" Lieutenant Colonels from World War I who had not yet received temporary promotions for merit. Practically all Majors and lower on the Regular Army lists were easily within the stated ages in grade. For this reason, there were literally hundreds of Regulars of this era who insisted and who still insist that the age-in-grade policy of 1941 was a Marshall-McNair design to shelve older Colonels who once had outranked them, to apply selection to a Seniority List and withal "to liquidate the Hump."

Reminded that the War Department releases specifically stated the policy was aimed primarily at the Guard and World War I Reserve officers, the typical retort from the old Regulars was voiced bitterly by one of them: "Whitey McNair and Marshall are merely using the Civilian Components as a screen, or a public excuse for executing some so-called reforms for which they could never get legislation without the Civilian Components officers as the excuse for the action."

Some Regulars, with both criticism and commendation, are of the opinion that Marshall and McNair were more than eliminating all they conceived to be "deadwood" from the Old Army lists and reducing the "Hump" from the past War. They further were seeking to preclude the creation of a new Hump at the end of the emergency. By sending back to civil life Guardsmen and Reservists over the designated age limits, there would be an orderly spread in the ages by ranks of those who might seek integration into the Regular officer corps in a future reorganization of an expanded standing Army, such as always had followed mobilizations and wars.

On the other hand, many Guardsmen devoutly insisted, and with equal plausibility, that the purpose was to write-off the leadership of the Guard to create vacancies for the young Regular Captains and Majors McNair alluded to in his interviews. Actually, the preponderance of evi-

434

dence now clearly suggests that the General Staff personnel planners, with Marshall's and McNair's enthusiastic approval, were shooting at both the Regular Army personnel problems, as they knew them to be, and the Guard problems as they conceived them to be. In short, for the Regular Army it placed the professional future career of every Colonel, Lieutenant Colonel and older-than-average Major in the hands of the General Staff with McNair and Marshall the last to review the lists. In Mark S. Watson's previously-mentioned history of the Chief of Staff and prewar planning, it is revealed clearly that General Marshall personally checked every list of promotions to General Officer rank and repeatedly rejected names from his personal knowledge of the officer. By January 1, more than 1,250 Regular Army officers (exclusive of 100 or more Guard and Reserve General Officers) had been promoted to General Officer grades or to ranks above Brigadier General, over General Marshall's signature.*

For the Guard the suddenly-announced age-in-grade policy was a hasty and belated procedure for washing-out of any Federal military status whatsoever of an estimated fifth of its officers of considerable service and experience. It was to be done without delay, notwithstanding the recent Congressional decision to continue the Guard on active duty for an additional six months. The statement to the Press, however, that it would adversely affect 20% of the Guardsmen, appears to have been an optimistic exaggeration of McNair's. It did hit the Lieutenants hardest, an appreciable number of whom were over 30 or 35. The story given the Press that over-age-in-grade officers of all components would be shifted to desk jobs was for many Guardsmen and Reservists an untrue euphemism. The desk jobs were for the rejects from among the Regulars. Some Guard officers who had readjusted their absence from civil life arrangements to meet the revised 18 months of active duty did immediately put in for Army desk assignments. Initially, nearly all were refused and summarily separated. Others wired their employers, business and professional partners they were coming home and to this end requested that their relief from active duty be expedited. They knew that in effect their Federal recognition for their further service in the Guard was being terminated without warning, by unilateral action and by arbitrary decision that had nothing to do with their expensively-gained military knowledge and skills, health, or other qualifications for leadership.

This was the status of affairs when the functioning of the policy

---

* Mr. Watson does not concede that Marshall occasionally may have been fallible, as in the case of Lloyd D. Brown. Furthermore, a story persists in Regular Army circles that the long-delayed promotion of such a brilliant commander as the later Gen. James A. Van Fleet was not through lack of recommendations by his immediate superior officers; it was because Van Fleet was in combat as a Colonel until Aug. 1944, before Marshall could be convinced he was not an officer with a similar name of whom Marshall retained adverse memories.

came to the attention of Major General Henry H. Arnold, Deputy Chief of Staff for Air, which under his masterful leadership was becoming rapidly an almost independent defense agency, though still a part of the Army. With a more flexible mind and far more imagination than his colleagues of the other Arms and Services, Arnold made it clear that his fast-burgeoning air bases and other ground installations and Headquarters could use many such out-of-age-in-grade officers from the Guard and Reserve. Many sought and accepted such assignments and rose rapidly to higher ranks under commissions in the Army of the United States than it was likely they could have achieved had they stayed in Guard units to be held to promotion only to vacancies in their strict Tables of Organization.

Many Guard officers who had sought and accepted immediate separation to return to civilian pursuits were at home on terminal leave (the unused leave time they had earned from active duty) when the sky fell at Pearl Harbor. Such leaves were cancelled summarily and immediately, the separation orders were revoked, and they were instructed to report in grade to the nearest Corps Area Headquarters for indefinite active duty and specific assignment.

Among the numerous Guard officers who had this amazing and certainly unplanned experience were Majors Stuart F. Brokaw, approaching age 48, and Forrest W. Edwards, only a matter of days over 47 when the age-in-grade policy was proclaimed. Both were former mathematics and science teachers who had risen to public school administrative positions in LaCrosse, Wisconsin. Both were outstanding troop leaders, brilliant Artillerymen in both theory and practice, and superb on Staff work. Both were eminently qualified for promotion and even were slated for Lieutenant Colonelcies to fill vacancies within the Division. Waiver of the rule in their favor, which, it was rumored, was being allowed within a nearby Regular Army Division, was sought. Results were negative. After Pearl Harbor, when it was learned in the Division that they were back on indefinite active duty, an effort was made to achieve their reassignment to the 32nd Infantry Division where their services were needed incident to vacancies and the impending reorganization into a "triangular" Division. Once again the results were negative. The War's end found both still wearing their cross cannon insignia along with the eagles of full Colonels, to which they had been promoted under Army of the United States commissions. But neither ever held again the Artillery assignment for which he had been so expensively trained and for which he was so well-adapted. The number of cases that they exemplify is undetermined, but they were by no means unusual.

Other Guard officers who had elected immediate deactivation, were completely out of the Service, with Federal recognition in their grades completely withdrawn, only a matter of weeks or days before Pearl

Harbor. A great many of these were so embarrassed at being sent home after a year of training just as hostilities erupted, that they sought Organized Reserve commissions, or A.U.S. commissions, in almost any grade or any assignment. Most were successful and those who were not too impetuous usually returned to active duty in the same or even higher rank. A few accepted spot commissions in the Navy, particularly in the Seabees. A Guard Medical Corps Captain who had left his Division in deep resentment immediately was offered and he accepted the two-and-a-half stripes of a Lieutenant Commander. He returned home at War's end with three stripes and a service record that included two amphibious landings. Not quite in the same category, but further illustrative of the officer chaos that immediately followed Pearl Harbor, was the case of Brigadier General Ralph M. Immell, Federally recognized as C.G., 53rd Cavalry Brigade. The Brigade had been broken-up in 1940 and its Regimental and lesser units were mobilized into active duty without him and his Headquarters. He was so embarrassed at home by not being in uniform after Pearl Harbor that he immediately sought and accepted a Colonelcy, Army of the U.S., with the promise of early overseas duty. In Italy he was promoted to Brigadier General and in France to Major General, A.U.S.

It also should be explained parenthetically that in the bitter warfare that followed, the unrealistic and artificial concept that one birthday too many made an officer incompetent for field service, was pretty much ignored in theory and practice. If a Regimental or Division Commander asked for a specific and eagerly combat-minded officer from the S.O.S. to fill a combat unit vacancy, the age-in-grade issue was no barrier to the transfer, if otherwise acceptable to the other interested commander. In France and Germany, few gave the matter a passing thought, though officers in combat did have birthdays and some often passed over the prescribed age limit. The meticulous Adjutant of a Group Headquarters during the Battle of the Bulge telephoned the V Corps Adjutant General, asking if he should process papers on a Field officer whom he belatedly had discovered was a month over age-in-grade. The response was a sarcastic query to the Group Commander as to who was suffering from combat fatigue: the over-age officer, the Adjutant, or both.

## DUPLICITY ON THE EVE OF PEARL HARBOR

*Fortune* Magazine for the month of December had been in the hands of its subscribers two or three weeks when blaring radios from every number on their dials shocked America with news of Pearl Harbor.

This particular issue of that always beautifully-ornate and brilliantly-written business and industrial periodical was dedicated largely to the Army and its growing pains. The frequent quotations and specially-posed pictures leave no doubt but that it was prepared not only with the full knowledge but the warm enthusiasm and full cooperation of General McNair and his Headquarters. The General and Special Staff in the War Department also appear to have participated. The general theme of the articles: "How Good is Our Army?"

The articles were loaded with frequent reassurances that a growth of the Active Army from 188,000 officers and men as of England's Dunkirk, May-June, 1940, to 1,588,500 as of publication date, betokened great progress. Ordnance and other equipment were reviewed and lack of same properly blamed upon the demands of Lend-Lease, including China and Russia. Design and calibers of tanks and guns that could rival the excellence of the German Army offered concern. But American professional military brilliance, joined with the know-how of American industry, could and would inevitably whip all these major and minor problems of materiel. Personnel was something else. The Selectees were a cross-section of American life. America was instinctively peace-loving. Its young men were correspondingly reluctant soldiers. Nevertheless, thanks to the progressive training of Army Ground Forces in general and General McNair in particular, progress was being made in spite of the National Guard. It was admitted regrettably that too many of the Selectees had to go to the Guard Divisions. There it had been a case of the blind leading the blind. If the Selectee, fresh from his initial three months of basic soldiering, "is reasonably bright, he has learned more about soldiering in the replacement training center than a good many Guardsmen know. Indeed, he probably knows more than some Guard officers."

There was optimism in gross figures of growth in men, installations and reorganization. Vigorous steps, even to the point of disqualifying some Regulars for field service through reclassifications and age-in-grade procedures, were being taken, the informants of *Fortune's* remarkably able interviewers and writers were assured. There was a conspicuous vagueness as to what the "cutting edge" of the burgeoning Ground Forces looked like. Indeed, it would have been difficult for the writers to have found an official answer. Quite wisely, the Troop and Station List section had been removed from the *Army Directory* after October 20, 1940. Nevertheless, the *Fortune* writers must have asked some searching questions. Among them must have been the query why a modernizing Army still was clinging to the obsolete, cumbersome, defensive type, "square" organization for the Guard Divisions, at a time when all doctrines and the recent maneuvers had indicated a demand for "triangular" Divisions of three Combat Teams, with no Brigade Headquarters intervening between the Division Commander and the firepower in his Regiments and Artillery Battalions.

One really would like to know specifically who answered that ques-

438

tion. It could have been any one of a half-dozen officers in high and responsible assignments in AGF Headquarters, including General McNair himself, for more than one Guard officer had heard from them informal lip service to the answer given. In any event, here is the question *Fortune* asked, complete with the reported answer:

Why hasn't the National Guard been given the reorganization it needed? Because the High Command shied away from stirring up a hornet's nest. Guard divisions are regional groups, and local pride could be counted upon to rise up in their defense. Reorganization would be unpopular with the Guardsmen, most of whom are eligible to vote by absentee ballot—and can write letters influencing votes back home. But the Army is at last taking action to reform the officer ranks.

The contemptible quality of this brazen and baseless, twisted, hypothetical lie already had been denied by the tide of events even before all the Guard units were mobilized. The reader is referred back to Chapter XV, page 366, in which is set forth the abolition of four National Guard Cavalry Divisions as such, followed by their complete redesignation, conversion, and reorganization into other combatant Arms and occasionally to field support Services. Most of them became Artillerymen. The same thing happened in one form or another to Battalion, Regimental and Brigade-size units, in addition to the Guard Cavalry Divisions, in the majority of the States.

There could have been an occasional squawk here and there. Could the typical horseman be expected to applaud swapping mounts for tractors and pistols for graphical firing tables? Could miners in Nevada, originally constituted as Combat Engineers, be expected to shout loud huzzahs for news that they suddenly had become Anti-Aircraft Coast Artillerymen? Nevertheless they readily accepted such sweeping and basic last-minute reorganizations. Moreover, these conversions and reorganizations were in an election year as a Presidential campaign was approaching its height. It was in a season of less sense of urgency than in 1941 after a year of drifting toward war. Had the Guard units in 1940 decided to kick-up a political rumpus over a matter of reorganization there would have been no need to mail in ballots and send in pressure telegrams. They were still civilians, at home, and could have put on the direct squeeze. And with the Presidential election mounting toward a climax the World would have known about it. But such did not happen.

If Guard units of such magnitude and numbers could be so readily discontinued, redesignated and so completely reorganized while in State status, in a season of less urgency and high political opportunism, by what sense of logical integrity or decency could the War Department General Staff and Ground Forces GHQ propose that there was political dynamite in mere "triangularizing" of the 18 "square" Divisions? They were already on active duty and thereby rendered mute and politically impotent. The "triangular" format basically required no more than detaching one Infantry Regiment and two Battalions of Artillery from each and a few other minor adjustments. Moreover, the War Department General Staff, General McNair and his Headquarters, knew the spurious quality of such a self-serving excuse to the public through the columns of a highly-respected periodical. The sweeping and organic reconversions and reorganizations at home stations in 1940 had been pursuant to their own planning and dictation! Thus the originators and responsible mouthers of the quoted, libelous, self-defense slanders could not have avoided knowledge of its utterly dishonest quality.

In the American Army, unlike some European establishments, Generals are responsible for their Staffs. If either General Marshall or General McNair, publicly or otherwise, ever sought to correct the fictitious excuses and quasi-official pronouncements such as appeared in the *Fortune* articles and in many instances and places elsewhere, such correction does not appear to be of record. Indeed, there is convincing evidence that McNair secretly nursed his phobia against volunteer National Guard troops until he left his Ground Force Headquarters for his FUSAG assignment in 1944. Until then he and his Headquarters directed all training of Army troops within the Continental United States.

The cited and quoted issue of *Fortune* was still on sale at news stands and in book stalls throughout the United States when the radios of America broke the incredible news that Japanese bombs were raining on Pearl Harbor. It marked the end of the whipping-boy and scapegoat slander that officially and unofficially had been heaped upon the Guard from the late Summer day, 1940, that an alert Congress unexpectedly tossed it into the Regular Army's unprepared custody and tutelage. *Pearl Harbor was one military disaster that could not be blamed on the Guard.* General Short, U.S.A., and his 24th (the old Hawaiian) Division and the recently-activated 25th Infantry Division, had no place to pass the buck except to the nearby Navy Headquarters. The Navy passed it right back, whereupon both Hawaiian Headquarters jointly tossed it to Washington. In the massive records of hearings, investigations and the growing literature of the subject, it has been batted back and forth like a badminton bird ever since.*

---

* The blame for Pearl Harbor never will be written to the full satisfaction of any thoughtful and trained historian; least of all to those who are so bold as to attempt the task themselves. The mass of evidence overwhelmingly indicates that in Washington the Departments of State, War and Navy, their several Secretaries, professional Staff chiefs and General Staff sections were utterly uncoordinated. Individually and collectively they bungled. Neither Adm. Husband E. Kimmel, U.S.N., nor Lt. Gen. Walter C. Short, U.S.A., was kept fully informed or clearly instructed. Nevertheless, they had sufficient information, wide enough latitude in their instructions, and sufficient

But in any event, no one has gotten around to blaming it on the National Guard—yet.

## THE ARMY'S "CUTTING EDGE," WHEN WAR CAME

Unlike World War I, there was no publicity clamor for this or that Division to be the first to leave American shores. There was no semi-controlled race for primacy between Division Staffs and their Commanders such as took place in 1917 in the two Guard Divisions (the 26th and the "Rainbow" Divisions) and the Regular Army's 1st Division. A different spirit pervaded America. A once-allied World power, France, had been vanquished and garrisoned. Two other powerful former allies were fighting for their existence at the brink of an abysmal disaster, whence there could be no recovery. A perfidious attack had deprived the American Navy of its vaunted battle line.

The Nation furthermore was confused and dispirited as to the status and condition of its Army, thanks to the self-serving, protective publicity of the War Department General Staff and Ground Forces GHQ. The American public and all the World were being told in that month's publications, and had been harangued liberally through the preceding 14 months, as to the worthless quality of the ground troops except for a too-few, presumably crack, Regular Army units. The Army Air Corps publicly was considered so lacking in fliers and modern equipment that it was pictured almost equally nonoperative. In the face of such widely-publicized, self-admitted, alibied impotence in every way except upon the seas, is there little wonder that the Japanese War Lords struck with such complete confidence that they could win a quick victory and reap its fruits behind a far-flung sea frontier defense, bastioned by distant island fortresses and airfields in the expansively-wide Pacific Ocean?

Is it strange that at the same time English military attaches and observers were sadly assuring their Imperial General Staff Headquarters that the American Army was in such deplorable condition it could not be counted upon for any material assistance even were America an open ally? It would be better, they argued, as late as November, 1941, to keep the flow of Lend-Lease supplies flowing to Russia and Britain (especially Britain) rather than divert it to American Ground Forces. In English opinion, the American Ground Forces had no "cutting edge."

---

men and means for greater insular security at their disposal to have done vastly better than they and their respective Staffs did. In 1812, Brig. Gen. William Hull, U.S.A., faced a court-martial and was sentenced to be shot (later remanded) for a similar debacle at Detroit. Perhaps Kimmel and Short, who merely were placed on the Retired List prematurely, were fortunate in being denied the day in court that they so vigorously sought. They could have fared worse than merely becoming official scapegoats on retired pay.

The price of the General Staff's protective coloring publicity was indeed exhorbitant. America would have been better served had Britain, Germany and Japan known the truth of America's rapidly-growing military might. It would have been a deterrent. The McNair alibi publicity line was an invitation to an attack. If an overseas enemy could wreck the Navy, he had a war four-fifths won, if official Ground Forces Headquarters opinion was valid. McNair had been telling the World that America was impotent for visiting upon them a counter-retribution by military means.

Actually, the American Ground Forces did have a cutting edge. It was small, in proportion to that month's strength of 1.7 million officers and men. But it was a sharp and competent cutting edge, given the equipment that had been going elsewhere. True, 18 Guard Infantry Divisions still awaited "triangularization". But that reorganization was largely a matter of detaching and regrouping component units already in the Guard Divisions. The Guard officers thoroughly knew the theory and practice back of the comparative formations.

As of December 8, 1941, the Army's uncommitted, battle front, Ground Forces, if the two unconverted horse Cavalry Divisions be ignored, consisted of 31 Divisions. They included the 1st, 2nd, 3rd, 4th and 5th Armored Divisions. Though the Guard had brought 18 armored non-divisional Battalions and no less than seven partially-Mechanized Cavalry Regiments into active duty, there were no Guard Armored Divisions. In Infantry, the Army could and did list as its very own the 1st, 2nd, 3rd, 4th, 5th, 6th, 7th, 8th, 9th, 24th, and 25th Infantry Divisions. There were also the unnumbered and so-called Philippine and Panama Divisions. Actually, the two unnumbered Divisions were task forces, which also included heavy, nondivisional, recent reinforcements by Guard units. Moreover, the 24th and 25th Divisions likewise were garrison troops for Hawaii. They were as certainly pinned-down as were the corresponding garrisons of the Canal Zone and Manila, or Luzon. Likewise, the 5th Infantry Division was pinned-down in Iceland by German naval and air threats. Hence, all the five Armored Divisions, consisting of 15 Armored Combat Commands, presumably were available for deployment elsewhere. Likewise, eight of the nine "triangular" Infantry Divisions, consisting of 24 Infantry Regiments (72 Battalions) and 32 Battalions of Field Artillery, were available immediately.

But the overwhelming percentage of a Ground Forces battle line potential was in the 18 National Guard "square" Divisions. They were numbered 26th to 45th inclusive, but exclusive of numbers 39 and 42. The Guard Divisions encompassed no less than 72 Infantry Regiments, for a total of 216 Infantry Battalions and 108 Battalions of Field Artillery. Thus the large and defensively-formed Guard Divisions represented 75% of the Infantry Battalions available for deployment

442

and 76.2% of the Divisional Artillery.* The tactics of World War II did not contemplate assignment of Armored Divisions to battle line sectors. Their use included defensive counterattacks, offensive breakthroughs and in exploitation of local gains or in an all-out pursuit. Offensive, cutting edge units, the Armored Divisions most certainly were.** Accordingly, if the percentages be considered in terms of Regimental Combat Teams, Infantry and Armored, and ignoring the 36 additional Guard Artillery Battalions, the percentages are different, but still strongly in favor of the semi-professional citizen-soldiers; i.e., 111 Regimental Combat Teams, of which 72, or 64.8%, were National Guard units, overwhelmingly commanded by National Guard officers and of which all the hard core of enlisted men and noncommissioned officers were National Guardsmen.

## GUARD DIVISIONS RUSHED OVERSEAS

But on December 8, 1941, the Operations Section of the General Staff had no time to ponder personnel sources. The essential facts were that it had 31 Divisions, five of them Armored. Eighteen of the 26 Infantry Divisions had not been streamlined into the "triangular" formations. The moment Hitler declared war, the broad outlines of Rainbow 5, the plan for all-out war on two fronts, became operative. What was more pertinent and immediately pressing, was President Roosevelt's commitment to Prime Minister Winston Churchill that American troops would leave immediately for the British Isles to underwrite the certainty of their air, naval and army base potential in future operations against the common European foe. It was to be, crush Germany first.

Though Hitler's armies were deep in Russia, more than 40 of his Divisions remained in Western Europe. Among them, and poised on the

---

* The reasons for Gen. McNair's failure to remould this powerful force to conform fully with the adopted doctrines of the "triangular" Divisions, the Companies, Battalions and Infantry Regiments of which already were "triangularized," has not been subjected to exhaustive research. What he may have had in mind for the future of the Guard Divisions did not happen, hence is hardly a part of this narrative. The following theories are worthy of investigation, though the author strongly discounts the second. (1) McNair was indecisive and exercised delay as long as possible. There is a body of unavoidable evidence in support of this. (2) Reorganization while on active duty would have left enough unassigned Regiments and Battalions for six additional Guard Divisions; the clamor for the creation of which, with resultant promotions for Guard officers, was the real "politics" that he feared in the *Fortune* article. This seems most unlikely. Never has a General Staff had both National politics and publicity under such complete and perfect control as from January 1, 1941, to December 8 of the same year. (3) McNair contemplated destruction of all Guard Divisions and the entire Guard as an A.U.S. component, Congress permitting, upon their return to home and State status at the end of their 18 months of active duty. There is documentary as well as oral evidence in support of this. A combination of some part of all three factors, or all of all three, could have prompted the wholly-unnecessary delay.
** Though highly-dramatic in their battlefield roles, battle casualties in engaged Tank Battalions were lower in percentage than within engaged Field Artillery Battalions.

Brest Peninsula, as if aimed at Ireland, were crack Parachute Divisions of the German Army. Hitlerian hopes for a diplomatic incident, perhaps one that could be contrived deceptively, that would trip neutral and highly-vocal and volatile South Ireland toward the Nazi orbit, were obvious. Though committed to the idea of fighting to the bitter end whichever belligerent might first violate its neutrality, the Irish Army was completely inadequate. Against such a threat, most likely an airborne and submarine-supported invasion near the mouth of the Shannon River, an entire English Army was pinned-down in North Ireland. Churchill wanted to pinch-out some of its Divisions immediately to reinforce the British Eighth Army in North Africa.

Accordingly, the 32nd Infantry Division (Wisconsin and Michigan), the 34th (Minnesota, Iowa, and North Dakota) and the 37th (Ohio) were alerted immediately. Before Christmas week, their advance detachments, including elements of their Engineer Regiments, were en route to Belfast, North Ireland. Meanwhile, the Divisions were being "triangularized," and given top priority for equipment, before and upon arrival at Ports of Embarkation. At the same time V Army Corps, Major General Edmund L. Daley commanding, was designated Force Headquarters. The Corps command was rounded-out further by assignment of the 1st Armored Division, the Regular Army's oldest, most experienced and best-equipped mechanized Division. Likewise, the 73rd Field Artillery Brigade, consisting of the 141st (Louisiana) and 166th (Pennsylvania) F.A. Regiments of 155mm Howitzers, the 190th F.A. Regiment of 155mm guns, and the 17th Field Observation Battalion, was alerted to become the Corps Artillery of the immediate overseas force. Complete with four Divisions, Corps Artillery, attached nondivisional tanks, Tank Destroyer, 102nd Mechanized Cavalry (New Jersey), Quartermaster, Signal, Ordnance, Hospital and Medical Regiments, it was no small command.

But two of the Divisions and some lesser components never reached Ireland. While they were in staging camps on the East Coast, the explosive, three-pronged Japanese offensive occurred. It threatened Alaska from Attu and Kiska. The Guadalcanal landings threatened the supply lifeline to Australia. The thrust Southward appeared to be aimed at the Australian mainland. The apparently uncertain results of the Coral Sea naval battle further filled American and British Empire strategists with alarm. General MacArthur, who had just opened a GHQ in Australia without benefit of field troops, sounded the tocsin of alarm. The 32nd and the 37th were entrained in their staging areas for Europe with the expectations of being in New York, or Boston, Ports of Embarkation within a matter of hours. The Pullman berths did occasion some discussion. The men awoke somewhere East of Chicago, with unmistakable evidence of being headed for San Francisco and the South Pacific.

444

On the 16th of September, elements of the 32nd Infantry Division were air-lifted from Port Moresby to New Guinea to extend an Australian flank in blocking Japanese invaders from Southward movement over the Kokoda Trail. Within another 30 days, these and additional elements of the 32nd Division seized the offensive, by fire and movement, to oust the Japanese from western New Guinea. This was the first offensive in the South Pacific, an initiative that never was lost.* The National Guard's 32nd Infantry Division and the simultaneously embattled Marines on Guadalcanal were the first American Infantry sent forth from the Continental United States after Pearl Harbor, to come under hostile smallarms fire in ground combat.

The 34th Infantry Division went to North Ireland with V Corps, as scheduled. For the great amphibious expedition concentrated against North Africa for simultaneous ship-to-shore assaults, Casablanca to Algiers, inclusive, November 8, 1942, the 34th Infantry Division was detached from V Corps to become assigned to the II Corps upon landing and taking its objective East of Algiers. It was assigned the most Eastern of all the North African beach assaults, and thereby deepest in hostile territory. Accordingly, the 34th found itself at the apex of the first American offensive to free North Africa of German domination, just as the 32nd had found itself on the nose of the first offensive in the South Pacific.

For the Divisional and non-divisional units of the National Guard, World War II had begun in earnest. Before the shooting had ended in the heart of Europe and on Okinawa, within easy bombing range of the Japanese home islands, all the Guard units, Divisional and non-divisional, and all 29 of the Air Corps Squadrons, were to find themselves embattled in a major Theater of War.

---

* It is known now that the Japanese had no all-out strategic intentions against either Australia or Alaska. In the Aleutians, at Guadalcanal and in New Guinea, they merely were staking-out their strategic defense perimeter in terms of garrison-defended air fields combined with naval base bastions. Behind all this the dream of a vast Empire of the Rising Sun—all China, Burma, the Philippines and modern Indonesia—would be materialized leisurely. Officially-inspired publicity had told them American had no ground forces, and could develop none in the foreseeable future, that could capture, occupy and defend such bastions for the island-hopping campaigns that did occur. With our Navy's battle line askew at Pearl Harbor, it was, in the light of available evidence, a Japanese G-2 estimate that would have rated a Superior mark in any staff or war college of that era.

# Bibliographical Note For Chapter XVII

Among the contemporary periodicals consulted, the *New York Times, Newsweek, Time, Life* and *Fortune* were used most frequently. Two volumes of the official series, *The United States Army in World War II,* are highly pertinent. They are Kent R. Greenfield, Robert R. Palmer, and Bell I. Wiley, *The Organization of Ground Combat Troops,* 1947, and Mark S. Watson, *The Chief of Staff: Prewar Plans and Preparations,* 1950. Both volumes suffer through lack of contact with or viewpoints from the field, which, by the nature of their purpose and scope is not so noticeable or even important in the latter as in the former. Moreover, official books written by a committee often suffer handicaps. Any one of the authors, all three of whom are superb historians, most likely would have written a better book had he been working alone, as was Mark S. Watson in writing the latter volume. Elting E. Morison, *Turmoil and Tradition: A Study of the Life and Times of Henry L. Stimson,* 1960, superbly reveals the chaos within the War Department as the Nation sought preparedness. E. J. Kahn, *McNair, Educator of an Army,* 1944, is a warm and sympathetic tribute by an excellent citizen-soldier and brilliant journalist. The *Annual Reports . . . War Department,* most particularly that from the National Guard Bureau, 1941, are, of course, indispensable. The previously-cited official *Army Almanac,* 1950, also offers a wealth of facts and figures in a most convenient form. Two Divisional histories are of some significance: Members of the 34th, *Story of the 34th Division from Louisiana to Pisa,* 1945, and Col. Russell L. Ramsey, *History of the 37th Infantry Division,* 1947. Maj. Gen. H. D. Russell, *The Purge of the 30th Division,* 1951, appears to be the only personal narrative dedicated entirely to the training period of a Division for World War II. See evaluation, footnote, p. 414. The author personally was acquainted with a number of the officers mentioned, and had enough personal contacts with most others to form some first-hand and not-always correct opinions. Gen. McNair he knew personally, enjoyed his comments and admired his scholarship. But pleasant memories of a personality never can be a basis for an honest historical review or evaluation.

CHAPTER XVIII

# The National Guard
# in World War II

THE PEARL HARBOR sneak attack brought a heavy, velvet pall of secrecy and censorship upon America. Among other things it had convinced every citizen as to the values of secrecy and surprise in warfare. Overnight it made Americans amenable to censorship. The mood was implemented immediately by the ever-sensitive master of public opinion in the White House. He had the hearty approval and able assistance of the State, War and Navy Departments. The dignified and austere mantle of the Supreme Court was brought forth to reinforce the black, official pall designed to cover a disaster that in England would have brought about the fall of a government overnight. But under our system of fixed-term elections, that could not happen in America. Moreover, in the White House was the most canny politician and domestic affairs statesman since Andrew Jackson. He had no intention of losing public esteem then or later if it could be avoided. Accordingly, President Franklin D. Roosevelt designated Supreme Court Justice Owen J. Roberts, accompanied by two Admirals and two General Officers from the Army, to proceed to Hawaii to investigate, assess responsibility and report without undue delay. It was designed to assuage and subdue an excited public rather than to inform.

447

The patriotic Supreme Court Justice cooperated so well and with such dignified restraint that by January 24, 1942, President Roosevelt happily released the Roberts Report on Pearl Harbor without editorial revision.

At the same time it was being made clear to editors and Press owners that publication of military and naval news without official clearance could be outright treason. Ship and troop movements immediately became Top Secret. The only people who seemed to know what Army units were moving to where, as, if and when, were the railroads' general passenger agents. They were telling their transportation personnel from one end of their lines to the other. Thus almost any alert Guardsman with local railroad station contacts could and often did scoop his own Division and Corps Headquarters by at least two weeks on troop movement information concerning themselves. Of course, the same news was equally available to newspapermen, but they were abstaining to the point of avoiding knowledge. They had no intention of having the treasonable-information-to-the-enemy label stuck on themselves or their publications.

In such an atmosphere of alarm, recrimination and uncertainty as to what was legitimate news, it was utterly impossible that there could be a highly-publicized, competitive spirit as to which Division should have the honor of being the first overseas, as was noted in an earlier chapter with reference to transoceanic movements in World War I.

Moreover, in World War II, the General Staff, under General George C. Marshall, had a much tighter, more centralized grip on the field forces than did Chief of Staff Hugh L. Scott and his successor, the transitory General Tasker H. Bliss of 1917-18. General Marshall furthermore intended to profit by the mistakes of his World War I predecessors. Most particularly he would avoid the division of authority that had plagued General Peyton C. March. Marshall would keep the lines of control closely gathered-in. There would be no Presidential letter of broad instructions to an A.E.F. Commander, with wide, expansive, discretionary powers, such as Woodrow Wilson had given General John J. Pershing, if the political-minded War Department General Staff could preclude it.

## THE FIRST TO LAND OVERSEAS

Under such a blanket of secrecy and under such highly-centralized management, the honor of being the first World War II Army Division to land in an overseas Theater of Operations fell to the 34th Infantry Division. It was composed entirely of National Guard units from Minnesota, North Dakota, South Dakota and Iowa. As noted in the preceding chapter, this Division was a part of the heavily-reinforced V Corps, the other Divisional elements of which were the 32nd (Wisconsin-Michigan), the 37th (Ohio) and the 1st Armored (U.S. Army). The code name was MAGNET FORCE. Its mission was (1) release of British units in North Ireland to the Middle East; (2) defense of Ireland, in conjunction with available British forces, should the German Army launch a diversionary, airborne and submarine-supported invasion of South Ireland from the Brest Peninsula; and (3) reception, further equipping and supply, utilizing "reverse Lend-Lease" when available, of additional Air and Ground Force units being scheduled for ultimate arrival in the British Isles.

The 34th Infantry Division commander, Major General Russell P. Hartle, U.S. Army, with an advance party of 35 or 40 officers and men, opened a temporary Headquarters in a Belfast hotel, January, 1942. Major General Edmund L. Daley, commanding V Corps and MAGNET FORCE, remained in the United States to expedite priorities on American equipment and supplies. He further sought to hasten the departure of the follow-up Divisions and lesser units of his large command from the hastily-designated East Coast staging stations for Atlantic Ports of Embarkation. Most of his troops were in Forts Devens, Dix and Camp Edwards. Other minor, improvised, supplementary staging installations, as far distant as Camp Sutton, North Carolina, were also hosts to some of his lesser units.

Because of the absence of realistic General Staff planning, to which both Guard and Regular Army Divisions by this date had become thoroughly accustomed, these staging stations promptly became bottlenecks to overseas movements. Well-trained field troops languished in them without opportunity for keeping their techniques sharp except by ceremonial formations, spit-and-polish discipline, combined with Company, Battery, Regimental and Staff schools for staying fresh on theories, if not practice. Practically all their field equipment had been sent direct to Ports of Embarkation for separate shipment in freighter convoys. Energetic Field Grade officers, often at their own expense, collected pamphlets, books and official and unofficial publications on allied and enemy armies to give realistic vitality to their improvised staging area schools. The Artillery officers, fully expecting soon to be issued British 25-pounders in lieu of the recently-adopted but scarce American 105mm howitzers, spent their spare time studying and teaching English weapons and equipment. Blackboard problems from 25-pounder range tables were considered constructive. Practicing deflection commands in degrees and minutes, rather than mils, proved to be much more confusing than English nomenclature. But the Guardsmen long since had learned to provide their own training and instruction if they wanted it to be really constructive.

Came May, 1942. It found three of General Daley's four Divisions and all of V Corps' 73rd Field Artillery Brigade (Pennsylvania-Louisi-

449

ana) still in the staging area bottlenecks. By that time General Daley, a restless, high-strung, dynamic, driving personality, was at the threshhold of a nervous breakdown from frustrations. Withal he had made sufficient nuisance of himself to the expanding Staff empires in the War Department that in May he was relieved. Thus ended one of the magnificent combat records from World War I, not to mention a reputation for outstanding performance in some of the highest Engineer Corps assignments in time of peace. Like many such Engineer officers, with wide civilian contacts from flood control and hydroelectric projects, General Daley had acquired horizons beyond the cloistered Army Posts and the War Department Staff conferences of his era. Certainly he was a far cry from the noncombatant General Staff types upon whom Generals McNair and Marshall had learned to rely and from among whose ranks they had risen. Daley's retirement the following September as a Brigadier General, "at his own request," pursuant to "Section 5, Act of 31 July 1935 as amended . . ." was perhaps justified. He obviously had lost the confidence of the War Department. He continued in the war effort, however, by accepting a quasi-military assignment for the State of New York.

## CRISIS IN THE SOUTH PACIFIC

Meanwhile, the situation in the Pacific had deteriorated faster than the war planning proponents of whip-Germany-first had thought possible. The President's promise of an early Second Front in Europe could not be validated until more pressing dangers were checked.

Japan had not waited until the surrender of Singapore, February 15, 1942, or until resistance ended in the Philippines, May 6, before fanning-out over the Pacific to seize, garrison, fortify and create operations bases upon selected strategic islands. On May 1 the explosively-expanding Japanese Empire had reached and occupied Tulagi and Guadalcanal, Westernmost of the Solomon Islands. It was an ominous threat to American supply lines to Australia. A few days later Japanese naval task forces with transports were seen approaching and achieving landings in western New Guinea. Almost simultaneously the islands of Attu and Kiska, in Alaska's Aleutian chain, were seized and occupied. American military installations in Alaska soon were to feel the force of the first hostile aerial bombardments in the history of North America. Though today recognized as a significant victory, the simultaneous uncertainties of the Coral Sea naval battle confused rather than reassured.

Troops afloat in a few transports to reinforce the Philippines when Manila was bombed and blockaded by the Japanese had been diverted to Australia. These and some Air Corps units were the principal components of the command that greeted General MacArthur when he arrived there from Bataan. The 41st Infantry Division, of Guard units from Washington, Oregon, Montana and Idaho, soon was sent him. It shipped-out in March, about the time the 34th Infantry Division, with the 107th Engineers of the 32nd Division, were counting all present in North Ireland.* Task Force 6814, a collection of National Guard Infantry Regiments, Artillery Battalions and other spare parts from the "triangularization" of the Guard "square" Divisions, simultaneously was en route from New York in a slow convoy to occupy and garrison New Caledonia, which was also in MacArthur's Theater. These islands were also a potential way station on the direct route to Sydney, Australia. The Task Force commander, Major General Alexander M. Patch, immediately organized most of his collection of National Guard oddments into the Americal Division. Not until November 26, 1954 did this historic National Guard Infantry Division acquire a number. It was redesignated, presumably to confuse future historians, as the 23rd Infantry Division and earmarked as a Regular Army Division.

But the never-inarticulate General Douglas MacArthur hardly had looked at his inventory of these and other prospective units before he cited the need for more. It was then that the General Staff planners took cognizance of the Divisions of MAGNET FORCE still languishing in staging areas for Atlantic seaboard Ports of Embarkation. They immediately detached the 32nd (Wisconsin, Michigan) and the 37th (Ohio) from V Corps of MAGNET FORCE and shipped them across the Continent in a vast cavalcade of Pullmans. It was, nevertheless, so secret that families knew not the whereabouts of their menfolk until they wrote from the Pacific instead of the British Isles. The 32nd went directly to Australia. The Ohio Guard Division disembarked at the Fiji Islands to set up additional outposts of containment against the madly-expanding "Empire of the Rising Sun."

The remainder of the much earlier-alerted MAGNET FORCE, consisting of the 1st Armored Division and V Corps non-divisional units, continued to North Ireland, pursuant to their assigned mission, with General Hartle as Corps Commander in Ireland. The 1st Infantry Division, and the 29th, National Guard, Virginia, Maryland, and District of Columbia, soon arrived in the British Isles in place of those diverted to the Pacific. The 34th Infantry, the 1st Infantry and 1st Armored Divisions, in October, were detached from the V Corps to participate in the great Anglo-American TORCH landings in North Africa, beginning November 8.

Meanwhile, prior to that date, the United States' Army's first offensive operation in World War II had been in progress for six weeks against

---

* The 107th Engineers were an advance party for the 32nd. When that Division was detached from V Corps, this Battalion was replaced by the 114th Engr. Bn. from Massachusetts, a spare part from the "triangularizing" 26th, or "Yankee," Division. Similar adjustments were not unusual in other Divisions.

the Japanese forces in Papua, western New Guinea. It was pretty much a one-Division show with the 32nd Division, flown to Port Moresby from Australia, playing the stellar role. It landed in Papua September 16, 1942. By early December the Division had captured Buna and had Papua well in hand. A more gruelling campaign is not of record in World War II.

The Navy's 1st and 2nd Marine Divisions, under Lieutenant General Alexander A. Vandergrift, U.S.M.C., had been on Guadalcanal since their first landings, August 8.* In their initial skirmish on the Tenaru River, August 21, they already had demonstrated themselves to be masters of defense and counterattack for holding Henderson Field and clinging to their beachhead. The U.S. Navy's series of sea victories over the Japanese transports and fleet, climaxed by the sea battles of November 14-15, underwrote America's holding the island, but they were not complete enough to stop the night flow of Japanese Army reinforcements to the Island.

To get the Marines out of the beleaguered and hotly-defended beachhead and to eliminate the 27,000 Japanese troops from further participation in that war, General Patch, from New Caledonia, with his Americal Division of Guard units, relieved Vandergrift and his 1st Marine Division on December 9, 1942. Much of the 2nd Marine Division remained for a time, under Patch, who was reinforced further by one Combat Team of the 37th Division (Ohio) and finally by the 25th Division, Regular Army and Guard, from Hawaii. Patch, ably supported by naval offshore gunfire and blocking operations, continued his offensive squeeze on what was left of the truly large Japanese jungle-based and darkness-supplied forces on Guadalcanal. But night runs by Japanese destroyer flotillas, when ultimate defeat was conceded, also made possible the evacuation of 11,706 officers and men of the Mikado's Army. Patch declared the victory won and the campaign ended as of February 9, 1943.

From the foregoing it is readily seen that shortly following the end of the first full year of hostilities, America was successfully ending two offensive campaigns in the Pacific—Guadalcanal and Papua. To Buna, the latter had been pretty much a joint operation of an Australian Brigade and the 32nd Division. To press the advance into western New Guinea, elements of the 41st Infantry Division (Washington, Montana, Oregon and Idaho) soon displaced Northward from Australia for coordinated operations with the 32nd. Both were joined later by the 43rd Infantry Division (Connecticut, Maine, Rhode Island and Vermont) from its earlier bases in New Zealand.

---

*In a strategic sense the slightly earlier Marine landings were part of a naval offensive. But the local tactical mission of the Marines was to occupy, defend and hold, which they did with magnificent courage. The Army's simultaneous Papuan campaign was offensive in both strategic and tactical missions.

It is further apparent that after 14 months of warfare in the Pacific, practically the entire Ground Forces capability of a sustained offensive reaction against the Bataan disaster had been found in the National Guard Divisions and in General Vandergrift's Marine task force that was thrown into the surprise occupation of the Guadalcanal beachhead. But with these Marine and the National Guard formations, the military initiative in the Pacific had been seized. New operational bases for ships and aircraft were made possible. The great, island-to-island, two-pronged, strategic offensives through Polynesia and through the Mariannas was on its way. Their inexorable advance was to humble Japan without the necessity of an invasion. But it naturally required more and more ships, planes and Ground Force Divisions.

This is no place to review the oft-told operational details of ships, Air Squadrons, and Army Divisions. The arrival of these early units in Europe and in the Pacific has been given in some detail to reflect the degree to which the stricken Nation, immediately following Pearl Harbor, was dependent upon its much-abused National Guard formations. The remainder of the Guard's participation in the Pacific, and in full comparison with all other comparable formations committed to those Theaters of Operations, can be told adequately by a chronological listing of all American Army Infantry Divisions that ultimately appeared in the Order of Battle lists of the Pacific.

Included with each are dates of activation and arrival overseas, and a statement of its campaigns and battle casualty statistics, and date of inactivation. It is readily conceded that these are not adequate yardsticks for the measurement of a Division's full record of sacrifice and service. This is particularly true in the Pacific, where the climate, jungle, lack of sanitation and other hazards to life and health often were more subtle enemies and actually created more non-battle casualties than did the battlefield contacts with the known and armed Japanese foe. It is conceded further that high battle casualties can occur in a brief period from special situations which may or may not be results of improper, or ill-advised, employment of troops. For example, it is doubtful if the unduly high casualties of the 96th Infantry Division (Army of the U.S. and Reserve) in the brief Okinawa containment and mop-up could be justified. Likewise, in the list of Divisions in the European Theater, the mass surrender of units in the 106th Infantry Division, with P.O.W. casualties exceeding 6,000, in only a few days of contact, could not have occurred in a better-trained and more ably-commanded Division.

Notwithstanding these obvious shortcomings of battle casualty statistics to reflect the full measure of service of a Division, they do, in close contiguity with dates of active duty, campaigns participated in and the date of their arrival overseas, give the reader a quick, comparative im-

453

pression as to the contributions of comparable National Guard, Regular Army and Army of the United States, Reserve, Ground Force units through World War II.


OVERSEAS DEPLOYMENT SEQUENCE, INFANTRY DIVISIONS, WORLD WAR II, AGAINST JAPAN, WITH THEIR CAMPAIGNS AND BATTLE CASUALTIES*

December 7, 1941—September 2, 1945

TRANS-PACIFIC, 1942:

41st Infantry Division (National Guard; Washington, Montana, Oregon, Idaho). Called from States to Federal service September 16, 1940. To Australia, April, 1942. Campaigns: *New Guinea; Luzon; Southern Philippines; Papuan.* KIA, 743; DOW, 217; TOTAL CASUALTIES, 4,260. Released from Federal service December 31, 1945 in Japan.

32nd Infantry Division (National Guard; Wisconsin, Michigan). Called from States to Federal service October 15, 1940. To Australia, May, 1942. Campaigns: *New Guinea; Papua; Leyte; Luzon.* KIA, 1,613; DOW, 372; TOTAL CASUALTIES, 7,268. Released from Federal service, February 28, 1946 in Japan.

23rd Infantry Division (National Guard; best known as The Americal Division) to New Caledonia as major elements of Task Force 6814 largely composed of National Guard Divisional surplus units resulting from Gen. McNair's myopic failure to "triangularize" the Guard Divisions before outbreak of hostilities. The Infantry Regiments of this Division were: 132nd (Illinois), 164th (North Dakota) and 182nd (Massachusetts). Date of activation in New Caledonia: May 24, 1942. Campaigns: *Guadalcanal; Northern Solomons; Southern Philippines; Leyte.* KIA, 981; DOW, 176; TOTAL CASUALTIES, 4,050. Released from Federal service December 2, 1945.

37th Infantry (National Guard; Ohio). Called from State to Federal service October 15, 1940. To Fiji Islands June, 1942. Campaigns: *Northern Solomons; Luzon.* KIA, 1,094; DOW, 250; TOTAL CASUALTIES, 5,960. Released from Federal service December 18, 1945.

43rd Infantry Division (National Guard; Rhode Island, Vermont, Maine, Connecticut). Called from States to Federal service February 24, 1941. To New Zealand, October, 1942. Campaigns: *New Guinea; Northern Solomons; Guadalcanal; Luzon.* KIA, 1,128; DOW, 278; TOTAL CASUALTIES, 6,026. Released from Federal service October 26, 1945.

---

* It is recognized that casualty figures in this tabulation of Divisions to the Pacific do not always agree with those of unit histories and occasional other early sources of official and semi-official character. The same is true of the subsequent and corresponding table of trans-Atlantic Divisions. Passage of time normally tends to refine and correct statistics. Hence, the most recent, published source was followed—*The Army Almanac*, edited by Brig. Gen. Gordon R. Young, U. S. Army (Ret.), copyright, 1959.

25th Infantry Division (Regular Army and National Guard). It was activated from miscellaneous units in Hawaii, October, 1941. One of its three Infantry Regiments was from the National Guard, the 161st Infantry Regiment (Washington). To Guadalcanal from Hawaiian garrison, December, 1942. Campaigns: *Central Pacific; Guadalcanal; Northern Solomons; Luzon.* KIA, 1,235; DOW, 262; TOTAL CASUALTIES, 5,432.

## TRANS-PACIFIC, 1943

7th Infantry Division (Regular Army, with one Infantry Regiment, the 184th, surplus from "triangularized" 40th Division, National Guard, California). Activated July 11, 1940. To Aleutian Islands and Hawaii, May, 1943. Campaigns: *Aleutian Islands; Eastern Mandates; Leyte; Ryukyus.* KIA, 1,948; DOW, 386; TOTAL CASUALTIES, 9,212. Remained on occupation duty in Korea and Japan with original personnel rotated home.

1st Cavalry Division (Regular Army). Active at peace strength from World War I. Without horses and motorized, it was actually an Infantry Division with vestigial terminology and organization from horse Cavalry. Its Combat Teams were organized on the 5th, 12th, 7th and 8th Cavalry Regiments, giving it the basic qualities of the old "square" Divisions.* It arrived in Australia July, 1943. Campaigns: *New Guinea; Bismarck Archipelago; Leyte; Luzon.* KIA, 734; DOW, 236; TOTAL CASUALTIES, 4,055.

24th Infantry Division (Regular Army) known from February, 1921, merely as "The Hawaiian Division"; redesignated August 26, 1941, as the 24th. It suffered slight casualties from Japanese aerial bombardment of Pearl Harbor December 7, 1941. It arrived in Australia, September, 1943. Campaigns: *Central Pacific; New Guinea; Leyte; Luzon; Southern Philippines.* KIA, 1,374; DOW, 315; TOTAL CASUALTIES, 7,012.

27th Infantry Division (National Guard; New York). Called from State to Federal service October 15, 1940. To Gilbert Islands, November, 1943, via Hawaii, May, 1942. Campaigns: *Central Pacific; Western Pacific; Ryukyus.* KIA, 1,512; DOW, 332; TOTAL CASUALTIES, 6,533. Released from Federal service December 31, 1945.

## TRANS-PACIFIC, 1944

40th Infantry Division (National Guard, California). Called from State to Federal service March 3, 1941. To New Britain, April, 1944, via Hawaii, September, 1942. Campaigns: *Bismarck Archipelago, Luzon, Southern Philippines.* KIA, 614; DOW, 134; TOTAL CASUALTIES, 3,025. Released from Federal service April 7, 1946.

---

* The Regular Army's one other Cavalry Division, the 2nd, was partially inactivated July 15, 1942 by transferring out units and personnel. It was reactivated February 25, 1943, with Negro enlisted personnel. It arrived overseas at Oran, North Africa, March 9, 1944. Compaigns: None. It was inactivated in Africa, May 10, 1944.

31st Infantry Division (National Guard; Mississippi, Louisiana, Alabama, Florida). Called from States to Federal service November 25, 1940. To New Guinea, April, 1944. Campaigns: *New Guinea; Southern Philippines; Western Pacific.* KIA, 340; DOW, 74; TOTAL CASUALTIES, 1,733. Released from Federal service December 21, 1945.

38th Infantry Division (National Guard; Kentucky, West Virginia, Indiana). Called from States to Federal service January 12, 1941. To New Guinea July, 1944, via Hawaii in January, 1944. Campaigns: *New Guinea; Leyte; Luzon.* KIA, 645; DOW, 139; TOTAL CASUALTIES, 3,464. Released from Federal service November 9, 1945.

6th Infantry Division (Regular Army). Activated October 12, 1939. To New Guinea, January, 1944, via Hawaii, July, 1943. Campaigns: *New Guinea; Luzon.* KIA, 410; DOW, 104; TOTAL CASUALTIES, 2,370. Inactivated in Korea, January, 1949.

93rd Infantry Division (Army of the United States, Reserve*). Activated in Army of United States, May 15, 1942. One Regiment, the 25th Infantry, was from the Regular Army. To Guadalcanal, February, 1944. Campaigns: *New Guinea; Northern Solomons.* KIA, 12; DOW, 5; TOTAL CASUALTIES, 133. Inactivated, February 3, 1946.

33rd Infantry Division (National Guard; Illinois). Called from State to Federal service March 5, 1941. To New Guinea, May 1944, via Hawaii, July, 1943. Campaigns: *New Guinea; Luzon.* KIA, 396; DOW, 128; TOTAL CASUALTIES, 2,426. Inactivated February 5, 1946 in Japan.

77th Infantry Division (A.U.S., Reserve). Activated in A.U.S. March 25, 1942. To Guam, July, 1944. Campaigns: *Western Pacific; Leyte; Ryukyus.* KIA, 1,449; DOW, 401; TOTAL CASUALTIES, 7,461. Inactivated March 15, 1946 in Japan.

96th Infantry Division (A.U.S., Reserve). Activated in A.U.S., August 15, 1942. To Leyte, July, 1944. Campaigns: *Leyte; Ryukyus.* KIA, 1,563; DOW, 473; TOTAL CASUALTIES, 8,812. Inactivated February 3, 1946.

98th Infantry Division (A.U.S., Reserve). Activated in A.U.S., September 15, 1942. To Japan, August, 1945. Occupation duty only. Inactivated February 16, 1946.

81st Infantry Division (A.U.S., Reserve). Activated in A.U.S., June 15, 1942. To Palau Islands, September, 1944. Campaigns: *Western Pacific, Southern Philippines.* KIA, 366; DOW, 149; TOTAL CASUALTIES, 2,314. Inactivated January 20, 1946, in Japan.

The foregoing listed and epitomized Divisions represent the entire Ground Forces commitment of *Infantry* Divisions against Japan. There

---

* Corresponds to the term National Army, of World War I. Many histories and tabulated compendiums refer to World War II units that are neither Regular Army nor National Guard as being AUS, or A.U.S., for Army of the United States. Such usage, without the word, Reserve, can be confusing. The Army of the United States is an-all inclusive term which covers all three of America's major military components: The Regular Army, the National Guard and the U.S. Army Reserve.

was in the Order of Battle, however, one Airborne Division that certainly fought as Infantry. It was the 11th Airborne Division, activated in the Army of the United States February 25, 1943 and designated as a Regular Army Division, November 15, 1948. Its campaigns were New Guinea, Leyte and Luzon, with 494 killed in action, 120 dying of wounds, and overall casualties of 2,431. It did not go overseas until May, 1944.

One other Army Division in the Pacific war should be mentioned also, though it was hardly a part of the overseas deployment listed above. It was the 12th Infantry Division (Regular Army, Philippine Scouts). It was not, however, so designated until after the Japanese capitulation. Historically, it was officially known from 1921 as "The Philippine Division (Square)." After Bataan, the Division (with its four Infantry Regiments, Field Artillery Brigade and lesser units) vanished from the Army lists until enough survivors emerged from Japanese P.O.W. installations for its reorganization and numbering as indicated above. Its casualties—killed, died of wounds, wounded, missing in action—included the entire Division, less a few escapees. Attached to it at the time were two National Guard Battalions of light tanks.

It is not to be inferred, of course, that so few Infantry Divisions and the Army Air Forces were alone in the humbling of the haughty Japanese Empire. They were ably assisted and abetted by the United States Navy, which included the 1st and 2nd Marine Divisions, most famous for their bitterly-contested beachhead on Guadalcanal. But it is too often overlooked that it was the National Guard's American Division, reinforced by the 147th Infantry (Ohio National Guard), that bailed the Marines out of the beachhead. Moreover, there was still some jumbled, jungle terrain to be mopped-up when the 25th Division arrived, a large segment of which, the 161st Infantry Regiment, was also of National Guard origin. Thus, if the Army was not alone in the Pacific, it is equally true that neither were the Marines and the Navy's ships at sea.

It is also of interest to note here that the Army sent not a single Armored Division against Japan, notwithstanding the tremendously stepped-up flow of such Divisions to Europe through 1944-45. The explanation is simple. In the Pacific theaters of action the only good operational areas for Armor were the broad, moist expanses of the wide Pacific Ocean. It offered a high-speed armored approach to every objective—as far as the beaches. Thus the naval strife of the American and Japanese warships constituted the fastest, greatest and longest-ranged armored combats in the history of warfare. But the American fleets and airplanes could not have operated without the Infantry to seize, occupy and hold the necessary, closing rings of bases. The Japanese

Navy and Air Squadrons were not pinned-down until their far-flung bases were torn from them by the Ground Force units.

Moreover, all elements afloat and ashore would have experienced more long and lonely moments than did come their way had General George C. Kenney's Fifth, Seventh and Thirteenth Air Forces been absent from the Pacific Order of Battle. The B29's from Okinawa and other offshore islands on strategic bombing missions for the Eighth and Twentieth Air Forces did much toward creating a climate of opinion for surrender within the Japanese homeland. In these there were Army Air Force units that stemmed from the 29 National Guard Squadrons from the States, inducted with the Guard Divisions in 1940 and 1941. But their story belongs to another chapter. Here we are primarily concerned with the Guardsmen in the Ground Forces.

The summarized records of the Pacific Divisions, alongside those of comparable units of the other Army Ground Forces components, certainly speak glowingly of and for the National Guard. It was the Guard units, in being and fully functional, that made possible a prompt reaction into effective, sustained offensives. Through the long, drab, dreary and depressed months following Pearl Harbor, it is impossible to overestimate the value of these first, modest, early offensive operations to the spirit and morale of the American people and Nation. This was particularly true within those proud States represented in the far Pacific effort by their own Guard formations.

## TRANS-ATLANTIC OFFENSIVE OPERATIONS

While the early offensives of the Marines and the National Guard Divisions in the far Pacific were floriating into early, heartening victories, the American planners were being confronted by divisive desires and advice from European allies. Russia was clamoring for more munitions via Vladivostok and the Persian Gulf plus an all-out Second Front to be created by an Anglo-American invasion of occupied France. Stalin, within diplomatic channels, and through his highly-articulate propaganda stooges in Britain and America, was demanding both, and at the same time. The Free French saw logic in the Second Front for the liberation of their homeland, but for most Frenchmen their vision stopped right there. Some did argue the quickest though more circuitous liberation route was via French North Africa. Free China, driven inland by the Japanese to Chungking, was in a receptive mood for anything so long as it achieved survival. With the victorious Japanese in Burma, even the back door to Free China was being closed. Thus China's needs were indeed many and desperate. England, still hopeful of salvaging an empire and with an historic eye on Suez and the Middle East, argued a first offensive could kill three pigeons with one arrow. A major offensive through North Africa, thence into Europe through the "soft underbelly," would please the French, take the pressure from the Russians, and magnificently keep the Empire, as well as Mother England, fully in the War.

Just who told England's Winston Churchill, the father of the phrase, that Europe had a "soft underbelly," is not of record. As a distinguished historian of things military and diplomatic, it safely can be assumed that he knew Italy, the predominately strategic, geographic factor in the Mediterranean approaches, had been conquered frequently from the North; but only once in the history of warfare had it been conquered from the South.* In other words, the "soft underbelly" eventually was to become conspicuous by its absence. But North Africa, notwithstanding English reverses Eastward from Libya, or Tripoli, was indeed ripe for the harvest. Thus the Washington planners were somewhat more than half-right when they hearkened unto the persuasive words of the most imaginative mind and greatest political mentality of the past hundred years, Winston Churchill. The decision was to "liberate" North Africa as a stepping-stone to driving German armies from Italy and France and the ultimate annihilation of Hitler's Germany. Operation TORCH was the result.

For its simultaneous landings, November 8-9, 1942, for the capture of Safi, Casablanca and Port Lyautey, on the Atlantic Coast of French Morocco, America mounted an unprecedently massive, transoceanic, amphibious attack force. Convoyed directly from the United States and supported by a mighty naval armada, the landing forces were composed of assault elements of the Regular Army's 3rd and 9th Infantry Divisions with a small number of Armored units from the 2nd Armored Division.

The amphibious attacks on North African French ports on the Mediterranean, Oran and Algiers, necessitating a transit from Gibraltar to their objectives under German observation and potential air and naval counterattacks, were to be executed by sea, air and ground task forces directly from the British Isles.

As noted earlier, MAGNET FORCE, largely consisting of V Corps, was arriving in the British Isles when the 32nd and 37th were suddenly and secretly detached to meet greater emergencies in the South Pacific. Their place soon was taken by the arrival in England of the 1st (Regular Army) and the 29th (Maryland-Virginia-D.C.) Infantry Divisions. It was decided to leave the V Corps, with Headquarters displaced to Bristol and publicly labeled as being "Reinforced," along with a few of its non-divisional Regiments and the 29th Infantry Division, as Intelligence cover for a mythical ground force buildup for early invasion of France. In reality the continuing flow to Great Britain

---

* By Emperor Justinian's Byzantine General Belisarius, 536-37, A.D.

was a gigantic massing of airmen and bombers in England for an application of the Douhet theory of subjugation of a nation and people by aerial bombardments. Meanwhile, the 1st Armored, 34th and 1st Infantry Divisions would be attached initially to Lieutenant General Sir Kenneth Anderson's First British Army (four Divisions) for the capture of the Mediterranean beaches, ports and the lesser North African Coast objectives.

Actually, the assault burden fell primarily upon the Americans. There was a pleasant theory that the French garrisons would not fire upon landing Americans with the same alacrity, accuracy and enthusiasm that they would upon attacking English formations. The sinking of a French fleet by English naval gunfire at Oran to keep the ships from falling under German control was still fresh in the minds of many French officers and men in North Africa. Consequently Sir Kenneth Anderson's English formations constituted a floating reserve until the landing Americans had firmly secured their assigned shore objectives. It was a handsome and logical theory that worked splendidly until the American Guardsmen of the 34th and Regulars of the 1st began wading ashore. Then and there the theory collapsed. The sturdy Guardsmen from Minnesota, the Dakotas and Iowa who led their men ashore just East of Algiers might as well have been from Yorkshire, London and Cornwall.*

Once ashore, beachheads joined, and the long battle line consolidated with one flank on the ocean and the other on the desert, the American Divisions passed to Lieutenant General Lloyd R. Fredendall's all-American II Corps. Toward the end of February, 1943, and following the Kasserine Pass reverse, General Fredendall lost the confidence of both his higher and subordinate commanders. He was relieved and followed by Major General George S. Patton. Meanwhile, new Divisions were arriving for the mop-up of North Africa and future operations against the so-called "soft underbelly." This was to be the role of the 45th (Oklahoma, New Mexico, Arizona and Colorado) and the 36th (Texas); the former against Sicily, July, 1943, and the latter against the Italian Boot at Salerno the following September.

The long, bitter Winter war in Italy of 1943-44, the Anzio "end run" disappointment, the continued clamor of the Russians for a "real Second Front," the insistence that France should be liberated without undue delay, the failure of the American and British air forces to achieve a subjugation of Germany through aerial bombardment and the eagerness of the Americans to end the war in Europe so that all effort be given to the defeat of Japan, all combined to commit England and

---

* Though amphibious warfare and beach landings are presumed to be a Marine Corps specialty, not so much as a Marine Corps Company was in assault forces. Likewise none were included in the greater landing operations in Normandy June 6, 1944.

America to OVERLORD—the cross-channel invasion of France, D-Day, June 6, 1944.

The buildup of ground forces in Britain for this operation was rapid. V Corps, Major General Leonard T. Gerow commanding, with Divisional units consisting of the 1st, 29th and 4th Infantry Divisions, was to lead the attack with assault forces for Omaha and Utah Beaches. The 4th was on the right (Utah), the 29th (Maryland-Virginia-D.C.) in the post of honor at center (right end of Omaha Beach) and the 1st Division was on the left. Incidentally, most of the non-divisional units in this greatest of all amphibious assaults were also National Guard units. Conspicuous among them were the 102nd Cavalry Group (Mechanized) and its two Squadrons—all from the New Jersey National Guard. V Corps' 1121st Combat Engineer Group and its organic Battalions were none other than the renumbered 112th Engineers (Ohio) that had spun-off in the "triangularization" of the 37th Division just prior to its leaving for the South Pacific. Also renumbered and merged in this group was the old 107th Engineers (Michigan) from the 32nd Infantry Division. Worthy of further mention in the Normandy assault were Guard units constituting the first non-divisional Artillery to land in France. They were the 190th Field Artillery Group (Pennsylvania); 190th Field Artillery Battalion (Pennsylvania); 200th Field Artillery Battalion (Pennsylvania); 186th Field Artillery Battalion (New York); and the 187th Field Artillery Battalion (New York).*

The Divisional and non-divisional reinforcements for the embattled Paratroopers and initial components of V Corps were necessarily rapid if the American sector of the lodgment area was to be held. The 2nd Infantry Division (Regular Army) was rushed ashore at Omaha Beach to fill the gap being created at Treviers by the planned, diverging and widening fronts of the 1st and 29th Divisions. Likewise, the 30th (Carolinas, Georgia and Tennessee) landed in approach march and attack formations to drive the counterattacking Germans inland from the Isigny area to link-up the Utah and Omaha Beach fronts.

Armored units, Tank Destroyers, Mechanized Cavalry, and full Armored Divisions streamed ashore under high priorities, because of the known German dispositions and capabilities with such equipment

---

* It is regretted that space precludes more than occasional and incidental mention of the 300 or more Battalion-size, non-divisional National Guard units in sundry Medical Corps, Engineer, non-divisional Infantry, Tank Destroyer, Field Artillery, Coast and Anti-aircraft Artillery formations. But the purpose of this chapter is to reflect the combatant contributions of the National Guard in its proportional relationship to comparable size units of the other components of the Army of the United States in World War II. For this purpose the Divisions are the conventional units of measurement. A mere listing of all the non-divisional National Guard Battalion-size units, their redesignations and often their new numerals with their Group and Regimental Headquarters, required no less than 27 printed pages of a War Department official report. Such a listing here would greatly distort the overall picture and further serve little purpose.

in France. But the high, thick hedgerows of Normandy's bocage country were equally restrictive upon both the attackers and defenders. The battle continued to be a slugging match between the Infantry-Artillery teams of the opposing armies.

Came time for the breakthrough at St. Lo, it was the smallarms fire, grenades, and bayonets of the 35th (Missouri, Kansas and Nebraska) and the heroic D-Day's 29th National Guard Infantry Divisions that created the great breach in the German lines to get the Armor out of the bocage hedgerows. Through the St. Lo gap, Patton's Third Army, heavy with Armor for sweeping across the more open country, flowed for the seemingly endless, dramatic hours of July 25-27, 1944. The 30th (Carolinas, Georgia and Tennessee) and 28th (Pennsylvania) Divisions were hard on the heels of the fast-flowing Third Army to join the 35th and 29th in shoring-up the shoulders of the breakthrough for the inevitable German counterattacks calculated to sever Patton's Third Army supply lines and leave his Infantry and Armor stranded in a strange land and vulnerable to destruction in detail. In resisting the War's most vicious German counterattack in a vain effort to separate the Third Army from the First Army at Mortain, both the 30th and 35th Guard Divisions bore the brunt of attack to play stellar roles in the complete victory that followed.

Meanwhile, for the Toulon-Cannes beach assaults in Southern France, the veteran 36th (Texas) and 45th (Oklahoma, Arizona, New Mexico, Colorado) were being teamed with the 3rd (Regular Army), likewise seasoned in Africa and Italy. Their highly-successful and victorious operations provided strategic protection to Patton's right flank as he swept Eastward, almost unopposed, across France. The invasion of France from the Mediterranean, though discounted by early planners, not only drew hostile Divisions away from the cyclonic advance of the American Third Army, but became the right flank of the Allied forces as they drove the retreating Germans into their fortified frontier— the Siegfried Line.

But, once again, space does not permit a review of the dramatic moments in the role of each National Guard Division that contributed to the European victory. A chronological listing, in the order of their arrival in Europe or Africa, of all Infantry Divisions that appeared in the European Order of Battle, with their pertinent statistics, again has the merit of putting them all on the same common denominator. The shortcomings of such a procedure are admitted again, but it appears to be the most effective technique for condensation and comparison.

# OVERSEAS DEPLOYMENT SEQUENCE, INFANTRY DIVISIONS WORLD WAR II, AGAINST GERMANY WITH THEIR CAMPAIGNS AND BATTLE CASULTIES

## TRANS-ATLANTIC, 1942

34th Infantry Division (National Guard; Minnesota, North Dakota, South Dakota, Iowa). Called from States to Federal service, February 10, 1941. To Ireland, January-March, 1942. Campaigns: *Tunisia; Naples-Foggia; Anzio; Rome-Arno; North Apennines; Po Valley.* KIA, 2,866; DOW, 484; TOTAL CASUALTIES, 16,401. Released from Federal status, November 3, 1945.

1st Infantry Division (Regular Army) Cadre Headquarters maintained from World War I at Fort Hamilton, N.Y. To England, August, 1942. Campaigns: *Morocco; Tunisia; Sicily; Normandy; Northern France; Rhineland; Ardennes-Alsace; Central Europe.* KIA, 3,616; DOW, 664; TOTAL CASUALTIES, 20,659. Returned to U.S., July, 1955.

29th Infantry Division (National Guard; Maryland, Virginia, District of Columbia). Called from States to Federal service, February 3, 1941. To England, October, 1942. Campaigns: *Normandy; Northern France; Rhineland; Central Europe.* KIA, 3,887; DOW, 899; TOTAL CASUALTIES, 20,620. Released from Federal service, January 17, 1946.

3rd Infantry Division (Regular Army). Cadre Headquarters maintained from World War I at Fort Lewis, Washington. To North Africa, November 8, 1942. Campaigns: *French Morocco; Tunisia; Sicily, Naples-Foggia; Central Europe; Rhineland; Ardennes-Alsace; Southern France; Rome-Arno; Anzio.* KIA, 4,922; DOW, 636; TOTAL CASUALTIES, 25,977.

9th Infantry Division (Regular Army). Activated August 1, 1940. To Africa, December, 1942. Campaigns: *Tunisia; Sicily; Normandy; Northern France; Rhineland; Central Europe.* KIA, 3,856; DOW, 648; TOTAL CASUALTIES, 23,277. Inactivated, January 15, 1947 in Europe.

## TRANS-ATLANTIC, 1943

36th Infantry Division (National Guard; Texas). Called from State to Federal service, November 25, 1940. To Africa, April, 1943. Campaigns: *Naples-Foggia; Anzio; Rome-Arno; Southern France; Rhineland; Ardennes-Alsace; Central Europe.* KIA, 3,131; DOW, 506; TOTAL CASUALTIES, 19,466. Released from Federal service, December 15, 1945.

45th Infantry Division (National Guard; Oklahoma, New Mexico, Arizona, Colorado). Called from States to Federal service, September 16, 1940. To North Africa, June, 1943. Sicily July 10, 1943. Campaigns: *Sicily; Naples-Foggia; Anzio; Rome-Arno; Southern France; Rhineland; Ardennes-Alsace; Central Europe.* KIA, 3,547; DOW, 533; TOTAL CASUALTIES, 20,993. Released from Federal service, December 7, 1945.

5th Infantry Division (Regular Army). Activated October 24, 1939. To England, Summer, 1943, via Iceland, May, 1942. Campaigns: *Normandy; Northern France; Ardennes-Alsace; Rhineland; Central Europe.* KIA, 2,298; DOW, 358; TOTAL CASUALTIES, 12,818. Inactivated, September 20, 1946.

2nd Infantry Division (Regular Army). Maintained as a peace-strength Division from World War I, Headquarters at Fort Sam Houston, Texas. To Ireland, October, 1943. Campaigns: *Normandy; Northern France; Rhineland; Ardennes-Alsace; Central Europe.* KIA, 3,031; DOW, 457; TOTAL CASUALTIES, 16,795. Returned to United States, July, 1945.

28th Infantry Division (National Guard; Pennsylvania). Called from State to Federal service, February 17, 1941. To Wales, October, 1943. Normandy July 28, 1944. Campaigns: *Normandy; Northern France; Rhineland; Ardennes-Alsace; Central Europe.* KIA, 2,316; DOW, 367; TOTAL CASUALTIES, 16,762. Released from Federal service, December 13, 1945.

8th Infantry Division (Regular Army and National Guard, 121st R.C.T. built on 121st Infantry, Georgia National Guard, surplus from 30th Division). Activated, July 1, 1940. To Ireland December, 1943. Utah, July 4, 1944. Campaigns: *Normandy; Northern France; Rhineland; Central Europe.* KIA, 2,532; DOW, 288; TOTAL CASUALTIES, 13,986. Inactivated, November 20, 1945.

88th Infantry Division (A.U.S., Reserve). Activated, July 15, 1942. To Casablanca, December, 1943. Campaigns: *Rome-Arno; North Apennines; Po Valley.* KIA, 2,298; DOW, 258; TOTAL CASUALTIES, 13,111. Inactivated, October 24, 1947 in Italy.

TRANS-ATLANTIC, 1944

4th Infantry Division (Regular Army). Activated, June 1, 1940. To England, January, 1944. Campaigns: *Normandy; Northern France; Rhineland; Ardennes-Alsace; Central Europe.* KIA, 4,097; DOW, 757; TOTAL CASUALTIES, 22,660. Inactivated, March 12, 1946.

30th Infantry Division (National Guard; Carolinas, Georgia, Tennessee). Called from States to Federal service, September 16, 1940. To England, February, 1944. Normandy, June 15, 1944. Campaigns: *Normandy; Northern France; Rhineland; Ardennes-Alsace; Central Europe.* KIA, 3,003; DOW, 513; TOTAL CASUALTIES, 18,446. Released from Federal service, November, 25, 1945.

35th Infantry Division (National Guard; Missouri, Kansas, Nebraska). Called from States to Federal service, December 7, 1940. To England, May, 1944. Normandy July 5, 1944. Campaigns: *Normandy; Northern France; Ardennes-Alsace; Rhineland; Central Europe.* KIA, 2,485; DOW, 462; TOTAL CASUALTIES, 15,882. Released from Federal service, December 7, 1945.

79th Infantry Division (A.U.S., Reserve). Activated, June 15, 1942. To England, April, 1944. Normandy June 12-14, 1944. Campaigns: *Normandy; Northern France; Ardennes-Alsace; Rhineland; Central Europe.* KIA, 2,476; DOW, 467; TOTAL CASUALTIES, 15,203. Inactivated, December 11, 1945.

83rd Infantry Division (A.U.S., Reserve). Activated, August 15, 1942. To England, April, 1944. Campaigns: *Normandy; Northern France; Ardennes-Alsace; Rhineland; Central Europe.* KIA, 3,161; DOW, 459; TOTAL CASUALTIES, 15,910. Inactivated, March 27, 1946.

90th Infantry Division (A.U.S., Reserve). Activated, March 25, 1942. To England, April, 1944. Campaigns: *Normandy; Northern France; Ardennes-Alsace; Rhineland; Central Europe.* KIA, 3,342; DOW, 588; TOTAL CASUALTIES, 19,200. Inactivated, December 27, 1945.

91st Infantry Division (A.U.S., Reserve). Activated, August 15, 1942. To North Africa, April, 1944. Italy, June, 1944. Campaigns: *Rome-Arno; North Apennines; Po Valley.* KIA, 1,400; DOW, 175; TOTAL CASUALTIES, 8,744. Inactivated, December 1, 1945.

80th Infantry Division (A.U.S., Reserve). Activated, July 15, 1942. To England, July, 1944. Campaigns: *Northern France; Rhineland; Ardennes-Alsace; Central Europe.* KIA, 3,038; DOW, 442; TOTAL CASUALTIES, 17,087. Inactivated, January 4, 1946.

94th Infantry Division (A.U.S., Reserve). Activated, September 15, 1942. To England, August, 1944. Campaigns: *Northern France; Rhineland; Ardennes-Alsace; Central Europe.* KIA, 1,009; DOW, 147; TOTAL CASUALTIES, 6,533. Inactivated, February, 7, 1946.

95th Infantry Division (A.U.S., Reserve). Activated, July 15, 1942. To England, August, 1944. Campaigns: *Northern France; Rhineland; Ardennes-Alsace; Central Europe.* KIA, 1,205; DOW, 167; TOTAL CASUALTIES, 6,591. Inactivated, October 15, 1945.

26th Infantry Division (National Guard; Massachusetts, New Hampshire, Maine, Vermont). Called from States to Federal service January 16, 1941. To Europe, September, 1944. Campaigns: *Northern France; Rhineland; Ardennes-Alsace; Central Europe.* KIA, 1,850; DOW, 262; TOTAL CASUALTIES, 10,701. Released from Federal service, December 29, 1945.

44th Infantry Division (National Guard; New Jersey, New York). Called from States to Federal service, September 16, 1940. To Cherbourg, France, September, 1944. Campaigns: *Northern France; Rhineland; Ardennes-Alsace; Central Europe.* KIA, 1,038; DOW, 168; TOTAL CASUALTIES, 5,655. Released from Federal service November 30, 1945.

102nd Infantry Division (A.U.S., Reserve). Activated, September 15, 1942. To Cherbourg, France, September, 1944. Campaigns: *Rhineland; Central Europe.* KIA, 932; DOW, 145; TOTAL CASUALTIES, 4,922. Inactivated, March 12, 1946.

104th Infantry Division (A.U.S., Reserve). Activated, September 15, 1942. To France, September, 1944. Campaigns: *Northern France; Rhineland; Central Europe.* KIA, 971; DOW, 143; TOTAL CASUALTIES, 4,961. Inactivated, December 20, 1945.

78th Infantry Division (A.U.S., Reserve). Activated, August 15, 1942. To Europe, October, 1944. Campaigns: *Ardennes-Alsace; Rhineland; Central Europe.* KIA, 1,427; DOW, 198; TOTAL CASUALTIES, 8,146. Inactivated, May 22, 1946, in Europe.

84th Infantry Division (A.U.S., Reserve). Activated, October 15, 1942. To Europe, October, 1944. Campaigns: *Rhineland; Ardennes-Alsace; Central Europe.* KIA, 1,284; DOW, 154; TOTAL CASUALTIES, 7,260. Inactivated, January 21, 1946.

92nd Infantry Division (A.U.S., Reserve). Activated, October 15, 1942. To Italy, October, 1944. Campaigns: *Rome-Arno; North Apennines; Po Valley.* KIA, 548; DOW, 68; TOTAL CASUALTIES, 2,997. Inactivated, November 28, 1945.

99th Infantry Division (A.U.S., Reserve). Activated, November 15, 1942. To England, October, 1944. Campaigns: *Rhineland; Ardennes-Alsace; Central Europe.* KIA, 993; DOW, 141; TOTAL CASUALTIES, 6,553. Inactivated, September 26, 1945.

100th Infantry Division (A.U.S., Reserve). Activated, November 15, 1942. To Southern France, October, 1944. Campaigns: *Rhineland; Ardennes-Alsace; Central Europe.* KIA, 883; DOW, 101; TOTAL CASUALTIES, 5,038. Inactivated, January 10, 1946.

103rd Infantry Division (A.U.S., Reserve). Activated, November 15, 1942. To Southern France, October, 1944. Campaigns: *Rhineland; Ardennes-Alsace; Central Europe.* KIA, 720; DOW, 101; TOTAL CASUALTIES, 4,558. Inactivated, September 20, 1945.

106th Infantry Division (A.U.S., Reserve). Activated, March 15, 1943. To England, November, 1944. Campaigns: *Rhineland; Ardennes-Alsace; Central Europe.* KIA, 417; DOW, 53; TOTAL CASUALTIES, 8,627. Inactivated, October 2, 1945.

66th Infantry Division (A.U.S., Reserve). Activated, April 15, 1943. To England, November, 1944. Campaigns: *Northern France.* KIA, 795; DOW, 5; TOTAL CASUALTIES, 1,452. Inactivated, November 8, 1945.

75th Infantry Division (A.U.S., Reserve). Activated, March 15, 1943. To England, November, 1944. Campaigns: *Rhineland; Ardennes-Alsace; Central Europe.* KIA, 817; DOW, 111; TOTAL CASUALTIES, 4,324. Inactivated, November 14, 1945.

87th Infantry Division (A.U.S., Reserve). Activated, December 15, 1942. To England, November, 1944. Campaigns: *Rhineland; Ardennes-Alsace; Central Europe.* KIA, 1,154; DOW, 141; TOTAL CASUALTIES, 6,034. Inactivated, September 21, 1945.

42nd Infantry Division (A.U.S., Reserve). Activated, July 14, 1943. To France, December, 1944. Campaigns: *Rhineland; Ardennes-Alsace; Central Europe.* KIA, 553; DOW, 85; TOTAL CASUALTIES, 3,971. Inactivated, July 13, 1946, in Austria.

85th Infantry Division (A.U.S., Reserve). Activated, May 15, 1942. To Italy, April, 1944, via North Africa. Campaigns: *Rome-Arno; North Apennines; Po Valley*. KIA, 1,561; DOW, 175; TOTAL CASUALTIES, 8,774. Inactivated, August 25, 1945.

69th Infantry Division (A.U.S., Reserve). Activated, May 15, 1943. To England, December, 1944. Campaigns: *Rhineland; Central Europe*. KIA, 341; DOW, 42; TOTAL CASUALTIES, 1,506. Inactivated, September 18, 1945.

76th Infantry Division (A.U.S., Reserve). Activated June 15, 1942. To England, December, 1944. Campaigns: *Ardennes-Alsace; Rhineland; Central Europe*. KIA, 433; DOW, 90; TOTAL CASUALTIES, 2,395. Inactivated, August 31, 1945, in Germany.

10th Infantry Division (Regular Army). Activated as 10th Light Division July 15, 1943. To Italy, January, 1945. Campaigns: *North Apennines; Po Valley*. KIA, 872; DOW, 81; TOTAL CASUALTIES, 4,072. Redesignated 10th Mountain Division November 6, 1944. Inactivated, November 30, 1945.

63rd Infantry Division (A.U.S., Reserve). Activated, June 15, 1943. To Europe January, 1945.* Campaigns: *Rhineland; Central Europe*. KIA, 861; DOW, 113; TOTAL CASUALTIES, 4,504. Inactivated, September 27, 1945.

65th Infantry Division, (A.U.S., Reserve). Activated, August 16, 1943. To Europe, January, 1945. Campaigns: *Rhineland; Central Europe*. KIA, 233; DOW, 27; TOTAL CASUALTIES, 1,230. Inactivated, August 31, 1945.

70th Infantry Division (A.U.S., Reserve). Activated, June 15, 1943. To Europe, January, 1945. Campaigns: *Rhineland; Ardennes-Alsace; Central Europe*. KIA, 755; DOW, 79; TOTAL CASUALTIES, 3,919. Inactivated, October 11, 1945.

TRANS-ATLANTIC, 1945

89th Infantry Division (A.U.S., Reserve). Activated, July 15, 1942. To Europe, January, 1945. Campaigns: *Rhineland; Central Europe*. KIA, 292; DOW, 33; TOTAL CASUALTIES, 1,029. Inactivated, December 17, 1945.

71st Infantry Division (Regular Army and A.U.S., Reserve; two of three Regimental Combat Teams built on 5th and 14th Infantry Regiments of Regular Army). Activated, July 15, 1943. To Europe, February, 1945. Campaigns: *Rhineland; Central Europe*. KIA, 243; DOW, 35; TOTAL CASUALTIES, 1,114. Inactivated, March 11, 1946.

97th Infantry Division (A.U.S., Reserve). Activated, February 25, 1943. To Europe February, 1945, and to Japan, October, 1945. Campaigns: *Central Europe*. KIA, 188; DOW, 26; TOTAL CASUALTIES, 979. Inactivated, March 31, 1946, in Japan.

---

* As in the case of a few other Divisions, Infantry and Artillery elements of the 63rd were in action against the enemy before the Division as such was given a sector and a mission. Regiments of the 63rd arrived in Marseille, France December 8, 1944, a month ahead of the Headquarters of the Division. As a result of the Battle of the Bulge, the early-arriving elements were committed to action as Task Force Harris, December 22, 1944. The Division did not take over an operational sector until February 6, 1945.

86th Infantry Division (A.U.S., Reserve). Activated, December 15, 1942. To Europe, March, 1945, and to Philippines, August, 1945. Campaigns: *Central Europe.* KIA, 136; DOW, 25; TOTAL CASUALTIES, 785. Inactivated, December 30, 1946, in the Philippines.

## NATIONAL GUARD UNITS AND THE ARMORED FORCE

Notwithstanding the imposing array of American Army Infantry Divisions that went to the European Theater of Operations, proportionally the Pacific was much more of an Infantryman's war than was Europe. Compared with the Pacific, there was in Europe a most lavish use of Armor and Field Artillery in the Ground Forces.

Armor in Divisional-strength units entered the stage of American military history July 15, 1940. The German Blitzkrieg had just prostrated France and folded around the British Expeditionary Force at Dunkirk. It was not until then that the War Department General Staff decided the slow, awkward steel coffins of World War I were not the final military lesson on that subject. On the above date, the more-or-less experimental Mechanized Cavalry Brigade at Fort Knox, Kentucky, that General Mac-Arthur as Chief of Staff had insisted upon in the early '30's, was expanded and activated as the 1st Armored Division. As of the same date, the 2nd Armored Division was created officially from Armored oddments at Fort Benning, Georgia. A few days earlier, the Armored Force, with then Brigadier General Adna R. Chaffee as its first Chief, had been born. The Chief of the infant force immediately acquired control of all Armored units in being and tried to expand his nascent empire and achieve the semi-independence of the separatist-minded Army Air Corps. There were dreams of Armored Corps and an Armored Army. This was too much for the reactionary Chief of GHQ Ground Forces, General McNair, and the General Staff conservatives in the War Department G3 Section. McNair compromised by allowing a wide range of freedoms, particularly in training, but was successful in keeping Armor within his orbit.

Even so, just prior to the induction of each of the 18 "square" National Guard Divisions, their organic tank units, along with their organic Air Corps squadrons, were declared non-divisional GHQ Troops. As such the Air units went to the Air Corps for materiel, maintenance, administration, doctrines and techniques, and likewise the National Guard tank units passed into the small but burgeoning domain of the Armored Force. But the threat to the Philippines from an already-expanding and bellicose Japan was so appallingly apparent that the clamor from the Manila Headquarters for a more balanced field force (more planes and some tank units) could not be ignored. As the oldest, most experienced, and best-equipped separate Armored units in being,

General Chaffee's eye naturally fell upon the Guard units for the Philippine assignment. Thus the National Guard tank units of California, Minnesota, Kentucky, Ohio, Illinois and Wisconsin, with far-from-modern equipment, embarked for the Philippines long in advance of the Pearl Harbor disaster. Their story is a part of the tragedy that befell the earlier-mentioned 12th (Philippine) Infantry Division and the other participants in the Bataan surrender, and after. The 12 remaining National Guard organizations that were separated from their parent Divisions at the time of induction were merged into the Armored Force. They were so repeatedly drawn upon for promotion to higher ranks and for cadres in the formation of new units in the rapidly-expanding Force, that they, like the Air Observation Squadrons taken into the Air Force, soon lost their identity, and in most cases even their designation and number.

At the same time that the Armored Force was expanding into the hell-on-wheels that the Germany Army soon learned it to be, General McNair, from his ivory tower on the Potomac, was clinging to his doctrine that the answer to tanks was not other tanks but highly mobile unarmored anti-tank artillery. From reserve positions, they would be rushed to the paths of an impending tank attack, dug-in and camouflaged in blocking positions whence the roaring column of hostile behemoths would be ambushed. His Staff talked him out of this application of Indian warfare to the modern battlefield.

The compromise was the "tank destroyer." Actually, it was a thin-skin, fast tank with a high-muzzle-velocity, flat-trajectory gun. Tank destroyers were organized into non-divisional Battalions. When the Guard's "square" Divisions were being reorganized and "triangularized," each, except that of the 41st Division, was required to create from surplus units one Tank Destroyer Battalion. They were numbered in a 600-series with the last two digits indicating the Division whence they came; the 626th Tank Destroyer Battalion was from the 26th Infantry Division, and the 645th from the 45th, for example. There were seven additional Tank Destroyer Battalions pinched from each of the seven Brigades of National Guard Corps Artillery. Theirs was a 700-series with the number of the Brigade the source of the last two digits; the 773rd Tank Destroyer Battalion having come from the 73rd Field Artillery Brigade. Though GHQ Troops and part of the Armored Force, just as Signal Corps Battalions were in the domain of the Chief Signal Corps officer, some of these National Guard Battalions went oversea as an attachment to the parent unit, and to all practical purposes were organic throughout the Theater of Operations. Most became separated, to have sundry adventures overseas, while others were redesignated to become a part of an Armored Division or inactivated for the personnel to become similarly merged with a larger Armored Force unit. Guard officers often volunteered individually into the Armored Force, which was looking for officers throughout its tremendous expansion through 1942-43. Guard Artillery officers with a fondness for direct laying or "hip shooting" from observed fires but who had no patience for instrument surveys of gun positions and meteorological corrections for unobserved fires, were particularly attracted to the Armored formations. Such shooting also appealed to ambitious young enlisted Guardsmen who sought A.U.S. commissions. They often put in for the Armored Force Officer Candidate School. Accordingly, in the Armored Divisions activated and organized after Pearl Harbor there were often as many former Guardsmen on the officer rosters as there were Regulars, but Reserve officers normally outnumbered both the two older components in most Armored Divisions.

Pearl Harbor caught the American Army with only four complete Armored Divisions in being. Two of them, the 3rd and 4th, were less than nine months old. The 5th Armored Division was in the process of being organized at Fort Knox. Beginning February 15, 1942 and at a rate of one each six weeks, the 6th to 14th Armored Divisions, inclusive, were activated, the last-numbered in November of 1942. All of these ultimately arrived in Europe, as did the 20th and 16th Armored Divisions activated in March and July, 1943, respectively. But all Armored Divisions that arrived in Europe after Patton's sweep across France were considered late-comers. Their light casualty lists usually said as much.

The average total casualties for all 16 Armored Divisions in Europe, including the 1st, which remained in Italy, were 3,895 per Division. Most of these occurred in the Infantry formations and self-propelled Field Artillery Battalions that were organic within the Armored Divisions. Thus, notwithstanding the drama of Armored movements, from an overall view of the record it is quite apparent that the business of taking and holding terrain for an ultimate conquest and victory was still pretty much an Infantry-Artillery team job throughout World War II, whether the engagements were in the Pacific or in Europe. Moreover, the longest and heaviest fighting was performed by the 19 early-available National Guard Divisions and the nine Infantry Divisions and the four Armored Divisions of the Regular Army. The Armored Divisions, 5th to 20th inclusive (all of them activated after Pearl Harbor), were rated as Army of the United States, Reserve Divisions.

## THE AIRBORNE DIVISIONS IN EUROPE

Because of their dramatic roles in Europe, a comparative word should be added concerning the three Airborne Divisions that saw action in Europe. The 13th Airborne, activated August 13, 1942, arrived in Europe early enough in 1945 for a campaign credit, but was too late for a casualty list. The 17th was activated April 15, 1943, participated in the last three campaigns with total killed and wounded casualties of 6,745. The 82nd was activated March 25, 1942 and redesignated an Airborne Division August 15, 1942. With two campaigns in Sicily and Italy and four additional credits from Normandy Westward, it was the most active and experienced. Its total casualties in all campaigns were 9,073. But, thanks to the fight for Bastogne, the slightly less-experienced 101st Airborne had the longer casualty list by a thin margin: 9,328. It was activated August 15, 1942.

All four of these Airborne Divisions, like the 11th in the Pacific, were classified as Army of the U.S., Reserve Divisions. Some since have been reactivated as Regulars. Actually these famous Divisions, like the separate Battalions of Rangers, were composed of officers and men from all components who voluntarily sought or eagerly accepted Airborne assignments. Anyone who early changed his mind and wanted other duty was transferred out. Therein was their power for dramatic, strenuous duty. It was also the strength of the Guard and Regular Army Divisions. The leadership at all levels, Corporals to Colonels, was there because that was where they insisted upon being. Even after some Regiments and Divisions had lost, by transfers, sickness and battle casualties, so many that the flow through of replacements exceeded the original strength, that hard core of officer and N.C.O. leadership remained.* Anyone who argues, as did General March from World War I, that mergers, reorganizations, transfers, augmentations and replacements had early erased discernible differentiations between Divisions and lesser units of the three components—Regular Army, Guard and National Army (A.U.S. Reserves)—most likely was also similar to General March in that he was not there himself. If he was there and observed no difference, it was because the nature of his assignment permitted no comparative observations, or he was a man of extremely low perceptive power. General Patton wisely insisted that Divisions and Regiments are not animated Tables of Organization but literally have a collective soul the same as a human being has an individual soul. Men acquire the soul of the unit through service in it, Patton added.

The comparatively light casualty lists of the Airborne compared with Infantry Divisions through the same campaigns are attributed to two primary reasons: (1) the Airborne Divisions of specialized Infantrymen were numerically smaller than the conventional Infantry outfits, but (2) more significant than that was the doctrine of pulling them out of action for future specialized missions as soon as conventional Infantry Divisions could be found to take their places in the line. Thus

---

* The 30th was the most heavily-cadred Division in the Army. Briefly in September, 1942, it was down to 2,100 officers and men from providing key personnel to other units being activated. The 31st, to 7,000, and the 33rd, to 8,000 in the same season, were the next most heavily-drawn-upon.

they spent months as Theater reserves while conventional Infantry Divisions were hammering-out victories in the hedgerows and forests.

## READINESS FOR COMBAT

Reference to the list of overseas Divisions reveals at a glance the National Guard Divisions were committed to both Atlantic and Pacific Theaters on equal or higher priorities than was the case with comparable Regular Army units. This has precipitated occasional discussions as to readiness for combat of all Divisions.

It is an ages-old question that invites subjective opinions, unprovable assertions and invidious comparisons. On the whole, the question merely promotes idle speculation. If units accomplish their missions, history records they were ready for combat. When they failed, more tangible reasons are sought but seldom found. A Staff writes the report and damns the units. The verdict and the Staff alibi routinely are: "The Regiment, or Division, was not ready for combat." Some cautious Generals and higher Staffs have been prone to cover themselves with advance apologias against possible failures. When failure came, the advance professional opinions as to unreadiness of the units for combat became proven facts in official reports and subsequent memoirs, if any. Major General Edward Braddock, for example, never having been in battle himself, naturally had doubts about himself secretly and even more grave doubts about his unseasoned Regiments. History records that Braddock was right on both counts. At First Bull Run, 1861, two utterly unseasoned, untrained and poorly-equipped armies clashed. One of them had to win. Fortune, with a bit of help from Beauregard, smiled on the Southern formations. So thorough, unanimous and completely logical were the self-protective apologias of Northern commanders that the myth lingers unto today that the Southern victory was due to "preparedness" of gallant Southern units, while the Northern defeat was due to "unpreparedness" and worthless Regiments.

Accordingly, there were many more-or-less honorable precedents for Major General Robert L. Eichelberger's critical misgivings as to combat-readiness of his formations as he launched the Papuan offensive. MacArthur had told him to capture Buna or not return alive. An advance alibi for his possibly premature demise was legitimately instinctive. Letting the recorded opinions stand in postwar memoirs could further increase the stature of the General and his Headquarters. His memoirs are in sharp contrast to those of the more modest, or perhaps the less apprehensive General Walter Krueger, who often commanded the same units in alternate offensive operations. In the North African operations, Major General L. F. Fredendall, C. G. of II Corps, before and after his relief to be succeeded by General Patton, was highly critical of the combat-readiness of Infantry and Armor under his command. But if the highly successful Lieutenant General L. K. Truscott be accepted as a reliable witness, Fredendall and his Headquarters must have been far more conspicuously unready for combat. Truscott was Deputy Chief of Staff and in charge of General Eisenhower's advanced Command Post at the time. The same Regular Army and Guard Regiments and Divisions of Armor and Infantry that Fredendall rated unready proved to be sufficiently combat-ready to establish Patton's reputation as a General Officer with a future. In other words, the Guard Divisions and lesser units were as ready for combat as were their Corps and Army field commanders, with their Staffs, that were handpicked from among the Regulars by Marshall and McNair for those high leadership assignments.

From the Normandy beaches to Central Europe, German officer prisoners-of-war usually knew the American Divisions on their front by their shoulder patches and often by their number and States of origin. If they indicated a qualitative difference between the hostile American Divisions they had fought, the one just before the last usually was better than the one to which they had surrendered. When asked why they surrendered to the second-rate outfit, the normal excuse was that day's failures of their own Air Force to provide adequate, if any, cover and the high mobility and ever-close support of American Artillery, which, they always insisted, had inexhaustible supplies of ammunition.

Most German Generals orally and in postwar writings have been unanimous in making Hitler, his high command and the Nazi party the scapegoats for all their troubles and ultimate defeat.* Even in defeat, these quirks of Teutonic military pride suggest they clung to the myth that theirs were the best Infantry and Armored Divisions in the World.

American officers in Europe in non-divisional assignments, such as Engineers, Corps Artillery, Corps and Army Staffs, often had a broad basis for qualitative comparison. For example, across France and Germany, representing all components, 17 Infantry Divisions, one Airborne Division and seven Armored Divisions were assigned to V Corps for various types of operations. Most of them saw their first day of combat under orders from V Corps Headquarters and in conjunction with V Corps Artillery. Qualitative differences among Divisions were often subjects of discussion. The collective opinion at the time appeared

---

* Japanese Generals had no Hitlerian usurper to whom they could attribute their grim defeats. Gen. Tomoyuki Yamashita, victor at Bataan, Corregidor, Malay and Singapore, but loser to Gen. Walter Krueger from Leyte to the surrender of Luzon incident to MacArthur's "Return," not only conceded the quality of his opposition but rated the comparative quality of his enemy's deployed Divisions. According to then Col. Horton V. White, Sixth Army G2, and further quoting from Gen. Krueger's *From Down Under to Nippon:* "General Yamashita indicated that he considered the 32nd Division the best his troops had encountered both at Leyte and on Luzon. He mentioned the 38th Division favorably and expressed admiration for the end run of the 1st Cavalry Division to Manila."

to be that the late 1944 and 1945 arrivals in the European Theater were better-equipped when they reached the battle zones, but the officers, men and Staffs were not nearly so well-trained and seldom had the same enthusiasm for getting the job done with which the early Divisions initially had gone into battle.

The most common explanation among those who speculated upon this was the constant thinning-out of the leavening influence of the original yeast of early volunteers resulting from a sense of service, combined with vocational and avocational interests and a spirit of adventure. These were the factors that had kept the Regulars, Guardsmen and active Reserve officers in uniform between the wars and which had swelled their ranks through 1940 as war clouds gathered. Battalions, Regiments and Divisions that were activated through 1942 were increasingly dependent upon non-volunteers with higher and higher percentages of the junior officers from among Selectees whose willingness to go to Officer Candidate Schools for quick commissions was predicated largely upon better pay and higher status. To provide higher officer cadres and NCO cadres for the new Divisions, all the older units not overseas, or scheduled for early sailings, frequently were drawn upon. Thus a comparatively heavy sprinkling of Guardsmen and Regulars was found in all the upper echelons of the new Divisions and Combat Teams.

It naturally followed that the few late-arriving Regular and Guard Divisions, such as the 26th (New England) and the 44th (New Jersey and New York) in Europe and the 6th (Regular Army) in the Pacific had been called upon for cadres so frequently that the percentages of the original personnel were constantly diminished. With major or minor degree, however, this was true of all Divisions and lesser units. But even though the old Corporals became Sergeants, the old Lieutenants became Captains, and the Majors became Colonels, the hard core of Sergeants, unit Captains, Lieutenant Colonels and Colonels with their respective Staffs remained. It was these who gave the Regular and Guard Battalions, Regiments and Divisions their personality, basic leadership, pride of origin and *elan*.

It is true that many Staff planners, personnel experts and operators of the Draft and Selectee machinery have accepted and occasionally have written on the theory that a drafted soldier is as good as any, but few, if any, well-seasoned combat soldiers believe it. Major General Henry W. Halleck once gave voice and pen to that idea. He was one of the more conspicuous though less competent General Officers of the Civil War. But bookish Halleck had bought the idea second-hand from Napoleon's Jomini. Later, but before the war was finished, he was to write his friend, General William T. Sherman, as to why the Draft was a failure in the crisis of the Union's life.

Common sense should have told Halleck and his modern Pentagon successors that there is no complete substitute for the volunteer soldier, professional or avocational, who is in a combat formation pursuant to a decision prior to a war, or upon the first rumbles of impending warfare, in which his Country is becoming involved. This self-evident truth is axiomatic in the thinking and experience of observant men who saw battle service in either World War I or II. These are the only American wars in which there has been a full basis for experience and conclusions. Moreover, it was only from National Guard and Regular Army formations that personnel initially were available for overseas service. That reason, and that alone, is why National Guard and Regular Army Divisions were so conspicuously early and brilliantly significant in the overseas battle efforts of America in World Wars I and II.

## OFFICERS OF THE NATIONAL GUARD

Inasmuch as a chronic criticism of the National Guard officer personnel was a favorite theme from some sources prior to Pearl Harbor, a review of the National Guard in World War II would be incomplete without some special attention to this subject. Because the so-called political Generals from the States were the most frequent targets of these barbs, they merit first consideration.

It hardly could be expected that these avocational, part-time volunteer citizen-Generals would be selected-up for such assignments as Chief of Staff or even deputy Chief, or as a Theater Commander. Such posts naturally were preempted by professionals whose careers permitted selection-up because of years of advance study to diplomas from their Arms schools, Command and General Staff at Fort Leavenworth and the War College in Washington. Courses of comparable length were not so much as open to National Guard and Reserve officers; not even in the case of wealthy citizen-soldiers for whom the serious business of earning a living was irrelevant and immaterial to their pursuit of the avocational, military hobby. Thus the primary yardstick of service must be in collective comparison with professionals of like rank as of the 1940 through early 1941 mobilization season to the end of the war. What did they do collectively for their Country through the pay-off period of actual war years? A soldier's reason for being is service through such crises. Moreover, it is his duty, irrespective of his component, to serve wheresoever he may be assigned and in such station or rank as he may be of service, barring bona fide disabilities or death. Such a commitment is inherent in the long-continued acceptance of an officer's commission of either a vocational or avocational character.

Collectively and as a group, the Major Generals on the Permanent Lists of the National Guard and the Regular Army offer comparative ease of statistical comparison. There were exactly 21 Regulars in the permanent, Promotion List rank of Major General, according to the semi-annual directory dated October 20, 1940. This list included one temporary four-star General (Marshall) and six temporary Lieutenant Generals. These higher temporary ranks were held then by virtue of assignments calling for those grades. As of January 1, 1945, with six months of fighting yet to be done, only five, or 23%, remained on the active list of the Army.* Of these, only one, Walter Krueger, commanded troops in battle. He was continued in command of the Sixth Army to the end of operations against Japan for more than a year beyond his statutory retirement age of 64. What happened to the remaining 16 Major Generals on the permanent Promotion List of the Regulars? Disabilities, physical or otherwise, statutory retirements for age, premature retirements for cause, such as that of Walter C. Short for his share of the Pearl Harbor debacle, and retirements at own request such as that of Campbell B. Hodges, explain practically all the reliefs of these Regular Army Major Generals from the Active List *during hostilities.*

Oddly enough, the number of National Guard Permanent List Major Generals was also exactly 21; one for each of the 18 Infantry Divisions inducted; one from each of the two Cavalry Divisions that had been granted a fully-organized Headquarters, and the National Guard Major General serving as Chief, National Guard Bureau. As of the close of the Fiscal Year ended June 30, 1945, according to National Guard Bureau records, nine, or 42%, of the 21 National Guard Permanent List Major Generals were still on active duty. One was serving in the grade of Colonel, a privilege not conceded to Walter C. Short, after Pearl Harbor. The remaining eight avocational Guard Major Generals inducted in grade beginning September 16, 1940, were on active duty in assignments appropriate to their grade as of the War's end. What happened to the remaining 12? The same thing that happened to the 16 Regular Army Permanent List Major Generals who did not finish the hostilities course. At least one Guard General Officer, however, was like General Krueger in that he was retained beyond the statutory age of 64 for ending active duty. He was the previously mentioned Major General Milton A. Reckord, of Maryland. One of the Guard Major Generals, Robert S. Beightler, of Ohio's 37th Division, commanded that Division from its date of Call to active duty until its inactivation at the close of hostilities. Rather than again pick up the broken threads of civil pursuits, he accepted integration into the Regular Army as a General Officer and continued active duty as a Major General until retirement in that grade. Other Divisions in combat were commanded by National Guardsmen, but they were promoted from the list of Brigadiers.

As of October 20, 1940, there were only 45 Brigadier Generals on the

---

* They were John L. DeWitt, Ben Lear, Walter Krueger, George C. Marshall and George Grunert.

Regular Army's Permanent Promotion List. Death, disabilities, physical and otherwise, compulsory and premature retirements had removed 19, or 42.2%, from the Active List by January 1, 1945, *with six months of the war remaining to be fought!* On June 30, 1945, with hostilities practically at an end, similar wayside losses from the list of 74 National Guard Brigadier Generals totaled 31. This results in a group comparison score of 41.9%, which is a statistical, hairline shadow under that of the Regular Army wayside group score, but so nearly identical that one might well consider the continuance and lossage scores of the Regulars and Guardsmen as being identical, except that the Guard figures are for *a six-months longer period.*

Among the Guardsmen Brigadiers who finished the war's full course, one, Raymond S. McLain, inducted as Artillery Brigadier, Oklahoma's 45th Division, was promoted to Major General, A.U.S., and Division Commander, thence to Lieutenant General and C. G., XIX Corps, in combat. Like General Beightler, at war's end he accepted integration into the Regular Army as a General Officer and died from natural causes while still on active duty as a three-star General. Kenneth F. Cramer, of Connecticut, inducted with the 43rd Division; Charles C. Haffner, Jr., of Illinois, 33rd Division, and Leonard F. Wing, Vermont's brilliant and heroic Artilleryman, exemplify additional Guard officers inducted as Brigadiers, but who were promoted to two-star rank, A.U.S., and assigned to Division commands; Cramer to the 24th, Haffner to the 103rd and Wing to the 43rd, with which he had been inducted. Other Guardsmen were promoted to higher ranks by virtue of military supply and administrative ability. Ralph M. Immell, Wisconsin Brigadier in 1940, for example, found himself passed-over for induction because his Cavalry Headquarters was broken-up and reorganized into a lower echelon. Came Pearl Harbor and he found himself a Federally-recognized Brigadier but without assignment, or even on active duty. He vacated the one-star rank for a Colonel's eagles and whatever assignment he might be given. As a Base Commander, Naples, Italy, he was promoted to Brigadier and in France to Major General, A.U.S.

The foregoing facts and figures certainly belie the myth that mass incompetence was the hallmark of National Guard General Officers. In terms of percentages, more of them carried the full weight of their induction ranks through the course of the entire War than did their contemporary Regular colleagues on corresponding lists in the same season of inductions.*

In group comparison and in terms of numbers and percentages on

---

* Be it said for the Regular Permanent List Brigadiers of 1940 that most of the 58% who did survive the stepped-up attrition rates incident to the more exacting and strenuous wartime service did rise rapidly and to high, temporary ranks. These included Courtney Hodges, Daniel I. Sultan and Jacob L. Devers.

the comparable Permanent Lists of Regular and National Guard Colonels who were able to carry the weight of their grade for the duration of the war, the avocational amateurs from civil life look even better. With the National Guard inductions of 1940 and early months of 1941, 273 full Colonels were taken into active Army service. They compared with the 705 Regular Permanent List Colonels in the Army Directory for October 20, 1940. At the end of the war, 148 Guard Colonels, 54%, were still on active duty in their permanent or higher temporary ranks. Only 273, or only 39% of the 705 Regular Colonels were still on active duty in their permanent or temporary higher rank, as of January 1, 1945, with six months of fighting yet to come.

The attrition rates in both groups are easily explained. It was not a lack of patriotism, desire, and, in many instances, not through any lack of knowledge, aptitude, skill or ability. But Colonels, like Generals, were then normally in an age group where attrition is comparatively high. Deaths from natural causes, annual physical examinations and required vigor for effective field service stepped-up the rates of attrition for military personnel in upper age groups compared with other occupations and professions. Thus the inactivated Colonels on both lists were results of McNair's age-in-grade policy (particularly for Guardsmen), disabilities, physical or otherwise, reclassifications, removals and forced premature retirements by the Craig Board and occasional deaths from natural causes, as well as statutory retirement for having reached age 64. But with 54% of the Guard Colonels "going all the way" and only 39% of their Regular Colleagues going beyond six months of the end, this should be sufficient to kill the myth that has grown purely by reiteration that the Federally-recognized and inducted National Guard Colonelcies of World War II were synonymous with State political patronage and military incompetence.*

The group records of the lower-ranking National Guard officers require less comment because they have been the victims of less public misunderstanding than the senior officers of the Guard. Here it is enough to say that of 1,100 Lieutenant Colonels mobilized with the Guard, two rose to the grade of A.U.S. Major General, three to A.U.S. Brigadier General, 321 to A.U.S. full Colonel, 383 continued in grade for the war, one accepted reduction to Major but finished the war; 217 failed to finish the duration-of-war hitch by reason of death in battle or from natural causes, health, and all reasons previously given for senior officers, with the age-in-grade policy just before Pearl Harbor causing more separations than for any other single cause. The comparable

---

* Likewise another myth is exploded by the same data. These figures for Regular Colonels and General Officers, along with the previously cited reclassifications, and by the Craig Board (see page 423) clearly indicate the absence of an instinctive "protective association" for the professionals that wilfully covered-up incompetence.

scores for the remaining ranks of the commissioned World War II Guardsmen are as follows: 1,379 Majors inducted; 190 promoted to colonelcies, A.U.S.; 663 to Lieutenant Colonelcies, A.U.S.; 129 served through war in grade; none accepted reduction; 250 were separated prior to end of war, with age-in-grade the largest single factor. Captains: 5,114 inducted; promotions to Colonel, 185; to Lieutenant Colonel, 1,183; to Major, 1,616; through war in grade, 383; accepted reduction to First Lieutenant, two; separated before end of hostilities, 726, with age-in-grade and field service casualties the major factors. First Lieutenants: 4,745 inducted; promotions to Colonel, 41; to Lieutenant Colonel, 825; to Major, 1,833; to Captain, 1,300; in grade through war 67; accepted reductions, 0; separated for reasons as above, 710. Second Lieutenants: 4,745 inducted; promoted through intervening ranks to Colonel, 7; to Lieutenant Colonel, 311; to Major, 1,086; to Captain, 2,092; to First Lieutenant, 349; in grade through the war, nine; separated for reasons mentioned above, 763.

All the above officers were inducted with their units and in the assignments specifically authorized by the applicable Table of Organization. In addition, there were 3,168 enlisted Guardsmen, mostly Sergeants, who held commissions in the National Guard Reserve. Acceptance of officers in civilian military components was hard enough for some old, hard-core Regulars through the prewar years, but these enlisted "reserve officers of a civilian reserve," as one between-the-wars Inspector haughtily termed them, often were viewed officially with more than passing disdain, if not professional, military concern. The training and war years score of these Company-grade Guard Reserve officers are thus of more than passing interest. Of the 3,168 enlisted Guardsmen who pinned on their bars upon induction to fill vacant slots incident to their Regiments and Battalions going to war strength, 13 were Captains. Of these, seven ultimately became Lieutenant Colonels, five became Majors, and one served in grade through the war. Of 213 National Guard Reserve First Lieutenants, one became a full Colonel, 19 became Lieutenant Colonels, 68 became Majors, 84 became Captains, and six served in their initial grade through the war. Of the 2,942 Second Lieutenants in this Guard Reserve category, 80 became Lieutenant Colonels, 490 became Majors, 1,401 became Captains, 463 had the one promotion to First Lieutenant, and four served in their initial commissioned grade through the war. Age-in-grade separations and field casualties fell heavily upon this group. Separations for all causes among these 3,168 commissioned, National Guard Reservists was 482.

Moreover, the above commissioned officer contributions, an overwhelming percentage of them in combat formations through their entire wartime tour, represent but a fraction of the commissioned manpower contribution of the National Guard to America's World War II effort. The Guard Divisions, Regiments, Battalions and separate Company-size units were hardly in camp before the expanding Army Air Corps, later redesignated the Army Air Force, began clamoring for officer material. Likewise, there were grave shortages of Lieutenants for expanding the newly-activated Ground Force formations, even prior to Pearl Harbor. The relatively large number of college men among the enlisted personnel of the Guard units were recognized immediately as an already well-oriented and at the same time a sort of captive collection of young men for profitable Officer Candidate recruiting. Accordingly, the Guard units at once began receiving directives to facilitate a flow of volunteers from their formations toward all Officer Candidate Schools in general and to Air Force O.C.S. installations in particular.

Upon graduation from the Officer Candidate Schools these young men were not commissioned back into their units as Guardsmen, but as Second Lieutenants, Army of the United States, on indefinite active duty. More than 75,000 enlisted Guardsmen were thus commissioned. No personnel analysis appears to have been made to establish the exact number. Data is not available as to the ranks they attained. At least one such enlisted Guardsmen is said to have ended his war years as a full Colonel. He could not be pinpointed, but in the Air Force, it could have occurred easily, and perhaps in more than one instance.

In the light of the foregoing record of men and representative units, the inestimable value of the National Guard to the Nation in her greatest of all wars cannot be challenged. The avocational, volunteer interest and spirit of potential service between the two World Wars kept an interest in matters military active at the grass roots of America in nearly 4,000 Cities, Counties and towns throughout the Nation. At the same time they kept equipped, functional units in being and awaiting a call. The delay in full mobilization of the military might of the Nation would have been delayed through a disastrous period that would have been measured in years and not in months had it not been for the Guard. And all of it, until Pearl Harbor, was achieved through the parsimonious allocation of aging World War I military stocks at home stations and in camps. Until the calls to fulltime active duty, a year before Pearl Harbor, the niggardly appropriations allowed but 48 drills a year and 15 days at Summer camps. Not in modern America has the Nation received so much value for the defense dollars spent. Guardsmen knew this and were justly proud of their record of service. Many others who have but partially understood the Guard, its traditions and achievements, have expressed high esteem.

In telling his appreciation of the Guard, Secretary of War Robert P. Patterson said: "The National Guard took to the field 18 infantry divisions, 300,000 men. Those State troops doubled the strength of the Army

480

at once, and their presence in the field gave the country a sense that it had passed the lowest ebb of its weakness . . . Nine of those divisions crossed the Atlantic to Europe and Africa and nine went to the far reaches of the Pacific. The soldiers of the Guard fought in every action in which the Army participated from Bataan to Okinawa. They made a brilliant record on every fighting front. They proved once more the value of the trained citizen-soldier."

Of course, the Secretary overlooked the Americal Division in the Pacific, the non-divisional combat formations, the stray Regiments from the States that found themselves in Regular Army Divisions, and the 29 Squadrons of Air National Guard fliers and ground crews. Moreover, many who served War Department tours under Mr. Patterson during Guard reorganization days often suspected there was much more he did not know concerning the Guard. But, Colonel Frederick G. Todd, historian and West Point Museum Curator, once said, or wrote, that few men, if any, ever could fully understand the Guard, or Guardsmen, without being a Guardsman. Hence any omissions reflected in the Secretary's remarks should be overlooked. There is ample other evidence that he did truly appreciate the National Guard, hence the quotation for its warmth, sincerity and spirit.

# Bibliographical Note For Chapter XVIII

Though often of more pictures than text and of unequal quality as to literary narration and selectivity of vital incidents and facts, the various unit histories of World War II National Guard Divisions are, of course, vital depositories of detailed information not available elsewhere. A few unit histories have real literary merit. Unfortunately, many of the titles no longer are available from the publishers. Local libraries often are able to arrange for temporary use of a copy of any title below through an inter-library loan from your State Historical Society. Some City libraries hold extensive collections of unit histories, particularly of those concerning Divisions in which the City or State was represented. The following is not a complete list of all unit histories consulted, but is representative. By Unit Members, *History of the 26th Infantry Division,* 1947; Unit Members, *History of the 27th Infantry Division,* 1947; Unit Members, *28th, Roll On,* 1945; Col. William J. Witte, *History of the 29th Division,* 1947; Robert L. Hewitt, *Work Horse of the Western Front—the Story of the 30th Division,* 1947; Unit Members, *31st Infantry Division in the Pacific,* 1947; Maj. Gen. H. W. Blakely, *The 32nd Division in World War II,* 1956; Unit Members, *Story of the 34th Division from Louisiana to Pisa,* 1945; *Roster of the 35th Division,* 1945; Division Association, *Campaigns of the 36th Infantry Division in World War II,* 1945; Stanley A. Frankel, *The 37th Division in World War II,* 1948; Unit Members, *History of the 38th Division, "Avengers of Bataan,"* 1947; Unit Members, *History of the*

*40th Division, the Years of World War II,* 1947; 1st Lt. W. F. McCartney, *History of the 41st Division,* 1947; Joseph Zimmer, *History of the 43rd Division, 1941-45,* 1946; Lt. Col. Edward Boherty, *History of the 44th Division,* 1947, and Historical Board, *The Fighting Forty-Fifth,* 1946.

Official publications such as *The Army List and Directory,* semi-annual publication, years 1939-40, and the *Official Army Register,* January 1, 1945, are indispensable but tedious sources relative to Regular Army commissioned personnel for group comparisons with corresponding groups of Guardsmen. The War Department *Annual Reports,* most particularly that of the Chief, National Guard Bureau, for the year ended June 30, 1946, are equally indispensable. The Department of the Army publication, *The Army Almanac,* 1950, and the privately-published, Stackpole edition, of the *Army Almanac,* 1959, are superb aids for statistical and condensed, tabulated information. For strategic analysis of and for major objectives within the several Theaters of War, particularly those in the Pacific, Rear Adm. Samuel E. Morison, *History of the U.S. Navy in World War II,* 15 vols., 1949-61, is the best in print. Army Divisions, however, are dropped from discussions once they are within beachheads. Ray S. Cline, *Washington Command Post,* 1957, reflects the strategic planning in Washington for the Army. This book is one of the 54 titles now in print, written and published under the auspices of the Historical Division, Department of the Army. A full list of titles available, which can be bought separately or as a set, may be procured from the Superintendent of Public Documents, Washington, D.C. While some of the 54 titles are dedicated to planning, supplies, etc., others give operations details down to Divisions and lesser units. George F. Howe, *Northwest Africa, Seizing the Initiative in the West,* 1957; Gordon Harrison, *Cross Channel Attack,* 1951; Martin Blumenson, *Breakout and Pursuit,* 1961; and, in the Pacific, John Miller, Jr., *Guadalcanal, the First Offensive,* 1949; Sam Milner, *Victory in Papua,* 1957; and Robert Ross Smith, *Approach to the Philippines,* 1953, are illustrative of these operational titles. The foregoing titles from this gigantic historical series are merely illustrative. They do include some of the best, detailed, expository writing on field operations that have been published since 1946. Memoirs of Generals often are revealing. Gen. Walter Krueger's *From Down Under to Nippon,* 1953, has a soldier's sharp eye for what units are doing what, where and when. Mark Clark, *Calculated Risk,* 1950, reflects the problems of a Theater Commander but throws little light on the Rapido River affair, in which a fellow Regular General Officer charged him responsible for unnecessary casualties in the 336th Infantry Division. But Lt. Gen. Lucian K. Truscott, *Command Decisions,* 1954, returns to the frank and forthright, name-calling evaluations of friend and foe which characterized the military memoirs of America's Civil War. The literature of World War II would be far richer if more Corps, Divisions and lesser unit commanders left memoirs in the same style. Too much of the postwar military literature had been views from high command and staff ivory towers or from correspondingly low worm's-eye views. Regrettably, the fictional self-pity and perverted morbidity of abnormal military worms that existed only in a novelist's imagination have attracted far more general attention and sold more books than have accurate historical narration and reporting from either the higher or lower echelons.

CHAPTER XIX

# Reorganization and Korea

THE AMERICAN MILITARY MIGHT in Europe began disintegrating almost as quickly as did that of the surrendering German armies. Some old-timers with sharp memories of the precipitate departure of General Pershing's A.E.F. for home and demobilization, occasionally muttered something about having seen this non-Shakespearean Comedy of Errors before and the new production was just as unrealistic and un-funny as the one of 1918-19. Others, endowed with greater optimism, could see considerable difference. History might be repeating itself, but there were sharper tones.

Had it not trickled-down through the command and Staff grapevine that General Courtney H. Hodges and his First Army Headquarters had been pinched-out immediately for transfer to the Pacific? The First Army team would become an Army Group command for the invasion of Japan as soon as the Okinawa mop-up could fold that campaign. Moreover, was it not common knowledge through contacts in Military Government, that at least one beefed-up Division, heavily reinforced with Armor for constabulary duty, would remain in Germany, along with similar English, French and Russian Divisions, to underwrite a future Democracy for Germany?

To this the more pessimistic old-timers yawned and recalled that a much larger American Army of Occupation, with Headquarters at Coblenz, had remained for that same purpose through the early 1920's. The grapevine also relayed rumors of two or three late-arriving Divisions being ticketed for transfer to the China-Burma-India Theater or to the Ground Forces strength buildup for the invasion of the Japanese home islands. At the same time, rumors from Manila held that older and seasoned combat units in that Theater were losing veterans on points rotation.

But what actually was happening to their own older, thoroughly battle-seasoned Divisions and lesser non-divisional units in Europe was not from the grapevine. They were losing veteran personnel of all ranks and ratings as fast as Battery and Company Clerks could check and authenticate individual Service Records. Each six months since sailing from the Port of Embarkation was good for a certain number of points. Each campaign ribbon and star were good for additional point values. Each wound and/or decoration carried point bonuses. Anyone who could add his service up to a designated minimum total was entitled to return home "without delay," which was the current military term for the reasonable delay inevitably present in all personnel affairs. These long-service, high-point, combat veterans in Europe and the Far East were being asked to sign a document of willingness to continue in service until the end of the hostilities in the Far East, following rotation home. Some units were overwhelmingly affirmative until it became known that the unit would not be transferred and redeployed as a unit, but that each officer and man would be reassigned to new or older units already in a Pacific Theater. Some asked for a change in time for a correction; others were too slow, or deliberately stood on their initial commitment.

Thus an old, discredited practice under a new name came back into American Army personnel policies: the principle of rotation. An elaborate system of staging camps, as personnel pipelines to Ports of Embarkation, came into throbbing activity as fast as the long-service units were being inactivated. Loss of combat personnel with the stipulated minimum of points was as high as 95% in some units. Their last batch of replacements, with short service and little or no combat experience, became replacements in retained late-arrival Divisions, scheduled for further combat service, or for older Regular Army units such as the 1st, 2nd or 3rd Infantry Divisions, Regular Army, the unbroken continuance of which the War Department General Staff long had fostered.

The extent to which the principle of rotation of individuals was a break with the immediate past should be noted. From the Revolution to the Civil War, inclusive, there had been an element of rotation, normally by short terms of service in units activated for a specific period, such as one year for the Mexican War; three months, six months, one year or three years for the Civil War. The three-year Regiments with the possibility of reenlistments and reorganization for additional terms had proved somewhat satisfactory in the eyes of Uptonian professionals, but were defective in having specific terms. A General could lose entire Regiments in the heat of a campaign.

An inexorable, unyielding concept of Upton's was that all troops the Nation might needfully train for a crisis should be held in arms "for the duration." For the Spanish War the terms of voluntary service had been for two years or the duration, whichever should come sooner. But by 1917 the teachings of the Uptonians had taken root. Service, whether by draft or by volunteering, was for the duration. Such was the philosophy and terms of 1940. But the course of the war, with volunteers and early Draftees in embattled overseas units more than two years from America, brought changes in public thinking. The people had an Army that grew rapidly to 7.7 millions, with more than half the growth most of the time conspicuously present within the Continental United States. With psychologists and psychiatrists explaining overseas "combat fatigue" with vague, mystifying, mouth-filling words, there is little wonder that Congressmen early caught a new trend of public thinking. From them the political-minded General Staff officers (whom Upton would have disowned scornfully) came up with "rotation" as the magic word.* Those careless commentators and writers who today solemnly claim all of Upton's principles have been adopted and he was thus the prophetic planner of today's American armies, have overlooked the impact of the word "rotation." Moreover, they have further revealed a lack of thoroughness in knowledge of Uptonian teachings in a number of other important points.

## THE FUTURE OF THE NATIONAL GUARD

Amid all these rumors and obvious activities toward letting those who might volunteer, plus the late-comer, ineligible-for-rotation, combat personnel continue the war against Japan, there was the natural specula-

---

* There is such a thing as "combat fatigue," even within rear area, overseas units that never have been in actual contact with the enemy. Nevertheless, precious few of the psychologists and psychiatrists who have expounded thereon evidence much first-hand knowledge of its causes, much less its cure. Most cases are extreme results of self-pity combined with old-fashioned homesickness, with the latter the predominant factor. The quickest and best cure is within the Theater of Operations rather than back home; i.e., immediate membership in and self-identification with a unit that is highly self-conscious of superbly doing a difficult and distasteful job. The unit, assocational feeling quickly creates a sort of home-away-from-home, and the sense of accomplishment removes the feeling of futility upon which self-pity feeds. Of course, men and/or units should be rotated away from the constant hammer of battle's beaten zone. Hot baths, clean clothes, two weeks' rest and occasional words of appreciation have permanently cured more cases of "combat fatigue" than advance rotation home. No physically fit officer or man should be rotated home merely for "combat fatigue."

tion as to the format of American peacetime defenses, come the dawn of the bright new day that would follow the subjugation of Japan. Letters and news clippings from home had told all who were interested that many hometown National Guard Armories had been filled by volunteer, uniformed, armed and drilling units composed of Selective Service rejects for physical disabilities, essential war workers, other citizenry with industrial exemptions, and public-spirited citizens well beyond compulsory military service ages.

These war emergency home defense units not only were available to State Governors for emergencies arising from storms, disasters and civil disorder, but they participated in bond drive parades and immediately responded to requisitions from Offices of Civil Defense for duty as waterfront security detachments, patrols to round-up escaped prisoners-of-war, guards for vital railroad yards and bridges, industrial plants and other likely targets for enemy saboteur efforts. Germany's sabotage record from World War I and the landing of saboteurs from submarines on the Atlantic Coast shortly after Pearl Harbor had given validity to these apprehensions and precautions. At their peak, the aggregate of these State Guard units, as they most often were officially designated, was approximately 110,000 officers and men.*

These known events at home, combined with the bitterly-deprecatory publicity that had been inspired from the War Department General Staff and General McNair's Ground Forces G.H.Q. against the National Guard units, convinced many older Guardsmen, with memories of 1920, that the demise of their component was definitely in War Department plans.

At least one junketeer to the combat Theaters from the Staff empires on the Potomac must have cheerfully passed the word to friends in London that no place could be found for the National Guard in the postwar scheme of things. Draft of personnel by Selective Service, in peace and war, had solved all military manpower problems. The war had demonstrated that Draft machinery could be so manipulated as to provide adequate Company- and Battery-level officers for an expansible Army of Draftees. Staff and command slots for this new postwar Selective Service Army would more than absorb all Regulars then in their temporary, higher grades. There thus would be no need for reductions to permanent Promotion List ranks such as had followed World War I.

It was good, morale-building patter for the combat-assigned Regulars

---

* Illinois Reserve Militia, Kentucky Active Militia, and Michigan State Troops were the only departures from the conventional State Guard designations. The New York State Guard was largest with a strength of 17,327 officers and men; North Dakota, smallest with 117 officers and men. Arizona, Montana, Nevada and Oklahoma did not bother to organize war emergency State Guard units. The aggregate of the Territorial Guards, Hawaii, Alaska and Puerto Rico, not included in the above total, was 5,500 officers and men.

in the European Theater. How many, if any, Regulars believed such charming and reassuring analyses of the bright New Day in the postwar peace is most uncertain. Knowledgeable Guardsmen and Reserve officers made mental note and darkly suspected someone was planning a highly-regimented future with thinly-limited choices for America's coming generation of military-age young manhood. Unfortunately, the outbreak of the wholly-unexpected Korean Affair, Summer of 1950, and the practical failures of the idealistically-conceived United Nations, followed by the inconceivable pressures of the Cold War, have brought a limited amount of truth to this anonymous rumor-monger's prophetic analysis. But from 1945 to 1950 he was basically in error. His proposal that there was no place for the National Guard in America's future was somewhat wide of the mark. Many Guardsmen said as much at the time.

Unknown to the Guardsmen overseas, however, there was a great fire of truth under the billowing smoke of rumors about doing away with the National Guard in its historic role as an American National defense institution. Within at least two States, leaders in the organization of the State Guard units for internal and civil defense had been told that they would not go out of existence with the return of the National Guard. The latter was to be merged into the postwar Organized Reserve Corps. Accordingly, a Federal Organized Militia would supplant the historic units of the States. At the same time, modern weapons, such as airplanes with transoceanic ranges, saboteur and Fifth Column operations had demonstrated the permanent necessity for home defense, i.e., State Guard, units trained in peace for home front duty. Also, in peace and war, they would be available to their State Governors for disaster and civil disorder calls to transitory active duty within their respective States. Thus would all physically-fit military manpower be released for volunteering or selective draft into expanding Field Armies for ending a future war by offensive operations.

Such ideas were floriating before and after Pearl Harbor. The demand for home front units merely fitted neatly into some Washington, General Staff ideas as to what should happen to the National Guard. General Marshall himself is believed by some to have been so influenced by Ground Forces G.H.Q. training reports and the inspired, anti-Guard publicity, that he had embraced the idea. But doubts as to the full validity of such reports must have arisen in his mind. It is of record that he felt the need of advice from a more objective, unselfish, scholarly source.

## GENERAL MARSHALL SEEKS ADVICE

To this end General Marshall called from retirement an old and trusted friend who long had outranked him and from whom he must have felt he had learned much. It was none other than Brigadier General

John McA. Palmer, U.S.A., Ret. As a Colonel he had been Pershing's key man in the Defense Act of 1920 legislative hassle with the National Guard and associated Reserve officers. Thus it was that, effective November 14, 1941, at age 71, Palmer returned to temporary active duty as a researcher and special adviser to the Chief of Staff on Civilian Components. Neither he nor Marshall could have suspected it then, but he was to continue on active duty without interruption until September 27, 1946. It was a service that was to add an Oak Leak Cluster to Palmer's earlier Distinguished Service Medal.

Following the legislative battle of 1920, reviewed in an earlier chapter, Palmer had returned to General Pershing's official family as Aide-de-Camp, 1921-23, whence he was detached briefly to represent the General as a part of the technical staff for the Conference on Limitation of Armament. While Aide to General Pershing, Colonel Palmer again was closely associated with then-Major George C. Marshall, who had reverted to his permanent rank. Marshall was also an Aide to Pershing through the same period.

Palmer was selected-up to the Permanent List of Brigadier Generals, 1923, and assigned to command the 19th Infantry Brigade in the Canal Zone. It was his first troop assignment since he had commanded in combat the Maryland-Virginia Brigade of the 29th (National Guard) Division in France. But the tropical duty broke General Palmer's health, which for years had been something less than robust. He was retired from this assignment for "disabilities incident to the service." But his splendid mental health more than offset any frailness of the body. Retirement allowed a return to his scholarly researches into American military history that had been interrupted by World War I. In addition to articles in sundry magazines, he completed *Statesmanship or War*, 1927; *Washington, Lincoln, Wilson—Three War Statesmen*, 1930; *General von Steuben*, 1937, and *America in Arms*, 1941. None but the last reached a wide public, but all were recognized by discerning reviewers as volumes of lasting value and some, or all, are found today in most City libraries and in practically all college and university holdings.

The enormity of change since he last had been on active duty, particularly the introduction of such complicated crew-served weapons as the long-range and high-speed battlefield attack planes and bombers, appears to have at first appalled the aging military student of things past. Could Guardsmen, committed to earning a living in civil life, maintain proficiency in the operation of such highly-technical equipment? As the war progressed the old scholar rapidly moved into the present and came to an affirmative answer. The Air National Guard in Korea and since proved him to be 100% correct.

His faith in the citizen-soldier, organized into periodic drilling and properly-equipped units, under command of citizen-soldier officers, in ranks sufficiently high to command the Guard units in being, remained undimmed. Any other structure would be contrary to the genius of the American people. Any effort to foist a European type of expansible army, such as Emory Upton and Peyton C. March had proposed, would be so contrary to the military customs and traditions of the people that it would be an invitation to failure.

For his known faith in the volunteer citizen-soldier and the unit structure in the organization of such volunteers, the leading National Guardsmen welcomed the news of his return to active duty. They knew him as a man of unselfish purpose and unswerving integrity, with whom they could talk. But they knew full well there would be tough arguments with him. There was no evidence that he had changed his mind in the slightest degree as to a partnership between the States and the Federal Government in National Guard affairs. They knew that in Palmer's thinking the Militia Clause guarantee and inalienable right to bear arms in the Bill of Rights was not a barrier to the Federal Government's annexation of the National Guard and merging it into an all-encompassing Federal Volunteer Militia to be known as the Army Reserve, or some such appropriate title in avoidance of the word "Militia," which Uptonian abuse had brought into disrepute.

## MARSHALL VIOLATES LAW ON FUTURE PLANNING

Notwithstanding the legalistic, Constitutional argument with Palmer that was certain to arise sooner or later, his return to active duty and in his particular assignment was absolutely the only flickering ray of sunshine through the long, dark months of late 1941 and 1943 when it appeared to the few informed Guardsmen remaining in the United States that their institution was doomed to death in the war to which it was contributing so much toward an ultimate victory. The fact that the National Guard Divisions and many lesser units had been snapped-up by the Operations Section of the War Department with highest movement priorities overseas and for earliest Army commitments to offensive field action had no impact upon the public favorable to the Guard's intrinsic value. This was natural, for the public did not know it, for reasons of security. Furthermore, such old, Uptonian devotees of the professionals as Generals McNair and Lear were still in highest Ground Forces assignments. They and their Staffs still were echoing their vintage 1939 preconceptions that Guard units were worthless, right while the Guardsmen were headed overseas and into action with highest priorities. Department policy on publicity in time of war did have the beneficial by-product of silencing their publicity smear campaign, the peak of which, as we have seen, had been on the newstands the weekend of Pearl Harbor.

As dark 1942 blended into the heartening victories of 1943, less thought was given to the rapidly-being-discredited maunderings of such officers, but, meanwhile, there was rising additional concern that General Marshall did not appear to be paying any attention to his chosen adviser, General Palmer. Worse yet, Marshall was wantonly invalidating the provision in Section 5 that had been Palmer's original and pet idea and which he personally had written into the National Defense Act of 1920. It was the stipulation that Guard and Reserve officers would serve on an advisory committee in all matters pertaining to organization, equipping and training the Civilian Components of the Army.

Such a committee still technically was in existence, but nothing was being referred to it. Its membership was scattered, and presumably had pressing duties in current active duty assignments which precluded its functioning. Certainly no National Guard voice was being heard in the War Department, unless it be that of the Chief of the National Guard Bureau. He and his Staff were being bypassed more frequently than otherwise, according to the Chief, Major General John F. Williams, of Missouri.

Major General George E. Leach of Minnesota was a former Chief of the National Guard Bureau. Out of active participation in Guard affairs since 1940, having reached statutory retirement at age 64, he was still mentally alert, physically vigorous and so active in his business and civic affairs that he was prevailed upon to serve as Vice-President of the National Guard Association through a part or all of the war. In that capacity, Leach wrote General Marshall a personal letter, January 6, 1942.

Leach considered it desirable that the Committee on National Guard and Reserve Affairs should become functional without further delay. If all experienced Guard officers were needed in more active assignments than such studies and deliberations, General Marshall was reminded that a competent panel could be created from experienced officers no longer on the active lists by reason of physical disabilities, or being out for age-in-grade.

There appears to be no evidence that Marshall considered the Leach letter more than an old soldier's desire again to be of service to his Country. In his reply there was little warmth for Leach and somewhat less for the idea.* But the letter unquestionably reminded Marshall of the existence of such a Committee and the fact that it was not getting

---

* Leach was a Douglas MacArthur man. As a Field Artillery Regimental Commander through World War I in the "Rainbow" Division, his combat service, which included a D.S.M. and the D.S.C., was thus entirely under MacArthur as Division Chief of Staff, and Division Commander. MacArthur was U.S. Army Chief of Staff while Leach was Chief of the National Guard Bureau. There could be some merit in the suggestion that Marshall had little interest in advice from a MacArthur disciple.

any work to do, and that lack of a panel of only five available, informed Guard officers was something less than a reasonable excuse.

In April following, National Guard representation within the War Department General Staff pursuant to Section 5 of the National Defense Act was suspended for the duration of the war. The Leach letter may or may not have triggered the subsequent illegal suspension. By that time Deputies, and Deputies of the Deputies, within the War Department General Staff, were making administrative decisions, processing the necessary Staff action papers and collecting mass approvals of buck sheets that included all sorts of major and minor decisions, both legal and illegal. But as Chief of Staff, Marshall necessarily bears the onus of the decision.

Meanwhile, a month earlier, the entire National Guard Bureau was removed from its position within the War Department Special Staff, with direct access to the Secretary of War. The Bureau was placed under the Commanding General, Army Service Forces. There its function was largely that of an office of records and the creation of the State Guard units briefly characterized above. This may or may not have been a violation of the Statutes, but it most certainly was a violation of their spirit and completely contrary to the Charter of the Bureau eagerly entered into by the General Staff a decade or more previously to keep the Guardsmen from writing the status of the Bureau, its scope and functions into law.

These two actions, more than any other, made truthful prophets of those Guardsmen after 1920 who consistently had insisted that many of the Regulars in the War Department General Staff were sheer, career opportunists whose word could not be trusted beyond the point where it might serve any interests other than their own. And, insofar as a few of them were concerned, this included General Marshall.* It is indeed improbable that the National Guard Bureau could have been dealt with so summarily in a rush of events and without his full knowledge and careful consideration. The National Guard Bureau was too big and too significant to have been shelved by the Deputy of a Deputy.

---

* Dr. Russell F. Weigley, in *Towards an American Army*, utilizes a biographical approach for a superb reexamination and presentation of American military philosophies, Generals George Washington to George C. Marshall, inclusive. The latter apparently gave him somewhat more difficulty in categorization than most. Dr. Weigley, with a hint of doubt, classifies him as a non-Uptonian along with General Palmer. There is little ground for basic disagreement. Marshall was non-Uptonian in one major and highly significant quality. From Palmer or someone he learned the difference between a purely military decision and a political decision in the realm of National policy and statecraft. Moreover, he knew and accepted the principle that in America the civilian politician, or statesman, always held the initiative and final voice as to what was a political decision and what was a purely military decision. Other than that, it is the current author's opinion (Hill's) that the pre-Pearl Harbor Marshall could have qualified as an enthusiastic Upton acolyte. Moreover, Marshall necessarily made many reappraisals of his prior ideas and on many things during the course of the war. Thus the end result was non-Uptonian, which leaves Dr. Weigley thoroughly correct in final effect.

This situation left the few Guard leaders remaining in Continental America one man with whom they could talk, General Palmer. And he did not appear to have enough influence to get a statute he had written himself properly observed. He did not rate so much as a swivel chair and a courtyard window in the Pentagon. His office was an over-size, front view, research cubicle on an upper deck of the Library of Congress. But talk to him the few Guard leaders frequently did.

They immediately attacked the theory that there existed any conflict of Constitutional interest in terms of welfare for National defense in a National Guard jointly owned by the States and the Nation, such as had evolved since the Civil War. Through the agency of Federal recognition, for example, the Federal Government had as much control over military qualifications of Guard officers as it did over issuance of commissions in the purely Federal Officers Reserve Corps. Moreover, the Guard was good; the overseas combat scores that were coming in clearly indicated as much. The alert but aging scholar listened and checked the records since World War I. He came into an agreement with their views, sometime in 1943 or early 1944; became an ally, in fact, but the Guardsmen were rather slow in finding it out.

## A POSTWAR POLICY FOR THE GUARD IS ADOPTED

Meanwhile, and before the late 1942 offensives in North Africa had been launched, the Special Planning Division of the War Department General Staff became active. Its scope was wide and, within certain assumptions, included all military needs for future security, which, of course, included personnel. The Special Planning Division was under the Directorship of Brigadier General William F. Tompkins, U.S. Army. He was an able officer from the Corps of Engineers. Out of West Point in the Class of 1915, he had commanded an Engineer Battalion in France through most of World War I, followed by tours of postgraduate study through the Army Service schools, including the War College. Like most Engineer officers of the era, he experienced a wide range of non-military assignments to large Federal engineering projects. From these he had professional and civic horizons far beyond the cloistered, between-the-wars Army Posts that had restricted the capacities of so many of the Regulars of his day.

But under the blanket of secrecy that enshrouded all actions, words and even thoughts in the War Department of 1942-43-44, National Guardsmen within the United States were just as much in the dark as to what the Special Planning Division was thinking and talking about as were those overseas. General Tompkins and his Planning Division, War Department General Staff, apparently took no one except higher echelons into their confidence.

In common sense and planning judgment it was as erroneous as it was

492

illegal. There was no security risk factor in discussions of the gross structure (without statistical estimates, of types and lists of proposed units) of military manpower following the victory. Indeed, with so much more war drama in the headlines, open hearings on the subject would not have rated two column-inches of news between patent medicine advertisements on page 21 of a Sunday issue. Reported in Japan and Europe, it could have done no more than reflect America's confidence of victory. Moreover, if Guardsmen and Reserve officers commanding units and serving on high Staffs overseas could share in the planning and be trusted with highly-sensitive information concerning the next campaign's objectives and the beaches where the landing assaults would be made, by what rule of common sense, or even within the muscle-bound logic then prevalent in the Pentagon, were equally patriotic citizen-soldiers on duty in the United States considered unfit to know, discuss, review and advise on mass manpower considerations within the Democracy that a great war was being fought to perpetuate? There were Reserve officer members of the Special Planning Division, but no Guard officer. Why? Guard graduates of the Staff College were available.

A referral of the Staff papers pertinent to the Civilian Components from the Planning Division to intermittent sessions of a Section 5 Committee, composed of at least five Guardsmen, five Reserve officers and five Regulars of appropriate ranks, with the Committee served by a permanent office and officer secretary for liaison and continuity with power to call meetings when volume of accumulated work or progress of higher planning appeared to justify same—in short, the simple compliance with the law—would have precluded much subsequent misunderstanding, abuse and recrimination. As it was, the entire situation was laden with warranted distrust.

The distrust of the National Guard leaders led to the election of Major General Ellard A. Walsh, Minnesota Adjutant General, to the Presidency of their Association in the Harrisburg meeting of April 1, 1943. It has been reviewed in an earlier chapter.* When Walsh found only deaf ears and mute tongues in the Pentagon, and none but John McA. Palmer in the Library of Congress with whom he could confer, simultaneous with a rising tide of additional reasons for viewing the situation with alarm, he spent the long cold nights of that Minnesota Winter preparing his earlier-characterized Philippic against the American military caste, or "Regular Army Samurai," to be condensed and delivered at the 1944 Conference of the National Guard Association.

Meanwhile, General Palmer was collaborating with his old friend from 1920, the former Senator James W. Wadsworth, in the writing of a peacetime Universal Military Training Bill. Wadsworth had been

---

* See pages 342-345.

defeated for return to the Senate from New York in 1926, but since 1933 had been in the Lower House, where he was to serve without interruption until 1950, and always with an intense interest in military affairs. Thus U.M.T., a Nationwide Draft for a period of time on all physically-fit young men, was indeed a basic assumption determined by General Marshall for the maintenance of the peacetime forces. Moreover, that assumption was a guiding principle for General Tompkins and his Planning Division. The more they planned the more it became a necessary keystone for their entire structure. But what would happen should U.M.T. fail in the war-weary America that would be electing new Congressmen? The less satisfactory but secondary objective would be some workable, force-producing, watered-down form of U.M.T. such as compulsory service for certain Draft Board-selected young men. What would Congress accept?

Many of the serving, highly-articulate Draftees, including officers and men who had opted for the Navy just ahead of a "valentine" from their Draft Boards, were writing letters home, and some to Congressmen, indicative of a dim view of any kind of compulsory service that the Nation could possibly get along without. Some were even hazarding the extremely modest opinion that if the present war was being won, it was being won without them, because they had done nothing constructive and had no prospect of doing such, since donning the uniform. The Planning Division was driven to an examination of the basic assumption. Question: Could either U.M.T., or a Selective Service Bill, be passed if also warmly opposed by returning, volunteer citizen-soldiers?

National defense in general and the Army in particular were again in need of friends. Except for the 1920 legislative differences, the Guardsmen consistently had been the best-informed, most warmly-sympathetic and always-effective civilian help to the professional Services—Army and Navy. What would be the attitude of the Guardsmen? Of the prewar Reserve officers? How many young men holding initial A.U.S. commissions would continue active voluntarily in a postwar Army Reserve? The outlook was disheartening. Palmer no doubt relayed his conversations with sundry Guardsmen, such as that with his old friend and comrade-in-arms from the Maryland-Virginia Brigade in World War I, General Reckord. He had told Palmer the National Guardsmen would support no Bill that did not continue the National Guard as the Nation's first-line Reserve Force, and with them organized into equipped and functional units under their own officers in advance of the call to active duty. Palmer had accepted the idea originally. As time wore on he had doubts.

The basic assumptions thus were falling like a row of upended dominoes when each falls in turn against the next. Would the Guard stand firm with the Regulars in a demand for compulsory military serv-

494

ice—U.M.T., or a watered-down form thereof? Meanwhile, it was quite clear from the embattled Theaters overseas that the National Guard Divisions and lesser units were bearing the brunt of offensives in the Pacific and were holding their own in Sicily and Italy with the oldest and most highly-touted 1st and 3rd Divisions of the Regular Army. There was also their exemplary comparison with the English formations that had been embattled since 1939. Generals McNair and Lear, plus their respective Staffs, could be wrong, or at least something less than objective. Tompkins and chosen members of his Special Planning Division at last decided to confer unofficially with some representative Guardsmen who were in Washington January 2, 1944, incident to a conference of State Adjutants Generals. There the Guardsmen were told that the page for the Guard had been left blank. If anything was written on it, the Guard would have to do the writing.

This was hardly honest and forthright, but Tompkins was leaving the door open until he could seek further instructions. The result was another conference in the National Guard Bureau offices February 28, 1944, attended by Tompkins and such of his Division as he saw fit to invite. Walsh was accompanied by Governor Martin of Pennsylvania, former C.G. of the 28th Division and Walsh's immediate predecessor as President of the Association. Three other Guard General Officers were present as was Lieutenant General Hugh A. Drum, U.S. Army, Retired, who had accepted command of New York's flourishing State Guard in its contemplated continuance into peace years. His presence spoke eloquently as to what was being planned for the Guard.

Walsh and his colleagues, Charles H. Grahl of Iowa, R. B. DeLacour of Connecticut, John F. Williams of Missouri and Edward Martin of Pennsylvania, gave a blunt, detailed statement of what Reckord already had told Palmer. They would accept nothing less than (a) the National Defense Act of 1920 as amended in 1933; (b) organization under the Militia Clause of the Constitution with the control thereof in time of peace by the States to remain unimpaired; (c) studies pertaining to the Guard to be made by the Chief of the National Guard Bureau of the War Department and (d) the stipulations of Section 5 of the Defense Act be complied with until there be National Guard representation in the Tompkins Special Planning Division.

Palmer sided with the Guardsmen. After they were gone he urged Tompkins to comply with the law and further to include the Guard in status quo for future planning. If the Guard had not been equipped and trained properly, the fault was not the system under the Militia Clause of the Constitution, but the fault of the Army for not having used the powers that it had enjoyed all along. Tompkins capitulated with a memorandum to the Chief of Staff, but the reasons he emphasized were those that Marshall and the General Staff had learned to accept as conclusive: i.e., political reasons. There would be another legislative Donnybrook in Congress if efforts were made to merge the Guard with the Organized Reserve Corps. Moreover, Palmer was there to remind him of what had happened to Peyton C. March's pet ideas when he tried to ignore "the genius of the American people" and their institutions, to borrow again one of Palmer's favorite terms. Marshall approved the principle and sent it to Secretary of War Stimson. In due time he signed it, more or less *pro forma*.

But no one appears to have told Walsh, the spokesman for the Guard, of the trends from this conference. He returned to his office in St. Paul, Minnesota, and continued honing the razor-keen edges of his barbed similes and metaphors relative to the caste-conscious and caste-serving "Regular Army Samurai." He read a condensed and concentrated version of the 145 pages (printed in full in the *Proceedings*) in the Baltimore Annual Meeting May 3-6 following.

No harm was done; indeed it was beneficial. The subsequent Pentagon plea that Tompkins and his Special Planning Division and General Marshall already had "saved the Guard" prior to the Walsh-engendered uproar is a perverted half-truth at best. Moreover, it had the effect of bringing the War Department General Staff back into compliance with the law concerning the Civilian Components. It further expedited constructive, realistic planning for reorganization of both the Guard and Organized Reserve by informed officers; i.e., Regulars and Guardsmen from the National Guard Bureau and the legally-constituted Section 5, General Staff Committees.

By August 24, 1944, Palmer had prepared to Marshall's satisfaction War Department Circular 347. It became the guidelines of the War Department and subsequently of the Department of Defense in matters pertaining to military manpower until the outbreak of hostilities in Korea. Much of it is still adhered-to.

Guardsmen in embattled areas overseas heard little or nothing of these developments until arrival back in America, when friendly Regulars congratulated them upon "Guard victories at home as well as abroad," to quote one combat Regular who had developed high esteem for Guard units. But actually it was more of a philosophical victory of Brigadier General John McA. Palmer over the teachings of Brevet Major General Emory Upton; a philosophy for the citizen-soldier and his local units versus the philosophy for unbridled professionalism in arms; a philosophy based upon thorough scholarship, learning, and understanding of "the genius of the American people" versus instinctive propaganda by distortion and reiteration for a military caste that is contrary to the laws, history, institutions and traditions of the American people. No single man, Guardsman or Regular, played a more significant role in the military reorganizations following America's two greatest wars than did John McA. Palmer. And in calling him out of retirement to act as his adviser, General Marshall did himself as well as his Country a distinct service. Until Palmer came into the picture and gained intellectual control of the General Staff thinking, Marshall, under the tutelage of the old, die-hard Uptonians, was headed down the same broad road of error that had broken Peyton C. March. Marshall, the most perceptive Chief of Staff in American military history, must have sensed as much in early November, 1941, when he began turning from McNair and Ben Lear to the old, scholarly doughboy in retirement—John McA. Palmer.

## THE EXPANDED NATIONAL GUARD

Thanks to General Marshall's cleanly-cut decision against the Uptonians in 1944 and the immediate activation of the principles of Section 5 of the existing Defense Act, combined with the green light to the National Guard Bureau to initiate detailed planning with the Adjutants General of the States, little time was lost after demobilization of the combat forces. In some States there was a purposeful lag. Time was needed to give all hands time to return to their homes, to become settled in their new, or old, localities, to become more-or-less accustomed to civilian clothes, and to learn whether or not they would have sufficient time for the avocational demands of volunteer service in a unit.

One difficulty immediately arose. The War Department quite properly gave all outgoing personnel lower than the grade of Colonel a terminal promotion to the next higher grade if he elected separation into an Organized Reserve status. In practically all instances, it was not only a just recognition of services well done, but it was calculated to hold a vast pool of officers and enlisted men until Federal Organized Reserve units, patterned as closely as possible after those of the Guard, could be created. In final analysis they could think of nothing better than the National Guard to imitate. Its record in two modern wars was convincing.

But in reorganizing the Guard units into rigidly-prescribed Tables of Organization units, it was frequently impossible to honor the highest grade a returnee had the full and just right to expect. A small City with one Infantry Company allocated occasionally had 10 or 12 worthy and well-qualified Captains, all ex-Guardsmen and eager to carry on as Company Commanders, but not a single First Lieutenant of Infantry in town and absolutely no Second Lieutenant of any Arm or Service available. The normal solution: A willing and surplus, terminally-promoted Major took a reduction, organized and commanded the Company, and recommended for the Lieutenancies those with the best combat records from among the eager-beaver Captains. Those chosen usually accepted, but not always. The same problem extended up to the rank of Colonel. Many took reductions in rank to serve in reorganization of the National Guard.

On the whole, it was good for the Guard. It immediately eliminated the indecisive from the decisive; the rank-conscious from the service-conscious. It immediately gave the postwar Guard a dedicated, hard core of officer leadership that is still present after nearly 20 years. But in the Summer of 1950, for the Korean Affair, many of these officers were back on active duty in grades lower than they had held at the end of World War II. It proved to be discriminatory, inasmuch as Reserve officers who had not been chosen for the Guard, or who had declined unit assignment in a Table of Organization Guard unit, often were recalled for Korea in their higher terminal promotion grades.

The reorganization of 1946-49 was a vast improvement upon that of the early '20's in one significant respect. After World War I the reorganization was from the bottom up. No Battalion Headquarters was allowed, for example, until there were four organic Companies in being, functional and Federally-recognized; no Colonel and Regimental Headquarters until there were three organic Battalions, etc. In 1946, the higher the Headquarters, the earlier it was organized. This not only increased the tempo but made for better selection of personnel and direction of effort. Under the earlier system, more than one Captain found himself a Battalion Commander merely because he was the best unit organizer rather than the best soldier and Unit Commander.

## THE REVISED TROOP STRUCTURE

The new National Guard Troop Structure followed historic lines in that combat units of all Arms received major emphasis. There were, however, a higher percentage of non-divisional and support elements. The most unique, or novel, additions were 12 Wing Headquarters, of Air National Guard; 24 Fighter Groups; three Light Bomb Groups; 12 Aircraft Control and Warning Groups; 12 Aircraft Control Squadrons; 24 Aircraft Control and Warning Squadrons; 72 Fighter Squadrons; 12 Communications Squadrons; 27 Air Service Squadrons; 84 Air Service Detachments; 12 Signal Light Construction Companies; 12 Radar Calibration Detachments; 84 Weather Stations; 84 Utility Flights; four Engineer Aviation Battalions; 12 Engineer Aviation Companies, and 12 U.S.A.F. Bands. Needless to say, this initial Troop Basis for the Air National Guard has undergone some significant and important modifications since 1946, but it is of historical interest as a part of the immediate postwar planning.

Likewise, Armored Divisions appeared for the first time in National Guard Troop Lists and the historic Cavalry shrank to a dozen or more Mechanized Squadrons. The 49th Armored Division was allocated to Texas; the 50th Armored to New Jersey. The remaining National Guard

498

Divisions continued in their traditional Infantry roles and as near as possible in their original State affiliations: 26th, Massachusetts; 27th, New York; 28th, Pennsylvania; 29th, Maryland, Virginia; 30th, North Carolina, Tennessee; 31st, Alabama, Mississippi; 32nd, Wisconsin; 33rd, Illinois; 34th, Iowa, Nebraska; 35th, Kansas, Missouri; 36th, Texas; 37th, Ohio; 38th, Indiana; 39th, Louisiana, Arkansas; 40th, California; 41st, Oregon, Washington; 42nd, New York; 43rd, Connecticut, Rhode Island, Vermont; 44th, Illinois; 45th, Oklahoma; 46th, Michigan; 47th, Minnesota, North Dakota; 48th, Florida, Georgia; 49th, California, and the 51st, South Carolina, Florida.

In addition to the 27 Divisions identified above, the initially-planned Troop Structure called for the National Guard to provide 21 Regimental Combat Teams; 33 Tank Battalions; 15 Mechanized Cavalry Squadrons; 123 Anti-Aircraft Artillery Battalions; 83 Coast Artillery Batteries; six Chemical Mortar Battalions; 14 Engineer Bridge Companies; 45 non-divisional Field Artillery Battalions; 21 Medical Battalions; 16 Military Police Battalions; 102 Ordnance Companies; 36 Quartermaster Companies; 13 Signal Battalions; 41 Radar Maintenance Units, and nine Army Security Units.

It was the most ambitious peacetime Troop Structure for units in being in American history. Such an ambitious program of military units to be created was contemplated for neither the Regular Army nor the Organized Reserve. It never was expected that these units would appear overnight. There were the usual progress phases and budget controls.

Indeed, one idea that neither General Tompkins, his Special Planning Division nor anyone else in the Pentagon through 1944-45 had bothered to question, was their assumption that all future sessions of Congress would vote funds to support anything that might be planned. The war years had gotten the Pentagon planners into the habit of being quite sure the money could and would come from somewhere to buy anything that was sufficiently planned in detail. This proved to be the basic assumption that was in gross error.

The Congress became highly money-conscious the day Japanese officers signed the capitulation papers aboard U.S.S. *Missouri*. Thus money suddenly became tightly budgeted instead of being dumped into a general war account with every Bureau head carrying bundles of no-limit blank checks—at least, that is the way it seemed so long as hostilities were in progress.

Thus the first unit of the new Guard to be Federally-recognized was on June 30, 1946, the night before the beginning of the new Fiscal Year. The unit was the 120th Fighter Squadron, Colorado Air National Guard. By December 31, 1948, the Guard was more than half-again larger than its strength in officers and men when inductions into Federal service begin in 1940. On that date it numbered 310,322 officers and men. They were distributed among 4,875 units in 4,000 cities and towns of the Nation and its Territories.

At the same time Congress and the public were beginning to ask whence could come the money to pay for these and all other ambitious plans for Armed Forces when there was no war. The Guard was approaching the day when it would be confronted by discharges to meet cutbacks in units where attrition would not keep the Guard within its allotted share of funds available. That day came when the Guard's growth strength had reached 356,473, during the Fiscal Year ended June 30, 1949. The squeeze was put on to reduce to 341,000 without delay.

But military strengths of volunteer citizen-soldiers cannot be played like an accordion. When the contraction is forced, it is impossible to stop on a nice, neat, budgetary note of 341,000, but the Guard fluctuated toward but under that figure until the outbreak of hostilities in Korea, the first week of June, 1950. The 4,597 units in being were then at functional strengths, better-equipped, and, thanks to the heavy percentage of combat veterans in commissioned and NCO grades, far more experienced and better-trained than those inducted in 1940-41. In numbers, however, they were considerably short of the 80% of war strength that had been idealistically planned, without regard to costs, back in 1944-45.

But the National Guard, among the defense agencies,* was not alone in feeling the Budget Bureau's knife. The downward impetus of a similar cutback from a strength of 677,000 to a revised budgeted strength of 630,000 had actually carried the Regular Army down to 591,487, as of June, 1950. At the same time, only 68,785 officers and 117,756 enlisted men of the Army Organized Reserve were in activated, training and drilling units. They were distributed among 10,629 units, compared with 324,761 Ground Forces Guardsmen in slightly less than 5,000 units as of the same date.

---

* Inevitably, the National Guard was caught-up in the turmoil over defense policies and defense reorganization which followed World War II. With so-called "unification" of the military forces as a goal, Congress enacted the National Security Act of July 26, 1947. It created a National Military Establishment, separated the Air Force from the Army, and established co-equal Departments of the Army, the Navy, and the Air Force, all under a Department of Defense. In theory, the latter was to have been a small, coordinating agency; as events proved, it was to grow enormously and assume operational functions reaching down into minute details of each of the Military Department's operations. The strain of adjudicating conflicting claims of the rival Services for roles and missions—and for their slice of the all-important appropriations pie—drove the first Defense Secretary, James V. Forrestal, to suicide, May 22, 1949. Among other things, there had been bitter conflict occasioned by efforts, in the guise of advancing the cause of "unification," to Federalize the Guard, both Army and Air. Meantime, effective Oct. 1, 1948, the National Guard Bureau had been reorganized to consist of an Army Division and an Air Force Division, each headed by a General Officer of the Guard, the whole being under the Chief of the Bureau itself, also a Guardsman. The reorganized Bureau was placed in *both* the Dept. of the Army *and* the Dept. of the Air Force—an arrangement which, despite some early skepticism, has worked very well, indeed.

There were an additional 390,961 non-training Organized Reservists about equally divided between officers and enlisted men. Conventionally they were participating in no military activity and for whom the War Department had no effective address lists. Many of them considered themselves completely out, to all practical purposes, but had not gotten around to requesting transfer to the Honorary Reserve. This category had become the catch-all list for thousands who had accepted Reserve status and the terminal promotion, but whose work and other duties in the new postwar World obviously precluded volunteering for any kind of service short of another all-out call and Draft of all Obligors. Indeed, the rotation idea, planted before the end of hostilities, had taken deep root and had floriated rapidly. Outside of the retained volunteers in the fractionally-paid units of the Guard and the Organized Reserve, plus the greatly-diminished fulltime Active Army, the only legally strong source for masses of manpower as fillers for depleted units was the newly-enacted Selective Service law.

The Air National Guard also was feeling the Budget pinch at 45,000 officers and men. They were in transition to new equipment and applicable organizational modifications. Nevertheless, no less than 20 Fighter Squadrons already were in jets.

In truth, America had diminished her military strength to a dangerously low point. The situation was even worse than the figures suggest. "Parkinson's Law," which is but little more than a witty professor's whimsical explanation of a phase of the law of diminishing return, was in full operation throughout the Armed Forces in general and in the Department of the Army in particular. Typically, throughout this immediate postwar period, the War Department, and its successor Department of the Army, carried on its payrolls slightly more than 300,000 civilian employes, 275,000 of them within the Continental United States, in addition to the Regular Army figure given above. Thus with nearly a million people, in and out of uniform, on the Department of the Army fulltime payrolls, as of December 31, 1949, the Army's *actual cutting edge* was down to a mere 10 Divisions (seven of Infantry, two Airborne, one Armored), four Armored Cavalry Regiments, five Regimental Combat Teams, two Infantry Regiments, 43 AAA Battalions, four Heavy Tank Battalions, 11 nondivisional Field Artillery Battalions and one Engineer Special Brigade.

Moreover, these cutting-edge units were far from war strength in most instances, even though they were dispersed from Okinawa to Berlin; from Alaska to the Panama Canal Zone. The 1st Division, its three associated Armored Cavalry Regiments (Constabulary duty) and single AAA Battalion in Germany, was nearest war strength of any. In Japan the 1st Cavalry (at last organized as Infantry), 7th, 24th and 25th Infantry Divisions and their seven associated AAA Battalions, were all under war strength with some Battalions and lesser units having stored their combat equipment, so their personnel could be transferred to beef-up other Battalions. As late as June, 1950, following some Draft legislation and a recruiting drive to strengthen the field formations, the four Divisions in Japan were each two or three thousand understrength when the North Koreans began hostilities.*

Though the World War II Draft legislation had been permitted to expire, on President Truman's recommendation, March 31, 1947, the conscription machinery had been kept intact on a sort of standby basis. The rising tensions with Russia, dramatized by the Berlin Airlift, were the impetus back of Public Law 759, 80th Congress. This new Selective Service measure, which became effective June 24, 1948, was to expire automatically June, 1950. It was calculated to give the Selective Service machinery a sort of test run which, in turn, would greatly expedite voluntary recruiting, not only for the Active Armed Forces, but for the National Guard and Organized Reserves of the Army, Air Force, Navy, Marine Corps and Coast Guard. Neither the Congress nor the Administration was yet in a frame of mind to appropriate funds for much more armed and active personnel than they had already.

The Act registered 8,500,000 young men, 18 through 25 years of age. Eighteen-year-olds could volunteer for one year of active duty, to be transferred thence to membership in a Reserve unit for not more than one month of refresher training active duty in any one year. They could thereby get off the immediate recall hook within six years, or at age 24. Failing to exercise this option prior to age 19, the registrant became vulnerable to 21 months of active duty followed by a recall obligation within the following five years. Lack of adequate appropriations practically nullified the law, but it did expedite recruiting for the Active Army, as well as for the Navy and Air Force, to the budgeted strength of each, and fielded about 30,000 actual Selectees into Army Training Centers and units stationed within the Continental United States. This was the situation when the first gunfire in Korea, 0400, June 24, 1950, signaled the invasion of South Korea by 90,000 North Korean field troops, spearheaded by 150 Russian T-34 tanks. This event not only breathed new life into this expiring, putative Draft Law, but quickly launched the Department of Defense into personnel studies and legislative programs while fighting a war.

---

* As Maj. Gen. William F. Dean's 24th Infantry Division (Regular Army) was in movement to halt the aggression, 2,108 men were transferred to it from the other three more distant Divisions to bring the 24th to its war strength of 15,965. Until receiving these reinforcements and the calling-in of personnel from deached duties incident to occupation chores, guard duty and housekeeping details, some of the Infantry and Artillery units of all four Divisions had been skeletonized to records-keeping detachments with their heavy weapons and artillery pieces in storage. The 24th was chosen for initial commitment to Korea because it was in Southern Japan and nearest Korea.

In the Department of the Army there was apparently an erroneous initial decision. The commitment to it quickly became so firm that change appeared politically inexpedient to the White House, hence impossible, assuming General of the Army Omar N. Bradley as Chairman of the Joint Chiefs of Staff and General J. Lawton Collins as Army Chief of Staff ever had any desire for the change.* As in most military situations, General Collins could, on advice and details provided by his General Staff, presumably choose any one of a few general lines of action, or perhaps a combination of two or more. The three major choices of possible personnel policies may be summarized as follows:

(1) To exhaust the possibilities of volunteer units and manpower for the duration with recourse to drafted Selectees for fillers if and when necessary. Announcement of the last recourse could be counted upon to stimulate volunteering. Such was the historic formula and which then existed within preamble and spirit of the current legislation. This decision would have meant that the entire National Guard be activated without delay, and its units and those of the Regular Army at once filled by active volunteering for the duration. Any resulting shortages could be filled for the duration through slight modification of existing Selective Service laws, which from the outset would expedite volunteering. The Federal units of the Organized Reserve of the Army immediately needed, and not available elsewhere, would be activated. Additional officers and enlisted specialists needed would be drawn from the Organized Reserves weekly drill pay status; thereafter by Military Occupational Specialty needs from voluntarily-available Reservists, commissioned and enlisted, from the great unassigned pool remaining from World War II. Having thus activated the needed Reservists (who at one time had volunteered or they would not have continued being Reservists), the Draft would be used to fill units for the Korean duration only in case recalls of volunteers and new volunteering did not fill the units. Dependence for future Reserve manpower strength, should the situation worsen into World War III, would be heaviest upon Selective Service machinery, uncalled Reserves, Officer Candidate Schools, and stepped-up creation of units and drafted Trainees. Meanwhile, America, the only

---

* From an historical viewpoint, it is too soon to assess any individual responsibility for errors and virtues (if any) in the personnel policies through the so-called Korean Police Action in the name of the United Nations. The entire policy from the beginning and throughout may have been pursuant to political directives. But from within the Pentagon, at the time, the atmosphere and impression prevailed that the Secretary of Defense, the Chiefs of Staffs of the Armed Forces and their departmental General Staffs had enjoyed and held the initiative in planning throughout, and thoroughly approved what was being done, and that the Administration was going along with them happily, rather than vice versa.

holder of nuclear bombs, had a massive deterrent against a World War III independent of immediately-available, massive manpower.

(2) Another option was to hold a large, semi-active strategic reserve, equipped, functional and in being, against the situation worsening into World War III, and to fight the entire police action with the Regular Army formations immediately beefed-up to war strength by volunteers for the duration and by orders to willing officers and enlisted men of the Organized Reserve by MOS. Any additional units needed for logistical duties to be called from among the more than 10,000 Organized Reserve units, with utilization of Selective Service and Replacement Training Centers for fillers for the duration. This would have meant leaving all the National Guard Divisions and Army Reserve combat units in status quo as the strategic reserve against the evil day of another World War III. Such ostentatious joining of Ground Forces in strategic reserve, along with airpower and the atomic bomb (which the Russians did not have), would have greatly impressed the Foreign Offices of all nations.

(3) For the immediate problem and for the long-range military health and posture of the Nation and with a popular tide running strong for Universal Military Training, a third option could be to build-up a vast backlog of militarily-trained young manpower, each young officer and man with an MOS number, or numbers, address, and telephone numbers neatly set up for IBM-type business machines, all of them obligated to compulsory active duty for varying terms of years into the future. Therein would be the makings of a future triumph over Russia's 175 active and well-equipped Divisions should the dreaded World War III come. To this end and in the name of the popular idea of rotation, the officers and men already in hand (Regulars, Guardsmen, part-pay Organized Reservists) should be utilized as little as possible; the Korean fighting should be held on a limited liability basis, utilizing as few units as practicable for contact with the enemy and for training, and flow through them the mass of individuals being rotated. Should the situation worsen into World War III, the machine records would purr; orders could be machine-printed, folded, enveloped and mailed. The millions of needed officers and men would appear on schedule at a stipulated place and date, each officer and man in his proper MOS slot, to constitute without delay the scores of Divisions and hundreds of lesser units essential for fighting Russia's 175 Divisions through a World War III. Meanwhile, the overseas Regulars would be joined by the Guard Divisions, from the strategic reserve of units in being, powerfully beefed-up by machine-selected trained men, to cope with the situation until the machine records-created Divisions of Korean-trained reserve manpower shook-down and flowed to the Theater, or Theaters, of Operations.

The comparative merits and disadvantages of each line of personnel

504

policy are obvious. Of the three, the last option was the most pessimistic. It could only envision such certain need in the foreseeable future for such a mass of militarily-trained manpower that a maximum number of men within the military ages should be trained, card-indexed by MOS numbers and regimented into a callable citizen-army of paper Divisions. Preparation of manpower for a bigger war becomes primary; immediate victory in Korea becomes secondary and an excuse for World War III preparedness, if this option be chosen.

The second choice was the most optimistic. It implied that the Army's 300,000 fulltime civilian employes, and 591,487 officers and men in the Active Army, with the support of willing and available Army Reservists, could and would maintain enough cutting-edge formations to assist the South Koreans in a field victory over Communism in Korea. Such a decision would have left all National Guard units at home stations and disturbed the fewest number of civilians in their normal pursuits. *But it would have assumed a far more efficient utilization of existing, full-time, payroll manpower than the Department of the Army was then achieving with its cutting edge of only 10 under-strength Divisions.*

The first-mentioned personnel policy option was the most tradition-ally American; i.e., quick and thorough defeat for the active enemy in the field. The quicker the victory, the more effective the deterrent against teetering neutrals and pseudo-neutrals, with the less likely future need for any strategic Ground Force reserves. Moreover, neither by sea nor by air did any potential enemy, or combination of enemies, in 1950, have the capability for destroying the massive, strategic, potential in in-dustry and manpower that America twice had demonstrated within the memories of all the leading European and Asiatic statesmen of that year.

Accordingly the first option should have been adopted forthrightly and without delay. Prompt victory should have been achieved. When the myth of Chinese volunteers was invoked by the Other Side to prolong the War (for such it truly was), comparable forces from another valid American ally, Nationalist China, should have been put on the Korean battlefront. Their place in Formosa could have been taken-over by a few American Divisions as a potential striking force for a highly-limited objective such as liberation of a significant Communist seaport on the Chinese Mainland. The thought of a cankering, Capitalistic sore on the side of Asiatic Communism would have brought home in jig-time Mao Tse-tung's "volunteers" to North Korea without such a "liberation" ever being necessary. Thus a quickly-unified Korea could have emerged with the North boundary on the historic line of the Yalu River. A fuller faith would have been kept with two Asiatic allies and there would have been no confusing World propaganda as to who won and lost in Korea.

But the Joint Chiefs of Staff, in the first few hours of the crisis, aided and abetted by a timid State Department, and under a President who was prone to leave details to departmental and bureaucratic professionals, appear to have staked-out the most limited objectives possible with an intent of handling the police action within the optimistic limits of the second choice. The rapidity of the North Korean advance and early restriction of American forces to the thinly- and desperately-held Pusan perimeter imposed upon them personnel policies that borrowed from all three, but most heavily from the highly pessimistic third option. As often happens when combinations of diverging major options are adopted, the Department of Defense appears to have fallen between the chairs and with considerably less-than-fortunate results.

## LEGISLATION FOR ROTATION

The first move, of course, was to breathe new life into the expiring Selective Service Act of 1948. The Selective Service Extension Act of 1950 (Public Law 599, 81st Congress) was the immediate result. It further empowered the President to order Reserve Components of any and all the Armed Services to involuntary active Federal service for not to exceed 21 months. This later was extended to July 1, 1953, and the period of service increased from 21 to 24 months (Public Law 51, 82nd Congress). Cognate legislation likewise extended expiring enlistments in the Active Armed Forces for an additional 12 months with subsequent extensions of this authority until July 1, 1953. The initial impact of this legislation upon the National Guardsmen was identical with that upon the Organized Reserve and non-training Volunteer Reserve, but for one major exception. The Guardsmen would be called as units. Most of the Army Reserves, or Federal Militia, eventually would be called as individuals.

The indecisive quality of the General Staff, Pentagon leadership in this crisis is reflected by the hot-and-cold attitudes toward the Guard. Although there was the prompt reminder that functional Guard units were immediately available, the initial and informal word was that Army units and Headquarters were not needed—just individuals as fillers and perhaps some Service of Supply units to be activated from the Organized Reserve. The retreat from Seoul to the Pusan Perimeter quickly changed that tune. Oklahoma's 45th Infantry Division, Major General James C. Styron, and California's 40th, Major General Daniel H. Huddleston, were alerted at home stations in July. They were Federalized September 1 and quickly beefed to war strength with Selectees. Pennsylvania's 28th, Major General Daniel B. Strickler, and the 43rd, Connecticut, Rhode Island and Vermont, Major General Kenneth Cramer, likewise were alerted. These two additional Divisions were Federalized four days later, September 5, 1950.

As the military tides ebbed and flowed, Pusan to the Yalu and back to Seoul, and grinding counteroffensives followed, four additional National Guard Divisions were ordered into Federal service. They were the 31st, Alabama and Mississippi, Major General Alexander G. Paxton; 44th, Illinois, Major General Harry L. Bolen; 37th, Ohio, Major General Leo M. Kreber, and 47th, Minnesota and North Dakota, Major General Norman E. Hendrickson.

Nor were these all. Twenty-two combat Wings of the Air National Guard, with their combat support units to a total of 84% of the National Guard Air arm were Federalized in the first weeks of the conflict. Practically all personnel of the Air Guard units saw early and continuous service in Korea. Also phased into the Korean Affair were additional Ground Force units: three Regimental Combat Teams and 714 Company-size Guard units to an aggregate of 34% of the Guard Ground Forces being mobilized, for an aggregate strength of Air Guardsmen to 45,000 officers and men, and in the Guard Ground Forces, 138,600 officers and men.

Most of the early-alerted Air National Guard and non-divisional Ground Force units were deployed quickly to Korea. They were followed by California's 40th and Oklahoma's 45th Infantry Divisions. But Pennsylvania's 28th and New England's 43rd were rushed to Germany, and Tennessee's 3rd Battalion, 178th Infantry Regiment, found itself the nucleus of a prospective defense force for Iceland. The Guard Divisions and non-divisional units that remained in the States for less spectacular training roles quickly found themselves constantly decimated by long order lists of individual officers and men to proceed to the Far East to become replacements in the embattled Regular Army Divisions. Most Guardsmen thus arrived in Korea as individual replacements. A comparatively small percentage were sent even to Alaska, Panama Canal Zone and to Europe to sustain rotation of Active Army personnel policies in those areas. In brief, no less than four of the National Guard Divisions quickly became personnel-receiving, unit training, and pumping stations in the pipeline maze of service options and short-term rotations into which the Pentagon bureaucrats, both in and out of uniform, were stumbling as fast as they could request the legislation.

The eight activated Guard Divisions, heavy as they were in Staff and command teams of officers and men in all ranks and ratings for their respective types of combat units, would have been far more valuable to the Nation had they been kept intact, filled with personnel for the duration and strategically positioned in the Far East Theater, or deployed on the line in Korea, for a prompt, field solution to that unwanted imbroglio. All their officers, except some of the Lieutenants, and the key enlisted personnel, had seen service, many in cutting-edge units, in one to seven campaigns, representing all Theaters, of the recently-ended World War II.

Indeed, all the National Guard units and as many as needed of the partial pay status personnel of the Organized Reserve, should have been mobilized without delay and for the duration, as contemplated in earlier legislation and planning. *It was for such that they had volunteered.* Had this been done and the units beefed to war strength by additional volunteering, stimulated by prospective drafts, much confusion and subsequent unnecessary expense could have been avoided. But this suggestion at the time brought the outraged complaint that it would result in excess units of some types and leave shortages elsewhere. Consolidations and transfers for the creation of needed units would result in officers and men in assignments out of line with their Military Occupation Specialty skills and numerals, it was argued.

This logical but spurious argument not only sold-short the often-demonstrated versatility of the citizen-soldier, but ignored the patent fact that it is easier, quicker and more efficient to redesignate and convert an existing unit to a new purpose than to create a unit from scratch. The rapidity and ease with which Cavalry units, for example, had been converted to Field Artillery in the two previous wars, was completely ignored. As one Staff wit of the era remarked: "An existing Laundry Company can be expanded and trained into a Foot-Washing Battalion for close Infantry support quicker than machine records can find, select-out and order to camp, process and group the required number of men with MOS numerals indicative of skills as Chiropodistical Assistants; and after groupment they still would not be a functional unit." But neither the suggestion nor the humor was appreciated in the Pentagon. The General Staff dream of a great mass of young, individual citizens, each trained and card-indexed to a military skill, associated as much as possible with a civilian trade, transitional skill or a profession, had captured imaginations. It could be done by short terms of compulsory service of not more than 24 months in the name of rotation and future long-term vulnerability to recall to active duty.

There was also the urge within the Defense Department to get the Reservists of all the Armed Services into one legislative package. It was considered synonymous with unification of the Services. Thus came into existence the Armed Forces Reserve Act of 1952, approved July 9. Actually the Act codified many previous statutes concerning Reserves of the Armed Services; and provided and equalized pretty much across-the-board various benefits for all Reservists. At the same time it retained many earlier concepts and practices peculiar to each Armed Service. Basically, it provided that each of the Armed Forces should maintain a Ready Reserve, a Standby Reserve and a Retired Reserve. Within this broad structure, with its stipulated degrees of future vulnerability to call, there were seven Reserve Components for all the Armed Forces.

They were:
1. The Army National Guard of the United States.
2. The Army Reserve.
3. The Naval Reserve.
4. The Marine Corps Reserve.
5. The Air National Guard of the United States.
6. The Air Force Reserve.
7. The Coast Guard Reserve.

With each of the foregoing subdivided into Ready, Standby, and Retired Reserves (except the Army and Air Guard components which are 100% in the Ready Reserve status with no "Standby"), the Armed Forces found themselves in position to offer more options to a vulnerable Selective Service registrant, than an alert life insurance salesman could propose to a reluctant prospect. They were calculated to get him to volunteer for his own choice of a Service ahead of the hot breath of the Draft Board. The shorter his choice for active duty, the longer he would be on a high-priority, Reserve hook, combined with home and Summer training periods and subject to recalls as a member of the Ready Reserve. The longer the period of active duty for which he volunteered and served, the sooner he would pass into the status of an almost invulnerable-to-recall member of the non-training Standby Reserve. The Retired Reserve largely consisted of long-service officers and enlisted men from active units of the Ready Reserve.

From the beginning of the Korean hostilities, the non-flying, base support elements of the Air Force and the reasonably-comfortable naval shore stations and ships, proved to be far more attractive to volunteers than were the Army options. Thus, quite early in the game, the former two Armed Forces were able to jack-up entrance requirements for all who presented themselves at recruiting stations. At times admission to an Ivy League university seemed less demanding. For training within certain skills, four-year enlistments were required. This in turn shortened the reserve obligation. None but the Marine Corps and the Army found it necessary to use Draftees as fillers. These usually elected the 24-months minimum. The popularity of this choice was increased when it became apparent that Reception Centers, basic training, unit training, specialty training, travel and pipeline time with two months' terminal leave time, often reduced the two-year period to a few months overseas and a matter of weeks in the presence of the enemy, if at all.* In the Pentagon, this "revolving door" personnel plan for fighting a "brushfire"

---

* This option was made even more palatable by the educational benefits of $110 to $160 a month for 36 months of post-active duty educational or vocational training benefits. Indeed, the more than 2,000,000 young men whose college education most likely is due to the Korean Affair, are now America's principal residual asset from that imbroglio.

war was justified by the theory that a vast backlog of recallable manpower had to be created just in case Russia promoted the Korean hassle into World War III. At the same time, wartime restrictions were reimposed upon some strategic materials such as structural steel. There is little wonder that Stalin cherished fond dreams of bankrupting American Capitalism with such ungearing harassments. Moreover, it could be that Stalin was succeeding better than he dreamed, for it was during this period that Russia largely closed the gap between herself and America in atomic weapons and soon was able to surpass America in rocket thrusts for space exploration.

## STATISTICS FROM THE "REVOLVING DOOR" POLICY

Admittedly, the battle casualty rate in Korea was not exorbitant. In the 37 months between June 25, 1950, and July 27, 1953, the American battle deaths in Korean fighting totaled 33,629, compared with the 53,402 for the 14 months that American troops were in combat during World War I. Deaths from automobile accidents in the United States for the three years, 1951-53, inclusive, totaled 115,090. Hospitalizations from auto accidents in the same period probably bear the same ratio to the 103,284 wounds, less than mortal, from the Korean conflict. This suggests the crippling and injuring American traffic accidents in a comparable 37 months must have wounded 345,000. Consequently, one hardly can argue that the price was excessive in terms of blood and tears, assuming that the auto is causing Americans to become accustomed to sudden and violent deaths and disabilities. Certainly the American casualty lists from Korea could be no measure of the damage the Kremlin hoped to do America via Korea.

The picture of disrupted manpower, waste of productive effort, and the gross inefficiency from the rapid rotation of hastily- and superficially-trained and seldom battle-experienced personnel was something else. Compared to the once-thought inefficiencies of World War I, the comparative combat yield that was *not* (repeat not) derived from the Korean mobilization is truly appalling. For the Army, Navy and Marine Corps in World War I, America put 4,734,991 Americans in uniform. Of these, 4,057,101 wore the high-collared Army blouse. In addition to the Army's Services of Supply at home and in France, the cutting-edge yield from these 4,000,000 soldiers totaled no less than 54 Divisions of approximately 27,000 officers and men each. Forty-two of these American Divisions landed overseas. In addition to the 12 that the Armistice found still in the States and well advanced in their training, four Divisions were in process of organization. Came the stillness of Armistice Day in France, 1918, and 29 of these Divisions were actually in combat on the Western Front, fighting as Divisions. Along with them were the non-

510

divisional Regiments and smaller units of combat troops directly under Corps and Field Army Commanders.

For the so-called Korean Police Action, and in striking contrast with the foregoing, America mobilized 5,720,000 officers and men. Their distribution among the Armed Services was as follows: Air Force, 1,285,000; Navy, 1,177,000; Marines, 424,000, and the Army, 2,834,000. The Army's combatant, cutting-edge yield, in terms of Divisions and proportional numbers of non-divisional, field support units, was a mere 20 Divisions with a combat strength of approximately 16,000 each. The support units, generally speaking, were also proportionally smaller than their corresponding units for World War I. Of the above-mentioned 20 Divisions, only eight, plus one Marine Corps Division, ever actually were committed to the Korean zone of operations.* The Department of the Army's slice of manpower shown here ignores the presence of more than a half-million civilian employes on the Department of the Army payrolls throughout most of the three years of the Korean Affair. In his Semiannual Report for the period ended June 30, 1953, the Army Secretary proudly reported that the civilian employe "reduction goals set by the Department of Defense were bettered by more than 100 per cent." The reduction was "from 543,853 to 504,490" civilians.**

The explanation for such a mass of manpower being "payrolled," if not mobilized, for such a small operation and productive of such a small combatant cutting-edge, was a result of several factors.

(1) The commitment to an almost absolute reliance upon the Draft with short-term rotation of personnel taking priority over the achieve-

---

* They were the 2nd, 3rd, 7th, 24th, 25th and the 1st Cavalry Division, which is actually an Infantry outfit. The remaining two, the 40th and 45th, were National Guard Infantry Divisions. Also in Korea was the 1st Marine Division and about a third (187th Regimental Combat Team, Reinforced) of the 11th Airborne Division, most of the operations of which were as Infantry. Also in the Order of Battle lists from the beginning were eight Korean Divisions of about 8,000 each; two reinforced Infantry Brigades plus air and naval units from England, and sundry oddments such as the Turkish Brigade and even smaller U.N. token forces from other countries. As a peninsula, Korea was most vulnerable to off-shore bombardments and air strikes from carriers and U.S. Air Force bases in Japan as well as in Korea. Without such support, undreamed-of in World War I, so few Ground Force Divisions could not have done so much. But in proportion to the manpower, ships and planes fielded and with less of a rotation and turnover problem, one may well wonder if they were any more efficient in terms of results than was the Department of the Army.

** On February 4, 1953, the Department of Defense and Armed Forces civilian employe lists were "frozen at 1,330,000." By June 30, 1953, the figure had been reduced by 73,000. The above statistics for the Army indicate more than half of the reduction was at the expense of the Department of the Army. The Navy's share of civilian employes at the end of the Fiscal Year, June 30, 1953, was 448,478; that of the Air Force, 302,200. These totals suggest that not more than 2,000 civilians were directly under the Office of the Secretary of Defense, whose duties then were largely policy-making and coordinative over the three Armed Forces Secretaries. Increasing ratios of civilian employes to the men actually in uniform have been an Armed Forces headache since 1900. The conventional, and often-justified explanation: Personnel with the essential education, experience, technical knowledge and skills can be neither employed nor retained within the pay scales and promotion policies of the uniformed Armed Services.

511

ment of a victory was most significant. As one combatant Army officer explained: "We were creating real combat units from the Pusan Perimeter to the Yalu and in the recoil from Chinese aggression. It was then that someone set up the Revolving Door at all ports of embarkation and disembarkation. You can't maintain Squad, Platoon, Company, Battery, Battalion and Divisional teams with constantly-rotating personnel. Key officers and men, combat-seasoned, melted away according to the calendar. Some successors came and went before they had become fully accustomed to living under static, combat conditions, not to mention actually fighting. Repple-Depple replacements normally arrived, with OCS junior officers as well as men actually counting their days of vulnerability to field service on their fingers until the calendar would rotate them back, out, and away from it all. There was no knitting of a mutual confidence in one another through association in strife and danger, through fire and movement, such as one gets in realistic peacetime field work or actual combat. Without that mutual confidence and trusting interdependence all the way, up and down, there are no truly aggressive and effective field units." According to this officer and others, officers of all grades, including Generals, apparently often were rotated for no better reason than to give others in the same grade "the experience of command in the field." "Between calendar-watching," another added, "and the frustrations of uncertain missions (Were we there merely to get nominal combat experience or to win a war?) we did not have the unit combat-effectiveness for offensive operations after the Summer of 1951 that we developed before and after the Inchon Landings and counter-attacks following the truly masterful retreat from the Yalu." These off-the-record officer opinions concerning the policy of reluctant Selectees and rotation summarize this factor quite adequately.

(2) The operation of "Parkinson's Law" within the great American bureaucracy in general and within the Armed Forces in particular can hardly be ignored. The above figures for payrolled personnel, in and out of uniforms, speak more eloquently than words. Never in the history of warfare have so few combatants been serviced, managed and commanded by so many. And never was it so difficult to center responsibility. With electronic speed, responsibility "bucks" sparked back and forth along chains of command between combat unit commanders and the Pentagon, with the White House occasionally becoming a crackling terminal. General MacArthur's reluctance to field all "bucks" that came his way from Washington led to his dramatic relief by an irritated White House incumbent.

And the final factor was (3) the Army's erroneous adoption of the industrial concept that military operational skills can be fragmented into small occupational specialties in which each man makes the prescribed movements, applies the stipulated tools in the manner designated in

512

the Technical Manuals, and adjusts his speed to the pressure flow of an assembly line. The corollary followed that given enough thousands of such card-indexed men, all with essential military occupational skills and in proportion to and cognate with one another, an army of functional units of all sizes results. The ghastly error is in the basic truth that a battle line is not an assembly line. Army men and units cannot be geared to the flow of a production line; they are chained to a flow of field events affecting teamwork at varying speeds, down to and including Infantry Squads and Platoons. Moreover, approximately 50% of the events are from the secret designs of a fielded, enemy army—not from the neatly-scaled and easily-read blueprints of a factory chief. It could be that some Army General Staff specialists took the wrong leaf from a Navy notebook. Admittedly, the Navy is correct in training personnel for "billets" aboard floating, fighting machines. There, jobs and skills can be fragmented as in a factory. When a Destroyer Captain orders flank speed, rudder right and a closure of range to 4,000 yards, he knows the crew is going along, with each man in his battle station, performing his brief skills as a living organism within and geared to a vibrant machine. But land fighting is vastly different. The dispersal of men and essential material in the presence of modern weapons makes it even more so than was the case in bygone wars.

Military skills and knowledge are not difficult to acquire. They have become more complicated, but the level of mass education and transferable civilian knowledge and skills make it as easy to convert a modern civilian into a soldier as it was in George Washington's day.* But, then, and even more so today, the teamwork in all units at all levels, understanding of one another's job, problems and missions, combined with mutual confidence of members of the team, are of paramount importance. These can be achieved only through existence as units, training as units and association as units. The unit purpose and atmosphere, if at functional strength and properly equipped, as are most Guard units, motivate and accelerate speeds and precision in equipment skills far more effectively than do military classrooms of a Replacement Training Center. The officers and men further develop early an interchangeability of duties and skills. And any Company, Battery, Battalion or Division in which officers and men cannot function with precision, if

---

* It is realized that this statement is contrary to general opinion. But consider a few fundamentals. Some of Washington's officers and many of his enlisted men could not read. Their knowledge of mathematics and the most elementary laws of science, such as an inertial force resulting from a uniform motion, was an absolute blank. Washington had to issue an order against any of his troops trying to salvage enemy cannonballs before they stopped rolling; broken ankles were putting too many of his men on crutches. The American Chief of Artillery, then hoarding ammunition for an ultimate attack on Boston, thoughtlessly had announced a reward (perhaps a tot of rum) for all and sundry who retrieved and turned in a cannonball that had been shot at American positions by the British defenders of Boston. Warfare truly has become more scientific and technological, but so have the American civilians.

with less speed, in a number of assignments and military skills and thereby immediately adjust themselves to the demands of teamwork in spite of casualties—that unit is courting disaster. Had the Army units in Korea been fighting the Germans or the Japanese instead of the North Koreans and Chinese, the American Army would not have been allowed the expensive luxury of the great, short-term, rotation experiment.

A statistical picture of the Army as of a given date is revealed by gross figures for the last 12 months preceding the signing of the Armistice July 27, 1953. According to the Semiannual Report of the Secretary of the Army for the last half of the Fiscal Year ended June 30, 1953, the strength of the Army was being reduced from 1,596,419 officers, men and Cadets at West Point, to 1,533,815. The force structure consisted "of 20 divisions, 18 separate regiments and regimental combat teams, over 100 antiaircraft battalions, and more than 150 other combat battalions." Approximately 746,000 men entered the Army and about 809,000 were released; more than 650,000 had no prior service. Only 1.5% of all Army personnel on active duty June 30, 1953, were volunteer National Guardsmen and Reservists.

Never in American military history has such limited use been made of willing and voluntarily-available citizen-soldiers. Never in American history have so many willing and unwilling men and women been mobilized into organized military effort (5,720,000 in uniforms of the Armed Services, mostly for short terms, and a level of 1¼ million civilian employes throughout the period) for what most agreed was a minor war; and never in American history, not even in the dubious years of 1812-1814, has America fallen so far short of a victory. American and Republic of Korea Divisions still are garrisoning the Cease-Fire Line.

# Bibliographical Note For Chapter XIX

For postwar reorganization, the *Annual Reports of the Chief of the National Guard Bureau* for 1946 through 1954 are essential. Of equal value are the *Proceedings of the National Guard Association of the United States,* 1946 through 1954, and Chapter V of Martha Derthick's ms. *History of the National Guard Association,* as well as the *Semiannual Reports of the Secretary of Defense* for each last half of the Fiscal Years beginning with that for January 1 to June 30, 1949, through 1954. The last named also include the *Semiannual Reports* of the Secretaries for the three Armed Forces through the corresponding dates. The Federal *Statutes* covering the military legislation of the period are, of course, highly pertinent. The legislation, however, is exceptionally well-digested and evaluated in Eilene Galloway, *History of the United States Military Policy on the Reserve Forces, 1775-1957.* It is a 60-page public document (Government Printing Office, Washington, 1957) originally prepared for Subcommittee No. 1, Committee on Armed Services, House of Representatives, with its principal emphasis and space devoted to recent legislation. Mrs. Galloway's bibliography, which emphasizes other public documents, such as *Hearings* and *Reports* by and from Congressional Committees and Subcommittees, is a most convenient guide to even more detailed sources. A definitive, comprehensive history of the Korean War that interlocks all factors—economic, political, diplomatic and military—remains to be written. For a convenient digest of military facts and dates, "The Korean War," in the *Army Almanac* (1957), pp. 614-629, is a good compendium. The same is true of Chapter XX, pp. 654-695, of Colonels R. Ernest Dupuy and Trevor N. Dupuy, *Military Heritage of America,* 1956. Roy E. Appleman, *South of the Naktong, North to the Yalu, June to November, 1950,* from the Office of the Chief of Military History, Department of the Army, 1961, is a superb first volume of a new military series on the Korean operations by the Ground Forces. Other significant titles that merit the attention of military students of this period are Samuel L. A. Marshall, *The River and the Gauntlet,* 1953; James G. Westover's *Combat Support in Korea,* 1955; and C. Joseph Bernardo and Eugene H. Bacon, *American Military Policy,* 1955. Courtney Whitney, *MacArthur: His Rendezvous with History,* 1956, is disappointing. The Congressional investigation of General MacArthur's relief, published by the Government Printing Office under the title, *The Military Situation in the Far East,* has the virtues and weaknesses of most investigative reports. Though there has been since 1946 considerable growth in military literature analyzing the present and looking toward the future, there has been a tendency to neglect the problems offered by military personnel, both in the Active Army and the Reserves, as well as military manpower in general. The scholarly and legalistic monographs from the Government Printing Office prepared and released by the Selective Service System merit the attention of anyone interested in the manpower problem in terms of both the past and the present.

## CHAPTER XX

# The Air National Guard

MONSIEUR J. A. C. CHARLES, the French physicist, hardly had arrived back in Paris from Man's first free flight in a hydrogen-filled balloon, December, 1783, before at least one military theorist began advocating aeronautical reconnaissance. The youthful Captain Lazare N. M. Carnot, Corps de Genie, French Army, immediately wrote an essay on the subject. Came the French Revolution, and imaginative, free-wheeling, Anti-Monarchist Carnot quickly found himself Deputy for the Pas de Calais district. Just as suddenly he was the *de facto* French Minister of War with an impending invasion on his hands. An early move in his preparedness was the activation of an aeronautics school and balloon units for field duty. He deployed them on the Belgian frontier. The balloonists were credited with a major role in Carnot's climactic victory of Fleurus, 1794. Napoleon soon supplanted Carnot in French affairs military. His doctrines of fast marches and light baggage eliminated the further evolution of military aeronautics in that era. The

517

leadership of the armies of Europe through the Crimean War, 1854-56, was by professionals who had learned all they knew (and had forgotten nothing) from fighting against, or under, the great Napoleon.

It thus remained for the citizen-soldiers of America's Civil War to rediscover the balloon as a battlefield instrument. Major General George B. McClellan, erstwhile soldier and railroad President, was a most open-minded man when it came to equipment. Professors Joseph Henry and T. C. S. Lowe easily prevailed upon him to add a Balloon Section to his Army for the Peninsula Campaign. It consisted of two officers, 50 enlisted men, horses and vehicles, complete with two portable hydrogen generators, an acid cart and two balloons. McClellan made little use of them, though Major General Fitz-John Porter, whose bright military star was soon to set in a scapegoat court-martial following Second Bull Run, is said to have flown enough missions both in captive balloons and floating free over enemy lines to have rated him an Air Medal under World War II Regulations. At the same time Confederates also were experimenting with a balloon of many colors made of donated silk attire of Richmond ladies. American military aeronautics languished after the fast movements incident to the Antietam and Gettysburg campaigns. Moreover, the ease with which spies passed through Confederate and Federal lines made Civil War ballooning seem unnecessarily expensive and strenuous.

But military aeronautics made a dramatic comeback during the Franco-Prussian War, during the siege of Paris, 1871. More than 60 free flights carried passengers and carrier pigeons out of Paris to become the only means of communication between the beleagured City and the remainder of the World. But this merely categorized the air as a one-way street leading nowhere in particular except "out." Nevertheless, General Shafter took an Aeronautical Detachment with his Headquarters to Cuba for the Santiago Campaign. It was miserably handled. The narrow ford of a rapid river was chosen as the site for a captive balloon ascension. It drew so much fire and created so many needless casualties among crossing Infantry columns that a balloon on a battlefield became synonymous with a skunk at a lawn party.

This was the status of military thinking when the Wright brothers harnessed a gasoline engine and propeller into a big box-kite with vertical and lateral rudders plus built-in wingtips that could be curved or flattened for an aileron effect. It obviously converted the atmosphere into a two-way street, but the professionals viewed it with an even more jaundiced eye. Even so, it was an invention that initiated the World's third and greatest military revolution. Europe's discovery of the stirrup made the armored knight master of the battlefields for several centuries. Gunpowder took him off the horse and in our own day has banished that noble animal from military Tables of Organization.

518

Military aeronautics has greatly expanded the speed and scope of war but it has not rendered either the battlefield or the soldier obsolete. Nor is it possible for the missile to make the airman obsolete. Warfare has the quality of stripping mankind down to fundamentals at the same time that so-called new weapons are being perfected and adopted. No weapon, be it most elemental, ever is abandoned entirely. The hand grenade is no more than an explosive rock; the gun's projectile is merely a vastly-improved arrow. These improvements, like the airplane and the transoceanic missiles, are children of a man-made civilization, hence the proposition that Man can become obsolete within a man-made civilization is absurd on the face of it. It is remotely conceivable that Man can destroy himself as a race. But in that case, there will be no one to record his obsolescence, for the language also will have vanished. But before this dreary destiny will have been achieved, battles will have been fought, perhaps with sticks and stones, between defenders seeking to deny intruders the meager fruits of victory to be found in a devastated land. The group, or army, best disciplined and organized for teamwork, will survive longest, other factors being equal. Warfare reduces mankind to fundamentals at the same time that it is stimulating mankind to perfect and utilize increasingly-complex families of weapons. A major reverse easily can and occasionally does ungear and render almost impotent the interlocked and complex weapons systems, as did the loss of the Navy's battle line at Pearl Harbor and the destruction of MacArthur's airplanes on Luzon, but with less sophisticated weapons, the Army's opening battle continued for months on Bataan.

## GUARDSMEN LOOK SKYWARD

But the Great Debate on military aeronautics did not begin the December day, 1903, that the Wright brothers' first successful plane lifted from the beach at Kitty Hawk, North Carolina. Those initial flights were measured in feet and seconds. It was not until 1908, when the longer flights of the perfected planes and engines, in America by Orville Wright and in France by Wilbur Wright, startled a long-doubting World. Meanwhile, a well-educated young Italian, age 20, and burning with enthusiasm for anything that might get off the ground, arrived in New York from Turin. For convenience he changed his name from Mario Terenzio Enrico Casalegno to Henry Woodhouse, and began grinding-out articles on aeronautics. He and his writings were massively ignored by all except a few members of an embryonic association that styled itself the Aero Club of America, and a few New York City National Guardsmen who were habitues of the 71st New York Regiment's Armory. Admittedly some of the interest of the latter stemmed from the thought that an off-Broadway balloon ascension might stimulate recruiting.

But from all motives there was interest enough for the Aero Club members to get through the door and feel at home. Some Aero Club men became Guardsmen, particularly after May 1, 1908. That was the day the 1st Signal Company, New York National Guard, began receiving instruction, with a 35,000-cubic-foot balloon owned by A. Leo Stevens. "The lesson was the official beginning of the plan to make aeronautics a part of the study and work of the signal corps" of the National Guard of New York, according to the New York *Herald* of that date. To that end an aeronautic unit of 25 men, commanded by Major Oscar Erlandson, had been organized as an integral part of the State's Signal Corps. There was a growing and sustained interest. Hudson Maxim and a Columbia University professor were among their instructors in 1911. Under modern bureaucratic centralization, with its outflow of directives and supervision, such initiative would be impossible.

Heavier-than-air craft soon captured their imagination. The 1st Signal Company financed, to the extent of $500, a do-it-yourself, home-constructed airplane. It was with the Company at the Pine Camp, Summer of 1910, through the field instruction period. A copy of an early Farman type, it was built by Private Phillip W. Wilcox, a student at Columbia University. For reason of weather or facilities, it was not flown at Pine Camp. Wilcox later crashed it at Mineola and walked away from the debris to achieve the rank of Major in the burgeoning Air Corps of World War I.

Notwithstanding this initial reverse with an airplane, by August, 1912, the unit definitely was flying missions in training maneuvers. But most missions were by a Curtiss-owned plane accompanied by a well-known early bird test pilot then carried on the Guard roster and so reported in the Press as being Private Beckwith Havens.

In that Summer, the National Guard units of New England and New York concentrated on opposite sides of the lower stretches of the Housatonic River for a brief war between the Blues, West and defending, against the Reds, from the East and invading. The Regular Army participated and there was wide interest in the maneuvers. Most attention was attracted by a Lieutenant Benjamin D. Foulois, U. S. Army. The reporter misspelled his name, but since he was still some years short of two stars and Chief of the Air Corps, it is not likely that the editor made an issue of it. Foulois's claim to fame through those maneuvers was a forenoon flight in which he rose to an altitude of no less than 3,080 feet, flew "all the way to Bridgeport," located every hostile troop camp or concentration, and was back on the ground within an hour and 15 minutes. Even so, Private Havens' flying stunts were what most Guardsmen present remembered longest.

After 1912, the New York Guard began clamoring for planes, but the Army would give it nothing. Hat in hand, the Guardsmen went back to their old friends in the Aero Club. By this time, Henry Wood-house was flourishing as editor of *Aircraft* and founder and publisher of *Flying* and *Aerial Age*. Through him they found vast sympathy, much publicity and some money. Forward-looking men were deciding that the airplane had come to stay.

Among them was Guardsman Raynauld Cawthorne Bolling, a native of Arkansas with a law degree from Harvard, who, at the age of 35, was doing quite well in the Big City. He was General Solicitor for the U. S. Steel Co., and a Director and President of lesser corporations. At Pine Camp Summer training he flew missions that convinced General O'Ryan that New York's Division (later the 27th) merited a separate Aeronautics unit. It was activated as the 1st Aero Company, N.G., N. Y., November 1, 1915. It proved to be a precursor of the 2nd Aero Company, N.G., N. Y., that was organized in Buffalo the following year.*

The two New York Aero Companies were called into Federal Service in July, 1916, and stationed at Mineola Aviation Field, Long Island. The Balloon Section of the Divisional Signal Corps unit does appear on the Mexican Border Station List, but Lieutenant Raynauld C. Bolling's heavier-than-air command served but 10 weeks and spent that time in training within the limits of their initial station. The Buffalo Company was mustered-out September 8, 1916, and never reorganized at home station. The 1st Aero Company stayed on until November 2 of the same year, but some of the officers of both Companies completed their training on their own time and expense through the following Winter.

In truth, the Regular Army did not want them on any terms, even though they had taken into service as unit property their own planes, which, for the most part, were of the type most widely-known later as "Jennies." They also had two DH, open-cockpit bombers, a type already in production in America for export to the embattled Allies of World War I. Their only aid toward procurement of such flight equipment appears to have been the Woodhouse-inspired $12,500 from the Aero Club and $5,000 from the State of New York. The Army particularly looked askance at such a small unit that had on its rolls a dozen or more officers and men of the position and caliber of U. S. Steel Attorney Bolling and James E. Miller, Vice-President of the Columbia Trust Company. When America entered the War, April, 1917, the War Department decision promptly was made that there would be no National Guard aviation units. The New York 1st Aero Company was disbanded and most of its personnel tendered their services as individuals. Almost

---

* There were stirrings toward aviation units in other States. Simultaneous with those in New York, most particularly in Ohio and Pennsylvania where occasional officers integrated their interest in flying with their military service. In Ohio a Lt. Col. Winder was particularly active, but his flying was as an individual rather than through association with an aeronautical unit of the Guard. There was similar interest among State Naval Militiamen in "hydroplanes" that resulted in unit efforts.

without exception they at once were taken into the Officers Reserve Corps, authorized in the legislation of the preceding year, and were given initial Reserve ranks higher than they had held in the Guard. As a full Colonel, Bolling was killed in France, oddly enough, while on a ground reconnaissance. Miller's death was in one of the conventional plane duels that characterized early aerial combat. Bolling Field, Washington, D. C., and Miller Field, on Staten Island, commemorate their voluntary service and sacrifice.*

The foregoing brief survey of early enthusiasms for modernity of thought and action in New York dramatizes the short-sightedness of the War Department General Staff of that era. The same interest and latent enthusiasm were extant in the National Guard Headquarters of other States, but they had neither the funds nor the equipment available to cultivate it. There were instances where far-sighted, imaginative State Adjutants General lent a degree of official sanction and semi-official sponsorship to air enthusiasts without the slightest degree of War Department monetary, material or other support. For example, a month after California's Major General E. A. Forbes saw the famed Eugene Ely land his Curtiss biplane aboard the cruiser, U.S.S. *Pennsylvania,* the first ship in history to receive a plane, in March, 1911, he organized the Aeronautical Detachment of the 7th Company, Coast Artillery Corps, National Guard of California—with Ely as a Private! Immediately afterward, three members of the Company were detailed to the Curtiss Aviation School at San Diego, they to pass-along their lore to the other members of the Detachment. Commissioned a Second Lieutenant in the California National Guard on July 27, 1911, Ely was killed, a matter of weeks later, in an exhibition flight at Macon, Ga. History is silent as to what eventually happened to this early bird organization, but on December 11, 1915, 22 men were mustered into an Aeronautical Section of the State Naval Militia—men who financed the purchase of their own biplane. Three of their number had qualified for pilots' licenses. The Section was inducted into World War I service with the Navy on April 6, 1917, and disappeared into history. The California Naval Militia was not revived after the war.

A less reactionary and backward-looking Headquarters of General Staff officers than those then busily playing National politics with Preparedness would have harnessed that enthusiasm and vast potential. The volunteer manpower, the 1915-16 urge for Preparedness, and the planes in production for Europe, were present for giving America a forceful role in the air effort against Germany after America's entry. As

---

* Raynauld C. Bolling and James E. Miller were Guardsmen who caught the vision of aviation's future in warfare rather than aviation *aficionados* who turned to the Guard as a vehicle for a new interest. Their National Guard service records dated from February 8, 1907, and April 30, 1906, respectively. Initially they were Cavalrymen in which Bolling served six years before making Sergeant. At the end of his first five years, Miller was still a Private.

it was, American ground forces throughout World War I were almost entirely dependent upon French and British aviators. These not-always-cooperative allies often were flying American-built planes. But American field commanders were dependent upon them for most of the air cover, aerial reconnaissance and primitive bombing missions flown over American sectors in France.

Not even at war's end did General Pershing have a fully-balanced combat force in Europe. The Air Arm was largely missing. Pershing's apparent success without one, there being no warmth for giving either the French or the English credit for doing much of anything after the Spring of 1918, merely increased the resistance of the Army professionals to accepting aviation following World War I. Indeed, from 1911 to 1917 was a regrettable era in which there was a flat refusal in Washington to recognize, expand and capitalize upon the potential of the National Guard for furthering the modernity of America's preparedness for war. But it is almost normal for bureaucratic thinking, if any, to lag behind that of the intelligent and often inspired avocational amateurs.

## GUARD AVIATION SQUADRONS RECEIVE
## FEDERAL RECOGNITION

The hasty demobilization of 1919, the delay in military reorganization while Congress debated the National Defense Act of 1920, and the dire prophecies about gas warfare depopulating the Earth in the next war, detracted attention from suggestions that there should be National Guard Air units in the postwar pattern. Indeed, the conventional professional view was that such advanced engines of war as airplanes were beyond the capabilities of mere weekend warriors in the Civilian Components. No War Department General Staff action was taken toward salvaging World War I training by utilization of such talent in the Organized Reserve. Such would have been the fate of the reorganizing Guardsmen within the States had the matter been left to the dominant, groundling opinions of the Army as then constituted.

Be it said in behalf of the few rated Air officers then in the Regular Army, under the leadership of such men as Brigadier General (Temporary) William ("Billy") Mitchell, and his successors, such as James E. Fechet, Benjamin D. Foulois, Oscar Westover and H. H. Arnold, there was the warmest and most friendly feeling toward the National Guard.* They knew they had no future insofar as the deeply-entrenched,

---

* The now almost-legendary Billy Mitchell began his colorful military career at the age of 19 by enlisting in Co. M, 1st Wis. Infantry, May 14, 1898. He continued on active duty for the Philippines pacification as a Lieutenant, U.S. Volunteers, and was integrated into the Regular Army as a Signal Corps 1st Lt., February 2, 1901. Mitchell, as a temporary Brig. Gen., in 1921-24, was only Assistant to the Chief of the Air Service. The Chief, 1921-27, was an aging, unimaginative but popular, temporary Maj. Gen., Mason M. Patrick, from the Corps of Engineers. He received the assignment to carry him through to retirement, avoiding reversion to his permanent rank as Colonel of Engineers.

unimaginative General Staff was concerned. With full knowledge of the General Staff's proclivity for palace politics and its willingness to respond to Congressional and White House opinion, Mitchell saw the National Guard as another pathway to an informed public opinion that would jar the groundlings into a revision of their ideas. But, as will be noted later, Mitchell did not sense this opportunity until Guardsmen arrived in Washington demanding Federal status for a unit already organized. He was indeed quick in seeing its potential, provided the citizen-soldiers could make a go of it. Moreover, Mitchell was to carry his idea of public appeal much further and to the point of inviting a court-martial in 1926. He entered the Court on grounds from which he must have known he could not escape a technical conviction (suspension from duty and pay for five years) but which he might convert into a sounding-board for additional appeals to the public. In this he was but partially successful. He might have accomplished more had he remained in the Service, but, in any event, his successors continued his esteem for the National Guard.

Unto the present day, Air Force leaders have demonstrated and are demonstrating far more confidence in and a willingness to support Air Guard units with more funds and resources than their opposite numbers in the Department of the Army have been toward supporting the post-World War II Army National Guard. There is ample evidence that the U. S. Air Force has fully accepted the obvious truth that as fast as the techniques of warfare and defense progress, likewise and to the same degree there is developed such a corresponding educational level and technical knowledge and skills within the civilian population of the Nation that produced such weapons. Accordingly, part-time civilian-soldiers, sailors and airmen can and should be organized into fully-functional units trained for the early operations with such weapons when National security is challenged.

But in 1920, as the post-World War I Guard units were reorganizing, Billy Mitchell had hardly begun his fight. The restless young war birds, back in civil life from France or from home front training fields, and who were eager to continue their camaraderie and flight interests, found no welcome mat at the War Department threshold. Among the most eager to get organized and doing something were the erstwhile New York Guardsmen who were home with Reserve commissions and nothing they could do with them. They yearned for a place in the fast-burgeoning 27th Infantry Division, should the slowly-emerging Tables of Organization make such a thing possible.*

Meanwhile, out in Minnesota, a dedicated and relentless early bird-man was nursing the idea that he could sell Curtiss Airplanes in St.

* More than 100,000 young officers and men returned to civil life in 1919 from training in flight and/or aviation mechanics and maintenance. The Air Service had on hand 3,500 American airplanes, 5,000 foreign airplanes and hundreds of balloons. No initiative was taken to gear these resources to National Guard enthusiasm.

Paul and Minneapolis. Because his Ohio boyhood dreams had taken wings, he saw no reason why the same should not happen to all others. In early 1916, his first earnings had gone into private flight lessons at $90 an hour. The price could have been why he soloed after the third hour. For him, World War I ended in a flight training base near Newport News, Virginia, which he left with a commission as a Reserve Lieutenant with Pilot's wings and nothing to fly. That was when he took the job as a Curtiss Airplane salesman in Minnesota's Twin Cities.

In St. Paul, Ray S. Miller met Major W. C. Garis, Assistant Adjutant General for the State of Minnesota. As had Bolling, Miller became obsessed with thoughts of a properly-equipped and functional Air unit in the National Guard. With the State's blessing, by the Summer of 1920 he had the officers and men lined-up, a meeting hall, and nothing more. From Major Garis and Lieutenant Miller, Brigadier General Walter F. Rhinow became infected with the Air fever. Miller later wrote: "Considerable correspondence was had with the War Department relative to the practicability of such a unit. . . . Finally the State of Minnesota rented a three-place Curtiss Oriole to fly to Washington to present more forcefully our plans. . . . We [Rhinow, Garis and Miller] arrived in Washington on schedule and explained our proposal to none other than General Billy Mitchell, who was quick to recognize the feasibility of our plans and gave us authorization. . . . With this encouragement, we returned to St. Paul, again on schedule and without a hitch. Incidentally, we flew by way of Chicago, Albany, N. Y., with many stops in between. I believe the only landings we made at what might possibly be called airports were at Chicago and Bolling Field, which then was some distance from downtown Washington."*

Some of the same factors that had defeated the early efforts of New York's Captain Bolling and his contemporaries were, in the postwar period, operating in favor of Minnesota's Lieutenant Miller. Among the multitudinous items of war surplus hardware and military gadgetry of the era, there were more space-consuming, crated, and uncrated airplanes and spare parts than there were funds for storage. Unlike many other entries in the inventories of surplus supplies, there was absolutely no commercial market for the aviation items. At the same time, the War Department planning committees were studying operational reports, complaints and alibis from the demobilized "square" Infantry Divisions that had fought in France. Their purpose was to ascertain what might be done advantageously were those Divisions fighting that same war again. There was a growing opinion that Division Commanders in the future

---

* As has happened to many Guardsmen, Miller's salaried and assigned duties with the Curtiss corporation took so much time from the Guard that he had to quit the corporation and go into the insurance business on his own. In this he created a small fortune, and at the same time gave his Country more than 40 years of uninterrupted and distinguished service through peace and war. He died at home, a Brigadier General, in retirement, 1961.

might well enjoy the luxury of Air officers in their Intelligence Sections and one organic Squadron of observation planes for close-in reconnaissance, identification of remunerative targets and photographic missions within the Division sector. Whether such Squadrons should actually be organized for the National Guard Divisions, or merely carried as paper units to be supplied after a future M-Day, was debated, with heavy opinion in favor of the latter. But the availability of so much surplus aviation property tipped the scales in favor of functional Guard Squadrons actually in being, in case the citizen-soldiers actually could accomplish the mission of creating and keeping Air units in being. It was against this background and the enthusiasm from the field that the Assistant to the Chief of the Air Service,* Billy Mitchell, was able to validate his promise to Minnesota.

Meanwhile, other States were writing assurances that such units could be created and kept in being within the Guard structure. There was the further insistence by some State Adjutants General that something be done before all the available flying talent was lost through diversion to other avocational interests. Such was the plea of the Minnesota team of Rhinow-Garis-Miller and the distance, with mode of travel, evidenced the faith in Air that appealed to Mitchell. As a result, the 109th Observation Squadron (St. Paul), as an organic element of the 34th Infantry Division, was the first aviation unit to be Federally-recognized, duly-equipped and fully-operational in training programs at home station. The official date of Federal recognition was January 17, 1921, following the interview with Mitchell the preceding September.

This honor and distinction could have gone easily to New York. No State was richer in officer talent. Thanks to Bolling and his prewar associates, more of New York's airmen had seen service overseas. Some had triumphed in sufficient numbers of aerial duels to be officially designated as Aces. A group of 20 or more met often at informal dinners and talked of alternate plans for continuing in a military aviation activity. They were under the leadership of Major Kenneth P. Littauer, D.S.C., Order of Leopold, Croix de Guerre, and Captain George Vaughn, D.S.C. and also a combat Ace. But unlike the St. Paul group, they did not organize enlisted personnel.

New York's Military Department had promised to redesignate and reorganize a conveniently-located Artillery Battery or Infantry Company into such Squadron enlisted personnel, if and when the War Department made up its mind in favor of an Observation Squadron for each of the National Guard Infantry Divisions. Moreover, the New York Adjutant General more than kept his word. Upon getting the green light from

---

* The Air Service was a separation from the Signal Corps in 1918. In 1926 it was elevated to the Air Corps, thanks to Billy Mitchell. In 1941, under Gen. H. H. Arnold, it became the Army Air Forces, and, in 1941, the U.S. Air Force.

Washington, he designated the Hempstead, Long Island, Infantry unit as the 102nd Observation Squadron and transferred to the Air arm, as non-flying personnel, the Company's entire roster of officers and men.

The procedure was somewhat less than satisfactory. Upon achieving Federal recognition, November 4, 1922, three of the officers and all the enlisted men of the Squadron reverted to Company K, 14th New York Infantry. Had the flight-rated officers of the 102nd Observation Squadron (27th Division) recruited their own maintenance and support teams, they may or may not have been recognized ahead of the Minnesota unit, but they certainly would have done better and faster. As it was, five other States had followed Minnesota's lead and organized their Observation Squadrons to achieve Federal recognition prior to the above date for New York. They were the 104th, 29th Division, Baltimore, June 29, 1921; the 113th, 38th Division, Indianapolis, August 1, 1921; the 101st, 26th Division, Boston, November 18, 1921; the 105th, 30th Division, Nashville, December 4, 1921, and the 106th, 31st Division, Birmingham, January 21, 1922. Subsequent organization of Observation Squadrons for the National Guard Divisions was more deliberate and spread through a number of years. By 1930 all the Guard Divisions of the era had their Air units, each consisting of the Squadron and associated Photographic Sections and Medical Detachments, fully recognized and functional.*

It is further significant that by 1930 the War Department was looking to the National Guard for more than Divisional Observation Squadrons. With smaller budgets and diminishing personnel lists and all the time under the impact of the publicity crusade by the air-minded officers for more appreciation of the future potential of Air units, it was inevitable that the National Guardsmen would be called upon to do more and more. In 1925, Little Rock, Arkansas, had evidenced a potential for supporting a unit. But the Arkansas Guardsmen happened to be in non-divisional units and the Divisions in the Deep South and neighboring Texas had Air units assigned and in being. Arkansas received the signal to come in, and her 154th Observation Squadron at once was designated as non-divisional and assigned to the VII Corps.

It was the beginning of a trend. In time, the 152nd and the 153rd Observation Squadrons, Hillsgrove, Rhode Island, and Meridian, Mississippi, respectively, appeared on the Federally-recognized Troop Lists of the National Guard as "Corps Aviation Troops." With the gathering of war clouds in Europe, the War Department, in contrast with the negative decisions of the Department in 1917, became almost frantic for National

---

* The remaining National Guard Observation Squadrons of this decade, their parent Divisions and home stations were as follows: 103rd, 28th Division, Philadelphia; 107th, 32nd Division, Detroit; 108th, 33rd Division, Chicago; 110th, 35th Division, St. Louis; 111th, 36th Division, Houston; 112th, 37th Division, Cleveland; 115th, 40th Division, Los Angeles; 116th, 41st Division, Spokane; 118th, 43rd Division, Hartford; 119th, 44th Division, Newark; 120th, 45th Division, Denver; 154th, non-divisional, Little Rock, Ark.

Guard aviation units. Under this impetus, in late 1939 and 1940, there were organized and Federally-recognized the 121st Observation Squadron, District of Columbia; the 122nd, Louisiana; 123rd, Oregon; 124th, Oregon; 125th, Oklahoma; 126th, Wisconsin; 127th, Kansas, and 128th, Georgia.

Accordingly, when the whistles blew for the mobilization of the National Guard for World War II, through the late Fall and Winter of 1940-41, the National Guard of the States sent no less than 29 properly-organized and fully-functional aviation Squadrons into active Federal service. The typical Guard unit, as of the date of induction, consisted of 20 to 30 rated Pilot officers and 140 to 150 enlisted men. Within modern terms of reference, it was not a significant force. But compared to what the Army did not have but should have had as of that date, these Guardsmen were a powerful reinforcement.*

## THE AIR GUARDSMEN BETWEEN THE WARS

Mere Federal recognition with its initial issue of World War I surplus aviation equipment and supplies by no means solved all problems for the early National Guard Observation Squadrons. The initial issue normally consisted of eight JN4H trainers with boxes and boxes of miscellaneous, unassorted and ill-chosen spare parts. Since the typical State had located none of its Armories on or near an airport, the problem of housing was paramount from the beginning. Nearby barns, abandoned airport shacks and collapsing World War I temporary hangars often were utilized. One unit literally improvised shelter for typewriters and office supplies from the crates whence came the arriving JN4H planes. All these problems soon were solved through local civic and State channels. Like their prophet, Billy Mitchell, most of the early Air Guardsmen proved to be instinctive masters of publicity and its twin brother, public relations; hence the speed of cooperative achievement.

Some nostalgic old-timers insist everything was better in those days. True, there were few airfields, no radar, not even radio. Aids to navigation were few. The "iron compass," or main line of the railroad leading to the destination, was considered the most trustworthy. State maps torn from school geographies and commercial atlases told which branch of a railroad junction should be followed. There were no weather reports, no Technical Orders, no War Department Regulations—just the aircraft, local initiative, and magnificent improvisations.

There was great enthusiasm for cross-country flight missions in the

---

* In April, 1939, the Air Troop List of the Regular Army consisted of no more than three Balloon Squadrons; 15 Bombardment Squadrons; 10 Observation Squadrons, 14 Pursuit Squadrons; eight Reconnaissance Squadrons and eight Attack Squadrons. Their support came from five Air Base Squadrons; three Staff Squadrons; 11 School Squadrons; one Depot Squadron; three Communications Squadrons; three Weather Squadrons, and four Transport Squadrons.

interest of international amity and goodwill. Northeastern units happily helped the Canadians photo-map the St. Lawrence waterway. The Royal Canadian Air Force at Winnipeg often needed free advice. Pilots of the 111th at Houston, Texas, could be counted upon to volunteer for Rio Grande patrol missions in behalf of the Immigration Service or the Texas Rangers. But when, during the Havana racing season, two Guard pilots crash-landed and walked away from a plane on one of the Florida keys, without having checked in or out of Key West, there was a lingering suspicion in the War Department that such international amity might be inspired by the Volstead Act and the Eighteenth Amendment. It was then, some old-timers insist, that the Chairman of the Spoil-Sport Committee of the War Department General Staff began dreaming-up unprecedented Regulations.

Billy Mitchell's expectation that aviation units in the National Guard might contribute toward making America more air-minded in military matters was fully justified, and his fondest hopes were far exceeded. The Guard aviators endlessly organized, attended and competed in one another's air shows. The New York Squadron's first air circus, in 1924, pulled 43,378 people through the turnstiles. It attracted only 73 entries, most of whom were other Guardsmen. The next year the entries were more than doubled and the attendance approximated 70,000. Because of the nature of flight, millions must have witnessed some part of the stunt flights, races and simulated air duels, or "dog fights." Among the less spectacular but headline-making events was a race with highly-bred and carefully-trained carrier pigeons to Washington, D.C. The aviators proudly announced a triumph over the pigeons by more than two hours.

The hangars of all Guard units were aeronautical hostels to every lonely, free-lance birdman whether he happened to have military status or not. Wing-patching, complete with glue-pot, fabric, struts and steel wire salvaged from a local crash, were usually free to any such grounded air travellers as might be in bad luck. As a result, the Guard unit's aviation publicity often became associated with some of the most colorful and adventurous names in the early history of flight. Indeed, the most sensational, headline-creating, dramatic, long-distance solo flight in aviation was made by Captain Charles A. Lindbergh, 110th Observation Squadron, Missouri National Guard. His flight in the privately-owned plane, *Spirit of St. Louis*, non-stop, New York to Paris, May 20-21, 1927, in $33\frac{1}{2}$ hours, unleashed the admiration, ovations and imaginations of more people than did any other single incident between the invention of the airplane and the recent Globe-girdling flights of Russian and American astronauts.

Less dramatic in terms of publicity appeal, but even more appreciated by the persons and communities favorably affected, were the voluntary and often hazardous mercy missions flown by Air Guardsmen.

Incidentally, it is a tradition the modern generation of pilots cherish and fully sustain. These missions were in the nature of almost every conceivable form of search, assistance and rescue. The unfortunates could be other fliers hours overdue; children lost in a forest who later were found accidentally locked in the attic of a neighboring vacant house; trappers and hunters lost, and/or snowbound in genuine distress. There were food-drop missions to isolated and distressed families; flights bearing essential serum to a distant, epidemic-ridden village, and the saving of entire communities through immediate, spot location of forest fires in time for regaining their control and ultimate extinction.

Such more-or-less dramatic incidents always made local headlines and occasionally created news from Coast to Coast. They were not only a boon to military aviation but they brought to the entire National Guard a beneficial and changing image. Quite often it was the nearest non-aviation unit of the National Guard that went into action for the final rescue or to fight the threatening forest fire for which the airmen had done the initial locating. Thanks to this and other factors, a more appreciative public esteem for the National Guard as a domestic and civic institution, as well as an agency for National defense, was a happy result even prior to the mobilization for World War II.

Notwithstanding these multitudinous non-military activities, each Observation Squadron had the same drill and training periods that were required of all other units. The Squadrons normally accompanied their Division Headquarters into Summer camps of instruction. They participated in the same field training, Staff and supply activities that fell to the lot of all others. Summer field camps further compounded the airmen's troubles. Between the wars, it was seldom that the entire Division would be in the field at the same time. The camps were lacking in tentage and utilities, including sanitation and water. Moreover, most Divisions were split between States with separate camps. Sequential training segments of a "square" Division in those days normally would be Division Headquarters, some spare parts, and one of the two Infantry Brigades, followed two weeks later by the other Infantry Brigade and the remaining Divisional spare parts. The Summer training season would end with the Field Artillery Brigade usurping the entire camp and area for exercises and service ammunition practice. It naturally followed that each of the Brigadier Generals commanding one of these sequential and successive training camp periods of the Division demanded that a part or all the airplanes of the Division's Squadron be present for a week or more. Administrative flights, orientation of Staff flights, photograph flights to expose faulty camouflage by the ground troops, flights for training ground troops in air-ground communications, and flights for artillery fire adjustments, were the conventional demands of all. Moreover, a part or all of the Squadron usually flew in to execute

530

some or all of missions desired by each commander of the series of three or four successive field camps of the entire Division. It meant the flight personnel of the Divisional Observation Squadron were tied-down for most of the entire Summer, for which they seldom drew pay for more than two weeks.

One may well conclude that no peacetime avocational activity ever has been more demanding of its devotees than was service in the early Observation Squadrons of the National Guard during the years 1922 until 1940. The most convincing proof of this proposition is the number of vacancies in the ranks of Captain and First Lieutenant each Squadron usually, and of necessity, carried in its rosters of flight-rated officers. The Tables of Organization in 1933 called for rated officers as follows: one Major, five Captains, 11 First Lieutenants, and 14 Second Lieutenants. Only a First Lieutenant commanding the Photo Section and the Medical Detachment Commander were non-rated. A stipulated time-in-grade and proficiency time and skills were required for promotion even though higher rank vacancies might exist. Accordingly, the 110th Observation Squadron, St. Louis, was almost typical of the era when it showed two vacant Captaincies, seven vacant First Lieutenancies, and two vacant Second Lieutenancies. Most units showed more vacancies in the lowest grade, but the total figure for the rated officer shortage was about the same in all Squadrons.

All were constantly in the same struggle; the constant striving for and retention of officers who could qualify as fliers. As the reservoir of pilots from 1917-18 ran dry, flight enthusiasts who had learned to fly at their own expense often were recruited and commissioned from the ranks. Others learned to fly as enlisted men in the unit and under tutelage of their own National Guard officers and thereby commissioned from the ranks. Other junior officers had been fortunate enough to finish the Air Corps Flying Cadet course, followed by a brief tour of extended active duty as Reserve Lieutenants in the Army. Meanwhile, loss of Guard- and Army-trained pilots from the Observation Squadrons to budding airlines and the aviation industry was almost constant. One of the grave oversights of the Regular Army was failure to give the National Guard units a reasonable number of slots in the pilot training program for complete officer replacement at all times. The Army's side of the problem was easy to state. Its Squadrons likewise were short of rated pilots or they would not have been dragging-in for extended active duty every flight Reserve officer who would agree to serve for a year or more, and further taking recourse to temporary ranks for their own Regulars to fill the essential command assignments in Field Grade and higher. The situation was not materially alleviated until 1940.

There must have been much fun in the old Guard Squadrons, with their freedom for air circuses, jumping across national boundaries, and other, irresponsible, cross-country junketing. But everything was not always beer and skittles, or there would not have been the unending struggle to get and hold officer personnel against the blandishments and aviation opportunities elsewhere. The evidence is conclusive that the hard core of Air Guard leaders, through the formative years between the wars, were men devoted to and dedicated to their avocation—to the Guard in general and to the National Guard Observation Squadrons in particular.

## THE AIR GUARDSMEN IN WORLD WAR II

The Air Guardsmen called to active duty with their 29 Observation Squadrons through the Winter and Spring of 1940-41 no longer were equipped with the "Jennies" of World War I. Those obsolete crates had been worn-out on endless junkets and as basic trainers through the early '20's. They had been replaced by O-38B's and O-38E's. Some Squadrons were even in possession of the new, low-wing, three-place O-47's in the late '30's, which all of them carried into the mobilization. The Observation Squadrons did not remain organic within their mobilizing Guard Infantry Divisions. The War Department was in alarm over the extent to which mechanized Armor and military aviation had been neglected. In a desperate, eleventh-hour effort to remedy the situation, all the National Guard Divisional Tank units and the Divisional Air Observation Squadrons were ordered to active duty as non-divisional troops and quite often sent to a different camp, or even a different Corps Area, from that of the parent Division.

This more-or-less overnight acquisition of 29 Observation Squadrons created an organizational imbalance of unit types within the Air Corps. Came Pearl Harbor as a harbinger of a long and gruelling war, and there were wholesale redesignations and change-overs to other types of Squadrons. Most of the Guard Squadrons already had been bled white for detached service, training cadres for new units and flight school assignments. But in the redesignations every one of them ceased being Observation Squadrons and at least a third of them even lost their original numerals. The 101st Observation Squadron, for example, became the 39th Tactical Reconnaissance Squadron; the 104th, the 489th Fighter Squadron; the 119th, the 490th Fighter Squadron; the 122nd, the 885th Bombardment Squadron, Heavy; the 123rd, the 35th Reconnaissance Squadron; the 126th, the 34th Photo Reconnaissance Squadron; the 128th, the 840th Bombardment Squadron, Heavy; the 152nd, the 37th Photo Reconnaissance Squadron, Long Range, Weather.

All other National Guard Squadrons retained their original numbers but acquired new names to conform to design and equipment for vastly different missions. Some did not even finish the hostilities in their new status. Inactivations from one category and redesignations into an-

532

other unit type continued through 1944. For the most part, the net result was a complete loss of original State and type of unit identity. Air Guard officers were promoted rapidly. When one found himself commanding a Wing, or a Group, he occasionally was able to wangle Staff assignments in his Headquarters for a few buddies he had known in the National Guard, old home town, aviation outfit. Except for a few, rare vestigial situations of that character, concerning which someone might mention the Headquarters as being run by a few old-timers out of the National Guard, one seldom heard the term in connection with air operations. That all the individual members, officers and men, of the erstwhile 29 Observation Squadrons from the Guard had to be dispersed as a leavening agent in the vast expansion of the Air Force, was inevitable. The Nation could not afford retention of so much talented initiative and know-how in so few small, highly-specialized and at the same time rapidly-becoming-obsolescent units.

The gross statistics of the Air Force expansion for World War II reveal the necessity for such dispersal of the individuals of the Guard's Air Observation Squadrons more eloquently than can the most carefully-chosen words. In 1939, Cadet Pilot training programs were being madly-accelerated. All available Air Corps Reserve officers, whether rated, grounded or never had been rated, were being called to the Colors individually. An active recruiting campaign was being conducted among vocational school students for mechanically-inclined enlisted men. Through these means, the Air Force had attained a strength of 22,387. In 1940 the Guard units, most of them recruited to the authorized induction strength, began augmenting the active duty Army Air Corps. That year the aggregate active duty strength rose to 51,185. Further officer and pilot training, recruiting, arrival and assignment of the first drafted Selectees to the Air Force combined wth completion of the induction of the Guard Observation Squadrons, raised the aggregate active duty figure in 1941 to 152,125. Even this comparatively preliminary expansion skyrocketed promotions of all experienced officers and men to the upper Field Grades so rapidly that waggish bartenders, courting the Infantry-Artillery officer trade, posted placards back of their bars which read: "Air Force officers below rank of Colonel will not be served hard liquor unless accompanied by parents."

But the Army Air Corps expansion (and the essential promotions) had just begun. In the peak year of 1944, 2,372,292 officers and men were wearing the insignia of the Army Air Forces. They were 31% of all personnel then in the Army uniform. Under such expansion, accompanied by improved equipment, new techniques and necessary but kaleidoscopic changes of organization within units and emphasis upon Troop Structures, it was utterly impossible for any of the Guard Squadrons to retain any degree of their peacetime heritage and complexion, as did the National Guard Regiments and Divisions of the Ground Forces through the same war.

## THE AIR GUARD SINCE WORLD WAR II

The esteem that the Army Air Force commanders had for the Guardsmen while on active duty through World War II is best evidenced by their immediate postwar professional Service attitudes. Though they were forceful and forensic in their secession from the Army to become a separate Air Force that would be all their own, they were equally insistent that they also have a sizeable chunk of the National Guard in their new scheme of things. Moreover, they were not settling for a mere reorganization of an historic 29 Squadrons with 1,500 officers and 4,500 enlisted men such as they had received from the States in 1940-41. The requested Troop Structure and proposed strengths were most flattering to the Guard, but the Air Force finally decided to be satisfied with a budgetary estimate for 49,500 officers and men distributed among 514 units operating from 79 Air Bases. They were under a National Guard State structure and included 12 tactical Air Wings; 24 combat Groups, Fighter, three combat Groups, Bomb; 27 Air Service Groups; and 84 Squadrons.

When hostilities broke out in Korea, Summer of 1950, they had their command structure and lesser units in being. Recruiting was still active, but the actual strength was 6,669 officers, 78 warrant officers and 37,981 airmen, for a total of 44,728, in June, 1950. The command and Troop Structure then and since necessarily have changed as rapidly as newer weapons became available and old equipment became obsolete. There is little need here to go into all the technical details of changes and transformations within the decade of the '50's. Nor is it necessary to repeat what has been reviewed in the preceding chapter concerning all components of the National Guard through the so-called Korean Police Action.

Sundry agencies of the Air Force have prepared operational critiques, analyses of strengths and weaknesses of various types of equipment, factors in speed of call-up and deployment, and lessons learned from the enemy, his practices and equipment. They are abundant in historical interest. They are classified. There are also a few printed historical studies of the highest order and digesting much of the foregoing that might well be drawn upon to embellish this chapter. But, unfortunately, the best and most interesting of these materials likewise still are classified. Though a few have been downgraded as low as a mere "Confidential" and fragments of others in higher classifications have been heard in speeches and alleged in the Press, it is the better part of wisdom for the historian to leave such a body of source material until everything can be told with all events and interpretations in proper relation to one another. Unlike the journalist and the orator, the historian can afford to wait. It should not be too long, for the wraps are being removed by downgrading in a progressive and orderly manner.

Here it should be emphasized, however, that since the Navy and the Air Force proved to be more attractive during the Korean Affair than did the Army, the Air National Guard was likewise a beneficiary of the wide range of choices available to the Selective Service registrant, or "Obligor," as the Pentagon chose to call him. Volunteering for the Air Guard rose rapidly, filling the units to approximate war strength as fast as they were alerted for induction. A peak of 52,298 was reached in late Autumn of 1952, by which time nearly all the Air Guard was in Federal service. Incidentally, some Wings and Squadrons, assigned to the Air Defense Command, were able to serve their deployment mission without actually leaving their home stations. But this does not mean that most of their flight personnel, and many of their ground personnel, did not go overseas. The service rotation concept, previously discussed, facilitated their flow to and from the overseas Theaters* as individual replacements.

So successful was the Air National Guard through the Korean Affair that it was called upon to assume increasing responsibilities through the continuance of the Cold War. The post-Korean objectives contemplated larger units with more officers, men and aircraft. Increasing percentages would be in combat elements with jet-propelled planes and, in some Wings and Squadrons, prepared to fight with atomic weapons. The budgeted objective quickly became 72,000 officers and men, modernly equipped. The Air Force Department had asked for more.

Actually, the Air Guard was short of that figure by 1,180 men at the end of Fiscal Year 1960, largely through "the high loss of newly recruited airmen. Careful screening," the *Annual Summary* noted, "prior to enlistment of recruits should do much to improve this situation." An airman's or an officer's removal from home station or to another State for business, employment or personal reasons, it might be noted, is a basis for discharge, as it always has been in the National Guard, whether Army or Air. Nevertheless, a remarkable feature of Guard personnel, Army and Air, is a lower turnover of personnel than often occurs in neighboring Regular units. Citizen-soldiers and airmen who like the Guard often consider their continuing relations with their unit a reason why better jobs elsewhere should be rejected; hence the admonition to Unit Commanders to screen recruits more carefully.

But the shortage of only 1.6% of the objective was not enough to keep the men and units from being fully functional and "prepared for

---

* The reader is reminded that there was a strong buildup of American strength in overseas areas other than the Far East, most particularly in Western Europe, the North Sea approaches, and the Mediterranean.

immediate service whenever required and ready to join with the active duty Air Force in providing a D-Day Force with which to conduct air defense, air offense and joint action with surface forces," to borrow the terms of their stated peacetime mission.

To achieve this mission, units of the Air Guard that year, 1960, were organized into three categories with Wings, Groups, Squadrons and lesser units assigned and equipped for the purposes of each category. They were:

## I. COMBAT FLYING ORGANIZATIONS
  1. Air Defense—Fighter-interceptors
     (a) 11 Wings
     (b) 30 Groups
     (c) 40 Squadrons
  2. Tactical Fighters
     (a) 7 Wings
     (b) 5 Groups
     (c) 22 Squadrons
  3. Tactical Reconnaissance
     (a) 4 Wings
     (b) 1 Group
     (c) 14 Squadrons
  4. Troop Carriers
     (a) 4 Squadrons
     (b) 4 Air Base Squadrons

## II. NON-TACTICAL FLYING ORGANIZATIONS
  1. Air Transport (Heavy)
     (a) 2 Wings
     (b) 4 Groups
     (c) 6 Squadrons
  2. Aeromedical
     (a) 1 Group
     (b) 5 Transport Squadrons
     (c) 1 Air Base Squadron (Aeromedical)
     (d) 1 USAF Dispensary (Aeromedical)
  3. Air Transport (Medium)
     (a) 1 Squadron

## III. GROUND SUPPORT ORGANIZATIONS
  1. Communications
     (a) 3 Communications Group Headquarters
     (b) 16 Communications Squadrons
     (c) 11 Ground Electronics Engineering Installation Agency
         units
     (d) 5 Radio Relay Squadrons
     (e) 1 Communications Squadron (Special)
  2. Tactical Control and Aircraft Control and Warning
     (a) 3 Tactical Control Groups
     (b) 3 Tactical Control Squadrons
     (c) 21 Aircraft Control and Warning units

3. Army Airways Communications System
   (a) 2 Squadrons
   (b) 9 Flights
4. Weather
   (a) 30 Flights

The aggregate inventory of active aircraft then in possession of the Air Guard units totaled 2,269. Of these, 1,566 were jet fighters, 226 were jet reconnaissance, and 217 were jet trainers. Represented in these inventories were type-models such as: B/RB57's, F102's and 104's, F86D/L's, F89's, F84F's, F86H's and F100's. Service type craft included C123's, SA16's, C97's, C119's, and the jet trainers of types appropriate to the unit.

The organization and the equipment clearly reflect the sense of urgency that dominates the Air National Guard. It is the same feeling of immediacy that created the military phrase "Minute Men" during the French-and-Indian War but more commonly associated with the Revolution because of the beginning of the Revolutionary War, Lexington and Concord. Pursuant to this Minute Man concept, the Air Guardsmen contemplate no time to mobilize and train. This further invokes a high-performance consideration for both personnel and materiel. Planes, weapons and electronic systems must be modern. Skills and teamwork of the personnel must be as precise and as fast as the modernity of the equipment. Maintenance of the increasingly-complex weapons, aircraft and allied instruments of aerial warfare must be at the maximum at all times.

As a result of these factors, and the essential readiness of the personnel, an unprecedentedly high percentage, compared with the historic Ground Force National Guard units, necessarily are retained under fulltime employment. In 1960, no less than 19%, or just short of one-fifth, of the commissioned and enlisted strength of the Air National Guard were under fulltime employment as "Air Technicians," and most of them—at least 65% of these Technicians—are in aircraft, equipment, instrument, and weapons maintenance. But all are Guardsmen, with tactical and operational duties through their weekend and Summer field training. It naturally follows that their operational assignments take advantage of their fulltime employment, knowledge and skills as "Air Technicians."

Because of this high percentage of Guardsmen constantly on the Air Base as fulltime employes, the modernity of equipment and the completeness of it issued and in the hands of the units, Air Guard Fighter Squadrons often have been aloft and mission-bound, in response to surprise alerts, faster than have been Regular Air Force Squadrons utilizing the same strips of their shared Air Base. This has been particularly true at Air Bases on which the Regulars did not have housing (barracks and homes) for all their key personnel to live on the Base. At least, that has been the conventional alibi of the red-faced Regulars following such alerts.

Herein, by the way, is found the answer to an often-recurring question in the Department of the Army's section of the Pentagon. The question: Can Army National Guard Divisions and lesser units be brought to the same state of constant combat-readiness as comparable units of the Regular Army? From the records and results of the Air Wings, Groups and Squadrons, the answer is an obvious and indisputable affirmative for the Army units just any time the Departments of the Army and of Defense and the Congress have sufficient sense of urgency to pay the price in personnel costs and for full issuance of actually modern equipment in all categories.

Officers and men in the Civilian, or Reserve, Components of the Armed Forces fully respond to the objective of constant and complete combat-readiness only when they know they actually have in their units today the very weapons and full field equipment they will fight with should war come with tomorrow's dawn. Moreover, some Army equipment in complexity and sophistication is approaching that of the Air Force. But many Army weapons still are comparatively simple, rugged, easily-maintained and easy to operate. Hence the same high ratio of full-time Technicians and officers and men for key slots should not be as essential to complete combat-readiness of an Army Guard unit as for an Air Guard unit of the same personnel strength. But the margin of difference cannot be too wide, particularly if the Army Guard unit has an on-site mission. The Army National Guard can do what the Air Guard is doing, but to date neither the Department of the Army nor of Defense has been willing to face-up to the price tag for that much of that kind of volunteer service. They have been too satisfied with the Draft Laws, and Selective Service, MOS numbers, punch cards and machine records for recall of "Obligors" as the final answer to their manpower problems. For inviting and fighting a prolonged and bloody war, these are indeed magnificent arrangements. Few will admit it, but that seems to be what the General Staff is planning. Otherwise there would be more support toward Army Guard readiness.

At the end of Fiscal Year 1960, the entire Federal investment in the Air National Guard, for equipment, buildings, land, improvements, miscellaneous construction and aircraft, was two-and-a-fifth billion dollars, with a little more than a billion-and-a-third of that sum tied-up in the aircraft. The training operations and maintenance for the entire Air National Guard for the Fiscal Year was 169 million, in contrast with which the actual pay of the 72,000 officers and airmen, including the Air Technicians, was only 48 million. In National Guard peacetime operations, one may well conclude that manpower is becoming a more-or-less minor item in that phase of preparedness costs.

For a brief but more intimate picture of an Air National Guard Group, let us examine briefly the components of such a command during a weekend training period, for which there are 48 drill credits. Long weekend periods, however, occasionally are invoked for four drill credits, hence in many cases, 12 long weekends retire minimum home Air Base training requirements for the year. A typical organization of units on one Air Base would comprise a Group Headquarters with its associated administrative, supply, maintenance and flying elements. There would be 20 to 25 fighter, or tactical, planes, with a minimum of 18 fully operational at all times. The Group most likely also will have a transport aircraft and jet trainers appropriate to type and mission. One also should find about 100 officers and 650 enlisted airmen on the Base and busy. All are in proper Air Force attire for their duties and at their proper stations incident to the flight operations or training in progress.

These officers and men would represent from 95 to 98% of the Group's complete roster as of that date. All of these 750 officers and airmen are civilians and 575 of them earn their living as accountants, mechanics, school teachers, salesmen, etc., within the nearby City's economy. The remaining civilians are employes of the State of California, New York, Oklahoma, or the State in which the Air Base is located. When they are not drilling through a weekend with their avocational teammates, they are the Air Technicians who not only keep the planes flying, spare parts on hand, and the communications net in constant repair, manned and functioning, but they handle the problems of supply, administration and supervision. It is from these people that the Air National Guard gets its basic stability in personnel. The total personnel costs of this mixture of fully-employed and partially-employed volunteer Air Guardsmen *is one-sixth the cost of the same personnel on fulltime active duty in the Regular Air Force.* This is not written in criticism, but rather points-out the advantage the Air Guard has in a stabilized mission with stabilized personnel and drawing upon the avocational interests of trained pilots, mechanics and crews who earn their living in civilian pursuits.

# Bibliographical Note For Chapter XX

There is a surprising amount of widely-scattered literature on early military aeronautics, particularly in books and magazine articles written by Englishmen and Frenchmen. The long article under "Aeronautics," Vol. 1, of the Eleventh Edition of the *Encyclopedia Britannica*, 1911, is the best, widely-available digest of that literature. The biographies of Carnot that emphasize the military vision of this first of all air-minded Generals are in French. A. Picaud, *Carnot, L'Organisateur de la Victoir*, 1887, and Henry Carre, *Le Grande Carnot*, 1947, may be found in the larger libraries. Thaddeus S. C. Lowe, the father of American military aeronautics, left a first-hand account, "Observation Balloons in the Battle of Fair Oaks," *Review of Reviews*, Vol. 43, pp. 186-90, February, 1911, and further amplified by him in Vol. 8 of *Photographic History of the Civil War*, 1911. More, if less interesting details, may be found in the previously-cited Series I of the *Official Records . . . War of the Rebellion*. (See bibliographical notes for the Civil War chapters). Richard Harding Davis, the war correspondent, in *The Cuban and Porto Rican Campaigns*, 1898, as usual second-guessed and out-generaled the professionals on how a balloon should not have been used in Cuba. We are indebted to Don Anderson, Airman 1st Class, New York National Guard Headquarters, for a superb collection of normally fleeting materials on the early aeronautical activities of the National Guard in his State. His biographical data on Col. Raynauld C. Bolling, and his photostatic excerpts from contemporary newspapers, pamphlets, magazines and other sources, made possible this chapter's highly-condensed account of the citizen-soldier vision that culminated in the 1st Aero Squadron, N.G., N.Y. We likewise are indebted to Lt. Col. Leo C. Goodrich, Minnesota Air Guard, and to Mrs. Eva Miller, widow of the late Brig. Gen. Ray S. Miller, for the access to his papers, which revealed the continuing and successful efforts for the Federal recognitions that eventually came to the Post-World War I Guard Observation Squadrons. Sylvia Ronzone, "The National Guard Sprouts Its Wings," *The National Guardsman*, Vol. 8, 1954, tells the story of Eugene Ely and the California Guard's pioneering for military aviation. The largest collection of Army Air Force unit histories for World War II that was found and consulted was in the Library of Congress, Washington, D.C. Very few identified their unit with the State of National Guard origin. The remainder of this chapter largely rests upon continuing publications and annual reports of U. S. Government Departments and agencies mentioned in earlier chapter bibliographies, but with one additional title; *The Air National Guard Summary*, Fiscal Years 1954-62, is a brief, annual, Multilith, unbound, diagrammatic and graphical presentation of objectives, costs, shortcomings and achievements. It is compact and rich in vital information. It deserves a more lasting and permanent format.

CHAPTER XXI

# Present Organizational and Manpower Patterns

I N THE SAME WAY that the Air National Guard has found it
necessary to modify its unit structure and occasionally to accept new
equipment with resultant internal adjustments within Squadrons, Groups
and Wings, the Army National Guard also has felt the impact of new
equipment and transitory doctrines of ground warfare. This began immediately following the Cease-Fire in Korea and the return of the National
Guard Divisions and lesser units to home stations and State status.

The Department of the Army, for example, had arrived at an opinion
that an imbalance existed between Infantry and Armored Divisions.
When the 44th Infantry Division, Illinois, was inactivated from Federal
service, that State was encouraged to decline its reorganization. After all,
its historic relationship was not with Illinois but with New Jersey and
upstate New York. In lieu thereof, Illinois accepted a number of non-

divisional units. This made it possible to redesignate and transition non-divisional Mechanized Cavalry in Tennessee into elements of a new Armored Division. These were joined by Tennessee's share of the 30th Infantry Division to constitute within Tennessee the present 30th Armored Division. Meanwhile, non-divisional units in North Carolina similarly were being joined with that State's former share of the 30th Infantry Division to consolidate that entire command within that State. Thus the National Guard had lost one Infantry Division and emerged with three instead of only the two original Armored Guard Divisions of Texas and New Jersey authorized in 1947.

In further search for Armored strength, New York's historic 27th Infantry Division, and California's 40th Infantry Division, upon its return from Korea, were converted to Armored Divisions with retention of their original and historic numerals. For a sixth and last Armored Division, the Department of the Army went to Florida and Georgia. Their units were regrouped, redesignated and reequipped to form the 48th Armored Division. Thus, within the first 18 months following the Cease-Fire in Korea, the National Guard component of the Army of the United States had lost four Infantry Divisions and gained four of Armor, which, with the 49th of Texas and 50th of New Jersey, which had been Armored since World War II, made a total of six Armored Divisions and 21 Infantry Divisions. A number of Regimental Combat Teams were converted to Engineer, Artillery and Armor Battalions and Groups.

The foregoing changes were accomplished by the end of Fiscal Year 1956, but three years later, another reorganizational shuffle had been completed. All Infantry Divisions were reorganized under the five-Battle Group, so-called Pentomic Concept, each Division reduced thereby from 110 units to 88, the largest cut being in the Infantry component. The nondivisional units were reorganized Nationwide to absorb a total cut of units in excess of 900. This was indeed a meat-ax reduction and reorganization. An attempt to eliminate six Infantry Divisions was defeated.

Completed in 1959, this reshuffle was followed by another, only three years later, in the first six months of 1963. The 34th Infantry Division (Iowa and Nebraska), the 35th (Kansas and Missouri), the 43rd (Connecticut, Rhode Island and Vermont) and the 51st (South Carolina and Florida) have been "realigned." The Divisions retained their old numbered designations, each remaining as "Command Headquarters, Divisional," consisting only of the Headquarters and its Headquarters Company. At the same time, Florida yielded its portion of the 48th Armored Division, which became an all-Georgia organization. Nationwide, there were many other changes and, all told, the loss of several hundred Company-size units, just as there had been in the so-called "Pentomic" reorganization of Infantry Divisions five years earlier. True, not just the Army National Guard was singled-out for this pruning; the Army Reserve, which had started out in the brave, new post-World War II era with not only Infantry and Armored Divisions like the Guard, but Airborne, and which gradually had been whittled-down, also lost four of its remaining 10 Infantry Divisions (the Airborne and Armored long since had passed out of its Troop Structure) and many other units.

The alleged purpose was to achieve greater readiness by concentrating many of the personnel and "priority" Division Forces, to be maintained at 80% of war strength and with priorities for equipment, training and field training-assigned "Obligors" from the Ready Reserve Reinforcement Pool. The initial assignments of combat Divisions to these "priority" forces went to the Guard's 26th (Massachusetts), 28th (Pennsylvania), 30th (North Carolina) and 42nd (New York) Infantry and the 30th (Tennessee) and 50th (New Jersey) Armored Divisions. Wisconsin's 32nd Infantry and Texas' 49th Armored, which had enjoyed such high priority that they were tabbed for "Berlin Crisis" duty, 1960-1961, suffered severe personnel losses after their return to State status and were given routine priorities. Besides the six highest priority Divisions, the 38th (Indiana) and 47th (Minnesota) Infantry Divisions were announced by the Department of the Army as having been assigned to "special" missions.

At strength and equipment levels considerably below the eight "Division Forces" was the rest of the Army National Guard, in accordance with what was represented as a new approach to mobilization planning. Even a new terminology was coming into play: the distinctions, overall, were between an "Immediate Reserve" and a "Reinforcing Reserve." Presumably as a guide to more frequent and realistic reappraisal of units' relative readiness than could be gained from monthly strength returns and annual Armory and field training inspections, units were being called upon to submit a semiannual self-rating in terms of personnel strengths, equipment and spare parts levels, and training status; these reports to be audited by State Adjutants General and Army Area Commanders.

Meanwhile, both the Guardsmen and the Regulars in the field have been reorganizationally harassed by what one might call transitory doctrines and gropings for new terminologies. New words, phrases and terms seem to be associated with progress and modernity even though the basic equipment and its use remain little different, or even entirely unchanged. That it makes for good publicity and creates a favorable image for the Army cannot be denied. Moreover, there is the natural urge of intermittent Chiefs of Staffs, and the General Staff teams with which they are associated during their brief tours, to desire a record of having done some heavy thinking as well as heavy paper-pushing during their sojourns in the Pentagon.

Some such motives often were so interpreted in the field in connection with General Maxwell D. Taylor's application of the "Pentomic Concept" to Divisional reorganizations. The basic idea seemed to be that future ground warfare would, like the ultra-modern theater, be "in the round." But instead of having the theatrical audience all around the stage, the embattled Division would be surrounded by the enemy, hence the five-sided Division composed of five "Battle Groups," instead of the three existing Infantry Regiments,* was adopted. Since the Division thus might be deployed on a five-sided and enclosed front whence it might well be rescued, if at all, by atomic bursts, some semantics shark came up with the quoted concept and Divisions of Regulars and Guardsmen thus were reorganized into so-called "Pentomic" Divisions. A hard-bitten General Officer with a brilliant field command record, but who would not care to be quoted by name, studied the new Pentomic Tables of Organization and opined: "Those poor, distracted paragraph soldiers in the Pentagon have run in circles so long through the corridors of that big, five-sided building that they have decided it is the normal way of military life and now they are planning to fight a war in that pattern." His proposition does have the merit of logic if not of fact.

After a few seasons of Staff College war games and field maneuvers, a school of military thought developed informally that a Pentomic Division could and would render a good account of itself in a purely defensive situation. But offensively and strictly on its own power, it would be hard put to punch its way out of a sagebrush flat surrounded by Yaqui Indians. It is with little surprise that the Department of the Army now has engaged upon another reorganization of Infantry Divisions, Regulars and Guardsmen.

This newest transformation is known as "ROAD," the abbreviation for "Reorganization Objectives Army Divisions." The "ROAD" Divisional frame is much the same for all Divisions whether Infantry, Mechanized, Armored or Airborne. It is the equipment and resulting internal organization of the lesser units that constitute the principal difference. The "ROAD" Infantry Divisions, which are to be most prevalent in the National Guard, bear a striking resemblance to the "triangular" Division of 1942 without the conventional attachments and reinforcements that were common to most Divisions in the European Theater through-

* The publicity and semantics experts in the Pentagon seem to be afraid of certain words that might have an adverse connotation. "Regiment" is one of them. It does have an unpleasant association with that horrible civilian word "regimentation." But substitution of a double-barrel term like "Battle Group" is not the solution. Some years ago many schools and colleges sought to improve janitor morale with the redesignation of "custodian." When the public became aware of this switch, janitorial morale again was upgraded by substitution of "Maintenance Helper" as the official classification. The net result is that the present public thinks anyone on a college payroll who is not a Professor must be a Janitor. The colleges and the Pentagon should stick to fundamental words for fundamental meanings and quit trying to achieve devious ends through abstruse terminology.

544

out World War II. The three Infantry Regiments of that era have been replaced by three Brigades that might well have a further striking resemblance thereto except for a higher degree of flexibility as to the number and types of combat Battalions attached to the Brigades. These obviously are to be adjusted to the Division's environment and mission. In a given situation an Infantry Division might be assigned as few as eight combat Battalions, six of Infantry and two of Armor within the Brigades. In another situation the same Division could have 15 combat Battalions, 11 of Infantry, two Mechanized Infantry and two of Armor.

In terms of organization, the field soldier of World War II would feel thoroughly at home in one of the new ROAD Divisions. Only the newer and wider variety of equipment would excite his attention, and in most instances, his unbounded admiration. But the Guard Divisions complain that they are not getting their share. And nothing dampens any soldier's interest, especially a Guardsman's, more completely than being told that the weapons he has are not those with which he will be fighting. Since the retention of the volunteer citizen-soldier is strongly predicated upon his personal and continuing interest, this is of much higher importance than generally is appreciated among the professional soldiers. In 1963 the "priority aggregate strength" was pegged at 400,000.

Meanwhile, what is the effect of these periodic and expensive reorganizational harassments? For the Staff officers and Service school faculties, from the War College down, whose brain cells are kept active studying and arguing in Staff papers and studies the merits of this and that, they are highly beneficial. There should be a less costly method of achieving the same intellectual stimuli. But for the officers and men in the field formations, whether they be Regulars, Guardsmen or Army Reservists, these widely-publicized, periodic and expensive public demonstrations of chronic indecision at the highest Army level are hurtful. Indecision destroys confidence. Lack of confidence in leadership is the threshhold of fears. These are destroyers that have no place during either peace or war in any army that intends to win.

But from a standpoint of expense alone they should be avoided. Complete field tests with fully-manned and equipped provisional units in tentative organizational patterns should prove, or repudiate, every theory, concept or assumption before it is perpetrated upon all ranks and ratings in the Companies, Batteries, Battalions, Brigades and Divisions of the entire Army of the United States. These tests should be continuing and constant through all seasons. Findings should not become springboards for eye-catching publicity and ballyhoo. At the same time there is no point in holding in top secrecy something which would appear readily in a Field Manual should it be adopted. Indeed, publication in a professional manner of the successes and failures of such experimentation and tests would be beneficial. Once a theory has been tested and proved valid, the appropriate change should be gradual and as fast as the associated equipment becomes available. To be sure, changes must be made in the interest of military progress, but the Pentagon's way through the past decade has not been the right way.

## THE NATIONAL GUARD AND SELECTIVE SERVICE

In theory, the United States has a Universal Military Training Act. But the only thing about it that is actually universal, in the all-inclusive sense of the word, is the possibility of military obligation that confronts every healthy young man between the ages of 17 and 26. But in facing-up to this possibility, the young man has more choices than are found in the fine print of a womb-to-tomb life insurance policy, complete with its alternatives for built-in savings or a financed college education; an early endowment or an old-age annuity.

First, there are the choices of Armed Services. Which is to be preferred: Air Force, Navy, Army, Marine Corps, or Coast Guard? Within each there are additional options. The longer the period, two to six years, for which he enlisted in one of the Regular Establishments, or the longer the period he acecpted active duty as a Selectee, the sooner he would be out of the Ready Reserve or "off the hook," and thence into the far less vulnerable and absolutely inactive Standby Reserve. Conversely, the more brief the period of active duty in the Armed Service, the longer he is on the hook as a Ready Reservist.

Here we are interested only in the Army and Air National Guard. Conventionally the young high school graduate not destined for college is encouraged by local Draft Boards and Recruiting Officers to enlist as a Regular, Army or Air Force, for at least four years, which is enough to take him off the hook, without further ado, into the "paper" Standby Reserve, where he remains for only two years. This bothers him little, as the Standby Reservist is sheltered against all but major mobilizations. But that eventuality most likely will bring a revision of the law that makes everyone up to age 45, with or without prior training, highly vulnerable; in which case his four years' prior training would be to his great advantage.

Moreover, his entry into the Regular Establishment pleases both the chosen Armed Service and his Draft Board. The Regular Service is the beneficiary of his expensive training for an average of three of the four years, at the end of which time he may become an enlisted careerist in that Service. The man's Draft Board and State are credited with him in their quotas as long as he is with the Colors. Thus no Recruiting Officer of any one of the Armed Services at the local Post Office, or in a regional Federal building, feels any compulsion to suggest an Army or Air National Guard unit as an alternative for two or more years in a Regular

Establishment, preferably that of the Recruiting Officer giving the advice.

Accordingly, the most effective recruiting for the Guard is by the Guardsmen who naturally trade upon the *camaraderie*, traditions and prestige of their local unit and the opportunity for full service with a minimum of interruption of civil life pursuits. The Army National Guard offers a choice that requires as little as four months with the Colors in active duty for training status. At the same time it concedes the justice of the Guardsman remaining on the Ready Reserve hook and as an active participant in Armory training for a longer, overall period. This extended liability is further made more acceptable to the recruit with the proposition that if a National crisis comes, a young man of spirit and sense of duty will want to get in on the chance for prompt service anyway. The Army or Air National Guard are his opportunity to plan and choose his slot and learn the skills it requires. Moreover, Nathaniel Greene, to become famous as General Greene of George Washington's Continental Line, could say no more than this to prospective recruits for his "Kentish Guards," of East Greenwich, Rhode Island Volunteer Militia, during the Cold War years with England prior to Lexington and Concord.

Though many Guardsmen voluntarily serve much longer than the minimums for getting off the Ready Reserve hook, the young man can join the Army Guard or the Air Guard, go to an Active Army training site or to an Active Air Force Base, for a number of months of active duty training, then return to his home town unit and participate in its Armory or Air Base training assemblies and annual field training for a fixed number of years before phasing-out into "Standby" status.

These programs are integrated with opportunities for NCO, specialists' ratings and officer opportunities for those qualified. Twenty to 40 years of prompt and faithful service now carry a nominal and pro-rated retirement benefit upon arrival at age 60 that will augment in a small way such other civilian savings, investments or industrial retirement benefits as he may have earned. But this feature has not proved to be the lure to sustained service which many assumed it might become. The long-termers in the modern National Guard have proved to be men who enjoy the Military as a pleasing, avocational interest geared to a strong sense of public service.

There are more-or-less similar options available to young men who wish to utilize the Army Reserve, the Naval Reserve, U.S. Marine Corps Reserve and the Coast Guard Reserve for the retirement of a part or all of their military obligations.

## PARTIAL MOBILIZATION OF 1961-62

Since Korea, there has been but one minor test of the efficacy of the present system. In the Summer of 1961, Russia moved toward a major crisis over the status of Berlin. For a broader choice than "massive re-taliation," or doing nothing at all, there was a decision for an overnight beefing-up of conventional strengths for the possibility of less-than-nuclear warfare. This resulted in the activation of Army Guard units and Army Reservists to the number of 150,000 officers and men for one year, more or less, dependent upon Soviet reactions. By the target date of October 1, 1961, 21,000 Air Guard officers and men also had been transitioned from civilian to full active duty status. Eleven of their Fighter Squadrons, with the necessary support units, were deployed in Europe. This largest mass overseas flight in peacetime history, by part-time fighter pilots only a month from their civilian jobs—and without loss of a plane or man—seemed to make an enormous if intangible im-pression upon the Air Force, the Department of Defense, and the Nation. If anything could erase the last trace of feeling that the Air Guard repre-sented a glorified flying club, or "48 little Air Forces," it was this dramatic performance. The result was an almost overnight reinforcement of the Seventeenth Air Force by no less than 260 high-performance jet aircraft. The 32nd Infantry Division (Wisconsin), 49th Armored Division (Texas), 150th Armored Cavalry Regiment (West Virginia), and scores of non-divisional lesser units were on active duty and in training prepared to replace the 2nd Armored and the 4th Infantry Divisions in their home posts at Fort Hood, Texas, and Fort Lewis near Seattle, should it become necessary for a similar overnight strengthening of the Seventh Army in Germany.* Two additional Guard Divisions were alerted to probabilities of an early call to active duty.

The entire need for so much as this minor, partial mobilization was challenged immediately on the floors of both houses of Congress. It became at once controversial. With these doubts as sounding-boards, a few self-serving politicians emitted the plaintive wail that the young manhood of their States were being burdened with the duty of all. Any mobilization, small or large, should fall equally upon all, they insisted. Theirs was a cavalier disregard of the fact that Korea's initial mobiliza-tion did not fall equally upon all alike, and furthermore, in both in-stances, the Guardsmen affected had volunteered for service in just such a call. These vote-seeking Congressional plaints were more embarrassing than helpful to American diplomacy and the units being activated in support of a non-nuclear deterrent.

Inevitably, there were rough spots in the minor mobilization. The Guard units never had been budgeted-for, or authorized in peacetime and at home stations, to go to the enlisted war strength tables of their units. As of the date of their induction into Federal active duty, their

---

* Army heavy equipment, for issue to the two Regular Army Divisions upon arrival in Europe by air, was stockpiled to make possible a mass airlift of the per-sonnel, should the situation worsen. It did not. Indeed, Russia's Premier Nikita Khrushchev promptly became quite reasonable on the subject of Berlin.

ceiling strengths were about 70% of the war strength ideal and ultimate, field service objective. A major aspect of the plan for meeting this shortage was to set the punch-card sorting machines in progress and recall to active duty, by their needed Military Occupational Specialty (MOS) numbers, the specific, individual Reservists needed to bring each National Guard unit to its war strength. Those individually called in this manner were obligated, non-participating Ready Reservists (not members of an Armory training unit) in their middle or late 20's who had been drafted for two years with the Colors and reverted home into the Army Ready Reserve Reinforcement pool. Most of them had considered themselves entirely off the hook before they actually were, merely because no one had been bothering them about anything. It was a part of the evil fruit of the implanted rotation concept and practice during the Korean affair. The mournful moans of their "Why me?" chorus obscured the splendid manner in which many Ready Reservists of all ranks and ratings readily fitted themselves into their assigned National Guard units and happily cooperated on every occasion toward proudly making it a highly-effective war strength unit.

It would have been a manpower miracle instead of a mobilization had not a wide variety of the recalled and unready Ready Reservists appeared with no knowledge of how they possibly could have been certified as skilled within the scope of their MOS card and number. Men with bulldozer and drag-bucket skills appeared in their MOS roles as Cooks. The worst case was a Reservist with MOS credentials as a top-rated, highly-skilled Signal Corps specialist on installation, maintenance and major repair of electrical cables and teletypewriter equipment. His actual technical knowledge, it soon was learned, began and ended with tire-changing ability and fan belt maintenance for a two-and-a-half-ton truck. Except for a few, such as the alleged cable expert, these sundry MOS errors tended to cancel one another so that the men affected finally were more-or-less slotted into assignments compatible with their actual skills. But before this happy end was achieved, some abiding faith in MOS cards had been jolted and some validity had been achieved in support of the "Why me?" plaints. Nevertheless, the operation demonstrated once again that men who initially were drafted Selectees could be assigned advantageously to volunteer National Guard units being inducted into Federal service.

A puzzled Congressman raised the query as to why the Air National Guard units inducted for the partial mobilization functioned so smoothly in comparison with the inducted Army Guard units. The full answer: (a) At home airports the Air Guard units were fully-equipped for immediate combat and at near war strength and with volunteer personnel. As noted above, neither of these conditions prevailed in the Army Guard units because of budgetary limitations. (b) Every fifth officer and man

(19% to be exact) in the Air Guard inducted units was a fulltime, civilian, air equipment Technician and Administrative Assistant, employed by the State with Federal funds to work for and to serve in the Air National Guard. That is indeed a strong and highly effective cadre. In contrast the Army Guard units had 3% of their members as Technicians and Administrative Assistants in a similar fulltime employment status.* Once again it is conspicuously true that modern equipment and warfare have required an increasing Federalization of the National Guard and further that the Army National Guard can become as instantly ready for immediate deployment and combat as is the always-alert Air Guard, but only if and when the Nation similarly experiences such a sense of urgency that it is willing to pay the cost.

The foregoing are the answers to the Congressional query. It can be added that the *challenge* of today is a combining of the advantages of Federalization without loss of the inherent virtues of decentralization in military personnel affairs. There must be a stronger bid to and appreciation of the willing volunteer, as in the Air National Guard; a stronger feeling of continued obligation through the Ready Reserve period imposed upon the non-volunteer after he has been "rotated-out," as many of them so consider it when they have been returned to civil life from their initial tour of training with the Colors. Through close adherence to the decentralized design of Major General Enoch Crowder in the first Draft Law, 1917, and in further close cooperation with the States, General Hershey and his Selective Service machinery have performed smoothly and in a distinctly superior manner in getting young men into the uniform. Perhaps the scope of that machinery and organization can be expanded to the trained but less-than-willing "Obligors" in the great pool of non-participating, Ready Reservists, who think they were off the hook the day of their release from the Colors to civil life pursuits. In such a program the National Guard, both Army and Air, necessarily would play an even more vital role in the Nation's defense. And they have nothing for which to apologize now. If there are weaknesses in America's defense posture through these recent Cold War years, it is because less spirited and less responsible civilian elements in America's free society have not reacted to the dangers from a foreign foe with the same alacrity as have the Volunteer Organized Militiamen of today—the National Guardsmen of the States, Army and Air.

On the whole, the recent, little partial mobilization was a marked success. It certainly accomplished its purpose, and that is all any mobilization ever did—with or without subsequent hostilities. Indeed, the

---

* In the preceding chapter an Air National Guard Group was described in which there were 750 officers and men, of whom 150, or 20%, were fully-employed Air Technicians and Administrative Assistants. In an entire Pentomic Infantry Division, with a home station, peace strength total of 9,000 officers and men, only 270, or 3%, were fully-employed Technicians, Supply and Administrative Assistants.

most successful are those without the casualty lists. Nevertheless, a Pentagon Staff officer in friendly criticism opined a fundamental weakness was the multiplicity of military options available to America's young manhood before and after registration with his local Selective Service Board. Their variety and number keep the young men and the public constantly and completely confused, he thought.

It is a tenable theory for purposes of argumentation but one with which the author and many others thoroughly and completely disagree. A society committed to freedom, that always has looked to its free citizenry for the military manpower with which to protect those freedoms, must allow its militarily-obligated citizenry a maximum of freedoms of choice as to the manner in which they serve toward the National purpose and cause. If the Pentagon cannot reach the people (and the larger the centralized bureaucracy, the greater are its handicaps to this end) with satisfactory clarity and understanding of the people, the job should be turned-over entirely to Selective Service and the National Guardsmen of the States. The ability of these agencies, when unshackled from centralized, bureaucratic restraints, to reach the people with sound thinking on the subject of one's military obligation, has been proved again, again, and again since the days of the Colonial Minute Men, and after Enoch Crowder corrected the gross errors that created the Civil War Draft Law debacle.

However, there are some other attractive, non-military options available to the modern young men as they approach the age at which they necessarily ponder the implications of a notice from their local Selective Service Board. These options are not neatly tabulated in the Government's information literature. They are collectively known to cynical high school Counsellors, to the apprehensively fond parents and even to their less-than venturesome young men as "finessing the Selective Service trick."

A "Jack-high finesse," as should be expected, is uncertain and often accompanied by unpleasant revision of vocational plans. It consists of immediate initiation of a vocational training or an educational program for early admission to a sheltered trade or profession or an employment area of defense and manpower shortages. Satisfactory progress in such programs leads to sequential deferments through or beyond the highly-vulnerable ages 21 to 26.

The "Queen-high finesse" is initially quite attractive, though thoughtful young men often ponder its long-range potential for unhappiness far more than do their nervously, overly-apprehensive and possessive parents. The Queen finesse calls for the "Obligor's" early marriage and a quick baby well in advance of a possibly crucial conversation with his Draft Board. Normally, this is a sure win for the "Obligor," because the Draft Board seldom holds more than a lightly-guarded King in the trump suit.

551

And, of course, the "Obligor" who can offer both the Queen and the Jack protected by two or three small ones can triumph against even the rarely-encountered Ace-King combination in the hands of a Draft Board.

Some pessimistic moderns view these self-evident trends with lifted eyebrows of alarm that are hardly justified. Men of low spirit and small sense of service were finessing the same tricks with the same cards when England's Alfred the Great organized volunteer bands of armed men in each town, pledged to rendezvous at previously-designated tactical stations when the "hue and cry" of an alarmed countryside identified hostile barbarians on one of the conventional approaches to the town or community. The same was inevitably true on the first Indian frontiers.

Generals George Washington, Nathaniel Greene and their followers often encountered the Queen-high and Jack-high finesse through their long seven years to a delayed triumph. These options were often apparent, North and South, through the ordeals of Secession and Reunion. Need one be surprised or disheartened by their recurrence in our own century? Indeed, many of these young men are of spirit and with keen sense of duty once they are convinced their Country really needs them. To them, the option exercised is a decision of immediate priority, but one never recognizes the less selfish qualities in them until the emergency arises, and by that time they find themselves of far more limited value to their Country than would be the case were their military responsibility faced forthrightly without delay and at the conventional age.

Meanwhile, and by the same historic tokens, America always has had and, there is reason to believe she will always have, a high percentage of young men of high spirit and a keen sense of service. It is they who grow to become middle-aged and older leaders of sterling worth who always will constitute the continuing cadre of the National Guard. And as long as volunteer citizen-soldiers, sailors and airmen are America's principal asset for defense, there will be a National Guard. True, a future generation might change its name, even as the long-standing terms "Train Bands" and "Volunteer Militia" gave way to the modern term. But the Guard, in terms of its purposes and ideals will continue in America until the much-talked-of but always more distant dawn of the Pacifistic Millenium. Accordingly, Wisconsin's Judge Kenneth S. White, then an officer of the 120th Field Artillery, was thoroughly prophetic, as well as irritatingly facetious, when he offered a toast to a friendly but unduly zealous, nit-picking Inspector with: "Regulations may come and Regulations may go. But the Guard goes on forever!"

# Bibliographical Note For Chapter XXI

Treatment of subjects of such contemporary interest necessarily rests heavily upon interviews, opinions and such ephemera as daily news reports, editorials, Congressional reactions, and Departmental and Selective Service information bulletins, and Armed Services releases and informational pamphlets. The avalanche of magazine articles and comments is too varied for characterization, but more were deeply concerned with the International tensions of the Berlin situation rather than the unduly-magnified petty discontents of a militarily-obligated, personnel minority. George Fielding Eliot's *Reserve Forces and the Kennedy Strategy*, 1962, is a thin but highly-perceptive and up-to-date volume.

# The Author

JIM DAN HILL commenced a colorful career as a youthful Texas ranch-hand. Along the way to his present position as President of Wisconsin State College, he served as a sailor in the U. S. Navy, as a merchant seaman and college professor. There was time out for college and post-graduate work leading to a Ph.D. in history and government.

The Army and writing are hobbies of long standing. He began his military career as a Second Lieutenant in the Organized Reserve Corps of the Army in 1923, retiring in 1956 as a Major General, having commanded the famed 32nd Infantry Division of the Wisconsin National Guard for 10 years. Graduated from the U. S. Army Command and General Staff College in 1940, he assumed command of the 120th Field Artillery Regiment of Wisconsin, later transferring to command of the 190th Field Artillery Regiment of Pennsylvania. He served in the European Theater during World War II and wears five combat stars and an Arrowhead (for assault landing on Omaha Beach in Normandy) on his European Theater medal. His other combat decorations include the Air Medal; the Bronze Star Medal, for leading Task Force Hill in the capture and occupation of Leipsig by the U. S. V Corps; and the Legion of Merit, for service during the Battle of the Bulge. He also was awarded the French Croix de Guerre with Palm and Chevalier, Legion d' Honneur.

During the Korean War, General Hill was Chairman of the Army's General Staff Committee on National Guard and Reserve Policy and later he served as a member of the Department of Defense Reserve Forces Policy Board. In those positions he was frequently on active duty in the Pentagon.

The author of two other books, *Sea Dogs of the Sixties* and *The Texas Navy*, both now available in paperback editions, he has written since 1950 a weekly newspaper column, *Let's Look At the Record*, which is published by a number of newspapers.

# Index

154th (Little Rock, Arkansas) non-divisional, 527n; assigned to VII Corps, 527;

489th and 490th Fighter, 532;

840 and 885th Bombardment, 532;

34th Photo Reconnaissance Squadron, World War II, 532;

35th Reconnaissance Squadron, World War II, 532;

37th Photo Reconnaissance Squadron (Long Range Weather), World War II, 532;

39th Tactical Reconnaissance Squadron, World War II, 532

Alabama, military strength during Civil War, 93; readmitted to Union, 107; within the IV Area, 355; 31st Infantry (Dixie) Division, 271, 507; 106th Observation Squadron (Birmingham), 527; see also Divisions, Regiments and lesser units, Air Wings and Squadrons

*Alabama, C.S.S.;* see Civil War, maritime aspects of

Alaska, within IX Corps Area, 359; Territorial Guards after Pearl Harbor, 486n; see also Divisions, Regiments and lesser units, Squadrons

Aleutian Islands, occupied by the Japanese, 450

Alexander, Gen. William L., Sec. of N.G. Constitutional Convention, 321-2; biographical sketch, 323

*Alfonso XII;* see Spanish-American War, Spanish ships in

Alger, Russell A., biographical sketch, 154-55

*America in Arms,* by Brig. Gen. John McA. Palmer, 241, 488

Americal Division; see Divisions

*The American Army,* by Maj. Gen. William H. Carter, mentioned, 204

*American Campaigns,* by Lt. Col. Matthew F. Steele, mentioned 250n

American Defense Society, 227

American Expeditionary Force (AEF); see World War I

America's Active Army; see "The Active Army"

Ames, Adelbert, carpetbagger Gov. of Miss., 47n, 111n, 116

Anderson, Lt. Gen. Sir Kenneth, commands First British Army, 460

Anderson, Maj. Robert, U.S.A., surrenders Fort Sumter, 41, 47n

Anglo-American TORCH Landings in North Africa; see World War II

Ansell, Lt. Col. Samuel T., adds penal clauses to Draft Bill, 252-3; see also Legislation

Anthony, Kansas Representative, questions effect of R.A. on the Guard, 301-2

"Appointments Board," actually a "Removal Board," 423

Arizona, activation of Nat. Gd. in 1916, 222; 40th (Sunshine) Division, 272; part of VIII Corps Area, 358; mentioned, 486n; see also Divisions, Regiments and lesser units, Air Wings and Squadrons

Arkansas, military strength during Civil War, 93; readmitted to Union, 107; Brooks Baxter War, see Civil War Reconstruction; 39th Infantry (Delta) Division, 272; part of IV Corps Area, 355; 154th Observation Squadron (Little Rock), 527, 527n; see also Divisions, Regiments and lesser units, Air Wings and Squadrons

Armed Forces Reserve Act of 1962; see Legislation

Armored Divisions; see Divisions

Armored Force, creation of, 468

"Armory Associations," purpose of, 198

Army, definition of term; 26; see also U.S. Army

Army Air Forces, 1941, forerunner U.S. Air Force, 526n

Army Appropriations Bill, March 2, 1867; see Legislation

Army Corps, established by Pershing, 279; components of 280-1 Nat. Gd. Regiments and Corps, Aviation Squadrons as elements of an Army Corps prior to 1940-1; note table 364-5

Army General Staff, attitude toward Nat. Gd., 369; 5 Rainbow Plans, description of, 370n; see also War Dept., General Staff

Army GHQ Reserve of Nat. Gd. Cav. Divisions, Brigades and Regiments, Infantry and Artillery prior to 1940-1, note table, 362-3; reorganization policy, 543

Army League, 215

Army Reserve Corps, a child of the Nat. Gd., 340

Arnold, Maj. Gen. H. H., Chief of Air Corps, 365n; welcomes out-of-age-in-grade officers from Guard and Reserve, 436; Air Corps becomes Army Air Forces, 526n; mentioned, 523

Astor Place Riot, 1849, quelled by New York 7th Infantry Regiment, 46-7

**B**

Bacon, Sen. A. O., protests use of "immune volunteers," 166

Brigades, normally organic within divs., hence *see also* Divisions. Selected separate brigades: Excelsior Brig. (N.Y., Civil War), 72; Iron Brigade (Wis., Mich. Ind., Civil War), 60; Duffield's Brig. (Mich., Spanish-American War), 167; 56th Cav. Brig. (Texas, 1922-40 Mobilization), 362; 73rd F.A. Brig., Separate (Louisiana, Pa.), 377, 444, 449, 469

"Brindle-tails;" *see* Civil War, Reconstruction

British Regulars, 2

British Territorials, 28

Britton, Col. Edward, Chairman of National Guard Executive Committee, 184

Brokaw, Lt. Col. Frank E., 411

Brokaw, Col. Stuart F., 436

Brooks, Maj. Gen. John R., at Arroyo, Puerto Rico, 168-9

Brooks-Baxter War; *see* Civil War Reconstruction, 112-3

Brown, Maj. Gen. Jacob, 17

Brown, Maj. Gen. Lloyd D., against Nat. Gd., 414-5; commands Pa. 28th Inf. Div., 415; mentioned, 435n

Brownlow, William G. (Parson), Scalawag Gov. of Tenn., 111n; biographical sketch, 116-7

Bryan, William Jennings, 222

Buchanan, James 38, 41

"Buckeye," 37th National Army Division, 266

Buell, Maj. Gen. Don Carlos, 69

Bull Run, battle of, exaggerated importance of, 62; unifying effect on the South, 67; myth concerning Northern defeat over First Bull Run, 1861, 472; mentioned, 44, 63, 82, 83, 94

Bullard, Lt. Gen. Robert Lee, opposed segregated Divisions in World War I, 121, 121n

Bullock, Rufus R., restores Militia rights in Georgia, 109-10

Bureau for Colored Troops, 86

Burke, Sen. Edward R., aid in preparedness legislation, 371

Burnside, Ambrose E., 47n

Butler, Maj. Gen. Benjamin F., 26n, 55, 57, 111n

C

Cadwallader, Maj. Gen. Thomas, member of Barbour Board, 320

California, military strength during Civil War, 92; 49th Inf. Div., 272, 281, 333, 506; San Francisco Teamster Strike,

July 1, 1934, 132n; part of IX Corps Area, 359; 115th Observation Squadron (Los Angeles), 527n; *see also* Divisions, Regiments and lesser units; Air Wings and Squadrons

Cameron, Simon 57

Camp Barkeley, Abilene, Texas, conditions in Sept., 1940, 407

Camp Blanding, Florida, maintenance costs, 417

Camp Bowie, Fort Worth, Texas, 265

Camp Edwards, Massachusetts, 479

Camp Grant, Rockford, Illinois, 273

Camp Greene, North Carolina, 267, 270

Camp Jackson, South Carolina, conditions at, Stp. 16, 1940, 408-9

Camp Logan, Houston, Texas, 265

Camp MacArthur, Waco, Texas, 265

Camp Meade, Maryland, 417

Camp Mills, Long Island, New York, 272

Camp Murray, Washington, conditions Sept., 1940, 408

Camp Ramsey, Minnesota, 160

Camp Shelby, Mississippi, 419

Camp Stuart, training center, "1st Squadron, Virginia Cavalry," 235

Camp Sutton, North Carolina, 449

Camp Upton, New York, 265n

Camp Wadsworth, Spartansburg, South Carolina, 277

Canby, Maj. Gen. E.R.S., U.S.V., 73

"Can Do," 15th U.S. Inf., 360

Carnot, Capt. Lazare N.M., Corps de Genie, French Army, balloon essayist, 517

Carranza, Venustiano, 230, 240; *see also* Mexican Revolution 1911-7

Casalegno, Mario Terenzio, Enrico; *see* Woodhouse, Henry

Carson, Kit, serves in Santa Fe Battalion, 24n

Carter, Brig. Gen. Jesse M., commands 11th Div., 298; Chief of the Militia Bureau, 298; admits to discrimination against Nat. Gd., 295-6; opposes Frelinghuysen Bill, 308; mentioned, 300

Carter, George W.; *see* Civil War, Reconstruction, Warmoth-Carter Feud

Carter, Maj. Gen. William H., advocates Upton's theories, 172; biographical sketch, 204; plans 30 U.S.V. Regiments, 180; mentioned, 186

Casualties, see Statistics and Strengths

Catledge, Turner, columnist for *N. Y. Times*, 341

Cavalry Divisions; *see* Army, GHQ Reserve of Nat. Gd. Cav. Divs., Brigs., etc.

Colored Units, casualties in, 277-8; *see also* Confederate States of America; Divisions, Colored; Negro; Spanish-American War; immune Regiments; U.S. Volunteer Regiments, U.S. Colored Troops, U.S.C.T.

Columbus, New Mexico, 13th U.S. Cavalry base, 230

Combat fatigue, attitudes towards, 485, 485n

Command and General Staff College, Fort Leavenworth, Kansas; *see* Service Schools

Commissions in U.S. Volunteers, definition of term, 30

"Companies," definition of term, 90n

Confederate States of America, formation of, 39; bound by Militia Acts of 1792, 1795, 39; constitution formulated, 39; legislation resulting in a Provisional Army, 40; military legislation, 43-4; basis of solidarity, 44-5; States admitted to the Confederacy, 54-5; recruitment policy, 67-8, 94; military promotion policy, 93; Negroes in, 121; *see also* Provisional Army, Confederate States of America (PACS); Secession

Connecticut, military strength during the Civil War, 92; part of I Corps Area, 354; 43rd Inf. Div., 506, 542; 118th Observation Squadron (Hartford), 527n; *see also* Divisions, Regiments and lesser units; Air Wings and Squadrons

Conscription, consideration of, 18-9; *see also* Colored Draftees; Draft Legislation; Draftees; Legislation; Obligors; Selective Service

Constitutional Government of the United States; *see* Wilson, Woodrow

Continental Army, relationship to the U.S. Regular Army, 8

"Continental Army" idea; *see* War Department

"Continental Army" Plan; *see* War Department

Coolidge, Calvin, 196

Cooper, Gen. Samuel, Confederate Army, 84

Corps Areas, as a manpower organization plan, 353; description of Corps Areas I, II, III, IV, V, VI, VII, VIII, IX, 354-60; Nat. Gd. Regiments and aviation Squadrons within each, 364

Couch, Gen. Darius N., commands Department of the Susquehanna, 66

Continental Army program, 241, 247

Continental Congress, status of military commissions made by, 25

Continental Line, prototypes of the

Organized Militia, 6; disbanded, 7; mentioned, 2

Coral Sea, naval battle, World War II, 450

Corps Areas, as a manpower organization plan, 353

"Corps Aviation Troops;" *see* National Guard Observation Squadrons

*Corps d' Afrique; see* U.S. Volunteer Regiments

Craig, Gen. Malin, Chief of Staff, 1935-9, 365n; career sketch, 391n; chairman of "Appointments Board," 423

Cramer, Maj. Gen. Kenneth F., career sketch, 477; commands 43rd Infantry Division, Federalized, 506

Crane, Stephen, war correspondent, 238, 328

"Crime of '99," 178, 194; *see also* "The Hump"

Crimean War, 48

Cripple Creek Massacre, 127

Crittenden, Col. Thomas T., commands 6th Indiana Volunteers, 58

Crowder, Brig. Gen. Enoch H., biographical sketch, 250-3; gains support for a draft bill, 254; draftees become organized, 266; decentralized design of first draft law, 1917, 550, 551; mentioned 284

Crown commissions, 2

Crown troops, 2

C.S.A.; *see* Confederate States of America

Custer, Lt. Col. George A., 47n, 100n

"Cyclone," Division, 38th (Indiana, Kentucky, West Virginia) Infantry, 271; *see also* Divisions

## D

D-Day, June 6, 1944; *see* World War II, European Theater; OVERLORD

Daley, Maj. Gen. Edmund L., commands V Army Corps Force Headquarters and MAGNET FORCE, 444, 449; relieved of duty, 449-50

Daniel, Beverly, 320

Darlington, Dr. T., sent to Southwest by N.Y. State, 241

Davis, Henry Winter, Radical Republican, 101

Davis, Col. Jefferson, commands 1st Miss. Rifles, 25-6; inaugurated Provisional President, 39; works toward expansion of P.A.C.S. Volunteers, 66; 1st call for volunteer troops, 75; mentioned 40, 43, 44, 49-50, 53, 74, 81, 111n

Davis, Richard Harding, critical of Army, 167-8; as war correspondent, 215, 238, 328; mentioned, 227

pany, Coast Artillery Corps, Nat. Gd. of Calif., 522

Forrest, Lt. Gen. Nathan B., 47n, 84

Forrestal, James V., 1st Defense Secretary, 500n

Forsyth, George A., 186n

Fort Adams, 354

Fort Benning, 334, 355

Fort Bliss, 358

Fort Cook, 358

Fort Des Moines, 358

Fort Devens, 354, 449

Fort Dix, 335, 408, 449

Fort Dodge, 273

Fort Donelson, 67

Fort Duquesne (Pittsburgh), 8

Fort Ethan Allan, 354

Fort Francis E. Warren, 358

Fort Henry, 67

Fort Hood, 548

Fort Knox, 356

Fort Leavenworth, 358

Fort Lewis, 548

Fort McHenry, 13

Fort Riley, 193, 358

Fort Sam Houston, 358

Fort Sheridan, 357

Fort Sill, 334, 407-8

Fort Snelling, 358

Fort Sumter, 40-2, 44, 53, 66

Foster, Brig. Gen. J. Clifford R., Pres. of Nat. Gd. Assn. of U.S., 1926, 329

Foulois, Lt. Benjamin D., U.S. Army, 520, 523

Fox, John, Jr., war correspondent, 328

Fox, Col. William F., 84

France, invasion of; see World War II, European Theater; OVERLORD

Franco-Prussian War, offered technical interest, 133

Franklin, Benjamin, commissions foreigners, 5; as a Pennsylvania Colonel organizes "military associations," 186

Fraser, Col. G. Angus, Pres. of Nat. Gd. Assn. of U.S., 127-8, 330

Fredendall, Lt. Gen. Lloyd R., commands II Corps, North African Campaign, 460; ideas on combat, 472

Freedmen; see Civil War; Reconstruction

Freedmen's Bureau Bill, July 16, 1866; see Legislation

Fremont, John C., 47n

Frelinghuysen, Joseph S., 307

Frelinghuysen Bill; see Legislation

French and Indian War, 4, 186

Fry, Maj. Gen. James B., U.S.V., 68, on failures of the Civil War Draft, 251, 251n

Fugitive Slave Act, 48

Funston, Maj. Gen. Frederick, as a Guardsman in the Philippines, 177; or C.G. on Mexican Border, 219, 226, 233, 239

FUSAG; see First United States Army Group

## G

Garde Nationale, 29

Garfield, Col. James A., appointed by Gov. Dennison, Ohio, 63

Garis, Maj. W. C., 525

Garrison, Lindley Miller, Sec. of War, plans to limit the Nat. Gd. to a home front, 211; explains meaning of a Reserve, 212-13; rejects Nat. Gd. as a manpower source, 216; follows General Staff's policy, 220n; hassle over the Philippines Resolution, 229; resigns as Sec. of War, 229; mentioned 215, 241, 247, 250, 314

Gates, Horatio, renounces a Regular Major's commission, 5

General Headquarters Reserves; see Army, GHQ Reserves of

General von Steuben, by Brig. Gen. John McA. Palmer mentioned, 488

General Staff; see War Dept., General Staff

Georgia, military strength during the Civil War, 51, 93; Militia Rights restored July 1, 1870, 109; 31st Infantry (Dixie) Division, 271; part of IV Corps Area, 355; 30th Division, 408-9, 461, 462; 128th Observation Squadron, 527; see also Divisions; Regiments and lesser units; Air Wings and Squadrons

German officers, attitudes toward American Divisions, 473

Gerow, Maj. Gen. Leonard T., commands V Corps, OVERLORD operation, 461

Geronimo, 209

Gettysburg, 66

Gibbons, Floyd, biographical sketch 238-9; reports on Nat. Gd. operations in the Southwest, 238-9

Gignilliat, Brig. Gen. Leigh R., 352

Gilbert, Edward, 322

Gompers, Samuel, labor leader, 126

Gordon, Lt. Gen. John B., Confederate Army, 47n, 84

Grahl, Charles H., 495

Grant, Gen. Ulysses S., success at Forts Henry and Donelson, 67; advises against use of Organized Militia in Reconstruction, 103-4; Presidential candidate, 107; recognizes Gov. Baxter, 113; mentioned, 47n, 72, 112, 116, 133

Grant, Ulysses S., III, 418

Great Railroad Strike of 1877, 125, 126, 128, 129

Greble, Maj. Gen. Edwin St. John, commands 36th Nat. Gd. Division, 265

Green, Maj. Gen. John T., Confederate Army, 47n

Greene, Maj. Gen. Nathaniel, 547, 552

Greenlaw, Brig. Gen. Albert, 268n

Gregory, Brig. Gen. Stanford W., 339

Grenadier Guards, 4

"Grenadiers," 11, 12, 195; see also Organized Militia, peacetime (National Guard) units

Grigsby, Col. Melvin, commands 3rd Regiment U.S. Volunteer Cavalry, 156

Gruenther, Gen. Alfred M., as example of promotions problem caused by "the Hump," 390

Grunert, Maj. Gen. George, 476n

Guantanamo Bay, 143; see also Spanish-American War

Gubernatorial Honorary Commissions, confusion arising from, 396-7

H

Haan, Gen. William G. (Bunker), commands 32nd Infantry Division, 275; favors continuance of Nat. Gd. system, 292; mentioned, 281

Haffner, Maj. Gen. Charles C., Jr., Illinois Guardsman commands Division in combat, 477

Halleck, Maj. Gen. Henry W., on quality of drafted soldiers, 474; mentioned 47n, 71

Hamilton, Alexander, organizes the N. Y. Artillery Battery, 8

Hamilton, Maj. Gen. Charles B., 60-1

Hampshire, H. M. S., 226n

Hancock, Maj. Gen. Winfield Scott, commands I Veteran Corps, 73; mentioned, 89

Hard, Brig. Gen. Dudley A., President of National Guard Association of America, 1930-31, 330

Hardee, Lt. Gen. William J., Confederate Army, use of Union prisoners, 96

Harding, Maj. Gen. Edwin F., commands 32nd Inf. Div., 411n

Harding, Pres. Warren G., 219

Harrison, Maj. Gen. William H., Jr., President of National Guard Association of the U.S., 1957-63, 345

Hartford, U.S.S., 36

Hartle, Maj. Gen. Russell P., U. S. Army, commands 34th Inf. Div., 341, 449; commands V Corps in Ireland, 451

Hartman, Lt. Col. John D. L., commands Virginia's 1st Provisional Regiment, 235, 236

Harvey, Philip F., 160

Harvey, William, 30n

Havana, Cuba, 143

Havens, Pvt. Beckwith, 520

Hawaii, armed forces in, as of 1936, 359; Nat. Gd. as of 1939, 364; Nat. Gd. after Pearl Harbor, 486n

Hay, James, chairman of Home Military Affairs Committee, 218; feud with Garrison, 229; author of National Defense Act of June 3, 1916, 231, 240; Hay Bill of April 2, 1914; see Legislation

Hayes, Col. Rutherford B., commissioned by Gov. Dennison, 63; presidential campaign of 1876, 118

Hayes-Tilden election controversy, 129

Haymarket Riot and Bombing, 126

Hayward, Col. William, commands 15th N. Y. Inf. (Colored), 277

Haywood, "Big Bill," Communist labor leader, 127

Hazzard, Capt. Russell T., 177

Heavy, Brig. Gen. John S., 298

Heil, Julius (the Just), Gov. of Wis., issues Honorary Colonelcies, 397

Hendricks, Sen. Thomas A., opposes Southern Militia rights, 108

Hendrickson, Maj. Gen. Norman E., commands 47th Inf. Div., federalized, 507

Henry, Joseph, balloonist, 518

Herkimer, Maj. Gen. Nicholas, New York citizen soldier, 8, 349

Hershey, Maj. Gen. Lewis B., as Director of Selective Service, 337, 350; attends Nat. Gd. conference, April 1, 1943, 342

Hill, Maj. Gen. Daniel Harvey, Confederate Army, 47n, 76, 84

Hitler, Adolf, 365, 418, 443

History of the American People, by Woodrow Wilson, mentioned, 227

Hobbs, Maj. Gen. Leland S., commands 30th Division, 415n

Hodges, Maj. Gen. Campbell B., 476

Hodges, Gen. Courtney H., 477n, 483

Hoffman, Maj. Gen. Roy, Oklahoma Nat. Gd., commands 93rd Inf. (Colored) Div., 278

Holmes, Brig. Gen. T. M., at Bull Run, 63

Home Guard, 6, 7, 12, 72

Hones, Lt. Col. William, 411

Honolulu, as seapower base in 1936, 359

Hood. Gen., Confederate Army, 84

Hooker, Joe, 47n

Hoover, President Herbert, 196

Hopkins, Harry L., WPA Chief, 365n
Huddleston, Maj. Gen. Daniel H., California's 40th Inf. Div., federalized, 506
Huerta, Victoriano, overthrow of, 226; *see also* Mexican Revolution, 1911-17
Huidekoper, Frederic L., Pres. of Army League, 215; attitudes toward World War I preparedness, 227, 227n
Hulings, Col. William J., commands 16th (Pa.) Inf. in Puerto Rico, 169
Hull, Brig. Gen. William, court-martial of, 441n
"The Hump": reason for in promotion list, 398-90; causes age-in-grade policy, 434; mentioned, 194, 388
Hunt, Gen. L. F., at Nat. Gd. Convention, 321

## I

Idaho, 41st (Sunset) Infantry Division, 272, 408; part of IX Corps, 359; *see also* Divisions; Regiments and lesser units
Illinois, military strength during the Civil War, 92; organized Militia in Spanish-American War, 157; Chicago's Black Horse Troop, 217; 1st Illinois Cavalry, 236; 33rd N. A. Division formed from Nat. Gd., 265; 8th Infantry (Colored) Division, 273; part of VI Corps Area, 356; 44th Infantry Division, inactivated, 507, 541; 108th Observation Squadron (Chicago), 527n; *see also* Divisions, Regiments and lesser units; Air Wings and Squadrons
Immel, Maj. Gen. Ralph M., A.U.S., 477; Adjutant General, Wis., 403; military career following Pearl Harbor, 437, 477
"Immunes," Regiments of, 156, 225; *see also* Spanish-American War
Indiana, military strength during the Civil War, 92, 169; 38th (Cyclone) Division, 271; part of V Corps Area, 356; 113th Observation Squadron (Indianapolis), 527; *see also* Divisions; Regiments and lesser units; Air Wings and Squadrons
Influenza; *see* World War I, influenza
International Longshoremen's Association, 732n
International Working Peoples' Association, 126
Interstate National Guard Association, 327; *see also* National Guard Association of the United States
Invalid Corps; *see* Provisional Army, Confederate States of America (PACS); and U. S. Veteran Reserve Corps

Iowa, military strength during the Civil War, 92; Keokuk's Company L, Nat. Gd., 240; 34th (Red Bull) Division, 271, 542; part of VII Corps Area, 357-8; part in World War II, 444; *see also* Divisions; Regiments and lesser units; Air Wings and Squadrons
"Iowa Mormon Volunteers," 24
"Irrepressible Conflict," 79; *see also* Civil War
*Isabel II; see* Spanish-American War

## J

Jackson, Maj. Gen. Andrew, force strength at New Orleans, 16; in Regular Army following War of 1812, 17; Florida campaign, 152
Jackson, Maj. Gen. Nathaniel J., of Maine, 58
Jackson, (Stonewall) Thomas J., 47n, 64, 76, 84
Jefferson, Thomas, attitude toward Regular Army, 8
Jefferson, Barracks, 356
Jeffreys, Herbert, commander of King's First Guards, 4
Johnson, Pres. Andrew, recognizes the provisional, or "Ten Percent Governments," 102-3; biggest mistake in Reconstruction policy, 103; criticism of, 104-5; problems arising from Army Appropriations Bill, March 2, 1867, 106; mentioned, 108
Johnson, Capt. Hugh S., co-author of Draft Bill, 250; *see also* Legislation
Johnson, Louis A., 370
Johnston, Gen. Joseph E., Confederate Army, 47n, 63, 76, 81, 84

## K

Kahn, Julius, 309
Kahn Bill; *see* Legislation
Kaiser, 222
Kansas, 1st Kansas Colored Infantry, 87; military strength during the Civil War, 92, 35th (Santa Fe) Division, 271, 461-2, 542; part of VII Corps Area, 357-8; 127th Observation Squadron, 528; *see also* Divisions; Regimental and lesser units; Air Wings and Squadrons
*Kearsarge, U.S.S.,* 140-1
Keehn, Maj. Gen., Roy B., Pres. of Nat. Gd. Assn. of the U.S., 1934-35; 330
Kellogg controversy, 114; *see also* Civil War, Reconstruction, Louisiana Governorship controversy, 1872-4
Kelly, Col. Reginald H., 411

Kenney, Gen. George C., commands 5th, 7th, 13th Air Forces, 458

Kent, Frank R., columnist for *Baltimore Sun*, 341

Kentucky, military strength during the Civil War, 92, 93n; Nat. Gd. strength by 1903, 185; 38th (Cyclone) Division, 271; part of V Corps Area, 356; *see also* Divisions; Regiments and lesser units; Air Wings and Squadrons

Key, Maj. Gen. William S., commands (Oklahoma) Nat. Gd. Div., 407

Key, Philip Barton, killed by Sickles, 56

Kimmel, Adm. Husband E., U.S.N., role in Pearl Harbor disaster, 440-441n

King, Brig. Gen. Rufus, commands Wisconsin's 2nd Regiment, 60

King George's War, 4

King William's War, 4

King's First Guards, 1st Regiment of British Regulars in America

Kitchener, Field Marshal Horatio, attitude toward World War I preparedness, 226n

Knights of Labor, 126

Know Nothings, 46

Knudsen, Lt. Gen. William S., commissioned by Pres. Franklin Roosevelt, 8

Korean Police Action, strength of Armed Forces at outbreak, 501-2; outbreak June 24, 1950, 502; official title of the Korean War, 503n; recruitment policies, 503-6; effect of retreat from Seoul to Pusan, 506; rotation policy interferes with efficiency, 508; educational or vocational training benefits resulting from, 509n; casualties, 510; Air Nat. Gd. units and non-divisional Ground Force units in, 507-10; example of extreme waste, 510-14; Divisions participating in, 511, 511n; explanation for mass of "pay-rolled" manpower, 511-3; Armistice, July 27, 1953, 514; survey of Air Force strength, 534-5; mentioned, 22

Korean War; *see* Korean Police Action

Krag magazine rifle; *see* Military Weapons

Krag-Jorgensen repeaters; *see* Military Weapons

Kreber, Maj. Gen. Leo M., commands 37th (Ohio) Inf. Div., federalized, 507

Kreuger, Gen. Walter, commands Third Army, 395, 413; exemplary cooperation, 424; commands "Blue" forces in great maneuvers, 431; assigned to South Pacific, May, 1942, 433; mentioned, 433n, 472, 473n, 476, 476n

Kuhn, Brig. Gen. Joseph E., 253

## L

Labor Battalions, 274

Lafayette, coins phrase *Garde Nationale*, 29

LaFollette, Senator of Wisconsin, 254

Lamont, Daniel S., Sec. of War, 130

Lawrence, Capt. James, 394n

"Lawrence Minutemen," voluntary association, 19

Lawton, Gen. H. W., suppresses Aguinaldo's Tagalog Rebellion, 163

Lawton's Cavalry, pursues Geronimo, 209

Leach, Maj. Gen. George E., Pres. of Nat. Gd. Assn. of the U.S., 1937-38, 330; motorized Guard Artillery Regiments, 338; sends letter to Gen. Marshall, 490-1; career sketch, 490n

Leadville District Strike; *see* Colorado

Lear, Lt. Gen. Ben, resents army reorganization scheme of 1920, 392; assignment criticized, 394-5; hostile toward Nat. Gd., 395, 489; opposes Maj. Gen. Russell, 415n; commands Second Army (Red) 431; mentioned, 433n, 476n

Lee, Charles, renounces a Regular Lieutenant Colonelcy, 5

Lee, Edward Brooke, student of military legislation, 1940, 341

Lee, Gen. Robert E., Confederate Army, 47n, 62, 71, 76, 81, 84, 133

Legislation:

Federal Militia Act of 1792, based on State sovereignty, 9; effect of amending law of 1808, 10; actual purpose of, 10; effect on manpower by 1811, 11; restrictions of, 21; basis for Civil War mobilization, 43-4; superseded by the Dick Act, 186; mentioned, 45, 180, 188

Militia Act of Feb. 28, 1795, basis for Civil War mobilization policies, 43-4

Conscription Act, Apr. 16, 1862, provisions of, 68; amendments, 68; effect of C.S.A. Act on North, 69; superiority of the C.S.A. Draft Law, 69

Federal Act, March 3, 1863, background of, 69; provisions, 69-70; effect of hired-substitute provision, 70; results of the Union Draft law, 71; mentioned, 57, 69

Wade-Davis Bill, July 2, 1864, 102

Civil Rights Bill, April 9, 1866, 105

Freedmen's Bureau Bill, July 16, 1866, 105

Reconstruction Act of March 2, 1867, 105

Army Appropriations Bill, March 2, 1867, 106

Lovett, Robert M., Special Asst. to Sec. of War Stimson, 423; attitude toward War Dept., 423n

Lowe, Prof. T. C. S., Civil War Balloonist, 518

*Lusitania, R.M.S.*, 222, 243

## M

MacArthur, Brig Gen. Arthur, U. S. A., serves as Major General, U. S. V. in the Philippines, 177; suppresses Tagalog Rebellion, 163; mentioned, 47n

MacArthur, Gen. Douglas, favors Nat. Gd. in 1916 mobilization, 242; commands "Rainbow," 84th Infantry Brigade, 269; favors continuance of Nat. Gd. system, 292; idea of an All-American "Rainbow" Division, 297-8; Chief of Staff, 1930-5, 356, 365; Field Marshal of the Philippines, 1935, 360; career sketch, 391n; receives 41st, 32nd, 37th, Infantry Divisions, 451; returns to Philippines, 473n; relieved from duty, 512; mentioned, 335, 490

McClellan, Maj. Gen. George B., commands Ohio's Organized Militia, 61, 63; West Virginia campaign, 62; Peninsula Campaign, 64-5; adds a Balloon Section to Army, 518; mentioned, 47n, 67, 84

Macomb, Brig. Gen. Alexander, 17

McCormick, Col. Robert R., 247

McDowell, Maj. Gen. Irvin, defeat at Bull Run, 61-3; mentioned, 84

McEnery, John, 114; *see also* Civil War, Reconstruction, Louisiana; Governorship controversy, 1872, 74

Machine Gun Companies; *see* National Guard

McKinley, William, criticism of, 153; biographical sketch, 155; calls Organized Militia, April 23, 1898, 157; mobilization policy, 170; underestimated ease of Spain's defeat, 171; mentioned, 209

McLean, Brig. Gen. Milton R., Treasurer, National Guard Association of the U.S., 331; career sketch, 477

MacMahon, Marshal, 133

McNair, Brig. Gen. Lesley J., on value of horse drawn Artillery, 333; C. G., Army Ground Forces, 342, 344; resents Army personnel policy of 1920, 392-4; career sketch, 394-5; opposition to Nat. Gd., 395, 440, 443n, 489; promotion practices, 413-14, 425; opposes Maj. Gen. Russell, 415n; attitudes on training, 423-4; indoctrinates *Fortune* Magazine

interviewers, 438-9; FUSAG assignment in 1944, 440; weakness publicity an invitation to an attack, 442; dampens aspirations of Armored Corps, 468-9; effect of his age-in-grade policy, 478

Macready, English actor, 46-7

MAGNET FORCE; *see* World War II, European Theater

Mahan, Rear Admiral Alfred T., U. S. N., on importance of sea power, 133

Maine, military strength during Civil War, 92; part of I Corps Area, 354; *see also* Divisions; Regiments

*Maine*, battleship, sinking of, 151-2

Manila Bay, battle of, 152

Mann, Brig. Gen. William S., Chief of the Militia Bureau, 297; commander of "Rainbow" Division, 298

Manson, Col. Mahlon D., 59

March, Gen. Peyton C., Chief of Staff, World War I, 254n, 263, 284; career sketch, 292n; advocates U. M. T., 293; opposed by Nat. Gd., 293; One Army Manifesto, Aug. 7, 1918, 298; Army Reorganization Bill, 301-2; opposes Frelinghuysen Bill, 308; concept of a large professional Army, 314; favors European type expansible Army, 489; mentioned, 281, 300, 305, 309

Marshall, Gen. George Catlett, Jr., overestimates strength of Japan, 170; graduate, 178; Chief of Staff, 196, 365n, 448; age-in-grade directive, 341; attitude toward Nat. Gd. in 1940, 369; revises Protective Mobilization Plan, 371-3; career sketch, 391n; errors in personnel judgment, 395n; visits Camp Jackson, 409; requests advice of Brig. Gen. John McA. Palmer, U.S.A., Ret., 487-8; ignores Palmer's advice, 490; suspends Nat. Gd. representation within the War Dept., 491; removes Nat. Gd. Bureau from War Dept. Special Staff, 491; categorized as non-Uptonian, 491n; attitude toward U.M.T., 494; mentioned, 22, 292, 342n, 370, 372; 417-8, 433n, 476n

Martin, Maj. Gen. Edward, President, National Guard Association of the U.S., 1940-3, 330; career sketch, 337-8; commands 28th Division, World War II, 341; Governor of Pennsylvania, 342; confers with Nat. Gd. leaders, 342, 495; views in 1944, 497

Martinsburg, West Virginia strike, 125

*Maryland Line*, 2

Marx, Karl, 126n

Maryland, military strength during Civil War, 92, 93n; 29th Nat. Gd. Division,

Chief, 312n; duties of, 333; renamed "National Guard Bureau," in 1933, 334; *see also National Guard Bureau*

Militia Rights Bill 648, March 2, 1869; *see* Legislation

Miller, James E., 522n

Miller, Maj. Gen. Ray S., efforts to obtain a Minn. Nat. Gd. Air Unit, 525n; mentioned, 339, 526-7

Miller Field, Staten Island, 522n

Mills, Brig. Gen. Albert L., heads Militia Bureau, 210; rejects Nat. Gd. proposals, 211

Milroy, Col. Robert H., 9th Indiana Volunteers, 58

Mineola Aviation Field, Long Island, N.Y., 521

Minnesota, military strength during Civil War, 92; typical role of a State in Spanish-American War mobilization, 159-65; 34th (Red Bull) Infantry Division, 271, 444, 215th Coast Artillery (Anti Aircraft) Brigade, 366; part of VIII Corps Area, 357; 205th Infantry Regiment redesignated Anti-Aircraft Coast Artillery, 366; 101st Coast Artillery Brigade, 366; 206th Infantry Regiment redesignated Harbor Defense Regiment, 366; 47th Infantry Division, 507, 543; 109th Observation Squadron (St. Paul), 526; *see also* Divisions; Regiments and lesser units; Air Wings and Squadrons

*Minnesota, U.S.S.,* steam frigate, 36

Minute Men, equivalent of modern Nat. Gd., 215; definition of term, 28-9

Mississippi, military strength during Civil War, 93; Militia rights restored, July 1870, 109; 31st Infantry Division, 507; 39th Infantry (Delta) Division, 272, 507; part of IV Corps Area, 355; 153rd Observation Squadron (Meridian), 527; *see also* Divisions; Regiments and lesser units; Air Wings and Squadrons

*Mississippi, U.S.S.,* 36

Mississippi, steamboat; *see* Civil War Reconstruction, Governorship controversy, 1872-4

Missouri, military strength during the Civil War, 92, 93n; 35th (Santa Fe) Division, 271, 461-2, 542; part of VII Corps Area, 357-8; 110th Observation Squadron (St. Louis), 527n; *see also* Divisions; Regiments and lesser units; Air Wings and Squadrons

*Missouri, U.S.S.,* Japanese capitulation aboard, 499

Mitchell, Burton J., 177

Mitchell, Brig. Gen. William ("Billy"),

authorizes plan for Minn. Nat. Gd. Air Unit, 525-6; elevates the Air Service to Air Corps, 526n

*Mohawk, U.S.S.,* screw gunboat, 36

"Molly McGuires," 126

Moltke, Helmuth von, captures Paris, 133

Monroe Doctrine, basis of American foreign policy, 100, 134, 152

Montana, 41st (Sunset) Division, 272, 408, 486n; part of IX Corps Area, 359; *see also* Divisions; Regiments and lesser units; Air Wings and Squadrons

Montgomery, Richard, 5

*Montgomery, U.S.S.; see* Maryland Naval Militia

Morale problem, 427-9, 431

Morgan, Edwin D., Gov. of N.Y., 26n, 37, 55

Morton, O. P., Gov. of Indiana, 60, 62

MOS; *see* Military Occupational Specialty

Moseley, Captain V. H., author of 1915 Draft Law, 246-7; 250

Moss, Brig. Gen. Harvey J., President of National Guard Association of the U.S., 329

Most, Johaan, founds International Working People's Association, 126; biographical sketch, 127n; mentioned, 131

Muehlberg, Hermann, Adjutant General of Minnesota, 158

Mustering days, 19

## N

Napoleon III, withdraws from Western Hemisphere, 100, 151

Nash, Frederick O.; *see* Civil War, Reconstruction, Governorship controversy in Louisiana, 1872-4

*Nation at War,* by Gen. Peyton C. March, mentioned, 254n

National Army of World War I, 2, 31

National Association for Universal Military Training, 247

National Defense Act, 1916; *see* Legislation

National Defense Act, 1920; *see* Legislation

National Guard; *see* National Guard of the United States

National Guard Air Corps Squadrons, organization of, 367; *see also* Air Wings and Squadrons

National Guard Air Units, factors detracting attention from, 523; struggle for Federal status, 524

National Guard Association of America; *see* National Guard Association of the United States

National Guard Association of the United States, origin of, 129-30, 320; campaign for nationwide publicity, 182-3; Elihu Root addresses the Association, 1903, 192; stresses joint reorganization of Regulars and Guard, 201; St. Louis conference, 1897, 327; 1919, 304; importance of, 320; first elected officers, 322; report of Special Committee concerning Federal legislation, 323-4; attitude on officer training, 324-5; method of electing officers, 329-31; Executive Council, 331; desirous of place for Guardsmen in Army schools, 334; *see also* Interstate National Guard Association

National Guard co-ordination, prior to 1860, 319-20

National Guard Bureau, replaces Militia Bureau, 210, 211, 332, 334; by-passed by War Department, 490; placed under the Commanding General, Army Service Forces, 491; conference of February 28, 1944, 495; reinstatement established, 496-7

"National Guard Cadets," 48

National Guard Conference, April 1, 1943, 342

National Guard, General Headquarters Reserves, 361-4

National Guard Machine Gun Companies, need for expressed, 202-3; refused place in Federal Service by War Dept., 202

National Guard Memorial Building, Washington, D.C., 345

National Guard of the United States:

Appropriations and equipment; comparison of appropriations, 1803 and 1883, 129; in 1913, 217; armaments through Dick Act, 194; outdated equipment, 199; lack of appropriations, 325-6; 480-1; unites with Regular Army to secure adequate budget, 335; effect of curtailed budget, 500

Attitudes toward, criticism of, 127-8, 214-5, 238-41; constitutionality of overseas duty, 205, 207; anti-Guard propaganda, 216-7; vindication of, 284; discrimination against, 299; citizen attitude toward Guard Federalization, 381-2; public attitude by 1940, 385-6; by Regular Army, 399, 403, 420; summarized, 404-5; denouncement by *Time* Magazine, 419-20; propaganda target of *Fortune* Magazine, 438-9

Definition of term, 2, 29

Organization policies, reorganization following 1889-99, 184-6; reorganization policy of 1903, 201; absenteeism comparison by States, 200; Regiment renumbering policy, 202, 265-6, 363n; nationalization of, 221-2; reorganization in Wisconsin, Michigan, Iowa, 237; loss of component identity, 263; Divisions become "National Army Divisions," 263, 266; replacement Divisions, 280-1; opposition to reorganization following World War I, 300; description of annual conferences, 331-3; conflict over motorization at expense of horse, 333; cooperation policy toward all Armed Services, 340; reorganization following World War II, 344; mobilization of 1940-1; increment plan, 373; unit, home States, training stations, total strengths and dates of federalization for each of the 22 increments, note tables 374-80; localized character of the Guard units, 400; promotion practices, 400-3; merit determination, 403; opposition to "triangularizing" of "square" Divisions, 439-40; identity threatened by becoming a Federal Organized Militia, 487; reorganization of 1946-9 through reduction in rank, 497-8; troop structure as of 1946, 498-9; reorganization of October 1, 1948, 500n

Part in legislation: modification of Root's Bill, 184; advantages in Dick Act destroyed, 207; amends New Volunteer Act of 1914, 218; importance of 1919 legislation, 242; charged with lobbying, 291-2; criticism of induction procedure under 1917 Draft Law, 297; recognition through Defense Act of 1920, 311-13; reasons for legislative triumph, 314-5; personnel benefits through Act of April 3, 1939, 335; support of the Selective Training and Service Act of 1940, 335; criticism of Selective Service Act, Sept. 16, 1940, 371

Part in peace and war; activity during Reconstruction, 103; revival following Civil War Reconstruction, 119; part in Great Railroad Strike of 1877, 126; part in Spanish-American War, 157; part in Philippines, 163, 177, 327; criticized for law and order enforcement against labor, 127; effect of World War I Declaration on volunteering, 257; strength at time of World War I, 261; commendable record of trained volunteers, 1940-41, 373; reason for significance of Guard Divisions in World War I and II, 475

573

Division, 264n, 275; part of II Corps Area, 355, 366; aeronautics unit of 1st Signal Company Corps, 520; 102nd Observation Squadron (New York City), 527n; 42nd Nat. Gd. Division, 543; *see also* Divisions; Regiments and lesser units; Air Wings and Squadrons

New York Naval Reserve, Naval Battalion organized October 28, 1889, 141; *U.S.S. Yankee*, 142-4; dual status of, 147

Newton, Captain Harry W., 177

Nickerson, Capt. Hoffman, 30n

Nihilistic philosophy, effect on labor, 126-7; *see also* Bakunin, Mikhail

NIKE-AJAX; *see* Defense of U.S.

NIKE-HERCULES; *see* Defense of U.S.

"Non-Promotion List Services," explanation of term, 351n

Normandy Assault; *see* World War II, European Theater, OVERLORD

North African Campaign; *see* World War II, European Theater, Operation TORCH

North Atlantic Treaty Organization (NATO), 148n

North Carolina, military strength during the Civil War, 93; readmitted to the Union, 107; 30th (Old Hickory) Division, 271, 408-9; 461-2; part of IV Corps Area, 355; *see also* Divisions; Regiments and lesser units; Air Wings and Squadrons

North Dakota, 34th (Red Bull) Division, 271n, 444; 41st (Sunset) Division, 272; part of VII Corps Area, 357-8; Nat. Gd. after Pearl Harbor, 486n; 47th Infantry Division, 507; *see also* Divisions; Regiments and lesser units; and Air Wings and Squadrons

Norwich University, as training center, 76

O

Oakes, Lt. Col. James, does research for an improved draft law, 71, makes a study of Civil War Draft, 251; mentioned, 252

Oakley, Annie, 71

"Obligors," definition of, 533-5; variety of available options, 546-7, 551-2; mentioned, 543, 550; *see also* Conscription; Legislation; and Selective Service

Observation Squadrons, 527; *see also* Air Wings and Squadrons

"Office of Naval Militia"; *see* Navy Department

Officers Reserve Corps, training camps, 257n; groups within the division of Reserve officer lists, 351; status of commanding officers, 352; adversely viewed

by Regulars, 352-3; target of War Dept. propaganda, 421-2; mentioned, 2

Officers Reserve Corps and Enlisted Reserve Corps, definition of term, 31

Officers Reserve Corps of World War I, origin of, 85

Ohio, military strength during Civil War, 40, 92; Organized Militia in Spanish-American War, 157, 37th Nat. Gd. Division, 266, 444, 507; part of V Corps Area, 356; 112th Observation Squadron (Cleveland) 527n; mentioned, 521n; *see also* Divisions; Regiments and lesser units; and Air Wings and Squadrons

Oklahoma, Guardsmen of, in 36th Nat. Gd. Division, 265; part of VIII Corps Area, 358-9; 45th Nat. Gd. Division, 407; hostile Indian machine gunners, 426n; 125th Observation Squadron (Oklahoma City), 528; mentioned, 486n; *see also* Divisions; Regiments and lesser units; and Air Wings and Squadrons

"Old Hickory," Division, 30th Infantry, 271; *see also* Divisions

Operation TORCH; *see* World War II, European Theater

Orchard, Harry, hired killer, 127, 131

Ordway, Maj. Gen. Albert, 327

Oregon, military strength during Civil War, 92; 41st (Sunset) Division, 272, 408; part of IX Corps Area, 359; 123rd Observation Squadron, 528; *see also* Divisions; Regiments and lesser units; Air Wings and Squadrons

Organized Militia, definition of term, 2, 28; Ranger Companies, 10, 12; as voluntary military associations, 11; during the War of 1812, 12, 15-6; Regiments, Battalions, Companies, and Batteries in Mexican War, note table, 24; Pre-Civil War dependence on, 45; foreigners in, 48; strength c. 1860, c. 1897, 50-2; Regimental organization, 58n; method of troop replacement in Wisconsin, 59-60; as training for leadership, 76; effect of restoration in South, 108; as shock troops of political campaigns, 117-8; reorganization in North and West following 1865, 122-4; identified in the Dick Act, 187

Organized Reserve Corps, 55, 72-3, 300

O'Ryan, Maj. Gen. John F., commands N.Y. Nat. Gd. 27th Division, 264n, 275, 304, 419-20; supports General Staff Plan, 292; favors Nat. Gd. reorganization as a Federal force, 304; attitude of Nat. Gd. toward, 310; opposes March-Baker Bill, 342n; mentioned, 306, 521

Otis, Maj. Gen. Ewell, 47n
Otis, Maj. Gen. Harrison G., in Philippines, 177
OVERLORD: see World War II, European Theater

P

PACS; see Provisional Army, Confederate States of America
Paine, Ralph D., war correspondent, 238, 328
"Palace Regulars," 212, 219, 230; see also War Department General Staff
Palmer, Brig. Gen. John McA., U.S.A., counters Upton's erroneous opinions, 84; condemns "Continental Army" scheme, 241; attends Nat. Gd. conference, 1943, 342; confers with Gen. Marshall, 371; advises Chief of Staff on Civilian Components, 1941-6, 488-9; career sketch, 488-9; scholarly writings, 488-9; staunch supporter of Nat. Gd., 489; conference regarding U.M.T., 493-4; prepares military manpower circular, 496; achieves recognition of Nat. Gd., 496-7; mentioned, 203, 306-7n; 309, 342n
Panama Canal Zone, defense force in 1936, 359
Panzer Divisions, 365
Papuan Campaign; see World War II, Pacific Theater
Paratroopers, first in American history, 431
Parker, Maj. Gen. James (Galloping Jim), organizes 32nd Infantry Division, 237, 285; relieved for age from 32nd Infantry Division, 275; commands mentioned, 236, 237
"Parkinson's Law," as applied within the Armed Forces, 501, 512
Parsons, Albert R., 126, 131
Patch, Maj. Gen. Alexander M., 451-2
Patrick, Maj. Gen. Mason M., Chief of the Air Service, 523n
Patterson, Robert P., Secretary of War, praises the Nat. Gd., 480-1
Patton, Gen. George S., confers with Brig. Gen. Lesley J. McNair, 393; commands landing force, N. African Campaign, 460; commands Third Army in OVERLORD Operation, 462; mentioned, 340, 390
Paxton, Maj. Gen. Alexander G., commands 31st Division, 507
Pearl Harbor, as seapower base in 1936, 359; impact of bombing on personnel planning, 436-7; marks end of scapegoat

slander for Guard, 440; blame for disaster, 440-1n; mentioned, 41
Peire, Maj. H. D., commander, 7th U.S. Infantry, 16n
Penn, D. B., in La. politics, 114-6
Pennsylvania, military strength during Civil War, 50, 92; Organized Militia in Spanish-American War, 157; First City Troop, 217; 28th Infantry Division, 265n, 266, 415, 506; part of III Corps Area, 355; 73rd Field Artillery Brigade, organization of, 366, 377, 444; 190th F.A. Regiment (Group), 366, 444, 461; 103rd Observation Squadron (Philadelphia), 527n; 28th Nat. Gd. Infantry Division, 543; mentioned, 521n; see also Divisions; Regiments and lesser units; and Air Wings and Squadrons
Pennsylvania Line, 2
Pentomic Concept, explanation of, 542; regards Divisional reorganizations, 544; matter of semantics, 544
Pershing, Gen. John J., punitive campaign in Mexico, 219, 221-2, 230-1, 233, 235, 239-40; proponent of "Square Divisions," 263-5; commands American Expeditionary Force, 278; alleged opposition to Maj. Gen. F. S. Strong, 281; criticizes Regular Army's attitude toward Nat. Gd., 305; as presidential candidate, 342n; eulogized by the Army, 420; mentioned, 293, 306, 309, 523
Philippine Constabulary, 350n
"The Philippine Division (Square)," 457
Philippine Occupation, after Spanish-American War, 176-7; during World War II, 360, 450; Bataan disaster, 453; see also Divisions
Philippine Scouts, definition of term, 350n, 360; 12th Infantry Division, 457
Phisterer, Captain Frederick, personnel statistician, 66, 90-2
Pierce, Brig. Gen. Franklin, 25-6
Pinchback, P. H. S., La. Lt. Gov. under Warmoth, 114-5; opposes the Radicals in 1876, 119
Planche's Battalion, 16
Pioneer Infantry Regiments, 282
Polk, Maj. Gen. Leonidas, 81
Porter, Lt. Gen. Ray E., exemplary attitude toward Nat. Gd., 413
Porter, Maj. Gen. Fitz-John, balloonist during Civil War, 518
Powderly, Terence V., dedicated labor leader, 126
Powell, Maj. Gen. Clifford R., commands 44th Nat. Gd. Division, 408

"Prairie" Division, 33rd Infantry, 275; see also Divisions

*Prairie, U.S.S.,* (Massachusetts); see Spanish-American War, maritime aspects of

Price, Col. Sterling, organizes "Santa Fe Battalion," 24, 24n, 81

Price, Maj. Gen. William G., President, National Guard Association of the U.S., 1926-7, 330

Protective Mobilization Plan (PMP), contemplated in 1936, 368; revision of, 371-3

Provisional Army, Confederate States of America (PACS), manpower call, February 2, 1862, 94; manpower amending act of January 23, 1862, 94; Invalid Corps, 95, citizen soldier volunteers in, 96

Puerto Rico, capture of Ponce, 1898, 143; Regiments in, 360, 364; Guard units after Pearl Harbor, 486n; see also Spanish-American War

Pullman Strike, 126

### Q

Queen Anne's War, 1701-13, 4

Quin, Percy E., Mississippi representative, questions effect of Reg. Army on the Guard, 301-2

### R

"Raccoon Roughs," voluntary association, 19

*The Radicals; see* Civil War, Reconstruction

"Rainbow," Division, 42nd Infantry, 271; see also Divisions

Rainbow Plans, 370n

Randall, A. W., Gov. of Wisconsin, 60

Ranger Companies; see Organized Militia

Reckord, Maj. Gen. Milton A., favors dual enlistment oath, 304; biographical sketch, 304n; leads Nat. Gd.'s legislative battle, 305, 337; aids in defeating Peyton March and Wadsworth Bills, 329; President, National Guard Association of the U.S., 1923-5, 330; commands 29th Division, World War II, 341; age-in-grade policy exception, 341-2; attends Nat. Gd. conference, April 1, 1943, 342; criticizes Selective Service Act of September 16, 1940, 371; proposal for Nat. Gd. recruitment, 430; attends conference regarding U.M.T., 494; mentioned, 273, 476

Reconnaissance Squadrons; see Air Wings and Squadrons

Reconstruction; see Civil War

Reconstruction Act of March 2, 1867; see Legislation

Reconstruction Governors; see Civil War, Reconstruction

"Red" Army, Second Army Order of Battle, 431

"Red Arrow" Division, 32d (Michigan, Wisconsin) Infantry, 271; see also Divisions

"Red Bull" Division, 34th (Minnesota, Nebraska, Dakotas, Iowa) Infantry, 271; see also Divisions

Reed, Gov. Harrison, biographical sketch of Florida's Reconstruction Governor, 110

Reese, Gen. J. N., President of National Guard Association of America, 327

Regiment, definition of term, 90; organization of Colored Regiments, 73; numbering method, 161n; see also U.S. Veteran Volunteers; U.S. Volunteer Regiments

Regiments and lesser units, National Guard, Mexican War, 24; Civil War, 90-3; Spanish-American War, 160-5; system of numbering for World War I, 266; non-divisional units at home stations between World Wars, 361-67; units in active duty call of 1940-1, 374-80

Regiments of Pioneer Infantry, 274

Regular Army, definition of term, 2; birthright in the Federal Constitution, 8; expansible plan, 14, 18; strength, War of 1812, 14-16; strength in 1860, 36, 92; reorganization in 1866, 101; thoroughness of physical exams, 341n; in the Philippines, 350n; Infantry Divisions as of 1940, 369; between World Wars I and II, 360-1; attitude toward C.C.C., 384; serial numbers explained, 390n; unpreparedness in 1940, 416n; effect of curtailed budget, 500; see also Divisions; and U. S. Army

Replacements for A.E.F., 279-81

Republican Party, beginning of, 38

Resaca de la Palma, Mexican offensive action, 20

"Reserve Militia," defined in the Dick Act, 187; see also "Military manpower pool"

Reserve Officers, opposition to age-in-grade policy, 434-5

Reserve Officers Training Corps (ROTC), 221, 388, 401

*Resolute, U.S.S.,* (New Jersey); see Spanish-American War, maritime aspects of

a court-martial, 17-18; father of American military professionalism, 18; chairman of Barbour Board, 320; mentioned, 25

"Sea Fencibles," 12; *see also* Organized Militia, peacetime (Nat. Gd.) units

Secession, Northern attitude toward, 38; first States to secede, 39

"Second American Revolution," name given the Civil War, 79

*Selectees,* 2

Selective Service, based on Common Law principle, 7; opposed by volunteer citizen soldiers, 494; *see also* Conscription; Draft Legislation; Draftees; Legislation; Obligors

Selective Service Act of 1948; *see* Legislation

Selective Service Draft Law; *see* Legislation

Selective Service Extension Act of 1950; *see* Legislation

Selective Training and Service Act of 1940; *see* Legislation

Seminole War, 1836-42, 19, 20, 128

Service of Supply (S.O.S.), 280, 343

Service Schools, Naval War College, Newport, R.I., 133; Command & General Staff College, Fort Leavenworth, Kansas, 134

Shafter, Maj. Gen. William R., commands V Corps, Spanish-American War, 154, 166-7, 328, 518

Shandrew, Col. John C., 162

Shelby Avengers, 68

Sheridan, Gen. Philip A., 133

Sherman, Gen. William Tecumseh, commands California Organized Militia, 47, 47n; West Point career officer, 133; as a presidential candidate, 342n

Shiloh, battle of, 67, 94

Shoop, Brig. Gen. Clarence A., commands Air National Guard, California, 339

Short, Lt. Gen. Walter C., U.S.A., C.G. in Hawaii during Pearl Harbor Disaster, 392, 415, 440-1n, 476

Sickles, Maj. Gen. Daniel E., organizes New York's "Excelsior Brigade," 55-6; proposes New York's units be federalized, 56, 56n; military career, 57n; mentioned, 72, 86

Singapore, surrender of, 450; *see also* World War II, Pacific Theater

Singleton, Dr. Otis A., makes a study of Southern Organized Militia abuses, 104, 118

Sirois, Maj. Gen. Edward D., 339

Slaves, military status of, 67-8; *see also* Civil War; and Negro

Slocum, Henry W., 47n

Smith, Gen. E. Kirby, 84

Smith, Capt. John, as a revered prototype, 2; military status compared to Capt. Robert Clive, 3

Smith, William H., biographical sketch of Alabama's Reconstruction Governor, 110

Snyder, Hon. J. Buell, 343

"Soft underbelly," significance of the phrase, 459

Solomon Islands, occupation by Japanese, 450; *see also* World War II, Pacific Theater

*Somers, U.S.S.; see* Maryland Naval Militia

Somerville, Lt. Ben. Brehon G., controversy with Brig. Gen. Lesley J. McNair, 393

South Carolina, initiates secession, 39; Regular Army of, 40-1; military strength during Civil War, 51, 93; readmitted to Union, 107; 30th Infantry (Old Hickory) Division, 271, 408-9, 461, 462; part of IV Corps Area, 355; 51st Infantry Division, 542; *see also* Divisions Regiments and lesser units; and Air Wings and Squadrons

South Dakota, 34th (Red Bull) Division, 271n; 41st (Sunset) Division, 272; part of VII Corps Area, 357-8; *see also* Divisions; Regiments and lesser units; Air Wings and Squadrons

Spanish-American War, 58-63; 141-4; declaration of war, April 24, 1898, 154; El Caney, 167, 167n; El Pozo, 167-167n; equipment of Reg. Army and Nat. Gd. Regiments, 152-3; journalistic influence, 153-4; *Maine,* sinking of, 151-2; Manila Bay, 152; maritime aspects and Naval Militia, 142-4; U.S. Volunteer Regiments, 155-6; Immunes Regiments, 156, 165; Organized Militia, 157; Shafter's V Corps, 165, 166-7; Nat. Gd. and Federal U.S. Volunteers, 165; Regular troops, 166; American and Spanish forces, 170; Nat. Gd. units engaged in Philippines, 163-4; Puerto Rico Invasion, 168-9; recruitment for Reg. Army expansion methods, 154-8; termination of war by speed of decisive action, 172; terms of service required by units, 485; "Round Robin Incident," 167, 170, 170n; San Juan Hill, 167, 167n; Santiago de Cuba, 158, 165n, 168; Spanish ships in, 143; *see also* Philippine Occupation

Special Planning Division; *see* War Department General Staff

579

Spies, August, 126, 131

Spirit of St. Louis; see Lindbergh, Capt. Charles A.

"Spotswood's Americans," Colonial Regiment, 4

Springfield Rifle; see Military Weapons

"Square Divisions" concept, 263-5

Stackpole, Maj. Gen. Edward J., battlefield historian of Civil War, 339

Standish, Capt. Miles, Mayflower Compact as a basis of authority, 3

Stanford, Col. Albert C., 412

Stanton, Edwin M., effect of War Dept. Order, August 4, 1862, 65; failure of his Draft Order, 69; mentioned, 68, 73

Stark, Maj. Gen. John, hero of Revolution, Vermont, 349

Starke, Col. Alexander N., 235

Starkweather, Brig. Gen. John C., 59, 61

State Constabularies, creation of, 131-2

*Statement of a Proper Military Policy for the United States,* War Department pamphlet, 220

*Statesmanship or War,* by Brig. Gen. John McA. Palmer, 488

Statistics and strengths, Regular Army force in 19th Century American Wars, 14; War of 1812, Battle of New Orleans, 16; Mexican War, 22-23; 1860 Land and Sea forces, 36-37, 42-43; 1860 Organized Militia Force, 50; Union forces at time of Civil War, 74, 80, 83, 90-92, 100; U.S. Regular Army at time of Civil War, 75-6; Provisional Army, Confederate States, 81-82; U.S. Volunteer Regiments (U.S.C.T.), 87; total forces, North and South, 94-5; note table of Union and Confederate Armies State Regiments, Companies, Batteries, 92-3; decline after Civil War, 100-101; Army and Guard strengths to 1903, 120, 123-4, 129, 136, 153, 157, 177, 184-5; Mexican Border and World War I mobilizations, 216, 231, 238, 242, 262, 258n, 347, 271n, 283-4, 264, 264n, 300-1, 300n, 308n, 347; casualties, 285-6; see also Divisions, World War II; military strengths and expenditures, 1920-39, see table 348, 349-51; Officers Reserve Corps in 1936, 351; Nat. Gd. mobilization 1940-41 increment plan, Tables, 374-80; Reg. Army, total line structure as of October 20, 1940, 390, 391n; Active Army strength, 1939-41, 430; American Ground Forces as of December 8, 1941, 442-3; Air Force expansion during World War II, 533-4; Air National Guard during and after

Korea, 535, 536-7; Army force as of June 30, 1953, 514

Steele, Lt. Col. Matthew F., 250, 250n

Stevens, Thaddeus, Radical Republican, 101

Stewart, Maj. Gen. Thomas J., President, National Guard Association of the U.S., 1909-16, biographical sketch, 328-9

Stilwell, Maj. Gen. Joseph W. (Vinegar Joe), attitude toward War Dept., 423n; mentioned, 395n

Simpson, Henry L., Sec. of War, 1911-13, 1940-45, compared to Root, 196; biographical sketch, 196-97; opposes Gen. Ainsworth, 203; opposes Nat. Gd. as a defense institution, 204; reverses attitude toward Guard, 211-12; favors du Pont Bill, 212; Chief Quartermaster in "T. R. Division," 243; mentioned, 208, 209, 247, 370

"Stonewall Brigade," 1st Brigade, 1st Division, Left Wing, Army of Northern Virginia, 80

Strickler, Maj. Gen. Daniel B., commands Pennsylvania's 28th Infantry Division, 506

Strong, Maj. Gen. F. S., commands 40th Infantry Division, 281

Stuart, J.E.B., 47n

Stull, Capt. J. I., commands "Georgetown Rifles," 13

Styron, Maj. Gen. James C., commands Oklahoma's 45th Infantry Division, 506

Sultan, Maj. Gen. Daniel Isom, commands 38th (Nat. Gd) Division, 419, 477n

Sumner, Charles, Radical Republican, 101

Sumner, William H., member of Barbour Board, 320

"Sunset," Division, 41st Infantry, 272; see also Divisions

"Sunshine," Division, 40th Infantry, 272; see also Divisions

Sweetzer, Brig. Gen. E. LeRoy, President of National Guard Association of the U.S., 1916-17, 329

*Sylvia, U.S.S.; see* Maryland Naval Militia

## T

Taft, Howard, attitude toward Nat. Gd., 196; places Militia affairs in the offices of the Sec. of War, 209; mentioned, 195-6, 197, 204

Tampico Incident; see Mexican Revolution, 1911-17

Tariff of 1828, 38

Taulbee, Capt. Joseph F., 235

Taylor, Gen. Zachary, depends on volunteer Organized Militia, 20; near Brownsville, 20; mentioned, 25

Taylor, Gen. Maxwell D. applies "Pentomic Concept," 544

Taylor, Lt. Gen. Richard, Confederate Army, 47n, 73, 84

Ten Percent State Governments, 120

Ten Regiments of Immunes, 156, 165

Tennessee, military strength during Civil War, 92n, 93; 30th Infantry (Old Hickory) Division, 271, 408-9; 461-2; part of IV Corps Area, 355; 105th Observation Squadron (Nashville), 527; *see also* Divisions; Regiments and lesser units; Air Wings and Squadrons

Terror: *see* Spanish-American War, Spanish ships in

Texas, military strength during Civil War, 92n, 93; Militia rights restored, 1870, 109; Nat. Gd. strength in 1903, 184-5; activation of Nat. Gd. in 1916, 222; 36th Division, 265; part of VIII Corps Area, 358-9; 111th Observation Squadron (Houston), 527n; 49th Armored Division, 543; *see also* Divisions; Regiments and lesser units; Air Wings and Squadrons

Theodosius the Great, 213

Thomas, Maj. Gen. George H., organizes 1st Regiment of Engineers, U.S.V.V., 88

Thomas, Brig. Gen. Lorenzo, 68

Tientsin, China, 15th U.S. Infantry in, 360

Tilden, Samuel J., in campaign of 1876, 118

Tinley, Maj. Gen. Matthew A., President of National Guard Association of the U.S., 1933-34, 330

Todd, Col. Frederick P., 45, 581

Todd, Brig. Gen. Henry D., commands 58th Field Artillery Brigade, 272; biographical sketch, 273; mentioned, 274, 275

Tompkins, Brig. Gen. William F., U.S.A., directs Special Planning Division, 492; career sketch, 492; confers with Guardsmen, 495

*Towards an American Army*, by Dr. Russell F. Weigley, 491n

Trainbands, of England, forerunner of modern National Guard, 3; replaced by the Colonial Organized Militia, 4; definition of, 28; mentioned, 2, 552

Training cantonments, comparison of Nat. Gd. and Nat. Army troop facilities, 1916, 258

Traub, Brig. Gen. Peter A., 268

Travis, Brig. Gen. Robert H., President of National Guard Association, 1931-2, 330; commands 30th Division Artillery Brigade, 409

"Tree Army"; *see* Civilian Conservation Corps

Treviño, General, 231; *see also* Mexican Revolution, 1911-17

"Triangular Division," 264, 544

"Troop," defined, 90n

Truman, Harry S., Chairman, Senatorial investigations of defense planning inefficiencies, 417; Selective Service policy, 502

Truscott, Lt. Gen. L. K., ideas concerning combat readiness, 473

Tumulty, Joseph P., Wilson's White House Secretary, 227

Twiggs, Gen. David E., surrenders at San Antonio, 42; mentioned, 36, 83

Tyler, Brig. Gen. Daniel, 47n

Tyndall, Maj. Gen. Robert, commands 38th Division, 419; target of anti-Guard propaganda, 420-21, 421n

## U

U.M.T.; *see* Universal Military Training

"Union Clubs"; *see* Civil War Reconstruction

Units; *see* Regiments and lesser units; and Divisions

U.S. Air Force, historical background, 526n

U.S. Army, definition of term, 2, 30; *see also* Civil War; Spanish-American War; Statistics and strengths; Divisions, all components; War of 1812; World War I; World War II

U.S. Army Reserve, 2, 85, 90; *see also* Divisions, all components; Officers Reserve Corps; Statistics and strengths; War Department

U.S. Constitution, 55, 56n, 65, 101

U.S. Foreign Relations, Great Britain following the Civil War, 101

United States Naval Reserve, created by National Guardsmen, 139; *see also* Naval Militia

U.S. Naval Reserve Force, 144, 146

U.S. Navy, strength in 1860, 35-36, 36n; training concept, 147-48

U.S. Volunteer Regiments, differentiated from State-created Volunteer Regiments, 85; total force, 85; 1st Regiment of Infantry, 85; 2nd Sharpshooters, 85; 1st Regiment consolidates with the 2nd, 86; U. S. Veteran Volunteers, 2, 85, 88-9; U.S. Veteran Reserve Corps, 2, 85-6; Corps d'Afrique and U.S. Colored Volunteers, 85, 86; U.S. Colored

from West Point, 216; opposed by Brig. Gen. John McA. Palmer, 489; seeks to ignore Nat. Gd. as a source of manpower, 215; *see* Legislation

War Department General Staff, views concerning the Nat. Gd., 181-2, 208, 217, 233, 300, 344, 492-3; permits combined instruction program for Reg. Army and State Units, 193-4; considers federalizing the Nat. Gd., 194; Uptonian influence, 203; plan of August 12, 1912, 213; age-in-grade policy, 341-2; 433-4, 437; March-Baker Bill, 342n; realizes importance of tanks and artillery, 365; recruitment policy as of June 30, 1941, 370; promotion policy, 377-8; assignment duties for surplus Army Officers, 388; purge of incompetents, 422; ponders personnel sources December 8, 1941, 443; attitude toward Nat. Gd. aviation units, 521, 523

War Department "Plattsburg Movement," 215, 227

War Department Special Planning Division, 492-3

"The War for Southern Independence," 79; *see also* Civil War

War Games in Louisiana, Lear's Second Army vs. Krueger's Third Army, 431-3

War of 1812, manpower policies, 3; Organized Militia in, 12; Washington, D.C., burned, 12; King's Own Regiment, 13; Fort McHenry bombardment, 13; Detroit-Niagara-Lake Champlain frontier, 16; maritime aspects of, 140

"War of the Rebellion," 79; *see also* Civil War

War with Spain; *see* Spanish-American War

Warmoth, Henry Clay, biographical sketch of Louisiana's Reconstruction Governor, 113

Washington, 41st (Sunset) Division, 272, 408; part of IX Corps Area, 359; 116th Observation Squadron (Spokane), 527n; *see also* Divisions; Regiments and lesser units; Air Wings and Squadrons

Washington, General George, seeks commission in the King's Regulars, 4, 9; commands Virginia's 1st Regiment, 4; Eight-Months Army captures Boston, 5; commissioned Lt. Gen., 8; death of, 9, mentioned, 8, 552

Washington, Capt. Lawrence, commissioned in "Spotwood's Americans," 4

*Washington, Lincoln, Wilson—Three War Statesmen*, by Brig. Gen. John McA. Palmer, 488

Watson, Mark S., clarifies intent of Public Law 190 (purge of incompetents), 422; reviews promotion policies of Marshall and McNair, 435, 435n

Wellington, Duke of, 246

West, Mae, commissioned an honorary Colonel, 396

West Point, New York, Hamilton's N. Y. Battery stationed at, 8; as leading Military Academy, 76

West Virginia, formation of, 62; military strength during the Civil War, 92; 38th (Cyclone) Division, 271; railroad strike of 1877, 320-1; part of V Corps Area, 356; *see also* Divisions; Regiments and lesser units

Western Federation of Miners, 124

Westover, Maj. Gen. Oscar, 523

Wheaton, Maj. Gen. Lloyd, 47n

Wheeler, Maj. Gen. Joe 166

Whig Party, disintegration of, 38

Whiskey Insurrection, 1794, 37

White, Maj. Gen. George A., commands 41st Nat. Gd. Division, 408

White, Col. Horton V., Sixth Army G2, 473n

White, Kenneth S., pays tribute to Nat. Gd., 552

White, Col. King, 112; *see also* Civil War Reconstruction, Brooks-Baxter War

White, Brig. Gen. Miller, U.S.A., attends Nat. Gd. conference, April 1, 1943, 342

White House Conference, November 14, 1938, 365n

White League; *see* Civil War Reconstruction, Governorship controversy, 1872-4

Wilcox, Maj. Phillip W., constructs airplane at Pine Camp, New York, 520

Wild, Private Dell P., 250

Wilkinson, Gen. James, relations with Winfield Scott, 17

Williams, Maj. Gen. John F., Chief of the National Guard Bureau, 343; reports as to morale and attitudes of Guardsmen, 428; attends conference at Nat. Gd. Bureau, February 28, 1944, 495; mentioned, 490

Wilson, Col. Guy M., President of National Guard Association of the U.S., 1921-2, 329, 330

Wilson, Maj. Gen. J. H., 168-9

Wilson, Maj. Gen. Winston P., 339

Wickersham, George W., decision as Attorney General adverse to Guard's position, 205; proposes to withdraw Nat. Gd. funds, 212; myth concerning use of Nat. Gd. outside of United States, 242; mentioned, 208

Winder, Lt. Col., 521n

Wing, Maj. Gen. Leonard F., 477

Wingate, Brig. Gen. George W., first President of National Guard Association of the U.S., 322; seeks Congressional support, 326, 326n

Winslow, Capt. John A., 140-1, 141n

Wisconsin, military strength during the Civil War, 50, 92; 32nd Infantry (Red Arrow) Division, 265, 271, 444, 543; part of VI Corps Area, 356; 126th Observation Squadron, 528; *see also* Divisions; Regiments and lesser units; Air Wings and Squadrons

Wood, Gen. Leonard, biographical sketch, 156, 156n, 208-9; appointed Chief of Staff, 197; opposes Gen. Ainsworth, 203; incites wrath of Guardsmen, 205, 218, 293; opposes Nat. Gd. as an American Army component, 208-9; publicity campaign, 1912-13, 215; political aspirations, 219; attitude toward World War I preparedness, 226; proposes guarantee of Volunteer rights in Draft Bill, 254; plans regimentation of all American Youth, 291; ideas concerning manpower, 303; concept of a large professional Army, 314; as a Presidential candidate, 342n; mentioned, 212, 233, 242, 386

Wilson, Woodrow, aided by Oakes' research, 71; inauguration of, 215; pacifistic idealist, 225; scholarly pursuits, 227-8; speaks at Manhattan Club, New York, November 4, 1915, 228; opposes the "Continental Army" plan, 228; calls Nat. Gd. units of Texas, New Mexico and Arizona, 231; policy of "watchful waiting," 232; decides on need for Draft, 250; mentioned, 241, 253, 255, 269, 284

Woodhouse, Henry, prolific writer on aeronautics, 519; as editor and publisher 521

Woodring, Harry H., Sec. of War, 370

World War I, influenza outbreak, 170; attitudes regarding preparedness, 225-7; effect of Declaration on volunteering, 257; reorganizing of American Expeditionary Force, 265-6; Pershing's manpower replacement plan, 278-9; call for replacements November 2, 1918, 282; part of Reg. Army Divisions in replacement, 282; part of National Army Divisions in replacement, 282; Pioneer Infantry Regiments, 282; victory through united effort, 282; military force at time of Armistice, 284; Nat. Gd. campaigns and casualties by Divisions, note table, 285; National Army campaigns and casualties by Divisions, note table, 286; Regular Army campaigns and casualties by Divisions, note table, 286; return of American Expeditionary Force, 1917-18, "Bridge of Ships," 289

World War I aftermath, General Staff Plan, 289-92; Divisions participating overseas, 298; isolation policy and economy, 348; quality of military manpower, 350; effect of economic depression on manpower and expenditures, 351; administrative plan for adequate manpower, 353; terms of service required in units, 485; personnel yield, 510-11

World War II, vaccine casualties 1941-2, 170-1, 170n, 171n; censorship policy, 447-8; terms of service required in units, 485; Air Troop List of the Regular Army strength, 1939, 528n; Air Force expansion statistics, 533-4; *see also* Divisions; Squadrons, Fighter; and Squadrons, Tactical Reconnaissance

World War II, European Theater, MAGNET FORCE (V Corps), 448-9, 459-60; TORCH, Anglo-American landings in North Africa, November 8, 1942, 451, 459; European offensive plans, 458-62; OVERLORD cross channel invasion of France, 461, 461n; American Army Infantry Divisions in, note tables 463-8; basic difference from Pacific Theater of Operations, 468; Armored Divisions, 469-70; Airborne Divisions, 470-2

World War II, Pacific Theater, Papuan Campaign, Army's first offensive, 1942, 411n, 451-2; Japanese three-pronged offensive, 444; Marines on Guadalcanal, 445, 452, 457; Japanese aggression in the Pacific, 450; two-pronged strategic offensive through Polynesia and the Mariannas, 453; details of American Army Infantry Divisions in, note tables 454-6; Nat. Gd. importance of, 454-8; Armored Divisions not needed, 457; Air Forces, 5th, 7th, 13th, 458; Airborne Divisions, 471

World War II aftermath, military demobilization, 483; rumors of divisional transfers to the Pacific, 484; rotation system following inactivation, 484-5; plan to destroy the Nat. Gd. as a separate defense institution, 487; Air Force reorganization plan, 534; Army National Guard reorganization, 541-2; Army Reserve reorganization, 543; crea-